YELLOWSTONE & GRAND TETON

DON PITCHER

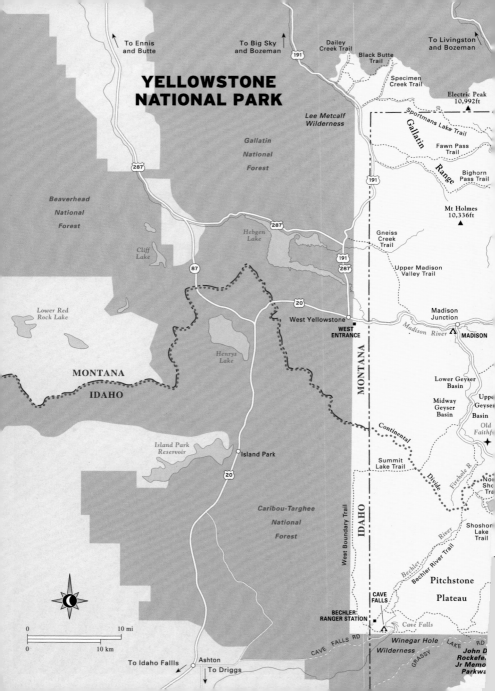

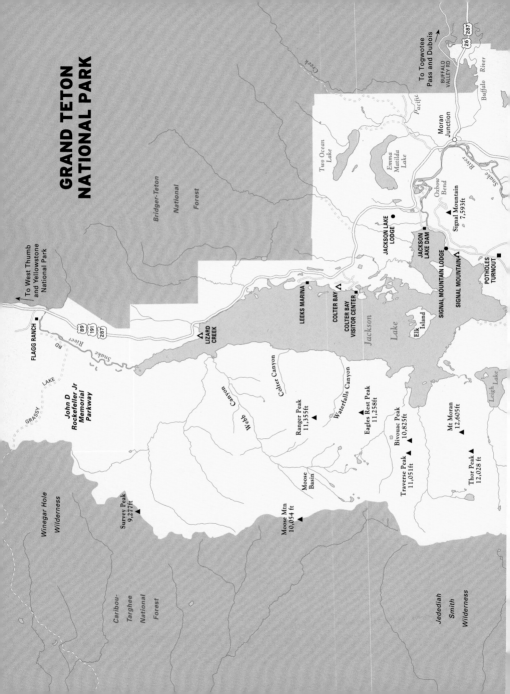

GRAND TETON NATIONAL PARK

To Togwotee Pass and Dubois

BUFFALO VALLEY RD

Buffalo River

26 287

Moran Junction

Pacific Creek

Snake River

Oxbow Bend

Signal Mountain 7,593ft

Two Ocean Lake

Emma Matilda Lake

Bridger-Teton National Forest

JACKSON LAKE LODGE

JACKSON LAKE DAM

SIGNAL MOUNTAIN

SIGNAL MOUNTAIN LODGE

POTHOLES TURNOUT

Elk Island

Jackson Lake

LEEKS MARINA

COLTER BAY

COLTER BAY VISITOR CENTER

To West Thumb and Yellowstone National Park

FLAGG RANCH

89 191 287

Snake River

LIZARD CREEK

John D Rockefeller Jr Memorial Parkway

GRASSY LAKE RD

Leigh Lake

Colter Canyon

Webb Canyon

Ranger Peak 11,355ft

Waterfalls Canyon

Eagles Rest Peak 11,258ft

Bivouac Peak 10,825ft

Mt Moran 12,605ft

Moose Basin

Traverse Peak 11,051ft

Thor Peak 12,028 ft

Moose Mtn 10,054 ft

Survey Peak 9,277ft

Winegar Hole Wilderness

Caribou-Targhee National Forest

Jedediah Smith Wilderness

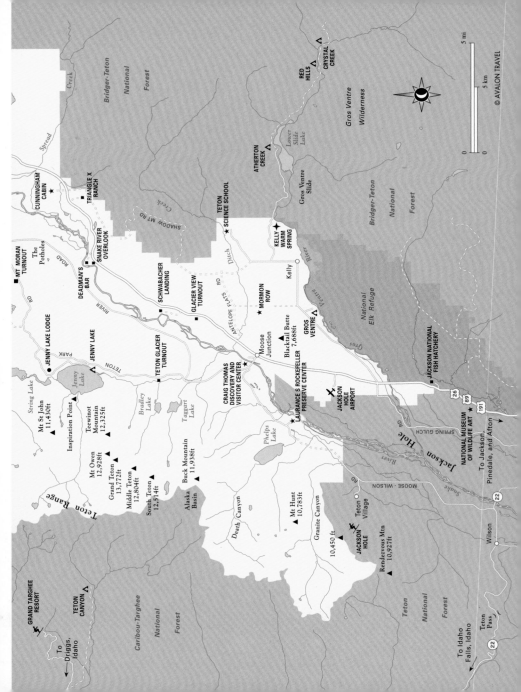

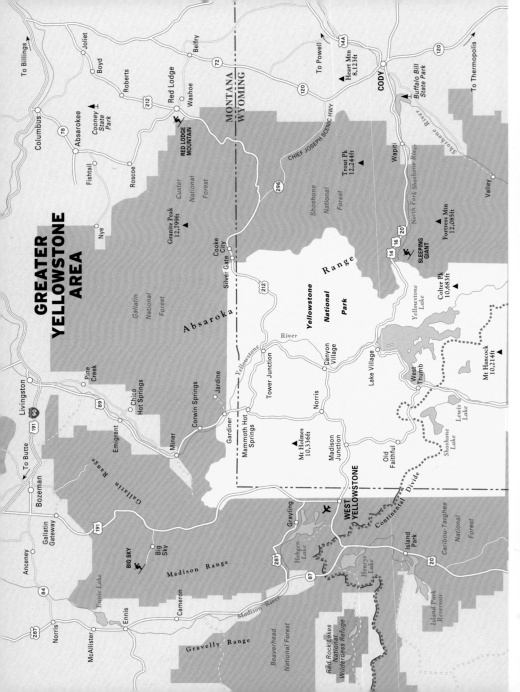

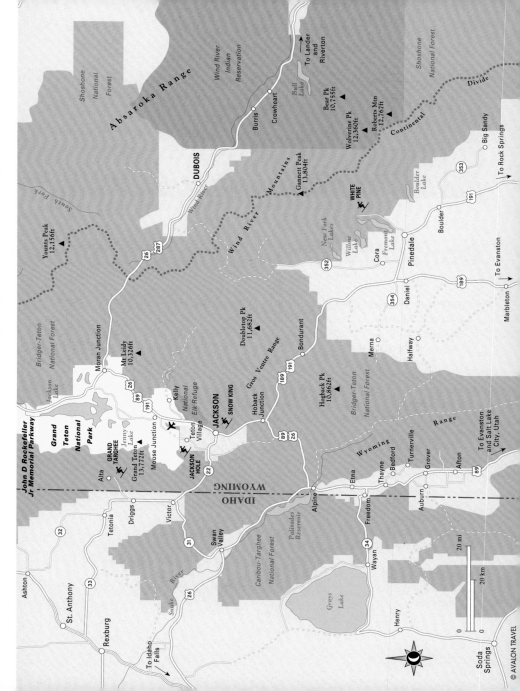

Contents

Discover Yellowstone & Grand Teton

If ever a place deserved the term "Wonderland," it would have to be the northwest corner of Wyoming. In this spectacularly scenic region lies the world's oldest national park – Yellowstone – along with one of the most stunning mountainscapes on the planet, Grand Teton National Park. Jackson Hole is a prosperous and bustling center for recreation and commerce; it's one of the most popular vacation destinations in North America. Beyond these three renowned areas are a wealth of attractions to please those who love the great outdoors and the West, including a world-class museum complex in Cody, gorgeous badlands topography near the Old West town of Dubois, and several delightful mountain settlements surrounding Yellowstone National Park. The region attracts more than three million visitors each year from around the globe.

The Greater Yellowstone Ecosystem is a mountainous region bisected by the Continental Divide. Several peaks – including Grand Teton – top 13,000 feet. Powerful geological forces crafted this landscape; their energy is especially visible in Yellowstone. The park sits atop a geologic hotspot that caused three stupendous volcanic eruptions in the last two million years, covering thousands of square miles with ash and affecting the global climate for years thereafter. There's no evidence that it will erupt anytime soon, but the heat from this seething cauldron

creates the geysers, hot springs, and fumaroles for which Yellowstone is famous. Despite all this heat, ice and water have also played important roles. Glaciers carved out valleys such as Jackson Hole, and rivers eroded the colorful Grand Canyon of the Yellowstone.

The Teton Range provides an incredible skyline that rises abruptly above Jackson Hole, a relatively flat basin through which the Snake River flows. In summer, the sagebrush flats are a garden of flowers set against the mountain backdrop. Autumn turns the cottonwoods and aspens into swaths of yellow and orange, and winter transforms everything a glorious, sparkling white.

With activities ranging from mountain biking to river rafting to gourmet dining, it's impossible to be bored here. The country is so beautiful that you may just want to kick back, tip back your new cowboy hat, and sip a Teton Ale while taking it all in. Welcome to one of the world's great wonderlands. You may never want to go home.

Planning Your Trip

▶ WHERE TO GO

Yellowstone National Park

Yellowstone's famed Old Faithful has predictable eruptions that delight crowds every 90 minutes or so, while Mammoth Hot Springs features an ever-changing palette of pastel-colored springs. Bucolic Lamar Valley in the northeast corner is the best place to see wolves and other wildlife. Grand Canyon of the Yellowstone may be the park's most spectacular feature, with the river plummeting 308 feet over Lower Falls. South of here is Yellowstone Lake, the largest high-elevation lake in North America.

Grand Teton National Park

Capped by 13,772-foot Grand Teton, the Teton Range rises abruptly from the valley floor, with the Snake River winding sinuously beneath ragged peaks. Craig Thomas Discovery and Visitor Center provides a great introduction to the park. Three of the most picturesque areas are Jenny Lake, the old barns of Mormon Row, and Jackson Lake for fishing and boating.

Jackson Hole

Wyoming's preeminent tourist town, trendy Jackson occupies the southern end of the valley called Jackson Hole. Four arches created from hundreds of elk antlers frame Town Square, host to faux shoot-outs and farmers' markets all summer. Jackson is crowded with dozens of galleries, and the National Museum of Wildlife Art is just north of town. Winter sleigh rides draw visitors to the National Elk

IF YOU HAVE . . .

- **ONE DAY:** Visit Yellowstone National Park.
- **TWO DAYS:** Add Grand Teton National Park.
- **THREE DAYS:** Add Jackson.
- **ONE WEEK:** Add Cody.
- **TWO WEEKS:** Add West Yellowstone, Cooke City, or Dubois.

Grand Teton National Park

Refuge, while skiers challenge the slopes of Jackson Hole Mountain Resort. All sorts of summer fun fill the calendar, from river rafting to classical music.

Gateways to Yellowstone

The Montana towns of West Yellowstone, Gardiner, Cooke City, and Silver Gate border Yellowstone, and visitors use them as bases for park explorations. The Wyoming towns of Cody and Dubois, east and southeast respectively from Yellowstone, are close enough for a long day trip into the park. Cody is home to both the acclaimed Buffalo Bill Historical Center and the Cody Nite Rodeo, with scenic Wapiti Valley to the west.

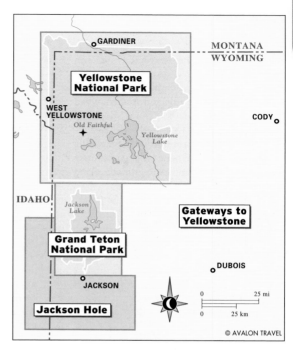

Old Faithful Geyser

▶ WHEN TO GO

Yellowstone summers start late (June) and are relatively short. The vast majority of visitors to Yellowstone and Grand Teton arrive in the hectic months of July and August, when the snows are gone, temperatures are warm, skies are often clear, local businesses and attractions are all open, and wildlife are readily visible. Anyone arriving at other times may find closed facilities and campgrounds, along with minimal Park Service staffing.

Fall is a favorite time to visit the parks. The crowds have diminished, most businesses and campgrounds are still open, and on crisp mornings the air is filled with the bugling of elk. Temperatures drop as fall progresses and the snow gradually moves down the mountains; most Yellowstone National Park roads are closed by early November.

Yellowstone winters are cold, snowy, and starkly beautiful. Park access is by snowcoach or guided snowmobile. Jackson Hole is a major winter destination, with three ski resorts and a wide range of winter activities. West Yellowstone is popular with snowmobilers and cross-country skiers, while Gardiner serves as a base for wolf-watchers.

Park Access

Entrance to Yellowstone costs $25 per vehicle ($12 by bicycle, foot, skis, or bus). The pass includes entrance to both Yellowstone and Grand Teton National Parks for seven days. For longer stays, an annual pass ($50) covers both parks and the Interagency Annual Pass ($80 per year) is good for all national parks.

Most roads in Yellowstone close on the Monday after the first Sunday in November and usually open again by mid-May. Only the road between Mammoth and Cooke City is kept plowed all winter. Plowing begins in early March, with the roads connecting Mammoth to West Yellowstone opening first (typically mid-April). Most campgrounds and visitor centers are open May–September.

north entrance to Yellowstone National Park, Gardiner, Montana

A herd of RVs plays follow the leader.

► BEFORE YOU GO

The vast majority of visitors arrive by car, though there are daily flights into Jackson from many major cities. You can also fly into a regional airport such as Salt Lake City, Utah or Billings, Montana and rent a car. Buses and vans provide connections between Jackson Hole and Salt Lake City. Most national chains offer car rentals in Jackson, with fewer options in the towns of Cody and West Yellowstone. Public transportation within the parks is nonexistent.

Lodging reservations are highly recommended for midsummer travel throughout the region, especially over holiday weekends. Reserve well ahead of your trip for the best options. Winters can also be busy, particularly in Jackson over the Christmas–New Year's holiday period. Some of the most in-demand lodges fill months ahead of time.

Explore Yellowstone & Grand Teton

▶ BEST OF YELLOWSTONE & GRAND TETON

This summertime trip provides a wonderful introduction to the region, starting in Jackson Hole and taking in the popular town sights before heading north into Grand Teton and Yellowstone National Parks. Jackson is accessible by nonstop flights from Denver and Salt Lake City, and car rentals are available at the airport.

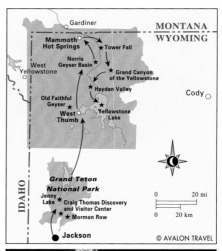

Day 1

Fly or drive in to the bustling town of Jackson and you'll quickly see why it's such a popular destination. Stop by the sod-roofed Jackson Hole and Greater Yellowstone Visitor Center for a plethora of brochures and a helpful staff to answer your questions. You can't miss shady Town Square with its four elk-antler arches, but you may need to park in the big lot a couple of blocks to the north. Evening shoot-outs are a summer favorite activity, and several dozen art galleries (and many other businesses) fill nearby shops. Just north of town is the outstanding National Museum of Wildlife Art. Downtown, travelers will find an amazing variety of dining choices. For dinner and a great beer, join the throngs at Snake River Brewing Company. Don't miss the Million Dollar Cowboy Bar with its saddle barstools and nightly country-and-western bands.

Day 2

Drive north into Grand Teton National Park to take in the mountain vistas and explore a few of the sights. Stop first at the Craig Thomas Discovery and Visitor

Million Dollar Cowboy Bar, Jackson

The three most popular attractions in Yellowstone are Old Faithful, Mammoth Hot Springs, and the Grand Canyon of the Yellowstone. One could easily spend a full day in each of these areas, but it is possible to make quick visits to all three while circling through the park. The following itinerary assumes you are coming in from West Yellowstone. Get an early start on the day, since you'll need to cover a lot of ground and the park speed limit is only 45 miles an hour.

Old Faithful: Your first stop will be the world's best-known geyser, which erupts approximately every 90 minutes. Drop by the visitor center to see the next predicted eruption and to learn about the natural world. Paved paths lead to nearby geysers, hot springs, and other features. Several interesting buildings are in the area, most notably **Old Faithful Inn,** built more than a century ago and still one of the largest log structures in the world.

Mammoth Hot Springs: Drive north from Old Faithful Geyser, stopping briefly to see the colorful bubbling mud and active small geysers at **Fountain Paint Pot.** You might also have time for fascinating **Norris Geyser Basin,** the hottest such basin in North America. When you reach Mammoth Hot Springs, take a quick tour of Albright Visitor Center, then turn your car east for the drive to **Tower Fall,** where a steep trail leads 0.5 mile downhill to the base of this pretty waterfall.

Grand Canyon of the Yellowstone: The road south from Tower Fall crosses 8,859-foot Dunraven Pass before dropping to this spectacular canyon. The most famous vista point (don't miss this one) is **Artist Point** on the south side, but others on both sides provide more options, including a steep trail that leads to the top of Lower Falls (twice the height of Niagara Falls).

Now it's time to circle back to your starting point. If it's already late in the day, drive directly back to West Yellowstone via Norris and Madison, but if there are still a couple of hours of daylight, continue south to **Lake Yellowstone** for a big dinner or sunset drink at historic **Lake Yellowstone Hotel** before continuing on to the town of West Yellowstone.

Lower Falls of the Yellowstone River from Artist Point

Schwabacher Landing along the Snake River, Grand Teton National Park

Center for an orientation to the park and its history. For a great half-day adventure, book an easy float or rollicking whitewater raft trip down the Snake River; a dozen local companies offer trips. You can also rent a bike and head up the paved bike path to Jenny Lake, a wonderful jumping-off point for hikes. Spend the night at a park campground (Jenny Lake is especially notable) or at Jenny Lake Lodge.

Day 3

This is a day to explore Grand Teton. Starting from Jenny Lake, take the park road north to Jackson Lake. Stops along the road include the photo-perfect barns of Mormon Row, and spectacular turnouts facing the Tetons, including Snake River Overlook (where Ansel Adams took his famous photo), and the view at Oxbow Bend, a great place to look for wildlife. At Jackson Lake, Colter Bay Marina offers scenic cruises, boat and kayak rentals, and guided fishing on this large reservoir. Not far away is grandiose Jackson Lake Lodge, built at the behest of John D. Rockefeller (who also played a big role in establishing Grand Teton National Park), where you will spend the night. A nice evening drive

is the winding road to the 7,593-foot summit of Signal Mountain, where the panorama encompasses the majestic Teton Range, Jackson Lake, Snake River, and the long valley called Jackson Hole.

Day 4

Spend today exploring Yellowstone by driving north to West Thumb, where you may want to stop for a brief look at the hot springs and other features before turning west to visit famous Old Faithful Geyser and Upper Geyser Basin area. Be sure to take time to wander around majestic Old Faithful Inn and the modern Old Faithful Visitor Education Center. It will probably be mid-afternoon by this point. There's no camping at Old Faithful, but excellent lodging options are available at Old Faithful Inn or Old Faithful Lodge.

Day 5

Another full day in Yellowstone begins by heading north from Old Faithful to Norris Geyser Basin. Take in the Back Basin loop to see if Echinus Geyser is active, or head down Porcelain Basin to enjoy the ever-changing colors. Continue on to Mammoth

Hot Springs and stroll the boardwalks at the colorful terraces, check out historical photos in the visitor center, and get lunch inside the hotel. In the afternoon, drive to Roosevelt Lodge, where cabins and delightful Old West cookouts are available (book in advance). Take an evening drive into nearby Lamar Valley, one of the finest places for wildlife-viewing. Wolves and bison populate this scenic corner of Yellowstone.

Day 6

A few miles south of Roosevelt Lodge is Tower Fall, a dramatic 132-foot waterfall. Farther south, the road winds over Dunraven Pass, where Mt. Washburn trails are popular in late summer. Be sure to take time to explore Grand Canyon of the Yellowstone, with its spectacular waterfalls and multihued canyon walls. An evening hike along one of the rim trails is a great way to end the day. Lodging and campsites are available in Canyon Village; Dunraven Lodge is the nicest.

Day 7

Drive south through lush Hayden Valley (pull out your binoculars to glass for bears or wolves) to Yellowstone Lake. Spend your final day in the park exploring the Yellowstone Lake area, where you can take a one-hour boat cruise and enjoy lunch at historic Lake Yellowstone Hotel. From here, it's a leisurely three-hour drive south to your starting point in Jackson Hole.

▶ WHERE THE BUFFALO ROAM

Yellowstone and Grand Teton provide world-class opportunities to see wildlife, and many visitors consider the chance to see bison, elk, wolves, bears, moose, and other large mammals the highlight of their trips. Early morning and early evening usually provide the best wildlife-viewing opportunities in the summer. At other times of the year the animals tend to be equally visible in the middle of the day. Bring a pair of binoculars and telephoto lenses for a close-up view, but make sure your behavior isn't disturbing the animal or causing it to move away. Check with Yellowstone and Grand Teton visitor centers for details on

bison, Grand Teton National Park

SAY CHEESE: TOP 10 PHOTO OPS

Okay, this one's rather subjective, but the following are good starting points for your photo safari.

- **Grand Canyon of the Yellowstone** from Artist Point
- **Old Faithful** at sunset
- Colorful **Palette Springs** at Mammoth Hot Springs
- **Bugling elk** in the fall within Grand Teton National Park
- Early morning at **Schwabacher Landing** along the Snake River
- **Moulton Barn** on Mormon Row
- **Snake River Overlook**
- **Oxbow Bend** and **Mt. Moran** with fall colors
- Horses at **Triangle X Ranch**
- **Elk antler arch** in downtown Jackson (with your kids, of course)

recent wildlife sightings and handouts showing where you're most likely to find them. Below are a few of the best spots.

Yellowstone National Park

NORTHEAST CORNER

In the remote northeast corner of Yellowstone, Lamar Valley is a great place to look for wildlife of all types, from the ubiquitous ground squirrels to an occasional grizzly. Elk, pronghorn antelope, and large herds of bison are commonly seen, and coyotes are often sighted, but the main attraction is wolves. Several wolf packs occupy this area, and wolf aficionados hang out on nearby slopes for a glimpse of them. You can rent a spotting scope in Silver Gate, just outside the park's northeast boundary.

MAMMOTH AREA

Despite the crowds of people at this popular corner of the park, Mammoth is also a good place to find wild animals. Elk are almost always somewhere in the area, particularly in the fall, when the males' bugling keeps hotel guests awake at night. Pronghorn antelope

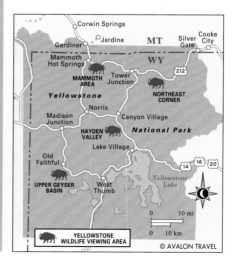

bighorn sheep

vegetation beneath. Both elk and bison spend considerable time along the Firehole River and in the hot springs areas to stay warm when temperatures plummet.

Grand Teton National Park
OXBOW BEND AND WILLOW FLATS

Near Moran Junction, this slow-moving loop off the Snake River is a great place to watch for swimming beavers, muskrats, and river otters, or for moose browsing on willows along the shore. Also keep your eyes open for birds—bald eagles, white pelicans, ospreys, and others. The best times to see animals are in the early morning and at dusk. Rent a canoe from Dornan's in Moose to paddle around Oxbow Bend. Another excellent place to scan for moose and elk is Willow Flats, a marshy area just up from Jackson Lake Dam.

MORMON ROW

This part of the park is best known for the photo-friendly barns backdropped by the Tetons, but you will often find a herd of bison in the open country nearby. The back roads

are fairly common, particularly along the one-way Old Gardiner Road, and bighorn sheep are often seen on steep hillsides between Mammoth and Gardiner. Look for moose in the Willow Park area 10 miles south of Mammoth, especially in the fall.

HAYDEN VALLEY

This lovely open valley south of Canyon is a mix of grasses and sage, with occasional lodgepole pines. It's a great place to see grazing bison and elk, plus the occasional grizzly, especially on the east side of the valley. Waterfowl, including Canada geese, trumpeter swans, pelicans, and many kinds of ducks, are plentiful in marshes and along the Yellowstone River. Stop at LeHardys Rapids in June and July to see spawning cutthroat trout.

UPPER GEYSER BASIN

Elk and bison are almost always visible near Old Faithful and in other parts of the Upper Geyser Basin, and the slow-moving bison often create traffic jams when they decide to use the main roads as trails. In the winter this is a great place to watch bison plowing snow with their massive heads to get at the

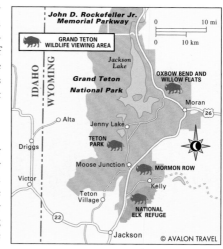

John D. Rockefeller Jr. Memorial Parkway

0   10 mi
0   10 km

GRAND TETON WILDLIFE VIEWING AREA

Jackson Lake

Grand Teton National Park

OXBOW BEND AND WILLOW FLATS

IDAHO | WYOMING

Moran
26

Alta

Jenny Lake

TETON PARK

Driggs

Moose Junction

MORMON ROW

Victor

Kelly

Teton Village

22

NATIONAL ELK REFUGE

Jackson

© AVALON TRAVEL

connecting Mormon Row with Kelly are excellent places to find pronghorn antelope.

TETON PARK ROAD

This scenic road follows a beautiful sagebrush-covered plateau with stands of lodgepole pines and aspens. Pronghorn antelope and Uinta ground squirrels are here, along with elk (especially in the fall) and some bison. Southwest of the visitor center is the narrow and winding Moose-Wilson Road (not for RVs), where you may encounter moose, mule deer, or an occasional black bear.

NATIONAL ELK REFUGE

In the summer this is a good place to see trumpeter swans, particularly near the Jackson Hole Visitor Center. You may see elk and other animals in the summer here, but winter is the main attraction, with horse-drawn sleighs carrying visitors among thousands of elk on the feeding grounds.

► CAMPING AND HIKING IN THE TETONS

This five-day tour is perfect for families and those who prefer to camp in the great outdoors. Jackson Hole and the Grand Tetons have a wonderful diversity of day hikes as well as backcountry adventures. Most campgrounds are open May–September; advance reservations are recommended.

Day 1

Choose from five campgrounds within Grand Teton National Park or several others in nearby Bridger-Teton National Forest. A quiet, out-of-the-way choice is Gros Ventre Campground in the park, but many visitors prefer Jenny Lake Campground for its central location and wonderfully scenic setting. Once you're set up, drive to the park's Craig Thomas Discovery and Visitor Center for details on the park, maps, brochures, and guidebooks. Just across the river in Moose are several Dornan's shops, offering groceries, wine, inexpensive meals, and outdoor gear, including bike and canoe rentals. Stop off at pretty Chapel of the Transfiguration and explore the 0.5-mile Menor's Ferry Trail before returning to your campsite.

Chapel of the Transfiguration, Grand Teton National Park

OFF THE BEATEN PATH

Triangle X Ranch, Grand Teton National Park

As one of America's most-loved natural areas, Yellowstone and Grand Teton National Parks attract millions of visitors annually. Yet despite the crowds, it can be surprisingly easy to escape to the natural world. Here are a few ways to avoid the hordes and have the parks to yourself.

- **Visit in the off-season,** especially autumn. Fall colors come late to the region, typically peaking the first week of October. The town of Jackson is still busy, but it's much quieter than in midsummer. Lodging rates are lower, the elk are bugling, and hiking trails are uncrowded.

- The 10,947-foot **Beartooth Pass** cuts through a wide-open landscape northeast of Yellowstone with knife-edged peaks, alpine lakes, pretty campgrounds, and miles of hiking trails.

- The **Heart Mountain Interpretive Center,** north of Cody, commemorates the thousands of Japanese-Americans who were incarcerated here during World War II.

- The 15-mile **River Road** provides an alternative route through the sagebrush of Grand Teton National Park, and is a good place to see elk in the fall.

- Take the dirt road into **Whiskey Basin** to find herds of Rocky Mountain bighorn sheep in winter and spring.

- The mostly gravel road into **Gros Ventre Valley** east of Kelly extends 30 miles into red-rock badlands.

- Take a backcountry hike to two of the wildest parts of Yellowstone: the **Bechler River** area and the **Thorofare** region.

- Looking to escape the Old Faithful madhouse? Directly behind the geyser, Observation Point Loop Trail climbs up **Geyser Hill,** with a view over the entire area.

- Most folks just ride up Jackson Hole Ski Resort's popular **tram** and then head back down, but several excellent alpine trails fan out from here for short hikes or multi-night wilderness treks.

- In winter, book a trip to a **rustic tent cabin** along Grand Canyon of the Yellowstone River, a fine base camp to explore by ski or snowshoe.

- Elude the Jackson Hole winter scene with **hut-to-hut ski trips** that lead to remote yet comfortable yurts.

- An hour southeast of Jackson, **Granite Hot Springs** is a delightful spot for a soak.

Day 2

Spend today hiking into the Tetons. Many short—and long—hikes are available including one of the most popular, to Inspiration Point. This one begins with a shuttle boat ride across Jenny Lake. It's a 0.5-mile hike to Hidden Falls, followed by another steep 0.5-mile climb to the top of a 400-foot hill overlooking the lake. From there, paths continue to nearby lakes or high into the Tetons.

Day 3

Head north from Jenny Lake and take a side road to Signal Mountain, with its panoramic vistas across Jackson Hole and the Tetons. Continue on to Jackson Lake, where a myriad of boating and fishing options await. Stop in at the Colter Bay Visitor Center for a trail map and escape the summertime crowds, looking for moose and trumpeter swans instead. South on U.S. Highway. 26/89/191, pull off for the view at Oxbow Bend. Beyond this are the old Cunningham Cabin and a couple of spectacular turnouts facing the Tetons. A gravel road drops down to Schwabacher Landing, popular with photographers at dawn and dusk. Return to Jenny Lake where you began the day.

Day 4

Spend today playing in the town of Jackson. Directly behind Jackson is Snow King Resort, with a summertime lift that's great for hikers and mountain bikers, plus a kids-love-it alpine slide. Twice-weekly rodeos are another favorite family activity, as are evening "shootouts" on Town Square. Take the scenic route back to Jenny Lake by driving to Teton Village to check out the activities,

Teton Village trail rides

including hourly horseback rides, an all-summer classical music series, a pop-jet fountain, and jaw-dropping tram rides to the summit of 10,450-foot Rendezvous Mountain. Narrow and winding Moose-Wilson Road continues north from here into the park, providing potential hikes along the way and an opportunity to visit eco-friendly Laurance S. Rockefeller Center.

Day 5

Four days have barely scratched the surface of this fascinating and scenic place. You may want to return to a spot you missed, or check out something different such as remote Gros Ventre River Valley or Teton Pass for some high-country hiking, or head back into Jackson for a day of shopping and play.

YELLOWSTONE NATIONAL PARK

The words "national park" seem to stimulate an almost Pavlovian response: Yellowstone. The geysers, canyons, and bears of Yellowstone National Park are so intertwined in our collective consciousness that even 1960s American cartoons used the park as a model: Jellystone Park was where Yogi Bear and Boo Boo were constantly out to thwart the rangers. One source estimates that nearly one-third of the U.S. population has visited the park, and each year more than three million people roll through its gates.

There is something about Yellowstone National Park that calls people back again and again, something more than simply the chance to see the curiosities of the natural world. Generations of parents have brought their children to see the place that they recall from their own childhood visits. Other cultures have the Ganges River, Rome, or Mecca as places with deep spiritual meaning. In America, our national parks have become places for similar renewal, and as the nation's first national park, Yellowstone remains one of our most valued treasures.

So, into the park we come in our cars with our crying babies in the back—babies who suddenly quiet down at the sight of a bison or elk. I recall bringing relatives to Yellowstone after I had worked in the vicinity all summer and had become a bit jaded. Their emotional reaction surprised me, and more than a decade later they still tell stories of the bison calves, the astounding geysers, the rush of the waterfalls, and the night they spent at Old Faithful Inn. Yellowstone is a collective religious experience

© DON PITCHER

HIGHLIGHTS

◖ Norris Geyser Basin: Yellowstone's hottest and oldest geyser basin is home to the world's tallest geyser – but don't wait for an eruption, or you may be here for years (page 44).

◖ Mammoth Hot Springs: Ever-changing, with water trickling over multihued terraces, Mammoth is a moving watercolor painting. Albright Visitor Center houses an interesting museum (page 47).

◖ Wildlife-Viewing: Peaceful and away from the big Yellowstone sights, the Northeast Corner is not only a good place to see bison and elk, but wolves as well (page 54).

◖ Tower Fall: Located in the northern end of the park, this very accessible 132-foot waterfall is a short walk from the parking lot (page 55).

◖ Grand Canyon of the Yellowstone: No adjectives can really describe the power and beauty of this painted canyon where the Yellowstone River drops over two high waterfalls. Lots of viewpoints from all angles, but acrophobics should avoid the Brink of the Lower Falls (page 55).

◖ Mud Volcano Area: Think of this as a bad case of geological heartburn. The names tell all: Dragon's Mouth Spring, Churning Caldron, and Sulphur Caldron (page 58).

◖ Yellowstone Lake: America's largest high-elevation lake occupies an ancient volcanic caldera. Boat tours and fishing are popular, or just relax with a drink inside historic Lake Yellowstone Hotel's Sunset Room (page 58).

◖ Old Faithful: This is the big enchilada. The eruptions are more-or-less predictable, always crowded, and always fun. But don't miss the many other sights in the area, particularly Riverside Geyser and Morning Glory Pool. The new visitor center is an attraction in its own right (page 63).

◖ Old Faithful Inn: This massive log structure is Yellowstone's most majestic lodge and a delightful place to soak up the ambience. Don't miss it (page 67).

◖ Midway Geyser Basin: The featured attractions are spectacular Great Fountain Geyser and brilliantly colored Grand Prismatic Spring, Yellowstone's largest at 370 feet across (page 70).

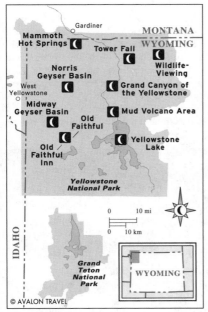

LOOK FOR ◖ TO FIND RECOMMENDED SIGHTS, ACTIVITIES, DINING, AND LODGING.

that sends us back to our roots in the natural world. The smell of wood smoke from a campfire, the picnic lunch on the shore of Yellowstone Lake, the backcountry horseback ride, the hike down to the lip of Lower Falls, the quick strike of a trout on the line, the gasp of the crowd as the first spurt of Old Faithful jets upward, the herds of bison wading Firehole River, the evening piano tunes drifting through the air at Lake Yellowstone Hotel, the howl of a distant wolf, and even the cheesy Yellowstone trinkets—all of these things combine to leave an indelible mark on visitors to Yellowstone National Park.

PLANNING YOUR TIME

America's first and most famous national park, Yellowstone is the primary regional destination. Travelers often take a cursory tour of the park in a single day, but try to set aside a minimum of three days to discover this diverse and geologically fascinating place. If you have only a day or two, pick a couple of spots and see them right. Don't just check out the views everyone else sees; find a nearby trail and do a little exploring on your own. It would be easy to spend a full week in Yellowstone, plus another week in nearby Grand Teton National Park and Jackson Hole. Before visiting, contact Yellowstone (307/344-7381, www.nps.gov/yell) for a copy of the park newspaper and other information.

The vast majority of Yellowstone visitors come June–August; anyone arriving at other times may find closed facilities and campgrounds, along with minimal Park Service staffing. Campgrounds that remain open year-round are often surprisingly busy since travelers have limited options. To avoid surprises, it's wise to make camping reservations well ahead of your trip, even in the off-season. The upside for off-season travelers is an abundance of wildlife and the lack of crowds.

For geyser action, check out the **Norris Geyser Basin,** home to Steamboat Geyser, which blasts 300 feet into the air on its extremely rare eruptions. **Old Faithful** is the most famous of dozens of geysers, hot springs, and other geothermal features that fill Upper Geyser Basin, the largest concentration of geysers in the world. The equally acclaimed **Old Faithful Inn** is a delightful century-old log structure. Stay for a meal or a night, or just step inside to soak up the ambience. Five miles north of Old Faithful, take time to visit **Midway Geyser Basin** with its massive Grand Prismatic Spring, the park's largest hot spring.

Mammoth Hot Springs, home to park headquarters and a small, interesting museum, is famous for its ever-changing palette of softly colored springs. The bucolic **northeast corner** is a good place to see bison, elk, and wolves, and nearby **Tower Fall** provides a great photo op.

The park's most spectacular feature may be the **Grand Canyon of the Yellowstone,** with the river plummeting 308 feet over Lower Falls. South of here is Hayden Valley (look for bison, elk, and occasional bears), along with the belching geysers and hot springs of **Mud Volcano,** and **Yellowstone Lake,** the largest

visitors at Canary Spring

© DON PITCHER

YELLOWSTONE

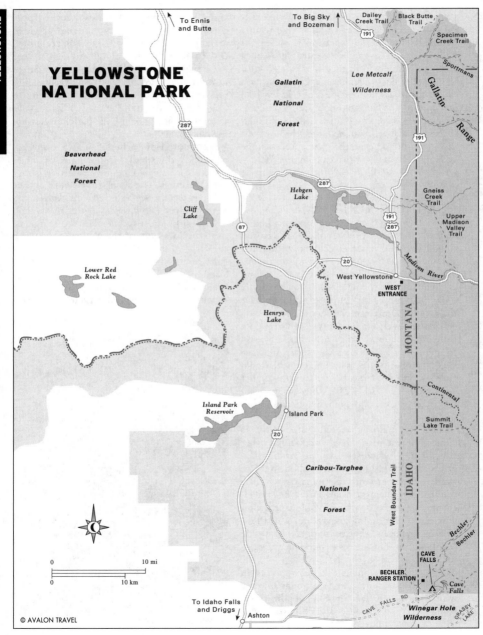

To Ennis
and Butte

To Big Sky
and Bozeman

Dailey
Creek Trail

Black Butte
Trail

191

Specimen
Creek Trail

YELLOWSTONE
NATIONAL PARK

Gallatin

National

Forest

Lee Metcalf

Wilderness

Sportmans

Gallatin

Range

287

191

Beaverhead

National

Forest

287

*Hebgen
Lake*

Gneiss
Creek
Trail

*Cliff
Lake*

87

191

287

Upper
Madison
Valley
Trail

20

*Lower Red
Rock Lake*

West Yellowstone

**WEST
ENTRANCE**

Madison River

*Henrys
Lake*

MONTANA

Continental

*Island Park
Reservoir*

Island Park

20

Summit
Lake Trail

IDAHO

Caribou-Targhee

National

Forest

West Boundary Trail

Bechler

Bechler

0   10 mi

0   10 km

**CAVE
FALLS**

**BECHLER
RANGER STATION**

Cave
Falls

To Idaho Falls
and Driggs

Ashton

CAVE FALLS RD

*Winegar Hole
Wilderness*

GRASSY LAKE

© AVALON TRAVEL

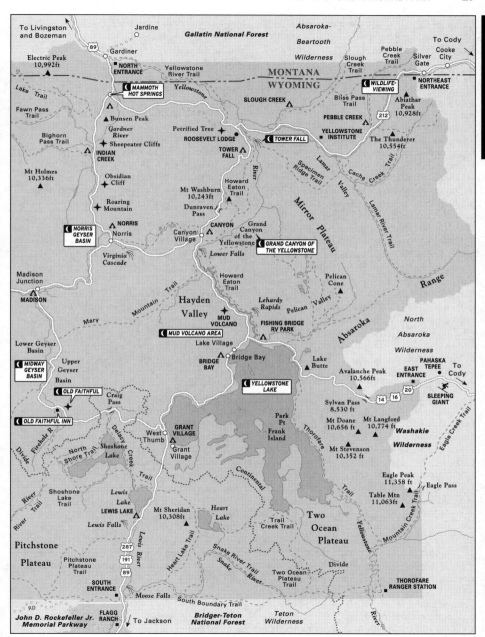

high-elevation lake in North America. On its north shore is the picturesque and graceful Lake Yellowstone Hotel.

THE SETTING

On a map, Yellowstone appears as a gigantic box wedged so tightly against the northwest corner of Wyoming that it squeezes over into Montana and Idaho. The park measures 63 by 54 miles and covers 2.2 million acres, making it one of the largest national parks in the Lower 48 (although it is dwarfed by Alaska's Wrangell–St. Elias National Park and Preserve, which covers almost six times as much land). The United Nations has declared Yellowstone both a World Biosphere Reserve and a World Heritage Site.

The park is accessible from all four sides, and a loop road provides easy access to all of the best-known sights. Because of its popularity as a destination, tourist towns surround Yellowstone: Jackson to the south, Cody to the east, Gardiner and Cooke City on the northern margin, and West Yellowstone on its western border. Also because so many people visit Yellowstone, there is a well-developed network of facilities inside the park, including visitor centers, campgrounds, hotels, restaurants, a hospital, gift shops, ATMs, Wi-Fi, cell phone access, espresso stands, and other supposed necessities of modern life. Although less than 2 percent of the park is developed, Yellowstone contains more than 2,000 buildings of various types. In some spots (most egregiously around Old Faithful), these developments have grown to the point that the natural world seems simply a backdrop for the human world that pulls visitors in to buy T-shirts or to watch park slide shows on wildlife or geysers while missing the real thing just outside the door.

More than any other national park, Yellowstone seems to provide the oddities of nature, creating, as historian Aubrey L. Haines noted, "a false impression that the park is only a colossal, steam-operated freak show." Yellowstone is a mix of the real and the unreal, a place where our fantasies of what nature should be blend with the reality of crowds of fellow travelers and the impact we have on the place we love so much. In midsummer, a trip into Yellowstone can be something less than a natural experience. Long lines of cars back up behind RVs creeping up the narrow roads, and throngs of visitors crowd the benches around Old Faithful Geyser waiting for an eruption, while dozens of others cluster around bewildered elk to get photos to email their friends. Despite this crowding—or perhaps because most folks prefer to stay on paved paths— many parts of the park remain virtually uninhabited. In the Yellowstone backcountry, one can still walk for days without seeing more than a handful of other hardy hikers.

A Place of Controversy

Yellowstone National Park evokes a torrent of emotions in anyone with a knowledge of and concern for the natural world. Perhaps more than any other wild place in America, the park seems to be in a perpetual state of controversy, be it over fire policies, bison and wolf management, snowmobile use, or some other issue; there's always something getting folks stirred up. Perhaps it is because so many Americans have visited the park that we feel a vested interest in what it means to us. Writer Paul Schullery, in his wonderful book *Searching for Yellowstone,* put it best when he noted, "Caring for Yellowstone National Park brings to mind all the metaphors of growth and change; it is a process more organic than political; a crucible of ideas, ambitions, dreams, and belief systems; a cultural, intellectual, and spiritual crossroads at which we are forever debating which way to turn." As visitation has risen in recent decades, more and more folks have begun to suggest some sort of limit on numbers to preserve the experience and protect the park. Don't-tread-on-me Westerners consider the idea of limits an example of environmental extremism among the elite, but as visitation increases, conflicts and controversies are natural outcomes.

GEOLOGY

Yellowstone is, without a doubt, the most geologically fascinating place on this planet. Here,

FIREHOLE RIVER AREA, 1839

At this place there is also large numbers of hot Springs some of which have formed cones of limestone 20 feet high of a Snowy whiteness which make a splendid appearance standing among the ever green pines Some of the lower peaks are very serviceable to the hunter in preparing his dinner when hungry for here his kettle is always ready and boiling his meat being suspended in the water by a string is soon prepared for his meal without further trouble...Standing upon an eminence and superficially viewing these natural monuments one is half inclined to believe himself in the neighborhood of the ruins of some ancients City whose temples had been constructed of the whitest marble.

Mountain man Osborne Russell

the forces that elsewhere lie deep within the earth seem close enough to touch. They're palpable not only in the geysers and hot springs but also in the lake that fills part of an enormous caldera, the earthquakes that shake this land, the evidence of massive glaciations, and the deeply eroded Grand Canyon of the Yellowstone.

Fire and Ice
THE YELLOWSTONE HOT SPOT

When geologists began to study the Yellowstone area in depth, they found a surprising pattern. Extending far to the southwest was a chain of volcanic fields, the most ancient of which—16 million years old—lay in northern Nevada. In addition, geologic fault lines created a 100-mile-wide semicircle around the Yellowstone area, as if some deep-seated force

were pushing the land outward and upward the way a ripple moves across a pond.

Both the volcanic activity and the wavelike pattern of faults are caused by the same source: a plume of superheated material moving up from the core of the planet through a narrow tube, creating a hot spot beneath the earth's crust. As the North American continent slid to the southwest through the eons, this plume traced a line of volcanoes across the West, and as the land continues to move, the plume causes massive deformations in the crust that show up as mountain ranges, fault lines, and earthquakes. It's a little like somebody tugging a piece of cloth across a candle. Approximately 40 such hot spots are known to exist around the globe, but most are beneath the seas. Other than Yellowstone, the best-known example is the chain of Hawaiian Islands. The earth has been moving over the Yellowstone hot spot at the rate of 15 miles per million years for the last 10 million years, and on the present track, the spot might eventually end up in Hudson Bay in 100 million years or so.

TAMBORA ON STEROIDS

The volcanic activity revealed by Yellowstone's geysers, hot springs, and fumaroles is not always benign. Within the last two million years there have been three stupendous volcanic eruptions in the area, the most recent taking place 640,000 years ago. The largest of these eruptions occurred two million years ago and created an event beyond the realm of imagination: 600 cubic miles of ash were blasted into the atmosphere! This eruption—probably one of the largest to ever occur on earth—ejected 17 times more material than the massive Tambora eruption of 1815, an explosion that was heard 1,600 miles away. The first Yellowstone event was 2,400 times as large as the 1980 eruption of Mount St. Helens, and it carried ash east to Iowa, north to Saskatchewan, south to the Gulf of Mexico, and west to California. This titanic infusion of ash into the atmosphere undoubtedly affected the global climate for years to follow.

The process that creates these explosions starts when molten rock pushes up from the center of the earth, causing the land to bulge upward into an enormous dome. Eventually the pressure becomes too great and fractures develop around the dome's margins, sending hot gases, ash, and rock blasting into the atmosphere. After the most recent eruption (640,000 years ago), the magma chamber collapsed into a gigantic, smoldering pit reaching 28 by 47 miles in surface area and perhaps several thousand feet deep. Through time, additional molten rock pushed up from underneath and flowed as thick lava over the land. The most recent of these lava flows was 70,000 years ago.

Two resurgent domes—one near Old Faithful and the other just north of Yellowstone Lake near LeHardys Rapids—have been discovered by geologists. Measurements at LeHardys Rapids showed that the land rose almost three feet from 1923 to 1985, before subsiding until 2004, when the land began to rise rapidly—as much as 17 cm (6.7 inches) in just three years. This upsurge is raising the outlet of Yellowstone Lake, creating new beaches on the north shore while flooding forests along the lake's southern margins. Obviously, Yellowstone's volcanism is far from dead, and scientists believe another eruption is possible or even likely, although nobody knows when it might occur.

The **Yellowstone Volcano Observatory** (http://volcanoes.usgs.gov/yvo)—a partnership of the USGS, Park Service, and University of Utah—monitors Yellowstone's ever-changing volcanic system and produces an excellent small publication about the park's geologic origins; find it in visitor centers.

GLACIATION

Not everything in Yellowstone is the result of volcanic activity. The entire Yellowstone region has undergone a series of at least eight major glaciations during the last million years, the last of which—the Pinedale Glaciation—began about 70,000 years ago. At its peak, the Pinedale Glaciation covered almost all of Yellowstone and reached southward into Jackson Hole and north much of the way to

Livingston, Montana. Over Yellowstone Lake, the ice field was 4,000 feet thick and covered 10,000-foot mountains. This period of glaciation ended about 15,000 years ago, but trees did not appear in the Yellowstone area until 11,500 years ago, and it wasn't until about 5,000 years ago that the landscape began to appear as it does today.

Geysers

Yellowstone is famous for geysers, and geyser-gazers will not be disappointed. At least 60 percent of the world's geysers are in the park, making this easily the largest and most diverse collection in existence. Yellowstone's more than 300 geysers are spread throughout nine different basins, with half of these in Upper Geyser Basin, the home of Old Faithful.

Geysers need three essentials to exist: water, heat, and fractured rock. The water comes from snow and rain falling on this high plateau, while the heat comes from molten rock close to the earth's surface. Massive pressures from below have created a ring of fractures around the edge of Yellowstone's caldera. This is one of the hottest places on the planet, with heat flows more than 60 times the global average.

HOW THEY WORK

Geysers operate because cold water is dense and sinks, while hot water is less dense and rises. The periodic eruption of geysers is caused by constrictions in the underground channels that prevent an adequate heat exchange with the surface. Precipitation slowly moves into the earth, eventually contacting the molten rock. Because of high pressures at these depths, water can reach extreme temperatures without vaporizing (as in a pressure cooker). As this super-heated water rises back toward the surface, it emerges in hot springs, fumaroles, mud pots, and geysers. The most spectacular of these phenomena are geysers. Two general types of geysers exist in Yellowstone. Fountain geysers (such as Great Fountain Geyser) explode from pools of water and tend to spray water more widely, whereas cone-type geysers (such as Old Faithful) jet out of nozzlelike formations.

In a geyser, steam bubbles upward from the superheated source of water and expands as it rises. These bubbles block the plumbing system, keeping hot water from reaching the surface. Eventually, however, pressure from the bubbles begins to force the cooler water above out of the vent. This initial release triggers a more violent reaction as the sudden lessening of pressure allows the entire column to begin boiling, explosively expelling steam and water to produce a geyser. Once the eruption has emptied the plumbing system, water gradually seeps back into the chambers to begin the process anew. Some of Yellowstone's geysers have enormous underground caverns that fill with water; in its rare eruptions, massive Steamboat Geyser can blast a million gallons of water into the air!

As an aside, *geyser* is one of the few Icelandic terms in the English language; it means "to gush forth." There are probably 30 active geysers in Iceland, many more on Russia's Kamchatka Peninsula, and a few in New Zealand, where geothermal development has greatly lessened geyser activity.

A fine online source with details about Yellowstone's geysers—and others around the globe—is maintained by the nonprofit **Geyser Observation and Study Association** (www.geyserstudy.org). The GOSA website has frequent postings of geyser activity, and volunteer observers are often present in the park during the summer, particularly at Grand Geyser in Upper Geyser Basin.

PROTECTING THE GEYSERS

Unfortunately, some of Yellowstone's geysers have been lost because of human stupidity and vandalism. At one time, it was considered great sport to stuff logs, rocks, and even chairs into the geysers for a little added show. Chemicals were also poured into them to make them play. As a result of such actions, some geysers have been severely damaged or destroyed, and some hot springs have become collection points for coins, rocks, sticks, and trash. Such actions ruin these thermal areas for everyone and destroy something that may have been going on for hundreds of years.

Other Geothermal Activity

Although geysers are Yellowstone's best-known features, they make up only a tiny fraction of perhaps 10,000 thermal features in the park. **Hot springs** appear where water can reach the ground surface relatively easily, allowing the heat that builds up in the chambers of geysers to dissipate. When less groundwater is present, you may find **fumaroles,** vents that shoot steam, carbon dioxide, and even hydrogen sulfide gas. **Mud pots** (also called paint pots) are essentially wet fumaroles. Hydrogen sulfide gas combines with water to produce hydrosulfuric acid. This acid breaks down surrounding rocks to form clay, and the clay combines with water to create mud. As gas passes through the mud, it creates the bubbling mud pots. Probably the best examples of these different forms are at Fountain Paint Pot in Lower Geyser Basin, where geysers and hot springs are found in the wetter areas below, while mud pots and fumaroles sit atop a small hill. Hydrogen sulfide is,

hot springs along Firehole River

© DON PITCHER

YELLOWSTONE

of course, poisonous, and toxic fumes sometimes kill bison and elk that cluster around the geothermal areas in the winter. Scientists joke that Norris Geyser Basin would be considered an EPA Superfund site if it weren't within a national park!

The colors in Yellowstone's hot springs come from a variety of sources, including algae and bacteria as well as various minerals, particularly sulfur, iron oxides, and arsenic sulfide. The algae and bacteria are highly temperature-specific and help create the distinct bands of colors around many hot springs. Interestingly, many of these algal species are found only in hot springs, although they exist around the world. The bacteria have proven of considerable interest to science because of their ability to survive such high temperatures. One such organism, *Thermus aquaticus,* was discovered in a Yellowstone hot spring in 1967, and scientists extracted an enzyme that was later used to develop the increasingly important technique of DNA fingerprinting. Above 194°F, even these hot-water bacteria, archaea (a single-celled microorganism), and algae cannot survive, so the hottest springs may appear a deep blue because of the water's ability to absorb all wavelengths of light except blue, which is reflected back into our eyes.

A couple of other terms are worth learning before heading out to see the sights of Yellowstone. **Sinter** (also called "geyserite") is a deposit composed primarily of silica. The silica is dissolved by hot water deep underground and brought to the surface in geysers or hot springs. At the surface the water evaporates, leaving behind the light gray sinter, which can create large mounds (up to 30 feet high) around the older geysers. The rate of accumulation is very slow, and some of the park's geysers obviously have been active for many thousands of years. The other precipitate that is sometimes deposited around Yellowstone's hot springs and geysers is **travertine,** consisting of calcium carbonate that has been dissolved underground.

A NOTE OF WARNING

The surface around many of the hot springs and geysers is surprisingly thin, and people have been killed or seriously injured by falling through into the boiling water. Stay on the boardwalks in developed areas, and use extreme caution around backcountry thermal features. If in doubt, stay away!

Exploring Yellowstone

Yellowstone is perhaps the most accessible large national park in America. Nearly all of the famous sights are within a couple of hundred feet of the Grand Loop Road, a 142-mile figure-eight through the middle of the park. Whatever you do, *don't* see Yellowstone at 45 miles per hour; that's like seeing the Louvre from a passing train.

For all too many visitors, Yellowstone becomes a checklist of places to visit, geysers to watch, and animals to see. This tends to inspire an attitude that treats this great national treasure as a drive-through theme park, where the animals come out to perform and the geyser eruptions are predicted so everyone can be there on time. If you're one of this crowd, give yourself a giant kick in the rear and take a walk, even if it is just around Upper Geyser Basin where can you see something beyond Old Faithful.

PARK ACCESS

Entrance to Yellowstone (307/344-7381, www.nps.gov/yell) costs $25 per vehicle, or $12 for individuals entering by bicycle, foot, skis, or as a bus passenger. Motorcycles or snowmobiles are $20. The pass covers entrance to both Yellowstone and Grand Teton National Parks and is good for seven days. If you're planning to be here longer or to make additional visits, get an annual pass covering both parks for $50, or the Interagency Annual Pass—good for all national parks—for $80 per year. An Interagency Senior Pass for all national parks is available to anyone older than 62 for a one-time fee of $10, and people with disabilities can get a free Interagency Access Pass. Both of these latter passes also give you 50 percent reductions in most camping fees.

Upon entering the park, you'll receive a Yellowstone map and a copy of *Yellowstone Today,* a quarterly newspaper that describes facilities and services and provides camping, fishing, and backcountry information. This is the best source for up-to-date park information. It's also packed with enough warnings to scare off a platoon of Marines. Examples include cautions against falling trees, bathing in thermal pools (hydrogen sulfide poisoning and meningitis), unpredictable wildlife, improper food storage, health problems from the altitude, narrow roads, theft, imitating wolf howls, leaving side mirrors attached when not pulling trailers, and scalding water. And, oh yes, "swim at your own risk." **Pets are prohibited on trails, hydrothermal areas, or boardwalks anywhere in Yellowstone.** Kennel facilities

are not available in the park but can be found in Jackson and Cody.

If you are planning a trip to Yellowstone, request a copy of the annual *Yellowstone National Park Trip Planner* booklet for an overview of sights, visitor centers, what to do, services, camping, and more. It's also available on the park website, www.nps.gov/yell/planyourvisit. Call 307/344-2113 for a recorded **park weather** forecast.

VISITOR CENTERS

The Park Service maintains visitor centers at Mammoth Hot Springs, Norris Geyser Basin, Old Faithful, Canyon Village, Fishing Bridge, and Grant Village. All of these sell maps and natural-history books covering the park and surrounding areas. In addition, you'll find smaller information stations at Madison and West Thumb and a Park Service ranger at the West Yellowstone Visitor Center.

Open daily, the **Albright Visitor Center** (307/344-2263) at Mammoth is the only year-round visitor facility in Yellowstone.

New in 2010, the 26,000-square-foot **Old**

© DON PITCHER

northeast entrance station

Faithful Visitor Education Center (307/545-2750) is open daily mid-April–early November and mid-December–mid-March. Don't miss this state-of-the-art building where tall windows frame eruptions of Old Faithful.

The modern **Canyon Visitor Education Center** (307/242-2550) is another must-see, with fascinating exhibits detailing park geology; it's open daily early May–September.

Grant Visitor Center (307/242-2650, daily late May–Sept.) houses informative exhibits and a film on the role of fires in the park. **Fishing Bridge Visitor Center** (307/242-2450, daily late May–Sept.) contains decrepit exhibits of birds, animals, and geology.

Park Service personnel also staff the **West Yellowstone Visitor Information Center** (406/646-7701, daily late May–Oct.), just outside the park.

TOURS

During summer, most people come into Yellowstone in private cars or RVs, but there *are* other ways of getting around. An interpretive bus tour provides a quick overview of the park while leaving the driving to an expert. This is especially true for RVers, who can park at Fishing Bridge RV Park or Bridge Bay Campground and then don't need to worry about traveling on narrow park roads.

Unfortunately, public transportation—other than the tours—does not exist within Yellowstone. There is, however, daily van service to West Yellowstone and Jackson Hole from Salt Lake City, and winter-only service between Bozeman and West Yellowstone.

In-Park Tours

From mid-May–late September, Xanterra Parks and Resorts (307/344-7311 or 866/439-7375, www.yellowstonenationalparklodges.com) guides full-day bus tours from Canyon Lodge, Lake Yellowstone Hotel, Old Faithful Inn, Fishing Bridge RV Park, Bridge Bay Campground, and Grant Village. Tours of the lower loop road are $63 adults or $32 ages 3–11 (free for younger kids). A longer "Yellowstone in a Day" tour (not recommended unless you're

into sensory overload and more than nine hours of riding around) costs $70 for adults or $35 for kids. The in-a-day tour is available only from Mammoth or Gardiner. Also available are professionally taught four-hour **Photo Safaris** ($81 adults, $41 kids) daily out of Old Faithful Inn and Lake Hotel.

The most distinctive park tour offerings are classic **Historic Yellow Bus tours.** Built in the 1930s, these lovingly refurbished vehicles get almost as much attention as the scenery; the top of the buses open for safari-style wildlife viewing. Tours head in a multitude of directions throughout the day, including half-day "Wake up to Wildlife" tours ($75 adults, $38 kids) in search of Lamar Valley wolves, and two-hour "Twilight on the Firehole" tours ($32 adults, $16 kids) of the Old Faithful area.

Other Park Tours

Upper or lower loop tours are available out of West Yellowstone from **Buffalo Bus Touring Co.** (406/646-9564 or 800/426-7669, www.yellowstonevacations.com, $65 adults or $49 kids for the lower loop, $120 adults or $98 kids for both loops). Park entrance fees are extra.

Summertime bus tours of Yellowstone are available several times a week from **Gray Line of Jackson Hole/Alltrans** (307/733-3135 or 800/443-6133, www.graylinejh.com). Tours last 11 hours and cost $115 (rates for kids are half-price) plus a $12 park entrance fee.

Karst Stage (406/388-2293 or 800/287-4759, www.karststage.com) has summertime tours departing from Livingston, Montana and continuing to Bozeman, Old Faithful, Lake Hotel, Canyon Village, Mammoth, Gardiner, and Emigrant, before returning to Livingston. The cost is $85 per person, with a four-person minimum. Call at least three days ahead of your travel date.

A multitude of other companies—at least 75 at last count—provide guided park tours from West Yellowstone, Cody, Jackson Hole, and other towns. The Yellowstone National Park website (www.nps.gov/yell) has a complete listing of permitted tour operators.

RETURN OF THE OLD YELLOW BUSES

After a 50-year hiatus, Yellowstone visitors can again step onboard a vintage yellow bus to tour the park. Built in the 1930s by the White Motor Company, these photogenic low-slung 13-passenger buses were used by the Yellowstone Park Transportation Company until the 1950s. The buses traveled to train depots, providing the primary means of transport as visitors stopped in a different park hotel each night. At their peak in 1940, some 98 yellow buses were in the Yellowstone fleet, but as private vehicle usage increased, the old buses fell out of favor and were sold and dispersed across the country.

The buses ended up in private collections, most notably that of the Skagway Streetcar Company in Alaska, where eight of them were used for tours until 2001. In that year – some 50 years after the buses left the park – Xanterra bought these buses for $38,000 apiece,

spending another $1.9 million to totally refurbish them. The buses were painstakingly rebuilt using retro-style instruments, reupholstered seats, yellow and black paint and decals to match the originals, new convertible tops, and a Ford E-450 chassis with automatic transmissions and modern 5.4-liter engines.

Xanterra began offering park tours in the yellow buses in 2007, and travelers can now choose from several different options led by knowledgeable drivers, including half-day photo safaris, morning wildlife adventures, and twilight trips. The buses are always an attention-grabber, and the open roof is great for watching wildlife and taking in Yellowstone's sights. They're a delightful step back in time to a simpler era. Contact **Xanterra Parks & Resorts** (307/344-7311 or 866/439-7375, www.yellowstonenationalparklodges.com) for details on yellow bus tours.

© DON PITCHER

historic yellow bus at Old Faithful Inn

Natural History Tours

In addition to traditional classes, the **Yellowstone Association Institute** (406/848-2400, www.yellowstoneassociation.org) leads a popular series of **Lodging and Learning** packages. These four- to six-day programs blend education, recreation, and comfortable lodging. Naturalist guides from the association lead excursions, and participants are provided accommodations in park hotels, plus breakfasts and lunches. The programs include special ones for families, winter ski treks, winter wildlife, and hiking. For the private touch, the institute offers **Yellowstone Ed-Ventures,** where a wildlife biologist accompanies you in your own vehicle. It's sort of like having a personal trainer for Yellowstone.

For a listing of licensed tour operators offering wildlife, natural history, and photography tours in the park, contact the Park Service (307/344-7381, www.nps.gov/yell). Operated by the highly respected Teton Science School, **Wildlife Expeditions** (307/733-2623 or 888/945-3567, www.wildlifeexpeditions.org) leads a variety of wildlife-viewing safaris throughout the region, including multi-day wildlife tours into Yellowstone. Also highly recommended are naturalist Carl Swoboda's **Safari Yellowstone** (800/723-2747, www.safariyellowstone.com), geologist Dr. Keith Watts of **Earth Tours** (307/733-4261, www.earthtours.com), and **Tory and Meredith Taylor** (307/455-2161), who lead personalized wolf-viewing tours in the winter.

Other companies with guided van tours into Yellowstone include **Ana's Grand Excursions** (307/690-6106, www.anasgrandexcursions.com), **Brushbuck Guide Services** (888/282-5868, www.brushbuckphototours.com), **Callowishus Park Touring Company** (307/413-5483, www.callowishus.com), **EcoTour Adventures** (307/690-9533, www.jhecotouradventures.com), **Upstream Anglers and Outdoor Adventures** (307/739-9443 or 800/642-8979, www.upstreamanglers.com), **The Hole Hiking Experience** (307/690-4453 or 866/733-4453, www.holehike.com), **Yellowstone Safari Co.** (406/586-1155 or 866/586-1155, www.yellowstonesafari.com), **Yellowstone Yearround Adventures** (406/585-9041, www.yellowstoneyearround.com), and **Yellowstone Country Adventures** (406/581-7476, www.yellowstonecountry-adventures.com).

ROADS

The speed limit on all park roads is a vigilantly enforced 45 mph (or less); exceed this and you're likely to get a ticket! Be especially cautious on the south side of the park, where rangers seem to wait most evenings and the relatively straight road makes it easy to speed. During summer you're not likely to approach the speed limit, because long lines of traffic form behind monstrous RVs or when wildlife is visible.

Gas stations are at Old Faithful, Canyon Village, Mammoth Hot Springs, Fishing Bridge, Grant Village, and Tower Junction, and repair services are available at all of these except Mammoth Hot Springs and Tower Junction. Additional service stations are in towns surrounding the park.

Seasonal Road Closures

Most roads in Yellowstone close on the Monday after the first Sunday in November and usually open again by mid-May. Only the road between Mammoth and Cooke City is kept plowed all winter; other roads are groomed for snowmobiles and snowcoaches (snow conditions permitting) by mid-December. Plowing begins in early March, and the roads reopen in sections. The roads connecting Mammoth to West Yellowstone open first (typically mid-Apr.), while Dunraven Pass is plowed last. Spring storms may cause closures or restrictions on some park roads, so get current road conditions at entrance stations and visitor centers, or by calling 307/344-7381. (I've seen crowds of stranded travelers as passes were closed over a snowy Memorial Day weekend!)

The Construction Maze

Yellowstone's roads have long been a source of irritation. Much of the roadbed was built at the turn of the 20th century, when horses

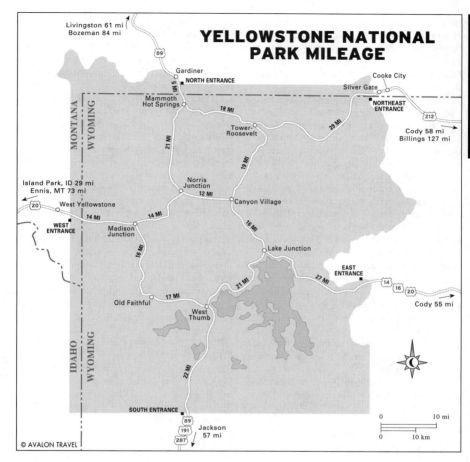

YELLOWSTONE NATIONAL PARK MILEAGE

Livingston 61 mi
Bozeman 84 mi

89

Gardiner
NORTH ENTRANCE

Cooke City
Silver Gate

Mammoth
Hot Springs

NORTHEAST
ENTRANCE

212

Cody 58 mi
Billings 127 mi

MONTANA
WYOMING

18 MI

Tower-
Roosevelt

29 MI

21 MI

19 MI

Island Park, ID 29 mi
Ennis, MT 73 mi

20

Norris
Junction

12 MI

West Yellowstone

Canyon Village

14 MI

14 MI

16 MI

WEST
ENTRANCE

Madison
Junction

Lake Junction

16 MI

EAST
ENTRANCE

21 MI

27 MI

14

16 20

Cody 55 mi

Old Faithful

17 MI

West
Thumb

IDAHO
WYOMING

22 MI

SOUTH ENTRANCE

89

191

287

Jackson
57 mi

0   10 mi
0   10 km

© AVALON TRAVEL

and carriages were the primary means of travel. Increasing traffic and larger vehicles contributed to the deterioration of park roads, as did stretched-thin park maintenance budgets. Yellowstone is now nearing completion on a massive two-decade, $300 million reconstruction program, and each summer you'll find a different section undergoing rebuilding. Be ready for delays of up to 30 minutes somewhere during your journey. Fortunately, all this work means that the roads are vastly better than they were in the 1980s. Contact the park's 24-hour hotline at 307/344-2117 for the latest on the road situation and this year's construction delays, or check the park newspaper. Road construction details can also be found online at www.nps.gov/yell/planyourvisit/roadclosures.htm.

WILDLIFE VIEWING

Yellowstone provides a marvelous natural setting in which to view bison, elk, moose, wolves, coyotes, pronghorn antelope, bighorn sheep, and other wild animals. One of the easiest ways to find wildlife is simply by watching for the brake lights, the cars pulled half off the road, and the cameras all pointed in one direction.

Inevitably, you'll find an elk or a bison placidly munching away, trying to remain oblivious to the chaos that surrounds it. Be sure to bring binoculars for your trip to Yellowstone. A spotting scope is also helpful in searching for distant bears and wolves.

Because of the constant parade of visitors and the lack of hunting, many of Yellowstone's animals appear to almost ignore the presence of people, and it isn't uncommon to see visitors approach an animal without respecting its need for space. Although they may appear tame, Yellowstone's animals really are wild, and attacks are not uncommon. Those quiet bison can suddenly erupt with an enormous ferocity if provoked by photographers who come too close. Between 1983 and 1994, four people were killed by bison in Yellowstone and Grand Teton National Parks. Stay at least 25 yards away from bison and elk and at least 100 yards away from bears. Do not under any circumstances feed the park's animals. This creates an unnatural dependency, is unhealthy for the animal, and may even lead to its death. You'll find some entertaining (and simultaneously scary) safety videos of wildlife encounters with foolish tourists on the Yellowstone website (www.nps.gov/yell).

The Park Service has a free pamphlet showing where you're most likely to see wildlife in Yellowstone. Pick one up at any visitor center. During summer, the best wildlife-viewing hours are early in the morning and in the late afternoon to early evening.

Bears

Both black and grizzly bears are found throughout Yellowstone, but the days of bear jams along the park roads are long past because rangers actively work to prevent bears from becoming habituated to people. Most bears have returned to their more natural ways of living, although problems still crop up with occasional bears wandering through campgrounds in search of food. You're more likely to encounter a bear in the backcountry areas, and some places are closed to hiking for extended periods each year for this

reason. The best places to watch for grizzlies along the road system are in the **Hayden** and **Lamar Valleys,** near **Mt. Washburn,** and from **Fishing Bridge to the East Entrance.** Black bears may be seen in forested areas throughout the park.

Stay at least 100 yards away from bears. Safety in grizzly country is always a concern, but statistically you are considerably more likely to be hurt in a traffic accident than to be mauled by a bear. There were just 22 bear-caused injuries in the park between 1980 and 1997—one injury for every 2.1 million visitors! Most of these injuries took place in backcountry areas and involved female bears with cubs or yearlings, and nearly all attacks took place after a surprise encounter with a bear. Three people were killed by Yellowstone bears in the last three decades of the 20th century, including a 1986 fatality caused when a photographer approached too close to an adult female grizzly. In 2010, a camper was killed in a nighttime attack at a Forest Service campground just outside the northeast corner of Yellowstone.

Bighorn Sheep

About 250 bighorns live within Yellowstone National Park, with much larger populations in the surrounding national forests. Look for bighorn sheep on cliffs in the **Gardner River Canyon** between Mammoth Hot Springs and the town of Gardiner. Ewes and lambs also frequently appear just off the road on **Dunraven Pass** north of Canyon, and day-hikers commonly encounter rams up close on the slopes of **Mt. Washburn.** Another place to see bighorns is along **Specimen Ridge.**

Birds

Trumpeter swans—beautiful white birds with seven-foot wingspans—are a fairly common sight in Yellowstone, particularly on the Madison and Yellowstone Rivers and on Yellowstone Lake. Many trumpeter swans winter in hot-spring areas. These are some of the largest birds in America, weighing 20–30 pounds. Another large white bird here is the ungainly-looking and bulbous-billed **white pelican,** a common sight on Yellowstone Lake and near Fishing Bridge. More than 350 pairs of pelicans nest on the Molly Islands in Yellowstone Lake; this is one of the largest white-pelican breeding colonies in the Rockies. **Bald eagles**—America's national bird—and **ospreys** have managed comebacks in recent years and are frequently seen along the Yellowstone River and above Yellowstone Lake. Look for **golden eagles** flying over the open grasslands of Lamar Valley or Hayden Valley.

Bison

Bison are found in open country throughout Yellowstone, including **Hayden, Lamar,** and **Pelican Valleys,** along with the **Firehole River Basin** (including Old Faithful). A favorite time to see bison in Yellowstone is late May, just after the new calves have been born. The calves' antics are always good for laughs. Be sure to use caution around bison; many people have been gored when they've come too close. *Always stay at least 25 yards away, preferably farther.*

Coyotes

Although wolves get the media attention, visitors to Yellowstone are probably more likely to see another native of the dog family: the coyote. Keep your eyes open for coyotes anywhere in Yellowstone but especially in open grassy areas, where they are most easily spotted. During summer, you'll often see them in small packs or alone as they hunt small mammals such as mice, voles, and pocket gophers. At other times of the year they prey on larger animals, including the calves of elk and pronghorn antelope, and scavenge carrion. Good places to look for coyotes are in the **Blacktail Plateau** area and Lamar Valley, along with the **Upper and Lower Geyser basins** near Old Faithful.

Deer

Mule deer (also known as black-tailed deer) are common in many parts of Yellowstone during summer, but most migrate to lower elevations when winter comes. They are typically found in open areas containing sagebrush or grass. Mule deer are named for their long

© DON PITCHER

Elk relax on the terraces at Mammoth Hot Springs.

mulelike ears. They also have black-tipped tails and a peculiar way of pogoing away when frightened.

The smaller **white-tailed deer** are far less common in Yellowstone. You are most likely to find them along rivers or in brushy areas at low elevations, such as around Mammoth Hot Springs or in Lamar Valley. Other places to watch for them are along Yellowstone Lake and in the Upper Geyser Basin.

Elk

One animal virtually every visitor to Yellowstone sees is elk. About 30,000 of these regal animals summer in the park, and approximately 15,000 remain through the winter, primarily on the north end of Yellowstone. In summer, look for elk in **Mammoth Hot Springs, Elk Park, Lamar Valley,** and **Gibbon Meadows,** but you're certain to also see them elsewhere. The bugling of bull elk is a common autumn sound in Yellowstone, as anyone who visits Mammoth at that time of year can attest. Winter snows push the elk to lower elevations on the north side of Yellowstone or out of the park into surrounding areas. *Stay at least 25 yards away from elk.*

Moose

The largest members of the deer family, moose are typically seen eating willow bushes in riparian areas inside Yellowstone National Park. The best places to look for moose are **Hayden Valley,** around **Yellowstone Lake,** the Willow Park area north of **Norris,** the southwestern corner along the Bechler and Falls Rivers, and along the Gallatin, Lamar, and Lewis River drainages.

Pronghorn Antelope

These speedy and colorful ungulates (hoofed mammals) are common sights on the plains of Wyoming, but most of Yellowstone doesn't provide adequate habitat. Pronghorn antelope are found only in sagebrush and grassy areas on the northern end of the park from **Lamar Valley** to the **Gardiner** area. The population totals about 200.

Wolves

The best place to look for wolves is the open terrain of **Lamar Valley,** where the Druid pack are visible at many times of the year. Another excellent spot is **Hayden Valley,** where members of Mollie's pack are commonly seen. Visit early in the morning or near dusk to increase your odds of seeing them. You may well hear their plaintive cry from your campground late at night, particularly at Slough Creek or Pebble Creek campgrounds. Binoculars or spotting scopes are helpful for roadside wolf-watching. Rent quality scopes from Silver Gate General Store (406/838-3043) in Silver Gate, Montana, just outside the park's northeast corner, or in Jackson from Teton Adventure Gear (307/203-2915, www.tetonadventuregear.com).

Wolf-watchers should follow the advice listed in the park newspaper. Noise can be a problem, especially in popular wolf-viewing areas, so avoid slamming car doors and keep other sounds to a minimum. And yes, it is illegal to imitate a wolf howl in the park. Do not follow the wolves around, because this may disturb them and affect their survival. Denning activity typically takes place early April–early May, with active denning areas closed to humans; check with the Park Service for closed areas.

Sights

The following tour of Yellowstone sights begins on the west side of the park (the most popular entrance is via West Yellowstone) and traces a more-or-less clockwise path around the Grand Loop, ending at the geyser basins north of Old Faithful.

MADISON

The tourist town of **West Yellowstone, Montana** is right outside the park's western boundary. The **West Entrance** is the busiest of all the park entry stations, handling more than one-third of the nearly three million people who enter Yellowstone each year. A 14-mile road heads east to Madison Junction, closely paralleling the scenic Madison River (a major tributary of the Missouri River), in which geese, ducks, and trumpeter swans are common. Bison and elk are other critters to watch for in the open meadows. The Madison River is open only to fly-fishing and is considered one of the finest places in the nation to catch trout (although they can be a real challenge to fool). On warm summer evenings, you're likely to see dozens of anglers casting for wily rainbow and brown trout and mountain whitefish.

At Madison Junction, the road splits, heading south to Old Faithful and north to Mammoth. This is where the Gibbon and Firehole Rivers join to form the Madison River. The 406,359-acre North Fork Fire of 1988 ripped through most of the Madison River country, but the land is recovering well in most places, and wildflowers are abundant in midsummer.

Madison Canyon is flanked by mountains named for two photographers who had a marked influence on Yellowstone. To the north is 8,257-foot **Mt. Jackson**—as in William H. Jackson, whose photos helped bring the area to national attention—and to the south is distinctive, 8,235-foot **Mt. Haynes,** named for the man who held the park photo concession for nearly four decades. These mountains and the surrounding slopes were created by rhyolite lava flows.

The Northwest Corner

From West Yellowstone, Montana, U.S. Highway 191 heads north to Bozeman, passing through a small corner of Yellowstone National Park en route. There are no entrance stations or developed facilities here, but the area provides backcountry access for hikers and horsepackers from several trailheads. The drive itself is scenic, and the road is wide and smooth. The road enters the park approximately 10 miles north of West Yellowstone and gradually climbs through stretches that were burned in the fires of 1988 before emerging into unburned alpine meadows near tiny Divide Lake. North of here, U.S. Highway 191 follows the growing Gallatin River downhill through a pretty mix of meadows, sagebrush, rocky outcrops, and forested hillsides with grassy carpets beneath. Approximately 31 miles north of West Yellowstone, the road exits Yellowstone and enters Gallatin National Forest. It's another 17 miles from here to the turnoff for Big Sky Resort or 60 miles from the park boundary to Bozeman.

Madison Junction to Norris

The **Madison Information Station** (307/344-2821) near Madison Junction is open daily 9 A.M.–6 P.M. late May–September and closed the rest of the year. A small bookstore is also here. Directly behind Madison Campground is 7,500-foot **National Park Mountain,** named in honor of a fabled incident in 1870. Three explorers were gathered around the campfire, discussing the wonders that they had found in this area, when one suggested that rather than letting all of these wonders pass into private hands, they should be set aside as a national park. Thus was born the concept that led to the world's first national park. The tale was passed on as the gospel truth for so long that the mountain was named in honor of this evening. Unfortunately, the story was a complete fabrication. Cynics may read something into the fact that National Park Mountain was torched by the fires of 1988.

North of Madison Junction, the road follows the Gibbon River nearly all of the 14 miles to Norris. It crosses the river five times and hangs right on the edge through Gibbon Canyon. The pretty, 84-foot-high **Gibbon Falls** is approximately five miles up the road and situated right at the edge of the enormous caldera that fills the center of Yellowstone. The 1988 fires consumed most of the trees around the falls, but the new lodgepoles are now topping 20 feet. Another five miles beyond this point, the road emerges from the canyon into grassy **Gibbon Meadows,** where elk and bison are commonly seen. The prominent peak visible to the north is 10,336-foot **Mt. Holmes.** On the west end of Gibbon Meadows is a barren area that contains **Sylvan Springs Geyser Basin.** No maintained trail leads to this small collection of pools and springs, but hikers sometimes head across the north end of the meadows at the Gibbon River Picnic Area. The path is wet most of the summer.

An easy 0.5-mile trail leads to **Artist Paint Pots,** filled with colorful plopping and steaming mud pots and hot springs. Although it's a short hike, the paint pots see far fewer visitors than roadside sites, making this a nice place to escape the crowds. The forest was burned in the North Fork Fire, so it's also a good place to see how the lodgepole pines are regenerating. Just south of the parking area for Artist Paint Pots is a trail to **Monument Geyser Basin,** where there isn't much activity, but the tall sinter cones form all sorts of bizarre shapes, including Thermos Bottle Geyser. The mile-long hike climbs 500 feet and provides views of the surrounding country. Another attraction is **Chocolate Pots,** found along the highway just north of Gibbon Meadows. The reddish-brown color comes from iron, aluminum, and manganese oxides. Just before you reach Norris, the road crosses through the appropriately named **Elk Park.**

◖ NORRIS GEYSER BASIN

Although Old Faithful and the Upper Geyser Basin are more famous, many visitors to Yellowstone find Norris Geyser Basin equally interesting. Norris sits atop the junction of several major fault lines, providing conduits for heat from the molten lava below. Because of this, it is apparently the hottest geyser basin in North America, if not the world; a scientific team found temperatures of 459°F at 1,087 feet underground and was forced to quit drilling when the pressure threatened to destroy the drilling rig! Because of considerable sulfur (and hence sulfuric acid) in the springs and geysers, the water at Norris is acidic; most of the world's acid geysers are here. The acidic water kills lodgepole trees in the basin, creating an open, nearly barren place. Norris Basin has been around at least 115,000 years, making it Yellowstone's oldest active geyser basin. It is a constantly changing place, with small geysers seeming to come and go on an almost daily basis.

The paved trail from the often crowded parking area leads to **Norris Geyser Basin Museum and Information Station** (307/344-2812, daily 9 A.M.–6 P.M. late May–Sept.), built of stone in 1929–1930. The small museum houses exhibit panels on hot springs and geothermal activity. Be sure to pick up the detailed brochure ($0.50) describing the various features at Norris. Ranger-led walks are given several times a day in the summer, and there's usually a ranger in the area ready to answer your questions. A little bookstore is housed in a nearby building. From the museum, the Norris Basin spreads both north and south, with two rather different trails to hike. Take the time to walk along both. The Norris Campground is only a quarter-mile from the geyser basin.

Porcelain Basin

Just behind the Norris Geyser Basin Museum is an overlook that provides an impressive view across the always-changing Porcelain Basin. The path descends into the basin, passing hissing steam vents, bubbling hot pools, and small geysers, including **Constant Geyser,** with frequent and sudden bursts to 20 feet or more. **Whirligig Geyser** is another one that is often active, spraying a noisy fan of water. (Watch your glasses and camera lenses in the

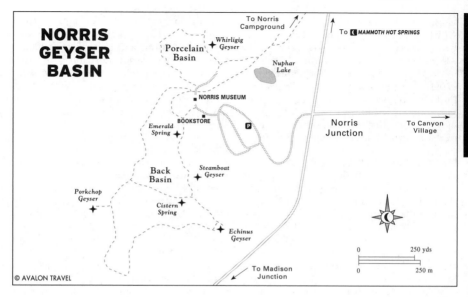

NORRIS GEYSER BASIN

To Norris Campground

To **MAMMOTH HOT SPRINGS**

Whirligig Geyser

Porcelain Basin

Nuphar Lake

NORRIS MUSEUM

BOOKSTORE

Emerald Spring

P

Norris Junction

To Canyon Village

Back Basin

Steamboat Geyser

Porkchop Geyser

Cistern Spring

Echinus Geyser

0   250 yds

0   250 m

To Madison Junction

© AVALON TRAVEL

steam; silica deposits can be difficult to remove.) For an enjoyable short walk, follow the boardwalk around the mile-long loop through Porcelain Basin. Stop to admire the bright colors in the steaming water, indicators of iron, arsenic, and other elements, along with algae and cyanobacteria.

Back Basin

A mile-long loop trail takes you to the sights within the Back Basin south of the Norris Geyser Basin Museum. Before heading out, check at the museum for the latest on geyser activity. Most people follow the path in a clockwise direction, coming first to **Emerald Spring,** a gorgeous green pool with acidic water just below boiling. A little way farther down the path is **Steamboat Geyser.** Wait a few minutes and you're likely to see one of its minor eruptions, which may reach 40 feet. On rare occasions, Steamboat erupts with a fury that is hard to believe, blasting more than 300 feet into the air—more than twice the height of Old Faithful—making this the world's tallest geyser. Eruptions can last up to 20 minutes

or more, enough time to pour out a million gallons of water, and the explosions have been heard up to 14 miles away. Steamboat's unforgettable eruptions cannot be predicted; a 50-year span once passed between eruptions, while several eruptions may occur in one year. If you ever see this one erupt, consider yourself incredibly lucky!

The path splits just below Steamboat; on the right is **Cistern Spring,** whose deep blue waters are constantly building deposits of sinter and have flooded the nearby lodgepole-pine forests, killing the trees. If you turn left where the trail splits, you'll come to **Echinus Geyser** (pronounced e-KI-nus). The name—Greek for "spiny"—comes from the pebbles that lie around the geyser; resembling sea urchins, they are a result of sinter accumulation. Sometimes Echinus settles into a regular pattern with frequent eruptions, but in the last decade or so they decreased, and it may stay dormant for weeks or months. When Echinus does erupt, the geyser sends explosions of acidic steam and water (pH 3.5) 40–60 feet. These generally last 3–5 minutes but sometimes continue for much longer. Unlike Old Faithful, this is one geyser where you can get up close and personal. Bench-sitters may get splashed, although the water is not hot enough to burn.

Continue along this trail beyond Echinus to see many more hot springs and steam vents. **Porkchop Geyser** was in continuous eruption for several years, but in 1989 it self-destructed in an explosion that threw rocks more than 200 feet, leaving behind a bubbling hot spring.

Norris Junction to Canyon

From Norris Geyser Basin to Canyon, the park road cuts across the center of Yellowstone on the high Solfatara Plateau, an area scorched in the 1988 North Fork Fire. The lodgepole pines had been uprooted in a wild 1984 windstorm, and four years later the wind-whipped fires arrived, creating a holocaust. Now, more than two decades later, the lodgepoles are a lush thicket of green.

Virginia Cascades Road is a 2.5-mile-long, one-way road that circles around this blow-down area and provides a view of the 60-foot-tall Virginia Cascade of the Gibbon River. Stop at the shady picnic area for lunch or to head across the meadow to fly-fish. Back on the main highway heading east, keep your eyes open for elk and bison as the road approaches Canyon. Also note the dense forest of lodgepole pines that was established after a fire burned through in 1955.

Norris Junction to Mammoth

The park road between Norris and Mammoth Hot Springs provides some interesting sights, although much of this country burned in the 1988 North Fork Fire. Just beyond the highway junction is the **Norris Soldier Station.** Built by the army in 1897 and modified in 1908, it is one of just three stations still standing in the park. The attractive log building now houses the small **Museum of the National Park Ranger** (307/344-7353, daily 9 A.M.–5 P.M. late May–late Sept.), with displays and a video on the history of park rangers.

Just up the road is **Frying Pan Spring** (named for its shape), where the water is actually not that hot. The bubbles are from pungent-smelling hydrogen-sulfide gas. **Roaring Mountain** is a bleak, steaming mountainside four miles north of Norris. In 1902, the mountain erupted into activity with fumaroles that made a roar audible at great distances. It is far less active today and is best seen in winter, when the temperature difference results in much more steam.

Obsidian Cliff

A stop at Obsidian Cliff offers an opportunity to see the black, glassy rocks formed when lava cooled rapidly. One mountain man (not, as many sources claim, Jim Bridger) told tall tales of "Glass Mountain," where his shots at an elk kept missing. When he got closer, he found he had actually been firing at a clear mountain of glass. The elk was 25 miles away, but the mountain was acting as a telescope to make the animal appear close. Obsidian Cliff was an important source of rock for Indians in making fine arrowheads and other tools. Obsidian from here was of such value that Indians traded it extensively; obsidian points made from this rock have even been found in Ohio and Ontario. (It is illegal to remove obsidian; leave it for future generations to enjoy.) North of here the countryside opens up along Obsidian Creek at **Willow Park,** one of the best places to see moose, especially in the fall.

Sheepeater Cliff and Golden Gate

Approximately 13 miles north of Norris, the park road passes Indian Creek Campground (one of the quietest in the park) and the basalt columns of Sheepeater Cliff, named for the Indian inhabitants of these mountains. North of this point, the country opens into Swan Lake Flats, where you get a fine gander at 10,992-foot Electric Peak nine miles to the northwest.

At Golden Gate the road suddenly enters a narrow defile, through which flows Glen Creek. Stop to look over the edge of **Rustic Falls** and note how the road is cantilevered over the cliff edge. If you're acrophobic, however, do

YELLOWSTONE

© DON PITCHER

road along Golden Gate near Mammoth

not stop here. Instead, have someone else drive, close your eyes, and say three Hail Marys.

Bunsen Peak and the Hoodoos

Bunsen Peak is an 8,564-foot inactive volcanic cone just south of Mammoth. Any chemistry student will recognize the name, because Robert Wilhelm Eberhard von Bunsen not only first explained the action of geysers but also invented the Bunsen burner. Parts of Bunsen Peak look like a chemistry experiment run amok. The North Fork Fire of 1988 swept through this area in a patchy mosaic, leaving long strips of unburned trees next to what are now just blackened telephone poles.

North of Golden Gate, the main road soon passes the Hoodoos, a fascinating jumble of travertine boulders leaning in all directions. The rocks were created by hot springs thousands of years ago and toppled from the east face of Terrace Mountain. Just before Mammoth, turn left onto Upper Terrace Drive, a 0.5-mile loop road providing access to the upper end of Mammoth Hot Springs. (No trailers or large RVs permitted.)

MAMMOTH HOT SPRINGS

Mammoth Hot Springs lies at an elevation of 6,239 feet near the northern border of Yellowstone, just five miles from the town of Gardiner, Montana. Here you'll find park headquarters, a variety of other facilities, and delightfully colorful hot springs. The Mammoth area is an important wintering spot for elk, pronghorn antelope, deer, and bison. During the fall, at least one bull elk and his harem can be seen wandering across the green lawns, while lesser males bugle challenges from behind the buildings or over the hill. The bugling may even keep you awake at night if you're staying in the Mammoth Hotel.

Origins

Mammoth Hot Springs consists of a series of multihued terraces down which hot, mineral-laden water trickles. This water originates as snow and rain that falls on the surrounding country, although some is believed to come from the Norris area, 20 miles to the south. As it passes through the earth, the water comes into contact with volcanic magma containing massive amounts of carbon dioxide, creating carbonic acid. The now-acidic water passes through and dissolves the region's sedimentary limestone, and the calcium carbonate remains in solution until it reaches the surface at Mammoth. Once at the surface, the carbon dioxide begins to escape into the atmosphere, reducing the acidity and causing the lime to precipitate out, forming the travertine terraces that are so prominent here. As the water flows over small obstructions, more carbon dioxide is released, causing accumulations that eventually grow into the lips that surround the terrace pools. The rate of accumulation of travertine (calcium carbonate) is astounding: more than two tons a day at Mammoth Hot Springs. Some terraces grow by eight inches per year. The first explorers were fascinated by these terraces; mountain man Jim Bridger noted that they made for delightful baths. A later operation—long since ended—coated knickknacks by dipping them in the hot springs! The springs are constantly changing as

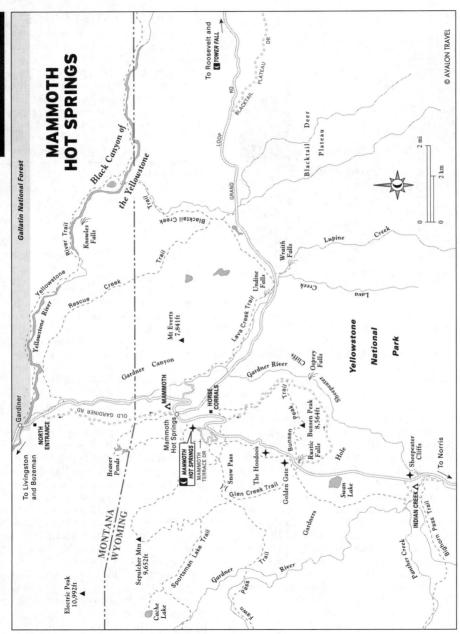

MAMMOTH HOT SPRINGS

Gallatin National Forest

Black Canyon of the Yellowstone

To Roosevelt and ◄ TOWER FALL

© AVALON TRAVEL

River Trail

Knowles Falls

Yellowstone River

Trail

Blacktail Creek

BLACKTAIL PLATEAU DR

LOOP RD

GRAND

Deer

Blacktail Plateau

Rescue

Creek

Trail

Wraith Falls

Lupine Creek

Yellowstone

Mt Everts 7,841ft ▲

Lava Creek Trail

Undine Falls

Lava Creek

2 mi

2 km

0

Gardner Canyon

Gardner River

Osprey Falls

Yellowstone

National

Park

Sheepeater Cliffs

Gardiner

OLD GARDINER RD

MAMMOTH

HORSE CORRALS

Bunsen peak Trail

Rustic Falls

Bunsen Peak 8,564ft ▲

Sheepeater

To Livingston and Bozeman

NORTH ENTRANCE

Mammoth Hot Springs ★

⌂ MAMMOTH

★ MAMMOTH HOT SPRINGS

MAMMOTH TERRACE DR

Snow Pass

The Hoodoos ★

Golden Gate ★

Glen Creek Trail

Hole

Swan Lake

Sheepeater Cliffs ★

To Norris

Beaver Ponds

MONTANA

WYOMING

Gardners

INDIAN CREEK ⌂

Bighorn Pass Trail

Sepulcher Mtn 9,652ft ▲

Sportsman Lake Trail

Gardner

Pass

River

Panther Creek

Electric Peak 10,992ft ▲

Cache Lake

Trail

Fawn

underground passages are blocked by limestone deposits, forcing the water in new directions. As a result, old dried-out terraces stand on all sides, while new ones grow each day. Areas that were active just a few years ago may now be simply gray masses of crumbling travertine rock, and new areas may appear and spread in a matter of days. Mammoth is guaranteed to be different every time you visit. One of the most interesting aspects of the hot springs here is the variety of colors, a result of the many different species of algae and bacteria that live in the water. Various factors, including temperature and acidity, affect the survival of different species; bright yellow algae live in the hottest areas, whereas cooler waters are colored orange and brown by other algae.

Visiting the Springs

Mammoth Hot Springs covers a steep hillside and consists of a series of colorful springs in various stages of accretion or decay. The area is accessible by road from below or above (Upper Terrace Drive), and a boardwalk staircase connects the two levels. At the bottom of Mammoth Hot Springs and off to the right is a 37-foot-tall mass of travertine known as **Liberty Cap** for its faint similarity to the caps worn in the French Revolution. The spring that created this formation no longer flows. (You may well think Liberty Cap shows a more striking similarity to something else a bit more—shall we say—masculine.)

The springs at Mammoth change continuously, and every visit brings something new. For details on currently active areas, pick up the Park Service's informative brochure ($0.50) from the box at the parking area. The most interesting areas in the last few years have been **Palate Spring** near the base and the very active **Canary Spring** in the vicinity of the overlook. Along Upper Terrace Drive, both **Angel Terrace** and **Orange Spring Mound** have started flowing again after decades of inactivity.

All of the water flowing out of Mammoth terraces quickly disappears into underground caverns. In front of the Mammoth Hotel are

© DON PITCHER

Canary Spring at Mammoth Hot Springs

two sinkholes from which steam often rises. Caverns above the terraces were once open to the public but were closed when it became apparent that they contained poisonous gases. Dead birds are sometimes found around one of the small pools in this area, appropriately named Poison Spring.

Historic Buildings

Mammoth contains several historic structures built during the army's tenure at **Fort Yellowstone.** The most distinctive are the six buildings (all in a row) constructed between 1891 and 1909 as quarters for the officers and captains. Most of the grunt soldiers lived just behind here in barracks, one of which is now the park administration building. The U.S. Engineers Department was housed in an odd stone building with obvious Asian influences; it's right across from the visitor center. The visitor center has an informative pamphlet ($0.50) that describes the Fort Yellowstone Historic District in detail. Displays around the grounds provide additional details.

Although one wing survives from a hotel built in 1911, most of the **Mammoth Hot Springs Hotel** was constructed in 1937. Step inside to view a large map of the United States built from 15 different types of wood. Mammoth also features a Yellowstone General Store, post office, gas station, restaurant, fast-food eatery, and medical clinic. Mammoth Campground is a short distance down the road. Just up the hill—less than a mile from the hotel—is the Mammoth corral, where horseback rides are offered. Also here is a small **cemetery** populated mostly by infants and a few civilians who died here in the early 1900s.

Albright Visitor Center

Named for Horace Albright—Yellowstone's first National Park Service superintendent— the Albright Visitor Center (daily 8 A.M.–7 P.M. late May–Sept., 9 A.M.–5 P.M. the rest of the year) is housed in the army's old bachelor officers' quarters. Spread over two floors are exhibits on park wildlife and history, but the real treats are the works of two artists who helped

bring Yellowstone's magnificent scenery to public attention. Twenty-three of painter Thomas Moran's famous Yellowstone water-colors line the walls (though they're hard to see in the dim lighting), and his studio has been re-created in one corner. Equally impressive are 26 classic photographs—including one of Thomas Moran at Mammoth Hot Springs—taken by William H. Jackson during the 1871 Hayden Survey. The paintings and photos are must-sees for anyone with an artistic bent. The center also has an information desk, videos about the park and Moran every half-hour, and racks of books. Check at the information desk for schedules of wildlife talks and frequent ranger-led walks to surrounding sights in the summer.

North Entrance Road

The main park road north from Mammoth Hot Springs follows the Gardner River, dropping nearly 1,000 feet in elevation before reaching the town of Gardiner, Montana. (Both the river and the misspelled town are named for Johnson Gardner, a ruthless trapper from the 1820s.) The river is a favorite of fly-fishing enthusiasts. A turnout near the Wyoming-Montana border notes the "boiling river" section of the Gardner; it's always worth a stop, and the 0.5-mile hike has a big reward at the end. Bring your swimsuit! Sometimes during the winter you can spot bighorn sheep on the mountain slopes just north of the river as you head down to Gardiner.

The "back way" to Gardiner is the **Old Gardiner Road,** a five-mile gravel road (great for mountain bikes, but not for RVs or trailers) that starts behind Mammoth Hot Springs Hotel. Traffic is downhill only, so you'll need to take the main road for your return into the park; mountain bikes can go in both directions. This is one of the best places to spot pronghorn antelope in the park, and it also provides a fine escape from the crowds at Mammoth.

Tower Junction

The 18-mile drive from Mammoth to Tower Junction takes visitors through some of the

© DON PITCHER

Albright Visitor Center, Mammoth Hot Springs

driest and most open country in Yellowstone. Two waterfalls provide stopping places along the way. Beautiful **Undine Falls** is a 60-foot-high double fall immediately north of the road. Just up the road is a gentle 0.5-mile path to the base of **Wraith Falls,** where Lupine Creek cascades 90 feet. Look for ducks and trumpeter swans in **Blacktail Pond,** a couple of miles farther east.

Blacktail Plateau Drive, approximately nine miles east of Mammoth, turns off from the main road. The rough seven-mile dirt road is a one-way route that loosely follows the Bannock Trail, a path used by the Bannock tribe on their way to buffalo-hunting grounds east of here. Their travois trails are still visible. The Bannocks used this route from 1838 to 1878, but it was probably used for hundreds or thousands of years by various tribes crossing the high plateau. Much of Blacktail Plateau Drive is through open sagebrush, grass, and aspen country, where you're likely to see deer and pronghorn antelope. The trees are very pretty in the fall. On the east end, the road

drops back into a forest burned by a severe crown fire in 1988 but now containing young aspen and lodgepole pines and abundant summertime flowers.

A two-thirds-mile boardwalk, **Forces of the Northern Range Self-Guiding Trail**, is six miles east of Mammoth Hot Springs. Half a mile beyond where Blacktail Plateau Drive rejoins the main road is the turnoff to the **petrified tree.** The 20-foot-tall stump of an ancient redwood tree (50 million years old) stands behind iron bars; a second petrified tree that used to stand nearby was stolen piece by piece through the years by thoughtless tourists. The **Tower Ranger Station,** originally occupied by the U.S. Army, is just before Tower Junction where the road splits, leading to either Northeast Entrance Road or Canyon.

NORTHEAST CORNER

Of the five primary entryways into Yellowstone, the Northeast Entrance is the least traveled, making this a great place to escape the hordes in midsummer. It is also one of the few places

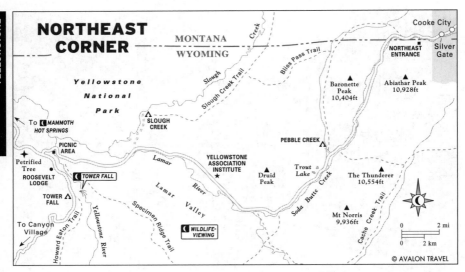

to see tall mountains in Yellowstone. The road heads east from Tower Junction and immediately enters **Lamar Valley,** an area of grass and sage along the sinuous Lamar River. Osborne Russell, who trapped this country in the 1830s, described it with affection:

We descended the stream about 15 mls thro. the dense forest and at length came to a beautiful valley about 8 Mls. long and 3 or 4 wide surrounded by dark and lofty mountains. The stream after running thro. the center in a NW direction rushed down a tremendous canyon of basaltic rock apparently just wide enough to admit its waters. The banks of the stream in the valley were low and skirted in many places with beautiful Cotton wood groves. Here we found a few Snake indians comprising 6 men 7 women and 8 or 10 children who were the only Inhabitants of this lonely and secluded spot. They were all neatly clothed in dressed deer and Sheep skins of the best quality and seemed to be perfectly contented and happy?.... We stopped at this place and for my own part I almost wished I could spend the remainder of my days in a place like this where happiness and contentment seemed to rein in wild romantic splendor surrounded by majestic battlements which seemed to support the heavens and shut out all hostile intruders?.... There is something in the wild romantic scenery of this valley which I cannot...describe; but the impressions made upon my mind while gazing from a high eminence on the surrounding landscape one evening as the sun was gently gliding behind the western mountain and casting its gigantic shadows across the vale were such as time can never efface from my memory.

Yellowstone River Picnic Area

Picnic areas don't generally merit a mention, but this one—1.5 miles east of Tower Junction on the Northeast Entrance Road—is an exception because of its proximity to a grand view. A two-mile trail takes off from here for Grand Canyon of the Yellowstone River. The hike is easy and provides a good chance to see bighorn sheep, but be careful to stay away from the canyon rim. For a loop hike (four miles round-trip), continue to the Specimen Ridge Trail, where you turn left and follow it back to your starting point.

Yellowstone Association Institute

The nonprofit Yellowstone Association Institute (406/848-2400, www.yellowstoneassociation. org) offers many classes out of Lamar Valley's historic Buffalo Ranch, approximately 10 miles east of Tower Junction. To augment the park's small wild herd, bison were brought here in 1902 from private ranches. The bison stayed in pens at night and were herded during the day. After 1915, they were allowed to roam freely in summer, although all of the park's bison were rounded up and driven here for winter. After 1938 the roundups ended, but the bison were fed hay every winter in Lamar Valley. Finally in 1952, even this practice was halted and the bison were allowed to roam throughout the park. The historic buildings are worth a look, or better still, take one of the institute's excellent classes.

Specimen Ridge

Just east of the historic Buffalo Ranch is a turnout across from Specimen Ridge, where explorers discovered the standing trunks of petrified trees that had been buried in volcanic ash and mudflows 50 million years ago. Through the centuries, the trunks literally turned to stone as silica entered the wood. The process was repeated through the centuries as new forests gradually developed atop the volcanic deposits, only to be buried by later flows. Scientists have found 27 different forests on top of each other, containing walnut, magnolia, oak, redwood, and maple—evidence that the climate was once more like that of today's Midwestern states. Erosion eventually revealed the trees, many of which are still standing. It's one of the largest areas of petrified trees known to exist.

There is no trail to the petrified forest, but during the summer, rangers lead hikes into the area. Check with the Albright Visitor Center for upcoming treks. Mark Marschall's *Yellowstone Trails* provides a description of the 1.5-mile route if you want to try it on your own. A lesser-known petrified forest in the northwest corner of Yellowstone is accessible via U.S. Highway 191.

© DON PITCHER

bison along the Lamar River in Lamar Valley

◖ Wildlife-Viewing

The Northeast Corner is still one of the best places in Yellowstone to view bison, with a gorgeous backdrop of open country and wooded mountains. Elk and mule deer are also commonly seen, and the reintroduction of wolves has added another dimension to wildlife-viewing. The valley contains several small ponds created when the retreating glaciers left large blocks of ice that formed "kettles." Erratic glacial boulders are scattered along the way. There are campgrounds at Slough Creek and Pebble Creek, and there is very good fishing in Slough Creek. But look out for one other critter: the ubiquitous ground squirrels that dart into the road, playing chicken with your tires.

Between the Slough Creek and Pebble Creek Campgrounds, wolf aficionados fill roadside turnouts each morning and evening, waiting patiently for members of the Druid Peak Pack (and other packs) to appear. Bring your binoculars and spotting scope! During the wolf denning season, the Park Service prohibits parking or walking along certain stretches of the road, but two turnouts are available.

Northeast Entrance

At the east end of Lamar Valley, the park road heads northeast up Soda Butte Creek and between the steep rocky cliffs of **Barronette Peak** (10,404 feet) and **Abiathar Peak** (10,928 feet). Stop at **Soda Butte,** where you'll find a substantial travertine mound similar to those at Mammoth. Although the springs are no longer very active, the air still reeks of hydrogen sulfide, the "rotten egg" gas. South of Soda Butte and several miles up a backcountry trail is **Wahb Springs,** found within Death Gulch. Here poisonous gases are emitted from the ground, killing animals in the vicinity. Early explorers reported finding dead bears that had been overcome by the fumes. Less than one mile north of Soda Butte is a pullout where a 0.5-mile trail leads to pretty **Trout Lake.** It offers a nice afternoon break from the crowds elsewhere in Yellowstone.

North of Pebble Creek Campground, the road squeezes through beautiful **Icebox Canyon,** past Barronette Peak, and into the (unburned) lodgepole pine forests. As befits the name, you're likely to see snow and ice here when surrounding areas are carpeted with greenery and flowers. The road follows Soda Butte Creek all the way to the edge of the park, crossing into Montana two miles before the park border. The **Northeast Entrance Station** is a classic log building built in 1935 and now designated a National Historic Landmark. The twin towns of Silver Gate and Cooke City are just up the road.

TOWER FALL/ROOSEVELT
Roosevelt Lodge

Lying at the junction of the roads to Canyon, Mammoth, and Lamar Valley, Roosevelt Lodge was built in 1920 and named for President Theodore Roosevelt, who camped a few miles to the south during his 1903 visit. A lifelong supporter of Yellowstone, Roosevelt helped push through legislation that clamped down on the rampant destruction of park wildlife early in the 20th century.

The Roosevelt area is a favorite of families, wolf-watchers, and anglers, many of whom return year after year. The main building has the rough-edged flavor of a hunting lodge and a peacefulness that you won't find at Old Faithful, Canyon, or Mammoth. Inside are two large stone fireplaces, and the porch out front has comfortable rocking chairs that are filled each evening. Folks plop their feet on the rail, nurse a beer, and watch the night roll in. Heavenly. Rustic cabins—most built in the 1920s—provide simple accommodations, and Roosevelt has a restaurant and little gift shop/general store, along with horseback rides. It's also the only place in Yellowstone to offer wagon rides and Old West cookouts; call well ahead for reservations.

Stop at the overlook to **Calcite Springs,** two miles southeast of the junction, where a walkway provides dramatic views into the canyon of the Yellowstone River, with steaming geothermal activity far below. The cliff faces contain a wide strip of columnar basalt, some of which overhangs the highway just to the south.

◖ Tower Fall

On summer afternoons, the parking lot at Tower Fall overflows with cars as folks stop to see Tower Creek plummet 132 feet before joining the Yellowstone River. The towerlike black rocks of the area are volcanic basalt. Nearby are a campground and a Yellowstone General Store. Tower Fall overlook is just a couple of hundred paved feet from the parking area, or you can follow the path 0.5 mile down the switchbacks to the canyon bottom. Unfortunately, the Park Service has closed the fascinating side trail to the base of the falls, but you do get a fine view of the river from the bottom of this path. A ford of the Yellowstone River—used by Bannock Indians in the 19th century—is just a quarter-mile away. For more than 100 years, a huge boulder stood atop Tower Fall; the water and gravity finally won in 1986.

Dunraven Pass and Mt. Washburn

As the park road climbs southward along Antelope Creek, it eventually switchbacks up the aptly named Mae West Curve. The North Fork Fire swept through this country in 1988, but the area is now verdant with new trees, grasses, and flowers. Ten miles south of Tower Junction, the old Chittenden Road turns off and leads a mile uphill to a large parking area and trailhead for popular day hikes up **Mt. Washburn,** the 10,243-foot peak that dominates this part of Yellowstone.

South of this is **Dunraven Pass** (8,859 feet), named for the Earl of Dunraven, who visited the park in 1874 and whose widely read book *The Great Divide* brought Yellowstone to the attention of wealthy European travelers. This is the highest point along any park road, even higher than the three other places where the road crosses the Continental Divide! Look for whitebark pines near the road, and be sure to stop just south of here for a view across to the distant Grand Canyon of the Yellowstone.

◖ GRAND CANYON OF THE YELLOWSTONE

Yellowstone is best known for its geysers and animals, but for many visitors the Grand Canyon is the park's most memorable feature. This 20-mile-long canyon ranges 1,500–4,000 feet across and has colorful yellow, pink, orange, and buff cliffs that drop as much as 1,200 feet on either side. The river itself tumbles abruptly over two massive waterfalls, sending up a roar that's audible for miles along the rims. Grand Canyon is accessible by road from both the north and south sides, with equally amazing views. The lodgepole pine forests around here escaped the 1988 fires.

Carving a Canyon

After a massive volcanic eruption 650,000 years ago, rhyolite lava flows came through what is now the Grand Canyon. The flows eventually cooled, but geothermal activity within the rhyolite weakened the rock with hot steam and gasses, making it susceptible to erosion. Through the centuries, a series of glaciers blocked water upstream, each time creating a lake. As each glacier retreated it undammed the stream, allowing the water in the lake to empty suddenly. The weakened rhyolite was easily eroded by these periodic floods of water and glacial debris, thus revealing pastel yellow and red canyon walls colored by the thermal activities. The **Lower Falls** are at the edge of the thermal basin, above rock that was not weakened by geothermal activity. The **Upper Falls** are at a contact point between hard rhyolite that does not erode easily and a band of rhyolite that contains more easily eroded volcanic glass. Today the canyon is eroding more slowly, having increased in depth just 50 feet during the last 10,000 years.

North Rim Vistas

A one-way road takes visitors to a series of extremely popular overlooks along the north rim of Grand Canyon of the Yellowstone. Farthest east is **Inspiration Point,** where the views of the canyon and Lower Falls are, well, inspirational. A wheelchair-accessible canyon view is available from the edge of the parking lot. **North Rim Trail** leads along the rim from Inspiration Point up to Chittenden Bridge, three miles away, and some sections of this

© DON PITCHER

Lower Falls of the Yellowstone River

brink! Just south of where the one-way road rejoins the main highway is a turnoff to the **Brink of the Upper Falls,** where a short walk leads to a less dramatic but still beautiful view of the 109-foot-high Upper Falls.

A party of prospectors wandered north into this country in 1867, following the Yellowstone River downstream without suspecting the canyon below. A. Bart Henderson wrote in his diary of strolling down the river and being:

very much surprised to see the water disappear from my sight. I walked out on a rock & made two steps at the same time, one forward, the other backward, for I had unawares as it were, looked down into the depth or bowels of the earth, into which the Yellow plunged as if to cool the infernal region that lay under all this wonderful country of lava and boiling springs.

Canyon Village

Canyon Village on the north rim is a forgettable shopping mall in the wilderness, complete with various stores and eating places, a post office, a gas station, cabins, lodges, and a campground. It's a good place to come on a rainy summer afternoon when the kids are starting to scream for ice cream. Horseback rides are available less than one mile south of here.

The real attraction at Canyon Village is the recently opened **Canyon Visitor Education Center** (307/242-2550). This must-see stop has fascinating exhibits detailing park geology, from geysers and hot springs to the supervolcano that powers everything. A room-size relief model illuminates the park's volcanic eruptions, ashfall, lava flows, and glaciers. Kids can turn the 9,000-pound rotating globe to find volcanic hot spots, and a giant lava lamp illustrates how magma rises in the earth. Upstairs, check out exhibits on earthquakes, including a seismograph showing today's temblors. There are all sorts of other high-tech exhibits, plus exhibits on lodgepole pine forests and grassland habitats. You could easily spend an hour here and will certainly come away

scenic and nearly level path are paved. Just a couple of hundred feet up from Inspiration Point, be sure to look for a 500-ton boulder deposited by a glacier during the glaciation that ended 15,000 years ago. The glacial erratic (as such rocks are called) originated in the Beartooth Mountains at least 30 miles north of here and was carried south atop a moving river of ice.

The one-way road continues westward to overlooks at **Grandview Point** and **Lookout Point.** From Lookout Point, a 0.5-mile trail drops 500 hundred feet to **Red Rock Point** for a closer view of Lower Falls—you can feel the spray. Farthest west along the one-way North Rim Road is the trail to the **Brink of the Lower Falls.** The trail is 0.5 mile long and paved, descending 600 feet to a viewing area where you can peer over the edge as the water plummets in a thunderous roar over the 308-foot precipice (twice the height of Niagara Falls). This is probably the most breathtaking sight in Yellowstone, but if you suffer from vertigo don't even think about peering over the

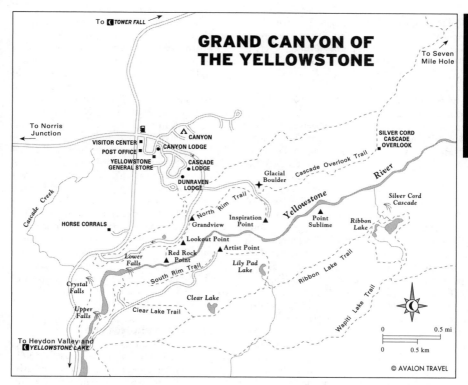

GRAND CANYON OF THE YELLOWSTONE

To ⟨ TOWER FALL

To Norris Junction

To Seven Mile Hole

VISITOR CENTER
POST OFFICE
YELLOWSTONE GENERAL STORE

CANYON
CANYON LODGE
CASCADE LODGE
DUNRAVEN LODGE

SILVER CORD CASCADE OVERLOOK

Glacial Boulder

Cascade Overlook Trail

Yellowstone River

Cascade Creek

HORSE CORRALS

North Rim Trail

Grandview

Inspiration Point

Point Sublime

Ribbon Lake

Silver Cord Cascade

Lookout Point

Red Rock Point

Artist Point

Ribbon Lake Trail

Lower Falls

South Rim Trail

Lily Pad Lake

Crystal Falls

Clear Lake

Wapiti Lake Trail

Upper Falls

Clear Lake Trail

To Heydon Valley and ⟨ YELLOWSTONE LAKE

0   0.5 mi
0   0.5 km

© AVALON TRAVEL

with a better understanding of Yellowstone's inner workings.

The visitor center is open daily 8 A.M.–8 P.M. June–September and 8 A.M.–5 P.M. in May and September–mid-October. It's closed in winter.

South Rim Vistas

The south rim of the canyon is lined with dramatic views into Grand Canyon. Cross the Chittenden Bridge over the Yellowstone River (otters are sometimes seen playing in the river below) and continue 0.5 mile to Uncle Tom's parking area, where a short trail leads to views of the Upper Falls and Crystal Falls. More unusual is **Uncle Tom's Trail,** which descends 500 feet to Lower Falls. The trail is partly paved, but it's steep and includes 328 metal

steps before you get to the bottom—good exercise if you're in shape. It was named for "Uncle" Tom Richardson, who, with the help of wooden ladders and ropes, led paying tourists to the base of the falls around the turn of the 20th century. Because there was no bridge, Uncle Tom also rowed his guests across the river near the present Chittenden Bridge. After his permit was revoked in 1903, visitors had to make do on their own.

One mile beyond Uncle Tom's parking area, the road ends at the parking area for **Artist Point,** the most famous—and crowded—of all Grand Canyon viewpoints. A short paved path leads to an astoundingly beautiful spot where one can look upriver to the Lower Falls or down the opposite direction into the canyon. Look for thermal activity far below. The point is apparently where artist Thomas Moran painted some of his famous watercolors. Avoid the crowds and afternoon thunderstorms by getting here early in the morning; it's almost always deserted at sunrise.

HAYDEN VALLEY

Just a few miles south of the Grand Canyon, the country abruptly opens into beautiful Hayden Valley, named for Ferdinand V. Hayden, leader of the 1871 expedition into Yellowstone. Reaching eight miles across, this relatively level part of the park was once occupied by an arm of Yellowstone Lake. The sediments left behind by the lake, along with glacial till, do not hold sufficient water to support trees. As a result, the area is occupied primarily by grasses, forbs, and sage. This is one of the best areas in the park to see wildlife, especially bison and elk. The Yellowstone River wanders across Hayden Valley, and streams enter from various sides. These waterways are excellent places to look for **Canada geese,** trumpeter swans, pelicans, and many kinds of ducks. **Wolves** are also frequently sighted; just look for the line of cars and the crowds with binoculars and spotting scopes. Although they are less common, **grizzly bears** can sometimes be found feeding at the eastern end of the valley. Because of the bears, hikers need to be especially cautious when tramping through the grasses and shrubs, where it is easy to surprise a bear or to be likewise surprised. On the north end of Hayden Valley, the road crosses **Alum Creek,** named for its highly alkaline water, which could make anything shrink. In the horse-and-buggy days, Yellowstone wags claimed that a man had forded the creek with a team of horses and a wagon but came out the other side with four Shetland ponies pulling a basket!

(Mud Volcano Area

The park road climbs south out of Hayden Valley to pass one of the most interesting of Yellowstone's many thermal basins. On the east side of the road, a turnout overlooks **Sulphur Caldron,** where a highly acidic pool is filled with sulfur-tinted waters and the air is filled

with the odor of hydrogen-sulfide gas. Directly across the road is the Mud Volcano area, where a two-thirds-mile loop trail provides what could be a tour through a bad case of heartburn. Pick up a Park Service brochure ($0.50) from the box for descriptions of all the bizarre features here. The area is in a constant state of flux as springs dry up or begin overflowing, killing trees in their path. **Churning Caldron** is a frothing pool where periodic jets send superheated water into the air. Just up the trail is one of the most interesting features, **Black Dragons Caldron,** where an explosive spring blasts constantly through a mass of boiling black mud. The wildest place at Mud Volcano is **Dragon's Mouth Spring,** which the Park Service notes is named for "the rhythmic belching of steam and water shooting from the cavernous opening." It's easy to imagine the fires of hell not far below this spring. The waters are 170°F. During winter (and often in summer), the Mud Volcano area is a good place to see elk or bison.

Along the Yellowstone

The park road parallels the Yellowstone River south of Mud Volcano. At **LeHardys Rapids,** a boardwalk provides an overlook where early-summer visitors see blush-red spawning cutthroats. In late summer, this part of the Yellowstone River is a very popular fly-fishing spot—some call it the finest stream for cutthroat fishing in the world—and a good place to view ducks and swans. Earlier in the year, it's open only to the bears that gorge on the cutthroats. By the way, the Yellowstone River, which begins at Yellowstone Lake, is the longest free-flowing (undammed) river in the Lower 48.

(YELLOWSTONE LAKE

When first-time visitors see Yellowstone Lake, they are stunned by its magnitude. The statistics are impressive: 110 miles of shoreline, 20 miles north to south and 14 miles east to west, with an average depth of 139 feet and a maximum depth of 390 feet. This is the largest high-elevation (over 7,000 feet) lake in North America;

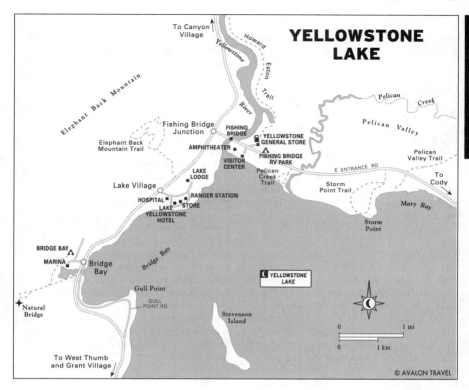

YELLOWSTONE LAKE

To Canyon Village

Howard Eaton Trail

Yellowstone River

Pelican Creek

Pelican Valley

Fishing Bridge Junction

FISHING BRIDGE

Elephant Back Mountain

Elephant Back Mountain Trail

AMPHITHEATER

YELLOWSTONE GENERAL STORE

FISHING BRIDGE RV PARK

VISITOR CENTER

LAKE LODGE

Lake Village

Pelican Creek Trail

E ENTRANCE RD

Pelican Valley Trail

To Cody

HOSPITAL

RANGER STATION

LAKE STORE

YELLOWSTONE HOTEL

Storm Point Trail

Mary Bay

Storm Point

BRIDGE BAY

MARINA

Bridge Bay

Bridge Bay

YELLOWSTONE LAKE

Gull Point

Natural Bridge

GULL POINT RD

Stevenson Island

To West Thumb and Grant Village

0   1 mi

0   1 km

© AVALON TRAVEL

Lake Tahoe is bigger, but lower. Yellowstone Lake can seem like a sheet of glass laid to the horizon at one moment and just a half-hour later be a roiling ocean of whitecaps and wind-whipped waves. These changeable waters can be dangerous to those in canoes or small boats; several people have drowned, including experienced park rangers. The water is covered by ice at least half the year, and breakup does not come until late May or early June. Even in summer, water temperatures are often only in the 40s. David Folsom, who was part of an exploration party traveling through the area in 1869, described Yellowstone Lake as an:

inland sea, its crystal waves dancing and sparkling in the sunlight as if laughing with joy for their wild freedom. It is a scene of transcendent beauty which has been viewed by few white men, and we felt glad to have looked upon it before its primeval solitude should be broken by the crowds of pleasure seekers which at no distant day will throng its shores.

Fishing Bridge

The area around famous Fishing Bridge (built in 1937) was for many years a favorite place to catch cutthroat trout. These same fish are a major food source for grizzlies, and this area is considered some of the most important bear habitat in Yellowstone. Conflicts between bears and humans led to the death of 16 grizzlies here. To help restore trout populations and to provide food for the grizzlies, the Park

Service banned fishing from Fishing Bridge in 1973 and tried to move the park facilities to the Grant Village area. Lobbying by folks from Cody (worried lest they lose some of the tourist traffic) kept some of the facilities at Fishing Bridge from closing. Remaining facilities include an RV park, Yellowstone General Store (gifts, groceries, and a snack bar), visitor center, amphitheater, and gas station. The bridge itself is still a popular stopping point and a good place to see large cutthroat trout in the shallows.

Fishing Bridge Visitor Center (307/242-2450, daily 8 A.M.–7 P.M. late May–Sept.) houses a few ancient bird displays and an information desk. Be sure to head out the back door for bucolic views across Lake Yellowstone.

Lake Yellowstone Hotel

Lake Yellowstone Hotel, the oldest extant park hostelry, was built in 1889–1891 by the Northern Pacific Railroad and originally consisted of a simple boxlike structure facing Yellowstone Lake. The hotel was sold to Harry Child in 1901, and two years later Robert Reamer—the architect who designed Old Faithful Inn—was given free rein to transform this into a more attractive place. Hard to believe that the same architect could create a grand log masterpiece and a sprawling Southern colonial mansion with distinctive Ionic columns in the same park! Lake Yellowstone Hotel is the second-largest wood-framed building in North America and requires 500 gallons of paint each year to keep it in shape. During the 1960s and 1970s the hotel fell into disrepair under the management of General Host Corporation, and in disgust, the Park Service bought out the concession and leased it to another company. Major renovations in the 1980s transformed the dowdy old structure into a luxurious grand hotel with much of the charm it had when President Calvin Coolidge stayed here in the 1920s.

Today, Lake Yellowstone Hotel is one of the nicest places to stay in the park, with fine vistas out over the lake and comfortable quarters. Relax with a drink in the sunlit **Sun Room**

while a pianist or a string quartet provides the atmosphere. Free 45-minute historic **tours of Lake Yellowstone Hotel** are given at 5:30 P.M. Monday–Friday early June–late September. The hotel also houses a restaurant, gift shop, and snack bar.

Be sure to take a walk along the lakeshore out in front of the hotel, where the Absaroka Range forms a backdrop far to the east. The highest mountain is Avalanche Peak (10,566 feet). Almost due south is the 10,308-foot summit of Mt. Sheridan, named for General Philip Sheridan, a longtime supporter of expanding the park to include the Tetons. Watch for the big white pelicans catching fish on the lake.

Just east of Lake Yellowstone Hotel is the **Lake Ranger Station,** built in 1922–1923 and now on the National Register of Historic Places. Inside the octagonal main room you will find a massive central fireplace, exposed log rafters, and rustic light fixtures. A short walk away is **Lake Lodge,** another rustic log structure, built between 1921 and 1929. It houses a reasonably priced cafeteria with grand windows fronting the lake. A Yellowstone General Store stands nearby, and dozens of plain cabins are behind it.

To West Thumb

The highway south from Lake Junction to West Thumb follows the lakeshore nearly the entire distance. A campground and boat harbor are at **Bridge Bay,** along with a ranger station, marina, and store. Stop here for hour-long boat tours of Yellowstone Lake, offered several times a day throughout the summer, or for guided fishing trips and boat rentals.

Back on the main road, keep your eyes open for Canada geese and trumpeter swans as you drive south. **Gull Point Drive,** a two-mile-long side road, offers views of **Stevenson Island** just offshore; farther south, **Frank Island** and tiny **Dot Island** become visible. The small **Potts Hot Springs Basin,** just north of West Thumb, is named for fur trapper Daniel T. Potts, one of the first white men to explore the Yellowstone country. His travels here in 1826 were described the following year in a

Philadelphia newspaper article. It was perhaps the first published mention of Yellowstone Lake and the hot springs.

East Entrance Road

The park road splits east from Fishing Bridge and follows the shore of Yellowstone Lake past country that escaped the 1988 fires. Three miles east of the bridge are Indian Pond—popular with birders—and the trailhead for Storm Point Trail. North of here, Pelican Valley is considered important grizzly habitat and is closed to all overnight camping year-round. Even daytime use is not allowed until July 4, and then only between 9 A.M. and 7 P.M. Before venturing out on the Storm Point Trail or into Pelican Valley, check at the Lake Ranger Station for current bear information. The 0.5-mile **Pelican Creek Nature Trail** starts one mile east of Fishing Bridge and provides an easy hike to a beach along Yellowstone Lake. Much of the way is on boardwalk over a marshy area.

At **Steamboat Point** the road swings out along the shore, providing excellent views across the lake and of a noisy fumarole. For an even better view (don't miss this one!), take the **Lake Butte Overlook** road, which continues one mile to a small parking area 1,000 feet above the lake. This is a fine place to watch sunsets and to get a feeling for the enormous size of Yellowstone Lake. Back on the main highway and heading east, you soon leave Yellowstone Lake behind and it is visible in only a few spots as the road climbs gradually, passing scenic **Sylvan Lake,** a nice place for picnics. Just up the road is tiny Eleanor Lake (little more than a puddle) and a steep trail to 10,566-foot **Avalanche Peak.**

Immediately east of Eleanor Lake, the main road climbs to 8,530-foot **Sylvan Pass,** flanked by Hoyt Peak on the north and Top Notch Peak to the south. Steep scree slopes drop down both sides. East of Sylvan Pass, the road descends quickly along Middle Creek (a tributary of the Shoshone River), providing good views to the south of Mt. Langford and Mt. Doane. **East Entrance Ranger Station** was built by the army in 1904. For many years, the road leading up to Sylvan Pass from the east took drivers across Corkscrew Bridge, a bridge that literally looped over itself as the road climbed steeply up the narrow valley. The road continues eastward to Cody through beautiful Wapiti Valley.

WEST THUMB AND GRANT VILLAGE

The South Entrance Station consists of several log structures right along the Snake River. Just 1.5 miles beyond the entrance is an easily missed turnout where you can walk down to 30-foot-high **Moose Falls.** Beyond this point, the road climbs a long, gentle ramp to Pitchstone Plateau, passing green forests of lodgepole pine. Stop at a turnout to look back at the majestic Tetons. Abruptly, this gentle country is broken by the edge of **Lewis River Canyon,** with rhyolite walls that rise to 600 feet. The fires of 1988 burned hot throughout much of this area, and dead trees line both sides of the canyon in all directions. Young trees are now carpeting many areas, but some remain almost barren more than two decades later.

The road parallels the river for the next seven miles. Nearly everyone stops for a look at 29-foot-high **Lewis Falls.** Camping is available at the south end of **Lewis Lake,** which—like the lake, falls, river, and canyon—was named for the Lewis and Clark expedition's Meriwether Lewis. Lewis Lake is the park's third-largest body of water (after Yellowstone Lake and Shoshone Lake) and is popular with canoeists, kayakers, and anglers. The clear waters contain brown trout and Mackinaw (lake trout). Approximately four miles north of Lewis Lake, the highway tops the Continental Divide, 7,988 feet above sea level. This is one of three such crossings that roads make within Yellowstone.

Grant Village

This odd scattering of buildings is named for President Ulysses S. Grant, who signed the act establishing Yellowstone and whose terms in office were marked by massive corruption scandals. Grant Village was built in the 1980s to replace facilities at Fishing Bridge, an area of important grizzly habitat. Unfortunately, instead of one bad development, Yellowstone now has two, because some of the buildings at Fishing Bridge still stand. Unlike some of the more historic places in Yellowstone where a natural rusticity prevailed, Grant Village has less charm than most Walmarts. An ugly steakhouse restaurant and waterside cafeteria face Yellowstone Lake, but the marina that was once here is closed. Also sprawled around Grant Village are a campground, rows of chintzy condos, a Yellowstone General Store, a visitor center, a gas station, and post offices. Much of the area around here was consumed in the 1988 Snake River Fire; unfortunately, the fire missed this scar on the Yellowstone landscape.

Grant Visitor Center (307/242-2650, daily 8 A.M.–7 P.M. late May–Sept.) houses an informative exhibit and film on the role of fires in the park, particularly the massive 1988 fires. These provide a good background for understanding the changes taking place as the burned areas recover.

West Thumb

If you look at a map of Yellowstone Lake, it's possible to imagine the lake as a giant hand with three mangled fingers pointing south and a gnarled thumb hitching west—hence the name West Thumb. This section of Yellowstone Lake is the deepest (to 390 feet) and is actually a caldera that filled with water after erupting 150,000 years ago. Considerable heat is still just below the surface, as revealed by **West Thumb Geyser Basin.** Get a Park Service booklet ($0.50) from the box for details on the area's geothermal origins and attractions.

THE LONE HIGHWAYMAN OF YELLOWSTONE

Because of its remote location, Teton Valley became a rendezvous place for rustlers and outlaws in the 1880s. Horses stolen from the soldiers at Fort Hall, along with cattle "liberated" from Wyoming and Montana ranches, made their way through Pierre's Hole to the railroads. Hiram C. Lapham was the first to try his hand at ranching in the valley, but his cattle quickly disappeared. With the help of a posse from Rexburg, Lapham tracked down the culprits, one of whom was killed in the ensuing gunfight. The others surrendered but escaped from jail when the wife of bandit Ed Harrington smuggled a gun to her husband in clothing worn by his baby. Harrington and partner Lum Nickerson were eventually tracked down and sent to jail.

Although Harrington was sentenced to 25 years, the governor pardoned him after just three. Harrington went on to become Teton Valley's first postman, but his criminal activity continued. Using the alias Ed Trafton, Harrington went on to rob stores throughout Teton Valley and eventually spent another two years behind bars. After getting out, he turned his attention to the tourism business in Yellowstone, but not in the standard way. Although it was never proven, he was suspected of being behind a string of stagecoach robberies in 1908 in which cash and jewelry were taken from tourists at gunpoint.

Harrington's most brazen feat came on July 29, 1914, when he single-handedly robbed 15 stages, earning the nickname "the lone highwayman of Yellowstone." The tourists were particularly impressed with his gentlemanly manner as he asked them to "please" hand over all their cash and jewelry. Harrington made off with $915.35 in cash and $130 in jewelry, but he made the mistake of posing for photos in the process. He was caught the following year and spent five years in Leavenworth Prison.

When Harrington died, a letter in his pocket claimed that he had been Owen Wister's model for the Virginian in the famous novel of the same name. Others suspected that he was more likely to have been Wister's model for the villain, Trampas.

A short loop trail leads past steaming hot springs and pools at West Thumb. Right on the shore is **Fishing Cone,** where tourists once caught fish and then plopped them in the cone to be cooked; after several clowning tourists were injured, the Park Service put a stop to this stunt. The **West Thumb Information Station** (daily 9 A.M.–5 P.M. late May–Sept.) houses a small bookstore, and in winter the station is used as a warming hut.

West Thumb to Upper Geyser Basin

The park road climbs over the Continental Divide twice west of West Thumb. Most of the forests here escaped the 1988 fires. A few miles beyond the eastern crossing of the divide is a turnout at **Shoshone Point,** where you catch glimpses of Shoshone Lake and the Tetons. In 1914, highwayman Ed Trafton (his real name was Ed Harrington) held up 15 stagecoaches as they passed by this point carrying tourists. He got away with $915.35 in cash and $130 in jewelry but made the rather obvious blunder of posing for photos! He was captured the following year and spent five years in Leavenworth. When he died, a letter in his pocket claimed that he had been author Owen Wister's model for the Virginian. Others suspected that he was more likely to have been Wister's model for the villain, Trampas.

Approximately 14 miles beyond West Thumb, pull off to see the Firehole River as it drops over **Kepler Cascades.** The western crossing of the Continental Divide is at **Craig Pass,** where a tiny pond (Isa Lake) empties into the Atlantic and Pacific Oceans at the peak of snowmelt following a big snow year.

OLD FAITHFUL AND UPPER GEYSER BASIN

Welcome to Upper Geyser Basin, home of Old Faithful, about 400 buildings of all sizes, and a small town's worth of people. For many folks, this is the heart of Yellowstone, and a visit to the park without seeing Old Faithful is like a baseball game without the national anthem. If you came to Yellowstone to see the wonders of

nature, you're going to see more than your share here, but you'll probably have to share your share with hundreds of other folks. On busy summer days more than 25,000 visitors come through the Old Faithful area! Fortunately, the Upper Geyser Basin contains the largest concentration of geysers in the world, and the adventurous will even discover places almost nobody ever visits. But be very careful: The crust can be dangerously thin around some of the hot springs and geysers, and people have been badly scalded and even killed by missteps. Stay on the boardwalks and trails.

You can approach Old Faithful from either direction; the two-lane park road will suddenly widen into four lanes, and a cloverleaf exit takes you to Yellowstone's most fabulous sight.

◖ Old Faithful

The one sight seen by virtually everyone who comes to Yellowstone is Old Faithful Geyser, easily the most visited geyser in the world. Old Faithful is neither the tallest nor the most

© DON PITCHER

Old Faithful Geyser

YELLOWSTONE

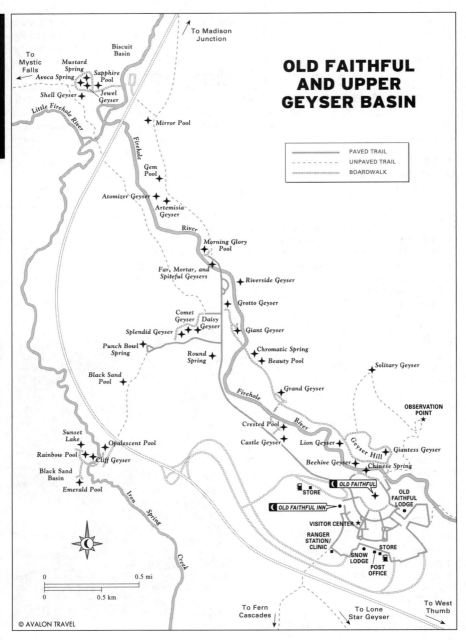

OLD FAITHFUL AND UPPER GEYSER BASIN

To Madison Junction

To Mystic Falls

Biscuit Basin

Mustard Spring

Avoca Spring

Sapphire Pool

Shell Geyser

Jewel Geyser

Little Firehole River

Firehole

Mirror Pool

Gem Pool

Atomizer Geyser

Artemisia Geyser

River

Morning Glory Pool

Far, Mortar, and Spiteful Geysers

Riverside Geyser

Grotto Geyser

Comet Geyser

Daisy Geyser

Splendid Geyser

Giant Geyser

Punch Bowl Spring

Round Spring

Chromatic Spring

Beauty Pool

Solitary Geyser

Black Sand Pool

Grand Geyser

OBSERVATION POINT

Firehole

River

Sunset Lake

Opalescent Pool

Crested Pool

Castle Geyser

Lion Geyser

Geyser Hill

Giantess Geyser

Rainbow Pool

Cliff Geyser

Beehive Geyser

Chinese Spring

Black Sand Basin

Emerald Pool

STORE

OLD FAITHFUL

OLD FAITHFUL LODGE

OLD FAITHFUL INN

VISITOR CENTER

RANGER STATION/ CLINIC

SNOW LODGE

STORE

POST OFFICE

Iron Spring

Creek

To Fern Cascades

To Lone Star Geyser

To West Thumb

	PAVED TRAIL
	UNPAVED TRAIL
	BOARDWALK

0   0.5 mi

0   0.5 km

© AVALON TRAVEL

© DON PITCHER

Old Faithful Inn

frequently erupting geyser in Yellowstone, but it always provides a great show and is both highly accessible and fairly predictable. Contrary to the rumors, Old Faithful never erupted "every hour on the hour," but for many years its period was a little more than an hour. It has slowed in recent years and is now averaging about 90 minutes per cycle, but varies from 51 to 120 minutes. In general, the greater the length of the eruption, the longer the interval until the next eruption. Check at the visitor center for the latest prognostications on this and other geysers in the basin.

An almost level paved path circles Old Faithful, providing many different angles from which to view the eruptions, although none of these is particularly close to the geyser because of the danger from hot water. Along the north side is **Chinese Spring,** named in 1885 for a short-lived laundry operation. Apparently, the washman had filled the spring with clothes and soap, not knowing that soap can cause geysers to erupt. One newspaper correspondent

claimed—although the tale obviously suffered from embellishment and racism—that:

The soap awakened the imprisoned giant; with a roar that made the earth tremble, and a shriek of a steam whistle, a cloud of steam and a column of boiling water shot up into the air a hundred feet, carrying soap, raiment, tent and Chinaman along with the rush, and dropping them at various intervals along the way.

Old Faithful provides a textbook example of geyser activity. The first signs of life are when water begins to splash out of the vent in what is called preplay. This splashing can last up to 20 minutes, but it's generally only a few minutes before the real thing. The water quickly spears into the sky, reaching 100–180 feet for 1.5–5 minutes before rapidly dropping. During a typical eruption, between 3,700 and 8,400 gallons of water are sent skyward.

On any given summer day, the scene at Old Faithful is almost comical. Just before the predicted eruption time, the benches encircling the south and east sides are jammed with hundreds of people waiting expectantly for the geyser to erupt, and with each tentative spray the camera shutters begin to click. Listen closely and you'll hear half the languages of Europe and Asia. Once the action is over, there's a mad rush back into the visitor center, the stores, and Old Faithful Inn, and within a few minutes the benches are virtually empty. A tale is told of two concessioner employees who once decided to have fun at Old Faithful by placing a large crank atop a box and putting the contraption near the geyser. When they knew it was ready to erupt, they ran out and turned the crank just as Old Faithful shot into the air. Their employer failed to find humor in the prank, and both were fired, or so the story claims.

Old Faithful Visitor Center

After years of planning, fund-raising ($27 million!), and construction, the magnificent 26,000-square-foot **Old Faithful Visitor Education Center** (307/545-2750) opened in 2010. A spacious lobby features ceiling-to-floor windows that frame eruptions of Old Faithful. Step into the exhibit hall to learn about hydrothermal areas within Yellowstone, with a focus on how geysers form. Other interactive exhibits describe hot springs, steam vents, and mud pots, including the unique microbes that survive in these superheated areas. Be sure to check out the video of active vents and odd spires at the bottom of Yellowstone Lake. Although it's geared to kids, the Young Scientist room is equally popular with adults, with all sorts of dynamic hands-on activities, including a life-size model of a geyser. (Did you know that animals that live near geysers suffer from tooth decay?) Most displays are in English, French, German, and Japanese. The building was constructed using many earth-friendly techniques and has gained Gold LEED certification.

In addition to the exhibits, the visitor center houses a state-of-the-art theater, where you can watch films about the park, and a Yellowstone Association bookstore selling books, maps, and other publications. At the information desk, rangers can answer questions—from where to see bighorn sheep to where to find the restrooms. Check the display for **predicted eruption times** of six major geysers in the area: Old Faithful, Grand, Daisy, Riverside, Great Fountain, and Castle.

The Old Faithful Visitor Education Center is open mid-April–early November and mid-December–mid-March. Hours are daily 8 A.M.–7 P.M. (information window till 8 P.M.) late May–early September and 8 A.M.–6 P.M. the rest of September. During the fall, winter, and spring when park gates are open, the visitor center operates daily 9 A.M.–6 P.M.

If you're not in the park but want to see the

YELLOWSTONE'S FIRST "TOURIST"

From the surface of a rocky plain or table, burst forth columns of water of various dimensions, projected high in the air, accompanied by loud explosions, and sulphurous vapors, which were highly disagreeable to the smell.... The largest of these wonderful fountains, projects a column of boiling water several feet in diameter, to the height of more than one hundred and fifty feet.... After having witnessed three of them, I ventured near enough to put my hand into the water of its basin, but withdrew it instantly, for the heat of the water in this immense couldron, was altogether to great for comfort, and the agitation of the water, disagreeable effluvium continually exuding, and the hollow unearthly rumbling under the rock on which I stood, so ill accorded with my notions of personal safety, that I retreated back precipitately to a respectful distance.

Angus Ferris in 1833

current situation at Old Faithful, check out the **live webcam** at www.nps.gov/yell/photosmultimedia/yellowstonelive.htm.

Old Faithful Inn

Matching one of the great sights of the natural world is one of America's most majestic hotels, Old Faithful Inn. Now more than a century old, the building was designed by Robert Reamer and built in the winter of 1903–1904. One of the largest log structures in existence, the inn has delighted generations of visitors and continues to enthrall all who enter. Its steeply angled roofline reaches seven stories high, with gables jutting from the sides and flags flying from the roof. Surprisingly, the hotel does not face the geyser. Instead, it was built facing sideways to allow newly arriving visitors the opportunity to view the geyser as they stepped from carriages. As you open the rustic split-log front doors with their hand-wrought hardware, you enter a world of the past. The central lobby towers more than 75 feet overhead and is dominated by a massive four-sided stone fireplace that required 500 tons of stone from a nearby quarry. Four overhanging balconies extend above, each bordered by posts made from gnarled lodgepole burls found within the park. Above the fireplace is an enormous clock designed by Reamer and built on the site by a blacksmith. Reamer also designed the two side wings that were added in 1913 and 1928.

On warm summer evenings, visitors stand out on the porch where they can watch Old Faithful erupting, or sit inside at the handcrafted tables to write letters as music spills from the grand piano. It's enough to warm the heart of even the most cynical curmudgeon. A good restaurant is on the premises, along with a rustic but comfortable bar, a gift shop, fast-food eatery, ice-cream shop, and ATM. Free 45-minute **tours** of Old Faithful Inn are given several times daily during the summer; check the activity desk for times. Old Faithful Inn closes during the winter; it would be hard to imagine trying to heat such a cavern when it's 30°F below zero outside! The building underwent a major renovation in the last few

inside the Old Faithful Inn

© DON PITCHER

years, with structural upgrades to protect it from earthquakes and a variety of other improvements. Today, it is open early May–mid-October.

Another nearby building of interest is **Old Faithful Lodge.** Built in 1928, this is the large stone-and-log building just south of the geyser of the same name. The giant fireplace inside is a joy on frosty evenings, and cafeteria windows face the geyser—unlike those at the inn.

Much newer, but an instant classic, is the award-winning **Old Faithful Snow Lodge,** which opened in 1999. This large building offers a sense of rustic elegance, with heavy timbers, a window-lined main entrance, a large stone fireplace, overstuffed couches, and handmade wrought-iron light fixtures and accents. It is one of just two Yellowstone lodges (the other being Mammoth Hot Springs Hotel) open in winter.

Cafeteria meals, espresso, and baked goods are available at Old Faithful Lodge, and Old

Faithful Snow Lodge houses a restaurant and snack bar. Both of these also have gift shops. In addition, the Old Faithful area has two gas stations, a post office, and a medical clinic.

Geyser Hill Area

Upper Geyser Basin is laced with paved trails that lead to dozens of nearby geysers and hot springs. The easiest path loops around Geyser Hill, just across the Firehole River from Old Faithful. Here are more than 40 different geysers. Check at the visitor center to get an idea of current activity and predicted eruptions, and while you're there pick up the excellent Upper Geyser Basin map ($0.50), which describes some of them. Several geysers are particularly noteworthy. When it plays, **Beehive Geyser** (it has a tall, beehive-shaped cone) vents water as high as 180 feet into the air. These spectacular eruptions vary in frequency; one time you visit they may be 10 days apart, while the next time you come they may be happening twice daily. **Lion Geyser Group** consists of four

different interconnected geysers with varying periods of activity and eruptions up to 80 feet. Listen for the roar when Lion is ready to erupt. **Giantess Geyser** may not be active for years at a time—or may erupt several times a year—but the eruptions are sensationally powerful, sending water 100–200 feet skyward. **Doublet Pool** is a beautiful deep-blue pool that is a favorite of photographers. Not far away is **Sponge Geyser,** which rockets water an astounding 2.29 billion angstroms into the air (that's nine inches, for the non-scientific crowd). It's considered the smallest named geyser in Yellowstone and gets its title by sending up a spurt of water big enough to be mopped up with a sponge.

Observation Point Loop Trail splits off shortly after you cross the bridge on the way to Geyser Hill and climbs to an excellent overlook where you can watch eruptions of Old Faithful. This is also a good place to view the effects of, and recovery from, the 1988 North Fork Fire. It's two miles round-trip to Observation Point from the visitor center. Another easy trail splits

Upper Geyser Basin

© DON PITCHER

off from this path to **Solitary Geyser,** which is actually just a pool that periodically burps four-foot splashes of hot water. This is not a natural geyser. In 1915, the hot spring here was tapped to provide water for Old Faithful Geyser Bath, a concession that lasted until 1948. The lowering of the water level in the pool completely changed the plumbing system of the hot springs and turned it into a geyser that at one time shot 25 feet in the air. The system still hasn't recovered, although water levels have been restored for many decades.

Firehole River Loop

An easy, paved path follows the Firehole River downstream from Old Faithful, looping back along the other side for a total distance of three miles. Other trails head off from this loop to the Fairy Falls Trailhead, Biscuit Basin, and Black Sand Basin. The loop is a very popular wintertime ski path, and sections are open to bikes in the summer.

Twelve-foot-high **Castle Geyser** does indeed resemble a ruined old castle. Because of its size and the slow accretion of sinter (silica) to form this cone, it is believed to be somewhere between 5,000 and 50,000 years old. Castle sends up a column of water and steam 75 feet into the air and usually erupts every 11–13 hours. Check at the visitor center for a guess at the next eruption.

Daisy Geyser is farther down the path and off to the left. It is usually one of the most predictable of the geysers, erupting to 75 feet approximately every 120–150 minutes. The water shoots out at a sharp angle and is visible all over the basin, making this a real crowd-pleaser.

Just east of Daisy is **Radiator Geyser,** which isn't much to look at—eruptions to two feet—but was named when this area was a parking lot and the sudden eruption under a car led people to think its radiator was overheating. A personal favorite, **Grotto Geyser** is certainly the weirdest of all the geysers, having formed around a tangle of long-petrified tree stumps. It is in eruption one-third of the time, but most eruptions reach only 10 feet.

Look for **Riverside Geyser** across the Firehole from the path and not far downstream from Grotto. This picturesque geyser arches spray 75 feet over the river and is one of the most predictable, with 20-minute-long eruptions approximately every six hours. The paved trail crosses the river and ends at famous **Morning Glory Pool.** For many years, the main road passed this colorful pool, which became something of a wishing well for not just coins but also trash, rocks, logs, and other debris. Because of this junk, the pool began to cool, and the beautiful blue color is now tinged by brown and green algae, despite efforts to remove the debris.

Turning back at Morning Glory, recross the bridge and head left where the path splits at Grotto Geyser. **Giant Geyser** is on the left along the river. Years may pass between eruptions of Giant (or it might erupt every week or so), but when it does go, the name rings true because the water can reach 250 feet. Cross the river again and pass **Beauty Pool** and **Chromatic Pool,** which are connected below the ground so that one declines as the other rises—very pretty.

Grand Geyser is a wonderful sight. The water column explodes in 1–4 towering bursts lasting 9–12 minutes and sometimes reaching 200 feet. It's the tallest predictable geyser on the planet; see the visitor center for the next eruption or wait with the crowds if the pool looks full. When Grand isn't playing, watch for smaller eruptions from nearby **Turban Geyser.** Hang around long enough in the summer and you'll almost certainly meet one or more of the "geyser-gazers," generally retirees with plenty of time to watch and make notes. Some of them spend their entire summer watching geysers, relaying geyser activity by radio back to the Old Faithful Visitor Center. Grand Geyser is a favorite because its behavior has been studied and follows a predictable pattern.

Two little fun geysers are a short distance to the south: **Sawmill Geyser** and **Tardy Geyser.** The latter is just 10 feet or so from the trail, providing an up-close look at a small but active geyser. Cross the river again just beyond these two geysers and pass **Crested Pool** on your

© DON PITCHER

Crested Pool, Upper Geyser Basin

way back to Castle Geyser. The pool contains deep-blue water that is constantly boiling, preventing the survival of algae.

Black Sand Basin

Black Sand Basin is a small cluster of geysers and hot springs, found just one mile west of Old Faithful. Most enjoyable is unpredictable **Cliff Geyser,** which often sends a spray of hot water 25–30 feet over Iron Spring Creek. Three colorful pools are quite interesting in the basin: **Emerald Pool, Rainbow Pool,** and **Sunset Lake. Handkerchief Pool** is now just a small spouter, but it was famous for many years as a place where visitors could drop a handkerchief in one end and then recover it later at another vent. In 1929, vandals jammed logs into the pool, destroying this little game. The pool was covered with gravel in subsequent eruptions of Rainbow Pool.

Biscuit Basin

Biscuit Basin is named for biscuitlike formations that were found in one of the pools;

they were destroyed in an eruption following the 1959 Hebgen Lake earthquake. From the parking lot, the trail leads across the Firehole River to pretty **Sapphire Pool** and then past **Jewel Geyser,** which typically erupts every 7–10 minutes to a height of 15–20 feet. The boardwalk follows a short loop through the other sights of Biscuit Basin. From the west end of the boardwalk, a one-mile trail leads to **Mystic Falls.** Biscuit Basin is three miles north of Old Faithful.

MIDWAY AND LOWER GEYSER BASINS

North of Upper Geyser Basin, the park road follows the Firehole River past Midway and Lower Geyser Basins, both of which are quite interesting. This stretch of the river is popular with fly-fishing enthusiasts, and several side roads provide access to a variety of hot springs and other sights.

◖ Midway Geyser Basin

Midway is a large and readily accessible geyser basin with a loop path leading to most of the sights. **Excelsior Geyser** is actually an enormous hot spring that pours 4,000 gallons per minute of steaming water into the Firehole River. The water is a deep turquoise. During the 1880s, this geyser was truly stupendous, with explosions that reached 380 feet in the air and almost as wide. These violent eruptions apparently damaged the plumbing system that fed them, and the geyser was dormant for nearly a century until smaller eruptions took place in 1985.

At 370 feet across, **Grand Prismatic Spring** is Yellowstone's largest hot spring. The brilliant reds and yellows around the edges of the blue pool are from algae and bacteria that can tolerate temperatures of 170°F. It's difficult to get a good perspective on this spring from the ground; see aerial photos to really appreciate its beauty.

Firehole Lake Drive

This road (one-way heading north) goes three miles through Lower Geyser Basin, the park's

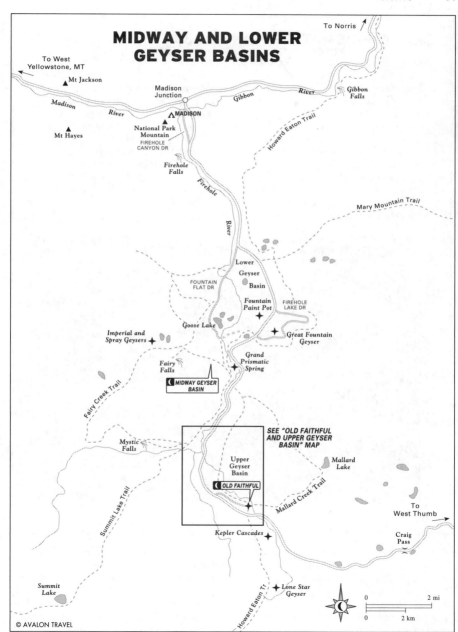

MIDWAY AND LOWER GEYSER BASINS

To Norris

To West Yellowstone, MT

Mt Jackson

Madison Junction

Madison River

Gibbon River

Gibbon Falls

△MADISON

Mt Hayes

National Park Mountain

FIREHOLE CANYON DR

Firehole Falls

Firehole River

Howard Eaton Trail

Mary Mountain Trail

Lower Geyser Basin

FOUNTAIN FLAT DR

Fountain Paint Pot

FIREHOLE LAKE DR

Goose Lake

Great Fountain Geyser

Imperial and Spray Geysers

Grand Prismatic Spring

Fairy Falls

MIDWAY GEYSER BASIN

Fairy Creek Trail

SEE "OLD FAITHFUL AND UPPER GEYSER BASIN" MAP

Mystic Falls

Upper Geyser Basin

Mallard Lake

OLD FAITHFUL

Mallard Creek Trail

Summit Lake Trail

To West Thumb

Kepler Cascades

Craig Pass

Summit Lake

Lone Star Geyser

Howard Eaton Tr

0   2 mi

0   2 km

© AVALON TRAVEL

GRAND PRISMATIC SPRING, 1839

At length we came to a boiling Lake about 300 ft in diameter forming nearly a complete circle as we approached on the south side The steam which arose from it was of three distinct Colors from the west side for one third of the diameter it was white, in the middle it was pale red, and the remaining third on the east light sky blue Whether it was something peculiar in the state of the atmosphere the day being cloudy or whether it was some Chemical properties contained in the water which produced this phenom-

enon I am unable to say and shall leave the explanation to some scientific tourist who may have the Curiosity to visit this place at some future period – The water was of deep indigo blue boiling like an imense caldron running over the white rock which had formed the edges to the height of 4 or 5 feet from the surface of the earth sloping gradually for 60 or 70 feet. What a field of speculation this presents for chemist and geologist.

Mountain man Osborne Russell

© DON PITCHER

Grand Prismatic Spring

most extensive geyser basin. **Great Fountain Geyser** is truly one of the most spectacular geysers in Yellowstone. Charles Cook, of the 1869 Cook-Folsom-Peterson Expedition, recalled his impression of the geyser: "We could not contain our enthusiasm; with one accord we all took off our hats and yelled with all our

might." Modern-day visitors would not be faulted for reacting similarly.

Great Fountain erupts every 10–14 hours (although it can be irregular) and usually reaches 100 feet, but it has been known to blast more than 200 feet. Eruptions begin 70–100 minutes after water starts to overflow from the crater and last for 45–60 minutes in a series of decreasingly active eruptive cycles; but don't leave too early or you may miss the real show! Eruption predictions are posted at the geyser and in the Old Faithful Visitor Center. While you're waiting, watch the periodic eruptions of **White Dome Geyser** just 100 yards down the road. Because of its massive 30-foot cone, this is believed to be one of the oldest geysers in the park. Eruptions typically occur every 15–30 minutes (but sometimes up to three hours) and spray 30 feet into the air.

Another mile ahead, the road literally cuts into the mound of **Pink Cone Geyser,** which now erupts every 6–20 hours and reaches a height of 30 feet. The pink color comes from manganese oxide. Just up from here at the bend in the road is **Firehole Lake,** which discharges 3,500 gallons of water per minute into Tangled Creek, which in turn drains across the road into **Hot Lake. Steady Geyser** is unusual in that it forms both sinter (silica) and travertine (calcium carbonate) deposits. The geyser is along the edge of Hot Lake and, true to its name, erupts almost continuously, although the height is only five feet. Firehole Lake Drive continues another mile to its junction with the main road right across from the parking area for Fountain Paint Pot. In the winter, Firehole Lake Drive is popular with skiers but is closed to snowmobiles.

Fountain Paint Pot

Always a favorite of visitors, Fountain Paint Pot seems to have a playfulness about it that belies the immense power just below the surface. Pick up a trail guide ($0.50) as you head up the walkway for the full story. **Silex Spring,** off to the right as you walk up the small hill, is colored by different kinds of algae and bacteria. The spring has been known to erupt as a geyser (to 20 feet) but is currently dormant.

Fountain Paint Pot is a few steps up the boardwalk and consists of colorful mud that changes in consistency throughout the season depending on soil moisture. The pressure from steam and gases under the Paint Pot can throw gobs of mud up to 20 feet into the air. Just north

of here are fumaroles that spray steam, carbon dioxide, and hydrogen sulfide into the air.

Continuing down the boardwalk, you come upon an impressive overlook above a multitude of geysers that change constantly in activity, including **Morning Geyser,** which has been known to erupt more than 200 feet. The most active is **Clepsydra Geyser,** which is in eruption much of the time. **Fountain Geyser** explodes in a stunning display that can last 30 minutes and reach up to 50 feet. Eruptions are unpredictable but impressive, particularly at sunset. The rest of the loop trail passes dead lodgepole pines that are being petrified as the silica is absorbed, creating a bobby-socks appearance.

Fountain Flat

Fountain Flat Drive provides access to meadows along the Firehole River and is a good place to see bison and elk. The paved road ends after one mile at a parking area, but hikers and cyclists (or skiers in winter) can continue another four miles on Old Fountain Freight Road to its junction with the main road again near Midway Geyser Basin. The road ends in a parking area near **Ojo Caliente**—a small hot springs with a big odor—right along the river. This is one of the most popular fly-fishing spots in the area. Several more hot springs are upstream from here, and the **Fairy Falls Trail** starts three miles south of the parking area.

Firehole Canyon Drive

This one-way road (south only) curves for two miles through Firehole Canyon, where dark rhyolite cliffs rise hundreds of feet above the river. The road begins just south of Madison Junction and was intensely burned in the 1988 North Fork Fire, giving the canyon's name a dual meaning. **Firehole Falls,** a 40-foot drop, is worth stopping to see, as is **Firehole Cascades** a bit farther up. Kids of all ages enjoy the popular hot springs–warmed **swimming hole** a short distance up the road. It's one of the few places along the Yellowstone road system where swimming is openly allowed (albeit not encouraged). No lifeguard, of course.

YELLOWSTONE

Hiking

Short nature trails (0.5 mile or less) accompany most of the major sights in the park, but Yellowstone also has a wonderful diversity of day hikes that are perfect for all levels of ability. Park visitor centers distribute free handouts for trails covering the Mammoth, Old Faithful, Grant Village, Canyon, Lake Yellowstone, Tower, and Bechler areas. You can also purchase a day-hike sampler pamphlet or various hiking books. Good ones are *Yellowstone Trails* by Mark C. Marschall and *A Ranger's Guide to Yellowstone Day Hikes* by Roger Anderson and Carol Shively Anderson.

The Park Service offers free naturalist-led programs and interpretive walks, along with excellent and free half-day **Ranger Adventure Hikes** most days; see your copy of *Yellowstone Today* for the current schedule. These hikes fill up quickly, so sign up in advance at any park visitor center.

MAMMOTH AREA
Bunsen Peak

- Distance: 4.2 miles round-trip
- Duration: 2–3 hours
- Elevation: 7,250 feet with a 1,300-foot climb
- Effort: moderately strenuous
- Trailhead: 5 miles south of Mammoth on the Mammoth-Norris Road, across from the Glen Creek Trailhead

This trail begins a short way up the Bunsen Peak Road (closed to motor vehicles) from the Golden Gate entrance and climbs through forest and meadow to the top of Bunsen Peak, where you'll find panoramic vistas of the entire region. Return via the same path.

Osprey Falls

- Distance: 8 miles round-trip
- Duration: 5–6 hours
- Elevation: 7,250 feet

- Effort: strenuous
- Trailhead: 5 miles south of Mammoth on the Mammoth-Norris Road, across from the Glen Creek Trailhead

This dirt track is open to hikers and mountainbikers but closed to cars. Follow it 2.5 miles to the Osprey Falls Trail, where a steep path (no bikes allowed) drops 700 feet in less than a mile to the base of this 150-foot waterfall. You'll need to climb back out the same way, so don't get too late a start.

Beaver Ponds Loop

- Distance: 5 miles round-trip
- Duration: 2–3 hours
- Elevation: 6,240 feet
- Effort: moderate
- Trailhead: between Liberty Cap and the stone house next to Mammoth Terraces

This trail begins with a 350-foot climb up and above Clematis Gulch. Turn right at the junction with Sepulcher Mountain Trail, and the trail soon levels out and rambles through meadows and aspen to a series of beaver ponds. Past here, the route loops back to Mammoth through forests and grassland. This trail provides a good opportunity to see mule deer, elk, pronghorn antelope, and moose, but it is best hiked in the spring or fall when temperatures are lower. Black and grizzly bears are sometimes seen along the way, so be sure to make noise while you walk.

Sepulcher Mountain Trail

- Distance: 11 miles round-trip
- Duration: 6–8 hours
- Elevation: 6,240 feet with a 3,400-foot elevation gain
- Effort: strenuous
- Trailhead: between Liberty Cap and the stone house next to Mammoth Terraces

Follow the Beaver Ponds Trail to the Sepulcher Mountain Trail junction and then climb sharply (you'll be sweating) through forest and meadows to the top of this 9,652-foot peak just northwest of Mammoth. Return the same way or via a loop trail that continues along the opposite side of the mountain through an open slope to the junction of Snow Pass Trail, which descends to the Howard Eaton Trail, and then back to Mammoth. You'll find abundant late-summer flowers in the expansive meadows on the south side of Sepulcher Mountain (named for several strange rocks at its summit). Before heading out, check at the visitor center to see if there are any major bear problems in the area and to get a topographic map and hiking tips.

NORTHEAST CORNER
Slough Creek Trail

- Distance: 4 miles round-trip
- Duration: 1–3 hours
- Elevation: 6,250 feet
- Effort: moderate
- Trailhead: on the dirt road toward Slough Creek Campground, where the road turns left

This trail—actually a wagon road—makes for a delightful day hike through Douglas fir forests and open meadows. The first mile gains 400 feet in elevation, but it's mostly downhill on the way back. The road continues all the way to the park boundary, 11 miles north of the campground, and is used for access to Silver Tip Ranch. This is the only way into the ranch, and because no motor vehicles are allowed, you may meet folks on a horse-drawn wagon during your hike. Day-hikers often go up the road as far as the first meadow, but more adventurous hikers continue to the second meadow (nine miles round-trip).

Pebble Creek Trail

- Distance: 4 miles round-trip
- Duration: 2 hours

- Elevation: 7,300 feet
- Effort: strenuous
- Trailhead: Warm Creek Picnic Area, 1.5 miles west of the Northeast Entrance station

This remote area is far from the crowds around Old Faithful or Canyon. The trail climbs 1,000 feet in 1.5 miles before dropping into flower-filled mountain meadows along Pebble Creek. A second trailhead at Pebble Creek Campground anchors the other end of this trail, but at 12 miles it's too long for most day-hikers. Backpackers use this route for longer trips into the area.

TOWER/FALL ROOSEVELT
Lost Lake Trail

- Distance: 4 miles round-trip
- Duration: 2–3 hours
- Elevation: 6,300 feet
- Effort: moderate
- Trailhead: behind Roosevelt Lodge

This trail climbs 300 feet in elevation through forested hills to Lost Lake, where you can either return via the Roosevelt Horse Trail or contour along the hillside to the Petrified Tree parking area, where another path loops back to the lodge. Black bears are often seen in the area, so stay alert.

Mt. Washburn

- Distance: 6 miles round-trip
- Duration: 3–6 hours
- Elevation: 8,850 feet with a 1,400-foot elevation gain
- Effort: moderately strenuous
- Trailheads: Dunraven Pass parking area (14 miles south of Tower Junction on the Tower-Canyon Road) or Chittenden Road parking area (9 miles south of Tower Junction)

This outstanding and extremely popular day hike is accessible from two different trailheads along the Tower-Canyon Road, both of which are equal in length and in elevation gained. Either route ascends 10,243-foot Mt. Washburn on a wide path, and the north end is open to mountain bikes. The summit provides commanding vistas in all directions, with a shelter at the base of the fire lookout (which has telescopes, water, and toilets). Many wildflowers bloom in midsummer, and **bighorn sheep** are frequently seen right along the trail. Bring warm clothes and rain gear because conditions on top may be much cooler and windier than below. Mornings are the best time to climb Mt. Washburn since afternoon thunderstorms often roll in during the summer. The Dunraven Pass parking area is often full, but space is generally available at the north trailhead.

CANYON AREA
Seven Mile Hole Trail

- Distance: 11 miles round-trip
- Duration: 6–8 hours
- Elevation: 8,000 feet
- Effort: strenuous
- Trailhead: Glacial Boulder pullout on the road to Inspiration Point

This trail provides fantastic views for the first mile or so, minus the crowds at nearby Inspiration Point. Look for **Silver Cord Cascade,** a thin ribbon of water dropping over the opposite wall of the canyon, but be careful not to go too close to the very loose edge—it's a very long way down! The trail switchbacks steeply to the Yellowstone River, passing odoriferous thermal areas en route (do not approach these). Many anglers come to Seven Mile Hole (it's seven miles downriver from Lower Falls), while other folks come to relax along the river. Save your energy for the strenuous 1,400-foot climb back up, and bring lots of drinking water. Three campsites are available near the base of the trail for those who want to make this an overnight hike (backcountry permit required).

South Rim Trail

- Distance: 6 miles round-trip
- Duration: 2–3 hours
- Elevation: 7,700 feet
- Effort: easy
- Trailhead: east end of Chittenden Bridge across from Wapiti Lake Picnic Area

This hike follows the almost-level and partly paved South Rim Trail two miles to Artist Point, providing many viewpoints en route, including an optional hike down Uncle Tom's Trail, a steep 500-foot drop to Lower Falls. The least-traveled part of the trail (it's called **Ribbon Lake Trail**) continues eastward along the top, providing an abrupt escape from the mob scene at Artist Point, as well as a chance to see the kaleidoscopically colored canyon, hear the roar of the river from far below, and watch for squirrels and birds. But be careful to stay away from the edge, where the rocks are loose. It's doubtful that anyone could survive such a fall, and I once came perilously close to testing that postulate. The trail continues to Lily Pad Lake, where a spur path leads uphill for a wonderful view of the canyon and **Silver Cord Cascade.** With a drop of 1,200 feet, Silver Cord is the highest falls in Yellowstone. You can return the same way or via a number of loop hikes in the area; get the park's *Canyon Area Trail Guide* for details. (As an aside, the old trail to Point Sublime has been closed because of unsafe conditions along the canyon rim.)

YELLOWSTONE LAKE AREA
Natural Bridge

- Distance: 3 miles round-trip
- Duration: 1–2 hours
- Elevation: 7,750 feet
- Effort: easy
- Trailhead: Bridge Bay Marina parking lot near the campground entrance road

This natural bridge is a 51-foot-high span of

rock that was carved by the waters of Bridge Creek. The trail meanders through the forest for 0.25 mile and then follows a paved road the rest of the way. A short, but steep, switchback trail to the top of the bridge starts in front of the interpretive exhibit but is closed to hiking the top of the bridge. Above the bridge, the trail crosses the creek and continues along the cliff before rejoining the road. Cyclists can ride bikes to Natural Bridge on a separate trail that begins south of the marina off the main road. The Natural Bridge area is closed in spring and early summer when bears are feeding on spawning trout in the creek.

Storm Point Trail

- Distance: 2.3 miles round-trip
- Duration: 1–2 hours
- Elevation: 7,800 feet
- Effort: easy
- Trailhead: Indian Pond pullout, 3 miles east of Fishing Bridge Visitor Center

This pleasant loop trail is essentially level and goes past a large colony of yellow-bellied marmots before reaching windswept Storm Point, where waves often pound against the rocks. Following the shoreline to the west, the trail eventually loops back through the lodgepole forest to Indian Pond. The trail may be closed in spring and early summer because of grizzlies, and mosquitoes may make a June or July trip less enjoyable.

Elephant Back Mountain Trail

- Distance: 3.6 miles round-trip
- Duration: 2–3 hours
- Elevation: 7,800 feet
- Effort: moderate
- Trailhead: pullout 1 mile south of Fishing Bridge Junction

This nice hike climbs 800 feet in elevation through dense lodgepole forests to panoramic views across Yellowstone Lake and into Pelican Valley. After one mile the trail splits into a loop, both sides of which join at the overlook.

Avalanche Peak Trail

- Distance: 4 miles round-trip
- Duration: 3–4 hours
- Elevation: 8,500 feet with a 2,100-foot elevation gain
- Effort: very strenuous
- Trailhead: across the road from the pullout at the west end of Eleanor Lake (8 miles west of East Entrance and 19 miles east of Fishing Bridge)

This trail begins on the east side of Middle Creek and climbs very steeply. It emerges from the forest halfway up at the base of a large bowl, and then it continues to the left and switchbacks over talus slopes to an open area below the summit. Follow the trail up the narrow ridgeline and cross it with extreme caution. At the summit, you can see most of the peaks in the Absarokas and Tetons, but snow is present on top until mid-July and afternoon thunderstorms bring the threat of lightning. Hiking isn't recommended here in September and October because of the presence of grizzly bears feeding on whitebark pine nuts.

WEST THUMB AND GRANT VILLAGE
Lewis River Channel and Dogshead Loop

- Distance: 11 miles round-trip
- Duration: 6–8 hours
- Elevation: 7,780 feet
- Effort: moderate
- Trailhead: Dogshead Trailhead just north of Lewis Lake on west side of road (5 miles south of Grant Village)

Choose between two trails—or combine them into a loop hike—to Shoshone Lake. The four-mile-long Dogshead Trail is more direct, while the seven-mile Lewis Channel Trail takes a much more scenic trek via the channel connecting Shoshone and Lewis lakes. This slow-flowing creek is popular with anglers who come to fish for brown and cutthroat trout during the fall spawning season, and it's also used by canoeists and kayakers heading into Shoshone Lake. Much of the Lewis Lake area was burned in the 1988 fires.

Yellowstone Lake Overlook

- Distance: 2 miles round-trip
- Duration: 30 minutes
- Elevation: 7,750 feet
- Effort: moderate
- Trailhead: on the right as you enter West Thumb Geyser Basin parking area

This fine day hike gains 400 feet in elevation in one mile, enough for a commanding vista across the lake, with the Absaroka Mountains behind.

DeLacy Creek Trail

- Distance: 6 miles round-trip
- Duration: 2–3 hours
- Elevation: 7,950 feet
- Effort: easy
- Trailhead: DeLacy Creek Trailhead (9 miles west of West Thumb Junction)

This trail provides access to Shoshone Lake—Yellowstone's largest backcountry lake—which is circled by more trails. Keep your eyes open for moose, sandhill cranes, and other animals in the meadows along the way.

OLD FAITHFUL AREA
Lone Star Geyser Trail

- Distance: 5 miles round-trip
- Duration: 2–3 hours
- Elevation: 7,600 feet
- Effort: easy
- Trailhead: Lone Star Geyser Trailhead 3.5

miles south of Old Faithful Junction (just east of Kepler Cascades)

A wide paved trail (actually an old road) leads to this popular geyser. It's a favorite of bicyclists in the summer and skiers in the winter. Lone Star Geyser erupts every three hours from a distinctive nine-foot-high cone, with eruptions generally reaching 45 feet and lasting for 30 minutes. Bikes are not allowed beyond the geyser. Hikers can also get to Lone Star via the Howard Eaton Trail out of Old Faithful (6 miles round-trip). For a longer hike, you can continue south from Lone Star on **Shoshone Lake Trail** to Shoshone Lake, eight fairly easy miles from the main road.

Mystic Falls Trail

- Distance: 2.5 miles round-trip
- Duration: 1 hour
- Elevation: 7,100 feet
- Effort: moderate
- Trailhead: at the back of the Biscuit Basin boardwalk (2 miles north of Old Faithful Junction)

This path follows a pretty creek to where the Little Firehole River cascades 70 feet over **Mystic Falls.** You can switchback farther up the trail to the top of the falls and then connect with another trail for the loop back to Biscuit Basin (3 miles round-trip). This is a very nice short hike and can be lengthened into a trip to **Little Firehole Meadows** (10 miles round-trip), where bison are often seen in the summer.

Fountain Freight Road/Fairy Falls

- Distance: 5 miles round-trip to Fairy Falls
- Duration: 2 hours
- Elevation: 7,250 feet
- Effort: easy
- Trailhead: 1 mile south of Midway Geyser Basin (4.5 miles north of the Old Faithful Interchange)

The four-mile-long Fountain Freight Road is closed to cars, but it's a great place for mountain bikers and those out for a relatively level walk. A steel bridge crosses the Firehole River at the southern trailhead, and the road soon passes the west side of spectacular **Grand Prismatic Spring;** rough trails lead up the hillside for a better view. One mile up from the trailhead you'll come to **Fairy Falls Trail** on your left. It's an easy walk to the falls, a 200-foot ribbon of water cascading into a large pool. The hike to Fairy Falls can be combined with longer treks to Little Firehole Meadow and Mystic Falls or to a pair of small peaks called Twin Buttes. Half a mile beyond Fairy Falls is **Imperial Geyser,** with periodic small eruptions. Nearby **Spray Geyser** erupts frequently, sending water six feet in the air. For a longer version of the hike to Fairy Falls (10 miles round-trip), start from the north end, where Fountain Flat Drive ends. The Fairy Falls area is closed mid-March–May due to bear activity.

BACKCOUNTRY HIKING

Most Yellowstone visitors act as though they were chained to their cars with a 100-yard tether—as if by getting away from their vehicles they might miss some other sight down the road. For the 2 percent or so who *do* abandon their cars, Yellowstone has much to offer beyond the spectacular geysers and canyons for which it is famous. Although many parts of the Yellowstone backcountry are heavily visited, regulations keep the sense of wildness intact by separating campsites and limiting the number of hikers. If you head out early or late in the season, you'll discover solitude just a few miles from the traffic jams.

Much of Yellowstone consists of lodgepole (or burned lodgepole) forests on rolling terrain. With a few exceptions, anyone looking for dramatic alpine scenery would probably be better off heading to Grand Teton National Park, the Beartooth Mountains, or the Wind River Mountains. The Yellowstone backcountry is still enjoyable to walk through, however, and

many trails lead past waterfalls, geysers, and hot springs. Besides, this is one of the finest places in America to view wildlife—including bison, elk, grizzlies, and wolves—in a setting other than a zoo.

Before August, when they start to die down, you should be ready for the ubiquitous mosquitoes. Ticks are a nuisance mid-March–mid-July in lower-elevation parts of Yellowstone. The fires of 1988 created some problems for backcountry hikers but also offer a good opportunity to see how the land is recovering two decades later.

A few two- to four-day backcountry hikes covering various parts of Yellowstone are possible. The park has more than 1,000 miles of trails, so this is obviously a tiny sampling of the various hiking options.

Before you head out, you will probably want to look over your hiking options. Two excellent source books are *Yellowstone Trails* by Mark Marschall and *Hiking Yellowstone National Park* by Bill Schneider. Get them from park gift shops or visitor centers, which also sell topographic park maps. The best maps are those produced by Trails Illustrated; these feature all of the major trails and show the severity of burn from the 1988 fires—a considerable help when planning hiking trips.

If you need a trailhead drop-off or pick-up, contact **Back Country Sports** (208/652-3385) out of Ashton, Idaho.

Rules and Regulations

The Park Service maintains more than 300 campsites in the Yellowstone backcountry, most of which have pit toilets and fire rings, along with storage poles to keep food from bears. Hikers may stay only at designated campsites. Wood fires are not allowed in many areas and are discouraged elsewhere, so be sure to have a gas stove for cooking. Bear-management areas have special regulations; they may be for day use only, include seasonal restrictions, or specify minimum group sizes (larger groups are safer). Pets are not allowed on the trails within Yellowstone, and special rules apply for those coming in with horses, mules, burros, and llamas. Because of wet conditions and the lack of forage, no stock animals are permitted before July.

A free **backcountry use permit** is required of each overnight party and is available in person from various Yellowstone ranger stations and visitor centers within 48 hours of your hike. Because of the popularity of backcountry trips, you should make reservations before your arrival in the park. (Some permits are available without advance reservations, but why take the chance?) Unfortunately, the Park Service has taken a lesson from the IRS and makes the process as complex as bureaucratically possible. Try to follow me here. Backcountry campsite reservations (not the same thing as a backcountry use permit) cost $20 per trip, and the reservation forms are available by calling 307/344-2160 or writing the Backcountry Office (P.O. Box 168, Yellowstone National Park, WY 82190). You can also download them online at www.nps.gov/yell. Campsite reservation requests must be mailed in, using these forms; reservations are not accepted by phone, fax, or over the Internet. For popular areas in the peak of summer, apply in March. You'll receive a confirmation notice by return mail and will exchange the notice for a permit when you get to the park; the permit must be obtained *in person* at a ranger station within 48 hours of your first camping date. Before receiving your permit, you will be given a lengthy rundown on what to expect and what precautions to take, and will be shown a bear-safety video. The ranger stations are generally open 8 A.M.–4:30 P.M. seven days a week June–August.

For backcountry rules, bear-safety tips, and suggestions for hiking and horsepacking, pick up Yellowstone's detailed *Backcountry Trip Planner,* which shows locations of campsites throughout the park and provides complete information on wilderness access and precautions. You should also pick up or request the free park pamphlet *Beyond Road's End.* Downloadable versions of both are available online at www.nps.gov/yell/planyourvisit/publications.htm.

Those interested in horsepacking or llama trips should contact the park (307/344-7381, www.nps.gov/yell/planyourvisit/stockbusn.htm) for a list of outfitters authorized to operate in Yellowstone. The outfitters offer everything from day trips to weeklong adventures deep into the backcountry.

Sportsman Lake Trail and Electric Peak

The land west of Mammoth is some of the most rugged in Yellowstone, with several peaks topping 10,000 feet. Several trails cut westward across this country, one of the most interesting being the **24-mile-long** Sportsman Lake Trail. The route begins at Glen Creek Trailhead five miles south of Mammoth and follows Glen Creek (a good place to see elk in autumn) for four miles before crossing into the Gardner River drainage. Along the way, a short spur trail leads to pretty Cache Lake. Considerably more challenging is a second side trip, the climb up 10,992-foot Electric Peak, the tallest mountain in this corner of Yellowstone. Many folks camp near Electric Peak and spend a day climbing. It's eight miles round-trip and you gain 3,000 feet on the way up, but the trail becomes harder to follow the higher you climb. See a park trail guidebook for details and precautions on this hike. It is possible to day hike to the top of Electric Peak from the Glen Creek Trailhead, but it's not recommended unless you have a masochistic streak, have done a lot of hiking, and are in great shape.

Beyond the side trail to Electric Peak, Sportsman Lake Trail crosses the Gardner River twice, and there are no bridges. The water can be dangerously deep early in the summer, so this hike is generally done in August or September. After you ford the river, the trail climbs to Electric Divide (watch for bighorn sheep) and then drops steeply to Sportsman Lake and down along pretty Fan Creek to the Fawn Pass Trailhead on U.S. Highway 191. Because this is a one-way hike you will need to set up some sort of vehicle shuttle. Another problem is bears. This country overflows with grizzly activity, and a party size of four or more is recommended for travel here. Off-trail travel is prohibited in some areas; see the Park Service for details.

Black Canyon of the Yellowstone

For an early-summer backpacking trip, it's hard to beat this **19-mile trek** along the northern edge of Yellowstone. Start at the Hellroaring Trailhead, 3.5 miles west of Tower, and follow the Yellowstone River Trail in a steep descent to the river, 600 feet below. A suspension bridge crosses the river, and from here on you remain on the north side all the way to Gardiner. One ford at Hellroaring Creek can be dangerous before August, but it can be avoided if you hike a mile or so upstream to a stock bridge crossing. After this point, the hike alternates between high ridges overlooking Black Canyon of the Yellowstone and quieter stretches where the trail drops down along the edge of the water. Dramatic Knowles Falls is a highlight. The trail is generally in good condition, but you may find it hot and dry in midsummer. Check with the Park Service for the latest on access to the west end of the Yellowstone River Trail, since it passes through private land near Gardiner and that portion may not be maintained or accessible.

Pebble Creek and Bliss Pass Trails

Pebble Creek Trail cuts through a section of Yellowstone that is far away from the geysers and canyons for which the park is famous. The crowds don't come here, but the country is some of the nicest mountain scenery to be found. The trail connects with the Northeast Entrance road at both ends, making access easy. You can start from either end, but if you begin at Warm Creek Picnic Area (1.5 miles west of the entrance station), you get to the high meadows more quickly. From the picnic area the trail climbs 1,100 feet in the first 1.5 miles, but beyond this it's all downhill. The best time to hike this trail is in late summer, when the water levels are lower (there are four fords) and the mosquitoes have abated. Hikers are treated to abundant alpine flowers and grand mountain scenery along the way, with the chance to see moose or elk in the meadows.

For a longer alternative hike, follow Pebble Creek Trail 5.5 miles from the picnic area and then turn west onto Bliss Pass Trail. The path crosses Pebble Creek (quite deep until late summer) before climbing 1,400 feet over Bliss Pass and then dropping 2,700 feet to Slough Creek Trail. From here it is an easy walk to Slough Creek Campground. Total distance from the Warm Creek Picnic Area to Slough Creek Campground is **20 miles.**

Shoshone Lake

The largest lake in the Lower 48 without direct road access, Shoshone Lake is probably the most visited part of Yellowstone's backcountry. Its shoreline is dotted with more than two dozen campsites, but most of these fill on midsummer nights with hikers, canoeists, and kayakers. Because of the lake's popularity, reserve well ahead for a summertime campsite. On-water access is via Lewis Lake and the Lewis River Channel. Anglers come to fish in the channel or lakes; Shoshone Lake has good numbers of brown, lake, and brook trout, all of which were planted here. Hikers reach Shoshone Lake primarily from the DeLacy Creek Trailhead on the north side between West Thumb and Old Faithful, or from the east side via Dogshead Trailhead. A **22-mile trail** circles Shoshone Lake, although it is away from the shoreline much of the distance. You may see moose or elk and are certain to meet clouds of mosquitoes before August. The finest lake vistas come from the east side, where the trail follows the lakeshore for four miles. On the west end of the lake, hikers will find Shoshone Geyser Basin, an area filled with small geysers, beautiful pools, and bubbling mud pots. Most of the lake escaped the 1988 fires, but trails from the east side (via Dogshead Trailhead) traverse burned stands of lodgepole.

Heart Lake

The Heart Lake area is another extremely popular backcountry and day-hiking area, offering easy access, a pretty lake, hot springs, and impressive mountain vistas. Heart Lake Trail begins just north of Lewis Lake (six miles south of Grant Village). The trail is fairly easy, climbing slowly through unburned forests for the first five miles and then following Witch Creek down past burned forests to Heart Lake, eight miles from the trailhead. Witch Creek is fed almost entirely by the hot springs and geysers scattered along it.

Near the Heart Lake patrol cabin the trail splits. Continue straight ahead another 26 miles to eventually reach the isolated and challenging Thorofare Trail on the southeast end of Yellowstone Lake; getting there requires fording the Yellowstone River, which may be waist deep even in late summer. For something a bit less remote, turn right and hike 0.5 mile to the Mt. Sheridan Trail, which heads west and climbs 2,800 vertical feet in three miles. Reaching the 10,308-foot summit will certainly leave you winded. A fire lookout at the top provides views across Yellowstone Lake and south to the Tetons.

At the base of Mt. Sheridan and just to the north is a small thermal area that contains Rustic Geyser (eruptions to 50 feet, but irregular) and Columbia Pool, among other attractions. Be very careful when walking here because of the overhanging rim at the pool edge.

Although many people simply hike to Heart Lake for an overnight trip, one could take many longer hikes out of here, including into the remote Thorofare. A complete loop around the lake is approximately **34 miles round-trip** but requires two Snake River fords that are at least to your knees in late July; check with the rangers for flow levels. The Heart Lake area is prime grizzly habitat and is closed until the first of July. Do not take chances in this backcountry!

Bechler River

The southwest section of Yellowstone is known as Cascade Corner, a reference to its many tall waterfalls; more than half of the park's falls are here. This scenic and wild country escaped the fires of 1988 and is popular with anglers.

Primary access is from either the Bechler Ranger Station (pronounced BECK-ler) or the Cave Falls Trailhead, both of which are well off the beaten path and must be reached via Cave Falls Road from the Idaho side. It's 22 miles in from Ashton, Idaho, the last 10 on a gravel road. As an alternative, Grassy Lake Road provides a narrow and rough gravel connection to Cave Falls Road. Grassy Lake Road begins at Flagg Ranch Resort near Yellowstone's South Entrance; see a good map for the exact route.

All hikers must register at the Bechler Ranger Station, even if they are heading out from Cave Falls Trailhead, three miles farther down the road. Cave Falls is a wide but not particularly tall drop along the Falls River. It's named for a cave on the west end of the waterfall. The Forest Service's **Cave Falls Campground** ($10) is open June–September.

A spiderweb of trails cuts across the Bechler country, leading to many waterfalls and past several hot springs. One popular hike goes from Bechler Ranger Station to the Old Faithful area, a distance of 30 miles; it's downhill much of the way if you hike it in reverse by starting at Old Faithful. From Bechler Ranger Station the trail cuts across expansive Bechler Meadows and then up narrow Bechler Canyon, passing Colonnade, Ouzel, and Iris Falls along the way. Many people stop overnight at Three River Junction to enjoy the hot springs–warmed water. Beyond this point, the trail punches over the Continental Divide and then runs west of Shoshone Lake to Lone Star Geyser and the trailhead at Kepler Cascades. It's best to hike this route in August or September after the Bechler River drops enough to be more safely forded. This also allows time for the meadows to dry out a bit (watch out for leeches) and for the mosquitoes to quiet to a dull roar. For the long trek between Bechler Ranger Station and Old Faithful you will need to set up some sort of vehicle shuttle, but shorter in-and-out loop trips can be created by reading the various Yellowstone hiking guides and studying topographic maps. **Back Country Sports** (208/652-3385) provides a shuttle service to the Bechler area from Ashton, Idaho.

The Thorofare

If any part of Yellowstone deserves the title "untamed wilderness," it has to be the Thorofare. Situated along Two Ocean Plateau and cut through by the upper Yellowstone River, this broad expanse of roadless country reaches from Yellowstone Lake into the Teton Wilderness south of the park. This is *the* most remote country anywhere in the Lower 48; at its heart you'd need to hike 30 miles in any direction to reach a road. Because of the distances involved, many people choose to traverse the Thorofare via horseback. There is considerable grizzly activity in this area, so various restrictions are in place. In addition, some major river crossings are impassable until late summer. Access to the Thorofare is via Heart Lake Trail, the Thorofare Trail, or through Teton Wilderness within Bridger-Teton National Forest.

The Thorofare Trail begins at Nine Mile Trailhead on the East Entrance Road and hugs the shore of Yellowstone Lake for the first 17 miles. This stretch was spared from the fires of 1988 and provides some incredible opportunities to watch sunsets over the lake, particularly from campsites near Park Point. The trail continues along Southeast Arm and then follows the broad Thorofare Valley upstream beside the Yellowstone River (great fishing). There are several difficult creek and river crossings before you reach the Thorofare Ranger Station at mile 32, but this is not even the halfway point! Civilization is another 36 miles away. To get there, follow the often muddy South Boundary Trail, which heads west over the Continental Divide, through four difficult creek or river fords, through forests burned in the 1988 fires, and past Snake Hot Springs before finally ending at the South Entrance Station.

Needless to say, trips into the Thorofare are only for those with a lot of stamina and extensive backcountry experience. Shorter variations are possible, of course, but most involve hiking in and out the same way. Check at the Lake Ranger Station for conditions in the Thorofare and study Yellowstone hiking guides before even considering a big trip here. It's spectacular and remote country, but that means you're on your own much of the time.

One way to cut nine miles off your hike into the Thorofare is by a boat ride across Yellowstone Lake. The folks at Bridge Bay Marina (307/242-3983) can drop you off at a few campsites on the east side, but this is a pricey option: $152 each way. Contact the Park Service's Backcountry Office (307/344-2160) to find out which campsites are accessible by motorboat. These sites tend to fill up fast, so you'll need to reserve well ahead.

Summer Recreation

Summer is the busy time for Yellowstone. Anyone who loves the outdoors will find all sorts of options, from fishing and hiking to wildlife watching and horseback rides.

FISHING

In the early years of the park, fish from Yellowstone Lake were a specialty at the various hotels, and because there was no limit on the take, up to 7,500 pounds of fish were caught each year. After commercial fishing was halted, park policy shifted to planting nonnative species. But by the 1970s, Yellowstone Lake had been devastated by overfishing, and new regulations were needed. Beginning in 1973, bait fishing was banned, Fishing Bridge was closed to anglers, and catch-and-release rules were put into place. Increased fish populations have been a boon for wildlife, especially grizzlies, bald eagles, and osprey. Because of these regulations, Yellowstone National Park has achieved an almost mythical status when it comes to fishing. Each year 75,000 visitors spend time fishing in the park. The most commonly caught fish in Yellowstone are cutthroat, rainbow, brown, lake, and brook trout, along with mountain

fly-fishing along the Firehole River

whitefish. Montana grayling are found at only a few small lakes within the park, most notably Grebe Lake.

The Yellowstone River is still considered one of the best places in the world to catch cutthroat trout, and the Madison River is a justifiably famous fly-fishing river with a wide range of conditions. Yellowstone Lake is where the lure anglers go to catch cutthroats and lake trout. Beginners may have luck in the Gallatin River, but they're less likely to do well in the Firehole River, where the fish are smart and wary. Peaceful Slough Creek in the northeast corner of Yellowstone is filled with fat rainbows and cutthroats, attracting fly-fishers from around the globe.

Several good books—available in local stores and visitor centers—provide tips on fishing Yellowstone waters. Try one of the following: *Bud Lilly's Guide to Fly Fishing the New West,* by Bud Lilly and Paul Schullery (Frank Amato Publications), *Yellowstone Fishes: Ecology, History, and Angling in the Park,* by John Varley and Paul Schullery (www.stackpolebooks.com),

or *Fishing Yellowstone,* by Richard Parks (www.falcon.com).

Trouble in Paradise

The last two decades were not at all kind to aquatic ecosystems in Yellowstone as a series of diseases and nonnative threats appeared. One of the greatest threats comes from **lake trout** (Mackinaw), a species that had been illegally planted—either accidentally or intentionally—in the 1980s or earlier. Lake trout were first discovered in Yellowstone Lake in 1994, and studies have since revealed that many thousands of them now inhabit the lake. A highly aggressive and long-lived species, lake trout feed on and compete with the prized native cutthroat, threatening to devastate the population. (The average lake trout eats 80–90 cutthroat trout per year in Yellowstone.) Cutthroat spawn in the shallow waters of the lake's tributary streams, where they are caught by grizzly bears, bald eagles, and other animals. Lake trout spawn in deeper waters that are inaccessible to predators, so fewer cutthroat and more lake trout could have an impact on grizzlies and eagles. Eradication of the lake trout is virtually impossible, but the Park Service has used gill nets to catch many thousands of them. There are no size or possession limits on lake trout caught in Yellowstone Lake, its tributaries, and the Yellowstone River, but any lake trout you catch in these lakes must be killed and reported.

Another problem is threatening trout, especially rainbow trout, throughout the Rockies. **Whirling disease,** a devastating parasite-caused disease, has seriously hurt populations of rainbow trout in parts of the Madison River outside Yellowstone. The disease was discovered in Yellowstone Lake cutthroats in 1998, and there are fears that it could spread to other lakes and rivers in the park. It is spread in part when mud or water is brought in from contaminated areas on waders, boats, and boots. Be sure to clean up thoroughly with a bleach solution before entering or leaving an area. Get details on whirling disease at www.whirling-disease.org.

As if the other problems weren't enough, **New Zealand mud snails** were discovered in park waters in 1995. These minuscule snails (natives of New Zealand) are now in the Firehole and Madison Rivers, where they can form dense colonies on aquatic plants and streambed rocks, crowding out native aquatic insects that are a food source for fish. It may be only a matter of time until other invasive exotic species—including **zebra mussels** and **Eurasian water-milfoil**—reach the Yellowstone ecosystem. Help prevent the spread of these pests by carefully cleaning boots, clothing, waders, gear, and boats. Find out more about preventing the spread of these and other invasive species in the park's *Fishing Regulations* brochure and online at www.cleaninspectdry.com and www.protectyourwaters.net.

Fishing Regulations

In most parts of Yellowstone, the fishing season extends from the Saturday of Memorial Day weekend in late May to the first Sunday of November, but Lake Yellowstone opens June 15, and the Yellowstone River above the falls opens July 15. Hayden Valley and some other areas are entirely closed to fishing, and only artificial lures and flies are allowed in the park. Lead cannot be used. All native species in the park—fluvial arctic grayling, cutthroat trout, and mountain whitefish—are catch-and-release only. Barbless hooks are required because they cause less damage and are easier to remove. Three rivers—Madison River, Firehole River, and Gibbon River downstream from Gibbon Falls—are open only to fly-fishing. For complete details, request the park's very detailed fishing regulations brochure, or find it online at www.nps.gov/yell/planyour-visit/publications.htm.

Fishing Fees

Anglers don't need a state fishing license but must obtain a special **Yellowstone National Park permit,** available from visitor centers, ranger stations, Yellowstone General Stores, and fishing shops in surrounding towns. The adult fishing fee is $15 for a three-day permit, $20 for a seven-day permit, or $35 for a season permit. Kids under age 15 can get a free permit, or can fish without a permit under the supervision of an adult who has one. Park visitor centers and ranger stations have copies of current fishing regulations.

BOATING

Bridge Bay Marina runs hour-long **Scenicruiser boat tours** of Yellowstone Lake ($14 adults, $9 ages 3–11) several times a day in the summer, providing a fine introduction to the area. Also available at the marina are **guided fishing charters** (starting at $152 for two hours for up to six people) and **boat rentals** ($10 per hour for a 16-foot rowboat; $47 per hour for an 18-foot motorboat with a 40-horsepower outboard). **Fly-fishing guides** are also available at $418 for two people per day.

The best Yellowstone Lake fishing is from boats rather than from the shoreline. If you're bringing your own boat or canoe to Yellowstone, pick up a park boat permit—and check out the regulations—at the Lake Ranger Station or Grant Village Visitor Center. Boat slips are available at Bridge Bay Marina. All streams are closed to watercraft, with the exception of the Lewis River Channel between Shoshone and Lewis Lakes. Motorboats are allowed only on Lewis Lake and parts of Yellowstone Lake.

Sea Kayaking

Several companies offer guided sea kayak trips in the park. **Snake River Kayak & Canoe School** (307/733-9999 or 800/529-2501, www.snakeriverkayak.com) leads a variety of trips in Yellowstone, starting with three-hour sunset paddles ($125 per person) on Yellowstone Lake and half-day paddles in the West Thumb area ($175), all the way up to six-day trips that leave the crowds behind as you explore the lake; these cost $1,250 per person, all-inclusive. The company also guides sea kayaking tours of Lewis and Shoshone Lakes and has a full range of kayaking classes in Jackson and Grand Teton National Park.

Jackson Hole Kayak School (307/733-2471, www.jacksonholekayak.com) has day tours of Yellowstone Lake or Lewis Lake for $195–295 per person (rate depends upon the number of fellow kayakers). They also offer multi-day treks, including three-day tours of Yellowstone Lake or Lewis and Shoshone Lakes for $875 per person. Multi-night trip prices include transportation from Jackson, kayaking and camping gear, supplies, and all meals.

O.A.R.S. (209/736-4677 or 800/346-6277, www.oars.com) offers half-day sea kayak trips from Grant Village for $95 adults or $70 kids. These can typically be booked the day before. In addition, they guide multi-day trips in the Yellowstone–Grand Teton region, including a six-day paddle, float, and hike adventure for $1,540 adults or $1,385 kids. Tents are included, and sleeping bags are available for rent if you lack one.

BICYCLING

Cycling provides a unique way to see Yellowstone up close. Unfortunately, park roads have narrow shoulders and traffic is heavy, making for dangerous conditions. These problems are exacerbated early in the year by high snowbanks, so bikes are not allowed on certain roads. Call 307/344-7381 for current road conditions. The Park Service produces a helpful *Bicycling in Yellowstone National Park* brochure with details on bicycle routes and safety, plus a map showing road conditions; get it from visitor centers or download a copy at www.nps.gov/yell.

If you're planning a cycling trip through Yellowstone, be sure to wear a helmet and high-visibility clothing. A bike mirror also helps. If you want to avoid some of the hassles and don't mind spring conditions, visit the park between late March and the third Friday in April, when motorized vehicles are usually prohibited from entering the park (except for park administrative vehicles). During this period, cyclists are allowed to ride only on the stretch between the West Entrance and Mammoth Hot Springs; other roads are closed to cycling because they're being plowed. Fall is also a good time to ride because traffic is much lighter than in summer. The best times to ride in summer are in the morning before traffic thickens or late in the afternoon before the light begins to fade and you become less visible to motorists. Special **hiker/biker campsites** are available at most park campgrounds for just $5.

Where to Ride

The best main park roads to ride (less traffic or better visibility and shoulders) are the following sections: Mammoth to Tower, Tower to Cooke City, Canyon to Lake, and Lake to Grant Village. Bikes are not allowed on backcountry trails or boardwalks inside Yellowstone. Several relatively short but fun mountain-bike rides are available around the park, including:

- The paved trail from Old Faithful to Morning Glory Pool (two miles)
- The partly paved trail to Lone Star Geyser in the Old Faithful area (two miles)
- Fountain Freight Road to the vicinity of Midway Geyser Basin (six miles)

- The old Chittenden Road up Mt. Washburn (three miles each way, but gaining 1,400 feet on the way up)
- Bunsen Peak Road near Mammoth (six miles and steep in places)
- The Old Gardiner Road from Mammoth to Gardiner (five miles)
- The abandoned railroad bed along the Yellowstone River between Gardiner and the park boundary at Reese Creek (five miles)
- Blacktail Plateau Drive (seven miles) east of Mammoth

Of these routes, cars are allowed only on the Old Gardiner Road and Blacktail Plateau Drive, but traffic is light on these two.

Bike Rentals and Tours

Rent bikes inside Yellowstone at Old Faithful Snow Lodge (307/545-4825, $8 per hour or $35 for 24 hours) and in the surrounding towns of West Yellowstone, Jackson, and Cody. **Backroads** (800/462-2848, www.backroads.com) has six-day multi-sport trips into

Yellowstone and Grand Teton that include biking, hiking, rafting, and kayaking. These are offered as either camping trips ($2,000–2,300 per person including meals) or trips on which you stay at local inns ($2,900–3,300 per person including meals). Trips take place weekly June–August.

Teton Mountain Bike Tours (307/733-0712 or 800/733-0788, www.wybike.com) leads all-day tours of the Old Faithful area for $150. The park website (www.nps.gov/yell) has a list of other permitted bicycle-tour operators.

HORSEBACK RIDES

Summertime trail rides are available from the corrals at Mammoth Hot Springs, Canyon Village, and Roosevelt Lodge. These cost $38 for one hour or $58 for a two-hour ride. Kids must be at least eight years old and 48 inches tall, and there is a 250-pound weight limit, much to the relief of the horses. Roosevelt also has **stagecoach rides** ($12 adults, $6 ages 3–11) several times a day in the summer. In addition, **Old West dinner cookouts** at

Horseback riding is a fun way to explore Yellowstone.

Roosevelt combine a horseback or wagon ride with a filling steak dinner.

For details on trail rides, contact Xanterra Parks and Resorts (307/344-7311 or 866/439-7375, www.yellowstonenationalparklodges.com). Several outfitters provide backcountry pack trips inside Yellowstone; get a list from Park Service visitor centers (307/344-7381, www.nps.gov/yell).

HOT SPRINGS

Many people are disappointed to discover that there are no places in Yellowstone where you can soak in the hot springs. Not only is "hot-potting" illegal, but it can also be dangerous because temperatures often approach boiling and bathers can cause severe damage to these surprisingly fragile natural wonders. Legal

bathing pools are found in cold-water streams that have hot springs feeding into them. You're not allowed to enter the source pool or stream itself. Families often stop for a swim in the Firehole River along Firehole Canyon Drive near Madison. The Park Service doesn't encourage this, and there are no lifeguards, so parents need to watch children closely.

Thirty miles north of Yellowstone in the little burg of Pray, Montana, is **Chico Hot Springs** (406/333-4933 or 800/468-9232, www.chicohotsprings.com). If you're staying in the Mammoth Hot Springs area of Yellowstone, a side trip to Chico may be worthwhile. The large outdoor pool is a great place to relax, the gourmet restaurant serves some of the best dinners anywhere around, and the classic old hotel is a favorite.

Winter Recreation

Winter transforms Yellowstone into an extraordinarily beautiful place where the fires and brimstone of hell meet the bitter cold and snow of winter. The snow often averages four feet in depth but can exceed 10 feet on mountain passes. The snow is usually quite dry, although late in the season conditions deteriorate as temperatures rise. Early in the winter or after major storms, backcountry skiing can be difficult because of the deep powder. Temperatures are generally in the 10–25°F range during the day, while nights frequently dip below zero. (The record is -66°F, recorded on February 9, 1933.) Winds can make these temperatures feel even lower, so visitors should come prepared for extreme conditions.

The thermal basins are a real wintertime treat. Hot springs that are simply colorful pools in summer send up billows of steam in the winter, coating nearby trees with thick layers of ice and turning them into "ghost trees." The geysers put on astounding displays as boiling water meets frigid air; steam from Old Faithful can tower 1,000 feet into the air! Bison and elk gather around the hot springs,

soaking up the heat and searching for dried grasses, and bald eagles are often seen flying over the heated waters of Firehole River. The bison are perhaps the most interesting to watch as they swing their enormous heads from side to side to shovel snow off the grass. Grand Canyon of the Yellowstone is another place transformed by the snow and cold. Although the water still flows, the falls are surrounded by tall cones of ice, and the canyon walls lie under deep snow.

The **Winter in Wonderland website**—www.winterinwonderland.com—provides a portal to all sorts of winter activities, lodging, tours, ranger-led programs, field seminars, and information. It's jointly maintained by the National Park Service, Yellowstone Association, and Xanterra.

SNOWMOBILING
Historical Winter Use

During Yellowstone's first 75 years as a park, winter visitation was almost unknown. The only people in the park were caretakers, who spent months at a time with no contact with the

PHOTO COURTESY OF XANTERRA PARKS & RESORTS® IN YELLOWSTONE

Old Faithful Snow Lodge in the winter

world outside. This began to change in 1949, when snow-plane tours were first offered from the West Entrance. The planes skimmed over the surface and could hold only two people—the driver and a passenger—so visitation barely topped 30 people that winter. In 1955, snow-coaches were permitted to enter Yellowstone, and more than 500 people visited, although few stayed overnight.

Snowmobiling Changes Everything

The first snowmobilers arrived in 1963, when the machines were still a novelty. As snowmobiling became increasingly popular, communities around Yellowstone benefited economically and began promoting the park as a winter wonderland. In the winter of 1971–1972 the Park Service began encouraging snowmobile use by grooming the roads and opening Old Faithful Snow Lodge. By the end of that winter, more than 25,000 people had visited, and by the early 1990s the number had rocketed to more than 140,000 people, with the park admitting more snowmobiles than all other national parks combined. Noise and air pollution from the two-cycle engines became a serious problem as 1,600 snowmobiles flooded into Yellowstone on busy days.

In the heavy-snow winter of 1996–1997 large numbers of bison moved out of Yellowstone, some of them along the groomed snowmobile road out the west side of the park. Nearly 1,100 bison were killed that year as part of Montana's effort to protect cattle from brucellosis (bison use the groomed-for-snowmobiling roads to find their way out of the park, potentially carrying brucellosis to cattle on surrounding ranches). The slaughter precipitated a lawsuit by the Fund for Animals that forced the Park Service to rethink its winter-use policies. To address the effects of snowmobiles and other uses, the Park Service under President Clinton attempted to ban snowmobiles from the park. Industry groups and others successfully fought the closure, with support from the snowmobile-friendly Bush administration.

Snowmobiling Today

After a decade of heated debate, the Park Service adopted a new winter use plan in 2007 that allows a maximum of 540 snowmobiles and 83 snowcoaches per day. All snowmobiles must be commercially guided and meet best-available emission and noise requirements (i.e., four-stroke engines). The new rules have significantly reduced snowmobile trips into the park.

Snowmobiles are available for rent from all four sides of the park and inside Yellowstone at Mammoth and Old Faithful, with the majority of snowmobilers—all guided, of course—coming in from West Yellowstone, where prices are usually a bit lower and access is quicker. Contact chamber of commerce offices in West Yellowstone or Jackson for companies offering snowmobile tours.

SNOWCOACHES

The easiest and most enjoyable way to get into Yellowstone in the winter is on the ungainly snowcoaches—machines that look like something the Norwegian Army might have used during World War II. Most were actually built by a Canadian company, Bombardier. They can be noisy, and the windows fog up (hence the spray bottles of antifreeze). But despite their ancient condition and spartan interiors, these beasts still work well and can carry 10 passengers, gear (two suitcases per person), and skis. You will also see (or ride in) a variety of other over-snow vehicles, including vans on tracks.

Snowcoach Tours

A variety of snowcoach tours are provided by Xanterra Parks and Resorts (307/344-7311 or 866/439-7375, www.yellowstonenational-parklodges.com). All snowcoach tours and transportation are half price for kids ages 2–11 and free for toddlers. Adult per-person rates to Old Faithful are $140 round-trip from Flagg Ranch (where the plowing ends just south of Yellowstone), $114 round-trip from West Yellowstone, and $140 round-trip from Mammoth. Xanterra also provides all-day tours several times a week from Mammoth to

Canyon for $125 round-trip and Old Faithful to Canyon for $130 round-trip. Half-day tours from Mammoth to Norris Geyser Basin cost $57. If you're just looking for transportation, express snowcoach runs (no tours) are $55 each way between Old Faithful and West Yellowstone.

Shorter snowcoach tours depart two or three times a week from Old Faithful for the Firehole River/Fountain Flats area (three hours; $33 round-trip). Three-hour winter wildlife bus tours to the Lamar Valley ($38 with a box breakfast) depart daily from Mammoth, providing a great opportunity to see wolves. Visit the Xanterra website (www.yellowstona-tionalparklodges.com) for details on these and other winter treks from Mammoth and Old Faithful. For any of these trips, be sure to make reservations well in advance.

During the winter, **Gray Line of Jackson Hole/Alltrans** (307/733-3135 or 800/443-6133, www.graylinejh.com) has daily bus runs from Jackson to Flagg Ranch for $106 round-trip, arriving in time to meet the snowcoach departures for Yellowstone. Reservations are required.

Yellowstone Alpen Guides (406/646-9591 or 800/858-3502, www.yellowstoneguides.com) leads snowcoach tours from West Yellowstone. All-day trips are $110 adults, $100 seniors, $90 kids to either Grand Canyon of the Yellowstone or Old Faithful. Guests on the latter run have an option of getting dropped at Biscuit Basin, where they can ski to Old Faithful and meet the rest of the group for the return trip. Ski or snowshoe rentals are available. The company's eight classic Bombardier snowcoaches (one built in 1953) have been modernized but are still a charming anachronism.

Snowcoach Yellowstone/Buffalo Bus Touring Co. (406/646-9564 or 800/426-7669, www.yellowstonevacations.com) operates modern snowcoach vans, with all-day tours from West Yellowstone to Old Faithful ($109 adults, $89 kids) or Canyon ($119 adults, $99 kids). Park entrance fees are additional.

Triangle C Ranch (307/455-2225 or 800/661-4928, www.trianglec.com) also provides all-day snowcoach trips, in a converted Ford Excursion from either Jackson or Dubois into Yellowstone, with pickups directly from your hotel. These head to either Old Faithful or Canyon for the day, departing at 7 A.M. and returning by 6 P.M. The cost is $265 per person ($300 to Canyon) including lunch, entrance fee, and guide.

For a truly unique experience, book a trip with **Yellowstone Expeditions** (406/646-9333 or 800/728-9333, www.yellowstoneexpeditions.com). The company has day tours from West Yellowstone using converted vans, but is best known for a remote base camp near Canyon that's perfect for those who want to really explore Yellowstone in winter. Guests stay in eight heated tent cabins, with two yurts providing a central kitchen and dining/social area. These trips start at $1,900 for two people for three nights and four days, and go up to $3,000 for two people for seven nights and eight days. The price includes lodging, food, bedding, round-trip transportation from West Yellowstone to the base camp near Canyon, and backcountry ski

guides. Ski and snowshoe rentals are extra. Days are spent skiing or snowshoeing in the Canyon area or along trails around Hayden Valley, Norris, or Mt. Washburn. Showers are available and the cedar sauna is perfect after a long day in the backcountry. This is the only overnight accommodation in the Canyon area during the winter.

SKIING AND SNOWSHOEING

Cross-country skis and snowshoes provide the finest ways to see Yellowstone in the winter. Rent them from Old Faithful Snow Lodge or Mammoth Hot Springs Hotel. Both places also provide lessons and guided tours for groups or individuals. The towns surrounding Yellowstone also have shops that rent skis and snowshoes. The Old Faithful area is the center for skiing within Yellowstone, with trails circling the Upper Geyser Basin and leading to nearby sights. You'll find similar ski trails (not always groomed) in the Tower Fall, Canyon, and Mammoth areas. Get free ski-trail maps at park visitor centers. Old Faithful Snow Lodge is open in winter, providing an excellent base

skiing at Mammoth Hot Springs

for day trips into nearby areas or for a snow-coach tour of the park.

Skiers and snowshoers sometimes assume that they can't possibly cause problems for Yellowstone's wildlife, but studies show that elk and bison often move away from skiers, which forces the animals to expend energy they need to survive through the bitterly cold winters. It's best to stay on the trails and to keep from skiing into areas where elk or bison may be disturbed by your presence.

For more on skiing and winter visitation in the park, see Jeff Henry's *Yellowstone Winter Guide* (www.roberts-rinehart.com), or *Winter Tales and Trails: Skiing, Snowshoeing and Snowboarding in Idaho, the Grand Tetons and Yellowstone National Park* by Ron Watters (Great Rift Press, www.ronwatters.com).

Skier Shuttles and Tours

Xanterra Parks and Resorts (307/344-7311 or 866/439-7375, www.yellowstonenational-parklodges.com) operates **skier snowcoach shuttles** ($15) from Mammoth southward to Golden Gate and Indian Creek, where you can ski downhill to Mammoth. Snowcoaches also shuttle skiers from Old Faithful to Fairy Falls Trailhead or the Continental Divide area for $15, and you can ski back on your own to Snow Lodge. The eight-mile Continental Divide run is primarily downhill.

In addition, Xanterra provides all-day Grand Canyon snowcoach-and-guided-ski tours five times a week from Old Faithful ($130 round-trip) and on Saturdays from Mammoth ($140). **Afternoon ski-daddies** are guided five-hour ski tours from Old Faithful to Fairy Falls or DeLacey Creek; they're offered on Wednesday and Saturday for $45.

Guided three-hour **snowshoe tours** ($32 with snowshoes) are available twice weekly from Old Faithful. They're a great way to explore the country. Besides these concessioner-run tours, park naturalists sometimes lead ski trips from Old Faithful to nearby sights; stop by the visitor center for details.

Safety on Skis

Before your trip, call Yellowstone (307/344-7381) to request the informative *Winter Backcountry Trip Planner*, with details on trails, equipment, weather, and avalanche safety. Online at www.nps.gov/yell/planyourvisit/backcountrytripplanner.htm, find an 11-minute winter backcountry video. Yellowstone's roads are traveled by snowmobiles and snow-coaches, making for potential conflicts with skiers. Be sure to keep to the right while skiing. Most trails are identified by orange metal markers on the trees. If you're planning a back-country trip, pick up a use permit from one of the ranger stations. A thorough understanding of winter camping and survival is imperative before you head out on any overnight trip, and avalanche safety classes are a wise investment.

Get avalanche-safety information from the **Gallatin National Forest Avalanche Center** (406/587-6981, www.mtavalanche.com) in Bozeman. The recording does not cover the entire park, but it does include the Washburn Range and areas near Cooke City and West Yellowstone. It's updated daily in the winter. Call 307/344-2113 for the latest park weather forecast.

WINTER PRACTICALITIES
Accommodations

Only two places offer wintertime lodging inside Yellowstone. **Mammoth Hot Springs Hotel,** on the north end of the park, is the only accommodation accessible by road and has ski and snowshoe trails nearby, while the modern **Old Faithful Snow Lodge and Cabins** puts you close to the geysers and many miles of ski trails. Each has a restaurant, lounge, gift shop, and rental of skis and snowshoes. Mammoth has a couple of advantages over Old Faithful: far fewer snowmobiles so it's much quieter, and road access to the Lamar Valley where wolves, bison, and elk are major attractions. You might even see a pack of wolves take down an elk.

A wide variety of multi-night **Winter**

Getaway package trips are available out of Mammoth and Old Faithful, including a "Nordic Heaven" trip ($678 d) that includes two nights' lodging, snowcoach transportation, breakfasts, plus ski and skate rentals. In addition, the Yellowstone Association Institute has excellent **Lodging and Learning** packages throughout the winter, notably a four-night "Winter Wolf Discovery" trip ($1,300 d) that includes lodging at Mammoth Hotel, plus breakfasts and lunches, naturalist-led treks to Lamar Valley, snowshoes, hot tub access, and evening programs. Get details on various winter lodging, learning, and play options from Xanterra Parks and Resorts (307/344-7311 or 866/439-7375, www.yellowstonenationalpark-lodges.com).

The only **wintertime camping** spot is Mammoth Campground, where temperatures are milder and the snow lighter.

During winter, the most popular—and crowded—times to visit Yellowstone are around Christmas and New Year's and the Presidents' Day weekend in February. If you plan to arrive at these times, make lodging reservations six months in advance. The rest of the winter, you should probably reserve at least three months ahead.

Services

Only the Mammoth and Old Faithful visitor centers are open during winter. Free ranger-led activities include evening programs at Mammoth and Old Faithful. Check the winter edition of *Yellowstone Today* for details, or find it on the web at ww.nps.gov/yell.

Xanterra Parks and Resorts (307/344-7311 or 866/439-7375, www.yellowstonenational-parklodges.com) offers a variety of guided ski and snowmobile tours and provides wildlife bus or van tours. In addition, the **Yellowstone Association Institute** (406/848-2400, www.yellowstoneassociation.org) has outstanding winter classes.

The **Mammoth Clinic** (307/344-7965) is open daily 8:30 A.M.–5 P.M. June–August, and weekdays—except Wednesdays—in the winter for medical emergencies.

The Yellowstone General Store at Mammoth is open for groceries and supplies year-round, but only meals and gas are available at Old Faithful. **Warming huts** are at Old Faithful, Madison Junction, Canyon, West Thumb, Fishing Bridge, and Indian Creek (south of Mammoth Hot Springs). They contain restrooms and snack machines (except Indian Creek and West Thumb), and all are open 24 hours (except for Old Faithful, where other facilities are available). The huts at Madison and Canyon also have snack bars selling hot chili or soup. Park rangers are often at the warming huts during the middle of the day.

Roads

Most of Yellowstone's roads officially close to cars on the Monday after the first Sunday in November and remain shut down all over except for the 56 miles between Mammoth and Cooke City. Roads don't open for cars again until sometime between mid-May and early June. The roads are groomed for snowmobiles and snowcoaches mid-December–mid-March. The rest of the winter you'll find only skiers and park personnel on the roads.

Accommodations

Yellowstone accommodations vary from extremely basic cabins with four thin walls starting at $65 up to luxury suites that will set you back $545. Following a fine old Park Service tradition, the rooms do not have TVs, and most lack phones. Web access is limited to slow phone connections (where available). What they do offer is the chance to relax in comfortable accommodations and explore the magical world outside. Most are open early June–late September, with additional winter lodging at Mammoth Hot Springs Hotel and the Old Faithful Snow Lodge. Several hundred more motels and other places to stay operate outside park boundaries in the towns of Jackson, Cody, West Yellowstone, Gardiner, and Cooke City.

Xanterra Parks and Resorts (307/344-7311 or 866/439-7375, www.yellowstonenationalparklodges.com) is Yellowstone's lodging concessioner. **Make Yellowstone lodging reservations six months ahead** for the park's prime hotels, or you may find that the only rooms available are in Grant Village, the laughingstock of park lodges. Those traveling with small children should request cribs when making reservations. Wheelchair-accessible (ADA-compliant) rooms are available at most of the park's cabins and hotels. (As an aside, several Web-based companies purport to make reservations for hotels and lodges inside Yellowstone, but all of these charge a service fee. Save yourself money and hassles by going directly to Xanterra.)

At the turn of the 20th century, most visitors to Yellowstone stayed in park hotels rather than roughing it on the ground. Three of these wonderful old lodging places remain: Old Faithful Inn, Lake Yellowstone Hotel, and Mammoth Hot Springs Hotel. Standard motel rooms can be found at Grant Village. In addition, three nicer places opened in the 1990s: the Old Faithful Snow Lodge and two small lodges at Canyon Village. All told, more than 2,200 rooms and cabins provide overnight accommodations in Yellowstone.

Not all lodging options inside the park are nearly as pleasant, however. Hundreds of simple boxes are clustered in the Lake, Mammoth, Old Faithful, and Roosevelt areas. Most of these cabins offer a roof over your head, simple furnishings, and communal showers, but the more expensive cabins are considerably nicer, and four of them even include private hot tubs. Fortunately, prices are fairly reasonable for all of the cabins, and the park concessioner is gradually renovating the oldest units.

Lodging rates are listed for two people; children under age 12 stay free. Add $11 per person for additional older kids or adults in the hotel rooms or cabins. Prices at some park lodgings are lower in May when snow still covers much of the park, but you need to book before April 1. Also available are a variety of winter and summer package deals that include lodging, tours, hikes, and more. Especially noteworthy are the multi-day **Lodging and Learning** packages that combine tours, educational activities, and hikes led by naturalist-guides from the **Yellowstone Association Institute** (406/848-2400, www.yellowstoneassociation. org) with accommodations in park hotels, plus breakfasts and lunches.

Rates listed are without tax, which is 6 percent on the south half of the park (inside Teton County—including Old Faithful, Grant Village, and Lake Village) and 8 percent on the north half (inside Park County—including Roosevelt, Mammoth Hot Springs, and Canyon Village).

MAMMOTH HOT SPRINGS

The rambling **Mammoth Hot Springs Hotel** sits in the northwest corner of Yellowstone near park headquarters in the settlement of Mammoth. Built in 1937 (one wing was constructed in 1911 and the original hotel was built even earlier), the hotel has 211 rooms in

PHOTO COURTESY OF XANTERRA PARKS & RESORTS® IN YELLOWSTONE

Mammoth Hot Springs Hotel

a variety of configurations. Elk are a common sight on the grounds, and in the fall the bulls' bugling may wake you in the morning. There's live piano music downstairs in the **Map Room** most summer evenings as a counterpoint to the elk songs. (The room is named for a distinctive map of the United States crafted from 16 types of wood; it's on the northern wall.) Also just off the lobby is a gift shop. Just steps away are Park Service headquarters, the fine Albright Visitor Center, and other historical buildings, along with places to eat and buy groceries, gas, and trinkets.

The hotel rooms are comfortable but modest. Walls are not entirely soundproof, furnishings show some wear, and the hallway floors squeak, but baths are large and the hotel exudes a graceful aura that befits the setting. Several rooms on each floor provide low-cost accommodations ($87 d) with communal baths down the hall, but most have two queen beds and private baths ($117 d); ask for a corner room if available. The hotel also houses two luxury suites ($439 d). It is open mid-May–mid-October and mid-December–early March.

Early-season discounts are available, and winter rates are below those in summer. In the winter, "Frosty Fun" packages are a good bet, including one that provides two nights' lodging, two breakfasts, hot tub access, and ice skates, at $268 for two people. Winter-only hot tub rentals are available, offering a great way to relax after a day of cross-country skiing. Mammoth Hotel and Old Faithful Snow Lodge are the only wintertime hotels inside the park.

Behind the hotel are 116 **《 Mammoth Cabins,** including **Budget Cabins** ($79 d) with a shared bathhouse, and delightful **Frontier Cottages** ($107 d) with small porches and private baths. Most of these accommodations were built in 1938, and all contain two double beds. Some are duplex units that can be joined for families or friends traveling together. Dozens of ground squirrels populate the grounds, providing endless entertainment

© DON PITCHER

Mammoth Cabins

for the kids. Four units also have private outdoor **hot tubs** and are the finest cabins in Yellowstone ($213 d). The Mammoth cabins are open mid-May–mid-October.

ROOSEVELT LODGE

At the junction of the roads to Canyon, Mammoth, and Lamar Valley, 【 **Roosevelt Lodge** is *the* place to escape the crowds and return to a quieter and simpler era. The lodge is decidedly off the beaten path to the major Yellowstone sights, and that suits folks who stay here just fine. Named for President Theodore Roosevelt—perhaps the most conservation-minded president ever—the lodge has the well-worn feeling of an old dude ranch, and many families treat it as such. More than a few folks book cabins for several weeks at a stretch, enjoying the wolf-watching, fly-fishing, horseback and wagon rides, and barbecue cookout dinners. (Cookouts book up six months ahead, so reserve your space when you make a Roosevelt Lodge reservation.)

The main lodge features two large stone fireplaces, a family-style restaurant with no-table meals, a lounge, a gift shop, a little general store, and a big front porch with old-fashioned rocking chairs. Surrounding it are 82 utilitarian cabins, most of which were built in the 1920s. Most basic—and just a step up from camping—are the sparsely furnished **Roughrider Cabins** with one, two, or three beds, a writing table, and a woodstove (the only ones in any Yellowstone lodging). These cabins share a communal bathhouse, cost $65 d, and fill quickly. Call far ahead to reserve one of these classics! Nicer **Frontier Cabins** with hardwood floors, one or two double beds, and private baths go for $108 d. All of these cabins can get stuffy in midsummer, and some windows lack screens. Two of the Roosevelt cabins are wheelchair-accessible. The Roosevelt Lodge and cabins are open mid-June–early September.

CANYON VILLAGE

Centrally situated **Canyon Lodge** is just 0.5 mile from Grand Canyon of the Yellowstone,

Lake Yellowstone Hotel

one of the park's premier attractions. The main lodge is part of a late-1950s complex of ugly structures built around a large parking lot. The area has all the charm of an aging shopping mall from an era when bigger meant better. The lodge itself covers the space of a football field and houses a dining room, cafeteria, lounge, and snack shop, but no guest rooms. Cabins at Canyon Village are open early June–late September.

Behind the lodge in the trees (at least the setting is peaceful), the road circles past three sprawling clusters of cabins, all with private baths and double or queen beds. You'll find 480 cabins here. The simplest **Pioneer Cabins** cost just $70 d and aren't much to look at outside but have been renovated and are actually fairly roomy and comfortable. Two newer types of cabins are available at Canyon: the **Frontier Cabins** for $96 d and the attractive **Western Cabins** with two queen beds for $166 d.

Providing far better accommodations are two 1990s additions: **Dunraven Lodge** and **Cascade Lodge.** Rooms at both of these attractive log- and rock-trimmed structures are furnished with rustic lodgepole pieces and have two double beds and private baths. Rooms in the lodges cost $166 d. The cabins and lodges at Canyon are open June–mid-September.

LAKE VILLAGE

The Lake Village area has a full range of lodging options for travelers, with a central location and good services.

Lake Yellowstone Hotel

The fascinating Southern colonial–style **Lake Yellowstone Hotel** delivers a magnificent view across Yellowstone Lake. Begun in 1889, the building expanded and changed through the decades to yield its current configuration of 158 guest rooms. The hotel has been lovingly restored and exudes a grandeur and charm rarely found today. It's the sort of place where Fred Astaire and Ginger Rogers would have felt comfortable dancing.

The Lake Yellowstone's inviting hotel rooms all contain updated furnishings, private baths, and in-room phones. Standard units cost $204 d on the back side or $219 d facing the lake, and a delightfully spacious two-bedroom presidential suite is the most elaborate (and expensive) accommodation in the park at $545 for up to six people. For the best vistas, ask for a third-floor room on the lake side when making your reservations.

Downstairs is a good restaurant (reservations required for dinner), along with a fast-food eatery; the cafeteria at Lake Lodge is only a short walk away. The real treat at Lake Yellowstone Hotel is the **Sun Room,** where rows of windows front the lake. The room's ambience is further enhanced by period wicker furnishings and evening piano or chamber music. It's a great place to sip a martini or write a postcard. The hotel is open late May–September.

Annex and Frontier Cabins

Out back is the **Lake Yellowstone Hotel Annex,** where rooms cost $145 d. There's no view, but each modern room has two double beds, phones, a bath, and pleasant furnishings. Some of these rooms are wheelchair-accessible.

Also behind Lake Yellowstone Hotel are more than 100 units originally built in the 1950s, jammed together in row after identical row to create the **Frontier Cabins.** Fortunately, they were nicely restored several years back and are surprisingly comfortable, clean, and cheap: $130 for up to four. Units are small, with just enough space for two double beds and a private bath. Cabin guests can pretend they're traveling on a more ample budget by spending time in the adjacent Lake Yellowstone Hotel dining room and the Sun Room. Lake Yellowstone Hotel Cabins are open mid-May–September.

Lake Lodge Cabins

A short distance east of Lake Yellowstone Hotel is **Lake Lodge.** Built in the 1920s, this archetypal log building has a gracious lobby containing two stone fireplaces, comfortably rustic furnishings, an open ceiling where the supporting log trusses and beams are visible, and a delightful front porch. One end of the

building houses a large and reasonably priced cafeteria with picture windows framing Lake Yellowstone, and the other end contains a recreation hall for employees. Lodging options at Lake Lodge are not nearly as gracious, consisting of plain-vanilla **Pioneer Cabins** from the 1920s and 1930s, each with a double bed and private bath for $68 d; renovated **Frontier Cabins,** built in the 1950s and 1960s (but renovated in 2011), that include two double beds and private baths with showers for $166 d. The 186 cabins at Lake Lodge are open early June–September. Guests here often walk over to the nearby Lake Yellowstone Hotel for fine dining and the chance to relax in the Sun Room.

GRANT VILLAGE

The southernmost lodging in Yellowstone, **Grant Village** has condo-type units from the 1980s, each with a parking-lot vista. These buildings would be completely out of place in *any* national park, especially Yellowstone. Six hideously ugly lodge buildings contain motel-type units for $149 d; make sure to request a remodeled room. All of these have two double beds and private baths, and several wheelchair-accessible rooms are available. A park visitor center and campground are in the area, along with a variety of concession facilities, including a restaurant, waterside café, general store, lounge, snack shop, and gift shop. Grant Village is open late May–September and has 300 units.

OLD FAITHFUL

The Old Faithful area contains a plethora of lodging options, including two large hotels and several dozen cabins.

Old Faithful Inn

Built in 1903–1904, timeless 【 **Old Faithful Inn** is easily the most delightful place to stay inside Yellowstone—if not in all of America. I wouldn't trade it for a thousand Hiltons. If you're able to get a room at OFI during your visit to the park, do so; you certainly won't regret it! The inn's 329 rooms are located in three parts of the building: Old House rooms are in the original structure, and the East and West Wings were added in the 1910s and 1920s. Each section has its own character, but even those staying in the simplest budget rooms here will enjoy the five-star lobby with its towering stone fireplace, the old-fashioned writing tables, cushy overstuffed chairs, a classy bar and restaurant, and evening piano music. Old Faithful Inn is open early May–mid-October.

Most rooms in the **Old House** section of the hotel are cramped spaces with a brass queen bed, dresser, log walls, robes, an in-room sink, and communal baths down the hall; these go for $96 d, with two-room units without bath for $179. Of the cheap rooms, the best ones (these are often reserved a year ahead) are the dormer rooms on the second floor—particularly room 229—but those who stay there must walk past folks in the lobby to take a shower! Mid-range rooms in the Old House contain private baths and one or two queen beds: $122 d; request numbers 46, 148, 154, or 240.

Many other types of rooms are available throughout this sprawling hotel. The **West Wing**'s standard rooms (also called "high-range rooms") are comfortable, with one or two queen beds and private baths for $145 d. Note, however that some of these lack even a parking-lot view. Attractively appointed rooms in the **East Wing** (also called "premium rooms") are very comfortable, containing two queen beds, phones, and tub baths with colorful tiles. Premium rooms vary in price from $205 to $239 d, with higher rates for those facing the geyser. Good choices include numbers 1002, 2002, 3002, 1004, 2004, 3004, 1024, 2024, and 3024; all have notable Old Faithful vistas, but 2024 and 3024 have the best dead-on views. If you have the cash, rent a six-person suite for $400–502; ask for suite numbers 1002, 2002, or 3002.

Old Faithful Lodge

Although it is an attractively rustic building that would be a major focal point almost anywhere else, **Old Faithful Lodge** is overshadowed by its grand neighbor, Old Faithful Inn. The lodge does not contain guest rooms but houses a large cafeteria (open for lunch and dinner only), recreation hall, gift shop, bake shop, ice-cream stand, espresso cart, and showers. Unlike the inn, the lodge has enormous windows that face the geyser, providing those eating in the cafeteria with dramatic views of the eruptions. The lodge's massive fir logs and stone pillars add to a feeling of permanence. Behind and beside Old Faithful Lodge are approximately 130 moderately priced but cramped cabins. These contain older (but functional) furnishings, and most have two beds. The simplest **Budget Cabins** share communal bathhouses and cost just $66 d; they're some of the cheapest rooms in Yellowstone and just a few steps from Old Faithful. Slightly nicer (but still small) **Frontier Cabins** have one or two beds and private baths and cost $108 d. There is even a pair of handicapped-accessible cabins here. The cabins at Old Faithful Lodge are open mid-May–September.

Snow Lodge

Built in 1999, the 100-room **C Old Faithful Snow Lodge** provides accommodations in both summer and winter (Mammoth Hot Springs Hotel is Yellowstone's only other wintertime hotel). Both inside and out, Snow Lodge evokes the spirit of "parkitecture" from the early 1900s. The building blends the past and present, with timbers (recycled from old buildings), hardwood floors, a central stone fireplace, custom-designed overstuffed couches, and wrought-iron accents, along with all the modern conveniences you expect from a fine hotel—unless you're expecting TVs, which no park hotels contain. Rooms are beautifully appointed and comfortable, and all have private baths. The hotel also houses a restaurant, snack shop, lounge, and gift shop, along with a ski shop and snowmobile rentals in winter. Rates are $197 d.

In addition to the hotel, 34 four-plex Snow Lodge Cabins are available behind the building, costing $143 d. Built in 1989, these **Western Cabins** have standard motel furnishings, with two double beds and a full bath. Duplex **Frontier Cabins** provide simple accommodations with bath for $96 d. The Snow Lodge and Cabins are open early May–late October

and mid-December–early March. Rates are the same in summer and winter. "Frosty Fun" packages are a better deal, including one that provides two nights' lodging, two breakfasts, ice skates, and a round-trip snowcoach transport to Old Faithful at $578 for two people.

Camping

Camping is available at a dozen sites scattered along the Yellowstone road network. Most of these campsites are open from at least late May–mid-September, but only Mammoth Campground remains open throughout the year. Generators are allowed in more than half of the campgrounds but can be used only between 8 A.M. and 8 P.M. Roadside or parking-lot camping is prohibited, and rangers vigorously enforce this rule.

Reservations are available—and advised—for five concessioner-managed campgrounds: Bridge Bay Campground, Canyon Campground, Grant Village Campground, Madison Campground, and Fishing Bridge RV Park. Contact **Xanterra Parks and Resorts** (307/344-7311 or 866/439-7375, www.yellowstonenationalparklodges.com) for reservations (no extra charge). The other seven (Park Service–managed) campgrounds inside Yellowstone are available on a first-come, first-camped basis with no reservations. You can pay with cash, checks, or credit cards. Historically, the Park Service increases rates annually by a small percentage every March or April. Call to confirm rates before booking.

During July and August, virtually all campsites in Yellowstone fill *before noon,* so get there early or reserve a space! The busiest weekends are—not surprisingly—around July 4 and Labor Day, but Yellowstone's most popular campgrounds fill up even in late fall and early summer. Call the Park Service at 307/344-2114 for a recording noting which campgrounds are full.

MADISON
Madison Campground
Sixteen miles north of Old Faithful, this is the closest campground to Yellowstone's most famous attraction. West Yellowstone is 14 miles to the west. The campground is near the confluence of the Gibbon, Madison, and Firehole Rivers and makes a fine base for exploring all the park's main attractions. All 277 campsites at Madison fill early in the day throughout the summer. Generators are allowed 8 A.M.–8 P.M., and the campground has flush toilets and a dump station, but no showers. It's open early May–late October and costs $20. Contact **Xanterra Parks and Resorts** (307/344-7311 or 866/439-7375, www.yellowstonenational-parklodges.com) for reservations (highly recommended). Group sites are available.

NORRIS GEYSER BASIN
Norris Campground
One of Yellowstone's most dramatic geyser basins is just a quarter-mile from Norris Campground. The campsites fill early most days, and the campground has flush toilets. Food and supplies are available at Canyon Village, 12 miles east of Norris. Generators are permitted 8 A.M.–8 P.M., and the campground is open mid-May–late September. The 116 sites cost $14. No reservations.

MAMMOTH HOT SPRINGS
Mammoth Campground
This extremely popular campground is near a residential area and along the busy park road, but just a short walk from the hot springs,

visitor center/museum, shops, horseback rides, and eating places in Mammoth. Generators are permitted 8 A.M.–8 P.M., and road traffic can be noisy, so this isn't the most peaceful spot. It has flush toilets and is the only park campground that remains open year-round. The 85 sites (all pull-through) cost $14. Reservations are not accepted, so get there early to be assured of a spot—even in winter and spring.

Indian Creek Campground

This quiet campground generally fills late in the day. It is just eight miles south of Mammoth, where you'll find food and other services. There are generators, and it has vault toilets. It sits alongside pretty Indian Creek and is open mid-June–mid-September. The 75 sites go for $12 each. No reservations.

TOWER-ROOSEVELT AREA
Pebble Creek Campground

This campground makes a good base for wildlife-watching in Lamar Valley and for exploring the scenic Icebox Canyon area. It's in a quiet corner of the park, seven miles from the Northeast Entrance. Food and limited supplies are available at Tower Fall and Roosevelt. Pebble Creek Campground has vault toilets and is open mid-June–September. The 32 campsites are $12. No reservations.

Slough Creek Campground

This fairly small 29-site campground is especially popular with anglers who come here to fly-fish for cutthroat trout and with wildlife enthusiasts who watch the bison, elk, and wolves of Lamar Valley. Good local hiking is nearby, too. Food and limited supplies are available at Tower Fall and Roosevelt. The campground is open late May–October and has vault toilets. Campsites are $12. No reservations.

Tower Fall Campground

Close to a dramatic waterfall on Tower Creek, this campground has 32 sites and vault toilets. Limited groceries and supplies are available

© DON PITCHER

Mammoth Campground

at the nearby general store, with meals at Roosevelt Lodge. The campground is open mid-May–September. Campsites cost $12. No reservations.

CANYON VILLAGE
Canyon Campground

This exceptionally popular camping area is close to the dramatic overlooks at Grand Canyon of the Yellowstone. A park visitor center, Yellowstone General Store, restaurant, cafeteria, post office, gas station, and other lodgings are a short walk away. Not surprisingly, the campground's 250 sites fill early most summer days. It has coin-operated washers and dryers, coin-operated showers, flush toilets, and a dump station. Generators are permitted 8 A.M.–8 P.M. Canyon Campground is open early June–early September and costs $20. Contact **Xanterra Parks and Resorts** (307/344-7311 or 866/439-7375, www.yellowstonenationalparklodges.com) for reservations—highly recommended.

LAKE VILLAGE
Bridge Bay Campground

This camping area is adjacent to the Bridge Bay Marina on the north side of Lake Yellowstone and also near a ranger station and store. Meals are available at Lake Yellowstone Hotel and Lake Lodge, just a few miles from here. This 425-site campground (the largest in Yellowstone) fills quickly most summer days. Generators are permitted 8 A.M.–8 P.M., and it has flush toilets and a dump station, but no showers or laundry. The campground is open late May–mid-September and costs $20. Contact **Xanterra Parks and Resorts** (307/344-7311 or 866/439-7375, www.yellowstonenationalparklodges.com) for reservations—highly recommended. Group sites are also available.

Fishing Bridge RV Park

On the north end of Yellowstone Lake, this very crowded 325-site campground is open only to hard-sided RVs, with a 40-foot maximum length. No tents, pop-ups, or other campers that bears might break into easily are allowed. Sites with full hookups cost $28 for up to four people, and generators are permitted 8 A.M.–8 P.M. Bathhouses have coin-op showers, flush toilets, washers, and dryers. Dining is available a few miles away at Lake Yellowstone Hotel and Lake Lodge. The RV Park is open mid-May–September and fills early most days. Contact **Xanterra Parks and Resorts** (307/344-7311 or 866/439-7375, www.yellowstonenationalparklodges.com) for reservations—highly recommended.

GRANT VILLAGE
Grant Village Campground

Near the south end of Yellowstone Lake and 19 miles southeast of Old Faithful, this campground fills early and offers more than 400 woodsy sites. It has coin-op showers nearby, flush toilets, washers and dryers, and a dump station. Generators are permitted 8 A.M.–8 P.M. Nearby are restaurants, a park visitor center, and a general store. The campground is open late June–September and costs $20. (Grant Village Campground opens later than others due to bear activity early in the summer.) Contact **Xanterra Parks and Resorts** (307/344-7311 or 866/439-7375, www.yellowstonenationalparklodges.com) for reservations—highly recommended. Group sites are available.

Lewis Lake Campground

On the southeast end of Lewis Lake, this 85-site campground is the southernmost in the park. It fills early and is open mid-June–early November. It has vault toilets, and a boat ramp is nearby. Campsites are $12. Food and other services are available at Grant Village to the north or Flagg Ranch to the south. No reservations.

CAMPING OPTIONS

When everything else is packed, folks head to campgrounds on surrounding Forest Service and Grand Teton National Park lands or to private campgrounds and motels in the gateway towns. The farther you get from Yellowstone, the more likely you are to find space. If you reach Nebraska, you should have no trouble at all. Campers can take showers ($4) at Old Faithful Lodge, Mammoth Hotel, Grant Village, Fishing Bridge RV Park, and Canyon Village Campground.

Food

Yellowstone's dining options are surprisingly varied. The cafeterias and fast-food joints cater to families and others looking for something predictable, but you can also try something more distinctive such as the Old West cookouts at Roosevelt Lodge. Both Old Faithful Inn and Lake Yellowstone Hotel have memorable dining rooms where the setting is half the experience. All restaurants, cafeterias, and lounges in Yellowstone are entirely nonsmoking.

RESTAURANTS

You'll find restaurants at Mammoth Hot Springs, Lake Yellowstone Hotel, Old Faithful Inn, Old Faithful Snow Lodge, Grant Village, Roosevelt Lodge, and Canyon Lodge. All of these are open for three meals a day throughout the summer, typically mid-May–September. Make dining reservations for any of the park restaurants at 307/344-7311 or 866/439-7375. Complete information, including menus, is available online (www.yellowstonenational-parklodges.com).

The enormous **((Old Faithful Inn Dining Room** (daily in summer 6:30–10 A.M., 11:30 A.M.–2:30 P.M., and 5–10 P.M.) is a wonderful option, with all-you-can-eat buffets for breakfast ($12 adults, $6 kids), lunch ($14 adults, $7 kids), and dinner ($24 adults, $11 kids); the dinner menu features bison burgers, beef tenderloin, chicken Oscar, and vegetarian chimichangas ($13–22 entrées). The Cozy Bear Pit Lounge serves single-malt scotches, tequilas, and cognacs.

Yellowstone's fine-dining choice is the **((Lake Yellowstone Hotel Dining Room** (307/242-3899, daily mid-May–early Oct. 6:30–10 A.M., 11:30 A.M.–2:30 P.M., and

5–10 P.M.), with breakfast buffets ($14 adults, $6 kids) and upscale lunches and dinners that emphasize seasonal and organic foods such as blackened wild Alaska salmon, bison osso buco, sautéed duck breast, and lamb. Most dinner entrées cost $20–30; reservations are required. Box lunches ($9) are available if you're heading out for a day of exploring.

Meals in other restaurants throughout the park are also fairly priced ($15–29), but the quality can vary from so-so to quite good. Typical menus include steaks, burgers, seafood, pasta, chicken, salads, and limited vegetarian dishes. Park restaurants are open for three meals daily throughout the summer. Hours vary a bit from place to place, but are typically 6:30–10 A.M. for breakfast, 11:30 A.M.–2:30 P.M. for lunch, and 5–10 P.M. for dinner. In winter (mid-Dec.–early Mar.), only the Mammoth and the Snow Lodge restaurants are open; their hours are 6:30–10 A.M. for breakfast, 11:30 A.M.–2:30 P.M. for lunch, and 5:30–8 P.M. for dinner.

The filling breakfasts (buffet also available) and decadent sundaes at **Mammoth Hot Springs Dining Room** (daily 6:30 A.M.–10 P.M. in summer, till 9 P.M. in winter, $11–22 dinner) are noteworthy, while **Roosevelt Lodge Dining Room** (daily 7 A.M.–9 P.M., $15–23) emphasizes down-home cowboy fare such as barbecue ribs, beef brisket, rib-eye steaks, and crispy fried chicken. Reservations are not accepted. The dinner menu at **Grant Village Dining Room** (daily 6:30 A.M.–10 P.M., $10–24) includes bison meatloaf, prime rib, and a surprisingly good mac' and cheese with four artisan cheeses. It also has a substantial breakfast buffet ($12 adults, $6 kids) and lunch-time pizzas, burgers, and sandwiches ($8–11). The

Old Faithful Inn Dining Room

building's high windows face Lake Yellowstone, although trees obscure the view. Reservations are advised for dinner, unless you want to wait quite awhile. **Grant Village Lakehouse Restaurant** (daily 6:30 A.M.–10:30 P.M., $15–23) has breakfast buffets and a casual dinner menu, but is closed for lunch.

Old Faithful Snow Lodge's **Obsidian Dining Room** has a fun Western flair. In addition to an extensive breakfast menu, the restaurant serves specialty burgers, steaks, and seafood. Unfortunately, the quality isn't stellar. Obsidian is open for breakfast daily 6:30–10:30 A.M., with dinner 5–10:30 P.M.; there is no lunch in the summer. In winter, it is open daily for breakfast, lunch, and dinner 6:30 A.M.–9:30 P.M. ($16–28).

Dinner reservations are *required* for Old Faithful Inn Dining Room (307/545-4999), Lake Yellowstone Hotel Dining Room (307/242-3899), and Grant Village Dining Room (307/242-3499), and they should be made before your arrival. For a dinner table at Old Faithful Inn, reserve a week ahead if you want a choice of seating times.

CAFETERIAS AND FAST FOOD

Yellowstone has always catered to families, and several park cafeterias provide reasonably priced meals. Hours vary a bit, but are typically 6:30–10 A.M. for breakfast, 11:30 A.M.–2:30 P.M. for lunch, and 5–10 P.M. for dinner. Your kids' noise will almost certainly be drowned out by racket from the rest of the hoi polloi (I'm speaking from experience here). You shouldn't, however, come here expecting a memorable meal; sometimes the food is downright awful. **Lake Lodge Cafeteria** is an especially notable structure, with big windows facing Lake Yellowstone. Similarly impressive is **Old Faithful Lodge Cafeteria,** housed in a grand stone-and-timber building. Head to the side porch for delightful Old Faithful Geyser views from the big rocking chairs. Less distinguished is **Canyon Lodge Cafeteria,** with a 1960s design that hasn't aged well. Call in the bulldozers! In Mammoth, **Terrace Grill** is an old family favorite for burgers, veggie burgers, sandwiches, espresso, and ice cream. You'll find snack shops or delis selling similar fare at

Old Faithful, Lake, and Canyon. All these eateries can also put together picnic lunches.

A number of Yellowstone cafeterias open surprisingly late in the season, so not all places may be open if you arrive before June. Check your copy of *Yellowstone Today* for details on seasonal openings and closings. The last dining places to open are Canyon Lodge Cafeteria (early June) and Lake Lodge Cafeteria (second week of June).

Many of the park's **Yellowstone General Stores** have food services of the burger, fries, and milkshake variety, and can create box lunches for a to-go meal.

COOKOUTS

The **C Old West Wagon Cookouts** at Roosevelt Lodge are a longtime family favorite and so popular that you'll need to make reservations at least six months ahead. Cookouts take place nightly mid-June–early September, and you either hop on board the horse-drawn wagons or astride a horse for a saunter into history. They take place in Pleasant Valley, three miles from the lodge, and include cowboy music, a campfire, and a big buffet with charbroiled steak and all the trimmings: baked beans, coleslaw, potato salad, corn, corn muffins, watermelon, fruit crisp, and beverages. Top it off with a cup of cowboy coffee. The staff can make vegetarian substitutions with advance notice, and covered seating is available in case of rain.

Wagon rides with dinner last 3–4 hours round-trip and cost $55 adults, $45 ages 3–11, or free for tots. Horseback riders can choose either a one-hour trail ride and meal for $66 adults, $56 ages 8–11, or a two-hour trail ride for $80 adults or $70 kids. Make reservations at 307/344-7311 or 866/439-7375, www.yellowstonenationalparklodges.com. If you're in the area and don't have a reservation, ask to get on the waiting list. You might get lucky and find a last-minute cancellation.

LOUNGES

Just because you're in a national park doesn't mean you can't tip back a gin and tonic.

Bear Pit Lounge inside Old Faithful Inn is a fine place for a drink in the evening. Beverage service is also available on the upstairs mezzanine and the outside deck facing Old Faithful. Another good place for a drink is **Firehole Lounge** at nearby Old Faithful Snow Lodge.

Lake Yellowstone Hotel's aptly named **Sun Room** fills a large wing of the lobby and is surrounded on three sides by picture windows. It exudes a casual elegance, making this a wonderful spot to while away the hours reading a book, writing postcards, or just listening to chamber or piano music with a drink in your hand.

Smaller bars are off the dining rooms at Mammoth Hot Springs, Roosevelt Lodge, Lake Lodge, Grant Village, and Canyon Lodge. The little corner bar at Mammoth has the only public TV inside Yellowstone; none of the in-park hotel rooms have televisions. Smoking is prohibited in all Yellowstone lounges (and in all buildings).

GROCERIES AND SUPPLIES

The park's 12 **Yellowstone General Stores** are at Mammoth, Canyon Village, Old Faithful, Fishing Bridge, Grant Village, Lake, Tower Fall, Bridge Bay, and Roosevelt. Each outlet has its own personality, and several of these—most notably the Lower Basin store at Old Faithful and the ones at Lake and Fishing Bridge—are grand old log structures. The Mammoth general store is another historic structure, here for nearly a century.

In addition to groceries, beer, and liquor, these stores sell a variety of merchandise, clothing, souvenirs, film and photo supplies, T-shirts, and accessories. The larger ones also have popular soda fountains with burgers, shakes, and other fast food. General stores at Canyon and Old Faithful deliver the best selection, and the Mammoth store is open year-round. The others are generally open mid-May–September and keep normal business hours. Yellowstone General Stores are managed by Delaware North Park Service (www.yellowstonegeneralstores.com).

Information and Services

RANGER PROGRAMS

Park naturalists lead slide shows, films, guided walks, kids' programs, campfire talks, and other activities at the campgrounds and visitor centers. These are always favorites of visitors, and on summer days you can choose from a multitude of Yellowstone activities, all of which are half-day. **Ranger Adventure Hikes** are offered most summer days. These hikes fill up very quickly, so sign up early at any park visitor center. Get a complete listing of ranger programs in the *Yellowstone Today* paper you receive upon entering the park or online at www.nps.gov/yell. Evening slide programs are also offered in winter at Mammoth and Old Faithful. For a more in-depth look at the park, take a class through the **Yellowstone Association Institute** (406/848-2400, www. yellowstoneassociation.org) or join one of its popular Lodging and Learning packages.

SUPPORTING THE PARK

The **Yellowstone Association** (406/848-2400, www.yellowstoneassociation.org) is a nonprofit organization that assists with education, research, publishing, and book sales inside the park. The organization also teaches dozens of classes through the acclaimed Yellowstone Association Institute.

The **Yellowstone Park Foundation** (406/586-6303, www.ypf.org) is another nonprofit group that works with the National Park Service by providing funds for projects and programs that would not be otherwise supported. Its biggest project was helping to raise $15 million for the new visitor center at Old Faithful. All funding comes from individuals and corporations, not from the government.

The primary environmental group involved with protecting Yellowstone and the surrounding public lands is the **Greater Yellowstone Coalition** (406/586-1593, www.greateryellowstone.org), based in Bozeman, Montana. This private nonprofit organization is involved in all sorts of environmental issues within the 10-million-acre Greater Yellowstone Ecosystem, including such hot-button issues as logging, gas development, winter use, and bison management. It represents more than 17,000 members and produces a monthly email newsletter detailing various issues. Annual membership costs $35.

SERVICES

For a complete directory of the many Yellowstone visitor services, see *Yellowstone Today*, which you receive upon entering the park. You can also download a copy at www.nps.gov/yell.

A year-round **post office** is in a 1930s-era stone building at Mammoth Hot Springs, with seasonal post offices at Old Faithful, Lake Village, Canyon Village, and Grant Village. **Worship services** are held at various Yellowstone locations all summer; details are available at any park visitor center.

Banking

You'll discover **ATMs** at most of the settled areas, including Old Faithful Inn, Old Faithful Snow Lodge, Fishing Bridge, Lake Yellowstone Hotel, Mammoth Hot Springs Hotel, Mammoth General Store, Canyon General Store, Canyon Lodge, and Grant Village. Park lodges and hotels are able to provide a limited **currency exchange** for international travelers Monday–Friday 8 A.M.–5 P.M.

Bookstores

The nonprofit **Yellowstone Association** (406/848-2400, www.yellowstoneassociation.org) operates bookstores within most park visitor centers, including those at Canyon Village, West Thumb, Mammoth, Norris, Old Faithful, and Madison. Concessioner stores also carry a limited selection of regional titles, and the surrounding towns have shops selling books.

Internet and Cell Phone

Cell phone users will find spotty service in

YELLOWSTONE ASSOCIATION

Founded in 1933, the nonprofit Yellowstone Association (406/848-2400, www.yellowstoneassociation.org) assists in educational, historical, and scientific programs. The organization publishes several natural-history publications and provides funds to produce trail leaflets and park newspapers, along with the excellent *Yellowstone Discovery* quarterly magazine. In addition, the association manages book sales at visitor centers, funds park exhibits and research, and otherwise assists the park in educating the public. The organization is best known for the **Yellowstone Association Institute,** operating just north of the park from a historic Gardiner, Montana building.

Instructors at the institute lead more than 100 different natural-history and humanities classes in the summer, along with several others in winter. Most of these last 2-5 days and typically cost about $100 per day – a real bargain. Courses cover the spectrum from wolf ecology to fly-fishing and provide a great way to learn about this wonderful wild place. Class size is small; most classes contain 10-15 students. Participants typically stay at the Buffalo Ranch in comfortable log cabins ($30 per person per night) and cook meals in the shared kitchen.

In addition to these classes, the Yellowstone Association Institute also offers **Lodging and Learning** programs, 2-5-day packages that blend education, recreation, and lodging. Naturalist guides from the association lead small-group excursions (12 people maximum), and participants are provided with accommodations in park hotels, plus breakfasts and box lunches. Its **Yellowstone for Families** program ($1,560 for two adults plus $455 per child) is especially popular, with a mix of activities for both kids and parents over four days: animal tracking, wildlife-watching, photography, painting, hiking, and more.

If you really want the personalized touch (and can afford it), the institute offers private tours in which a wildlife biologist travels with you in your vehicle for 6-8 hours, providing an introduction to park wildlife and ecology. The charge is $495 for up to five people.

A tax-deductible membership in the Yellowstone Association starts at $35 per year. Members receive discounts on classes taught by the Yellowstone Association Institute and can sign up early. They also receive quarterly newsletters and discounts for items sold by the association.

© DON PITCHER

Yellowstone Association Institute

many parts of Yellowstone—and it's nonexistent in much of the backcountry. There's no AT&T coverage at all, but Verizon users should get good reception near Old Faithful, Lake, Canyon, Grant Village, and Mammoth areas.

Internet access has improved substantially in the last few years. Wi-Fi service (free for hotel guests) should be available in Snow Lodge, Grant Village, Canyon Lodge, Lake Lodge Cafeteria, and a handful of other locations. To preserve the historic lodging experience, Wi-Fi is not available at Old Faithful Inn or Lake Hotel.

Laundry and Showers

In summer, find coin-operated washers and dryers at Fishing Bridge RV Park, Canyon Village Campground, and Grant Village Campground. Public showers ($4) are at Fishing Bridge RV Park, Old Faithful Lodge, Mammoth Hotel, Grant Village, Roosevelt Lodge, and Canyon Village Campground.

Medical

For medical emergencies 24 hours a day, the park manages **Lake Hospital** (307/242-7241), a 10-bed acute-care facility. It's open mid-May–mid-September; also here are a clinic and pharmacy. Outpatient services are available both here and at the **Old Faithful Clinic** (307/545-7325), open mid-May–early October. Open weekdays year-round and daily in the summer, the **Mammoth Hot Springs Clinic** (307/344-7965) has a physician available. Call 911 for emergencies anywhere in the park.

Publications

If you're planning a trip to Yellowstone, call the park at 307/344-7381 to request a copy of the *Yellowstone National Park Trip Planner.* It provides detailed up-to-date information on hiking and camping, fishing, services, road construction, safety issues, park highlights, and lots more. The same information (and much more) is available online at www.nps.gov/yell/planyourvisit/publications.htm. Also be sure to request the latest version of the park paper, *Yellowstone Today;* it's issued quarterly.

Several print and online sources provide unofficial information on Yellowstone. One of the better private sources is *Yellowstone Journal* (307/332-2323 or 800/656-8762, www.yellowstonepark.com). The publication comes out several times a year and is sold in stores inside and around the park. A good freebie publication called simply *Yellowstone Park* is published annually and is available online at www.billingsgazette.com. Find it in regional visitor centers outside the park. Also check out the Web-only *Yellowstone Traveler* (www.yellowstoneparktraveler.com).

Shopping

Nearly every road junction in Yellowstone has some sort of general store, gas station, or gift shop. **Yellowstone General Stores** (www.yellowstonegeneralstores.com) are especially interesting because they tend to be in rustic old log structures and staffed by friendly retired folks and fresh college kids. Although they were recently modernized, these stores still retain the historic charm from past eras. You'll find all of the standard tourist supplies and gifts, plus groceries, snack bars, booze, camping equipment, books, fishing supplies, and locally made arts and crafts. The largest general stores are at Old Faithful and Canyon.

The **Old Faithful Inn Gift Shop** is well worth a visit, with a good selection of items from apparel to artwork. It often has book signings and guest presentations during summer. **Old Faithful Lodge Gift Shop** features artists in residence creating paintings or pottery (for sale, of course). Additional gift shops can be found in the other hotel complexes at Old Faithful Snow Lodge, Lake Yellowstone Hotel, Lake Lodge, Mammoth Hot Springs, Roosevelt Lodge, Canyon Lodge, and Grant Village. Park gift shops are managed by Xanterra Parks and Resorts, which has further info on their website (www.yellowstonenationalparklodges.com). The Mammoth store is notable for its efforts at environmental sustainability; products include details on the carbon footprint of various purchases.

GRAND TETON NATIONAL PARK

Grand Teton National Park remains one of the preeminent symbols of American wilderness. The Tetons rise abruptly from the valley floor, their bare triangular ridges looking like broken shards of glass from some cosmic accident of creation. With six different summits topping 12,000 feet, plus some of the finest climbing and hiking in Wyoming, the Tetons are a paradise for lovers of the outdoors. They have long been a favorite of photographers and sightseers, and once even appeared in an ad promoting Colorado tourism! The Tetons change character with the seasons. In summer, the sagebrush flats are a garden of flowers set against the mountain backdrop. When autumn arrives, the cottonwoods and aspens become swaths of yellow and orange. Winter turns everything a glorious, sparkling white, set against the fluorescent blue sky.

Grand Teton National Park isn't only about mountains, of course. Boat rides on Jackson Lake and raft trips down the Snake River, along with photo-perfect Jenny Lake, the barns of Mormon Row, and the winding road up Signal Mountain, are all accessible to anyone with a vehicle. Two brand-new visitor centers—Craig Thomas Discovery and Visitor Center and the Laurance S. Rockefeller Preserve Center—provide exceptional introductions to the park. Bring your bike or hiking shoes to explore a multitude of trails and country roads, and keep your eyes open for bison and other wild creatures along the way.

© DON PITCHER

GRAND TETON

HIGHLIGHTS

◖ **Craig Thomas Discovery and Visitor Center:** This informative center has tall windows facing the Tetons and state-of-the-art exhibits on the natural world (page 118).

◖ **Chapel of the Transfiguration:** Built in 1925, this quaint log church has a back window that frames the Tetons. No one makes better wedding chapels than this (page 119)!

◖ **Jenny Lake:** You won't be the first – or last – person to discover this idyllic lake in the heart of Grand Teton National Park (page 122).

◖ **Signal Mountain:** Too narrow for RVs, but the road up Signal Mountain provides panoramic vistas of the Tetons; it's best at sunrise or sunset (page 123).

◖ **Teton Viewpoints:** Ansel Adams wannabes take note: This is where that famous photo of the Tetons was taken (page 128).

◖ **Mormon Row:** These historic farm buildings provide a picture-perfect setting and a good spot to view bison (page 129).

◖ **Inspiration Point and Hidden Falls:** Getting there is half the fun, with a shuttle boat trip across Jenny Lake followed by a half-mile hike to this scenic point. Expect a queue in midsummer, or just hike around the lake to avoid the crowds (page 132).

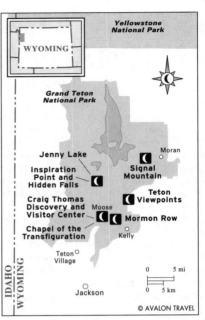

LOOK FOR ◖ TO FIND RECOMMENDED SIGHTS, ACTIVITIES, DINING, AND LODGING.

PLANNING YOUR TIME

Travelers to Grand Teton National Park typically see it at the same time they're visiting Yellowstone National Park and the town of Jackson. Backcountry hikers are attracted to the scenic canyons and alpine areas within the park, and the 13,772-foot Grand Teton is a goal of mountain climbers. Photographers can't resist the mountain-and-river **Teton Viewpoints** that captivated millions of earlier visitors, including Ansel Adams. A couple of days are sufficient to see park sights.

Jenny Lake is one of the most scenic areas in the park. Here a boat transports hikers to **Inspiration Point,** a base for longer

explorations into the Tetons. Historic Jenny Lake Lodge has upscale accommodations and gourmet meals; it's one of several good choices in the park.

Enjoy the view from the summit of **Signal Mountain,** and scan for moose in the sloughs at Oxbow Bend. Bison roam the flats near **Mormon Row,** which has some of the most photographed barns in America with a Teton Range backdrop to die for. Jackson Lake is popular for fishing and boating, and rafting the Snake River attracts thousands of people each summer.

The little settlement of **Moose,** on the south end of Grand Teton National Park, is home to park headquarters and the striking **Craig Thomas Discovery and Visitor Center.** Nearby is the **Chapel of the Transfiguration,** a rustic log church with a dramatic backdrop. The narrow and winding Moose-Wilson Road heads south to Teton Village, providing access to hiking trails and to the exhibits at the **Laurance S. Rockefeller Preserve Center.**

Before your visit, contact Grand Teton National Park (307/739-3600, www.nps.gov/grte) for publications and maps, or use the website to learn more about the area.

GEOLOGY
Building a Mountain Range

The precipitous Teton Range has perhaps the most complex geologic history in North America. Although the Tetons are ancient by any human scale, they are the youngest mountains in the Rockies, less than 10 million years old (versus 60 million years for the nearby Wind River Mountains). The Tetons are a fault-block range, formed when the earth's crust cracked along an angled fault. Forces within the earth have pushed the western side (the Tetons) up, while the eastern part (Jackson Hole) dropped down like a trapdoor. Geologists believe the fault could slip up to 10 feet at a time, producing a violent earthquake. All this shifting has created one of the most dramatic and asymmetric mountain faces on earth.

Unlike in typical mountain ranges, the highest parts are not at the center of the range but along the eastern edge, where uplifting continues. The western slope, which drops gently into Idaho, is much less dramatic, although the views are still impressive. This tilting-and-subsidence process is still going on today, pushed by the movement of a plume of magma beneath Yellowstone as the continental plate slides over the top. Because of this subsidence, the town of Wilson in Jackson Hole now lies 10 feet below the level of the nearby Snake River; only riverside dikes protect the town from flooding.

As the mountains rose along this fault, millennia of overlying deposits were stripped away by erosion, leaving three-million-year-old Precambrian rock jutting into the air above the

© DON PITCHER

the Teton mountain range

GRAND TETON

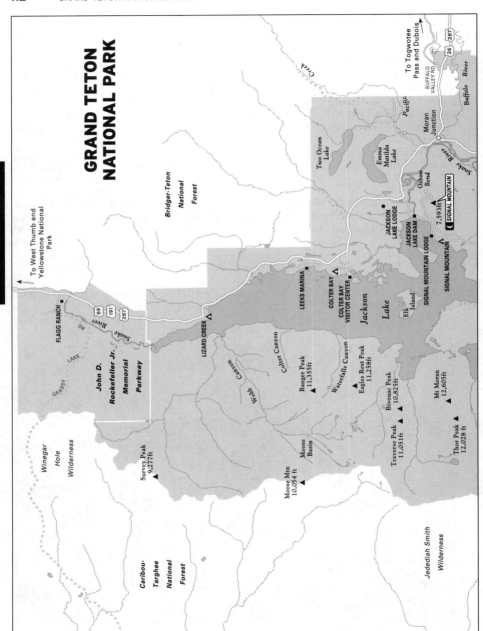

GRAND TETON NATIONAL PARK

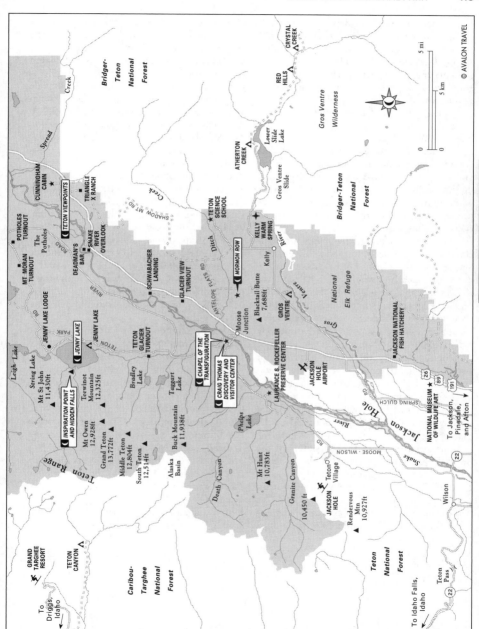

© AVALON TRAVEL

5 mi

5 km

more recent sedimentary deposits in the valley. Because of this shifting and erosion, sandstone deposits atop Mt. Moran match those 24,000 feet below Jackson Hole. Although the most recent major earthquake on the Teton Fault was at least 2,000 years ago, geologists are convinced that Jackson Hole could experience a major temblor at any time.

Rivers of Ice

In counterpoint to the uplifting actions that created the general outline of the Tetons, erosional forces have been wearing them down again. Glaciers, which are created when more snow falls than melts off, have proven to be one of the most important of these erosional processes. After a period of several years and under the weight of additional snow, the accumulated snow crystals change into ice. Gravity pulls this ice slowly downhill, creating essentially a frozen river that grinds against whatever lies in the way, plucking loose rocks and soil and polishing hard bedrock. This debris moves slowly down the glacier as if on a conveyer belt, eventually reaching the glacier's terminus.

When a glacier remains the same size for a long period, large piles of glacial debris accumulate at its end, creating what glaciologists call a terminal moraine. One of these created Jackson Lake, when a huge glacier dumped tons of rock at its snout. After the glacier melted back, this terminal moraine became a natural dam for the waters of the Snake River. Similar mounds of glacial debris dammed the creeks that formed Jenny, Leigh, Bradley, Taggart, and Phelps Lakes within Grand Teton National Park.

The earth has experienced cyclical periods of glaciation for hundreds of thousands of years, probably because of changes in the earth's orbit around the sun. During the colder parts of these cycles, glaciers appear and advance. The entire Yellowstone region has undergone a series of massive glaciations, the last of which is called the Pinedale Glaciation. It began about 70,000 years ago and had essentially disappeared by 15,000 years ago. At its peak, the Pinedale Glaciation covered all of Yellowstone and reached well into Jackson Hole.

Streams flowed from the ends of these glaciers, carrying along gravel, sand, silt, and clay. The cobbles and sands from these streams were dropped on the flat valley below, while the finer silts and clays continued downstream, leaving behind soils too rocky and nutrient-poor to support trees. Only sagebrush grows on this plain today, while the surrounding hills and mountain slopes (which were spared this rocky deposition) are covered with lodgepole and subalpine fir forests. Trees can also be found covering the silty terminal moraines that ring the lakes.

Other reminders of the glacial past are the "potholes" (more accurately termed "kettles") that dot the plain south of Signal Mountain. These depressions were created when large blocks of ice were buried under glacial outwash. When the ice melted, it left a kettle-shaped pond surrounded by glacial debris. Only a dozen or so small glaciers remain in the Tetons; the largest is the 3,500-foot-long Teton Glacier, visible on the northeastern face of Grand Teton. For a far more detailed picture of Teton geology, read *Interpreting the Landscape: Recent and Ongoing Geology of Grand Teton and Yellowstone National Parks,* by John Good and Kenneth Pierce (Grand Teton Association, www.grandtetonpark.org).

Exploring Grand Teton

Grand Teton National Park has fewer "attractions" than Yellowstone—its big sister to the north—and an easy day's drive takes you past the road-accessible parts of the park. The real attractions are the mountains and the incomparable views one gets of them from Jackson Hole. This is one backdrop you will never tire of seeing.

PARK ACCESS

Grand Teton National Park (307/739-3600, www.nps.gov/grte) has two entrance stations. One is just north of the Craig Thomas Discovery and Visitor Center on Teton Park Road, and the second is on U.S. Highway 89/191/287 at Moran Junction. Entrance to the park is $25 per vehicle or $12 for individuals entering by bicycle, foot, or as a bus passenger. Motorcycles and snowmobiles are $20. The pass covers entrance to both Yellowstone and Grand Teton national parks and is good for seven days. If you're planning to be here longer or to make additional visits, get an annual pass covering both parks for $50, or the **Interagency Annual Pass**—good for all national parks—for $80 per year. An **Interagency Senior Pass** for all national parks is available to anyone older than 62 for a one-time fee of $10, and people with disabilities can get a free **Interagency Access Pass.** The latter two passes also provide 50 percent reductions in most camping fees.

At the entrance stations, park visitors receive a copy of *Teewinot,* the park newspaper. It lists park facilities and services, along with interpretive programs, nature walks, and other activities. Family favorites for generations are the evening campfire programs held at campground amphitheaters throughout the summer. The park also produces a helpful accessibility handout with details on wheelchair-accessible visitor centers, trails, sights, picnic areas, activities, campsites, and accommodations.

GRAND TETON

© DON PITCHER

Craig Thomas Discovery and Visitor Center

VISITOR CENTERS

Grand Teton National Park headquarters is in the settlement of Moose near the southern end of the park. The striking **Craig Thomas Discovery and Visitor Center** (307/739-3399, daily year-round) in Moose provides an outstanding introduction to the park. Also noteworthy is the **Laurance S. Rockefeller Preserve Center** (307/739-3654, daily late May–Sept.), halfway between Moose and Teton Village on the Moose-Wilson Road.

Jenny Lake Visitor Center (307/739-3392) is open daily mid-May–September and closed the rest of the year.

On the east side of Jackson Lake, **Colter Bay Visitor Center** (307/739-3594) is open daily early May–mid-October.

Just north of Grand Teton, inside John D. Rockefeller Jr. Memorial Parkway, is **Flagg Ranch Information Station** (307/543-2372), open daily early June–early September.

TOURS

Grand Teton lacks any form of public transit, and most visitors arrive by car or onboard tour buses. Taxi services are available from Jackson, and bike rentals are available in Jackson and Moose.

During the summer, **Grand Teton Lodge Company** (307/543-3100 or 800/628-9988, www.gtlc.com) has three-hour bus tours of Grand Teton National Park ($38 adults, $18 kids under 12) on Monday, Wednesday, and Friday. Tours depart Jackson Lake Lodge (307/543-3100 or 800/628-9988, www.gtlc.com, late May–early Oct.) at 8:30 A.M. Summertime bus tours of Grand Teton and Yellowstone National Parks are available several times a week from **Gray Line of Jackson Hole/Alltrans** (307/733-3135 or 800/443-6133, www.graylinejh.com). Grand Teton tours last eight hours ($100 adults, kids $50, plus $12 entrance fee).

In winter, Gray Line has daily bus runs to Flagg Ranch Resort ($106 round-trip) that arrive in time to meet snowcoach departures for Yellowstone. Reservations are required. Taxi companies in Jackson can also provide shuttles to Flagg Ranch in the winter, including **Buckboard Transportation** (307/733-1112 or 877/791-0211, www.buckboardtrans.com, $100 for up to four people one-way).

Operated by Teton Science School, **Wildlife Expeditions** (307/733-2623 or 888/945-3567, www.wildlifeexpeditions.org) leads an array of wildlife-viewing safaris throughout the region, from four-hour sunset trips for $125 to four-day tours through Yellowstone and Grand Teton for $1,995. Their trips change seasonally—depending upon which animals are visible—and are offered in customized vehicles with multiple roof hatches for better wildlife-viewing.

Also highly recommended are naturalist Carl Swoboda's **Safari Yellowstone** (800/723-2747, www.safariyellowstone.com) and Dr. Keith Watt's **Earth Tours** (307/733-4261, www.earth-tours.com).

Other companies offering guided van tours of the park include **Ana's Grand Excursions** (307/690-6106, www.anasgrandexcursions.com), **Brushbuck Guide Services** (888/282-5868, www.brushbuckphototours.com), **Callowishus Park Touring Company** (307/415-5483, www.callowishus.com), **EcoTour Adventures** (307/690-9533, www.jhecotouradventures.com), **Upstream Anglers and Outdoor Adventures** (307/739-9443 or 800/642-8979, www.upstreamanglers.com), **Grand Teton Adventure Company** (307/734-4454 or 800/700-1558, www.grandtetonadventures.com), **The Hole Hiking Experience** (307/690-4453 or 866/733-4453, www.holehike.com), and **VIP Adventure Travel** (307/699-1077, www.vipadventuretravel.com).

ROADS

Grand Teton National Park is bisected by the main north-south highway (U.S. Hwy. 26/89/191) and by the highway heading east over Togwotee Pass (U.S. Hwy. 26/287), providing easy access to many of the most dramatic vistas and finest places to see wildlife. Both routes are kept open year-round through Grand Teton, although wintertime plowing ends at Flagg Ranch Resort, just south of the Yellowstone boundary. In addition, a paved

© DON PITCHER

heading west to the Tetons

during summer; look for them at dawn and dusk. (Grand Teton is the only national park outside of Alaska that allows hunting. The rules are pretty strange, however, requiring elk hunters to become temporarily deputized park rangers before they head out!) **Grizzlies** are becoming more common in Grand Teton, especially in northern portions of the park and around Signal Mountain. The Willow Flats area is closed in spring due to heavy grizzly use of the area (they prey on elk calves). **Black bears** are present in wooded canyons and riverbeds throughout the park. Other animals to look for are bald eagles and ospreys along the Snake River and trumpeter swans and Canada geese in ponds and lakes. Watch for **mule deer** in meadows and at forest edges, such as those near Colter Bay. **Beavers** can be seen at Schwabacher's Landing along the Snake River.

GRAND TETON

park road cuts south from Jackson Lake Dam to Jenny Lake and Moose. Only the southern end of this road is plowed in winter; the remainder becomes a cross-country ski or snowshoe route. South of Moose, a narrow, winding road (the Moose-Wilson Road) connects the park with Teton Village, nine miles away. It is rough dirt in places—no trailers or RVs—and is closed in winter. Get the latest on park road conditions by calling 307/739-3614.

WILDLIFE-VIEWING

Grand Teton National Park is an excellent place to look for wildlife, especially in the early morning or at dusk. **Moose** are often seen at Willow Flats along Jackson Lake just north of the dam, at Oxbow Bend, south of the settlement of Moose, and along the Snake River. Herds of **pronghorn antelope** are common on the sagebrush flats near Kelly. **Elk** are frequent sights in fall as they migrate down from the high country to the elk refuge near Jackson, but smaller numbers are in the park

Bison

Herds of bison (buffalo) are commonly seen in the Moran Junction area, in the Mormon Row area (Antelope Flats Road), and along Teton Park Road. Bison were present historically (hence the name Buffalo River) but had been extinct for perhaps a century when eight bison were released into Grand Teton National Park in 1969. The population grew slowly for the first decade until they discovered the free alfalfa handout at the elk refuge north of Jackson. Partly because of this winter feeding, the population has grown to almost 600 animals—much to the chagrin of the elk-refuge managers. A few bison are hunted outside the park to control their numbers.

Wolves

Wolves were reintroduced to Yellowstone National Park starting in 1995 and have continued to expand into surrounding areas, including Grand Teton National Park. They're most easily seen in winter, particularly on the adjacent National Elk Refuge where they prey on elk, but they may sometimes be seen during summer inside the park.

Sights

The following tour takes you past points of interest along the main roads. The route follows a general clockwise direction beginning in Moose and continuing to Jenny Lake, Signal Mountain, Jackson Lake, Colter Bay, and the eastern half of the park past Mormon Row and Blacktail Butte.

MOOSE
◖ Craig Thomas Discovery and Visitor Center

Begin your visit inside the dramatic new Craig Thomas Discovery and Visitor Center (307/739-3300, www.nps.gov/grte), where 30-foot-high windows pull your eyes outward for a spectacular Teton Range panorama. Inside, you'll find state-of-the-art exhibits showcasing the natural world; "video rivers" beneath your feet; a large three-dimensional map revealing the lay of the land, geology, and mountaineering displays; interactive child-friendly activities, and a Grand Teton Association bookstore. The spacious auditorium presents an excellent film, *Grand Teton National Park: Life on the Edge*, shown every half-hour. (I won't give away the surprise, but you're bound to be pleased when the curtain rises at the movie's end.) The visitor center is open daily 8 A.M.–7 P.M. early June–late September, and daily 8 A.M.–5 P.M. (except

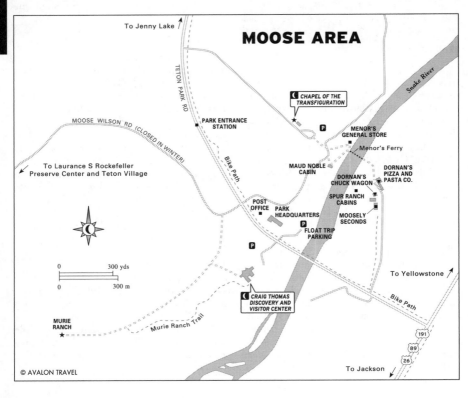

© AVALON TRAVEL

© DON PITCHER

GRAND TETON

The Chapel of the Transfiguration is a wonderful spot for a wedding.

Christmas) the rest of the year. There's free Wi-Fi, too.

The commercial center at Moose is across the Snake River bridge and just east of the visitor center. Here you'll find a plethora of operations run by **Dornan's** (307/733-2415, www.dornans.com): a general store, gift shop, lodging, fishing shop, restaurant and bar, wine shop, bike shop (with rentals), canoe and kayak rentals, and a chuck wagon eatery. Also here are the sporting-goods store **Moosely Seconds** (307/739-1801) and a fishing shop, **Snake River Angler** (307/733-3699, www.snakeriverangler.com). Moose has pretty much everything you might need for a day in the park.

Murie Ranch

Down a quiet dirt road just south of the visitor center is the home of Olaus and Mardy Murie, two giants of the environmental movement. Olaus was a pioneering biologist in Alaska's arctic regions, and founder of the Wilderness Society. In 1945, the Muries bought the old STS Dude Ranch in Moose, Wyoming, and made it their home. Together they worked to protect the Arctic National Wildlife Refuge, pushed for protection of wilderness areas, and

wrote the classic book *Wapiti Wilderness*. Olaus died in 1963, shortly before the Wilderness Act was passed, but Mardy—the first woman to graduate from the University of Alaska—lived until 2003 (age 101) at her little log cabin in Moose. She wrote several books, played an important role in passing the Alaska National Interest Lands Conservation Act, and received the Presidential Medal of Freedom for her conservation work in both Alaska and Wyoming.

Today, the historic ranch's 17 structures—built in 1927—are part of a National Historic District. Befitting the Muries' love of nature, they are managed as the **Murie Center** (307/739-2246, www.muriecenter.org), which puts on a variety of conservation seminars and events throughout the year. Also here are the Murie archive and library. Park rangers lead free summertime historical tours of the Murie ranch on Monday and Thursday at 2 P.M. Winter snowshoe tours are also offered.

Chapel of the Transfiguration

Just inside the South Entrance to Grand Teton National Park, a side road leads to the Chapel of the Transfiguration and Menor's Ferry. The rustic log church (built in 1925) is most notable for its dramatic setting. The back window faces directly toward the Tetons, providing ample distractions for worshippers (or wedding guests). The bell out front was cast in 1842. Episcopal services are held on summer Sundays, with Eucharist at 8 and 10 A.M.

Menor's Ferry

Menor's Ferry is named for William D. Menor, who first homesteaded here in 1894 and later built a cable ferry to make it easier to cross the river. His old whitewashed store still stands. You can cross the river in a reconstructed version of the old ferry when the water level is low enough; check out the ingenious propulsion mechanism that uses the current to pull it across. For many years, Menor's Ferry served as the primary means of crossing the river in the central part of Jackson Hole. Wagons were charged $0.50, while those on horseback paid $0.25. (William Menor's brother, Holiday, lived on the opposite side of the river, but the two often feuded, yelling insults across the water at each other and refusing to acknowledge one another for years at a time.)

Also here is the 0.5-mile **Menor's Ferry Trail;** a brochure describes historic points of interest along the path. Bill Menor's cabin houses a small **country store** that sells the old-fashioned supplies he stocked at the turn of the 20th century. It is open daily 9 A.M.– 4:30 P.M. late May–September; closed the rest of the year.

Menor sold out to Maude Noble in 1918, and she ran the ferry until 1927, when a bridge was built near the present one in Moose. The **Maude Noble cabin** now houses an excellent collection of historical photos from Jackson Hole. Maude gained a measure of fame in 1923 when she hosted the gathering of residents to save Jackson Hole from development.

Heading northwest beyond the Menor's Ferry area, the main road climbs up an old river bench, created by flooding from the rapid melting of the glaciers, and passes the trailhead to the turquoise waters of **Taggart Lake.** The land around here was burned in the 1,028-acre

Beaver Creek lightning fire of 1985, and summers find a riot of wildflowers.

The **River Road** (a.k.a. RKO Road) is a rugged 15-mile dirt-and-boulders route through open sagebrush country along the Snake River. (The road got its alter-ego name, RKO, when several RKO movies were filmed here in the 1940s and early 1950s.) It's a fine place to watch for bugling elk in the fall. Access the road off Teton Park Road from the south end near the Cottonwood Creek picnic area, and from the north end near Signal Mountain Road. The road is sometimes closed in early summer due to active wolf denning, and is virtually impassable for most rental cars; you'll need a high-clearance 4WD vehicle (or mountain bike) in the rocky draws. A highlight along the River Road is historic **Bar BC Ranch** (closed in 2010 for renovations), with its weathered log buildings and dramatic riverside setting. The ranch—the second dude ranch in the valley— was owned by Struthers Burt, who was instrumental in establishing the park.

MOOSE-WILSON ROAD

This narrow and winding road heads south from park headquarters in Moose, continuing nine miles to Teton Village. It is especially pretty in autumn when the aspens are turning. This is also a good place for wildlife-watching—look for moose and other animals in summer—or for easy cross-country ski adventures on a sunny winter day.

The road is paved most of the way, but a 1.5-mile section is dirt. Keep your speed down to reduce the amount of dust in the air and to keep the backseat passengers from getting ill from all the curves. Moose-Wilson Road is closed to vehicle traffic November 1–April 30, and is not plowed in the winter. No trailers or RVs are allowed.

Two backcountry trailheads—Death Canyon Trailhead and Granite Canyon Trailhead— are accessible from the Moose-Wilson Road.

Laurance S. Rockefeller Preserve

The Rockefeller family played a pivotal role in establishing Grand Teton National Park, but

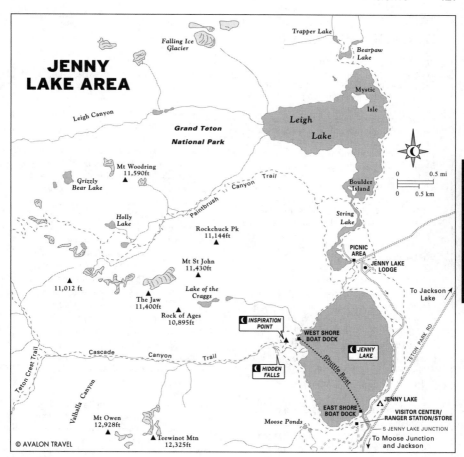

JENNY LAKE AREA

Falling Ice Glacier

Trapper Lake

Bearpaw Lake

Mystic Isle

Leigh Canyon

Grand Teton National Park

Leigh Lake

Boulder Island

Mt Woodring 11,590ft

Grizzly Bear Lake

Paintbrush Canyon Trail

0   0.5 mi
0   0.5 km

Holly Lake

String Lake

Rockchuck Pk 11,144ft

PICNIC AREA

JENNY LAKE LODGE

Mt St John 11,430ft

11,012 ft

Lake of the Craggs

The Jaw 11,400ft

Rock of Ages 10,895ft

To Jackson Lake

INSPIRATION POINT

WEST SHORE BOAT DOCK

JENNY LAKE

Cascade Canyon Trail

Teton Crest Trail

HIDDEN FALLS

Shuttle Boat

TETON PARK RD

Valhalla Canyon

Mt Owen 12,928ft

Teewinot Mtn 12,325ft

Moose Ponds

EAST SHORE BOAT DOCK

JENNY LAKE

VISITOR CENTER/ RANGER STATION/STORE

S JENNY LAKE JUNCTION

To Moose Junction and Jackson

© AVALON TRAVEL

for many decades they continued to own the JY Ranch, an inholding in the heart of the park. Laurance S. Rockefeller (1910–2004; grandson of John D. Rockefeller) donated the land to Grand Teton in 2001, and today this preserve is a wonderful place to relax and explore. The distinctive **Laurance S. Rockefeller Center** (307/739-3654, daily 8 A.M.–5 P.M. late May–Sept.) is down a side road off the Moose-Wilson Road halfway between Moose and Teton Village. Eight miles of trails lead from here through the preserve, across sagebrush meadows, through forests, and along the shores of Phelps Lake. Parking is quite limited, and the lot is often full 10 A.M.–3 P.M.

The visitor center itself is unlike any you've ever seen, with a minimalist feeling that reflects Laurance S. Rockefeller's Buddhist and emotional connections to nature. Instead of the usual array of things to see and gizmos to show you the inner workings of the planet, you'll find dramatic mountain views and large, high-ceiled rooms with a few memorable exhibits, including an amazing photo mosaic and a surround-sound space where you can sit and listen to a parade of nature noises—from

BEAVER DICK LEIGH

Around 1863, Richard "Beaver Dick" Leigh became the first white man to attempt a permanent life in Jackson Hole. An Englishman by birth, Beaver Dick lived in a log cabin with his Shoshone wife, Jenny, and their five children, scraping out the barest existence by hunting, trapping, and guiding. As guide for the 1872 Hayden Survey of the Jackson Hole area, Beaver Dick gained the respect of the surveyors, who named Leigh Lake for him and Jenny Lake for his wife. Reading his diaries and letters is a lesson in how difficult life was for early Wyoming settlers. On one terrible Christmas in 1876, Beaver Dick watched his entire family – Jenny, their newborn baby, and the four other children – all slowly die from smallpox. Their deaths left him badly shaken, as he related in a letter to a friend:

i got Dick in the house and to bed and Tom went over to get Mr. Anes. Wile Tom and Anes was sounding the ice to see if a horse could cross my wife was struck with Death. she rased up and looked me streaght in the face and then she got excited...and she sade she was going to die and all our childron wold die and maby i wold die...she was laying very quiet now for about 2 hours when she asked for a drink of water. i was laying downe with one of my daughters on eatch arme keeping them quiet because of the fever. i told Anes what she wanted and he gave hur a drink and 10 minuts more she was ded...i can not wright one hundreth part

that pased thrue my mind at this time as i thaught deth was on me. i sade Jinny i will sone be with you and fell asleep. Tom sade i ad beene a sleep a half hour when i woke up everything was wet with presperation i was very weak. i lade for 10 or 15 minuts and saw William and Anne Jane had to be taken up to ease themselves every 5 minuts and Dick Juner very restlas...Anne Jane died about 8 o clock about the time every year i used to give them a candy puling and thay menchond about the candy puling many times wile sick...William died on the 25 about 9 or 10 o clock in the evening...on the 26th Dick Juner died...Elizabeth was over all danger but this, and she caught cold and sweled up agane and died on the 28 of Dec about 2 o clock in the morning. this was the hardist blow of all...i shall improve the place and live and die near my famley but i shall not be able to do enything for a few months for my mind is disturbed at the sights that i see around me and [the] work that my famley as done wile thay were liveing.

But the human spirit is remarkably resilient. Beaver Dick later married a Bannock girl, raised another family, and guided for others, even meeting Theodore Roosevelt on one of his hunting trips. Beaver Dick Leigh died in 1899 and was buried on a ridge overlooking Idaho's Teton Basin.

frogs to thunderclaps. The resource room contains classic natural history books and a fireplace. The building itself was constructed with recycled materials (including old blue jeans for insulation), uses composting toilets, and is heated and cooled from deep geothermal wells. The visitor center evokes contrasting emotions from visitors. Some love its clean aesthetics and eco-friendly design; others find it sterile and bizarre. Love it or hate it, this is a must-see, and the extraordinary preserve itself is well worth exploring.

◖ JENNY LAKE

The most loved of all Grand Teton lakes is Jenny Lake, nestled at the foot of Cascade

Canyon and surrounded by a luxuriant forest of Engelmann spruce, subalpine fir, and lodgepole pine. Jenny Lake is named for Jenny Leigh, the Shoshone wife of Beaver Dick Leigh. A one-way loop road leads south past Jenny and String Lakes, providing excellent views of the **Cathedral Group:** Teewinot, Grand Teton, and Mt. Owen. This is the most popular part of the park, and day-hikers will find a plethora of trails to sample, along with crowds of fellow hikers. Paths lead around both Jenny and String Lakes, while another nearly level trail follows the east shore of **Leigh Lake** to several pleasant sandy beaches. **String Lake** is narrow but very pretty and makes a fine place for canoeing or swimming. Get supplies from the small store at Jenny Lake and information or guidebooks from the **Jenny Lake Visitor Center** (307/739-3392, daily 8 A.M.–7 P.M. early June–early Sept.; daily 8 A.M.–5 P.M. early May–early June and early–late Sept.). Coin-operated storage lockers are next to the store. **Jenny Lake Ranger Station** (307/739-3343)

is open daily 8 A.M.–5 P.M. mid-May–mid-September.

Shuttle boats (307/734-9227, www.jennylakeboating.com, $10 adults, $5 kids round-trip, mid-May–Sept.) provide hiking trail access every 15 minutes to the Inspiration Point and Cascade Canyon areas. This is one of the most popular day hikes in Grand Teton. One-hour scenic boat cruises ($15 adults, $7 kids) are offered nightly at 6:30 P.M. in the summer. You can also rent canoes and kayaks ($15 per hour).

Beautiful **Jenny Lake Lodge** (307/733-4647 or 800/628-9988, www.gtlc.com, late May–early Oct.) sits on the northeast end of the lake and provides the finest lodging in the park; the gourmet meals are legendary.

JACKSON LAKE
◖ Signal Mountain

As the park road approaches Jackson Lake, a paved but narrow side road (no RVs or trailers) turns east and leads to the summit of Signal

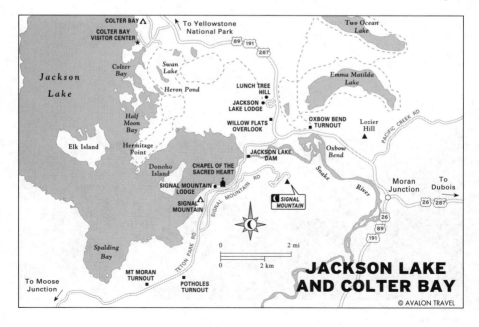

JACKSON LAKE AND COLTER BAY

© AVALON TRAVEL

Mountain, 800 feet above Jackson Hole. On top are panoramic views of the Tetons, Jackson Lake, the Snake River, and the long valley below. To the south lies **The Potholes,** a hummocky area created when retreating glaciers left behind huge blocks of ice. The melting ice created depressions, some of which are still filled with water. Signal Mountain was burned by a massive 1879 fire and offers a good opportunity to see how Yellowstone may look in 75 years.

Hugging the southeast shore of Jackson Lake, **Signal Mountain Lodge** (307/543-2831, www.signalmountainlodge.com) includes cabins and campsites, plus a gift shop, convenience store, gas station, marina with boat rentals, restaurant, and bar. Just east of the lodge is the **Chapel of the Sacred Heart,** a small Roman Catholic church that has summer services at 5:30 P.M. on Saturdays and at 5 P.M. Sundays. The road then crosses **Jackson Lake Dam,** which raises the water level by 39 feet, alters the river's natural flow, and inundates a large

area upstream. Many conservationists fought to have Jackson Lake excluded from the park, concerned that it would establish a bad precedent for allowing reservoirs in other parks. Nevertheless, once you get away from the dam, the lake appears relatively natural today (except in drought years, when it gets the "bathtub ring" effect).

Along Jackson Lake

A turnout near Jackson Lake Junction provides views over **Willow Flats,** where moose are frequently seen, especially in the morning. Topping a bluff overlooking the flats is **Jackson Lake Lodge** (307/543-3100 or 800/628-9988, www.gtlc.com, late May–early Oct.), built in the 1950s with the $5 million financial backing of John D. Rockefeller Jr. Architects are not thrilled about the design (one author termed it "the ugliest building in western Wyoming"), but the 60-foot-tall back windows frame an unbelievable view of the Tetons and Jackson Lake. Immediately across from the

Jackson Lake and the Teton Range from Signal Mountain

© DON PITCHER

lodge is a trail leading to **Emma Matilda** and **Two Ocean** Lakes. It is 14 miles round-trip around both lakes, with lots of wildlife along the way, including moose, trumpeter swans, pelicans, and ducks. You may have to contend with large groups on horseback.

Find your own inspiration at **Lunch Tree Hill,** a 0.5-mile hike from Jackson Lake Lodge. While visiting the area in 1926, John D. Rockefeller Jr. climbed this knoll for a picnic lunch with Horace Albright, then the superintendent of Yellowstone. They watched moose browsing below and took in the panoramic Teton Range vista. This visit helped crystallize Rockefeller's realization that he needed to act to protect this remarkable area from development. Park rangers lead hikes up Lunch Tree Hill most summer mornings. The trail begins in back of Jackson Lake Lodge; turn right for the path up the hill.

COLTER BAY

Colter Bay Village is one of the most developed parts of Grand Teton National Park, with a full marina, stores, a gas station, cabins, a campground, restaurants, and acres of parking. The **Colter Bay Visitor Center** (307/739-3594, daily 8 A.M.–7 P.M. early June–early Sept., 8 A.M.–5 P.M. early May–early June and early Sept.–mid-Oct.) has a big information desk, park films, and a fine bookstore.

For many years, the primary attraction here was David T. Vern's incredible collection of Indian arts—the finest of its kind in any national park. Unfortunately, the building did not adequately protect the collection and in 2011 it moved to Tucson for preservation. A brandnew facility is in the planning stages, but don't expect to see it for several years—at best. In the meantime, a handful of pieces remain on display, and Native artisans are present downstairs throughout the summer. Stop to chat with them about their paintings, beaded items, wood carvings, pottery, and weaving. Step out behind the visitor center to join the shoreside fun at **Colter Bay Marina,** where you can take tours of Jackson Lake or rent a canoe or boat.

ROCKEFELLER MEMORIAL PARKWAY

North of Colter Bay, the highway cruises along the shore of Jackson Lake for the next nine miles, providing some fine vantage points of the Tetons. The burned area on the opposite shore was ignited by lightning in the 1974 Waterfalls Canyon Fire, which consumed 3,700 acres. By late fall each year, Idaho spud farmers have drawn down water in the lake, leaving a long, barren shoreline at the upper end.

Shortly after the road leaves the upper end of Jackson Lake, a signboard announces your entrance into John D. Rockefeller Jr. Memorial Parkway. This 24,000-acre parcel of land was transferred to the National Park Service in 1972 in commemoration of Rockefeller's unstinting work in establishing Grand Teton National Park. The land forms a connection between Grand Teton and Yellowstone and is managed by Grand Teton National Park. Much of this area was severely burned by the 1988 Huck Fire, which began when strong winds blew a tree into power lines. Despite immediate efforts to control the blaze, it consumed 4,000 acres in the first two hours and later grew to cover nearly 200,000 acres, primarily within the Forest Service's Teton Wilderness. Dense young lodgepole pines now carpet much of the land.

Flagg Ranch

On the northern end of Rockefeller Parkway is **Flagg Ranch Resort** (307/543-2861 or 800/443-2311, www.flaggranch.com), where facilities include a gas station, convenience store, gift shop, cabins, restaurant (daily 7 A.M.–10 P.M., $14–34), and campground with RV hookups. The Park Service operates little **Flagg Ranch Information Station** (307/543-2372, daily 9 A.M.–3:30 P.M. early June–early Sept.). During the winter, Flagg Ranch is the jumping-off point for snowcoach and guided snowmobile trips into Yellowstone; the road isn't plowed north of this point.

Two nearby trails provide easy day hikes.

GRAND TETON

The nearly level **Polecat Creek Loop Trail** is 2.3 miles round-trip and follows a ridge overlooking a marsh and through conifer forests. **Flagg Canyon Trail** is five miles round-trip and provides views of a rocky canyon cut through by the Snake River.

Grassy Lake Road

Grassy Lake Road takes off just north of Flagg Ranch Resort and continues 52 miles to Ashton, Idaho. It's a scenic drive, but don't attempt this narrow and rough dirt road with a trailer or an RV. This route provides a shortcut to the Bechler River area of Yellowstone and is a popular wintertime snowmobile route. **Huckleberry Hot Springs,** a short hike north from the Grassy Lake Road bridge over the Snake River, was the site of a public swimming pool until 1983, when it was razed by the Park Service. The hot springs are accessible via an unmaintained trail, but you'll need to wade Polecat Creek to reach them. Although they remain very popular with hikers and cross-country skiers, it's worth noting that the

springs might pose a risk from high radiation levels and potentially deadly amoebae.

A few miles east of the Idaho-Wyoming border on Grassy Lake Road is **Squirrel Meadows Guard Station** (208/652-7442, www.fs.fed.us/r4/caribou-targhee), a two-room Forest Service cabin with bunk beds, a hand pump for water, and an outhouse. The cabin sleeps up to six for $35 (reservations at 518/885-3639 or 877/444-6777, www.recreation.gov, $9 fee). Wintertime access is via snowmobile or skis for the last 12 miles to the cabin from the Idaho side. Lodging is available just across the Idaho border at **Squirrel Creek Guest Ranch** (208/652-3972, www.idahoranch.com, $75–105 d).

JACKSON LAKE TO MORAN JUNCTION
Oxbow Bend

East and south of Jackson Lake, the park road passes Oxbow Bend, where a turnout is almost always filled with folks looking for geese, ducks, moose, and other animals. The oxbow was formed when the meandering river cut off

© DON PITCHER

the Tetons reflected in Oxbow Bend

an old loop. The calm water here is a delightful place for canoes, although the mosquitoes can be a major annoyance in midsummer. Come fall, photographers line the shoulder of the road for classic shots of flaming aspen trees with Grand Teton and **Mt. Moran** in the background. Mt. Moran is the massive peak with a flattened summit, a skillet-shaped glacier across its front, and a distinctive black vertical diabase dike that looks like a scar from some ancient battle. It rises 12,605 feet above sea level and is named for Thomas Moran, whose beautiful paintings of Yellowstone helped persuade Congress to set aside that area as the world's first national park.

Moran Junction

At Moran Junction you pass the park's Buffalo Entrance Station and meet the road to Togwotee Pass and Dubois. A post office and school are the only developments remaining here. The epic Western *The Big Trail* was filmed nearby in 1930, starring an actor named John Wayne in his first speaking role. (Wayne had never ridden a horse before this.) An interesting side trip is to head east from Moran on U.S. Highway 26/287 for three miles to **Buffalo Valley Road.** This narrow and scenic road leads to Turpin Meadow, a major entryway into the Teton Wilderness. It is very pretty, especially in early summer when flowers carpet the fields. Buck-and-rail fences line the road, and the pastures are filled with horses and cattle. Beyond Turpin Meadow, the road turns to gravel and climbs sharply uphill, rejoining the main highway a couple of miles below Togwotee Mountain Lodge. The Blackrock Ranger Station of Bridger-Teton National Forest is eight miles east of Moran Junction on U.S. Highway 26/287. Nearby is historic **Rosie's Cabin,** built early in the 20th century by Rudolph Rosencrans, an Austrian emigrant who was the first forest ranger in this part of the Tetons.

MORAN JUNCTION TO MOOSE

South of Moran, U.S. Highway 26/89/191 immediately crosses the Buffalo River (a.k.a.

Buffalo Fork of the Snake River), where bison were once abundant. With a little help from humans, bison have been reestablished and are now often seen just south of here along the road.

Cunningham Cabin

The turnoff to the Cunningham Cabin is six miles south of Moran Junction. The structure actually consists of two sod-roofed log cabins connected by a covered walkway called a "dogtrot." Built around 1890, it served first as living quarters and later as a barn and smithy. A park brochure describes the locations of other structures on the property.

Pierce Cunningham came here as a homesteader and, with his wife, Margaret, settled to raise cattle. Although this was some of the better land in this part of the valley, the soil was still so rocky that they had a hard time digging fencepost holes. Instead, they opted to build the buck-and-rail fences that have become a hallmark of Jackson Hole ranches. Cunningham Ranch gained notoriety in 1893 when a posse surrounded two suspected horse thieves who were wintering at Cunningham's place while he was away. Vigilantes shot and killed George Spencer and Mike Burnett in an example of "mountain justice." Later, however, suspicions arose that hired killers working for wealthy cattle barons had led the posse and that the murdered men may have been innocent. **Spread Creek** is just north of the Cunningham cabin; it gained its name by having two mouths, separated by a distance of three miles.

Triangle X Ranch

Triangle X Ranch is one of the most famous dude ranches in Jackson Hole. Although it's on park land, the Turner family has managed Triangle X for more than 60 years. (One of the owners, John Turner, was director of the U.S. Fish and Wildlife Service under the first President Bush.) Stop by just after sunup to watch wranglers driving 120 head of horses to the corrals. It's a scene straight out of an old Marlboro ad.

GRAND TETON

THE MAGIC OF THE TETONS

Somewhere at the eastern base of the Tetons did those hoofprints disappear into a mountain sanctuary where many crooked paths have led. He that took another man's possession, or he that took another man's life, could always run here if the law or popular justice were too hot at his heels. Steep ranges and forests walled him in from the world on all four sides, almost without a break; and every entrance lay through intricate solitudes. Snake River came into the place through canyons and mournful pines and marshes, to the north, and went out at the south between formidable chasms. Every tributary to this stream rose among high peaks and ridges, and descended into the valley by well-nigh impenetrable courses.... Down in the bottom was a spread of level land, broad, and beautiful, with the blue and silver Tetons rising from its chain of lakes to the west and other heights residing over its other sides.

From Owen Wister's *The Virginian*

Southwest from Triangle X, the road climbs along an ancient river terrace and passes **Hedrick Pond,** where the 1963 Henry Fonda movie *Spencer's Mountain* was filmed. Although the book on which the movie was based was set in Virginia, the producers found the Tetons a considerably more impressive location. Trumpeter swans are often seen on the pond. Hedrick Pond isn't visible from the road and there are no signs pointing it out, but you can get there by parking near the S-curve road sign 1.4 miles south of Triangle X. The pond is a good example of a kettle pond, created when retreating glaciers left behind a block of ice covered with gravel and other deposits. The ice melted, leaving behind a depression that filled to become Hedrick Pond.

◖ Teton Viewpoints

Several park road turnouts provide popular photo-opportunity spots, the most famous being **Snake River Overlook.** Ansel Adams's famous shot of the Tetons was taken here and has been imitated with less success by generations of photographers. Throughout the summer, a progression of different flowers blooms in the open sagebrush flats along the road, adding brilliant slashes of color. They're prettiest in late June; in the high country, the peak comes a month or more later than elsewhere.

Just north of Snake River Overlook is the turnoff to **Deadman's Bar.** A steep partially dirt road (not for RVs) drops to one of the primary river-access points used by river rafters. The river bar received its name from an incident in 1886. Four German prospectors entered the area, but only one—John Tonnar—emerged. Bodies of the other three were found along the Snake River, and Tonnar was charged with murder. The jury in Evanston believed his claim of self-defense and he was set free, an act that so angered locals that they vowed to take care of future Jackson Hole criminals with a shotgun. A skull from one of the victims is on display in the Jackson Hole Museum.

Schwabacher Landing sits at the end of a one-mile gravel road that splits off just north of the Glacier View Turnout. It's a pleasant place for riverside picnics, and some of the most famous Teton Range photos—the ones you see in local galleries—were taken just a few hundred yards upstream from the parking area. Schwabacher Landing was formerly a common starting point for rafting trips, but the river channel has shifted westward, making access difficult. Most floaters now put in at Pacific Creek or Deadman's Bar.

ANTELOPE FLATS LOOP

One mile north of the turnoff to Moose, **Antelope Flats Road** heads east along Ditch Creek. This road provides an interesting side loop to dramatic views of the Tetons and a great chance to see bison, elk, antelope, and other wildlife. Antelope Flats Road connects with other paved (and dirt) roads leading to Mormon Row, Teton Science School, Gros Ventre River Valley, and the town of Kelly. It forms a peaceful and beautiful out-of-the-way diversion from the crowds in other parts of the park.

Just south of the Antelope Flats junction is **Blacktail Butte,** a timbered knoll rising 1,000 feet over the surrounding sagebrush plains. It's a favorite of rock climbers and has a hiking trail up the back (east) side. Climbing access is from a parking area off U.S. 26/89/191.

◆ Mormon Row

You will want to stop at the much-photographed old farm buildings known as Mormon Row. The farmland here was homesteaded by predominantly Mormon settlers in the early 1900s, but was later purchased by Rockefeller's Snake River Land Company and transferred to the Park Service. Only one set of buildings—an acre of the Moulton Ranch—is still in private hands. The other buildings were allowed to decay until the 1990s, when the Park Service recognized their value and stepped in to preserve the structures. Herds of bison often wander past the old farmsteads in summer, providing one of the best places to view them. Also keep your eyes open for small groups of pronghorn antelope in the vicinity.

Shadow Mountain Area

This interesting area is found up a side road off Antelope Flats Road. Shadow Mountain Road (officially Forest Road 30340) is paved for the first mile or so but turns to gravel as it snakes rather steeply up the mountain. The road is definitely not recommended for RVs or trailers, or for any vehicles after rains, when some sections turn to slippery mud. Shadow Mountain (8,252 feet) is named for the shadows of the Tetons that fall across the mountain's face each evening. The views from the top are truly amazing, with the Tetons in all their glory. Several dispersed campsites can be found along this route on Forest Service land.

Teton Science Schools

Hidden away in a valley along upper Ditch Creek is Teton Science Schools (TSS, 307/733-4765, www.tetonscience.org), a fine hands-on school for both young and old. Founded in 1967 as a summer field-biology program for high-school kids, TSS has grown into a year-round program with classes that run the gamut from elementary-school level all the way up to intensive college courses and a graduate program. Summertime visitors of all ages will enjoy classes on such diverse subjects as bird-banding, canoeing, sunset hikes, and elk-watching. These classes fill up fast, so make reservations early to be sure of a spot. The school's excellent month-long wilderness emergency medical technician (EMT) course

Grand Teton from Shadow Mountain

© DON PITCHER

GRAND TETON

in early winter is one of the few programs of its kind in the nation.

Based at the old Elbo dude ranch (started in 1932), TSS includes two dormitories, a central kitchen, a dining area, and other log structures. Visitors to the school should visit the **Murie Natural History Museum,** which displays thousands of specimens of birds, mammals, and plants. Included are casts of animal tracks used by famed wildlife biologist Olaus Murie in producing his *Peterson's Guide to Animal Tracks*. It's open to the public, but call ahead to arrange an appointment.

Separately, the **Jackson Campus** of TSS occupies an 860-acre parcel west of town along Highway 22. This eco-friendly facility provides room for additional programs and lodging for guests, including those for "Road Scholars" (formerly Elderhostel). In addition, the school operates very popular **Wildlife Expeditions** (307/733-2623 or 888/945-3567, www.wildlifeexpeditions.org) with safaris throughout the Grand Teton and Yellowstone area.

KELLY

The small settlement of Kelly borders on the southeastern end of Grand Teton National Park and has log homes and a cluster of Mongolian-style yurts—certainly the most unusual dwellings in Wyoming. Folks living in the yurts share a common bathhouse and rent the land. The town has a shoebox-size post office and a couple of rental cabins, along with a real treat, **Kelly on the Gros Ventre** (307/732-9837, www.facebook.com, 7 A.M.–6 P.M. daily in summer, 7 A.M.–3 P.M. Tues.–Sat. in winter), serving sandwiches ($8), box lunches, and Jackson Hole's best espresso. The shop also has ice, beer, pop, and firewood—all the staples for camping (free Wi-Fi, too!). The Park Service's **Gros Ventre Campground** is three miles west of Kelly.

GROS VENTRE AREA

Gros Ventre Road leads east from the Kelly area, passing **Kelly Warm Spring** on the right. Its shallow and warm waters are a favorite place for local kayakers to practice their rolls or for

families to wade and hunt for frogs on a summer afternoon. A short distance up the road and off to the north (left) are the collapsing remains of the **Shane cabin,** where a scene from the classic 1951 Western was filmed. Beyond this point, the road enters Bridger-Teton National Forest and the Slide Lake area, where there is a Forest Service campground.

Gros Ventre Slide

One of the most extraordinary geologic events in recent Wyoming history took place in the Gros Ventre (pronounced GROW-vont, "Big Belly" in French trapper lingo) Canyon, named for the Gros Ventre Indians of this area. Sheep Mountain, on the south side of the canyon, consists of sandstone underlain by a layer of shale that becomes slippery when wet. Melting snow and heavy rains in the spring of 1925 lubricated this layer of shale, and on June 23 the entire north end of the mountain—a section 2,000 feet wide and one mile long—suddenly slid 1.5 miles downslope, instantly damming the river below and creating Slide Lake. A rancher in the valley, Guil Huff, watched in amazement as the mountain began to move, but he managed to gallop his horse out of the way as the slide roared within 30 feet. Huff's ranch floated away on the new lake several days later.

For two years folks kept a wary eye on the makeshift dam of rock and mud. Then, on May 18, 1927, the dam suddenly gave way, pushing an enormous wall of water through the downstream town of Kelly. Six people perished in the flood, and when the water reached Snake River Canyon nine hours later it filled the canyon to the rim with boiling water, trees, houses, and debris. Today a smaller Slide Lake still exists, and the massive landslide that created it more than 75 years ago remains an exposed gouge visible for miles around. Geologists say that, under the right conditions, more of Sheep Mountain could slide. Dead trees still stand in the upper end of Slide Lake. The Forest Service has a **Gros Ventre Geological Trail** 10 miles up Gros Ventre Road. This 0.25-mile path leads to an incredible viewpoint overlooking the slide and is marked with interpretive signs.

Gros Ventre Valley

A drive through Gros Ventre River Valley provides some fine views across to the Tetons. Gros Ventre Road turns to gravel above Slide Lake, becoming quite rutted in places. Surprising scenery makes the sometimes bone-jarring route easier to take. The landscape here is far different from that of the Tetons, with brilliant red-orange badland hills rising sharply above the Gros Ventre River. Two more Forest Service campgrounds (Red Hills and Crystal Creek) are four miles above Slide Lake, or you can camp in dispersed sites off the road. **Grizzly Lake Trail** starts at the Red Hills Campground and continues for 3.5 miles to this small mountain lake.

There are wonderful vistas of the Red Hills and Gros Ventre River Valley below.

The road continues another 15 beautiful miles along the river above the lake, getting rougher at the upper end. Several remote guest ranches are up here. Beyond Cow Creek Trailhead (29 miles from Kelly), the route is virtually impassable unless you have a high-clearance 4WD and are ready to get stuck. Hard-core mountain bikers sometimes continue up this road/trail and then drop into the Green River watershed north of Pinedale. Cow Creek Trail and other paths lead into the Gros Ventre Wilderness, which borders the south side of the road.

Hiking

The precipitous Tetons that look so dramatic from the roads are even more impressive up close and personal. Grand Teton National Park is laced with 200 miles of trails, and hikers can choose anything from simple day treks to weeklong trips along the crest of the range. Unlike nearby Yellowstone, where most of the country is forested, the Tetons contain extensive alpine scenery. This means, however, that many of the high passes won't be free of snow until late July and may require ice axes before then. Check at the visitor centers or Jenny Lake Ranger Station for current trail conditions. In addition, this high country can be dangerous when frequent thunderstorms roll through in summer. Several people have been killed by lightning strikes in the Tetons. Most storms hit in the afternoon, so it's good to get an early start to avoid them if possible. Besides, trailhead parking spots fill early, especially on warm summer weekends.

Get the helpful *Grand Teton Day Hikes* pamphlet from park visitor centers or online at www.nps.gov/grte. For the guided version, get a schedule of free ranger walks and hikes (including special ones for kids) from visitor centers or in the park newspaper. These are offered daily throughout the summer.

MOOSE AREA
Phelps Lake

- Distance: 4 miles round-trip to the lake
- Duration: 2 hours
- Elevation: 6,800 feet
- Effort: moderate to strenuous
- Trailhead: Death Canyon Trailhead (3 miles south of Moose off the Moose-Wilson Road)

This trailhead is a popular access point for backpackers heading into the wilderness, but shorter hikes are possible. It's 1.8 miles round-trip to **Phelps Lake Overlook,** where you get a view across this beautiful mountain lake 600 feet below. From Phelps Lake Overlook you can hike steeply down for a lakeside picnic on the sandy beach, and then back the same way.

Death Canyon Patrol Cabin

- Distance: 8 miles round-trip
- Duration: 6 hours

GRAND TETON

- Elevation: 6,800 feet
- Effort: strenuous
- Trailhead: Death Canyon Trailhead (3 miles south of Moose off the Moose-Wilson Road)

This challenging hike covers some of the same country as the Phelps Lake hike, but it continues beyond Phelps Lake Overlook to Death Canyon Patrol Cabin at the junction of Death Canyon Trail and Static Peak Trail. Getting to the cabin requires climbing 420 feet to the overlook, losing 400 feet in elevation, and then climbing 1,000 feet higher. And you've got to go back the same way. The small log cabin was built by the Civilian Conservation Corps in the 1930s and is still used by trail maintenance crews. Continue 0.5 mile beyond the cabin up Death Canyon Trail for a dramatic vista into Death Canyon.

JENNY LAKE AREA
◖ Inspiration Point and Hidden Falls

- Distance: 2.2 miles round-trip with boat shuttle; 5.8 miles round-trip by trail
- Duration: 2–4 hours
- Elevation: 6,800 feet
- Effort: moderate
- Trailhead: East Boat Dock on Jenny Lake

The fun trek to Inspiration Point is one of the most popular day hikes in Grand Teton

LIGHTNING SAFETY

Lightning is a significant hazard for travelers on foot or horseback in Wyoming, particularly in the high mountains, such as the Tetons, Wind River Range, Snowy Range, or the Big Horns. Three people were killed by lightning strikes in 1998 and 1999 in the Snowy Range west of Laramie, and others are hit almost every year around the state. In the 1990s, acclaimed writer Gretel Ehrlich was struck while riding a horse on her ranch at the foot of the Big Horns. Her long and excruciating recovery is detailed in *A Match to the Heart* (Random House, www.randomhouse.com). On July 22, 2010, a freak morning storm struck climbers heading up Grand Teton, killing one person and sending several victims to the hospital.

CREATING A THUNDERHEAD
Thunderstorms are created by a combination of convective forces, moisture, and unstable air. On sunny days as the ground warms, heat begins to rise convectively. When the air above is unstable (much cooler at higher altitudes than closer to the ground), the warm air rises rapidly. As it rises, the air cools enough that tiny droplets of moisture precipitate out, forming clouds that may grow into thunderheads if there is enough moisture and atmospheric instability. This rapid development of thunderheads generates enormous amounts of energy that is released as lightning, wind, hail, and rain. During a lightning strike, an electrical charge reaches toward the ground and is met by an opposite charge rising from the earth. They connect in a brilliant flash of light, heat, and noise as 35,000 amperes of charge are released.

PROTECTING YOURSELF
Nearly 100 people die each year from lightning strikes in the United States, and hundreds of others are injured. Statistically speaking, golfers are the most likely to get zapped, because they are often in open areas carrying metal golf clubs when a storm rolls in. Others at risk include softball and soccer players, mountain climbers, horseback riders, swimmers, and hikers.

Several factors are important in protecting yourself from lightning. One is to pay attention to building storms, even distant ones, and especially those that build quickly. Mountain thunderstorms – created when winds push air masses upslope against a mountain range – are five times more likely to occur than storms over adjacent valleys. The color of thunder-

National Park. The trail starts on the west side of Jenny Lake. It's 2.4 miles by foot from the Jenny Lake Ranger Station on the east side, or you can ride one of the summertime Jenny Lake Boating **shuttle boats** (307/734-9227, www.jennylakeboating.com, daily mid-May–Sept., $10 adults or $5 kids round-trip) that cross the lake every 15 minutes or so. Hours vary, but in peak season (July to mid-Aug.) it's 7 A.M.–7 P.M. Shuttle boat lines lengthen around 11 A.M., so get here early in the morning to avoid the crush and to better your odds at finding a parking spot. Boat tickets are not available in advance. Afternoon thunderstorms frequently build up over the Tetons, which is another good reason to start your hike early.

From the boat dock on the west side, the trail climbs 0.5 mile to picturesque Hidden Falls, and then continues steeply another 0.5 mile to Inspiration Point, which overlooks Jackson Hole from 400 feet above Jenny Lake. Avoid the crowds on the way down from Inspiration Point by following a second trail back to Jenny Lake. If you miss the last boat at 6 P.M., it's a 2.4-mile hike around the lake to the parking area.

Cascade Canyon

- Distance: 14–19 miles round-trip
- Duration: 7–11 hours
- Elevation: 6,800 feet
- Effort: strenuous to very strenuous

heads is another factor to watch; black bases mean significant amounts of moisture and may portend a more violent thunderstorm.

The most dangerous times are – surprisingly – before a thunderstorm comes directly overhead. Strikes can hit up to five miles in front of a fast-moving thunderstorm. In 1999, a Boy Scout was struck in the Tetons while watching a distant thunderstorm; overhead it was mostly blue sky! To determine your distance from an approaching storm, count the number of seconds between a lightning strike and the subsequent thunderclap, then divide by five to get the approximate distance in miles. If thunder arrives within five seconds, the storm is dangerously close, just one mile away.

Lightning experts warn that **there are no safe places outside in a thunderstorm,** and any actions you take will only slightly reduce the dangers. If you see a storm approaching, get off ridgetops and other high places, move out of open fields, and move away from trees or other tall objects and away from water. If you are in a forest, stay near a lower stand of even-size trees. If at all possible get to a car or house, especially one with plumbing or electrical wires that transmit electrical charges into the ground.

Lightning follows the path of least resistance, which usually means taller objects or those containing metal. If you can't get to a car or house, stay as low as possible. Put your ankles and knees together and crouch down with hands over your ears to protect your hearing from thunder. Move 15-20 feet from others in your group and avoid dissimilar objects such as water and land, rock and ground, or tree and ground. Horseback riders should dismount and move away from the horse. Metallic and electronic objects attract lightning, so stay away from power lines, fence posts, golf clubs, cell phones, climbing gear, or metal objects in your backpack. Even a metal cap rivet can attract lightning. If you're indoors when a storm hits, move away from windows, doors, appliances, pipes, and telephones.

If someone near you is struck by lightning, get immediate help by calling 911 and be ready to perform CPR. Injured people do not carry an electrical charge and can be handled safely. For additional lightning safety information, see the National Weather Service's lightning safety website (www.weather.gov/os/lightning) and The National Lightning Safety Institute's homepage (www.lightningsafety.com).

GRAND TETON

• Trailhead: East Boat Dock on Jenny Lake

Many day-hikers continue at least part of the way up Cascade Canyon beyond Inspiration Point. The trail climbs gradually, gaining 640 feet in the next 3.6 miles, and provides a good chance to fish for trout or watch for moose and other animals along Cascade Creek. Those with strong legs can make a *very* long day hike all the way up to Lake Solitude (14 miles round-trip with shuttle boat) or even Hurricane Pass (19 miles round-trip with shuttle boat, gaining almost 3,600 feet on the way up). If you're into hiking that far, it probably makes more sense to reserve a backcountry campsite and take things a bit more leisurely.

Taggart and Bradley Lakes

• Distance: 6 miles round-trip to both lakes
• Duration: 2–3 hours
• Elevation: 6,900 feet
• Effort: moderate
• Trailhead: Taggart Lake Trailhead at Taggart Creek parking lot (2 miles north of Moose)

A very popular day hike follows **Taggart Lake Trail** to the lake and then back via the **Beaver Creek Trail,** a distance of 4.4 miles round-trip. A side loop to Bradley Lake adds about 2 miles to this journey. These trails provide a fine way to explore the damlike glacial moraines that created the lakes. You can also continue beyond Bradley Lake on a trail that climbs to beautiful Amphitheater Lake, the primary access point for climbs up Grand Teton. (Climbers generally begin from Jenny Lake, however.)

Amphitheater Lake

• Distance: 10 miles round-trip
• Duration: 7 hours
• Elevation: 6,750 feet
• Effort: very strenuous
• Trailhead: Lupine Meadows Trailhead, accessible off Teton Park Road just south of Jenny Lake

Looking for a fast climb into the mountains?

Amphitheater Lake is only 5 miles up the trail but is 3,000 feet higher, making this the quickest climb to the Teton tree line. Many folks day-hike the Amphitheater Lake Trail to savor the wonderful vistas across Jackson Hole along the way. Camping is available at Surprise Lake, 0.5 mile below Amphitheater Lake, but you'll need a backcountry permit. The mountain behind this alpine cirque is 11,618-foot **Disappointment Peak,** directly in front of Grand Teton. It was named in 1925 by a group of climbers who mistakenly thought they were on the east face of the Grand.

COLTER BAY AREA
Colter Bay Trails

• Distance: 1–9 miles round-trip
• Duration: 1–4 hours
• Elevation: 6,800 feet
• Effort: easy
• Trailhead: Hermitage Point Trailhead at the south end of Colter Bay Visitor Center parking lot

A spiderweb of mostly level trails heads south from this trailhead, passing beaver ponds and willow patches where trumpeter swans, moose, and ducks are commonly seen. The longest destination is **Hermitage Point,** on the tip of a peninsula jutting into Jackson Lake. Get a map of Colter Bay trails from park visitor centers to see the various options. Shorter loop paths include the 2-mile **Lakeshore Trail** and the 3-mile **Swan Lake-Heron Pond Trail.** Find dramatic vistas of the Tetons at **Lunch Tree Hill,** a 0.5-mile hike from Jackson Lake Lodge. Head out the back door of the Lodge and turn right to find the trail.

BACKCOUNTRY HIKING

The most popular backcountry hiking area centers on the crest of the Tetons and the lakes that lie at its feet, most notably Jenny Lake. **Teton Crest Trail** stretches from Teton Pass north all the way to Cascade Canyon, with numerous connecting paths from both sides of the range. Three relatively short (two- to

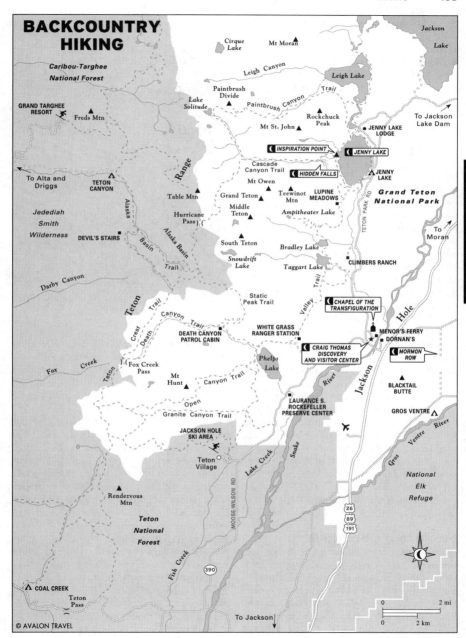

BACKCOUNTRY HIKING

Caribou-Targhee National Forest

Cirque Lake

Mt Moran ▲

Jackson Lake

Leigh Canyon

Leigh Lake

GRAND TARGHEE RESORT

Freds Mtn ▲

Paintbrush Divide

Lake Solitude

Paintbrush Canyon

Trail

Rockchuck Peak ▲

● JENNY LAKE LODGE

To Jackson Lake Dam

Mt St. John ▲

🌙 **INSPIRATION POINT**

🌙 **JENNY LAKE**

To Alta and Driggs

TETON CANYON ⌂

Range

Cascade Canyon Trail

🌙 **HIDDEN FALLS**

▲ JENNY LAKE

Alaska

Table Mtn ▲

Grand Teton ▲

Mt Owen ▲

Teewinot Mtn ▲

LUPINE MEADOWS

Grand Teton National Park

Jedediah Smith Wilderness

DEVIL'S STAIRS ▪

Hurricane Pass) (

Middle Teton ▲

Ampitheater Lake

To Moran

Basin

South Teton ▲

Bradley Lake

Darby Canyon

Trail

Snowdrift Lake

Taggart Lake

CLIMBERS RANCH ▪

TETON PARK RD

Static Peak Trail

Valley

🌙 **CHAPEL OF THE TRANSFIGURATION**

Jackson

Teton

Crest

Trail

Death

Canyon

Trail

DEATH CANYON PATROL CABIN ▪

WHITE GRASS RANGER STATION ▪

Trail

⌂ **MENOR'S FERRY**

DORNAN'S

Hole

Fox   Creek

Teton

) (Fox Creek Pass

Mt Hunt ▲

Canyon Trail

Phelps Lake

River

★ **CRAIG THOMAS DISCOVERY AND VISITOR CENTER**

🌙 **MORMON ROW**

Snake

BLACKTAIL BUTTE

Open

Granite Canyon Trail

JACKSON HOLE SKI AREA

LAURANCE S. ROCKEFELLER PRESERVE CENTER

✈

GROS VENTRE ⌂

Gros Ventre River

Teton Village ○

Lake Creek

MOOSE-WILSON RD

National Elk Refuge

Rendezvous Mtn ▲

Teton National Forest

Fish Creek

390

26 89 191

⌂ **COAL CREEK**

Teton Pass

To Jackson ↓

© AVALON TRAVEL

| 0 | 2 mi |
| 0 | 2 km |

GRAND TETON

three-day) loop hikes are possible. For more complete descriptions of park trails, see *Jackson Hole Hikes* by Rebecca Woods (Jackson: White Willow Publishing) or *Teton Trails* by Katy Duffy and Darwin Wile (Grand Teton Association, www.grandtetonpark.org). Get topographic maps at **Teton Mountaineering** in Jackson; best is the waterproof version produced by Trails Illustrated.

Permits

The backcountry trails of Grand Teton National Park are some of the most heavily used paths in Wyoming, and strict regulations are enforced. Backcountry-use permits are required of all overnight hikers, and you'll need to specify a particular **camping zone or designated campsite** for each night of your trip. Get permits and detailed backcountry brochures from the visitor centers in Moose or Colter Bay or the Jenny Lake Ranger Station. Get there early in the morning during summer for permits to popular trails. A limited number of backcountry permits can be reserved in advance January 5–May 15 online (www.nps.gov/grte/planyourvisit/bcres.htm). You can also request permits by faxing 307/739-3443. You'll need to pick the permit up in person and pay a $25 service fee for reservations. There's no charge for permits if you get them the day of your trip. Get additional information on permits and reservations by calling 307/739-3309. Be sure to also request the park's *Backcountry Camping* handout (online at www.nps.gov. grte) with details on regulations, snow conditions, minimizing impacts, and bear safety. On the back is a trail map that shows camping zones and access.

Safety in the Backcountry

Grizzlies and black bears roam throughout the park, particularly in the forested areas along the lakes. Special boxes are provided for food storage at backcountry campsites along Jackson, Leigh, and Phelps Lakes. Backcountry campers at other sites are required to use a **hard-sided food storage**

mules-ear wyethia flowers

© DON PITCHER

canister provided by the Park Service at no charge. Hanging of food is no longer allowed in the backcountry, and bikes are not allowed on trails anywhere inside the park. Campfires are not permitted at higher elevations, so be sure to bring a cooking stove.

Backcountry hikers (and day-hikers, for that matter) need to be aware of the dangers from summertime **thunderstorms** in the Tetons. A common weather pattern is for clear mornings to build to blustery thunderstorms in late afternoon, followed by gradual clearing as evening arrives. Lightning is a major threat in the park's exposed alpine country, and rain showers can be surprisingly heavy at times. Make sure all of your gear is wrapped in plastic (garbage bags work well), and carry a rain poncho or other rainwear. Many hikers carry cell phones for emergencies, but coverage is spotty in the mountains. Unfortunately, the phones can also create a false sense of security for those who are not familiar with backcountry travel. Don't head unprepared into the mountains thinking you can always call for a rescue if you sprain your ankle.

Cascade Canyon to Paintbrush Canyon

One of the most popular hikes in Grand Teton National Park is this **19-mile loop** trip up Cascade Canyon, over Paintbrush Divide, and down Paintbrush Canyon (or vice versa). The trip offers a little of everything: dense forests, alpine lakes, flower-covered meadows, and magnificent views of the Tetons. It is best done in late summer, because a cornice of snow typically blocks Paintbrush Divide until the latter part of July. Most folks do it as an overnight trip, but it's possible to do the entire loop in a single very long day if you're in good shape and have a masochistic streak. Be sure to bring plenty of water along.

Begin at the String Lake Trailhead and head south around Jenny Lake, stopping to enjoy the views (and crowds) at Inspiration Point before heading up along Cascade Creek. The trail splits at the upper end of this canyon; turning left takes you to Hurricane Pass and the Teton Crest Trail, where you'll discover wonderful views of the back side of Grand Teton. Instead, turn right (north) and head up to beautiful Lake Solitude. Behind you, Teewinot, Mt. Owen, and Grand Teton are framed by the glacially carved valley walls. Above Lake Solitude, the trail climbs sharply to Paintbrush Divide and then switchbacks even more quickly down into Paintbrush Canyon. The trail eventually leads back to String Lake. Be sure to stop at beautiful Holly Lake on the way down.

Death Canyon Loop

Another fine loop trip departs from the Death Canyon Trailhead, approximately three miles south of park headquarters on the Moose-Wilson Road. Many hiking options are available here, with trails leading to Phelps Lake, up Open Canyon, or into Death Canyon. (The name came about when a survey party was in the area in 1899 and one of the men disappeared. He was never seen again.) Despite the name, Death Canyon provides a wonderful **26-mile loop** hike that takes you over three high passes and into spectacular alpine country. From the trailhead, hike to Phelps Lake Overlook before dropping to a junction, where you turn right to hike up Death Canyon. Bear left at a patrol cabin built in the 1930s, and continue climbing all the way to Fox Creek Pass (9,520 feet). After this the going is fairly easy for the next three miles along Death Canyon Shelf to Mt. Meek Pass, where you drop into famous Alaska Basin. Return to your starting point by climbing east from Alaska Basin over Static Peak Divide (10,800 feet) and then switchbacking downhill to the CCC cabin and the trailhead. This is a late-season trek, because snow often blocks the passes until July; get snow conditions at the Jenny Lake Ranger Station.

Rendezvous Mountain to Death Canyon

This **23-mile-long loop** hike is different in that much of the way is downhill. Begin at the new Jackson Hole tram in Teton Village, where a $25 ticket takes you to the top of Rendezvous Mountain. From the summit, the trail leads down to a saddle, across the South Fork of Granite Creek, and up to Teton Crest Trail. Head north on this trail to Marion Lake—a popular camping site—and then over Fox Creek Pass. The trail splits, and the right fork drops sharply down into scenic Death Canyon. At the lower end of Death Canyon, cliffs rise nearly 3,000 feet on both sides. The trail forks at Phelps Lake, and from here you can either hike back to Teton Village via the Valley Trail or head to the trailhead at White Grass Ranger Station, 1.5 miles northeast of Phelps Lake.

Recreation

Summers in Grand Teton are ideal for outdoor play. The weather is typically warm and sunny, but with just enough variety to keep things interesting. For high adventure (literally), you could climb Grand Teton with a guide, or for something less challenging, sit back and watch the scenery float past from a river raft or ride horseback through the sagebrush.

CLIMBING

The Tetons are considered some of the premier mountaineering country in the nation, with solid rock, good access, and a wide range of climbing conditions. Hundreds of climbing routes have been described for the main peaks, but the goal of many climbers is Grand Teton, better known as "the Grand." At 13,772 feet, this is Wyoming's second-highest summit, exceeded only by 13,804-foot Gannett Peak in the Wind River Mountains.

First to the Top

In the climbing trade, first ascents always rate highly, but the identity of the first climbers to have scaled Grand Teton has long been a matter of debate. The official record belongs to the party of William Owen (as in nearby Mt. Owen), Bishop Spalding (as in nearby Spalding Peak), John Shive, and Frank Petersen, who reached the summit in 1898. Today, however, it appears that they were preceded by two members of the 1872 Hayden Expedition: Nathaniel P. Langford (first superintendent of Yellowstone National Park) and John Stevenson. In addition, another party apparently made it to the top in 1893. Owen made a big deal out of his climb and spent 30 years trying to work himself into the record books by claiming the Langford party never reached the top. The whole thing got quite nasty, with Owen even accusing Langford of bribing the author of a history book to gain top honors. In 1929, Owen convinced the Wyoming Legislature to declare his group the first on top. Few people believe it today, and the whole thing looks

pretty foolish because even seven-year-old kids have made it up the Grand.

Several thousand people climb the mountain each summer, many with no previous climbing experience (but with excellent guides and a couple of days of training). The record time is an unbelievable three hours, six minutes, and 25 seconds, for Bryce Thatcher in 1983. This time includes starting from—and returning to—the parking lot at the foot of the mountain! And just to prove that it could be done, in 1971 one fanatic actually skied the Grand (he's the ski-school director at Snow King Resort), followed in 1989 by a snowboarder. Both lived to tell the tale.

Getting There

Most climbing takes place after the snow has melted back (mid-July) and before conditions again deteriorate (late Sept.). Overnight mountain climbing or off-trail hiking requires a special permit available from the **Jenny Lake Ranger Station** (307/739-3343, daily 8 A.M.–5 P.M. late May–late Sept.). There's no need to register if you're climbing or doing off-trail hiking for the day only, just for overnight trips. (Still, it's a good idea to leave a detailed trip itinerary with a responsible person in case of an emergency.) Winter climbers should register at the **Craig Thomas Discovery and Visitor Center.** The climbing rangers—one of the most prestigious and hazardous jobs in the park—are all highly experienced mountaineers and can provide specific route information for the various summits. Call 307/739-3604 for recorded climbing information, or talk to staff at the ranger station for weather conditions, route information, and permits.

Many climbers who scale Grand Teton follow the Amphitheater Lake Trail from Lupine Meadows to its junction with the Garnet Canyon Trail. This leads to the **Lower Saddle,** which separates Grand Teton and Middle Teton. Exum and the Park Service have base-camp huts and steel storage boxes here. There are outhouses at Lower Saddle, and climbers are required to use high-tech carry-out bags for human waste—complete with a system that breaks down feces (www.whennature-calls.com).

Other folks pitch tents behind boulders in the extraordinarily windy mountain gap at Lower Saddle. See Park Service handouts for camping restrictions and recommendations in this fragile alpine area, where heavy use by 4,000 climbers each year has caused considerable damage. The final assault on the summit of Grand Teton requires technical equipment and expertise. No motorized drills are allowed for placing climbing bolts.

Mountaineers who have registered to climb the Grand can stay at **Climbers' Ranch** ($20 per night, early June–mid-Sept.), near Taggart Lake. Lodging is in small log cabins with 4–8 bunks; hot showers and a cooking shelter are close by, but you'll need to bring your own sleeping bag and food. Call 307/733-7271 after June 1 for reservation information, or visit the American Alpine Club's website

(www.americanalpineclub.org) for details and reservations. The ranch has space for 65, but 45 of these spaces are kept open for walk-ins. It's a good idea to reserve in April for July and August.

Climbing Schools

Jackson Hole is blessed with two of the finest climbing schools in North America: **Jackson Hole Mountain Guides** (165 N. Glenwood St., 307/733-4979 or 800/239-7642, www.jhmg.com) and **Exum Mountain Guides** (307/733-2297, www.exumguides.com); Exum has a summertime office at the south end of Jenny Lake near the boat dock. Both are authorized concessions of the National Park Service and the U.S. Forest Service and offer a wide range of classes, snow training, and climbs in the Tetons and elsewhere—even as far away as Alaska and the Himalayas. Exum has been around since 1931, when Glenn Exum pioneered the first solo climb of what has become the most popular route to the top of the Grand, the Exum Route. It's the only company

© DON PITCHER

climbers trying their moves on Blacktail Butte

permitted to guide all Teton peaks and routes throughout the year. Exum's base camp is in the busy Lower Saddle area, while Jackson Hole Mountain Guides' base camp is 450 feet lower in elevation in a more secluded location (it takes an extra hour of climbing on the day of your ascent). Exum has some of the most experienced guides in the world, and they take up to four clients in a group, while Jackson Hole limits its Grand Teton ascent parties to three clients.

During midsummer, you'll pay $1,000–1,500 per person (depending on the number of people in the group) for a Grand Teton ascent; this includes two days of basic and intermediate training followed by a two-day climb up the Grand and back. Food, gear, and shelter are also included. If you're planning to climb the Grand during the peak summer season, make reservations several months in advance to be assured of a spot. For July and August, try to make Grand Teton climbing reservations in the spring.

Reservations generally are not needed for the companies' single-day climbing schools. Also available are climbs of other faces, such as Baxter's Pinnacle, Symmetry Spire, and Cube Point, along with more advanced classes and climbs in the Wind River Mountains and up Devils Tower and other precipices throughout the Western states. In addition, both companies offer a multitude of **winter classes and expeditions**, such as avalanche safety, ski mountaineering, and ice climbing. Jackson Hole Mountain Guides has additional climbing operations in Cody, Lander, Red Rocks, and Moab. Exum also operates from City of Rocks, Devils Tower, and the Wind River Mountains.

On Your Own

If you already have the experience and want to do your own climbing, the most accessible local spot is **Blacktail Butte,** just north of Moose near Ditch Creek. The parking lot here fills on warm summer afternoons as hang-dogging enthusiasts try their moves on the rock face. Get climbing supplies at **Moosely Seconds**

Mountaineering (307/739-1801) in Moose, or in Jackson at **Teton Mountaineering** (170 N. Cache Dr., 307/733-3595 or 800/850-3595, www.tetonmtn.com). Both stores rent climbing shoes and other gear. **Enclosure Indoor Climbing Center** (670 Deer Lane, 307/734-9590, www.enclosureclimbing.com) has challenging indoor climbing walls where you can practice your moves.

For complete details on local climbing, see Reynold Jackson's *A Climber's Guide to the Teton Range* (The Mountaineers Books, www.mountaineersbooks.org), the smaller *Teton Classics: 50 Selected Climbs in Grand Teton National Park* by Richard Rossiter (Globe Pequot Press), or *Teton Rock Climbs* by Aaron Gams (www.tetonrockclimbs.com), a digital guidebook of routes. Mountain climbing is inherently dangerous, and even the best climbers have accidents on The Grand. Over the years, many people have died in the Tetons, and in 2008, George Gardner—an Exum guide with 28 years of experience—died in a fall while solo climbing.

RAFTING

Several rafting companies lead scenic half-day 10-mile float trips (around $60 adults or $45 kids) down the Snake River inside the park, putting in at Deadman's Bar and taking out in Moose.

Float It Yourself

The Park Service (307/739-3602, www.nps.gov/grte) has useful information on running the sections of the river inside Grand Teton; ask for a copy of *Floating the Snake River* (or download it online). Note that life jackets, boat permits ($10 for a seven-day permit), and registration are required to run the river through the park, and that inner tubes and air mattresses are prohibited. Floating the gentler parts (from Jackson Lake Dam to just above Pacific Creek) is generally easy for even novice boaters and canoeists, but below that point things get dicier. The water averages 2–3 feet deep, but it sometimes exceeds 10 feet and flow rates are often more than 8,000 cubic feet per second, creating logjams, braided channels, strong currents, and dangerous sweepers. Peak flows are between mid-June and early July. Inexperienced rafters or anglers die nearly every year in the river. Flow-rate signs are posted at most river landings, the Craig Thomas Discovery and Visitor Center, and the Buffalo Ranger Station in Moran, or call 800/658-5771. If you're planning to raft or kayak on the whitewater parts of the Snake River, be sure to contact the Bridger-Teton National Forest office in Jackson (307/739-5500, www.fs.fed.us/r4/btnf/teton/river) for additional information, including its *Snake River Canyon Floater's Guide.*

Excellent waterproof maps of the Grand Canyon of the Snake River are sold at the visitor center. In addition to showing the rapids, these maps describe local geology and other features.

Rent rafts and whitewater kayaks from **Snake River Kayak and Canoe School** (307/733-9999 or 800/529-2501, www.snakeriverkayak.com), **Leisure Sports** (1075 S. U.S. Hwy. 89 in Jackson, 307/733-3040, www.leisuresportsadventure.com), **Rendezvous River Sports/Jackson Hole Kayak School** (307/733-2471, www.jacksonholekayak.com), **Riding and Rafts** (307/654-9900, www.jacksonholerecreation.com) 35 miles southwest of Jackson in Alpine, or **Rent-a-Raft** (307/733-2728, www.rentaraft.net) in Hoback Junction 12 miles south of Jackson. Local taxi companies can provide shuttles.

BOATING

Canoeists will discover several excellent places to paddle within Grand Teton, particularly the Snake River Oxbow Bend, String Lake, and Leigh Lake. Canoes are available for rent both in the park at Colter Bay Marina and Signal Mountain Lodge and in Jackson.

Boaters within Grand Teton will need to buy a permit; seven-day permits cost $20 for motorboats, $10 for nonmotorized craft. Motorboats are allowed only on Jackson Lake, Jenny Lake (10-horsepower max), and Phelps Lake. Sailboarding, water-skiing, jet skis, and sailing are permitted on Jackson Lake, but no personal watercraft are allowed anywhere in the park. All boaters must purchase an **Aquatic Invasive Species** decal ($10), and must take precautions to protect waterways from the spread of potentially ruinous nonnative plants and animals. Details are available online (www.cleaninspectdry.com, www.protectyourwaters.net).

Jenny Lake Boating (307/734-9227, www.jennylakeboating.com) has a variety of services on the south end of this gorgeous, mountain-rimmed lake, including shuttle boats ($10 adults, $5 kids) to Inspiration Point, one-hour scenic boat cruises ($15 adults, $7 kids), and rentals of canoes and tandem kayaks ($15 per hour). The boats run daily mid-May–September.

Marinas

Jackson Lake has three marinas, all of which are generally open mid-May–late September. **Signal Mountain Lodge Marina** (307/543-2831, www.signalmountainlodge.com) rents a range of floating vessels, including sea kayaks, canoes, motorboats, runabouts, fishing boats, pontoon boats, and deck cruisers.

Colter Bay Marina (307/543-3100 or 800/628-9988, www.gtlc.com) is near a Park Service campground, cabins, and the Colter Bay Visitor Center. It's an exceptionally busy place in the summer, with motorboat, kayak, and canoe rentals, along with guides to take you to the hot fly-fishing spots. Scenic **Jackson Lake cruises** ($26 adults, $13 kids under 12) are also available from Colter Bay Marina, as are breakfast or evening cruise-and-dine trips ($36 adults, $22 kids for breakfast; $57 adults, $37 kids for dinner).

A short distance north of Colter Bay is **Leek's Marina** (307/543-2494, www.signalmountainlodge.com), a simple place with a couple of docks, a pizza restaurant, and gas pumps.

Kayaks and Canoes

O.A.R.S. (209/736-4677 or 800/346-6277, www.oars.com) offers multi-day sea kayaking trips around Jackson Lake—perfect for

GRAND TETON

beginning kayakers and families. You don't need any paddling experience for these trips, which are supported by a motorized skiff. Overnight trips cost $265 for adults or $215 for youths; two-night kayak trips are $422 adults or $340 kids. O.A.R.S. also has combination trips that include kayaking on the lake and rafting down the Snake River; a three-day multi-sport trip costs $659 adults or $554 youths. For the whole enchilada, check out their six-night combo trips that include kayaking on Yellowstone and Jackson Lakes, park tours, camping, and a raft trip down the Snake River for $1,539 adults, $1,385 youths. The company supplies kayaks, a guide, tents, and dry bags, with sleeping bags available for rent. Reserve several months ahead, since these popular adventures fill quickly.

Jenny Lake Boating (307/734-9227, www. jennylakeboating.com) rents canoes and tandem kayaks for $15 per hour. Canoes are also available at the Signal Mountain and Colter Bay marinas.

FISHING

Grand Teton National Park rivers and lakes contain cutthroat, lake, and brown trout, along with whitefish. Park anglers must have a valid Wyoming state fishing license, available for $14 per day to nonresidents. Kids younger than 14 don't need a license if they're with an adult who has a valid fishing license. Pick up a helpful handout describing fishing regulations and seasons from park visitor centers. Fishing licenses and supplies are available at park marinas and stores.

Yellowstone and Grand Teton have different fishing regulations and license requirements. If you're heading into Yellowstone to fish, you'll need to purchase a special Yellowstone National Park fishing license. Both parks prohibit the use of nonnative baitfish.

Located in Moose, **Snake River Angler** (307/733-3699 or 888/998-7688, www. snakeriverangler.com) sells and rents fishing supplies. Their guides offer learn-to-fly-fish lessons for beginners, along with boat-based guided fishing ($475 for two). Fishing guides

are also available from **Signal Mountain Lodge Marina** (307/543-2831, www.signalmountainlodge.com) and **Colter Bay Marina** (307/543-3100 or 800/628-9988, www.gtlc.com), along with many Jackson-based operations.

In Jackson, drop by Jack Dennis' Sports (50 E. Broadway, 307/733-3270 or 800/570-3270, www.jackdennisoutdoors.com) to pick up a free copy of *Jack Dennis Sports Fly Fishing Guide*, with descriptions of regional fishing areas and advice on which lures to try.

BIRDING

The diversity of habitat types within Grand Teton National Park means that bird-watchers can find everything from trumpeter swans to calliope hummingbirds. The park produces a free *Bird-Finding Guide* with descriptions of birding hot spots. A couple of the best places are Willow Flats and Blacktail Ponds. A checklist of park birds is also available from visitor centers.

BIKING

Grand Teton is becoming an increasingly cyclist-friendly park. A paved eight-mile pathway connects Moose with Jenny Lake, paralleling Teton Park Road and providing a safer alternative for bike riders. A second portion of the pathway—completed in fall 2011—continues south 12 miles to Jackson, where it connects with additional bike trails. This newest pathway crosses under the highway at Moose junction and follows the east side of U.S. 26/89/191, crossing the Gros Ventre River on its own bridge. Note, however, that much of the bike path between Moose and Jackson is closed October–April to prevent conflicts with migrating elk. All bike paths are also open to runners, rollerbladers, and strollers. Park bike paths are not plowed in the winter.

Pick up the park's bicycling pamphlet for details on cycling options. Bikes are not allowed on any trails within Grand Teton National Park, but you *can* ride mountain bikes on several wonderful dirt roads, including Two Ocean Lake Road (three miles), Grassy Lake Road (52 miles from Flagg Ranch to Ashton,

© DON PITCHER

bison and bicyclists on the road near Mormon Row

Idaho), and the River Road (15 delightfully remote miles in the heart of the park). In addition, the paved secondary roads in the Antelope Flats–Mormon Row–Kelly area see less traffic and provide the opportunity to see bison and spectacular mountain vistas. Shadow Mountain Road is an off-the-beaten-path dirt road that takes off from the Antelope Flats area and climbs through Forest Service land to splendid vistas. The primary north-south highway through the park—U.S. 26/89/191—is heavily trafficked, and cars often top the speed limit. Cyclist should avoid this route.

Teton Park Road is closed to cars and other motorized traffic until May, and during April it is plowed and open to cyclists, walkers, and inline skaters. When the weather warms up, this is a wonderful traffic-free way to see the park.

Rentals and Tours
Rent bikes from **Adventure Sports** (307/733-3307, www.dornans.com) at Dornan's in Moose; $28 for a half-day or $36 for all day.

They'll provide a map showing good mountain biking roads in the park. **Teton Mountain Bike Tours** (307/733-0712 or 800/733-0788, www.wybike.com) leads scenic half- or all-day bike trips through Grand Teton for all levels of ability, with prices starting at $60 for a four-hour ride in the Antelope Flats area.

HORSEBACK RIDING
Grand Teton Lodge Company (307/543-3100 or 800/628-9988, www.gtlc.com) has horseback rides at **Jackson Lake Lodge Corral** and **Colter Bay Village Corral;** they're $36 for one hour or $54 for two hours (same price for adults and kids). Located in Rockefeller Parkway between Grand Teton and Yellowstone, **Flagg Ranch Resort** (307/543-2861 or 800/443-2311, www.flaggranch.com) offers hour-long horseback trail rides in the summer for $38.

SWIMMING
Swimming is allowed in all park lakes, but they can be quite cold. Jenny, String, and Leigh Lakes all have delightful spots for swimming

on the east side, including some sandy or gravelly beaches. The Snake River is dangerous and swimming isn't recommended. Jackson Lake Lodge (307/543-3100 or 800/628-9988, www.gtlc.com, late May–early Oct.) has a large heated outdoor pool, but it's open only for guests at the lodge or nearby Colter Bay Village. In addition, the town of Jackson has a wonderful recreation center with pools, and the shallow pond at Kelly Warm Spring is a fun spot to splash around.

WINTER RECREATION

The snow-covered landscape of Grand Teton National Park draws cross-country skiers and snowshoers throughout the winter.

Skiing

Cross-country skiing is popular on park roads and trails in the winter. The main thoroughfare—Teton Park Road—provides stellar views of the Teton Range and is groomed weekly for both parallel and skate skiing (with sections for hikers and snowshoers) from Taggart Lake to Signal Mountain, a distance of 14 miles. Park three miles northwest of Moose at the Taggart Lake Trailhead, where plowing ends. More adventurous skiers will enjoy side trails to Jenny Lake (eight miles round-trip) or the more challenging Taggart Lake–Beaver Creek loop (three miles, with an elevation change of almost 400 feet).

Another fun area is the Moose-Wilson Road, an easy four-mile round-trip ski from the Granite Canyon Trailhead (where plowing stops). Just don't ski into the canyon, since avalanches are a hazard. A good optional side route is the trail to Phelps Lake overlook (five miles round-trip with an elevation change of 520 feet). Other enjoyable places to ski include Antelope Flats Road and trails at Taggart Lake, Flagg Ranch, and Colter Bay.

For unsurpassed vistas of the Tetons, try skiing to the top of 8,252-foot Shadow Mountain, 14 miles northeast of Jackson. From the town of Kelly, drive another five miles north to a parking area (the road isn't plowed beyond this point), and then ski up the nearby Forest Service road that snakes up the mountain. It's fairly steep in places and seven miles round-trip. Snowmobilers also use this road, so be ready to move out of the way quickly.

Most park ski routes (other than Teton Road) are not machine-groomed but are often well packed by other skiers. After a new snowfall, you'll need to break trail as you follow the orange markers. Pick up a brochure describing ski trails from the Craig Thomas Discovery and Visitor Center, or find the information on the park website (www.nps.gov/grte). If you're planning to camp overnight in the park, you'll need to get a free permit from the visitor center.

Snowshoeing

Park naturalists lead two-hour snowshoe hikes late December–March (snowshoes provided, $5 donation). No experience is needed. These daily hikes depart the **Craig Thomas Discovery and Visitor Center** at 1:30 P.M. Reservations are required; children must be eight or over. Call 307/739-3399 for details on these and other winter activities in the park.

Snowmobiling

Snowmobiles have very limited access to Grand Teton National Park. Grassy Lake Road within John D. Rockefeller Jr. Memorial Parkway is open to snowmobilers between Flagg Ranch and Ashton, Idaho. The only other snowmobile access is for ice fishing on Jackson Lake. For the latest, pick up the snowmobiling handout at the visitor center.

Accommodations

Several places provide concessioner lodging inside Grand Teton National Park. As in most national parks, none of the lodge rooms contains TVs, radios, or air conditioning. Some rooms contain phones, and Wi-Fi access is available in the lobby of Jackson Lake Lodge. Reserve at least nine months ahead to be sure of getting a room in the peak summer season. Dozens of additional accommodations are south of the park in Jackson. **Grand Teton Lodge Company** (owned by Vail Resorts Hospitality, www.gtlc.com) is the primary park concessioner, managing Jackson Lake Lodge, Jenny Lake Lodge, Colter Bay Village, and a variety of park services.

Grand Teton Lodge Company operates a **free shuttle bus** to Jackson from the park. It runs twice daily in the summer, stopping at Jackson Lake Lodge, Jenny Lake Lodge, Colter Bay Village, and downtown Jackson. The shuttle is only for guests staying at company lodges in Grand Teton.

MOOSE

Near park headquarters in Moose, **Dornan's Spur Ranch Cabins** (307/733-2522, www.dornans.com) has a dozen modern log cabins filled with handcrafted lodgepole pine furniture. One-bedroom cabins are $175 d or $205 for up to four people, and two-bedroom cabins cost $250 for up to six people. There's a three-night minimum stay in the summer. All cabins include full kitchens and are open most of the year (closed Nov. and Apr.). Off-season rates are 30 percent lower.

JENNY LAKE

For four-star accommodations a stone's throw from the Tetons, stay at ◖ **Jenny Lake Lodge** (307/733-4647 or 800/628-9988, www.gtlc.com, late May–early Oct.), where 37 comfortably appointed cabins surround a cozy Old West main lodge. This is a marvelous honeymoon or big-splurge place, and the $515 s or $599 d price includes horseback rides, bikes,

breakfast, and a five-course dinner. (Note, however, that the meals are served only at specific times, so you'll need to adjust your schedule accordingly.) For the ultimate in extravagance, choose the lodge's luxurious suites ($775–850 d).

JACKSON LAKE

Built on a grand scale, the 385-room **Jackson Lake Lodge** (307/543-3100 or 800/628-9988, www.gtlc.com, late May–early Oct.) occupies a bluff above Willow Flats on the southeast side of Jackson Lake. Sixty-foot-high windows look across to the Tetons and fireplaces flank the spacious central hall, which offers Wi-Fi (limited elsewhere in the hotel). Guest computers are available. Outside is a large swimming pool and kiddie pool (major attractions for families), and inside you'll find restaurants, a lounge, gift shop, newsstand, clothing shop, and ATM. All rooms contain two double beds and phones; some also have small fridges. Most guests stay in 348 cottage units surrounding the main building, but 37 guest rooms are available inside the lodge itself. Rooms in the lodge without a view (unless you count the parking lot) are $224 d, while those with windows fronting the Tetons are $319 d. Cottages cost $224–239, or $289–319 d for ones with mountain vistas. A separate modern structure facing Moose Pond houses some of the nicest rooms and suites ($599 d), while a single luxury suite in the lodge costs $775 d. Extra guests (beyond two) in any of these rooms are $10 per adult. Pets can stay in the cottages for $15 extra.

On the south shore of Jackson Lake, **Signal Mountain Lodge** (307/543-2831 or 800/672-6012, www.signalmountainlodge.com, early May–mid-Oct.) offers a variety of accommodations. Simple and rustic log cabins start at $132 d, up to $198 for a two-room unit that sleeps six. Motel-style rooms with fridges and microwaves are $175 for up to four people or

GRAND TETON

guests at Jackson Lake Lodge watch a Teton sunset

© DON PITCHER

$227 for a nicer room with a gas fireplace and king bed. The lodge's finest options include lakefront suites for $254–274, cozy bungalows with kitchens and private decks for $182 d, and a three-room cabin with fireplace in the living room, full kitchen, and laundry for $300.

COLTER BAY

Family-oriented **Colter Bay Village** (307/543-3100, ext. 1080, or 800/628-9988, www.gtlc.com) has 166 rustic cabins of varying sizes and types, some of which sleep six people. The most basic are canvas-and-log structures with outdoor grills and picnic tables, potbelly wood-stoves, and bring-your-own-linen bunk beds (a limited number of sleeping bags are available for rent). These tent cabins cost just $50 d ($6 for each additional person up to six). Tent cabins are open late May–early September. There are no phones or cooking facilities in any of these cabins. Restrooms are nearby, along with coin-operated showers.

Slightly nicer are little one-room cabins that share a bath for $60 d (two twin beds or one double bed). Cabins with a private bath start at $109 d for those with a double bed, up to $155 d for those with two double beds and a twin bed. Two-room cabins with a bath are $169 for up to four. Additional guests are $10 each in all of these, and the cabins are open late May–late September. Guests at Colter Bay Village can use the big outdoor swimming pool at nearby Jackson Lake Lodge.

ROCKEFELLER MEMORIAL PARKWAY

In Rockefeller Parkway just three miles south of Yellowstone, **Flagg Ranch Resort** (307/543-2861 or 800/443-2311, www.flagg-granch.com) has modern four-plex log cabins with patios and two queen beds or a king bed. Rates are $179–189 d, plus $10 for additional adults. The main lodge houses a convenience store, restaurant, gift shop, and central area with couches and a large fireplace. Flagg Ranch is open mid-May–late September and early December–early March, but lodging is available only in summer.

BUFFALO VALLEY

Several lodging places are in beautiful Buffalo Valley, east of Moran Junction on U.S. Highway 26/287.

Hatchet Resort

Eight miles east of Moran Junction, Hatchet Resort (307/543-2413 or 877/543-2413, www.hatchetresort.com) has year-round accommodations and a friendly staff in a country setting. Well-maintained log-walled motel rooms with kitchens and fireplaces go for $145–169 d, while modern log suites featuring vaulted ceilings, fridges, and microwaves, are $239–259 d; one has a jetted tub. Groups appreciate the A-frame house with five bedrooms, a gas fireplace, and full kitchen for $455. Hatchet also has five simple budget rooms with shared baths for $99 d. All guests can use the large outside hot tub, and the small resort also has Wi-Fi, a general store, and gas. Hatchet Grill serves breakfasts and lunches ($7–9), and The Whetstone has surprisingly good dinners—burgers, salads, steaks, trout, and more ($11–27). Both are open May–mid-October.

Buffalo Valley Ranch

Buffalo Valley Ranch (307/543-2062 or 888/543-2477, www.buffalovalleyranch.com) is adjacent to Heart Six Ranch (same owners) and is 12 miles east of Moran Junction. A triplex log building houses a pair of one-bedroom units ($159 for up to four), along with a spacious two-bedroom unit ($219 for up to nine guests), all with kitchenettes, private baths, washers, and dryers. The ranch affords fine views across Buffalo Valley to the Tetons, but book early since cabins fill in the summer. Also here is **Buffalo Valley Café** ($10), serving tasty meals three times daily.

Luton's Teton Cabins

You'll discover spectacular views of the Tetons from Luton's Teton Cabins (307/543-2489, www.tetoncabins.com), 36 miles northeast of Jackson (five miles east of Moran Junction). The modern duplex cabins have full kitchens, private baths, queen beds, and front porches facing the mountains. One-bedroom units cost $270 d, two-bedroom units are $395 for up to six people, and deluxe cabins sleep six for $433. Cabins are open May–October (no phones, but free Wi-Fi). Horse-lovers can use the corrals at no charge.

KELLY AREA
Anne Kent Cabins

For rustic accommodations with an unbeatable Teton view from the front deck, stay at Anne Kent Cabins (307/733-4773, www.annekentcabins.com, June–Sept.) in the quiet village of Kelly a dozen miles northeast of Jackson. These cabins are perfect for those who want a real taste of Wyoming from a family with a long local history. Two rental options are available. Your best bet is to request the very comfortable log house, which has bedrooms in the loft and basement, two baths, a complete kitchen, washer, and dryer (but no phone). Wi-Fi may be available. The home sleeps a maximum of 12 adults and kids for $250 (plus $25 per person for more than four guests). Next door are two cabins that rent together and sleep five guests for $200. The front one (built in 1939) includes a bedroom and kitchen, while the back cabin contains a second bedroom plus bath. The Anne Kent Cabins feature handmade lodgepole furniture created by co-owner Ron Davler, who crafts them at the adjacent Jackson Hole Log and Rawhide Furniture.

Moulton Ranch

Moulton Ranch on Historic Mormon Row (307/733-3749, www.moultonranchcabins.com, late May–Sept.) rents several cabins in one of Jackson Hole's most majestic locations. This is the only private property on Mormon Row inside Grand Teton National Park, and the much-photographed Moulton Barn—one of the prototypical Wyoming images—is just a few hundred feet away. The five cabins are cozy and not at all elaborate, but where else might you awake to a spectacular Teton vista with bison grazing outside your window? Rates start at $89 d for a tiny cottage with a separate bathhouse, up to $229 for a modern cabin with

GRAND TETON

Moulton Ranch along Mormon Row

space for six. The latter is especially popular and features a kitchenette, deck, and picture window facing the Tetons. No phones (your cell phone will probably work), but Wi-Fi is available in some cabins.

Budges' Slide Lake Cabins

Budges' Slide Lake Cabins (307/733-9061, www.jacksonholecabins.com, open year-round) are four secluded but modern cabins along Slide Lake, six miles east of Kelly. Each has a woodstove, full kitchen, patio, and phone (but no TVs or Wi-Fi). Rates are $245 d, plus $30 for each additional adult guest (maximum of eight). A small cabin in nearby Kelly sleeps two for $100, including a kitchen and bath, but no TV or phone. Also available is a comfortable three-bedroom, two-bath log home in Kelly with mountain vistas ($250 for up to six guests).

GUEST RANCHES

Within Grand Teton National Park, 25 miles north of Jackson, **(Triangle X Ranch** (307/733-2183 or 888/860-0005, www.

trianglex.com, May–Oct. and late Dec.–mid-Mar.) is a classic family-oriented ranch with unmatched Teton views. The ranch has been in the Turner family for more than 75 years, and the acclaimed author Barry Lopez once worked as a wrangler here. Horseback riding is the main focus, but it also offers kids' programs and nightly events such as Dutch-oven cookouts, naturalist presentations, square dancing, and campfire sing-alongs. All-inclusive weekly rates are $3,700 for two adults. In winter Triangle X goes upscale, with fewer guests (maximum of 35, versus 80 in the summer), a hot tub, and three gourmet meals a day. The nightly winter rate is $250 d, including lodging, meals, and use of cross-country skis and snowshoes. There's a two-night minimum stay in winter and a one-week minimum stay in summer (four nights in spring and fall). No credit cards accepted in the summer. In addition, Triangle X offers very popular Snake River float trips.

Wyoming's most elaborate—and expensive—guest ranch, **Lost Creek Ranch** (307/733-3435,

© DON PITCHER

horses at Triangle X Ranch

www.lostcreek.com, late May–mid-Sept.), is 21 miles north of Jackson. This showplace resort emphasizes fitness, with a spa facility that includes exercise classes, a weight room, steam room, sauna, and hot tub, along with massage and facials (extra charge). Guests stay in modern duplex log cabins and enjoy gourmet meals in the main lodge's patio overlooking the Tetons. Amenities include such nontraditional items as a heated swimming pool, tennis courts, and a skeet range, in addition to more standard horseback riding, kid programs, float trips, hiking, Yellowstone tours, and fly-fishing. It's all a bit too Disneyesque for my taste, and the prices are too Madison Avenue. Weekly all-inclusive rates run $5,400 for two people in a duplex cabin or an astounding $13,000 for up to four people in a luxurious two-bedroom, two-bath cabin with a living room and fireplace. Some consider this a small price to pay for such pampering. The ranch hosts a maximum of 60 guests at a time. There is a one-week minimum stay.

You might get lucky and find a space at historic **(¢ Moose Head Ranch** (26 miles north of Jackson, 307/733-3141 in summer or 850/877-1431 Oct.–May, www.mooseheadranch.com). This family ranch has room for 44 guests and receives so many repeat customers that it's almost always booked up. New guests should call for reservations in October for the following summer, but cancellations occasionally occur, even in midsummer. The 120-acre ranch is entirely surrounded by Grand Teton National Park and features modern log cabins, horseback riding, private trout ponds, fly-fishing lessons, and gourmet meals. There's a five-night minimum stay, and all-inclusive rates are $5,300 per week for two people. The ranch is open June–mid-August.

Buffalo Valley Ranches

A longtime favorite—it began taking guests in the 1920s—is **Turpin Meadow Ranch** (307/543-2496 or 800/743-2496, www.turpinmeadowranch.com). The ranch's Buffalo Valley location provides impressive Teton vistas, along with all of the traditional ranch activities: horseback riding, cookouts, fly-fishing, day trips to Yellowstone, and pack trips. Guests stay in modern cabins; summertime all-inclusive weekly rates are $2,800–3,800 for two people. The ranch is open May–October and December–March, and is a favorite snowmobiling spot in winter. Call for winter details and rates.

A classic family summer destination, **Heart Six Ranch** (307/543-2477 or 888/543-2477, www.heartsix.com) is in the heart of Buffalo Valley, 12 miles east of Moran Junction and 43 miles northeast of Jackson. Horseback rides are a star attraction, along with kids' programs, day trips to Yellowstone National Park and the Jackson Hole rodeo, and a range of evening activities including cookouts, nature programs, and Western music. Or, you can just relax in the hot tub while kids play in the outdoor pool. All-inclusive weekly rates are $4,000 for two people. The ranch takes in up to 50 guests at a time and is open year-round. Only weekly stays are available June–August, but at other times of the year the ranch offers nightly lodging ($75–250 d). This is a favorite base for snowmobilers mid-December–March.

Gros Ventre Ranches

Looking for a peaceful place to really relax? Twenty miles up a dirt road in undeveloped Gros Ventre Valley (30 miles northeast of Jackson), **Goosewing Ranch** (307/733-5251 or 888/733-5251, www.goosewingranch.com) is one of the most remote guest ranches in Jackson Hole. The well-appointed modern log cabins have fireplaces, private baths, and decks. Guests can use the outdoor hot tub all year

and the outdoor heated pool in the summer. Popular summertime activities include horseback excursions, fly-fishing, mountain-biking, hiking, and children's programs. All-inclusive weekly midsummer rates are $2,600 for two people. There's a three-night minimum stay, and the ranch accommodates a maximum of 30 guests. When winter arrives, the ranch becomes a favorite destination for snowmobiling, with a variety of packages available.

Situated up undiscovered Gros Ventre River Valley (15 miles northeast of Jackson near Slide Lake), **Gros Ventre River Ranch** (307/733-4138, www.grosventreriverranch.com, May–Oct.) is a small ranch with accommodations for up to 45 guests in modern log cabins and a homestead house and is known for its delicious meals. The main activities are horseback riding, world-class fly-fishing, cookouts, canoeing, and mountain-biking. The lodge has a pool table, table tennis, and large-screen television. Weekly all-inclusive rates are $3,370 for two people.

Along the rolling Gros Ventre River, **Red Rock Ranch** (307/733-6288, www.theredrockranch.com, June–mid-Sept.) faces spectacular orange-red badlands. The ranch is 32 miles northeast of Jackson, and the quiet location and drop-dead-gorgeous scenery are reason enough to stay here. Guests settle into comfortable log cabins with woodstoves, and take part in horseback riding, cookouts, and other activities. The ranch also features kids' programs, stocked fishing ponds, a large swimming pool, and a hot tub. There's space for a maximum of 30 guests, and a six-night minimum stay is required. All-inclusive rates are $3,700 for two adults for six nights.

Camping

Grand Teton National Park has five camp-grounds; all are $20 (half-price if you have an **Interagency Senior Pass** or **Interagency Access Pass**). These are available on a first-come, first-served basis with **no reservations** (except group sites). By mid-afternoon in the peak summer season most park campgrounds may be full, so get there early; Gros Ventre Campground almost never fills. The maximum stay is seven days at Jenny Lake or 14 days at other campgrounds. Camping and overnight parking are not allowed along roadsides, over-looks, or parking areas within the park. Off-the-road camping is restricted to specific sites and requires a special permit.

Grand Teton rangers lead popular evening **campfire programs** at all five campgrounds throughout the summer. All campgrounds have running water but no utility hookups. **Showers and a coin laundry** are available at Colter Bay Village. Several special **hiker/biker campsites** are at Jenny Lake and Colter Bay. Group sites can be found at Colter Bay and Gros Ventre campgrounds, but reservations are required.

All Grand Teton National Park camp-grounds are closed in winter, but limited tent camping and RV parking ($5; restrooms and water but no hookups) are available at the Colter Bay Visitor Center parking lot. Get re-corded park campground and lodging informa-tion at 307/739-3603, or find additional details online (www.nps.gov/grte).

Jenny Lake Campground
First to fill is always Jenny Lake Campground, with 49 tent sites (no RVs) near this wonder-fully scenic lake in the heart of the park. The campground is open mid-May–September and usually fills by 9 A.M. in midsummer. Not far away is a little general store, plus Jenny Lake Lodge with gourmet meals. The camp-ground has 10 walk-in sites ($8) for hikers and bikers.

Signal Mountain Campground
On the south shore of Jackson Lake, Signal Mountain Campground has 86 sites, a trailer dumping station, and room for RVs up to 30 feet long. It frequently fills by noon in midsum-mer and is open early May–mid-October. The campground is near Signal Mountain Lodge, which has a restaurant and general store. It's 32 miles from Jackson.

Colter Bay Campground
On the east side of Jackson Lake, Colter Bay Campground is one of the largest in the park, with 350 tent/RV, group, and walk-in sites, a dump station, and nearby coin-operated showers and laundry facilities. Also close by are the Colter Bay Visitor Center, a general store, a pair of eateries, and rustic cabins for rent. Leeks Marina, with a popular pizzeria, and Jackson Lake Lodge are just a few miles down the road. Colter Bay Campground is open late May–late September and typically fills by mid-afternoon in summer. The camp-ground has nine walk-in sites ($5) for hikers and bikers, and group sites can be reserved by calling 800/628-9988.

Lizard Creek Campground
This campground has 60 quiet campsites on the north end of Jackson Lake and is open early June–early September. These sites rarely fill, and RVs must be less than 30 feet. The nearest food and supplies are in Flagg Ranch or Colter Bay, both approximately eight miles away.

Gros Ventre Campground
With over 350 sites, Gros Ventre Campground is both the largest campground in the park and the last to fill (if at all). The campground is on the southern edge of the park along the Gros Ventre River near Kelly and is 10 miles from Jackson. It's open early May–early October and has a dump station and five group sites. There's a great little espresso shop in nearby Kelly, but

GRAND TETON

the nearest stores or restaurants are in Jackson or Moose. Group sites can be reserved by calling 800/628-9988.

CAMPING OPTIONS

In addition to the five NPS campgrounds, park concessioners maintain two seasonal RV parks with full hookups, showers, washers, and driers. **Flagg Ranch Resort** (307/543-2861 or 800/443-2311, www.flaggranch.com, late May–late Sept.) in Rockefeller Parkway has 100 pull-through RV sites with full hookups for $60, and 75 tent sites for $35. Reservations are highly recommended.

On the south shore of Jackson Lake is **Colter Bay RV Park** (307/543-3100 or 800/628-9988, www.gtlc.com, $55 RVs, late May–late Sept.). No tent spaces here, but evening nature programs are offered in the summer.

Grand Teton Park RV Resort (307/733-1980 or 800/563-6469, www.yellowstonerv.com, open year-round) is six miles east of the park along Highway 26/287. There are fine views of the Tetons, and facilities include a heated seasonal pool and hot tub, recreation room, and grocery store. The cost is $57 d for RVs with hookups, $40 d for tents. Simple camping cabins go for $72–79 d.

Food

Though more limited than your choices in nearby Jackson, Grand Teton National Park has a good variety of dining options, from the all-you-can-eat outdoor affairs at Dornan's to memorable Jenny Lake Lodge meals. Most places do not require reservations, though you may need to wait for a table on a busy summer evening.

RESTAURANTS AND LOUNGES
Moose

An old favorite with an egalitarian setting—look for the tepees—is **Dornan's Chuck Wagon** (307/733-2415 ext. 203, www.dornans.com, mid-June–mid-Sept.), offering reasonable meals every summer since 1948. Breakfasts (daily 7–11 A.M., $10) include pancakes, biscuits and gravy, and French toast. Sandwiches are the main lunch attraction (daily noon–3 P.M., $10), and dinners (daily 5–9 P.M., $17) include beef stew, mashed potatoes, beans, short ribs, bread, cobbler, and a big outdoor salad bar; add a few bucks for trout, steak, or BBQ chicken. Friday and Saturday dinners ($25) star prime rib or New York steak.

Across the street—and open all year—is Dornan's 【 **Dornan's Pizza and Pasta Co.** (307/733-2415 ext. 204, daily

11:30 A.M.–9:30 P.M. mid-June–mid-Sept., reduced winter hours, closed Apr. and Nov.), offering a wide range of homemade pizzas ($16), sandwiches (including a tasty chicken salad croissant for $9), calzones, salads, and pastas. Try the Teewinot pizza with Canadian bacon, artichoke hearts, sun-dried tomatoes, and feta cheese. Dining is available on the side patio or—more dramatically—on the big upstairs deck, where you can watch the rafts float past topped by can't-beat-the-view Teton vistas. (Because of its height, the deck is for adults only.) **Spur Bar** serves beer on draught and mixed drinks, along with monthly wine tastings ($10 for 10 wines) the first Sunday of each month. Monday-evening **Hootenannies** are a fun addition in winter; these move outside to the adjacent Chuck Wagon Restaurant when summer arrives. Musicians perform once or twice a month, and there's free Wi-Fi. Check out the plank on the wall next to the entrance. In 1944, local resident Farney Cole used the board to defend himself from a bear attack. He survived, as did the bear.

Jenny Lake

Marvelous old 【 **Jenny Lake Lodge** (307/543-3300 or 800/628-9988, www.gtlc.com, daily 7:30–9 A.M., noon–1:15 P.M., and

6–8:45 P.M. late May–mid-Oct.) has impeccable service, windows that face the Tetons, and a cozy setting. Five-course dinners are the featured attractions, and the wine list is extensive. Lunch is à la carte ($10–13), but breakfast and dinner are fixed price (and pricey: $72 for a five-course dinner, $22 for breakfast). This is a dress-up place, so a jacket and slacks are recommended for dinner. Reservations should be made a day or more in advance, since lodge guests have priority.

Jackson Lake

Several good dining options exist at Jackson Lake Lodge (307/543-3100 or 800/628-9988, www.gtlc.com, mid-May–Oct.), including the famed **◖ Mural Room** (daily 7–9:30 A.M., 11:30 A.M.–1:30 P.M., and 5:30–9 P.M., $18–38 dinner entrées) with its 60-foot windows fronting the Tetons. It's hard to imagine a more extraordinary setting for dinner! The restaurant serves three meals a day, including an impressive buffet breakfast with fresh waffles ($15 adults, $9 kids). Dinner reservations are advised for the Mural Room (call 307/543-3463 ext. 3463).

Across the lobby from the Mural Room is **Blue Heron Lounge** (daily 11 A.M.–midnight), offering equally impressive views. Musicians provide evening accompaniment for your cocktails.

Find casual meals and soda fountain specials at **Pioneer Grill** (daily 6 A.M.–10:30 P.M.) and **Pool Snack Bar,** next to the large outdoor swimming pool. A better bet is the **Pool BBQ** (daily 6–8 P.M. June–Aug., $24 adults, $12 kids), serving all-you-can-eat dinner buffets featuring hamburgers, brisket, carnitas, barbecue chicken, fruit cobbler, watermelon, cornbread, corn on the cob, coleslaw, and other Western grub. Live music nightly; reservations are recommended (call 307/543-3463 ext. 3463).

Signal Mountain Lodge (307/543-2831 or 800/672-6012, www.signalmountainlodge. com) houses **Trapper Grill** (daily 7 A.M.–10 P.M. early May–mid-Sept., till 9 P.M. late Sept.–Oct., $8–15), with casual fare and a popular

deck for alfresco dining. Burgers, salads, sandwiches, soup, elk meatloaf, and more are on the menu—but lots of folks just opt for a gigantic plate of their famous nachos ($15). Step into Deadman's Bar for legendary blackberry margaritas. Also here is the **Peaks Dining Room** (daily 5:30–10 P.M. early May–mid-Sept., till 9 P.M. late Sept.–Oct., $20–32), with an upscale menu and spectacular vistas of the Tetons. Reservations are not accepted. Deadman's Bar also serves a late-night pub menu.

Leek's Pizzeria (307/543-2494, www. signalmountainlodge.com, daily 11 A.M.–10 P.M., $9–23) is a very popular pizzeria that also serves calzones, sandwiches, salads, and beer on tap. Kids love the specialty-flavor ice creams. Open early May–mid-October.

Colter Bay

Colter Bay Village has two dining choices. The **Ranch House** (daily 6:30–10:30 A.M., 11:30 A.M.–1:30 P.M., and 5:30–9 P.M. May–Sept., $16–22) offers breakfast buffets, lunch sandwiches, and steaks, trout, chicken, and pasta for dinner. Find lighter fare at **John Colter Café Court** (daily 11 A.M.–10 P.M. June–Sept., $5–19), including chicken, burritos, sandwiches, salads, and snacks.

Rockefeller Memorial Parkway

The main lodge at **Flagg Ranch Resort** (307/543-2861 or 800/443-2311, www.flag-granch.com) houses Bear's Den Restaurant, serving three meals a day. Also here are a saloon and grocery store.

Buffalo Valley and Gros Ventre

Buffalo Valley Café (307/543-2062 or 888/543-2477, www.buffalovalleyranch.com, daily 7 A.M.–9 P.M. mid-May–Labor Day) is outside the park in this quaint valley three miles east of Moran Junction. The seasonal café serves breakfast, lunch, and dinner and is popular with campers, folks staying in nearby cabins, and locals who drive up from Jackson. Steaks are on the menu, but the buffalo burgers ($10) are the real attraction. Sit on the screened deck for Teton backdrops with your meal.

Kelly on the Gros Ventre (307/732-9837, www.facebook.com, 7 A.M.–6 P.M. daily in summer, 7 A.M.–3 P.M. Tues.–Sat. in winter, $5–10) serves sandwiches, box lunches, and espresso. There's also free Wi-Fi.

GROCERIES AND SUPPLIES

The best in-the-park store is **Dornan's Trading Post** (307/733-2415, www.dornans.com, open year-round), near park headquarters in Moose. The store is stocked with groceries, tasty deli sandwiches ($7), fresh baked goods, and camping supplies. The cart out front has espresso, and next door is **Dornan's Wine Shoppe,** with one of the biggest selections of fine wine and beer in Jackson Hole, including more than 1,700 different wines. Wine tastings take place here on the first Sunday of the month, October–June. Other nearby Dornan's operations include Moose Pizza and Pasta Co., the Chuck Wagon, and a gift shop. In winter, the gift shop rents cross-country skis, snowshoes, and pull-behind sleds.

Colter Bay General Store (307/543-3100) has a good choice of groceries and supplies, while convenience stores operate at Signal Mountain, Flagg Ranch Resort, and Jenny Lake. The store at Flagg Ranch Resort is open in both summer and winter seasons (mid-May–mid-Oct. and mid-Dec.–mid-Mar.). All of the others are open only in summer.

Information and Services

INFORMATION
Support Organizations

The **Grand Teton Association** (307/739-3403, www.grandtetonpark.org) operates bookstores in park visitor centers and the store at Menor's Ferry. It also has an online service for Grand Teton books and other publications. All profits finance new publications or assist the Park Service in its research and interpretive programs.

The nonprofit **Grand Teton National Park Foundation** (307/739-0629, www.gtnpf.org) provides support for park projects (including the new visitor center at Moose) that would not otherwise be funded, and all contributions are tax-deductible.

Kids in the Park

It's hard to imagine a more kid-friendly park than Grand Teton. Two marvelous new visitor centers—Craig Thomas Discovery and Visitor Center and Laurance S. Rockefeller Preserve Center—have a variety of fascinating exhibits, including the yes-you-can-touch variety. River rafting trips and horseback rides are fun for older kids, and everyone loves the boat rides across Jenny Lake to Inspiration Point. Park restaurants all have kid-friendly meals and Jackson Lake Lodge offers the perfect combo: a fun outdoor pool with a popular snack bar. If you have older kids (and a bike trailer), rent a bike and head out the back roads around Mormon Row and Kelly.

All sorts of ranger-led programs are listed in the park paper, including many family options. Grand Teton's **Junior Ranger** program is filled with educational activities for kids. It takes an hour or so, and is a great way to introduce children to the natural world. The "graduation" ceremonies are fun too. One of the joys of Grand Teton is its proximity to Jackson, providing all sorts of in-town options if your kids are getting bored, from the speedy alpine slide at Snow King to the noisy shoot-out on Town Square.

Ranger Programs

Check your copy of the *Teewinot* for details on several dozen options for talks, hikes, junior ranger classes, boat cruises, campfire programs, and historical lectures. You might learn about the legacy of Laurance Rockefeller at one talk, or how teepees were used at another. There's always something of interest, and many of these free programs are geared to families.

SERVICES

Gas is available year-round at Dornan's in Moose, summer and winter at Flagg Ranch Resort, and summer only at Colter Bay Village, Signal Mountain Lodge, and Jackson Lake Lodge. You'll find gift shops at Signal Mountain, Flagg Ranch Resort, Jackson Lake Lodge, Moose, and Colter Bay. Year-round **post offices** are in Moran, Moose, and Kelly. Get cash from **ATMs** at Dornan's in Moose, Jackson Lake Lodge, Colter Bay Village, Flagg Ranch Resort, and Signal Mountain Lodge.

Outdoor Gear

The little settlement of Moose has several businesses in addition to the Dornan's shops and eateries. **Adventure Sports** (307/733-3307, www.dornans.com) rents mountain bikes, canoes, and kayaks. Next door is **Moosely Seconds** (307/739-1801, www.skinnyskis.com, daily late May–Sept.), with deals on outdoor clothing and climbing gear. The shop also rents ice axes, crampons, rock shoes, trekking poles, approach shoes, plastic boots, and snowshoes. **Snake River Angler** (307/733-3699, www.snakeriverangler.com) sells and rents fishing supplies and camping equipment.

Medical

Get emergency medical assistance at the **Grand Teton Medical Clinic** (307/543-2514, daily 10 a.m.–6 p.m. May–Oct.) near the Chevron station at Jackson Lake Lodge. The nearest hospital is **St. John's Medical Center** in Jackson.

Pets

Dogs are allowed in Grand Teton National Park, but need to be on a six-foot or less leash. They are not permitted inside visitor centers or other facilities.

GRAND TETON

JACKSON HOLE

One of the most-visited slices of wild country in North America, Jackson Hole attracts well over three million travelers each year. They come here for a multitude of reasons: to camp under the stars in Grand Teton National Park, to play and shop in the New West town of Jackson, to hike flower-bedecked trails up forested valleys, to ride sleighs among thousands of elk, to raft down the Snake River, to ski or snowboard at one of three local resorts, or to simply stand in wonderment as the sun colors the sky behind the mountains. Many continue north to Yellowstone National Park, another place on everyone's must-see list. Drive north from Jackson toward Yellowstone and you'll quickly discover the biggest reason so many people are attracted to this place—its beauty. The Tetons act as a magnet, drawing your eyes away from the road and forcing you to stop and absorb some of their majesty. Welcome to one of the world's great wonderlands.

In the lingo of the mountain men, a "hole" was a large valley ringed by mountain ranges, and each was named for the trapper who based himself there. Jackson Hole, on Wyoming's far western border, is justifiably the most famous of all these intermountain valleys. Although Jackson Hole reaches an impressive 50 miles north to south and up to 16 miles across, the magnificent range of mountains to the west is what defines this valley. Shoshone Indians who wandered through this country called the peaks Teewinot (Many Pinnacles); later explorers would use such labels as Shark's Teeth or Pilot Knobs. But lonely French-Canadian trappers arriving in the early 1800s provided the

HIGHLIGHTS

◖ Visitor Center: Officially called the Jackson Hole & Greater Yellowstone Visitor Center, this large facility provides a one-stop introduction to the region, with information on the town, national forests, and the Elk Refuge (page 162).

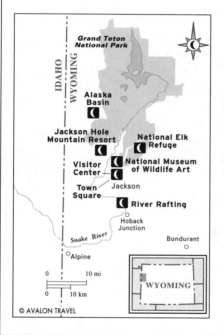

◖ Town Square: Where else could you mix three million tourists, hundreds of elk antlers arranged in arches, and a faux shoot-out on summer evenings (page 162)?

◖ National Museum of Wildlife Art: One of Wyoming's top museums, with works by all the American masters, from Alfred Jacob Miller to Robert Bateman (page 164).

◖ National Elk Refuge: Winter is the peak season, with thousands of elk and horse-drawn sleighs in a scene straight out of Currier and Ives (page 166).

◖ River Rafting: Running the Snake River is a major summertime attraction, with many companies providing the raft and guide for a whitewater rock-and-roll or a gentle float trip past the Tetons (page 170).

◖ Jackson Hole Mountain Resort: This famous ski area keeps on trucking with all sorts of winter and summer activities – including an all-summer classical music festival, pop-jet fountains, and the tram up Rendezvous Mountain (page 181).

◖ Alaska Basin: This one's for backpackers, with access from Driggs, Idaho to the heart of the Teton Range. It's a gorgeous alpine valley, where high trails lead into Grand Teton National Park (page 229).

LOOK FOR ◖ TO FIND RECOMMENDED SIGHTS, ACTIVITIES, DINING, AND LODGING.

JACKSON HOLE

name that stuck: les Trois Tetons (literally, the Three Breasts).

The valley—originally called Jackson's Hole—was named for likable trapper David E. Jackson, one of the men who helped establish the Rocky Mountain Fur Company. When Jackson and his partners sold out in 1830, they realized a profit of more than $50,000. Jackson's presence remains in the names of both Jackson Hole and Jackson Lake. Eventually, more polite folks began calling the valley Jackson Hole in an attempt to end the ribald stories associated

with the name Jackson's Hole. (It's easy to imagine the jokes, with both Jackson's Hole and the Tetons in the same place.) In 1991, a group calling itself the Committee to Restore Decency to Our National Parks created quite a stir by suggesting that Grand Teton National Park be renamed. A letter sent to the Park Service and various members of Congress noted: "Though a great many Americans may be oblivious to this vulgarity, hundreds of millions of French people around the world are not! How embarrassing that these spectacular, majestic mountains are reduced to a dirty joke overseas." After a flurry of letters in response, the hoax was revealed; it was a prank by staff members of *Spy* magazine.

PLANNING YOUR TIME

Wyoming's preeminent tourist town, Jackson is both an important access point for Yellowstone and Grand Teton National Parks and a destination in its own right. Visitors should probably plan on at least two days, but you could easily spend a couple of weeks just having fun in Jackson Hole (if your credit card doesn't get maxed out). Jackson has two peak seasons: summer, when families and international travelers stay here as part of a Yellowstone trip, and winter, when skiing and snowboarding are the big draws.

Prior to your trip, contact the Jackson Hole Chamber of Commerce (307/733-3316, www. jacksonholechamber.com) for brochures, or browse their website for links to hundreds of

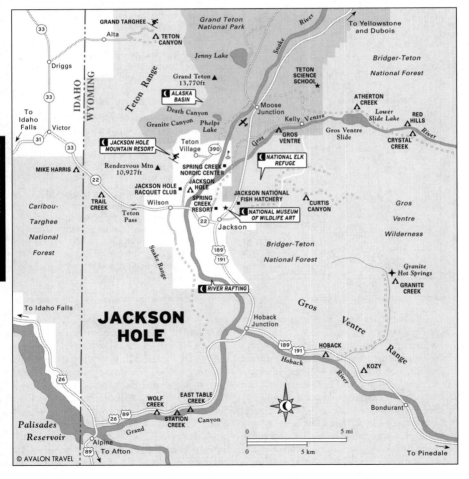

local businesses. Once in town, be sure to drop by the **Jackson Hole & Greater Yellowstone Visitor Center** (532 N. Cache Dr., 307/733-3316, www.jacksonholechamber.com, open daily) for publications, maps, and detailed area information.

Town Square in the heart of Jackson is shady and set with picturesque elk-antler arches on the corners, and a nearby street corner closes for entertaining shoot-outs most summer evenings. Acclaimed as one of the top artistic centers in the nation, Jackson has more than 30 **art galleries,** and the impressive **National Museum of Wildlife Art** perches along a hillside just north of town.

Visitors are drawn to the **National Elk Refuge** for its wintertime sleigh rides among the elk. Skiers and snowboarders enjoy the slopes at famous **Jackson Hole Mountain Resort,** smaller **Snow King Resort,** or on the deep powder of **Grand Targhee Resort,** a morning bus ride away on the west side of the Tetons. Jackson's restaurants are easily the finest (and most expensive) in Wyoming, and lodging varies from cozy old log units to ultra-luxurious hotels. In summer, the **Snake River** is a major center for whitewater rafting and fly-fishing, while mountain bikers and hikers head out on miles of paths. Horseback rides and chuck-wagon cookouts are other summertime favorites, as are the twice-weekly Jackson Hole rodeos. At Teton Village, visitors enjoy classical music performances during the Grand Teton Music Festival in July and August. More adventurous visitors head out on extended backcountry trips into Grand Teton National Park and national forest lands, including beautiful **Alaska Basin** on the west side of the Tetons.

Jackson

The town of Jackson (pop. 9,000) lies near the southern end of Jackson Hole, hemmed in on three sides by Snow King Mountain, the Gros Ventre Range, and East Gros Ventre Butte. At 6,200 feet in elevation, Jackson experiences cold, snowy winters, wet springs, delightfully warm and sunny summers, and crisp, color-filled falls. Jackson is unlike any other place in Wyoming; on a typical summer day more than 35,000 tourists flood the town. Sit on a bench in Town Square on a summer day and you're likely to see cars from every state in the country. Tourists dart in and out of the many gift shops, art galleries, fine restaurants, Western-style saloons, and trendy boutiques. The cowboy hats all look as if the price tags just came off.

In other parts of Wyoming, Jackson is viewed with a mixture of awe and disdain—awe over its gorgeous scenery, but disdain that Jackson is not a "real" town, just a false front put up to sell things to outsiders. Yes, Jackson is almost wholly dependent on the almighty tourist dollar, but as a result it enjoys a cultural richness lacking in other parts of the state. Besides, if you don't like all the commercial foolishness, it's easy to escape to a campsite or remote trail in the wonderful countryside of nearby Grand Teton National Park or Bridger-Teton National Forest.

Keep your eyes open around Jackson and you're likely to see well-known residents such as Hollywood stars Harrison Ford and Calista Flockhart, Danny DeVito and Rhea Perlman, Connie Stevens, and Sandra Bullock, along with former Secretary of the Interior James Watt (who resigned in disgrace in 1983), attorney Gerald Spence (of Karen Silkwood and Imelda Marcos notoriety), Yvon Chouinard (mountaineer and founder of Patagonia), industrial heir Charles DuPont, and members of the extended Rockefeller family. Former Vice President Dick Cheney has a luxury home in Teton Pines and is a frequent visitor, which explains all of the Blackhawk helicopters, Secret Service agents, and Suburbans with dark-tinted windows.

JACKSON HOLE

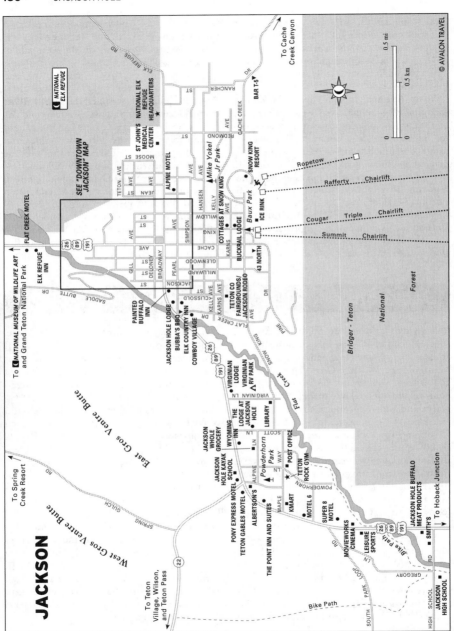

JACKSON

West Gros Ventre Butte

East Gros Ventre Butte

To Spring
Creek Resort

To Teton
Village, Wilson,
and Teton Pass

To Teton, Wilson, and Teton Pass

SPRING GULCH RD

To ◀ NATIONAL MUSEUM OF WILDLIFE ART
and Grand Teton National Park

SADDLE BUTTE DR

FLAT CREEK MOTEL
ELK REFUGE INN

NATIONAL
ELK REFUGE

ELK REFUGE RD

SEE "DOWNTOWN JACKSON" MAP

ST JOHN'S MEDICAL CENTER
NATIONAL ELK REFUGE HEADQUARTERS

MOOSE ST
TETON AVE
JEAN ST
AVE
AVE
AVE
ALPINE MOTEL
HANSEN AVE
KELLY AVE
WILLOW ST
KING ST
CACHE
GLENWOOD
MILLWARD
JACKSON
PEARL ST
DELONEY AVE
GILL AVE
BROADWAY
ST
ST
ST
AVE
SIMPSON AVE

26 89 191

PAINTED BUFFALO INN
JACKSON HOLE LODGE
BUBBA'S BBQ
ELK COUNTRY INN
COWBOY VILLAGE

FLAT CREEK DR
KARNS AVE
CLISSOLD AVE

TETON CO FAIRGROUNDS/ JACKSON RODEO

VIRGINIAN LODGE
VIRGINIAN RV PARK
VIRGINIAN LN

THE LODGE AT JACKSON HOLE
LIBRARY

JACKSON WHOLE GROCERY
WYOMING INN

JACKSON HOLE KAYAK SCHOOL

SNOW KING RD

FLAT Creek

SCOTT LN
SCOTT

Powderhorn
Park

POST OFFICE

TETON ROCK GYM

POWDERHORN LN

ALPINE LN

MAPLE WAY

PONY EXPRESS MOTEL
TETON GABLES MOTEL
ALBERTSON'S

THE POINT INN AND SUITES

KMART
MOTEL 6
SUPER 8 MOTEL

MOVIEWORKS CINEMA
LEISURE SPORTS
SMITH'S

JACKSON HOLE BUFFALO MEAT PRODUCTS

To Hoback Junction

26 89 191

Bike Path

GREGORY

HIGH SCHOOL RD
SOUTH PARK LOOP RD

JACKSON HIGH SCHOOL

Bike Path

22

ST JOHN'S MEDICAL CENTER

Mike Yokel Jr Park

Jr Park
REDMOND AVE
RANCHER ST
RANCHER DR

CACHE CREEK DR

BAR T-5 ▶

To Cache
Creek Canyon

SNOW KING RESORT
Baux Park
ICE RINK

COTTAGES AT SNOW KING
BUCKRAIL LODGE
43 NORTH

Ropetow
Rafferty   Chairlift
Cougar   Triple   Chairlift
Summit   Chairlift

PINE DR

Bridger - Teton

National   Forest

0.5 mi
0.5 km

© AVALON TRAVEL

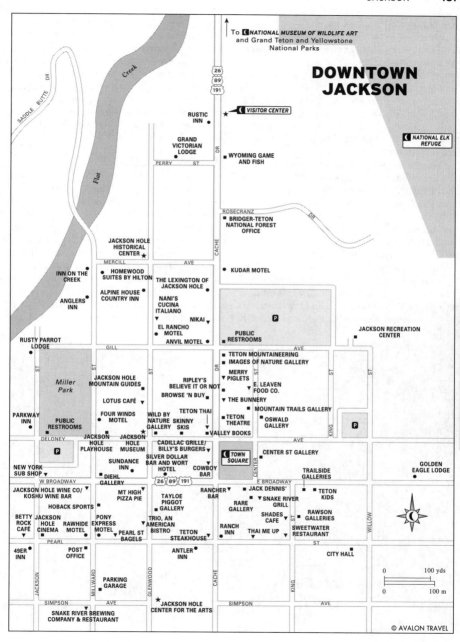

To **◖** *NATIONAL MUSEUM OF WILDLIFE ART*
and Grand Teton and Yellowstone
National Parks

DOWNTOWN JACKSON

◖ *VISITOR CENTER*

◖ NATIONAL ELK REFUGE

SADDLE BUTTE DR

Creek

26 89 191

RUSTIC INN

GRAND VICTORIAN LODGE

PERRY ST

WYOMING GAME AND FISH

Flat

CACHE AVE

ROSECRANZ

DR

BRIDGER-TETON NATIONAL FOREST OFFICE

JACKSON HOLE HISTORICAL CENTER ★

MERCILL AVE

KUDAR MOTEL

INN ON THE CREEK

HOMEWOOD SUITES BY HILTON

THE LEXINGTON OF JACKSON HOLE

ALPINE HOUSE COUNTRY INN

NANI'S CUCINA ITALIANO

NIKAI

EL RANCHO MOTEL

ANVIL MOTEL

ANGLERS INN

P

PUBLIC RESTROOMS

JACKSON RECREATION CENTER

RUSTY PARROT LODGE

GILL AVE

Miller Park

JACKSON HOLE MOUNTAIN GUIDES

LOTUS CAFÉ

FOUR WINDS MOTEL

RIPLEY'S BELIEVE IT OR NOT

BROWSE 'N BUY

WILD BY NATURE GALLERY

TETON THAI

SKINNY SKIS

TETON MOUNTAINEERING

IMAGES OF NATURE GALLERY

MERRY PIGLETS

E. LEAVEN FOOD CO.

THE BUNNERY

MOUNTAIN TRAILS GALLERY

TETON THEATRE

OSWALD GALLERY

KING ST

P

PARKWAY INN

PUBLIC RESTROOMS

VALLEY BOOKS

DELONEY AVE

JACKSON HOLE PLAYHOUSE

JACKSON HOLE MUSEUM

P

CADILLAC GRILLE/ BILLY'S BURGERS

SILVER DOLLAR BAR AND WORT HOTEL

CENTER ST GALLERY

◖ TOWN SQUARE

NEW YORK SUB SHOP

SUNDANCE INN

COWBOY BAR

TRAILSIDE GALLERIES

GOLDEN EAGLE LODGE

DIEHL GALLERY

W BROADWAY

26 89 191

E BROADWAY

JACKSON HOLE WINE CO/ KOSHU WINE BAR

MT HIGH PIZZA PIE

TAYLOE PIGGOT GALLERY

RANCHER BAR

JACK DENNIS'

TETON KIDS

HOBACK SPORTS

RARE GALLERY

SNAKE RIVER GRILL

BETTY ROCK CAFÉ

JACKSON HOLE CINEMA

RAWHIDE MOTEL

PONY EXPRESS MOTEL

PEARL ST BAGELS

TRIO, AN AMERICAN BISTRO

TETON STEAKHOUSE

SHADES CAFÉ

RAWSON GALLERIES

RANCH INN

THAI ME UP

SWEETWATER RESTAURANT

WILLOW ST

PEARL ST

49ER INN

POST OFFICE

ANTLER INN

CITY HALL

JACKSON

MILLWARD

PARKING GARAGE

GLENWOOD

CACHE

KING

0   100 yds

0   100 m

SIMPSON AVE

★ JACKSON HOLE CENTER FOR THE ARTS

SIMPSON AVE

SNAKE RIVER BREWING COMPANY & RESTAURANT

© AVALON TRAVEL

JACKSON HOLE

◖ VISITOR CENTER

Anyone new to Jackson Hole should be sure to visit the spacious **Jackson Hole and Greater Yellowstone Visitor Center** (532 N. Cache Dr., 307/733-3316, www.jacksonholechamber.com, daily 8 A.M.–7 P.M. late May–early Sept., 9 A.M.–5 P.M. the rest of the year) on the north side of town. (The phone is answered only on weekdays, but on weekends you can leave a message and you'll be mailed an information packet.)

The information center is a two-level, sod-roofed wooden building—jokingly called the "little prairie on the house"—with natural-history displays, a blizzard of free leaflets extolling the merits of local businesses, a gift shop selling regional books and maps, and a covered upstairs deck overlooking the National Elk Refuge. Ducks and trumpeter swans are visible on the marsh in the summer, and elk can be seen in the winter. Downstairs, the "bear cave" is a big kid draw. The information center is staffed by the Jackson Hole Chamber of Commerce, along with Fish and Wildlife Service, Forest Service, and other agency personnel in the summer. Free nature and history talks are generally given several times a week during the summer, or you can watch a video about the refuge.

In addition to the main information center, you'll find brochure racks at the airport, the stagecoach stop on Town Square, next to the public restrooms at Cache and Gill, and the Mangy Moose in Teton Village.

◖ TOWN SQUARE

In 1932, the local Rotary Club planted trees in the center of Jackson, adding four picturesque arches made from hundreds of elk antlers in the 1950s and 1960s. Today the trees offer summertime shade, and at any time of day or night you'll find visitors admiring or posing for photos in front of the arches that mark the corners of Town Square. During winter, the snow-covered arches and trees are draped with lights, giving the square a festive atmosphere. Surrounded by dozens of boardwalk-fronted galleries, bars, restaurants, factory outlets, and

stagecoach at Town Square, downtown Jackson

© KATHY ERICKSON /WILD ABOUT LIFE PHOTOGRAPHY

JACKSON HOLE IN 1835

This Valley is called "Jackson Hole" it is generally from 5 to 15 mls wide: the southern part where the river enters the mountain is hilly and uneven but the Northern portion is wide smooth and comparatively even the whole being covered with wild sage and Surrounded by high and rugged mountains upon whose summits the snow remains during the hottest months in Summer. The alluvial bottoms along the river and streams inter sect it thro. the valley produce a luxuriant groth of vegetation among which wild flax and a species of onion are abundant. The great altitude of this place however connected with the cold descending from the mountains at night I think would be a serious obstruction to growth of most Kinds of cultivated grains. This valley like all other parts of the country abounds with game.

Osborne Russell,
Journal of a Trapper 1834-1843

gift shops, the square is the focal point of tourist activity in Jackson.

During summer, **stagecoaches** wait to transport you on a leisurely ride around town, and each evening "cowboys" put on a free **shoot-out** for throngs of camera-happy tourists. The shoot-out starts at 6:15 P.M. Monday–Saturday nights all summer. They've been killing each other like this since 1957. With stereotypical players and questionable acting, the "mountain law" system seems in dire need of reform. Most folks love the sham; Canon and Olympus love it even more. Warning: The sound of blanks is surprisingly loud and can be frightening for small children.

ART

Artists have long been attracted by the beauty of Jackson Hole and the Tetons. Mount Moran, the 12,605-foot summit behind Jackson Lake, is named for Thomas Moran, whose watercolors helped persuade Congress to set aside Yellowstone as the first national park. The late Conrad Schwiering's paintings of the Tetons have attained international fame; one was even used on the Postal Service's Wyoming Centennial stamp in 1990. Ansel Adams's photograph of the Tetons remains etched in the American consciousness as one of the archetypal wilderness images. A copy of the image was included in the payload of the *Voyager II* spacecraft en route out of our solar system. Today many artists live or work in Jackson Hole, and locals proclaim it "Art Center of the Rockies," ranking it with New York, San Francisco, Santa Fe, and Scottsdale.

Jackson Hole Center for the Arts

If you have any doubts that Jackson Hole is an arts mecca, look no further than the modern Jackson Hole Center for the Arts (240 S. Glenwood, 307/734-8956, www.jhcenterforthearts.org). This 41,000-square-foot masterpiece has space for 15 different nonprofit arts organizations under one roof, with an amazing array of classes and workshops. Drop by to pick up a schedule of classes. Newly added in 2007, the 525-seat **Performing Arts Pavilion** is a lovely performance space. Call the box office for tickets, 307/733-4900, or find the online calendar of upcoming performances.

One of the primary tenants is the **Art Association** (307/733-6379, www.artassociation.org), offering dozens of classes and workshops year-round in everything from photography and ceramics to stained glass and woodworking. The on-site **ArtSpace Gallery** displays changing exhibitions by regional and national artists.

Dancer's Workshop (307/733-6398, www.dwjh.org) occupies much of the second floor, with dozens of classes weekly in modern, ballet, pointe, hip-hop, ballroom, jazz, country-and-western, and other dance forms. The facilities

Jackson Hole Center for the Arts

COURTESY OF CENTER FOR THE ARTS

also house Contemporary Dance Wyoming, the state's only professional dance company.

Also at the Center for the Arts, **Off Square Theatre Company** (307/733-3670, www.off-square.org) is a professional repertory company with comedies in the summer and a wide variety of productions and workshops throughout the winter.

◖ NATIONAL MUSEUM OF WILDLIFE ART

Jackson is home to the magnificent National Museum of Wildlife Art (307/733-5771 or 800/313-9553, www.wildlifeart.org), two miles north of town along U.S. Highway 26/89 and directly across from the National Elk Refuge. A monumental sculpture of five elk greets visitors at the base of the hill, and the building's Arizona sandstone exterior blends in with nearby rock outcroppings. Step inside the doors of this 51,000-square-foot museum to discover a marvelous interior. As visitors enter the main gallery, a larger-than-life bronze mountain lion crouches

above, ready to pounce. Kids will have fun in the hands-on Children's Discovery Gallery and can join hands-in-the-paint activities on Monday mornings. Adults will appreciate the artwork spread throughout a dozen galleries, along with the video theater, Rising Sage Café (tasty lunches), 200-seat auditorium, and gift shop. Cyclists and those on foot can access the museum from an underpass beneath the highway that connects with the bike path to Jackson. A sculpture garden is scheduled for completion in 2012.

The museum collection features pieces by Carl Rungius, George Catlin, Albert Bierstadt, Karl Bodmer, Alfred Jacob Miller, N. C. Wyeth, Conrad Schwiering, John Clymer, Charles Russell, Robert Bateman, and many others. Of particular interest are the reconstructed studio of John Clymer and the spacious Carl Rungius Gallery, where you'll find the most complete collection of Clymer's paintings in the nation. Also of note is the exhibit on American bison, which documents these once vastly abundant animals and their slaughter;

ART GALLERIES

More than 30 galleries crowd the center of Jackson. As the town has grown, local galleries have also evolved. You'll still find places selling ludicrously romanticized cowboy paintings and campy prints of sexy Indian maidens with windblown hair and strategically torn garments, but the town is increasingly filled with galleries that exhibit sophisticated and contemporary works.

The **Jackson Hole Gallery Association** (www.jacksonholegalleries.com) produces a helpful gallery guide; pick up one from local galleries or the visitor center. **Third Thursday Art Walks** are a monthly staple, when many galleries open for extended evening hours June–October. Tammy Christel of **Jackson Hole Art Tours** (307/690-1983, www.jacksonholearttours.com) leads informative gallery tours.

Excellent galleries with changing exhibits of modern art are **RARE Gallery** (60 E. Broadway, 2nd floor, 307/733-8726, www.raregalleryjacksonhole.com), **Diehl Gallery** (155 W. Broadway, 307/733-0905, www.diehlgallery.com), **Tayloe Piggott Gallery** (62 S. Glenwood St., 307/733-0555, www.tayloepiggottgallery.com), **Altamira Fine Art** (172 Center St., 307/739-4700, www.altamiraart.com), and **Teton Artlab** (307/690-0836, www.tetonartlab.com) inside the Center for the Arts at 240 S. Glenwood. All are well worth a visit, as is **Wild Hands** (265 W. Pearl Ave., 307/733-4619, www.wildhands.com), with functional and playful art and pottery.

In a quiet spot just a block off Town Square, the two-level **Trailside Galleries** (130 E. Broadway, 307/733-3186, www.trailsidegalleries.com) displays everything from grandiose Western works to impressionist and wildlife art. Other traditionalist galleries worth a look are **Mountain Trails Gallery** (150 N. Center St.,

307/734-8150, www.mtntrails.net), **Legacy Gallery** (75 N. Cache, 307/733-2353, www.legacygallery.com), **Joanne Hennes Gallery** (5850 N. Larkspur Dr., 307/733-2593, www.joannehennes.com), and **Wilcox Gallery** (165 Center St., 307/733-3950, www.wilcoxgallery.com).

Rawson Galleries (50 King St., 307/733-7306) features traditional watercolors, displayed in a crowded space; open July–October.

For a very different type of art, visit **By Nature Gallery** (86 E. Broadway, 307/200-6060, www.bynaturegallery.com), where unique furnishings have been created from fossilized fish, minerals, and more.

PHOTO GALLERIES

Many nationally known photographers live or work in Jackson Hole. Tom Mangelsen displays his outstanding wildlife and landscape photos at **Images of Nature Gallery** (170 N. Cache Dr., 307/733-9752 or 888/238-0177, www.mangelsen.com) and has galleries at 15 other locations around the country.

Inside **Wild by Nature Gallery** (95 W. Deloney, 307/733-8877 or 888/494-5329, www.wildbynature.com), photographer Henry H. Holdsworth shows strikingly beautiful wildlife and nature imagery.

In Gaslight Alley at 125 North Cache, **Brookover Gallery** (307/733-3988, www.brookovergallery.com) exhibits grandiose landscapes by photographer David Brookover, who works with an 8x10 camera.

At **Oswald Gallery** (165 N. Center St., 888/898-0077, www.oswaldgallery.com) the emphasis is on contemporary fine-art photography. There's always something visually challenging; this isn't the place to look for pretty nature scenes.

the museum's bison collection is the largest in the world. Six galleries showcase photography, painting, and other art that changes throughout the year. Spotting scopes in the cozy members' lounge (open to the public) are useful for watching residents of the adjacent National Elk Refuge.

Museum admission is $12 adults, $10 seniors, $6 ages 5–18; free for kids under five. Hours are daily 9 A.M.–5 P.M. in summer, and 9 A.M.–5 P.M. Monday–Saturday and 11 A.M.–5 P.M. Sunday mid-October–April. The museum is closed Christmas, Thanksgiving, and Columbus Day. Free audio tours detail works in the permanent collection, and you can watch films on wildlife.

Wildlife films, slide lectures, talks, concerts, kids' programs, and other activities take place throughout the year in the auditorium and galleries; pick up a schedule of upcoming events at the entrance desk or visit the museum website. One of the most popular events, **Western Visions,** comes in late September. It includes jewelry, photography, and the Miniature Show & Sale, with small works by 100 of the country's leading artists. A winter highlight is **Art After Hours/ Tapas Tuesdays** (5–9 P.M. Tues., Dec.–Mar.), when the museum opens for après-ski programs combined with tapas served by Rising Sage Café.

HISTORICAL MUSEUMS

The small **Jackson Hole Museum** (105 N. Glenwood, 307/733-2414, www.jacksonhole-history.org, noon–5 P.M. Sun., 10 A.M.–6 P.M. Mon.–Sat. late May–mid-Sept., closed the rest of the year) has a surprising homespun charm. Inside are displays and collections illustrating the days when Indians, trappers, cattlemen, and dude ranchers called this magnificent valley home. Check out the rock-encrusted flintlock musket, the old postcards, and a replica of the "Colter stone." Admission is $3 adults, $2 seniors, $1 ages 3–18, and $6 families. In the summer, the museum sponsors free hourlong **historical walking tours** of Jackson's downtown on Tuesdays and Thursdays at 10:30 A.M.

Also managed by the local historical society, the **Jackson Hole Historical Center** (105 Mercill Ave., 307/733-9605, 10 A.M.–5 P.M. Tues.–Fri. year-round, free) is a small research facility housing photo archives, a library of classic regional books, and rotating exhibits throughout the year.

◖ NATIONAL ELK REFUGE

Immediately north of Jackson is the National Elk Refuge (307/733-9212, www.fws.gov/nationalelkrefuge), winter home for thousands of these majestic animals. During summer, the elk range up to 65 miles away to feed on grasses, shrubs, and forbs in alpine meadows. But as the snows descend each fall, they move downslope, wintering in Jackson Hole and the surrounding country. The chance to view elk up close from a horse-drawn sleigh makes a trip to the National Elk Refuge one of the most popular wintertime activities for Jackson Hole visitors.

History

When the first ranchers arrived in Jackson Hole in the late 19th century, they moved onto land that had long been an elk migration route and wintering ground. The ranchers soon found elk raiding their haystacks and competing with cattle for forage, particularly during severe winters. The conflicts peaked early in the 20th century when three consecutive severe winters killed thousands of elk, leading one settler to claim that he had "walked for a mile on dead elk lying from one to four deep." Following a national outcry, the federal government began buying land in 1911 for a permanent winter elk refuge that would eventually cover nearly 25,000 acres.

About 5,500 elk (two-thirds of the local population) typically spend November–May on the refuge, administered by the U.S. Fish and Wildlife Service. Because development has reduced elk habitat in the valley to one-quarter of its original size, refuge managers try to improve the remaining land through seeding, irrigation, and prescribed burning. In addition, during the most difficult foraging period, the elk are fed alfalfa pellets paid for in part by sales of elk antlers collected on the refuge. During this time, each elk eats more than seven pounds of supplemental alfalfa per day, or 30 tons per day for the entire herd. Elk head back into the mountains with the melting of snow each April and May; during summer you'll see few (if any) on the refuge.

JACKSON HOLE

elk with sleigh, National Elk Refuge

Visiting the Refuge

The National Elk Refuge is primarily a winter attraction, although it's also an excellent place to watch birds and other wildlife—including nesting trumpeter swans—in summer. Refuge staff are on duty year-round in the Jackson Hole & Greater Yellowstone Visitor Center (532 N. Cache Dr., 307/733-3316, www.jacksonhole-chamber.com, open daily), leading nature talks, summertime wildlife viewing from the back deck, and theater programs. Visit the pictur-esque and historic (built in 1898) **Miller Ranch** on the east side of the refuge, 0.75 mile out Elk Refuge Road. It's open daily 10 A.M.–4 P.M. Memorial Day–Labor Day, with a naturalist available to answer questions about the refuge.

The main winter attraction here is the chance to see thousands of elk up close from one of the **horse-drawn sleighs** that take visitors through the refuge. The elk are accustomed to these sleighs and pay little heed, but people on foot would scare them. A tour of the National Elk Refuge is always a highlight for winter-time visitors to Jackson Hole. In December and January the bulls have impressive antlers

that they start to shed by the end of February. The months of January and February are good times to see sparring matches. You might also catch a glimpse of a wolf or two, because a pack now lives in the area year-round and hunts elk in winter. Morning is the best time to look for wolves.

Begin your wintertime visit to the refuge at the Jackson Hole & Greater Yellowstone Visitor Center, where you can buy sleigh-ride tickets ($18 adults, $14 ages 5–12, free for kids under age five). Reservations are available, but are not required, through Bar-T-Five (307/733-0277 or 800/772-5386, www.bart5.com), the folks who run the sleighs. The visitor center shows an interpretive slide show about the ref-uge while you're waiting for a shuttle bus to take you to the boarding area. Sleighs run daily 10 A.M.–4 P.M. mid-December–March (closed Christmas), heading out as soon as enough folks show up for a ride—generally just long enough for the early-comers to finish watching the slide show. The rides last 45–60 minutes. Be sure to wear warm clothes or bring extra lay-ers, because the wind can get bitterly cold.

Hatchery

Four miles north of town and adjacent to the elk refuge is the **Jackson National Fish Hatchery** (307/733-2510, http://jackson. fws.gov, daily 8 A.M.–4 P.M. year-round), which rears 400,000 cutthroat trout annually. There's also a small pond open for fishing on the grounds (fishing license required), a great spot for kids and novice anglers.

RAPTOR CENTER

Teton Raptor Center (307/203-2551, www. tetonraptorcenter.org, noon–4 P.M. Tues. and Thurs., 8 A.M.–noon Wed. in summer) is housed within the historic red barns of the Hardeman Ranch, seven miles from Jackson in the little town of Wilson. The center rehabilitates injured birds of prey and offers tours (by appointment, $10) several times weekly in the summer. This is a great chance for an up-close view of a golden eagle, red-tail hawk, and various falcons. The center also offers free weekly evening talks at Teton Village; their website features an osprey cam for live summer action on a nearby nest.

KITSCH

If you're a fan of the *National Enquirer,* check out the weird and wacky collection at **Ripley's Believe It or Not!** (140 N. Cache, 307/734-0000, www.conceptattractions.com, daily 9 A.M.–10 P.M. in summer, and noon–6 P.M. Sun., 11 A.M.–7 P.M. Mon.–Thurs., 10 A.M.–8 P.M. Fri.–Sat. the rest of the year; closed Tues.–Wed. Nov.–Dec.). Here you'll discover a shrunken head, six-legged buffalo calf, six-foot-long cigar, antique bedpan collection, and even art created from dryer lint. Who says art is only for the elite? Entrance costs a steep $11 adults, $9 ages 5–12, free for kids under five.

For more foolishness, have the kids drag you to the **Teton Maze** (307/734-0455) across from the Snow King chairlift. As the ads proclaim, it's a-Maze-ing.

Summer Recreation

Summer visitors to Jackson Hole can choose from an overwhelming array of outdoor options. Top favorites include float trips and whitewater rafting on the Snake River, mountain biking, hiking, and horseback rides, but kids love the alpine slide at Snow King, the fun pool at the rec center, and the tram rides at Jackson Hole Resort, not to mention the Town Square shoot-outs and evening rodeos that fill the summer calendar. If you've booked only a few days, you'll wish for more time to explore this fascinating place.

HIKING

The country around Jackson abounds with hundreds of miles of hiking trails, providing recreation opportunities for all levels of ability. Many of the most popular local trails are within nearby **Grand Teton National Park.** Notable in-the-park hikes are found in the Taggart Lake and Jenny Lake areas, at Colter Bay, and off the Moose-Wilson Road. The Information Center in Jackson has a brochure detailing these hikes, and a local outdoors shop, Skinny Skis (65 W. Deloney Ave., 307/733-6094 or 888/733-7205, www.skinnyskis.com), produces an excellent free summertime guide to hiking in the area called *Trailhead.*

For a fast trip to the alpine, take the **Jackson Hole Ski Resort tram** to the summit of Rendezvous Mountain ($25 adults, $12 kids), where trails fan out in various directions into Grand Teton National Park; the bird's-eye view is hard to beat. Visitors can also ride the free **Bridger gondola** (4:30–9 P.M.) to the 9,095-foot level, with access to additional hiking trails, as well as casual meals at the Deck or fine dining at Couloir Restaurant.

Snow King

Closest to town are the trails at Snow King (400 E. Snow King Ave., 307/733-5200 or 800/522-

5464, www.snowking.com), where you can either hike up the mountain or ride the chairlift ($12) to the summit and hike back down. Once on top, you'll find a 0.5-mile nature trail and wonderful across-the-valley views of the Tetons. Nearby is the **Cache Creek Trail,** which follows this pretty creek uphill for six miles along an old road that's closed to motor vehicles. It's a great family hike or mountain-bike ride. For an alternate loop back (four miles round-trip), turn onto the **Putt-Putt Trail** two miles up. Cyclists often use Cache Creek Trail to connect with Game Creek Trail for a loop around Snow King Mountain. All of the trails in the Snow King area are open to mountain bikes, and you can transport bikes on the chairlift.

Teton Pass

Ski Lake is a more challenging hike or bike ride, with spectacular views awaiting. It starts west of Wilson on Highway 22 at Phillips Canyon. Walk up the dirt road 0.5 mile and take the left fork in the road to the start of the trail. It side-slopes around to a viewpoint and then climbs through the forest to Ski Lake, nestled high in the alpine and three miles from your starting point. The **Black Canyon Overlook Trail** starts from the parking area at the top of Teton Pass, 10 miles west of Jackson. It follows Pass Ridge for two miles, with an abundance of wildflower meadows and forest along the way. You can continue from here down Black Canyon to the end of Trail Creek Road at the base of the pass for a longer hike, but will need a shuttle ride back up the pass.

Snake River Canyon

The Snake River Canyon south of Jackson is best known as a river-rafting destination, but a couple of good hikes are a landlubber's option. The **Cabin Creek Trail** begins 0.5 mile up a dirt road behind Cabin Creek Campground (17 miles from Jackson). The trail follows the creek uphill to a pass that is filled with late-summer wildflowers, and from here you'll be treated to delightful views of the Snake River drainage. Return the same way, or head back downhill along the **Dog Creek Trail** that ends near the junction of Wilson-Fall Creek Road with U.S. Highway 89/26. Either way, it's about six miles of hiking, but if you head back via Dog Creek Trail you'll need a shuttle back to your car.

Granite Creek

This beautiful valley has good hiking, a quiet out-of-the-way location, and the added bonus of a hot spring. Get here by driving south from Jackson 12 miles to Hoback Junction and then another 12 miles east on U.S. Highway 189 to the turnoff for Granite Hot Springs. The **Granite Creek Falls Trail** starts at the junction of Swift Creek and Granite Creek, eight miles up the road. It follows the creek upstream to impressive Granite Falls and then on to **Granite Hot Springs** (also accessible by road), where you can soak in the wonderful mineral pool for $6. Towel and swimsuit rentals are available. The trail is two miles long and quite easy, and there's a campground near the springs.

For a more challenging hike, try the **Shoal Falls Trail,** which starts from the same trailhead eight miles up Granite Creek Road and leads five miles to an overlook near Shoal Falls. Get trail details from the Forest Service.

Guided Hikes

Teton County Parks & Recreation Department (155 E. Gill St., 307/739-9025, www.tetonwyo.org/parks) sponsors a wide range of outdoor activities in the summer, including adult day hikes. For a break from the young'uns (1st–6th grade), take them to **Camp Jackson** summer day camp at Davey Jackson Elementary (200 N. Willow, 307/733-5302), available weekdays for $35 per day. You don't need to be a local resident to take part in any of these activities, but reserve ahead because some fill up. The Parks & Rec office also rents out volleyball, horseshoe, bocce ball, and croquet sets.

Educational nature walks into the mountains around Jackson are led by **The Hole Hiking Experience** (307/690-4453 or 866/733-4453, www.holehike.com). Rates start at $82 adults,

$65 for kids for a four-hour hike. Longer trips, including multi-night backpacking, are also available. For a free version, Grand Teton National Park offers guided walks and nature talks throughout the year.

For a different sort of guided hike, check out the excellent and free **historical walking tours** offered by the Jackson Hole Museum on Tuesday and Thursday.

◖ RIVER RAFTING

Jackson Hole's most popular summertime recreational activity is running Wyoming's largest river, the Snake. Each year more than 150,000 people climb aboard rafts, canoes, and kayaks to float down placid reaches of the Snake or to blast through the boiling rapids of Snake River Canyon. (The name "Snake" comes from the Shoshone Indians, who used serpentine hand movements as sign language for their tribal name—a motion trappers misinterpreted as a snake and applied to the river flowing through Shoshone land.)

Almost 20 different rafting companies offer dozens of raft trips each day of the summer. Although you may be able to walk up and get a raft trip the same day, it's a good idea to reserve ahead for any river trip in July and August. In general, try to book a trip three or four days in advance and at least one week ahead if you need a specific time, prefer an overnight float trip, or are traveling with a larger group. One or two people are more likely to get onboard at the last minute.

You may want to ask around to determine the advantages of each company. Some are cheaper but require you to drive a good distance from town; others offer more experienced crews; still others provide various perks such as fancy meals, U-paddle trips, overnight camps along the river, interpretive trips, or boats with fewer (or more) people. Several operators also lead seven-hour combination trips that include a lazy float followed by a meal break and a wild whitewater run.

The rafting companies generally operate mid-May–late September, and river conditions change throughout the season. Highest flows—and the wildest rides—are generally in May and June. Get a complete list of floating and boating outfits, along with descriptive brochures, from the visitor center in Jackson.

Float Trips

The gentlest way to see the Snake is by taking one of the many commercial float trips. Along the way, you'll be treated to stunning views of the Tetons and glimpses of eagles, ospreys, beavers, and perhaps moose or other wildlife along the riverbanks. Several companies—Barker-Ewing Float Trips, Will Dornan's Snake River Float Trips, Grand Teton Lodge Company, Signal Mountain, Solitude, and Triangle X—offer 10-mile scenic float trips along the quiet stretch **within Grand Teton National Park,** putting in at Deadman's Bar and taking out at Moose ($55–60 adults, $35–40 kids). (Grand Teton Lodge Company often puts in at Pacific Creek.) Triangle X offers a unique 12-mile park supper float-and-cookout with access to a private spot along the river.

Other rafting companies offer 13-mile **South Park float trips outside the park,** putting in at the bridge near Wilson and taking out above Hoback Junction ($45–60 adults, $40–50 kids, lunch included). Companies offering this trip are Barker-Ewing Whitewater & Scenic, Dave Hansen, Lewis & Clark, Sands, Will Dornan's Snake River Float Trips, Jackson Hole Whitewater, Snake River Kayak & Canoe School, Snake River Park, Solitude, Teton Whitewater, and Teton Expeditions. In-the-park trips are considerably more scenic, so know what you're getting before you sign up since the differences are not emphasized by the rafting companies (at least by those who don't operate inside the park). Given the choice, I would always choose the trip that passes below the Tetons over the one that skirts suburban Jackson. Some companies add options such as breakfast cookouts or overnight trips with camping along the way.

Age limits vary, but kids must generally be at least eight to float the river. Raft companies usually have folks meet up in either Jackson or Moose. A wide variety of special voyages are also available, including overnight camping and fish-and-float trips.

OUTFITTERS

The following rafting outfits offer a variety of float trips. Pick up their slick brochures at the visitor center or from their offices scattered around town.

- **Barker-Ewing Float Trips** (307/733-1800 or 800/365-1800, www.barkerewing.com)
- **Barker-Ewing Whitewater & Scenic** (307/733-1000 or 800/448-4202, www.barker-ewing.com)
- **Dave Hansen Scenic Float Trips** (307/733-6295 or 800/732-6295, www.davehansenscenicfloattrips.com)
- **Grand Teton Lodge Company** (307/543-3100 or 800/628-9988, www.gtlc.com)
- **Jackson Hole Whitewater** (307/733-1007 or 800/700-8238, www.jhww.com)
- **Lewis & Clark Expeditions** (307/733-4022 or 800/824-5375, www.lewisandclarkriverrafting.com)
- **Mad River Boat Trips** (307/733-6203 or 800/458-7238, www.mad-river.com)
- **Sands Wild Water** (307/733-4410 or 800/358-8184, www.sandswhitewater.com)
- **Signal Mountain Lodge and Marina** (307/543-2831 or 307/543-2831, www.signalmountainlodge.com)
- **Snake River Kayak & Canoe School** (307/733-9999 or 800/529-2501, www.snakeriverkayak.com) Snake River Kayak & Canoe School also has "rubber duckie" inflatable kayaks for a unique whitewater adventure.
- **Snake River Park Whitewater** (307/733-7078 or 800/562-1878, www.snakeriverwhitewater.com)
- **Solitude Scenic Float Trips** (307/733-2871 or 888/704-2800, www.solitudefloattrips.com)
- **Teton Expeditions** (307/733-1007 or 888/700-7238, www.tetonexpeditions.com)
- **Teton Whitewater** (307/733-2285 or 866/716-7238, www.tetonwhitewater.com)
- **Triangle X Float Trips** (a.k.a. National Park Float Trips, 307/733-5500 or 888/860-0005, www.trianglex.com)
- **Will Dornan's Snake River Float Trips** (307/733-3699 or 888/998-7688, www.jacksonholefloattrips.com)

As an aside, one of the oldest names in the business, **Barker-Ewing,** is actually two different operations with rather different agendas. Barker-Ewing originated in 1963 when Dick Barker and Frank Ewing started guiding clients down the Snake River. They went their separate ways in 1984, and today, the Barker family operates Grand Teton National Park float trips under the name Barker-Ewing Float Trips, while the Ewing family runs Snake River whitewater trips and South Park floats under the name Barker-Ewing Whitewater & Scenic. Both companies splash "Barker-Ewing" across the top of their brochures, adding to the confusion for many travelers. Despite any tension between the two companies, both are first-rate operations with some of the most experienced guides anywhere.

You can also float the river with any of the local fishing outfitters and combine angling with drifting downriver. One good company—it gives a really personalized tour—is **Wooden Boat River Tours** (307/732-2628, www.woodboattours.com, $400 for up to three passengers), which has classic wooden dories.

Note that a few of the raft operators are regarded as "training grounds" for other companies; recommended outfits with good records include Barker-Ewing Float Trips, Solitude, Dave Hansen, and Triangle X. Grand Teton Lodge Float Trips often use massive 15-person rafts with two oarsmen. Unfortunately, three people died in a 2006 accident when one of their rafts hit a tree that had been uprooted by high water, throwing all the passengers into the river. Use caution before booking a river trip when the river is running high following a heavy snowpack year.

Whitewater Trips

Below Jackson, the Snake enters the wild Snake River Canyon, a stretch early explorers labeled "the accursed mad river." The usual put-in point for whitewater "rapid-transit" trips is West Table Creek Campground, 26 miles south of Jackson. The take-out point is Sheep Gulch, eight miles downstream. In between, the river rocks and rolls through the narrow canyon, pumping past waterfalls and eagle nests and then over the two biggest rapids, Big Kahuna and Lunch Counter, followed by the smaller Rope and Champagne rapids. For a look at the action from the highway, stop at the paved turnout at milepost 124, where a trail leads down to Lunch Counter. The river changes greatly throughout the season, with the highest water and wildest rides in June. By August the water has warmed enough for a quick dip. Be sure to ask your river guide about the Jeep that sits in 60 feet of water below Lunch Counter!

Whitewater trips last about 3.5 hours (including transportation from Jackson) and cost about $60–65 adults, $50–55 children (age limits vary). Seven-hour combination trips covering 21 miles include a float trip, deli lunch, and whitewater run for $94–110 adults, $78–90 kids. You'll find discounted rates early or late in the summer.

One feature to consider is raft size. Many companies use smaller eight-person rafts (often called U-paddle), but trips on 14-person monsters are a few dollars cheaper. The U-paddle versions are more fun than letting the guide do all the work in an oar raft, and the smaller eight-person rafts provide the most challenging—and wettest—runs. Snake River Kayak & Canoe offers two-person "rubber duckie" kayak trips.

Note that this is not exactly a wilderness experience, especially in mid-July, when stretches of the river look like a Los Angeles freeway with traffic jams of rafts, kayaks, inner tubes, and other flotsam and jetsam. The river isn't as crowded on weekdays and early in the morning;

take an 8 A.M. run for the fewest people. Early in the season when the river is high and fast your trip can be quite short, sometimes just 45 minutes on the water.

Don't take a camera along unless it's waterproof; bankside float-tographers are positioned along the biggest rapids to shoot both commercial and private rafters. Stop by **Float-O-Graphs** (130 W. Broadway Ave., 307/733-6453 or 888/478-7427, www.floatographs.com) for a photo from your run. Another company with a similar service is **Snake River Whitewater Photos and Video** (140 N. Cache Dr., 307/733-7015 or 800/948-3426, www.snakeriverphotos.net). Both companies also post photos online.

OUTFITTERS

Most outfitters include round-trip transportation from Jackson. (Prices are a bit lower from Snake River Park Whitewater, but you'll need to drive to their office at Hoback Junction, 13 miles south of town.) Some companies also offer trips that combine an eight-mile scenic float trip through South Park with an eight-mile whitewater trip for about $85–90 adults or $75–80 kids.

Rafting companies provide wet suits and booties, but expect to get wet, so wear lightweight clothes and bring a jacket for the return ride.

The following outfitters offer whitewater raft trips. Recommended companies with good safety records and well-trained staff include Barker-Ewing, Dave Hansen, and Sands. The largest local rafting company, Mad River, has a reputation as a proving ground for novice guides (but its prices are typically lower than those of other operators).

- **Barker-Ewing Whitewater & Scenic** (307/733-1000 or 800/448-4202, www.barker-ewing.com)
- **Dave Hansen Whitewater** (307/733-6295 or 800/732-6295, www.davehansenwhitewater.com)
- **Jackson Hole Whitewater** (307/733-1007 or 800/700-7238, www.jhww.com)

- **Lewis & Clark Expeditions** (307/733-4022 or 800/824-5375, www.lewisandclarkriver-rafting.com)
- **Mad River Boat Trips** (307/733-6203 or 800/458-7238, www.mad-river.com)
- **Sands Wild Water** (307/733-4410 or 800/358-8184, www.sandswhitewater.com)
- **Snake River Kayak and Canoe School** (307/733-9999 or 800/529-2501, www.snakeriverkayak.com)
- **Snake River Park Whitewater** (307/733-7078 or 800/562-1878, www.snakeriver-whitewater.com)
- **Teton Whitewater** (307/733-2285 or 866/716-7238, www.tetonwhitewater.com)

Riding and Rafts (307/654-9900, www.jacksonholerecreation.com) has raft rentals ($100–115) if you want to float the rapids on your own.

FISHING

Jackson Hole has some of the finest angling in Wyoming, with native Snake River cutthroat (a distinct subspecies) and brook trout in the river, along with Mackinaw (lake trout), cutthroat, and brown trout in the lakes. The Snake is a particular favorite of beginning fly-fishing enthusiasts; popular shoreside fishing spots are just below Jackson Lake Dam and near the Wilson Bridge. Jackson Lake may provide higher odds for catching a fish, but you'll need to rent a boat from one of the marinas. This is the place parents take kids. Another very popular fishing hole is just below the dam on Jackson Lake. Flat Creek on the National Elk Refuge is an acclaimed spot for fly-fishing. Note that Wyoming fishing licenses are valid within Grand Teton National Park but not in Yellowstone, where you'll need a separate permit.

A variety of exotic plants and animals may threaten the Snake River and other waterways, including New Zealand mud snails, zebra mussels, and Eurasian water-milfoil. Help prevent the spread of these pests by carefully cleaning boots, clothing, waders, gear, and boats. More information is available online at www.clean-inspectdry.com and www.protectyourwaters.net.

Fishing Guides

Many local companies guide fly-fishing float trips down the Snake River and other area waterways. Two people (same price for one person) should expect to pay $400–450 per day for a guide, rods and reels, lunch, and boat. Your fishing license and flies are extra. The visitor center has a listing of local fishing guides and outfitters, and its racks are filled with their brochures. You'll also find links to many of these at www.jacksonholechamber.com.

On Your Own

If you'd rather do it yourself, pick up a copy of the free *Jack Dennis Sports Fly Fishing Guide,* which offers descriptions of regional fishing areas and advice on which lures to try. Find it at **Jack Dennis Sports** (50 E. Broadway Ave., 307/733-3270 or 800/570-3270, www.jack-dennisoutdoors.com). While there, you may want to buy a regional guide to fishing such as *Flyfisher's Guide to Wyoming* by Ken Retallic (Wilderness Adventures Press, www.wildadv-press.com) or *Fishing Wyoming* by Kenneth Lee Graham (Falcon Guides, www.falcon.com).

Jackson has several excellent fly-fishing shops, including the aforementioned Jack Dennis Sports. **Westbank Anglers** (3670 Teton Village Rd., 307/733-6483 or 800/922-3474, www.westbank.com) is a nationally known fly-fishing dealer with a slick mail-order catalog, excellent fishing clinics, and float trips. **High Country Flies** (185 N. Center St., 307/733-7210 or 866/733-7210, www.highcountryflies.com), **Orvis Jackson Hole** (485 W. Broadway Ave., 307/733-5407, www.orvis.com/jackson-hole), and **Will Dornan's Snake River Angler** (in Moose, 307/733-3699 or 888/998-7688, www.snakeriverangler.com) all offer fly-fishing classes and sell quality gear. Rent fishing rods, fly rods, float tubes, and waders from Jack Dennis, High Country Flies, or **Leisure Sports** (1075 S. U.S. Hwy. 89, 307/733-3040, www.leisuresportsadventure.com).

JACKSON HOLE

BOATING
Kayaking and Canoeing

In business for more than 35 years, **Snake River Kayak & Canoe School** (365 N. Cache, 307/733-9999 or 800/529-2501, www. snakeriverkayak.com) offers a wide variety of river kayaking and canoeing classes for all levels of ability, plus fishing trips and raft trips. Half-day private lessons include transportation, boats, paddles, wet suit, rubber booties, and life jackets ($250 for two students). Beginners may want to start out with one of the three-hour "rubber duckie" inflatable kayak river trips ($75). In addition, the school has sea kayak tours of all lengths in Yellowstone National Park. The shop rents practically anything that floats: canoes, sea kayaks, whitewater kayaks, inflatable kayaks, and rafts, all with paddles and roof racks included. Also available are dry bags and life jackets.

The folks at **Rendezvous River Sports/ Jackson Hole Kayak School** (945 W. Broadway Ave., 307/733-2471, www.jackson-holekayak.com) teach a wide range of kayaking courses from the absolute beginner level to advanced "hairboating" for experts. Classes include kayak roll clinics, river rescue, special women's clinics, and kids' classes, plus multi-day tours in Yellowstone. Private lessons are available, and the company rents sea kayaks and whitewater kayaks, plus inflatable kayaks and rafts.

Leisure Sports (1075 S. U.S. Hwy. 89, 307/733-3040, www.leisuresportsadventure. com) rents rafts, float tubes, canoes, inflatable kayaks, water skis, wet suits, dry bags, life vests, and all sorts of other outdoor equipment. Next to Dornan's in Moose, **Adventure Sports** (307/733-3307, www.dornans.com) also rents canoes and kayaks.

HORSEBACK RIDING
Trail Rides

Think of the Wild West and one animal always comes to mind—the horse. A ride on Old Paint gives city slickers a chance to saunter back in time to a simpler era and to simultaneously learn how ornery and opinionated horses can

be. If it rains, you'll also learn why cowboys are so enthralled with cowboy hats. In Jackson Hole you can choose from brief half-day trail rides in Grand Teton National Park all the way up to weeklong pack trips into the rugged Teton Wilderness. The visitor center has a brochure listing local outfitters and stables that provide trail rides and pack trips.

For rides by the hour or day ($30–40 for a one-hour ride, $45–60 for two hours, or $80–110 for a half-day), try **Teton Village Trail Rides** (in Teton Village, 307/733-2674, www. wagonswestwyo.com), **Jackson Hole Trail Rides** (behind Snow King Resort, 307/733-6992, www.jhtrailrides.com), **Spring Creek Ranch** (atop Gros Ventre Butte off Spring Gulch Road, 307/733-8833 or 800/443-6139, www.springcreekranch.com), **A/OK Corral** (in Hoback Junction, 307/733-6556, www.horsecreekranch.com), **Mill Iron Ranch** (10 miles south of Jackson, 307/733-6390 or 888/808-6390, www.millironranch.net), or **Goosewing Ranch** (25 miles east of Kelly near the Gros Ventre Wilderness, 307/733-5251 or 888/733-5251, www.goosewingranch.com).

Of these, Teton Village Trail Rides, Spring Creek Ranch, and Mill Iron Ranch are the most popular, but you probably won't go wrong with any of these companies. Mill Iron Ranch, Spring Creek Ranch, and A/OK Corral also offer rides that include breakfast or dinner cookouts. Farther afield are several companies offering trail rides, including four that operate out of Buffalo Valley (45 miles northeast of Jackson): **Buffalo Valley Ranch** (307/543-2062 or 888/543-2477, www.buffalovalleyranch.com), **Castagno Outfitters** (307/543-2407 or 877/559-3585, www.castagnooutfitters.com), **Turpin Meadow Ranch** (307/543-2496 or 800/743-2496, www. turpinmeadowranch.com), **Teton Horseback Adventures** (307/730-8829, www.horsebackadv.com), and **Yellowstone Outfitters** (307/543-2418 or 800/447-4711, www.yellowstoneoutfitters.com). More trail rides are offered at **Togwotee Mountain Lodge** (307/543-2847 or 800/543-2847, www.togwoteelodge.com), 48 miles northeast of Jackson on the way to

Togwotee Pass. The minimum age for horseback riding is typically 5–6; young children ride while the horse is being led around by a parent. Teton Village Trail Rides also offers unique **winter rides** at Teton Village ($55 for one hour on plowed trails).

In Alpine (35 miles southwest of Jackson), **Riding and Rafts** (307/654-9900, www.jacksonholerecreation.com) offers unguided horse rentals for $50 for a half-day ride; it's the only local place for do-it-yourselfers. (Pseudo-legal disclaimer from their website: "If you fall off and get hurt, you just have to lie there until you get better.")

Jackson Hole Llamas (307/739-9582 or 800/830-7316, www.jhllamas.com) leads day hikes and backcountry treks with these fascinating and gentle animals.

Chuck-wagon cookouts are a very popular family option in Jackson Hole during the summer. Guests travel in horse-drawn wagons (or by horseback) and are treated to a delicious all-you-can-eat meal and entertainment.

In the foothills eight miles south of Jackson, **Game Creek Ranch** (1500 Game Creek Rd., 307/733-7101, www.gamecreekranch.biz) has a huge indoor riding arena with Western or English riding lessons for all levels, a five-week ranch camp for kids, riding clinics, and horse boarding.

Wagon Trains

Two local companies lead overnight wagon-train rides (in wagons with rubber tires) into the country around Jackson Hole. Guests split their time between riding in the wagons and riding on horseback. **Wagons West** (307/543-2418 or 800/447-4711, www.wagonswestwyo.com) heads up into the Mt. Leidy Highlands for 2–6 days. The shortest trips (two days and one night) are $470 adults, $395 kids under 14. Four-day, three-night trips are $805 adults, $695 kids; and six-day, five-night trips run $1,025 adults, $895 kids. **Teton Wagon Train/ Double H Bar** (307/734-6101 or 888/734-6101, www.tetonwagontrain.com) charges $895 adults, $815 ages 9–14, and $765 ages 4–8 for a four-day, three-night package that includes horseback and wagon riding, meals, and camping gear.

Cowboy for a Day

One of the last working cattle ranches in Jackson Hole, historic **Snake River Ranch** (307/733-2674, www.tetonvillagetrailrides.com) has more than 3,500 head of cattle on a 5,000-acre spread. City slickers can join cowboys as they push cattle between pastures. This is real work and not for the timid, but a great opportunity at $100 for 3–4 hours. The ranch also has wagon tours and is a popular location for weddings.

BIKING

Jackson Hole offers all sorts of adventures for cyclists, particularly those with mountain bikes. Local bike shops provide maps of mountain-bike routes. Note that bikes are not allowed on hiking trails in Grand Teton National Park or in Forest Service wilderness areas. The main road in Grand Teton National Park is plowed but closed to cars and other motorized traffic during April. It's great for an easy and scenic ride.

Bike Paths

Jackson Hole is a wonderful place for bikes, and is fast becoming a destination for cycling enthusiasts, thanks in part to the **Jackson Hole Community Pathways** (307/732-8573, www.tetonwyo.org/pathways). This expanding network of paved paths covers 37 miles, connecting with eight more miles within Grand Teton National Park. Additional trails are being added, and eventually these trails will all be linked, providing continuous bike paths from Hoback Junction north through Grand Teton National Park and west into Teton Valley, Idaho. Visit the Community Pathways website (www.tetonwyo.org/pathways) for details and downloadable maps, or pick up one of their maps at the visitor center. Get additional details from Friends of Pathways (335 S. Millward St., 307/733-4534, www.friendsofpathways.org), a nonprofit advocacy group.

A paved trail heads north from Jackson along

U.S. Highway 26/89/191 into Grand Teton National Park. Built in 2011, the path follows the highway to Moose, where it joins the Park Service's bike path to Jenny Lake. With this connection, it's now possible to bike the entire 21 miles from downtown Jackson to Jenny Lake. Underpasses beneath the highway provide bike and pedestrian access to the National Museum of Wildlife Art and the settlement of Moose in Grand Teton.

A seven-mile paved trail parallels the highway south of Jackson to the Snake River bridge. For a fun loop ride, use this path to connect to the very popular Game Creek Trail, which meets Cache Creek Trail, circling back to Jackson behind Snow King. (Some of this route is not paved.) A paved bike path goes from the town of Wilson westward to the summit of Teton Pass (a gain of 2,000 feet in 3.5 miles), with a second arm continuing from Wilson to Teton Village and then north to Grand Teton National Park parallel to the Moose-Wilson Road. The gap between Jackson and the Snake River should be completed by 2013.

A four-mile path starts behind the main post office on Maple Way, crosses U.S. Highway 89, and continues past the high school before turning north to meet the road to Wilson (Hwy. 22). This road has wide shoulders but gets lots of traffic.

The trails at **Snow King Resort** (400 E. Snow King Ave., 307/733-5200 or 800/522-5464, www.snowking.com) are open to mountain bikers, and you can either pedal uphill or ride the chairlift with your bike ($12). **Jackson Hole Mountain Resort** (307/733-2292 or 888/333-7766, www.jacksonhole.com) has seven miles of bike trails on the lower sections of the mountain for all levels of ability, including a very popular all-downhill bike park with groomed trails, banked corners, and jumps for all levels of ability. Access is via the Teewinot chairlift ($10 adults, $6 kids); no charge if you've purchased a separate tram ticket.

Bike Rentals and Tours
Mountain and road bikes are available from several local shops, including the two best

places: **Fitzgerald's Bicycles** (245 W. Hansen St., 307/734-6886, www.fitzgeraldsbicycles. com, 10 A.M.–6 P.M. Mon.–Fri., 10 A.M.–5 P.M. Sat., 10 A.M.–3 P.M. Sun.) and over in Wilson at **Wilson Backcountry Sports** (1230 Ida Dr., 307/733-5228, www.wilsonbackcountry.com). Both of these are full-service pro shops with high-quality full-suspension mountain bikes. Fitzgerald's will even deliver bikes directly to your hotel.

Other area bike shops include:

- **Hoback Sports** (520 W. Broadway Ave., 307/733-5335, www.hobacksports.com)
- **The Edge Sports** (490 W. Broadway Ave., 307/734-3916, www.jacksonholeedgesports. com)
- **Grand Targhee Ski Resort** (in Alta, 307/353-2300 or 800/827-4433, www. grandtarghee.com)
- **Adventure Sports** (307/733-3307, www. dornans.com) in Moose

There are also three Teton Village shops: **Jackson Hole Sports** (307/739-2687, www. jacksonhole.com), **Teton Village Sports** (307/733-2181 or 800/874-4224, www.teton-villagesports.com), and **Wildernest Sports** (307/733-4297, www.wildernestsports.com). All of these rent standard or cruiser bikes with helmets for $25–42 per day, $15–25 per half-day, and some also have bike trailers, full-suspension mountain bikes, road bikes, hybrid bikes, child bikes, and car racks.

Half-day mountain-bike tours are available from **Fat Tire Tours/Hoback Sports** (307/733-5335, www.hobacksports.com). Options include an easy National Elk Refuge ride ($55) and a more adventurous one ($85) that includes a chairlift ride to the top of Snow King leading into nearby trails. **Teton Mountain Bike Tours** (307/733-0712 or 800/733-0788, www. wybike.com) has scenic half- or all-day bike trips through Grand Teton National Park, Bridger-Teton National Forest, Yellowstone National Park, and the National Elk Refuge. These trips are for all levels of ability, starting at $60 for a four-hour ride in the Antelope Flats area.

ALPINE FUN
Jackson Hole Resort

Take a fast and scenic nine-minute ride to the top of Rendezvous Mountain (10,450 feet) aboard the 100-passenger **aerial tram** (307/733-2292 or 888/333-7766, www.jacksonhole.com, daily 9 A.M.–6 P.M. late May–Sept., $25 adults, $20 seniors, $19 ages 13–17, $12 ages 6–12, free ages five and under) at Teton Village. The tram ride gains more than 4,000 feet in elevation—this is a sensational way to reach the alpine. On top is a small snack shop in Corbet's Cabin with made-to-order waffles and cocoa; bring a lunch if you need something more substantial. Several trails provide enjoyable hikes from the summit, but be sure to pack drinking water and a warm jacket. Dogs and bikes aren't allowed on the tram.

TRAM I AM

For four decades, the main attraction at Jackson Hole Resort was the 52-passenger aerial tram that climbed the summit of Rendezvous Mountain, providing jaw-dropping views across Jackson Hole. But all things must pass. In 2005, Jackson Hole Resort stunned local residents – and skiers around the country – by announcing that the aerial tram would be retired at the end of summer 2006. In operation since 1966, the tram had simply become too worn out to repair. The old one was demolished the following year, and work began on a new and much-improved tram. Opening day for the new $30 million tram came in 2008, much to the relief of skiers, boarders, and Jackson Hole businesses.

Manufactured in Switzerland and powered by 1,970-horsepower engines, the new fire-engine red tram holds 100 people – almost twice the capacity of the old one – and takes nine minutes to get to the summit (versus 12 minutes for the old tram). It can carry 600 passengers per hour, more than twice as many as before.

© DON PITCHER

tram at Jackson Hole Mountain Resort

JACKSON HOLE

Rendezvous Mountain is a favorite place for paragliders to launch. Tandem paragliding flights ($245) are available from **Jackson Hole Paragliding** (307/690-8726, www.jhparagliding.com). No experience is needed for these half-hour flights, accessed via the tram.

Summer visitors can also ride the *free* **Bridger gondola** (from 4:30–9 P.M.) to the 9,095-foot level. It doesn't reach the top of the mountain, but affords panoramic vistas over Jackson Hole with access to hiking trails and meals at The Deck and Couloir Restaurant.

Take mountain bikes up the **Teewinot chairlift** (mid-June–early Sept., $10 adults, $8 ages 13–17, $6 ages 6–12, free for younger kids), with seven miles of bike trails on the lower sections of the mountain.

In addition to alpine rides, Teton Village is home to a number of other summer activities on the **Village Commons** ($12 per ticket or $50 for five tickets), including a bungee trampoline and a 25-foot outdoor climbing wall. The big central plaza features a delightful pop-jet fountain, playground, and fire pit, plus an amphitheater for concerts, Teton Raptor Center demonstrations, and storytelling on summer evenings at 5 P.M. Horseback rides, bike rentals, and disc golf are nearby, and child care is available at Kids Ranch (307/739-2654). Stop by the Activity Center for a map and details on all the Teton Village options.

Snow King

At Snow King Mountain right on the edge of Jackson, the resort's main **chairlift** (400 E. Snow King Ave., 307/733-5200 or 800/522-5464, www.snowking.com, daily 9 A.M.–8 P.M. late May–early Sept., $12 adults, $8 ages 7–13, free for kids under 7) takes folks for a 20-minute ride to the summit of the 7,751-foot mountain. On top you'll find a short nature trail, panoramic views of the Tetons, and a myriad of longer hiking and biking trails. Rent a bike at the base of the mountain for a fun ride down.

Also at Snow King is the 2,500-foot-long **Alpine Slide** (307/733-7680 or 800/522-5464, www.snowkingmountain.com), a summertime family favorite. For anyone older than six, the

cost is $15 for one ride or $65 for five rides. For children ages 2–6 riding with an adult it's an additional $3 per ride.

Grand Targhee Ski Resort

On the other side of the Tetons at Grand Targhee Ski Resort (in Alta, 307/353-2300 or 800/827-4433, www.grandtarghee.com), you can ride the **chairlift** ($15 adults, $6 kids) to the 10,200-foot summit of Fred's Mountain, where Grand Teton stands just seven miles away. The lift operates daily late June–mid-September. Mountain bikers can bring a bike (or rent one) to ride the trails high up the slopes; the cost is $20 for an unlimited number of chairlift rides.

SWIMMING AND GYMS

Jackson is home to **Teton County/Jackson Recreation Center** (155 E. Gill St., 307/739-9025, www.tetonwyo.org/parks, 6 A.M.–9 P.M. Mon.–Fri., noon–9 P.M. Sat., noon–7 P.M. Sun.), which includes an indoor aquatics complex with a lap pool, 185-foot corkscrew water slide, and hot tub, plus a wading pool featuring a waterfall, slide, and water geyser. Basketball and volleyball courts are also inside the rec center, and after your workout, relax in the sauna and steam room. Nonresident prices are $7 adults, $5.50 ages 13–17, $4.50 seniors and ages 3–12, and $23 families; free for tots under three. The rec center also offers a variety of courses and activities, including yoga, toddler swimming, basketball, volleyball, and aerobics.

Out of the way is the wonderful hot mineral pool at **Granite Hot Springs** (307/734-7400, http://granitehotsprings.mountainmancountry.com, $6), 35 miles southeast of Jackson. The springs are open daily summer and winter.

Near the Aspens south of Teton Village, **Teton Sports Club** (4030 W. Lake Creek Dr., 307/733-7004, www.tetonsportsclub.com) offers aerobic classes, cardio machines, free weights, indoor and outdoor hot tubs, a sauna, and a summer-only outdoor pool. Day passes are $15. Massage therapists and personal trainers are available.

Jackson Hole Health & Fitness (838 W. Broadway Ave., 307/734-9000, www.jh-healthandfitness.com) houses a state-of-the-art center with machines, weights, bikes, treadmills, elliptical trainers with iPod connectivity, and flat-screen TVs. Day passes are $10.

SPAS

Jackson is a wonderful place to pamper yourself. Most of the top-end hotels provide spa facilities open to both guests and the general public, including Amangani, Rusty Parrot, Snow King Resort, Spring Creek Ranch, Snake River Lodge, Teton Mountain Lodge, Four Seasons Resort, and Hotel Terra. The visitor center has brochures from additional spas, acupuncture clinics, and yoga studios to center your soul. There's even a **Teton Wellness Festival** in early October to get in touch with your inner self (and outer self at the same time). Visit www.tetonwellness.org for links to local centers, from homeopaths to Pilates classes.

ROCK CLIMBING

Jackson Hole is home for two highly regarded climbing schools: **Jackson Hole Mountain Guides** (165 N. Glenwood St., 307/733-4979 or 800/239-7642, www.jhmg.com) and **Exum Mountain Guides** (307/733-2297, www.exumguides.com), with a summertime office at the south end of Jenny Lake. Both offer a wide range of classes—including those for kids and families—plus guided climbs up Grand Teton and wintertime courses in avalanche safety and ice climbing.

Largest indoor rock gym in the Rockies, **Enclosure Indoor Climbing Center** (670 Deer Lane, 307/734-9590, www.enclosureclimbing.com) has a huge diversity of climbing terrain, roped climbing areas, and bouldering, plus a fitness center and even child care. There's also an outdoor climbing wall in Teton Village and at Grand Targhee Resort.

AERIAL RIDES

Two local companies offer early morning hot-air balloon rides in the summer: **Wyoming Balloon Co.** (307/739-0900, www.wyomingballoon.com) and **Endeavor Ballooning** (307/699-1339, www.wyoming-hotair.com). Adult rates are $295 per person for these hour-long flights.

The top of the Jackson Hole Resort tram is a favorite place for paragliders to launch. Tandem paragliding flights ($225) are available from **Jackson Hole Paragliding** (307/739-2626, www.jhparagliding.com). No experience is needed for these 15-minute flights.

Cowboy Up Hang Gliding (307/413-4164, www.cuhanggliding.com) has tandem flights from Alpine (35 miles southwest of Jackson), using an ultralight to gain altitude for flights over the Salt River Range. These cost $169 for a flight that lasts at least 20 minutes.

Over the pass in Driggs, Idaho, **Teton Aviation Center** (208/354-3100 or 800/472-6382, www.tetonaviation.com) has glider flights, at $250 for a one-hour flight; they're a great way to come eye-to-eye with Grand Teton.

GOLF AND TENNIS

Like many resort areas, Jackson Hole has an abundance of tony golf courses, including five in the valley plus another six over the pass in Teton Valley. **Jackson Hole Golf and Tennis Club** (307/733-3111, www.jhgtc.com), one mile north of town, has a public 18-hole golf course designed by Robert Trent Jones Jr. and rated one of the 10 best in America. Also here are a private swimming pool, tennis courts, fitness center, and North Grille Restaurant (11:30 A.M.–close in summer) for patio dining.

Teton Pines Country Club (on Teton Village Rd., 307/733-1773 or 800/238-2223, www.tetonpines.com) is Jackson Hole's other golf spot open to the public. Its Arnold Palmer-designed 18-hole championship course is very challenging; 14 of the holes require over-water shots. The club also features a grand clubhouse, tennis courts, and a large (and private) outdoor pool, along with fine dining at The Pines restaurant. Both Teton Pines and Jackson Hole Golf and Tennis Club have rentals and lessons for golfers and tennis aficionados.

The Tom Fazio–designed 18-hole course **Shooting Star Golf Course** (307/739-3260 or 877/739-8062, www.shootingstarjh.com) opened in 2009 next to Teton Village. It is, however, only for members, and at $100,000 per, it's a bit beyond the range of most mortals!

For the dedicated miniature golfer, **Alpine Miniature Golf** (307/733-5200 or 800/522-5464, www.snowking.com, $8) has a Lilliputian 18-hole hillside course next to the Alpine Slide at Snow King Resort.

Public tennis courts are on the east end of the rodeo grounds along Snow King Drive, and within Miller Park at Deloney and Gill Streets.

TOWN PARKS

Eight parks are scattered around Jackson, including the famous Town Square. Several others are of note, particularly if you have children in tow. The largest, **Miller Park,** covers a grassy city block at Deloney and Gill Streets and includes basketball and tennis courts, a picnic shelter, restrooms, and a delightful playground. **Powderhorn Park,** on the west side of town near Powderhorn and Alpine Lanes, has additional playground equipment, a picnic shelter, and restrooms. **Mike Yokel Jr. Park,** on East Kelly Avenue near Snow King, features a sand volleyball court, horseshoe pits, a playground, a picnic shelter, and restrooms. **Baux Park** at the base of Snow King Mountain is similar, with a playground, horseshoe pits, and picnic tables. **Home Ranch Park** is next to the parking lot at Cache and Gill and has picnic tables and restrooms. **Owen Bircher Park** in Wilson includes a summertime roping arena (a good place to watch budding cowboys and cowgirls on summer afternoons) that becomes a wintertime ice rink. The park also has a sand volleyball court, a softball/soccer field, picnic tables, and restrooms.

In addition to those mentioned in the town parks, public restrooms can be found half a block south of Town Square on Cache Drive.

Winter Recreation

Jackson Hole has an international reputation as a winter destination. As access has become easier and the facilities more developed, many people have discovered the wonders of a Jackson Hole winter, especially one centered on a week of skiing or snowboarding. Three very different ski resorts attract the crowds: Grand Targhee for down-home, powder-to-the-butt conditions; Snow King for steep, inexpensive, edge-of-town slopes; and Jackson Hole for flashy, world-class skiing. All three places have rental equipment, ski schools, and special programs for kids. Snowboarders and telemarkers are welcome on the slopes. These resorts combine with an incredible abundance of developed and wild places to ski cross-country to make Jackson Hole one of the premier ski and snowboard destinations in America.

See a travel agent for package trips to any of the Jackson-area resorts. For daily ski reports, including information on both downhill and Nordic areas and the backcountry, listen to KMTN (FM 96.9) in the morning or visit resort websites. Both Jackson Hole Resort and Grand Targhee also post snow updates on Twitter.

DOWNHILL SKIING AND SNOWBOARDING

If you plan to spend more than a couple of days in the area, it is probably worth your while to join the **Jackson Hole Ski and Snowboard Club** (307/733-6433, www.jhskiclub.com). In return for a $30 membership, you receive an impressive number of premiums, including reduced rates for lift tickets and season passes, plus discounted lodging, meals, drinks, snowmobile trips, and shopping at local stores. Join online or at their office inside Snow King Resort (400 E. Snow King Ave.).

Grand Targhee Ski Resort (307/353-2300 or 800/827-4433, www.grandtarghee.com)—just five miles above Alta, Wyoming—is the main attraction for the Teton Valley, Idaho area. The resort offers excellent skiing and snowboarding in winter, along with a wide range of summer activities.

Ski and Snowboard Rentals

Rent or buy downhill skis and snowboards from **Hoback Sports** (520 W. Broadway Ave., 307/733-5335, www.hobacksports. com), **Boardroom of Jackson Hole** (225 W. Broadway Ave., 307/733-8327, www.board-roomjacksonhole.com), **The Edge Sports** (490 W. Broadway Ave., 307/734-3916, www. jacksonholeedgesports.com), **Gart Sports** (485 W. Broadway Ave., 307/733-4449, www. gartsports.com), **Jack Dennis Sports** (50 E. Broadway Ave., 307/733-3270 or 800/570-3270, www.jackdennisoutdoors.com; and in Teton Village, 307/733-6838), **Jackson Hole Sports** (in Teton Village, 307/739-2687, www.jacksonhole.com), **Pepi Stiegler Sports** (in Teton Village, 307/733-4505, www.pepistieglers.com), **Wildernest Sports** (in Teton Village, 307/733-4297, www.wil-dernestsports.com), or **Teton Village Sports** (307/733-2181 or 800/874-4224, www.teton-villagesports.com). Rentals are also available at all three ski areas.

◖ Jackson Hole Mountain Resort

Just 12 miles northwest of Jackson is Jackson Hole Mountain Resort (307/733-2292 or 888/333-7766, www.jacksonhole.com), the largest and best-known Wyoming ski area. A true skiers' and snowboarders' mountain, Jackson Hole is considered the most varied and challenging of any American ski area. The powder is usually deep (average annual snowfall is 38 feet), lift lines are short, the slopes are relatively uncrowded, and the vistas are unbelievable. First opened in 1965, Jackson Hole Mountain Resort has become one of the nation's favorite ski areas. The resort has invested many millions of dollars in the last decade or so, upgrading facilities, adding lifts,

expanding snowmaking, completing a spacious children's center, and building an ice rink and snowboarding half-pipe. These improvements have both enhanced the resort's reputation as an expert's paradise and added facilities that are friendlier to families and intermediate skiers. Jackson Hole Mountain Resort is owned by the Kemmerer family, whose ancestors founded the town of Kemmerer, Wyoming, and is one of the few major American ski resorts that is still independently owned. The resort is trying to become eco-friendly; it gets all its energy from renewable energy credits and recycling a third of all trash.

The mountain has one unusual feature that occurs in midwinter: A temperature inversion frequently develops over the valley, meaning that when it's bitterly cold at the base of the mountain, the top is 15–20°F warmer. Skiers often remain on the upper slopes all day to enjoy these warmer temperatures.

With an unsurpassed 4,139-foot vertical drop (longest in the United States), 2,500 acres of terrain spread over two adjacent mountains, runs that exceed four miles in length, and 24 miles of groomed trails, Jackson Hole Mountain Resort is truly a place of superlatives. Half of the resort's 60 runs are in the advanced category—including several of the notorious double-diamonds—but it is so large that even beginners will find plenty of bunny slopes on which to practice. (As a trivial aside, Montana's Big Sky Resort also claims the longest vertical drop of any American mountain—4,300 feet—but this involves taking three lifts and ending your run below where you start.)

The only way to the summit of 10,450-foot **Rendezvous Mountain** is aboard one of the 100-passenger aerial tram cars. Powered by 1,970-horsepower engines, they climb nearly 2.5 miles in nine minutes, offering jaw-dropping views across Jackson Hole. Rendezvous Mountain is where experts strut their stuff on these steep and fast slopes, and if you're not at least close to expert status you'll find your blood pressure rising as the tram heads up the mountain. More than a few skiers and boarders have taken the tram back down after seeing what lies below. Yes, those death-defying cliff-jumping shots are real; check out infamous **Corbet's Couloir,** a rocky gully that requires a leap of faith. Fortunately, intermediate skiers and boarders are not given short shrift at Jackson Hole Mountain Resort, particularly on the friendlier slopes of 8,481-foot **Après Vous Mountain.** Intermediate (and advanced) downhillers could spend all day playing on these slopes, and a high-speed quad here means that riders can blast to the summit of Après Vous in just five minutes. Because of the speed of this and other lifts, the wait at the base is usually just a few minutes.

In addition to these lifts, you can ride a gondola, five other quad chairs, two triple chairs, a double chair, and a Poma lift. Snowboarders will appreciate the half-pipe and boarders' terrain trail. The resort's **Kids Ranch** (307/739-2788, $89 per day) provides supervised day care, including a spacious play area; it's the only drop-off day-care center in Jackson Hole, and it's open seven days a week in winter. Not far away is a special "magic carpet" (a conveyer belt of sorts) for children learning to ski or snowboard.

Summer visitors to Jackson Hole Mountain Resort find an amazing variety of activities including horseback rides, music festivals, rock-climbing, paragliding, a mountain biking course, disc golf, playful pop-jet fountains, a bungee trampoline, shopping, or just soaking up the view while nursing a beer.

RATES AND SERVICES

Get to Teton Village from the town of Jackson by hopping on the START bus ($3 each way; 307/733-4521, www.startbus.com). This is the only inexpensive part of a visit to Jackson Hole Resort, where prices for lift tickets approach the stratosphere. Regular-season single-day tickets are $91 adults, $55 ages 6–14, and $68 seniors. Afternoon-only rates are $73 adults, $44 kids, and $55 seniors. Multi-day tickets—the most common kind bought—are $435 per week (five days of skiing) for adults, $260 for kids 5–14, and $325 for seniors. Lifts are open 9 A.M.–4 P.M. daily Thanksgiving–early April.

Skis and snowboards can be rented at shops in Jackson or Teton Village. The ski school offers a Kids Ranch program with age-specific skiing and boarding. Jackson Hole Resort even has special steep snowboarding and skiing camps, where you learn from extreme downhill fanatics. Tommy Moe—gold and silver medalist at the 1994 Winter Olympics—is a ski ambassador for the resort. A private day of guided skiing is available for $1,400 (intermediate and expert skiers only).

Ski hosts provide information and twice-daily tours from the front of Walk Festival Hall. Racers and spectators will enjoy NASTAR events, along with various other competitions throughout the winter.

Get recorded snow conditions by calling the **Snowphone** at 307/733-2291; messages are changed each morning before 5 A.M. The resort's website is packed with additional details, including the current weather and snow conditions, or visit www.jacksonhole.com/mobile from your iPhone.

Into the Backcountry

If you're looking for untracked powder, the Jackson Hole Mountain Resort (307/733-2292 or 888/333-7766, www.jacksonhole.com) can set up private lessons for access to parts of the mountain that are off-limits to mere mortals.

In lower Rock Springs Canyon, two miles south of the resort, **Rock Springs Yurt** has a backcountry location that's accessible by cross-country skis or snowshoes. It's only a two-mile trek, but you gain 1,000 feet along the way, making this a challenging trip. The fully equipped yurt is available for guided day trips and overnight stays. It sleeps eight for $425, including dinner and breakfast cooked by the "yurt meister." Contact Jackson Hole Resort (307/739-2663 or 800/450-0477, www.jacksonhole.com) for details. The yurt is also open to summertime hikers.

Powderhound skiers with a ton of cash will find unparalleled outback conditions accessible via **High Mountain Heli-Skiing** (307/733-3274, www.heliskijackson.com). Operating from Togwotee Mountain Lodge (307/543-

2847 or 800/543-2847, www.togwoteelodge. com) 48 miles northeast of Jackson, **Togwotee Snowcat Skiing** takes skiers and snowboarders into a wide variety of terrain with spectacular vistas of the Tetons en route.

Teton Village

At the base of Rendezvous Mountain is the Swiss-style Teton Village—alias "the Vill." Everything skiers and boarders need is crowded together here: lodges, condominiums, espresso stands, restaurants, après-ski bars, gift shops, groceries, ski, snowboard, and snowshoe rentals and lessons, storage lockers, car rentals, a sledding hill, child care, personal trainers, dogsled tours, and even a travel agency for escapes to Hawaii. Tune your radio to FM 100.1 "Teton Village Radio" for parking and transportation information.

On-the-mountain facilities include a fine-dining establishment (Couloir Restaurant) at the top of Bridger gondola, Casper Restaurant at the bottom of Casper Bowl, and snack bars at the base of Thunder chairlift and the top of Après Vous chairlift. Casper Restaurant serves a barbecue picnic most days and is a popular place to join friends for lunch.

Snow King Mountain

Snow King Mountain (307/734-3136, www. snowkingmountain.com) has three things that other local ski areas lack: location, location, and location. The resort sits directly behind town and just seven blocks from Town Square. This is the locals' place, Jackson's "town hill," but it also offers surprisingly challenging runs. It may not be the largest or fanciest place around, but the King's ski runs make up in difficulty what they lack in size. From below, the mountain (7,808 feet at the summit) looks impossibly steep and narrow. High atop the big chairlift, the vista provides a panoramic tour of Jackson Hole and the Tetons.

Snow King was the first ski area in Wyoming—it opened in 1939—and one of the first in North America. The original chapter of the National Ski Patrol was established here in 1941. The mountain has a 1,571-foot

vertical drop. You'll find more than 400 acres of skiable terrain at Snow King, with the longest run stretching nearly a mile. A triple chair, two double chairs, and a Poma lift climb the mountainside. Other features include snow-making, a tubing park, and a very popular terrain park for snowboarders. It's the only local resort with lighted runs.

RATES AND SERVICES

Prices for lift tickets at Snow King are well below those at other Jackson Hole resorts: $42 per day ($32 per half-day) for adults and $32 per day ($22 per half-day) for kids under 13 and seniors. Hours of operation are daily 10 A.M.–4 P.M., with **night skiing** (4–7 P.M. Tues.–Sat.) available on the lower sections of Snow King for an additional $20 adults or $15 kids and seniors. In addition, the King has special three-hour rates for lift tickets ($30 adults, $20 kids and seniors); these are perfect for skiers and boarders who arrive late in the afternoon and want to hit the slopes for a bit. With some of the best snowmaking in Wyoming, the resort usually opens by Thanksgiving and remains in operation through early April.

At the base of Snow King you'll discover a lodge with reasonable ski-and-stay packages. Also at Snow King are two restaurants, a lounge (called, not surprisingly, The Lounge), ski and snowboard rentals and lessons, plus a variety of other facilities, including an indoor ice rink and mountaintop snack shack. Jackson's START buses (307/733-4521, www. startbus.com) provide frequent service to town (free) or Teton Village ($3).

CROSS-COUNTRY SKIING

For many Jackson Hole residents, the word "skiing" means heading across frozen Jenny Lake or telemarking down the bowls of Teton Pass rather than sliding down the slopes of the local resorts. Jackson Hole has become a center for cross-country enthusiasts and offers an impressive range of conditions—from flat-tracking along summertime golf courses where a gourmet restaurant awaits to remote wilderness settings where a complete knowledge of snowpack structure, avalanche hazards, and winter survival techniques is essential. Beginners will probably want to start out at a Nordic center, progressing to local paths and the more gentle lift-serviced ski runs with experience. More advanced skiers will quickly discover incredible snow in the surrounding mountains.

Ski Rentals

Rent or buy cross-country skis from **Skinny Skis** (65 W. Deloney Ave., 307/733-6094 or 888/733-7205, www.skinnyskis.com), **Teton Mountaineering** (170 N. Cache Dr., 307/733-3595 or 800/850-3595, www.tetonmtn.com), or **Wilson Backcountry Sports** (Wilson, 307/733-5228, www.wilsonbackcountry.com). Local Nordic centers also rent equipment. Most places rent both classical cross-country skis and skate skis (much faster and a better workout), along with telemark and alpine touring skis.

Nordic Centers

Nordic skiing enthusiasts will find two different developed facilities near Jackson and a third at Grand Targhee in Alta, Wyoming. The largest is **Jackson Hole Nordic Center** (307/739-2629, www.jacksonhole.com) in Teton Village, with 15 kilometers of groomed trails—both set track and skating lanes—that cover a wide range of conditions. Call 307/733-2291 for the snow report. This is the best place to learn cross-country skiing. Daily trail passes are $14. Traditional cross-country skis, skate skis, and telemarking equipment are available for rent, and the center offers a wide spectrum of lessons and tours. Hours are daily 8:30 A.M.–4:30 P.M. You can exchange your alpine lift ticket at Jackson Hole Mountain Resort for one at the Nordic center (but, hey, it had better be for no extra charge since you've already dropped $91!).

Along Teton Village Road, **Teton Pines** (307/733-1005 or 800/238-2223, www.tetonpines.com) features 16 kilometers of immaculately groomed track (both classical and skating) on a summertime golf course. Daily trail passes cost $10 adults or $5 children and seniors. Ski rentals and lessons are available. Hours are daily 9 A.M.–5 P.M. The clubhouse here has a restaurant for gourmet après-ski lunches and dinners.

On the west side of the Tetons 42 miles out of Jackson, **Grand Targhee Nordic Center** (307/353-2300 or 800/827-4433, www.grandtarghee.com) has 15 kilometers of groomed cross-country ski trails (classical and skating) covering rolling terrain. Trail passes are $10 adults and $6 seniors and kids. Lessons and ski rentals are also available. Hours are daily 9:30 A.M.–4 P.M. Guests with Targhee lodging packages can ski free on the cross-country tracks.

On Your Own

Nordic skiers who would rather explore Jackson Hole and the mountains that surround it on their own will discover an extraordinary range of options, from beginner-level treks along old roads to places where only the most advanced skiers dare venture. Because Jackson has so many cross-country fanatics (and visiting enthusiasts), tracks are quickly broken along the more popular routes, making it easier for those who follow. For complete coverage of all these options, pick up a copy of the helpful free winter outdoors guide *Trailhead* at Skinny Skis (65 W. Deloney Ave., 307/733-6094 or 888/733-7205, www.skinnyskis.com). If you're heading out on your own, be prepared for deep snow (four feet in the valley) and temperatures that often plummet below zero at night.

Teton County Parks & Recreation (155 E. Gill, 307/739-9025, www.tetonwyo.org/parks) leads all-day cross-country ski and snowshoe outings in winter, as well as cross-country lessons. The department also grooms 30 kilometers of local pathways for cross-country and skate skiing in the winter; call 307/739-6789 for the grooming hotline with daily updates. **Friends of Pathways** (307/733-9562, www.friendsofpathways.org) produces a free map of local Nordic trails (including the grooming schedule) and has a downloadable version on their website.

JACKSON AREA

Even beginners will enjoy exploring several local spots. The closest place to Jackson for on-your-own cross-country skiing is **Cache Creek Canyon.** The trailhead is at the east end of Cache Creek Drive, where the plowing ends at a parking lot. The trail is groomed by Parks & Rec a couple of times per week. For a longer trip, take the Rafferty ski lift at Snow King and then ski west through the trees and down to Cache Creek, returning via the road. Ask at Snow King Resort (400 E. Snow King Ave., 307/733-5200 or 800/522-5464, www.snowking.com) for specifics and safety precautions.

Another popular local place is along the **Snake River dikes,** where Highway 22 crosses the river one mile east of Wilson. The dikes extend along both sides of the river for several miles, making for easy skiing. This is also a good place to watch ducks, moose, and other critters or to listen to the river rolling over the rocks. The northeast side is groomed for skate and touring skis on a regular basis but can get pockmarked by folks walking the trail.

GRANITE HOT SPRINGS

One of the most popular ski- and snowmobile-in sites is Granite Hot Springs (307/734-7400, http://granitehotsprings.mountainmancountry.com), a delightful hot spring–fed pool on Forest Service land. Get there by driving 25 miles southeast of Jackson into Hoback Canyon and then skiing 10 miles in from the signed parking area. The route is not difficult, but because of the distance it isn't recommended for beginners unless they're prepared for a 20-mile round-trip trek. The pool costs $6 adults, $4 ages 3–12, and is free for infants. It's open daily 10 A.M.–5 P.M. in winter. Bring your swimsuit or rent a suit and towel here. Ask the attendant about places to snow camp nearby.

TETON PASS

Locals head to 8,429-foot Teton Pass when they really want to test their abilities. The summit parking area fills with cars on fresh-snow mornings as everyone from advanced beginners to world-class ski mountaineers heads out for a day in the powder or a week of wilderness trekking in the Tetons. Snow depths of eight feet or more are not uncommon in midwinter. (The snow once became so deep on the pass that it took plows two weeks to clear the road!) The slopes around Teton Pass cover the full spectrum, but be sure you know your own ability and how to avoid avalanches. Check the previously mentioned Skinny Skis *Trailhead* winter guide for specifics on Teton Pass, or talk to folks at Skinny Skis or Teton Mountaineering. This is the backcountry, so you won't see any signs at the various bowls; ask other skiers if you aren't sure which is which. Avalanches do occur in some of these bowls, and it's possible to get lost up here during a storm, so come prepared.

Those without backcountry experience should contact **Rendezvous Backcountry Tours** (307/353-2900 or 877/754-4887, www.skithetetons.com), **Jackson Hole Mountain Guides** (307/733-4979 or 800/239-7642, www.jhmg.com), **Exum Mountain Guides** (307/733-2297, www.exumguides.com), or **Jackson Hole Nordic Center** (307/739-2629, www.jacksonhole.com) for guided ski tours at Teton Pass and elsewhere.

Ski Tours

Both **Jackson Hole Mountain Guides** (307/733-4979 or 800/239-7642, www.jhmg.com) and **Exum Mountain Guides** (307/733-2297, www.exumguides.com) run winter ascents of Grand Teton, plus avalanche safety courses and ski mountaineering trips. Longer winter trips, including a five-day Teton Crest tour, are also available.

Over on the western slopes of the Tetons, **Rendezvous Backcountry Tours** (307/353-2900 or 877/754-4887, www.skithetetons.com) maintains three Mongolian-style yurts in the Jedediah Smith Wilderness, each situated several hours of skiing (or hiking) from the next. These immensely popular huts can sleep up to eight and have kitchens, bunks, sleeping bags, and woodstoves; they're $375 per night on weekends ($325 on weekdays) plus $150 for a guide to take you in on the first day. You'll need to be experienced in backcountry skiing and have the necessary safety equipment and avalanche training. If you don't quite measure up, the company provides guided ski tours to the huts. A three-day, two-night catered trip is $695 per person including guide, porter service, meals, lodging, sleeping bags, and avalanche equipment. The backcountry yurts are available December–April, but call far ahead for reservations. The most popular one (Baldy Knoll) fills a year in advance! Rendezvous also has a close-in family yurt ($95 d or $150 for up to six guests). It's open year-round, with drive-up access in summer and a 0.5-mile walk in winter. The family hut has running water, a kitchen, and bath, while the backcountry yurts have outhouses.

Jackson Hole Nordic Center (307/739-2629, www.jacksonhole.com), at Teton Village, has guided ski tours into Grand Teton National Park; a half-day for two people costs $160.

ICE-SKATING

Each winter, the town of Wilson floods the town park for skating, hockey, and broomball. A warming hut stands next to the rink. In Jackson, the rodeo arena at the fairgrounds (552 S. Snow King Ave.) becomes a winter ice rink for broomball and open skating. Both rinks are free and lighted most winter evenings. Contact Teton County Parks & Recreation (307/733-5056, www.tetonwyo.org/parks) for details.

For the out-of-the-elements version, skate over to **Snow King Resort** (400 E. Snow King Ave., 307/733-5200 or 800/522-5464, www.snowking.com), where the indoor ice-skating rink is open in the winter and offers skate rentals and lessons. In addition, **Grand Targhee Ski Resort** (in Alta, 307/353-2300 or 800/827-4433, www.grandtarghee.com) has a skating pond with rentals.

SNOWSHOEING

Snowshoeing began as a way to get around in the winter, but the old-fashioned wood-and-rawhide snowshoes were bulky and heavy. In recent years snowshoeing has become a popular form of recreation, as new technology created lightweight and easily maneuverable snowshoes. Snowshoeing requires no real training: Just strap the snowshoes on, grab a pair of poles, and start walking. But be careful where you walk.

Rent snowshoes from **Skinny Skis** (65 W. Deloney Ave., 307/733-6094 or 888/733-7205, www.skinnyskis.com), **Teton Mountaineering** (170 N. Cache Dr., 307/733-3595 or 800/850-3595, www.tetonmtn.com), **Wilson Backcountry Sports** (in Wilson, 307/733-5228, www.wilsonbackcountry.com), or **Grand Targhee Ski Resort** (in Alta, 307/353-2300 or 800/827-4433, www.grandtarghee.com).

Guided Trips

Teton County Parks & Recreation (155 E. Gill, 307/739-9025, www.tetonwyo.org/parks) leads snowshoe tours periodically throughout the winter. Snowshoe walks into the mountains around Jackson are also offered by **The Hole Hiking Experience** (307/690-4453 or 866/733-4453, www.holehike.com), the only company permitted to guide snowshoeing trips in nearby national forests. Their most popular trips go to Shadow Mountain north of Kelly. Rates start at $95 adults, $75 kids for a four-hour snowshoe trek (minimum of three people).

Also check out A. J. DeRosa's **Wildlife Snowshoe Adventures** (307/732-2628, www.woodboattours.com), combining snowshoe hikes with lunch or dinner at a riverside teepee.

The Saddlehorn Activity Center at **Jackson Hole Mountain Resort** (307/733-2292 or 888/333-7766, www.jacksonhole.com) has snowshoe rentals and tours. In addition, a snowshoe trail parallels Nordic Center ski tracks, and Forest Service naturalists lead snowshoe hikes in the area on Wednesday and Saturday.

Free naturalist-led snowshoe tours are offered at **Grand Targhee Ski Resort** (in Alta, 307/353-2300 or 800/827-4433, www.grandtarghee.com). Additionally, naturalist-led snowshoe hikes are available in Grand Teton National Park.

SLEIGH RIDES

Several companies offer romantic dinner and horse-drawn sleigh rides in the Jackson Hole area mid-December–March. Make reservations well in advance for these popular trips. If you don't have the cash for one of these, take a daytime sleigh ride at the National Elk Refuge.

Jackson Hole Mountain Resort (307/733-2674, www.tetonvillagetrailrides.com, $80 adults, $70 children under 11, and free for infants) picks up Teton Village guests for a romantic 30-minute ride to Cascade Restaurant at Teton Mountain Lodge, where they are offered a variety of dinner options. Reservations are recommended. If you're just looking for a Teton Village sleigh ride, there is a 12-person sleigh ($35 adults, $25 kids) or a private ride on a romantic "Cinderella" sleigh ($100 for up to four people). Both options last approximately 30–40 minutes.

Spring Creek Ranch (307/733-8833 or 800/443-6139, www.springcreekranch.com) has 45-minute afternoon sleigh rides ($39 per person) at the top of Gros Ventre Butte. It also has packages ($89 per person for adults, $59 kids) that combine a sleigh ride with a meal at the Granary Restaurant. This is one of Jackson's finer restaurants, so bring your dress clothes and make reservations.

Mill Iron Ranch (307/733-6390 or 888/808-6390, www.millironranch.net, $85 adults, $60 kids) is a friendly family-run operation with evening sleigh rides in a down-home setting 10 miles south of Jackson in Horse Creek Canyon. Guests get a 45-minute ride that takes them past an elk herd to the lodge for a big T-bone steak dinner. In scenic Horse Creek Canyon, this is the most authentic of the local sleigh rides. Call for reservations.

Dinner sleigh rides are also offered at **Grand Targhee Ski Resort** (in Alta, 307/353-2300 or 800/827-4433, www.grandtarghee.com, $40 adults, $15 kids), where a horse-drawn sleigh transports you to a remote yurt for a Western-style meal.

TUBING

Two local ski areas have sliding parks with customized inner tubes and rope tows. At Snow King Resort the park is called **King Tubes** (307/734-8823 or 800/522-5464, www.jacksonholesnowtubing.com) and is available on weekday evenings and weekends after noon. Rates are $16 for one hour or $21 for two hours for adults; $13 for one hour or $18 for two hours for kids. The **Grand Targhee tube park** (307/353-2300 or 800/827-4433, www.grandtarghee.com) is open for après-ski fun only (after 5 P.M.) and costs $10.

DOGSLEDDING

Founded by eight-time Iditarod musher Frank Teasley, **Jackson Hole Iditarod Sled Dog Tours** (307/733-7388 or 800/554-7388, www.jhsleddog.com) has excellent half-day ($225 per person including lunch) and all-day trips ($295 per person including a big steak or trout dinner). The main destination is wonderful Granite Hot Springs (accessible only on all-day rides), but when snow conditions are right, the teams may run in the Cliff Creek, Grays River, Shadow Mountain, and Gros Ventre areas. All trips include round-trip transportation from Jackson to his base on the Hoback River.

Another Iditarod veteran, Billy Snodgrass, operates **Continental Divide Dogsled Adventures** (307/739-0165 or 800/531-6874, www.dogsledadventures.com), with dog teams at Togwotee Mountain Lodge (48 miles north of Jackson). Half-day tours in this gorgeous country are $224 per person, including lunch and transportation from Jackson. All-day tours are $270 and longer trips are also available, including a two-day adventure in which you stay overnight in a backcountry yurt or at luxurious Brooks Lake Lodge.

SNOWMOBILING

Snowmobiling is one of Jackson Hole's most popular wintertime activities. Hundreds of miles of packed and groomed snowmobile trails head into Bridger-Teton National Forest. Some of the most popular places include the Togwotee Pass area 48 miles north of Jackson,

JACKSON HOLE

Cache Creek Road east of town, and Granite Hot Springs Road 25 miles southeast. Only guided snowmobile groups are allowed into Yellowstone, with all-day tours to Old Faithful ($270 for one rider or $390 for two riders).

Tours to other areas are usually less expensive, and some motels offer package deals. The visitor center has brochures and a complete listing of local snowmobile-rental companies, plus maps of snowmobile trails.

Entertainment and Events

Jackson Hole has a wide range of entertainment options: cowboy bars where saddles double as bar stools, classical concerts beneath the stars, playful family musicals, rodeos and chuck-wagon dinners, and much more.

At the modern 525-seat theater within **Jackson Hole Center for the Arts** (307/733-4900, www.jhcenterforthearts.org) you might see everyone from Leo Kottke and Herbie Hancock to the Preservation Hall Jazz Band and Willie Nelson.

In 2009, Teton County instituted a no-smoking measure that prohibits smoking in restaurants, bars, and workplaces, along with many outdoor locations such as chairlift lines, restaurant patios, and sports arenas. Because of this, virtually all Jackson Hole restaurants and bars are now entirely smoke-free. The only exception is the smoky Virginian Bar (750 W. Broadway Ave.) on the south end of town. (This will change if the Virginian loses an ongoing lawsuit over the issue.) Jackson Hole Mountain Resort, Grand Targhee Resort, and Snow King Resort all prohibit smoking except in designated areas.

NIGHTLIFE

Barflies will keep buzzing in Jackson, especially during midsummer and midwinter, when visitors pack local saloons every night of the week. At least one club always seems to have live tunes; check Jackson's free newspapers to see what's where. Cover charges are generally $5 on the weekends, and most other times you'll get in free. See the free *Jackson Hole Weekly* (307/732-0299, www.planetjh.com) for upcoming music and other entertainment.

The famous **Million Dollar Cowboy Bar** (on the west side of Town Square, 307/733-2207, www.milliondollarcowboybar.com) is a favorite of real cowboys and their wannabe cousins. Inside the Cowboy you'll discover burled lodgepole pine beams, four pool tables (nearly always in use), display cases with stuffed dead bears and other cuddly critters, bars inlaid with old silver dollars, and bar stools made from old saddles. Until the 1950s, the Cowboy was Jackson's center for illegal gambling. Bartenders kept a close eye on Teton Pass, where messengers used mirrors to deliver warnings of coming federal revenuers, giving folks at the bar time to hide the gaming tables in a back room. Today the dance floor fills with honky-tonking couples as the bands croon lonesome cowboy tunes six nights a week (Mon.–Sat.). Looking to learn swing and two-step dancing? You can join an excellent free beginners' class at 7:30 P.M. every Thursday, and then dance up a storm when the band comes on at 9.

Silver Dollar Bar & Grill (50 N. Glenwood St., 307/732-3939, www.worthotel.com) inside the Wort Hotel offers a setting that might seem more fitting in Las Vegas: Gaudy pink neon lights curve around a bar inlaid with 2,032 (count 'em!) silver dollars. It tends to attract an older crowd with nightly drink specials (best martinis in Jackson), but Tuesday nights are the notable exception, when bluegrass bands and no cover attract a packed house of partying 20-somethings.

In Teton Village is **Mangy Moose Restaurant & Saloon** (307/733-4913, www.mangymoose.net) Jackson Hole's jumpingest pickup spot and *the* place to rock out. The Moose attracts a hip skier/outdoorsy crowd with rock, blues, or world beat bands (Wed.–Sat.,

© DON PITCHER

Jackson's famed Million Dollar Cowboy Bar

sometimes nightly) both summer and winter. This is also where you'll hear nationally known acts. Upcoming acts are listed on the Mangy Moose website. The on-site restaurant serves food until 10 P.M.

On the way to Teton Village, and next door to Calico Restaurant, **Q Roadhouse** (2550 Moose-Wilson Rd., 307/739-0700, www. qjacksonhole.com, daily 5–10 P.M.) is a cavernous, indestructible pub (concrete floors and an industrial décor), where the menu includes wings, blackened catfish, and jambalaya. Toss your peanut shells on the floor and join the happy crowds of locals listening to rock tunes (live bands Thurs. nights) and putting back the beers.

Jammed against the hill on the west end of town, **Sidewinders Sports Grill & Tavern** (802 W. Broadway Ave., 307/734-5766, www. sidewinderstavern.com, daily 11:30 A.M.–12:30 A.M.) is a bar/restaurant with pub grub, 30 beers on tap, and a couple-dozen flat-screen TVs for sports enthusiasts. Look for the enormous American flag out front. Downstairs is

trendy **Ignight** (307/734-1997, www.ignight-jacksonhole.com, $8–14), with freshly squeezed juice cocktails at the martini bar, along with sushi, ceviche, salads, and a variety of finger food. Live music (Thurs.–Sat. nights) enlivens the classy setting.

The Granary (307/733-8833 or 800/443-6139, www.springcreekranch.com) atop East Gros Ventre Butte has mellow jazz (Fri. nights) and piano tunes (Sat.).

Over in Wilson, **The Stagecoach Bar** (307/733-4407) is *the* place to be on Sunday nights 6–10 P.M., when locals call it "the church." In the 1970s, when hippies risked getting their heads shaved by rednecks at Jackson's Cowboy Bar, they found the 'Coach a more tolerant place. Today, tobacco-chewing cowpokes show their partners slick moves on the tiny dance floor as the Stagecoach Band (jokingly known as the "worst country-western band in the U.S.") runs through the country tunes one more time; the band has performed here every Sunday since 1969! Outside you'll find picnic tables and a volleyball court for pickup games in the summer, or pick up a cue stick and show off your billiard skills indoors. The Mexican-infused bar food comes from Pica's Taqueria, with burritos, tacos, burgers, quesadillas, and more. Also popular are the Thursday-night disco parties with a dance-club atmosphere and a fog machine; it's a great time to dress up in *Saturday Night Fever* garb.

THE ARTS

In addition to the bar scene, summers bring several lighthearted acting ventures to Jackson. For family musicals such as *Paint Your Wagon, Nunsense,* or *Annie Get Your Gun,* head to **Jackson Hole Playhouse** (145 W. Deloney, 307/733-6994, www.jhplayhouse.com). Shows take place Monday–Saturday evenings in a campy 1890s-style setting; tickets are $26 adults, $22 ages 13–18, and $19 ages 5–12. A family saloon (no alcohol; what kind of a saloon is that?) and restaurant are next door. More serious productions are offered in the winter.

A professional repertory group, the **Off Square Theatre Company** (307/733-3670, www.offsquare.org) stages Broadway comedies in the summer at the Jackson Hole Center for the Arts, with dramatic productions the rest of the year.

In existence for more than 50 years, the **Grand Teton Music Festival** (307/733-1128, www.gtmf.org) takes place at Walk Festival Hall in Teton Village, with performances of classical and modern works by a cast of 200 world-renowned symphony musicians. Concerts are at 8 P.M. from the first of July to mid-August each year, with free "Inside the Music" concerts on Tuesday, Wednesday-night spotlight concerts ($41 adults, $10 kids) featuring jazz, bluegrass, and Afro-Cuban music, and Thursday-night "musicians' choice" classical chamber music ($25 adults, $10 kids). Full festival orchestra concerts on Friday and Saturday are $52 adults, $10 kids. They also perform a free outdoor **Music in the Hole** patriotic concert on the Fourth of July for an audience that tops 8,000, plus special youth concerts and other events. Three-hour-long Friday-morning rehearsals are just $10.

CINEMA

Watch flicks downtown at **Teton Theatre** (120 N. Cache Dr.) and **Jackson Hole Twin Cinema** (295 W. Pearl St.), or south of town at **MovieWorks** (860 S. U.S. Hwy. 89). All three of these have the same movie line: 307/733-4939. Find this week's films online at www.jacksonholecinemas.com.

CHUCK-WAGON COOKOUTS

Jackson Hole is home to several chuck-wagon affairs offering all-you-can-eat barbecue cookouts and Western musical performances in the summer. Each has its own advantages, but reservations are highly recommended at all of these.

Run by the Thomas family since 1973, **Bar-T-Five** (790 Cache Creek Rd., 307/733-5386 or 800/772-5386, www.bart5.com, $43 adults, $36 ages 5–12, free for kids under five) is one of the best chuck-wagon feeds. Horse-drawn Conestoga-style wagons depart just east of Snow King, carrying visitors along Cache Creek past costumed mountain men, cowboys, and Indians. At the in-the-trees cookout site (chicken, roast beef, salad, rolls, corn, beans, dessert, and lemonade), cowboys serenade your meal, tell stories, and crack corny jokes that aren't entirely politically correct. It's great fun for families and busloads of Japanese tourists. It's open mid-May–September, with departures Monday–Saturday at 5 and 6:30 P.M. (closed Sun.).

Along the Teton Village Road near Teton Pines, the **Bar J Chuckwagon** (307/733-3370 or 800/905-2275, www.barjchuckwagon.com) does a land-office business throughout the summer, with seating for over 700 people in a cavernous building, including busloads of gray-haired Gray Liners. In existence since 1977, Bar J is famous for its first-rate musicians who fiddle (one is a two-time national fiddle champion), sing, yodel, and regale the audience with cornball jokes and dollops of cowboy poetry. Before the show everyone queues up for heaping servings of barbecued beef, roast chicken, pork rib, or rib-eye steak served with baked potatoes, beans, biscuits, applesauce, spice cake, and lemonade (but no alcohol). Amazingly, Bar

J manages to feed the entire crowd in a half-hour. The picnic-table seating is cramped, but after dinner you're treated to 90 minutes of rollicking entertainment. The cost is $20–30 for adults (depending on your meal), $10 for kids under eight, or free for tots. Bar J is open late May–September, with dinner at 7 p.m.; many folks arrive an hour or so earlier to get front-row seats for the show. It's a good idea to make reservations at least one week ahead. The Bar J does not offer wagon or horseback rides.

In beautiful Buffalo Valley, 45 miles northeast of Jackson, **Castagno Outfitters Covered Wagon Cookouts** (307/543-2407 or 877/559-3585, www.castagnooutfitters.com) start with a 30-minute ride in covered wagons. The wagons stop at an isolated aspen grove, where guests enjoy a dinner of steak, barbecued beans, baked potato, corn bread, watermelon, and dessert. Dinners cost $35 adults, $30 kids, and run mid-June–late August; closed Sunday. Call the day before for reservations.

EVENTS

Jackson Hole is packed with entertaining events almost every day of the year. Some of these are homegrown affairs such as the county fair, whereas others attract people from near and far. Of particular note are the International Pedigree Stage Stop Sled Dog Race (IPSSSDR), the Pole-Pedal-Paddle Race, the Elk Antler Auction, the Grand Teton Music Festival, and the Jackson Hole Fall Arts Festival. (In addition to the events listed, Grand Targhee Ski Resort has a year-round calendar of events on the other side of the Tetons.)

Winter

December is a particularly beautiful time in downtown Jackson. Lights decorate the elk antler arches, and a variety of events take place. Buy arts and crafts during the **Christmas Bazaar** early in the month, or take the kids to visit Saint Nick and his elves on Town Square starting in mid-December; they're there daily 5–7 p.m.

Kick the year off by watching (or participating in) the annual **torchlight ski parades** at all three local ski areas. Parades take place on New Year's Eve at Snow King (400 E. Snow King Ave., 307/733-5200 or 800/522-5464, www.snowking.com) and New Year's Day at Jackson Hole Mountain Resort (307/733-2292 or 888/333-7766, www.jacksonhole.com), where kids have a separate "glow worm" parade using glow sticks. Two parades occur at Grand Targhee Ski Resort (in Alta, 307/353-2300 or 800/827-4433, www.grandtarghee.com) on Christmas Eve and New Year's Eve.

In existence since 1996, the **International Pedigree Stage Stop Sled Dog Race** (IPSSSDR, pronounced IPS-der, 307/734-1163, www.wyomingstagestop.org) is the largest sled dog race in the lower 48 states and a qualifying event for Alaska's Iditarod. Unlike the Iditarod and most other mushing events, this one is run in short 30- to 60-mile legs, with teams operating from a different town each day. As with the Tour de France, it's the total time that counts in this stage race. The race is the creation of Iditarod musher Frank Teasley and nurse Jayne Ottman, who came up with the idea as a way to raise awareness of the need to immunize children; it's unofficially called "The Race to Immunize." IPSSSDR starts in Jackson and then goes on to Lander, Pinedale, Big Piney, Alpine, Kemmerer, and Evanston, before ending in Park City, Utah. The race boasts a $50,000 purse and has attracted some of the top names in dog mushing, including Iditarod winners Lance Mackey, Jeff King, and Rick Swenson. It's held over eight days in late January and early February.

Each February, local Shriners hold horse-drawn **cutter races** (307/733-4052)—essentially a wild chariot race on 0.25 mile of ice—at Melody Ranch, six miles south of Jackson.

Ski and snowboard races take place all winter long at local resorts; volunteer to work one of the gates at a downhill race and you get to ski free the rest of the day.

One of the most popular—and silliest—Jackson events is the **World Championship Snowmobile Hill Climb** (www.snowdevils. org), in which man (or woman) and machine

JACKSON HOLE

© KATHY ERICKSON/WILD ABOUT LIFE PHOTOGRAPHY

elk antler auction during Elkfest

churn up the slopes at Snow King Resort. The event takes place in late March.

The ski season ends the first weekend of April with the **Pole-Pedal-Paddle Race** (307/733-6433, www.polepedalpaddle.com), combining alpine skiing, cross-country skiing, cycling, and canoeing in a wild, tough competition. It's the largest such event in the West and great fun for spectators and contestants, many of whom dress up in goofy costumes.

Spring

Spring in Jackson Hole is the least favorite time of the year for many locals. The snow is going, leaving behind brown grass and trees; biking and hiking trails aren't yet passable; and the river is too cold to enjoy. For many folks, this is the time to load up the car and head to Utah for a desert hike in Canyonlands. Despite these conditions, April and May can be a good time to visit, especially if you want to avoid the crowds, need to save money on lodging, or are planning to stay for the summer and need a job and a place to live. (Housing gets progressively more difficult to find after April.)

Summer

Summer begins with a series of events during **Elkfest** (307/733-3316, www.elkfest.org) on the third weekend of May, including a **mountain-man rendezvous** and chili cook-off. The main event, however, is the world's only public **elk antler auction,** which attracts hundreds of buyers from all over the globe to Jackson's Town Square. Local Boy Scouts collect five tons of antlers from the nearby National Elk Refuge each spring, with 80 percent of the proceeds helping to fund feeding of the elk. This may sound like an odd event, but the take is generally more than $60,000! Prices average $9 per pound, and the bidding gets highly competitive; perfectly matched pairs can go for more than $1,500. The antlers are primarily used in taxidermy, belt buckles, and furniture.

Memorial Day weekend in May brings **Old West Days** (307/733-3316), complete with a mountain-man rendezvous, horse-drawn parade, brewfest, carriage show, and crafts fair. In late June, the **Jackson Hole Writers Conference** (307/413-3332, www.

© DON PITCHER

calf roping at Jackson Hole Rodeo

jacksonholewritersconference.com) attracts nationally known authors and wannabes to the Center for the Arts.

Fourth of July is another big event in Jackson, with a parade, rodeo, pancake breakfast, and an impressive fireworks show from Snow King Mountain. Another very popular Independence Day event is the free **Music in the Hole** (307/733-1128, www.gtmf.org) outdoor classical concert by the Grand Teton Music Festival orchestra.

If you have a burning desire for something hot, don't miss the **Jackson Hole Fire Festival** (www.vista360.org) on summer solstice (June 21), when the city partners with Fujiyoshida, Japan. You'll see traditional Japanese drumming, dancing, street torches, and food.

On Wednesday and Saturday nights in summer you can watch bucking broncs, bull riders, barrel racers, rodeo clowns, and hard-riding cowboys at the **Jackson Hole Rodeo** (307/733-7927, www.jacksonholerodeo.us, late May–early Sept., starting at 8 P.M., $14 adults, $9 ages 5–12, free for kids under five) on the Teton County Fair Grounds. Kids get to join

in the amusing calf scramble. Another ongoing event is the **Grand Teton Music Festival** (307/733-1128, www.gtmf.org), providing summertime classical music at Teton Village.

The **Art Fair of Jackson Hole** (307/733-8792, www.jhartfair.org) features more than 100 artisans displaying their works at Miller Park. This highly competitive, juried event takes place in mid-July and again in mid-August.

The last week of July brings an always fun **Teton County Fair** (307/733-5289, www.tetoncountyfair.com) with 4-H exhibits (from lambs to photography), pig wrestling in the mud, a horse show, pony rides and a petting farm, watermelon- and pie-eating contests, live music and comedy acts, a carnival, rodeos, and everyone's favorite: a bang-up **demolition derby** on the final Sunday night.

During the second weekend of September, the invitation-only **Jackson Hole One-Fly Contest** (307/203-2654, www.jhonefly.com) attracts anglers from all over, including several celebrity competitors. Another charity event is **Old Bill's Fun Run** (307/739-1026, www.oldbills.org) the second Saturday of September; it's raised more than $67 million over the last decade or so!

Fall

Jackson Hole is at its most glorious in the fall, as aspens and cottonwoods turn into a fire of yellow and orange against the Teton backdrop. Most tourists have fled back home, leaving locals and hardier visitors to savor the cool autumn nights. The peak time for **fall colors** is generally the first week of October—considerably later than most people expect.

The primary autumn event is the **Jackson Hole Fall Arts Festival** (307/733-3316, www.jacksonholechamber.com/events), which takes place over a 10-day period in September. Featured activities include exhibits at the National Museum of Wildlife Art and local galleries, a juried art fair, an art auction, Western fashion and furniture shows, a miniature art show, cowboy poetry and old-time cowboy music, "Taste of the Tetons" with delectable food from local restaurants, and tours of historic ranches. Also fun is a "quickdraw" in which artists paint, draw, and sculpt while you watch; the pieces are then auctioned off.

In early October, **Quilting in the Tetons** (307/733-3087, www.quiltthetetons.org) brings a week of exhibits, classes, workshops, and quilting demonstrations.

Shopping

If you have the money (or a credit card), Jackson is a great place to buy everything from artwork to mountain bikes. Even if you just hitchhiked in and have no cash to spare, it's always fun to wander through the shops and galleries surrounding Town Square.

Fans of classic Old West furniture should not miss **Fighting Bear Antiques** (375 S. Cache, 307/733-2669 or 866/690-2669, www. fightingbear.com), famed for its collection of Thomas Molesworth pieces. It's housed in a huge log structure a few blocks from Town Square. Owner Terry Winchell literally wrote the book on this creator of uniquely American furniture.

There are lots of T-shirt places in town, but **Lee's Tees** (80 W. Broadway Ave/, 307/733-6671, www.leestees.com) sells the high-quality versions.

OUTDOOR GEAR

Outdoor enthusiasts will discover several excellent shops in Jackson. Climbers, backpackers, and cross-country skiers head to America's oldest climbing shop, **Teton Mountaineering** (170 N. Cache Dr., 307/733-3595 or 800/850-3595, www.tetonmtn.com), for quality equipment, maps, and travel guides. They also rent tents, sleeping bags, pads, backpacks, climbing shoes, crampons, and ice axes in the summer, along with snowshoes and cross-country, telemark, and alpine touring skis in winter. Check the bulletin board for used items.

Jack Dennis Sports (50 E. Broadway Ave., 307/733-3270 or 800/570-3270, www.jackdennisoutdoors.com) is a large upscale store with fly-fishing and camping gear in summer and skis and warm clothes during winter. The store also rents almost anything: tents, stoves, lanterns, cookware, sleeping bags, fishing poles, fly rods, waders, float tubes, backpacks, skis, snowboards, snowshoes, and more.

Skinny Skis (65 W. Deloney Ave., 307/733-6094 or 888/733-7205, www.skinnyskis.com) has high-quality clothing and supplies, especially cross-country ski gear. Rent sleeping bags, tents, climbing shoes, ice axes, baby carriers, and backpacks here. The same folks run the summer-only **Moosely Seconds** (307/739-1801) in Moose, with climbing and outdoor gear, along with rentals of trekking poles, ice axes, crampons, rock shoes, approach shoes, plastic boots, and snowshoes.

Another place to rent outdoor gear of all

types—including fishing gear, tents, sleeping bags, kayaks, float tubes, dry suits, water skis, backpacks, camp stoves, and lanterns—is **Leisure Sports** (1075 S. U.S. Hwy. 89, 307/733-3040, www.leisuresportsadventure.com).

Teton Adventure Gear (220 E. Broadway Ave., 307/203-2915, www.tetonadventuregear.com) rents spotting scopes, binoculars, GPS units, bear spray, electric bear fences, tents, bike racks, avalanche air bags(!), and unique rooftop car tents.

Gart Sports (485 W. Broadway Ave., 307/733-4449, www.gartsports.com) is a large store with a variety of outdoor and sports gear.

The least expensive place to buy rugged outdoor wear, cowboy boots, and cowboy hats is **Boot Barn** (840 W. Broadway Ave., 307/733-0247, www.bootbarn.com).

BARGAINS

Buy used clothing and other items at **Browse 'N Buy Thrift Shop** (139 N. Cache Dr., 307/733-7524) or the more chaotic **Orville's** (385 N. Cache Dr., 307/733-2684).

BOOKS

Unlike many Wyoming towns where the book selection consists of a few bodice-buster romance novels in the local pharmacy, Jackson is blessed with several fine bookstores. **Valley Bookstore** (125 N. Cache Dr., 307/733-4533, www.valleybookstore.com) is the largest local bookshop, with a big choice of regional titles, plus occasional author signings and readings. **Main Event** (980 W. Broadway Ave., 307/733-7112) in the Powderhorn Mall sells new books and CDs and rents videos. A few doors away in the mall is **Jackson Hole Book Traders** (307/734-6001, www.jacksonholebooktraders.com), with a surprising selection of used and rare books. Find a great selection of regional and natural history titles at **Jackson Hole and Greater Yellowstone Visitor Center** (532 N. Cache Dr., 307/733-3316, www.jacksonholechamber.com).

Accommodations

As one of the premier centers for tourism in Wyoming, Jackson Hole is jam-packed with more than 70 different motels, hotels, and B&Bs, plus many more condominiums and guest ranches. Other lodging can be found just to the north within or near Grand Teton National Park. The Jackson Hole Chamber of Commerce's website (www.jacksonholechamber.com) has brief descriptions and Web links for most local places.

Because of the town's popularity, Jackson accommodations command premium prices. With a few exceptions, you'll pay at least $110 d during the peak visitor seasons of July–August and late December–early January. Rates can drop more than 50 percent in the off-season, so if you can visit March–May or late September–mid-December, you'll save a lot of cash. (The same Super 8 Motel rooms that go for $179 in July cost just $63 in early November!) In the town of Jackson, the highest rates are usually in July and August, while at Teton Village, skiers and snowboarders send room rates to their peak between mid-December and early January. You will need to add 6 percent in taxes to all the lodging rates below, and some hotels also add a 2 percent "resort impact fee" for regional marketing.

Reservations are highly recommended. For midsummer, book rooms at least two months ahead, or longer if you really want to be certain of a place. During the Christmas–New Year's period you should probably reserve six months in advance to ensure a spot. Summer weekends tend to be the most crowded, with many families driving up from Salt Lake City for a cooling break in the mountains.

If you're overwhelmed by all the lodging choices, try one of the reservation services, such as **Jackson Hole Central Reservations**

(307/733-4005 or 800/443-6931, www.jacksonholewy.com). Looking for other opinions? Tripadvisor (www.tripadvisor.com) has many reviews of Jackson Hole lodging places.

JACKSON HOTELS AND MOTELS
Under $100

Two older motels—The Cottages at Snow King and Alpine Motel—offer the cheapest rates in town and have the same owners. Both are located in quiet residential areas, but they don't take advance reservations and are often booked up by summertime workers. They're a good last-minute option if you roll into town without reservations and not a lot of cash. The modest rooms at **The Cottages at Snow King** (470 King St., 307/733-3480, $88–98 d) include one or two queen beds, a fridge, and microwave; full kitchen units ($120) sleep four. Pets are welcome at no extra charge. **Alpine Motel** (70 S. Jean St., 307/739-3200, $82–92 d, $110 for kitchen units) is just a few blocks from Town Square. The furnishings may not be the newest, but the rooms are clean, and a small outdoor pool (heated seasonally) is on the premises. Both motels rent rooms only on a monthly basis October–April.

Family-owned **C Kudar Motel** (260 N. Cache Dr., 307/733-2823, www.kudarmotel. com, $89 d, early May–early Oct.) is a holdover from a quieter era when Jackson's motels were simple and unpretentious. You'll find 14 basic motel units with queen- or king-size beds and TVs; three rooms contain the original 1950s furnishings. Of considerably more interest are Kudar's 17 rustic but nicely maintained and spotless log cabins ($109–129 d), built in 1938. The larger two-room cabins can sleep five. There are no phones in any of the units, but the cabins contain fridges, microwaves, air conditioning, and Wi-Fi. There's a large grassy center with shady trees. Travelers love Kudar's, with many returning year after year, including some who've visited annually since the 1950s.

$100-200

Many Jackson accommodations fall in the $100–200 range, with pricing factors being location, type of room, quality of furnishings, and presence of amenities such as pools and hot tubs. Most are comfortable midrange options, not corporate lodging giants, but they offer good value and down-home friendliness.

DOWNTOWN

Justifiably popular with families, **Elk Country Inn** (480 W. Pearl, 307/733-2364 or 800/483-8667, www.elkcountryinn.com) is a fine option. Choose from spacious motel rooms ($140 s or $146 d) with two queen beds, fridge, and microwave, or a room with three queen beds, one of which is in an upstairs loft ($166 d or $185 for six guests). (Add $10 to these prices for a kitchenette unit.) There's also a luxury suite ($210 d) with a king bed and kitchen. Out back are two dozen modern log cabins ($194–214 d) with full kitchenettes, including dishes and lodgepole furnishings. Guests appreciate the indoor hot tub, exercise room, shady picnic area with a small playground, Wi-Fi, plus a free wintertime shuttle to Teton Village. Elk Country is one of the better bargains in Jackson.

Located in a peaceful neighborhood six blocks from Town Square, family-owned **C Buckrail Lodge** (110 E. Karns Ave., 307/733-2079, www.buckraillodge.com, $111 d with one queen, $137 d with two queen beds) has faux-log-cabin units on immaculate parklike grounds; portions of Clint Eastwood's *Any Which Way You Can* were filmed here. Relax in the large outdoor hot tub, then plunk down for the night in one of the dozen lovingly maintained motel rooms, all decorated with Western-style furnishings. There are no in-room phones (use your cell phone) and the walls are thin, but the bathrooms are spacious and guests can use the computer in the lobby or open a laptop for Wi-Fi. Buckrail is closed mid-October–April.

At **Anvil Motel** (215 N. Cache Dr., 307/733-3668 or 800/234-4507, www.anvilmotel.com), stay in a little room with one queen ($128 d) or relax in a larger unit with two queen beds ($148 for up to four people). A Jacuzzi suite ($192) and family suite ($310) are also available. All rooms include a microwave, small fridge, and Wi-Fi. The same owners run the nearby **El Rancho Motel** (240 N. Glenwood Dr., 307/733-3668 or 800/234-4507, www.anvilmotel.com, $104–137 d) with older budget units and no air-conditioning.

Ranch Inn (45 E. Pearl St., 307/733-6363 or 800/348-5599, www.ranchinn.com) offers a wide variety of accommodations just one block off Town Square. These include standard rooms ($115 d), tower rooms with balconies facing Snow King, fridges, and microwaves ($160 d), and suites with king beds, wood-burning fireplaces, balconies, and jetted tubs ($180 d). Amenities include an indoor hot tub, Wi-Fi, and a continental breakfast. Some tower rooms are wheelchair-accessible.

Golden Eagle Inn (325 E. Broadway Ave., 307/733-2042 or 888/748-6937, www.goldeneagleinn.com) is a quiet, out-of-the-way family motel with standard rooms for $140 d, and larger rooms for $160–190 d. All include a microwave, small refrigerator, Wi-Fi, and access to a heated outdoor pool. Adjacent is a two-bedroom house with a full kitchen that sleeps four for $275. The same owner has **Four Winds Motel** (150 N. Millward St., 307/733-2474 or 800/228-6461, www.jacksonholefourwinds.com, $125 d), just a few blocks from Town Square and across the street from a city park (with a popular children's playground). The rooms are nothing fancy, but they're exceptionally clean and affordably priced. Free Wi-Fi. Both Golden Eagle and Four Winds are open April–November.

A couple of blocks off Town Square, cozy **Anglers Inn** (265 N. Millward St., 307/733-3682 or 800/867-4667, www.anglersinn.net, $140–160 d) has pleasant rooms with Western-style fixtures, lodgepole beds and chairs, and small baths. All rooms contain a fridge, microwave, and free Wi-Fi.

Find a diverse mixture of room styles at

Jackson Hole Lodge (420 W. Broadway Ave., 307/733-2992 or 800/604-9404, www.jacksonholelodge.com), where featured attractions are a large indoor swimming pool, a wading pool, two hot tubs, a sauna, Wi-Fi, a guest computer, and a game room on attractive grounds. Standard motel rooms cost $109–139 d. Condo-type units are much nicer, with an upscale decor that includes log furniture; they're $169 for a studio unit, $269 for a one-bedroom unit (sleeps four to six) with a living room, fireplace, and full kitchen. Two-bedroom units cost $329 for up to eight people.

Antler Inn (50 W. Pearl Ave., 307/733-2535 or 800/522-2406, www.townsquareinns.com) is a large 110-room property just one block off Town Square. Many units contain two queen beds ($150 d), but also available are a dozen large family rooms/suites ($190–275) with three beds and space for six people. Most of these have wood-burning fireplaces. Rounding out the options are attractive (but small) log-walled rooms ($130 d). All guests have access to an exercise room, sauna, large indoor hot tub, and Wi-Fi. There's a free winter shuttle to Teton Village.

Rawhide Motel (75 S. Millward St., 307/733-1216, www.rawhidemotel.com, $159 d) is a fine midtown place with large rooms containing handmade lodgepole furniture, plus Wi-Fi and fridges. Open early May–early October.

The rooms are a bit cramped, but guests appreciate the friendly service and extra touches at **Sundance Inn** (135 W. Broadway Ave., 307/733-3444, www.sundanceinnjackson.com). The motel is close to Town Square and serves a light homemade breakfast plus evening cookies and lemonade. Standard rooms cost $139–159 d ($129 for two twin beds), while two-room suites are $185 for up to four people. Wi-Fi is available.

On the north side of town, **Cache Creek Lodge** (390 N. Glenwood, 307/733-7781, www.cachecreekmotel.com) is another well-kept, moderately priced choice. All rooms

JACKSON HOLE

include full kitchens (with dishes and pans) and Wi-Fi. Standard units start at $140 d, with two-bedroom suites that sleep up to six for $185 d.

A large heart-of-town place is **49'er Inn and Suites/Quality Inn** (330 W. Pearl, 307/733-7550 or 800/451-2980, www.49erinn.com), with 142 rooms spread across several buildings. There are standard rooms ($165 d) with two queen beds and a nothing-special decor; newer and considerably nicer are five-person studio suites ($220, some include fireplaces); and two luxury suites ($245) with hot tub and fireplace. Final options include a three-bedroom apartment and two-bedroom house (both $339). All guests have access to outdoor and indoor hot tubs, sauna, and exercise room, plus a full breakfast and Wi-Fi.

SOUTHSIDE

On the south end of Jackson at the Y intersection of highways 89 and 22, **Pony Express Motel** (1075 W. Broadway Ave., 307/733-3835 or 800/526-2658, www.ponyexpressmotel.com) is an excellent family option. Kitchen units with a queen bed are $139 d, while family units with a queen bed and a bunk bed for the kids, plus microwave and fridge, cost $149. Free Wi-Fi, but the main attraction is a heated outdoor pool.

Right across the highway from Pony Express, **Teton Gables Motel** (1140 W. Broadway Ave., 307/733-3723, www.tetongables.com, $124 d) is another reasonably priced place with older rooms, all with microwave, fridge, and free Wi-Fi.

One of Jackson's better deals for standard motel rooms is—not surprisingly—**Motel 6** (1370 W. Broadway Ave., 307/733-1620 or 800/466-8356, www.motel6.com, $106 d), but even here the summertime rates are high. You'll find humdrum rooms and an outdoor pool; reserve six months in advance for July and August. Off-season prices ($40 d) are a much better bargain.

NORTHSIDE

Two mid-priced motels are adjacent to each other, one mile north of Jackson on U.S.

89. Both face the Elk Refuge (and the busy highway). **Elk Refuge Inn** (307/733-3582 or 800/544-3582, www.elkrefugeinn.com) is the smaller and more homey of the two, with a mix of rooms and friendly management. Rates are $135 d for downstairs rooms or $150 for upstairs units with kitchenettes and private balconies. A six-person family unit is $140. All rooms include drive-up access, fridge, microwave, continental breakfast, Wi-Fi, and guest computer.

Flat Creek Inn (307/733-5276 or 800/438-9338, www.flatcreekinn.com) is a large two-level motel just a few hundred feet north of Elk Refuge Inn. Rooms are functionally furnished, with microwaves and small fridges. Standard rooms are $169 for up to four guests, while spacious kitchenettes sleep up to five for $209. Three suites ($149–319) are more spacious, and the largest includes a separate bedroom with king bed, kitchen, flat-screen TV, and other comforts. Guests in the suites have access to an indoor hot tub, and all guests get a continental breakfast and Wi-Fi in the lobby.

Over $200

It should come as no surprise that tony Jackson Hole has several elaborate, pricey, and sumptuous places to stay, with rooms starting around $200 and hitting the stratosphere at $4,000 a night!

DOWNTOWN

Close to Town Square, the **Wort Hotel** (50 N. Glenwood St., 307/733-2190 or 800/322-2727, www.worthotel.com) has been a Jackson favorite since 1941. A disastrous 1980 fire—started by a bird that built a nest too close to a neon sign—destroyed the roof and upper floor. The hotel was completely restored within a year, and today it's better than ever, with such amenities as a fitness center, valet parking, Wi-Fi, a business center, and two small hot tubs. The lobby, with its grand central staircase and stone fireplace with crackling fire, makes a fine place to meet friends. The Silver Dollar Bar and Grill serves meals, or you can sidle up to the famous curving bar—inlaid with 2,032 uncirculated silver dollars from 1921. The Wort's spacious rooms are attractively decorated with a New West motif that includes lodgepole-pine beds and creative fixtures. Rates are $349 d for standard rooms (with two queens or one king bed), or $389 d for larger and more luxurious rooms. Spacious junior suites with king beds and wet bars cost $449, while the luxury suite will set you back $799 d.

Greatly expanded and updated in the last few years, **The Lexington at Jackson Hole** (235 N. Cache Dr., 307/733-2648 or 888/771-2648, www.lexjh.com) sprawls across four buildings with very comfortable guest rooms and a friendly staff. Large units with two queen beds or one king bed are $219 d, while two-room suites cost $269 d, or $289 d for units with kitchenettes; add $12 for each additional adult. Amenities include a small indoor family pool and hot tub, a filling hot breakfast, fridges, a computer in the lobby, and Wi-Fi.

An outstanding in-town choice is **Parkway Inn** (125 N. Jackson St., 307/733-3143 or 800/247-8390, www.parkwayinn.com). This immaculate, midsize lodge has a delightful Victorian ambience with antique furniture and quilts in many rooms, along with jetted tubs and flat-screen TVs in the some units. Guests will also enjoy a small indoor lap pool, two hot tubs, two saunas, and a gym in the basement, along with Wi-Fi. A light breakfast is served in the lobby. Rates are $249 d for standard rooms with two queen beds or a king bed, $329 for larger suites, or $369 d for two-room suites; $25 each for additional guests (maximum of four per room).

An excellent nine-room lodge just a few blocks from Town Square, **Inn on the Creek** (295 N. Millward, 307/739-1565 or 800/669-9534, www.innonthecreek.com) has a peaceful location beside Flat Creek. Standard rooms ($229–279 d) feature designer furnishings and down comforters. The deluxe rooms ($299–349 d) also include fireplaces and in-room hot tubs, while a gorgeous suite ($599) sleeps four and has a full kitchen, jetted tub, and private patio. A light breakfast is delivered to your door each morning, and there's a private backyard, Wi-Fi, and guest computer.

Another downtown option is **Grand Victorian Lodge** (85 Perry Ave., 307/739-2294 or 800/584-0532, www.grandvictorianlodge.com), a "boutique hotel with a bed and breakfast ambience." Choose from standard rooms ($199–219 d), deluxe rooms ($229–279 d), or a large two-room suite ($289 d) that features a four-poster king bed, jetted tub, and gas fireplace. A delicious full breakfast is a morning highlight, and guests can relax on the back deck or surf the Web wirelessly.

You'll find outdoorsy owners at **Alpine House Country Inn** (285 N. Glenwood, 307/739-1570 or 800/753-1421, www.alpinehouse.com); both Hans and Nancy Johnstone were skiers for U.S. Olympic teams and are highly knowledgeable about adventure options in the Tetons. The timber-frame lodge is just two blocks from Jackson's Town Square and has 22 guest rooms in two connected buildings. Both are bright and modern, accented by Swedish-style stenciling on the walls. All rooms have private balconies and deep soaking tubs, saunas, plus access to a central computer and Wi-Fi. A healthy full buffet breakfast is served. Rates are $175 d in the original rooms (no TV or air conditioning), or $215–260 d in the new building, which also features gas fireplaces in most rooms. The two suites cost $295 for up to four guests. The owners also manage four two-bedroom cottages ($400) nearby that sleep five comfortably; each cottage has two bedrooms, a sleeper sofa, washer, dryer, and kitchen. Closed in November and April.

Acclaimed **◖ Rusty Parrot Lodge and Spa** (175 N. Jackson, 307/733-2000 or 888/739-1749, www.rustyparrot.com) features sumptuous accommodations just two blocks from Town Square. All 31 rooms are highlighted with handcrafted furniture, original artwork, oversize tubs, and goose-down comforters; some also contain wood-burning fireplaces or jetted tubs. Rates are $400–475 d for standard rooms, or $635 d for the luxurious master suite, and include an unforgettable breakfast (it's never the same) served each morning in the cozy dining room. (Deduct $40 from the rate if you don't want the breakfast.) Guests can relax in the hot tub on a deck overlooking Jackson, borrow a book from the library, or pamper themselves with a massage, aromatherapy session, or facial from Body Sage Spa (extra charges). The lodge also serves epicurean dinners at Wild Sage Restaurant (daily 5:30–9:30 P.M.). It doesn't get much better than this.

One of Jackson's newest lodging places is **Homewood Suites by Hilton** (207 N. Millward St., 307/739-0808 or 800/225-5466, www.jacksonwy.homewoodsuites.com, $359–389 d). All units are two-room suites with separate living and sleeping areas, top-of-the-line beds, a fireplace, two TVs and phones, free airport shuttle, an indoor pool, fitness center, and hot tub, plus fully equipped kitchens, Wi-Fi, and a big breakfast buffet. Guests are served a light dinner Monday–Thursday evenings.

SOUTHSIDE

The Point Inn & Suites (1280 W. Broadway Ave., 307/733-0033 or 877/547-5223, www.thepointjh.com) has comfortable rooms at the south end of town. Standard rooms cost $189 d, while Western-style suites with fireplaces and hot tubs go for $239 d. Amenities include a light breakfast, large hot tub, fitness facility, sauna, Wi-Fi, guest computers, ski racks, plus microwaves and fridges in most rooms. (The hotel was formerly a Days Inn.)

A modern hotel with an ostentatious lobby and southside location, **Wyoming Inn of Jackson Hole** (930 W. Broadway Ave., 307/734-0035 or 800/844-0035, www.wyoming-inn.com) has large and comfortable rooms for $299 d, including a big hot breakfast. The finest rooms ($349 d) also include fireplaces and jetted tubs. Guests appreciate Wi-Fi, guest computers, laundry service (a big hit with families), and a free airport shuttle, all at no extra charge.

A three-story building sandwiched between strip malls on the south end of Jackson, **The Lodge at Jackson Hole (Best Western)** (80 S. Scott La., 307/739-9703 or 800/458-3866, www.lodgeatjh.com) has big guest rooms featuring a fridge, microwave, safe, Wi-Fi, and two queen beds (or a king) for $259 d. Hotel guests are treated to a buffet breakfast, a unique indoor/outdoor heated pool, hot tubs, and a sauna, plus access to the Jackson Hole Athletic Club and a free winter shuttle to Teton Village.

Log Cabin Motels

Several local motels offer log-cabin accommodations for a step back into the Old West while keeping such newer amenities as TVs, private baths, and Wi-Fi.

Set amid tall cottonwood trees along Flat Creek, **Rustic Inn** (475 N. Cache Dr., 307/733-2357 or 800/323-9279, www.rusticinnatjh.com) has a sprawling mixture of cozy log cabins, log-motel units, and newer log-sided units. The website details all cabin choices, ranging from older cabins (containing two queen beds and a fireplace for $229 d) to larger ones (with flat-screen TVs, fridges, and microwaves for $329 d), up to "superior" cabins with private decks, rain showers, flat-screen TVs, and king beds ($399 d). Add $10 per person for additional guests (max. four persons). All guests have access to the sauna, gym, outdoor pool, and hot tub, plus Wi-Fi, concierge service, and a hot breakfast. Guests sometimes complain of the lack of electrical outlets and limited storage for skis and other winter gear.

Near a busy Jackson intersection, **Cowboy Village Resort** (120 Flat Creek Dr., 307/733-3121 or 800/962-4988, www.townsquareinns.com) has 82 modern but jammed-together cabins with kitchenettes and sleeper sofas. The cabins cost $178–198 for up to four people in a studio unit with two queen bunk beds, or $218 for a cabin with a separate bedroom (one king or two queens). Two hotel rooms are available: one with a king bed ($208 d) and a larger unit with two queens, a bunk bed, and full kitchen ($278 for up to six). Guests have access to a covered outdoor pool, an indoor hot tub, office computer, and Wi-Fi. In winter a continental breakfast is available, along with a free shuttle to Teton Village.

TETON VILLAGE HOTELS AND MOTELS

Teton Village is 12 miles northwest of Jackson at the base of Jackson Hole Resort. The Village has a variety of lodging and dining options and year-round activities, and is perfect for skiers and snowboarders. Frequent START bus service makes it easy to get to town, even if you don't have a rental car. Most lodging and dining places are considerably more expensive than in Jackson, but the Village has a couple of lower-priced choices. In addition to hotels in this area, be sure to check out condominium rentals as a Teton Village option.

Under $100

Located in the heart of Teton Village, **The Hostel** (307/733-3415, www.thehostel.us) provides budget rates in a scenic location. Eight coed or single-sex hostel rooms are available for $32 per person; private rooms run $79 s or d, or $89 for up to four people. The tiny plain-vanilla rooms lack TV or phones, but there's a big central lounge for camaraderie; it includes TVs, DVD players, pay phones, pool table, table tennis, foosball, fireplace, microwave, refrigerator, games, Wi-Fi ($5 per day), and a ski-waxing room. Because of its Teton Village location at the foot of Jackson Hole Mountain Resort, The Hostel is very popular with skiers on a budget, so reserve two months ahead for midwinter rooms. Winter reservations require a four-night minimum stay. Space is typically available in the summer, with no minimum stay. Pets are accepted for a $10 fee.

$100-200

In the heart of Teton Village action, **Village Center Inn** (307/733-3990 or 800/443-8613, www.jhrl.com) charges $105 d for studio or loft units and $150 for two-bedroom units that sleep six. All units include full kitchens, but no Wi-Fi (though it's available nearby). Peak-season winter rates rise to $200 d for a one-bedroom unit, and up to $230 for two bedrooms. The decor is utilitarian, but other than The Hostel, this is the cheapest Teton Village accommodation. There is a two-night minimum stay in winter.

$200-300

Alpenhof Lodge (307/733-3242 or 800/732-3244, www.alpenhoflodge.com) exudes a European ambience, reflecting its Swiss and German owners. Summertime rates start at $239 d for the simplest rooms on the top floor with sloping ceilings, or $289 for rooms with Bavarian furnishings and space for four guests. A two-room suite is $549. A continental breakfast is included and guests have access to the heated year-round outdoor pool, hot tub, sauna, Wi-Fi, and computer. The resident golden retrievers are a bonus.

Another Teton Village option, **The Inn at Jackson Hole/Best Western** (307/733-2311 or 800/842-7666, www.innatjh.com) has standard rooms with log furnishings ($209–219 d), units with kitchenettes and fireplaces ($239–269 d), and family-friendly loft suites with fireplaces and kitchenettes ($329 for up to four guests). Guests can use the hotel's outdoor heated pool and hot tub, sauna, and ski lockers. There's an upscale restaurant and Wi-Fi.

Over $300

If you're looking for beautifully appointed accommodations, you can't go wrong at **Snake River Lodge and Spa** (307/732-6000 or 800/445-4655, www.snakeriverlodge.rockresorts.com). The lodge features a New West–style lobby with stone fireplaces and whimsically carved bears, plus rooms that follow the theme with rustic lamps, pine furniture, and colorful prints. A distinctive free-form indoor/outdoor heated pool has a cascading waterfall, and other attractions include indoor and outdoor hot tubs, a sauna, ski lockers, a ski-in concierge service, Wi-Fi, and a five-story spa and health club with exercise equipment, facials, manicures, hydrotherapy, massages, soaking tubs, and steam baths. Peak-season summer and winter rates are around $345 d for the guest rooms, $665 d for a one-bedroom suite or condo, up to $1,575 for a three-bedroom private home. Snake River

Lodge is owned by RockResorts; their website frequently offers multi-night specials that include breakfast.

Four Seasons Resort (307/732-5000, www.fourseasons.com/jacksonhole) includes a 124-room luxury hotel with ski-in access, an elegant restaurant (Westbank Grill), an après-ski bar for slope-side drinks, a gorgeous outdoor heated pool, three hot tubs, a full health club, spa, and concierge all under one roof. Summertime rates start at $695 d for not-so-standard standard rooms (king bed, marble bath and soaking tub, in-room safe, minibar, private terrace or gas fireplace). Also available are 32 condos and homes, including a five-bedroom place that rents for $7,500 a night in the ski season!

Another of Jackson Hole's upmarket lodging options (it gets a four-diamond rating from AAA), **Teton Mountain Lodge** (307/734-7111 or 800/801-6615, www.tetonmountainlodge.com) is a Western-style lodge at the base of the mountain in Teton Village. An impressive array of amenities and services are featured: indoor and outdoor heated pools, hot tubs (including an amazing adults-only rooftop version), a fitness center/spa, concierge service, valet parking, Wi-Fi, and underground parking. Guests can choose from lodge rooms or studios ($309–319 d), junior suites ($389 d), one-, two-, or three-bedroom suites ($529–1,330 d), all the way up to the penthouse suite ($1,830 nightly).

One of the newer high-end lodges in Teton Village, **Hotel Terra** (307/739-4000 or 800/631-6281, www.hotelterrajacksonhole.com) has a splashy modern design with an eco-boutique emphasis. Rooms are sumptuously appointed, with organic cotton sheets and bathrobes, Wi-Fi, safes, twice-daily maid service, and all sorts of techie treats, from "rain showers" in the bath and in-floor heating to iPod docking stations and flat-screen TVs. Guests have access to the pools, fitness center, and hot tubs at adjacent Teton Mountain Lodge (same owners). Standard rooms are $319–329 d, studios with kitchens cost $339

d, and suites start at $530–975 d, up to a magnificent three-bedroom suite for $1,545.

BED-AND-BREAKFASTS

Jackson hosts many fine B&Bs, where those who can afford it can relax in comfort at the homes of locals. Be sure to reserve space far ahead during the peak summer season, although you might get lucky at the last minute if someone cancels. The **Jackson Hole Bed and Breakfast Association's** website (www.jacksonholebnb.com) has links to a number of local B&Bs.

Teton Village

Near the Aspens along the road to Teton Village, **The Sassy Moose Inn** (307/733-1277, www.sassymoose.com, $159–189 d) is a modest log house with five guest rooms, each with private bath, TV, and Wi-Fi. The larger rooms have two beds and are fine for families. A full breakfast is served each morning. Guests can soak in the outdoor hot tub, and an on-site spa provides massage and other treats. Pets are welcome (a rarity for B&Bs).

On the way to Teton Village, **Teton View B&B** (2136 Coyote Loop, 307/733-7954, www.tetonview.com) features a guest room ($225 d) and suite ($259 d), both with private baths. Guests enjoy a big breakfast, Wi-Fi, and a dramatic view of the Tetons from both the indoor whirlpool tub and outdoor hot tub. The owners also offer a perfect-for-families cabin with a kitchen, wood-burning stove, and private bath ($325 d). For additional guests, add $25 per adult or $15 per child. A two-night minimum stay is required. Open June–October.

The rambling **Wildflower Inn** (307/733-4710 or 888/893-7910, www.jacksonholewildflower.com) sits on three acres of country land along Teton Village Road, with five bright guest rooms. Four rooms have private decks, and all contain private baths and handcrafted lodgepole beds. One of the rooms is actually a suite with a separate sitting room, hot tub, and gas fireplace. Ken and Sherrie Jern built and manage the B&B, and bring a wealth of local knowledge; both were ski instructors at Vail, and he's a longtime Exum climbing guide. Rates are $300–350 d ($380 d for the suite) and include a memorable family-style breakfast and a plant-filled solarium. Children are welcome, and Wi-Fi is available.

One of the most impressive local lodging options is **(Bentwood B&B** (307/739-1411, www.bentwoodinn.com), just north of the junction on the road to Teton Village. This massive 6,000-square-foot log home sits amid tall cottonwood trees and is a favorite place for weddings and receptions. The interior is filled with Western styling and English antiques. The grand living room is centered on a three-story stone fireplace, and each of the five elegant guest rooms has a fireplace, flat-screen TV, deck or balcony, jetted tub, and Wi-Fi. The loft room is perfect for families. Innkeepers Deborah and Lee Clukey are gracious hosts. Wine and hors d'oeuvres are served each evening, and morning brings a creative breakfast. Lodging rates are $350 d, or $450 for up to four in the family room. Children are welcome in this very special place.

Wilson

A personal favorite is **Teton Treehouse B&B** (307/733-3233, www.atetontreehouse-jackson-hole.com, $215–240 d) a gorgeous four-story hillside home in Wilson. This spacious open-beam B&B sits up 95 steps—needless to say, it's not accessible for people with disabilities—and contains six guest rooms with private baths. It really does offer the feeling of living in a tree house, and it's a great place for bird-watchers. Decks provide impressive views across the valley below, and guests enjoy a healthy full breakfast each morning along with Wi-Fi access and a popular evening fire pit. Young children are not permitted, and there's a three-night minimum stay in July and August. The B&B is open mid-May–September.

RESORTS
Jackson

At the base of Jackson's in-town ski hill, and just a few blocks from downtown, **Snow King Resort** (400 E. Snow King Ave., 307/733-5200 or 800/522-5464, www.snowking.com) includes more than 200 hotel rooms and 170 condos, plus such amenities as a year-round heated outdoor pool, hot tub, sauna, exercise facility, restaurants facing the slopes, a bar, concierge, business center, game room, spa, and Wi-Fi. A free shuttle provides connections to the airport and Teton Village (winters), and guests receive discounted passes for Snow King Ski Area. The lodge offers reasonable ski-and-stay packages starting at $140 per night for two people, including lodging, breakfast, and a ski pass in early winter. When the snow is gone, Snow King is a popular destination for meetings, offering 48,000 square feet of conference space. A winter ice rink is close by, and in summer a slide, horseback riding, chairlift, bike trails, and miniature golf course attract families. The main resort building has a 1970s feel, but guest rooms are comfortable and updated. Hotel rooms at Snow King cost $245 d in the summer, with condos starting around $300 d, up to an ultra-luxurious three-bedroom Love Ridge condo that will set you back $745 per night.

Some of the most dramatic vistas of the Tetons are from the luxurious **Spring Creek Ranch** (307/733-8833 or 800/443-6139, www.springcreekranch.com). On a 1,000-acre estate, the resort sits high atop Gros Ventre Butte four miles west of Jackson and includes a wide range of lodging options. Hotel rooms and studios are $340 d in the summer, and two-bedroom suites cost $360 for four people. One-bedroom condos run $340 d; two- and three-bedroom condos range from $410 to $1,400 nightly, with the largest sleeping eight comfortably. Also available are executive four-bedroom homes (one covers 6,500 square feet!) that cost a mere $2,250 per night. All rooms at Spring Creek Ranch contain fireplaces and lodgepole furnishings, and the condos and studios include full kitchens. Other amenities include a private pond, tennis courts, an outdoor pool, hot tub, fitness center, courtesy airport

Spring Creek Ranch

© DON PITCHER

transportation, and day spa with massage and other offerings (extra fee).

Atop Gros Ventre Butte near Spring Creek Ranch is stunning **Amangani** (307/734-7333 or 877/734-7333, www.amangani.com), the only representative of Amanresorts in America. (Most of the company's other lavish resorts are in Asia.) Aman groupies and business travelers know to expect the utmost in luxury, and they will certainly not be disappointed here, starting with dressed-in-black employees and spare-no-expenses construction. Guests who come here expect pampering, and the somewhat snooty staff obliges. The three-story sandstone-faced hotel contains 40 suites, each with a patinaed-metal fireplace, mountain-facing balcony, king-size bed, deep soaking tub (with a window view), minibar, and terrazzo dining table. Amangani's central lobby is particularly impressive, blending sandstone columns, redwood accents, custom furnishings, and soaring two-story windows. Outside, those soaking in a whirlpool and heated 35-meter pool enjoy a remarkable view of the Tetons. Among other amenities are a complete health center, a gourmet restaurant, a lounge, and courtesy airport transportation. Amangani's accommodations include suites ($875 d), three deluxe suites ($1,100 d), five large luxury suites with two baths and spacious balconies ($1,400–1,700 d), and a four-bedroom home ($4,800) for the utmost in sumptuousness. A three-night minimum is required in the summer. The health center and restaurant are open to the general public.

Teton Village

Four miles south of Teton Village, **Teton Pines Resort and Country Club** (307/733-1005 or 800/238-2223, www.tetonpines.com) features the amenities you'd expect in a year-round resort, including an 18-hole golf course, tennis center, and classy restaurant. Guests have access to the outdoor pool and hot tub, athletic-club privileges, concierge service, and an airport shuttle. Most of the resort's condos are privately owned, but three large (2,100-square-foot) three-bedroom town houses are offered on a nightly basis. Each includes a kitchen, dining room, two decks, three baths, a fireplace, hot tub, washer, dryer, and attached garage. These sleep up to eight for $1,050 per night. Golf packages are also available.

GUEST RANCHES

Several of Wyoming's best-known and most luxurious dude ranches are in Jackson Hole, providing wonderful places for families who are looking to rough it in style. Many more guest ranches are just over Togwotee Pass in the Dubois area and to the south in the Pinedale area. Grand Teton National Park has several of the most popular dude ranches, including:

- **Goosewing Ranch** (www.goosewingranch. com)
- **Gros Ventre River Ranch** (www.grosventreriverranch.com)
- **Heart Six Ranch** (www.heartsix.com)
- **Lost Creek Ranch** (www.lostcreek.com)
- **Moose Head Ranch** (www.ranchweb.com/moose-head-ranch)
- **Red Rock Ranch** (www.theredrockranch. com)
- **Triangle X Ranch** (www.trianglex.com)
- **Turpin Meadow Ranch** (www.turpinmeadowranch.com)

Flat Creek Ranch

At the base of Sheep Mountain, Flat Creek Ranch (307/733-0603 or 866/522-3344, www. flatcreekranch.com) is packed with history. The land was originally homesteaded by cowboy, hunting guide, and rustler Cal Carrington, but he sold it to his close friend, "Countess" Cissy Patterson, in 1923. Previously married to a Polish count, Cissy came from a wealthy Chicago newspaper family, but her love of the West and horses matched Cal's. For two decades Cissy and Cal were grist for the gossip mill, mostly during her trips to Wyoming, but also when she took him along on a grand tour of Europe. Cissy died in 1948, and her relatives now own the ranch. After a long hiatus and

extensive improvements, this historic ranch in a gorgeous setting is once again open for guests, with five renovated cabins and three gourmet meals daily. The emphasis is on fly-fishing in legendary Flat Creek; the ranch owns 1.5 miles along the stream. Other activities include horseback rides and hikes into the Gros Ventre Wilderness, canoeing, and a wood-fired sauna for chilly evenings. There's a three-night minimum stay in the summer ($675 for two people per night, all-inclusive). The ranch is 15 miles up a bumpy dirt road, but the ranch provides transportation (Mon. and Fri. only) if you don't have a four-wheel-drive with high clearance. Open late May–late September.

R Lazy S Ranch

Another historic dude ranch is R Lazy S Ranch (near Teton Village along the Moose-Wilson Rd., 307/733-2655, www.rlazys.com), with space for 45 guests, who enjoy horseback rides, fishing, and other Western adventures. A one-week minimum stay is required. All-inclusive rates range widely depending upon the cabin: $2,745–4,032 for two people per week. Lazy S is open mid-June–September. Tykes under age seven are not allowed.

Spotted Horse Ranch

On the banks of the Hoback River, 16 miles south of Jackson, Spotted Horse Ranch (307/733-2097 or 800/528-2084, www.spottedhorseranch.com) exudes a comfortable rusticity. The main lodge and cabins contain lodgepole furniture, and a maximum of 35 guests stay in log cabins with modern conveniences. Activities include horseback riding (some Appaloosas), fly-fishing, cookouts, and river trips, and you can unwind in the hot tub or sauna. A one-week minimum stay is required in the summer ($4,500 d per week, all-inclusive). Open mid-May–October.

MOUNTAIN RESORTS

East of Moran Junction at Togwotee Pass (9,658 feet), U.S. Highway 26/287 tops the Continental Divide and then slides eastward toward Dubois and the Wind River Valley. The

JACKSON HOLE

Togwotee Pass area is famous for luxuriously deep snow all winter and is a destination for snowmobilers, cross-country skiers, and dog-sledding enthusiasts. Just north of the pass is Teton Wilderness, a place to discover what solitude means. As you face west from the pass, the Teton Range offers a jagged horizon line. This entire area provides a delicious escape from hectic Jackson and is home to two noteworthy, attractive high-elevation resorts: Togwotee Mountain Lodge and Brooks Lake Lodge.

Togwotee Mountain Lodge

Forty-eight miles northeast of Jackson and just a few miles west of Togwotee Pass is Togwotee Mountain Lodge (307/543-2847 or 800/543-2847, www.togwoteelodge.com), a pleasantly rustic place to spend a night or a week. Owned by the conglomerate Aramark, the resort offers horseback rides, and the staff can set up mountain-bike trips, whitewater rafting, fly-fishing, backcountry pack trips, and other summertime adventures, along with wintertime snowmobiling (the primary winter activity), dogsledding, and cross-country skiing when the snow flies. Togwotee has a variety of accommodations, and guests will enjoy two large hot tubs. Summer rates are $170 d for rooms in the lodge, $200 d for family rooms with bunk beds for the kids, and $230 d for one-bedroom cabins. The mini-suites and cabins sleep up to six people ($10 per person for more than two). In winter, the resort specializes in package deals that include lodging, breakfast and dinner, snowmobile guide, and free airport shuttle. The resort also houses a restaurant ($15–27), bar, gas station, gift shop, and convenience store. Togwotee is closed early April–mid-May and mid-October–November.

Brooks Lake Lodge

Brooks Lake Lodge (307/455-2121, www.brookslake.com) may have the finest location of any Wyoming resort, with a placid lake in front and the cliffs of Pinnacle Buttes nearby. Built in 1922, it has long served travelers en route to Yellowstone, and its enormous great hall contains big-game trophies from all over

the world. Completely restored, the lodge is now on the National Register of Historic Places. Seven guest rooms are available in the main lodge, and eight attractive cabins hide in the trees; all are tastefully appointed with handmade lodgepole furniture. The cabins also have woodstoves.

The turnoff for Brooks Lake Lodge is 65 miles northeast of Jackson (34 miles east of Moran Junction) and another five miles off the highway via Brooks Lake Road. The lodge is open mid-June–mid-September and late December–mid-March. There's a three-night minimum stay, and rates are $650–750 per day for two guests in the lodge or cabins. The largest and most luxurious cabin has two bedrooms, a living room, kitchen, jetted tub, and more for $1,700 nightly. All rates include gourmet meals, horseback riding, guided hiking, canoeing, fly-fishing, and Wi-Fi in the summer. A stocked casting pond is available for working on your technique. The spa features a small workout room, sauna, and outdoor hot tub; massage and facials are extra. Winter stays include three meals, cross-country skis, ice-fishing, and snowshoes, plus spa access for $500–550 per day for two people (two-night minimum). Snowmobile rentals and dogsled tours are also available. Brooks Lake Lodge is open to the public for winter lunches (burgers, sandwiches, salads, and daily specials), making this a popular stop for snowmobilers and cross-country skiers.

RENTALS
Condominiums

Condominiums provide a popular option for families and groups visiting Jackson Hole. These privately owned places are maintained by several local property-management companies and vary from small studio apartments to spacious five-bedroom houses. All are completely furnished (including dishes) and have fireplaces, cable TV, phones, and mid-stay maid service if you remain more than five nights. The nicest also include access to pools and hot tubs and have balconies overlooking the spectacular Tetons. Many of the condominiums are in Teton Village (adjacent to the ski area) or a couple of miles south in Teton Pines or the Aspens; others are scattered around Jackson Hole, so make sure you get a place close to your interests.

Condo prices vary widely depending upon location and amenities, but during the winter holiday season (Christmas–early Jan.), expect to pay $190–230 per night for studio or one-bedroom condos (1–2 people). Two-bedroom units (up to four people) cost $280–320 per night, and full four-bedroom/three-bath condos (these sleep eight) run $375–520 per night. The most sumptuous places will set you back $4,800 nightly in the peak winter season, but if you're feeling flush with cash, rent one of the finest homes for a mere $28,000 a month! Summer and off-peak winter rates are often 35–50 percent lower, with spring and fall rates 50–70 percent lower than peak-season prices. In fall or spring, condos offer a real bargain for traveling families looking to stay several nights in the area. Minimum stays of 3–7 nights are required throughout the year, with the longest minimum stays required in the peak winter season.

If you have the luxury of time, do a little comparison shopping before renting a condo. Things to ask include whether you have access to a pool and hot tub, how close you are to the ski slopes, how frequent the maid service is, and whether the units include such amenities as Wi-Fi, DVD players, flat-screen TVs, washers, and dryers. Also be sure to find out what beds are in the rooms, because couples might not enjoy sleeping in twin bunk beds. Ask about the age and condition of the condos, since some are dated. The newest units are at Love Ridge (next to Snow King Resort) and White Buffalo Club (downtown). Fortunately, the rental companies provide helpful online photos, floor plans, and other details for the various styles of condos.

Contact the following companies for details:

- **Four Seasons Resort** (307/732-5000, www.fourseasons.com/jacksonhole)

- **Grand View Lodge & Spa** (at Snow King Resort, 307/733-3186 or 800/522-5464, www.grandviewlodgeandspa.com)
- **Jackson Hole Lodge** (307/733-2992 or 800/604-9404, www.jacksonholelodge.com)
- **Jackson Hole Reservations** (307/733-6331 or 800/329-9205, www.jacksonhole.net)
- **Jackson Hole Resort Lodging** (307/733-3990 or 800/443-8613, www.jhrl.com)
- **Love Ridge Resort Lodges** (at Snow King Resort, 307/733-5200 or 800/533-7669, www.loveridgelodge.com)
- **Mountain Property Management** (307/733-1684 or 800/992-9948, www.mpmjh.com)
- **OK Rentals** (307/733-8604 or 800/735-8310, www.jackson-hole-vacations.com)
- **Rendezvous Mountain Rentals** (307/739-9050 or 888/739-2565, www.rmrentals.com)
- **Snow King Resort Condominiums** (307/733-5200 or 800/522-5464, www.snowking.com)
- **Spring Creek Ranch** (307/733-8833 or 800/443-6139, www.springcreekranch.com)
- **Teton Pines Resort and Country Club** (307/733-1005 or 800/238-2223, www.tetonpines.com)

The largest of these businesses—and a good place to begin your search—is Jackson Hole Resort Lodging. Owned by Jackson Hole Mountain Resort, it manages about 200 places. Other large management companies include Rendezvous Mountain Rentals and Snow King Resort Condominiums. The last of these also owns (and can book condos at) Grand View Lodge & Spa and Love Ridge Resort Lodging.

Two resorts offer fractional-ownership condos in Jackson Hole: **The Residence Club at Teton Pines** (307/733-1005 or 800/238-2223, www.tetonpinesresidenceclub.com) and **The**

Teton Club (307/734-9777 or 866/352-9777, www.tetonclub.com). The Teton Club is right at the base of Jackson Hole Resort, making it perfect for skiers, while Teton Pines offers an upscale country club with a golf course and other amenities. Members typically share ownership and stay for 4–12 weeks per year. Also check out the **White Buffalo Club** (160 W. Gill Ave., 307/734-4900 or 888/256-8182, www.whitebuffaloclub.com), a member-only operation in the heart of Jackson.

Home Rentals and Swaps

Jackson Hole home rentals—both short- and long-term—are available from **Jackson Hole Reservations** (307/733-6331 or 800/329-9205, www.jacksonhole.net), **OK Rentals** (307/733-8604 or 800/735-8310, www.jackson-hole-vacations.com), **Mountain Property Management** (307/733-1684 or 800/992-9948, www.mpmjh.com), **Rendezvous Mountain Rentals** (307/739-9050 or 888/739-2565, www.rmrentals.com), **Mountain Haus** (307/690-1034, www.jhmountainhaus.com), and **Rocking-V Lodge** (307/733-7319, www.rocking-v.com).

Rancho Alegre Lodge (3600 S. Park Loop Rd., 307/733-7988, www.ranchoalegre.com) offers Jackson's most expensive lodging. On a 50-acre spread facing the Tetons, this 10,000-square-foot structure houses seven bedrooms (each with its own TV/VCR, phone, and fridge) and offers an upscale hunting lodge decor along with such amenities as concierge service, a private chef available for hire, seven fireplaces, extensive decks, a hot tub, and a pool table. Full-house rentals (up to 20 guests) are $2,600 per night, including continental breakfasts, with a four-night minimum stay in the summer (and four times $2,600 is $10,400...). At these prices, the lodge is primarily used for weddings, corporate retreats, large and wealthy families, and ski groups.

At the base of the mountains in Wilson, **Trail Creek Ranch** (307/733-2610, www.jacksonholetrailcreekranch.com) operated as a dude ranch for 50 years. Lodging on this 270-acre spread ranges from a double room with a king bed ($140; no kitchen) to a two-bedroom cabin ($270) with full kitchen that's perfect for friends. All units have private baths and limited Wi-Fi, but no distracting TVs. Families love the heated outdoor pool. Trail Creek is open June–September, with a three-day minimum stay.

In addition to the lodging places described, visitors to Jackson Hole may want to investigate a house exchange. Several online companies list homeowners in Jackson who are interested in a trade if you have an upscale home, especially one on the beach in midwinter! If you live in Hawaii or Costa Rica and want to go skiing, your home might be a hot property. If you live in North Dakota or Baghdad, good luck. Companies worth investigating include **Home Exchange** (310/798-3864 or 800/877-8723, www.homeexchange.com), **Home Link** (954/566-2687 or 800/638-3841, www.swapnow.com), and **Intervac** (415/839-9670 or 800/756-4663, www.intervac-homeexchange.com).

Another option is through one of the online vacation rental brokers, such as **Vacation Rentals by Owner** (www.vrbo.com), **CyberRentals** (www.cyberrentals.com), or **Vacation Homes** (www.vacationhomes.com).

Camping

Fully 97 percent of Jackson Hole is publicly owned, primarily within Grand Teton National Park and Bridger-Teton National Forest. So many options exist that campers can pitch their tent in a new campground every night for three weeks. Private RV parks are considerably more limited, but a half-dozen are scattered around the valley.

PUBLIC CAMPGROUNDS

Most public campgrounds on Forest Service and Park Service lands around Jackson Hole are on a first-come, first-camp basis with no reservations. In addition to these campsites, many people camp for free on dispersed sites on Forest Service lands; contact the agency for locations and restrictions.

Bridger-Teton Campgrounds

Bridger-Teton National Forest (307/739-5400, www.fs.fed.us/r4/btnf) has a number of campgrounds ($10–15; open mid-May–Sept.) located around Jackson Hole. Closest is **Curtis Canyon Campground,** seven miles northeast of Jackson up a gravel road with a fine view of the Tetons.

Three popular Bridger-Teton campgrounds are southwest of Jackson in the Snake River Canyon, with access via U.S. Highway 26/89. They include **East Table Creek Campground** and **Station Creek Campground,** both 24 miles south of Jackson and 11 miles southwest of Hoback Junction, along with **Wolf Creek Campground,** 26 miles southwest of Jackson and six miles from Hoback Junction.

Three more campgrounds are northeast of Jackson in the Gros Ventre Valley. **Atherton Creek Campground** sits along Slide Lake, 18 miles northeast of Jackson and seven miles northeast of Kelly up Gros Ventre Road. **Red Hills Campground** and **Crystal Creek Campground** are near each other along the Gros Ventre River, approximately 23 miles northeast of Jackson and 13 miles up the partly gravel Gros Ventre Road.

In the Buffalo Valley area 45 miles northeast of Jackson, pitch your tent at **Hatchet Campground,** eight miles east of Moran Junction; **Turpin Meadow Campground,** 10 miles east of Moran Junction; or **Box Creek Campground,** along Buffalo Valley Road.

Forty-nine miles north of Jackson, **Angles Campground** is a small site just uphill from Togwotee Mountain Resort on U.S. Highway 287. Another small camping place, **Sheffield Creek Campground,** 55 miles north of Jackson, is off U.S. Highway 89/191/287 near Flagg Ranch Resort (poor road access until late summer). Remote **Pacific Creek Campground** is 46 miles north of Jackson and nine miles up Pacific Creek Road, with access through Grand Teton National Park.

Two campgrounds are approximately 20 miles southeast of Jackson along the Hoback River: **Kozy Campground,** seven miles southeast of Hoback Junction, and **Hoback Campground,** eight miles east of Hoback Junction.

Close to Granite Hot Springs—a delightful place for a soak—**Granite Campground** is 35 miles southeast of Jackson and nine miles up the gravel Granite Creek Road.

Caribou-Targhee Campgrounds

Trail Creek Campground and **Mike Harris Campground** are in the **Caribou-Targhee National Forest** (208/354-2312, www.fs.fed.us/r4/caribou-targhee, $10) on the west side of Teton Pass, approximately 20 miles west of Jackson. Both are open mid-May–mid-September, with reservations ($9 fee) available at 518/885-3639 or 877/444-6777, www.recreation.gov.

RV PARKS

As land values have soared, the number of RV parks in Jackson has dropped. Today, only two RV resorts remain, with two more a dozen miles to the south and three more north of town in or near Grand Teton National Park.

The private RV parks around Jackson can be surprisingly expensive: Some places charge more for a tent space than it would cost to stay in a motel room in many Wyoming towns! Even more expensive is a ticket for parking RVs overnight on Jackson city streets. It's illegal to do so, and police strictly enforce the ordinance.

On the south end of town behind the Virginian Lodge, **Virginian RV Park** (750 W. Broadway Ave., 307/733-7189 or 800/321-6982 in summer or 800/262-4999 in winter, www.virginianlodge.com) is the biggest RV parking lot in the area. Full hookups at more than 100 sites (many pull-through spaces) cost $65; no tents. Guests at the RV park can use the Virginian Lodge's outdoor pool and hot tub. Wi-Fi is available in the hotel lobby. The park is open May–mid-October.

The best local option—by far—is **Jackson Hole Campground** (2780 N. Moose-Wilson Rd., 307/413-0495, www.jacksonholecampground. com, $35 tents, $65 RVs, open year-round), with a quiet, shady location near Calico Restaurant on the road to Teton Village. There's a shower house, cable TV, Wi-Fi, and a camp store, but no laundry. Call ahead for reservations.

Two private campgrounds are in the Hoback Junction area, 12 miles south of Jackson. **Lazy J Corral** (307/733-1554) is right on the highway at Hoback Junction, but the rates are low: RV sites with full hookups cost just $27. It does not have tent spaces but is open year-round.

Snake River Park KOA (307/733-7078 or 800/562-1878, www.snakeriverpark.com), 12 miles south of Jackson at Hoback Junction, has RV spaces for $43–59 d, tent sites for $38 d, and simple "kamping kabins" for $77–89 d. It's open early April–November. The KOA has a riverside location and a game room. Snake River Park Whitewater rafting company is also based here.

Food

Jackson stands out from the rest of Wyoming on the culinary scene: Chicken-fried steak may be available, but it certainly isn't the house specialty! You won't need to look far to find good food; in fact, the town seems to overflow with memorable (and even more memorably priced) eateries. If you stood in Town Square and walked in any direction for a block, you would find at least one restaurant that would be a standout in any other Wyoming town. More than 70 local restaurants do business here—in a town that contains just 9,000 people.

To get an idea of what to expect at local restaurants, pick up a copy of the free *Jackson Hole Dining Guide* at the visitor center, local restaurants, or online (www.focusproductions. com). The guide includes sample menus and brief descriptions of many local establishments. All local restaurants are now entirely smoke-free.

BREAKFAST

The best breakfast place in Jackson isn't in Jackson, but in Wilson, where **(Nora's Fish Creek Inn** (307/733-8288, 6:30 A.M.–2 P.M. and 5:30–9 P.M. Mon.–Fri., 6:30 A.M.–1:30 P.M. and 5:30–9 P.M. Sat.–Sun., $19–28) attracts a full house each morning. The food (including *huevos rancheros,* biscuits and gravy, and omelets) is great, the setting is authentically rustic, and the waitresses are friendly and fast. Nora's also serves tried-and-true lunches and dinners at fair prices, from patty melts ($7) to nut-crusted halibut ($25). Dinner reservations required in the summer.

A longtime morning standout is **The Bunnery** (130 N. Cache Dr., 307/733-5474 or 800/349-0492, www.bunnery.com, daily 7 A.M.–9 P.M. in summer, till 7 P.M. in winter, $7–10), with good omelets and fresh-squeezed juices, plus delicious sandwiches on freshly baked breads, salads, burgers, homemade soups, and espresso. There's plenty of space inside, with a patio deck for summer mornings. The Bunnery bakes a variety of pies, cakes, and other sweets, but it's best known for hearty-flavored OSM (oat, sunflower, and millet) bread—on the pricey side at almost $6 a loaf.

Teton Steakhouse (40 W. Pearl St., 307/733-2639, www.tetonsteakhouse.com, daily 6:30 A.M.–11 P.M.) serves a two-notches-on-your-belt breakfast buffet ($7), with pancakes, bacon, sausage, potatoes, fruits, and more (coffee and juice are extra).

Bubba's Bar-B-Que Restaurant (100 Blackcreek Dr., 307/733-2288, daily 6:30 A.M.–10 P.M. in summer, daily 6:30 A.M.–8:30 P.M. in winter, $5–9) is another cheap and tasty option, with a very filling worker's special ($7). Ask for it, since you won't find it on the menu.

In Teton Village, head downstairs at the Mangy Moose to **RMO Café** (307/734-9438, www.mangymoose.net, daily 7 A.M.–5 P.M., $5–8), offering killer breakfasts along with inexpensive burgers, pizza-by-the-slice ($3), and sandwiches, salads, and burgers for lunch.

E. Leaven Food Co. (175 N. Center St., 307/733-5600, www.eleavenfood.com, daily 7 A.M.–3 P.M. in summer, 8 A.M.–3 P.M. in winter, $6–9) has a bright location a block off the Square. Take a table beside the tall windows facing the leafy alley. Breakfast omelets, quiche, bagels, Belgian waffles, and monster cinnamon rolls are followed by lunchtime hot and cold sandwiches and salads. There's good espresso and box lunches, too.

COFFEE AND SWEETS

Housed in a tiny log cabin a block off the Square, **Shades Café** (25 S. King St., 307/733-2015, www.facebook.com, daily 7:30 A.M.–3 P.M.) has a shady summer-only side patio. Breakfasts feature eggs Benedict (recommended), muesli, and fresh-baked croissants, plus lattes, mochas, and other coffee drinks. Lunch standouts are salads, quiches, burritos, and panini. Shades is a relaxing place to hang out with the espresso habitués, although it does close early in the fall, winter, and spring.

Just off Town Square, **Jackson Hole Roasters** (145 E. Broadway Ave., 307/690-9318, www.jacksonholeroasters.com, 7 A.M.–7 P.M. Mon.–Fri., 8 A.M.–7 P.M. Sat.–Sun.) roasts organic, fair-trade coffees. Get a pound to go or have the barista craft an espresso *doppio* on their hi-tech Clover machine.

(Atelier Ortega (150 Scott Ln., 307/734-6400, www.atelierortega.com, 8 A.M.–8 P.M. Mon.–Sat., 9 A.M.–5 P.M. Sun.) is the creation of Mexican-born Oscar Ortega, a master pastry chef whose accolades include numerous international awards. Crème brûlée, truffles, and other luscious confections await true chocoholics. These are heavenly works of art, almost too perfect to eat.

LUNCH

One of the most popular noontime spots in Jackson—it's been here more than 35 years—is **Sweetwater Restaurant** (85 King St., 307/733-3553, www.sweetwaterjackson.com, daily 11:30 A.M.–3 P.M. and 5:30–10 P.M. in summer, 11:30 A.M.–3 P.M. and 5:30–9 P.M. in winter, $18–24). The historic log cabin has several tables on the front deck and a lunch menu ($10–12) of dependably good salads, homemade soups, and earthy sandwiches. For dinner, try cedar-plank wild salmon, elk osso bucco, or chicken-fried pork.

Better known as DOG, **(Down on Glen** (307/733-4422, daily 7 A.M.–2 P.M., 5:30–10 P.M. Fri.–Sun.) is a minuscule eatery next to Mountain High Pizza at Glenwood and Broadway with a schizophrenic personality. Locals—and in-the-know tourists—crowd in for tasty and cheap breakfast burritos (just $6), organic buffalo burgers, and Philly cheesesteaks early in the day. Owner Sange Sherpa's roots emerge weekend evenings, when DOG becomes **Everest Momo Shack,** serving Nepalese specialties ($10–13), including curry dishes, tikka masala, and momo dumplings, all with a side of naan bread. Delicious, but because everything is freshly made you'll need to wait—and sometimes quite a while. Primarily a to-go spot, DOG has a couple of picnic tables on the patio. Breakfast and lunch are served year-round, but Nepalese meals are available only in summer and winter.

A popular hole-in-the-wall just off the Square, **Backcountry Provisions** (50 W. Deloney St., 307/734-9420, www.backcountryprovisions.com, daily 7 A.M.–5 P.M., $7–8) creates tasty, healthy sandwiches. Try the Dolomite, with prosciutto, salami, provolone, red peppers, and red onion.

Betty Rock Café (325 W. Pearl, 307/733-0747, www.bettyrock.com, 10 A.M.–5 P.M. Mon.–Sat., till 10 P.M. Thurs., $7–9) is a great and noisy place for brunch, with delectable homemade breads, breakfast egg sandwiches, pastrami melts, turkey havarti panini, Thai wraps, salads, soups, and espresso. Drop by on Thursday nights for all-you-can-eat gourmet pizzas ($11, add $4 for Caesar salad). The waitstaff brings out different pizza variations throughout the evening.

A peaceful side-street location, an eclectic all-organic menu with vegan options, and fresh baked goods are all attractions for **Lotus Café** (145 N. Glenwood St., 307/734-0882, www.tetonlotuscafe.com, daily 7 A.M.–7 P.M. in summer, 8 A.M.–9:30 P.M. in winter, $6–11 breakfast and lunch, $13–22 dinner). The menu sprawls across an array of dishes and cuisines, from cinnamon French toast to coconut cashew *biryani*. Fresh-squeezed juices, espresso, and free Wi-Fi are available.

Off the beaten track in Wilson, **❰ Chippy's Kitchen** (307/690-3214, www.jacksonholecatering.com, daily 11:30 A.M.–6 P.M.) is a hidden gem. Owner/chef Chippy Sherman also operates a popular catering business. The tiny cabin gets slammed for lunch, with enormous sandwiches ($8–9) made from whatever is fresh in the kitchen—creations like jalapeño-cheddar corn bread with prosciutto, brie, and roasted asparagus. Daily specials feature soups, salads, and amazing desserts (try the ice-cream sandwich cookies). Check the cooler for dinners to go ($10–15). Closed mid-October–mid-November and mid-April–mid-May.

Find delicious sub sandwiches on tangy homemade bread at **New York City Sub Shop** (20 N. Jackson St., 307/733-4414, www.newyorkcitysubshop.com, 10 A.M.–7 P.M. Mon.–Fri., 10 A.M.–6 P.M. Sat., 10 A.M.–5 P.M. Sun. in summer, reduced hours in winter). It's a little pricey ($7 for a half hoagie or $12 for a whole), but the service is fast, and the hot sandwiches are vastly better than the Subway versions.

Pearl Street Bagels (145 Pearl St., 307/739-1218, daily 6:30 A.M.–6 P.M.) serves home-baked bagels on the small side, along with good espresso and juices. There's a second Pearl Street over in Wilson (307/739-1261); it's *the* groovy place to be seen in Wilson (okay, so are Nora's, Chippy's, and the 'Coach).

For lunches in the Teton Village area, stop by **Westside Store and Deli** (307/733-6202, daily 7 A.M.–9 P.M.) in the Aspens. The deli will be glad to pack you a big picnic lunch, and it also sells entrées (about $6) such as lemon-Dijon chicken, lasagna, and ribs.

The National Museum of Wildlife Art, two miles north of Jackson on U.S. Highway 26/89, houses a bright little restaurant with windows facing the National Elk Refuge. The **Rising Sage Café** (307/733-8649, www.risingsagecafe.com, daily 11 A.M.–3 P.M., $6–11) has a lunch menu of sandwiches (try the chicken salad croissant), buffalo burgers, homemade soups, chili, salads, and espresso.

AMERICAN

Jackson's most popular family eatery is **❰ Bubba's Bar-B-Que Restaurant** (100 Blackcreek Dr., 307/733-2288, daily 6:30 A.M.–10 P.M. in summer, 6:30 A.M.–8:30 P.M. in winter, $13–20). Each evening the parking lot out front is jammed with folks waiting patiently for a chance to gnaw on barbecued spare ribs, savor the spicy chicken wings, or gobble up the turkey plate. Get here before 6:30 P.M. for shorter lines at the big salad bar ($8). Lunch is a real bargain with great specials ($8). Drinks, including beer and wine, come in recycled Mason jars. There are cheap and tasty breakfasts, too.

Get great all-American burgers at the 1950s-style **Billy's Burgers** (55 N. Cache Dr., 307/733-3279, www.cadillac-grille.com, daily

11:30 A.M.–10:30 P.M.), adjacent to the more upscale Cadillac Grille. The Billy burger ($6) is a half-pound monster.

Next door to Billy's and in the basement of the bar of the same name, the **Million Dollar Cowboy Steakhouse** (307/733-4790, www. cowboysteakhouse.net, daily 5:30–10 P.M.) specializes in "casual Western elegance" and great steaks, from sirloin to filet mignon. In addition, the menu encompasses salads, shrimp scampi, pasta, ribs, and a few lonesome vegetarian specials. The bar offers a dozen different single-malt scotches, plus seasonal drink specials. The Steakhouse is not for kids and it's not cheap: steaks are $26–48. Reservations are advised.

Also recommended is **Gun Barrel Steakhouse** (862 W. Broadway Ave., 307/733-3287, www.gunbarrel.com, daily 5:30–10 P.M., closed in Nov.), where the meaty mesquite-grilled steaks, elk, and buffalo are served in a delightful hunting-lodge atmosphere with trophy game mounts; they came from a wildlife museum that previously occupied the site. You'll find lots of historic guns and other Old West paraphernalia around the Gun Barrel too, making this an interesting place to explore even if you aren't hungry. Gun Barrel is a bit on the pricey side, with entrées for $17–37. The bar has a wide choice of beers on draught.

Very popular with both locals and ski bums is famous **Mangy Moose Restaurant & Saloon** (Teton Village, 307/733-4913, www. mangymoose.net, daily 11 A.M.–10 P.M. for food, drinks till 2 A.M., $15–24). The menu changes weekly, but typically includes sirloin steak, black Angus prime rib, Alaskan halibut, and Idaho rainbow trout. Sprawling over two levels, it's a fun and lively place. There's free Wi-Fi, and live bands play several nights a week year-round.

The menu and setting at **Teton Steakhouse** (40 W. Pearl St., 307/733-2639, 6:30 A.M.–10 P.M. Sun.–Thurs., 6:30 A.M.–11 P.M. Fri.–Sat.) reflect this restaurant's previous incarnation as a Sizzler, but that doesn't faze anyone. The central location (one block off Town Square), stuff-yourself meals, and noisy,

kid-friendly setting bring a crowd every day, even if the food is nothing special. Line up to put in your order for steaks ($17–30), ribs, or chicken, or just sidle up to the big salad, soup, and dessert bar to fill your plate. There also is a breakfast buffet and free Wi-Fi. This place is very popular with hogs who park their Hogs (Harleys) and waddle in, along with swarms of motorcoach tourists.

Next to Albertson's on the south end of Jackson, **Rendezvous Bistro** (380 South U.S. Hwy. 89, 307/739-1100, www.rendezvousbistro.net, daily 5:30–11 P.M. in summer, closed Sun. in winter, $17–32) has a strong local following for all-better-than-mom's meatloaf, Jamaican jerked chicken, veal marsala, duck confit, and a rather pricey oyster bar. Definitely recommended.

ASIAN
Chinese
In Grand Teton Plaza on the south end of town, **Chinatown Restaurant** (850 W. Broadway Ave., 307/733-8856, 11 A.M.–9:30 P.M. Mon.–Fri., 5–10 P.M. Sat., 5–9:30 P.M. Sun., $9–14) serves good Chinese dishes—particularly the *mu shu* vegetables, lemon chicken, and pot stickers—and offers weekday lunch specials ($8).

Ocean City China Bistro (340 W. Broadway Ave., 307/734-9768, daily 11 A.M.–9:30 P.M., $9–13) provides a pleasant downtown setting and more than 120 choices—from honey walnut prawns with pork to Szechwan Three Delight. Weekday lunch combo plates ($8) are a bargain.

Hong Kong Buffet (826 W. Broadway Ave., 307/734-8988, 10 A.M.–10:30 P.M. Mon.–Sat., 11 A.M.–10 P.M. Sun.) has an enormous 50-item buffet: $8 at lunch or $12 for dinner and all day Sunday.

Japanese
Get delicious freshly rolled sushi—including vegetarian rolls and a unique hot spicy tuna roll—at **Masa Sushi** (307/733-2962, 6–10 P.M. Tue.–Sun., $18–25), located inside The Inn at Jackson Hole in Teton Village. The setting is intimate and inviting.

Long a favorite with locals and visitors, **Nikai Sushi** (225 N. Cache, 307/734-6490, www.nikaisushi.com, daily 6–9:30 P.M.) serves creatively prepared sushi as the main attraction, but also has a menu of Asian fusion items from the open kitchen, including miso-glazed black cod, coconut fried chicken, and *wakame* seaweed salad. The atmosphere is contemporary and stylish. Most items are priced $10–20, but you'll also find $6 rolls. Reservations are advised.

Housed within the Jackson Hole Wine Company, **Koshu Wine Bar** (200 W. Broadway Ave., 307/733-5283, www.koshuwinebar.com, daily 5:30–10 P.M., $10–32) serves pan-Asian cuisine nightly in a tiny but classy setting with a big summer-only covered deck. The menu changes often, but typically includes butter chicken, Thai beef salad, and Korean-style ribs. You can choose from more than a dozen wines by the glass, or buy a bottle from the shop's extensive selection (corkage fee). A DJ spins tunes Thursday and Saturday nights till 2 A.M.

Thai

In an alley across the street from Teton Theater, friendly ◖ **Teton Thai Restaurant** (135 N. Cache Dr., 307/733-0022, www.tetonthai.com, 11:30 A.M.–3 P.M. and 5:30–10 P.M. Mon.–Sat., $14–18) is a favorite spot for 20-something locals. Pick a rice, noodle, or curry dish and add your choice of chicken, beef, shrimp, or tofu. Vegan and gluten-free options are available. Service can be haphazard and it may take time to get served, but you'll be glad you waited. All seating is outdoors, though some is under a deck. The festive atmosphere amps up on Thursday and Friday evenings when a DJ spins tunes till 11 P.M. Everything moves inside the tiny eatery when winter comes, with customers crowding into a handful of stools along the counter. No credit cards or alcohol, but it's fine to BYOB.

Thai Me Up Restaurant & Brewery (75 E. Pearl St., 307/733-0005, www.thaijh.com, daily 11:30 A.M.–11:30 P.M., $14–17) has a gimmicky name and a U.S.-born chef, but the food is spicy, creative, and delicious. It has a few sidewalk tables, plus a tiny bar with offbeat drinks, including the Bigglesworth Typhoon, a blow-me-down 45-ounce blend of seven different alcohols that's set afire. The location is a bit quieter than places on the Square. Entrées include a good choice of vegetarian and gluten-free dishes. G-13, wide noodles in a coconut kaffir curry, is a not-too-spicy favorite. The bottle beer list features many unique European beers; you can also try several beers brewed on the premises, including Thai Me Up 2x4 Quadruple Pale Ale.

ITALIAN

Hidden away on the north end of town next to Anvil Motel, **Nani's Cucina Italiana** (242 N. Glenwood, 307/733-3888, www.nanis.com, daily 5–10 P.M., $19–25) is a longtime favorite. Flowers cover the exterior in summer, and inside it's quiet and romantic. In addition to the standards, Nani's features a menu of specialties from a different region of Italy each month. The wine bar (Enoteca Sicula) has an extensive choice of Italian and California vintages. Patio dining is available in the summer. Reservations are recommended.

Owned by acclaimed chef Roger Freedman—formerly of Snake River Grill— ◖ **Il Villagio Osteria** (307/739-4100, www.jhosteria.com, daily noon–2 P.M. and 5:30–10 P.M., $18–34) is housed within Teton Village's luxurious Hotel Terra. It specializes in Italian cuisine, including house-made gnocchi, asparagus ravioli, and wonderful pizzas ($18) and panini from the wood-fired oven. The 12-seat wine bar is less formal, with plenty of Italian wines available by the glass or bottle. There's also a big outside deck facing the Teton Village fun. Reservations are essential.

Several other pizza places stand out in Jackson. You'll find **Calico Italian Restaurant & Bar** (307/733-2460, www.calicorestaurant.com, daily 5–10 P.M. restaurant, 5 P.M.–midnight bar) in the garish red-and-white building 0.75 mile north on Teton Village Road. The menu has gone a bit upscale, but prices are still manageable: $14–26 entrées, including such faves as linguini with spinach and chicken or Italian sausage lasagna from the open kitchen. A 12-inch personal pizza is $12. The bar at Calico is a locals' watering hole, and kids love the two-acre lawn/playground, wraparound covered porch, and flower-bedecked patio affording Teton vistas. START buses stop right out front, making this an easy destination even if you're without a car.

Mountain High Pizza Pie (120 W. Broadway Ave., 307/733-3646, www.mh-pizza.com, daily 11 A.M.–11 P.M. in summer, till 10 P.M. in winter, $16) is a convenient tried-and-true downtown place offering all the usual toppings (and some not so, such as the Thai pie), plus calzones, subs, salads, and delivery to Jackson and Teton Village.

MEXICAN

For the fastest Mexican food in town (with the possible exception of Taco Bell), drop by **Pica's Mexican Taqueria** (1160 Alpine La., 307/734-4457, www.picastaqueria.com, daily 11 A.M.–10 P.M., $7–15). You'll find tasty tacos, bodacious burritos, enchanting enchiladas, and tempting *tortas* in a hip setting packed with locals. There's also a morning menu of breakfast burritos, huevos rancheros, and more on weekends. The shop is in the Buffalo Junction strip mall near Albertson's, with a second one inside Stagecoach Bar in Wilson.

In business since 1969, **The Merry Piglets** (160 N. Cache Dr., 307/733-2966, www.merrypiglets.com, daily 11:30 A.M.–10 P.M. in summer, 11:30 A.M.–9 P.M. in winter, $11–20) is a very busy place with a heart-of-town location. The menu features Tex-Mex meals, carne asada, fajitas, enchiladas, quesadillas, fish tacos, nachos, and cheese crisps—the house specialty. Excellent margaritas, pitchers of beer, and a skylit front section add to the appeal. Reservations are not accepted, so you'll find a long wait on midsummer evenings.

For a side of Jackson most tourists don't see, drop by **Alameda Tienda Mexicana** (975 Alpine Ave.) for Mexican pastries, meats, specialty groceries, and piñatas. The shop is hidden away in a tiny backstreet location.

FINE DINING

If you want fine continental dining and aren't deterred by entrées costing $25 or more, Jackson has much to offer.

Just off Town Square, **Snake River Grill** (upstairs at 84 E. Broadway Ave., 307/733-0557, www.snakerivergrill.com, daily 6:30–10 P.M.) is one of Jackson's finest gourmet restaurants—with prices to match ($21–42 entrées). Meals are exquisite, and the seasonal menu typically contains a variety of artfully presented seafood, free-range beef, and organic vegetables. The wine list is equally impressive, and there's a big rooftop deck (late June–Sept.) for alfresco dining on warm evenings. Reservations are a must; reserve two weeks in advance for prime-time seatings in the summer. Snake River Grill is a good place to scan for Jackson's best-known residents, Harrison Ford and Calista Flockhart. Closed November and April.

For views so spectacular they make it difficult to concentrate on your meal, don't miss **The Granary Restaurant** (307/732-8112, www.springcreekranch.com, daily 7–11 A.M., noon–2 P.M., and 5–9 P.M., closed Sun.–Tues. mid-Oct.–mid-Dec., $22–40), atop East Gros Ventre Butte west of Jackson with tall windows opening to the Tetons. This is also a great place for evening cocktails and romantic dining. Entrées include Idaho trout, Kobe beef sirloin steak, and a popular Cajun-spiced elk tenderloin. The separate lounge menu has lighter fare, including happy-hour specials 4–7 P.M. nightly, jazz on Friday, and a piano bar Saturday evenings.

Jackson's popular nouvelle cuisine restaurant—**C Cadillac Grille** (55 N. Cache on the square, 307/733-3279, www.cadillac-grille.com, daily 11:30 A.M.–3 P.M. and 5:30–10 P.M., $14–34)—serves creative meals, with a changing menu of seafood, filet mignon, buffalo burgers, and wild game. The art deco decor of the Cadillac helps make it one of the most crowded tourist hangouts in town, but it also attracts a devoted following of locals, especially during the nightly happy hour when two-for-one drinks are the draw. The restaurant includes a bar with lighter fare ($7–10 salads,

JACKSON HOLE

ribs, and chicken wings), Billy's Burgers, and a covered rear patio for summertime dining. Owned by a trio of local chefs, **Trio, An American Bistro** (45 S. Glenwood, 307/734-8038, www.bistrotrio.com, daily 11:30 A.M.–2:30 P.M. and 5:30–9 P.M.) is a trendy downtown eatery with high ceilings and a metallic decor. Start with sautéed mussels or arugula salad. House specialties include Tuscan grilled New York steak, wood-fired half chickens, and buffalo burgers. Be sure to order a side of their famous waffle fries with bleu cheese fondue. Most entrées are $15–30, but $12 will get you a simple mozzarella, marinara, and basil pizza. Reservations are advised.

Housed within Rusty Parrot Lodge, the acclaimed **(Wild Sage Restaurant** (175 N. Jackson, 307/733-2000 or 888/739-1749, www.rustyparrot.com, daily 5:30–9:30 P.M., $33–45) serves gourmet dinners in an intimate setting (just 26 seats). One of two AAA four-diamond restaurants in Jackson Hole, Wild Sage offers a delectable array of regional cuisine and fresh seafood. The menu changes, but typically includes pan-seared beef tenderloin, herb-crusted bison rib-eye, and ginger and citron crème brûlée, plus a fine choice of wines by the glass or bottle. Reservations are required; call a month ahead in midsummer. Breakfast (7–10 A.M.) is primarily for lodge guests, but is open to the public when space is available (more common in winter). The morning menu has several options, from a granola, yogurt, fruit, pastry, and coffee bar ($7) up to an all-you-can-eat spread ($15).

Located atop Bridger gondola at Jackson Hole Resort, **(Couloir Restaurant** (307/739-2675, www.couloirrestaurant.com) has gained accolades from both Condé Nast and *Food and Wine*. This special-occasion spot features views of Corbet's Couloir and the valley of Jackson Hole 2,800 feet below, with four-course dinners for $85 per person ($145 with paired wines). Signature dishes include an amazing house-smoked tenderloin of buffalo and a "locavore" salad from farmers' market vegetables and fruits. Desserts and cocktails are equally notable. The setting is contemporary, and dinner reservations are highly recommended (available at www.opentable.com). The gondola (free in summer, free for restaurant patrons only in winter) starts running at 4:30 P.M. The vistas from the big outside patio (The Deck) are especially pretty at sunset; a bar menu features appetizers, sliders, burgers, shared plates, and happy-hour specials. Summer hours for both Couloir and The Deck are 5–11 P.M. Sunday–Friday late June–early September (closed Sat.). The Deck closes for winter, but Headwall Deli opens for ski season downstairs from Couloir. During ski season, Couloir is open 5:45–10 P.M. Friday–Saturday and daily for lunch.

BREWERIES

Before Prohibition in 1920, nearly every town in Wyoming had its own brewery, making such local favorites as Hillcrest, Schoenhofen, and Sweetwater. After repeal of "the noble experiment," breweries again popped up, but competition from industrial giants such as Anheuser-Busch and Coors forced the last Wyoming operation—Sheridan Brewing—out of business in 1954. It was another 34 years before commercial beer-making returned. In 1988, Charlie Otto started a tiny backyard operation in Wilson. His **Grand Teton Brewing Company** (208/787-4000 or 888/899-1656, www.grandtetonbrewing.com) brews just over Teton Pass in Victor, Idaho, where you can sample Teton Ale, Old Faithful Ale, Howling Wolf Weisse Bier, Bitch Creek ESB, and Sweetgrass IPA. You'll find them on tap at many Jackson-area bars and restaurants and for sale in six-pack bottles throughout the region.

An old warehouse two blocks from Town Square has been beautifully transformed into **(Snake River Brewing Co. and Restaurant** (265 S. Millward St., 307/739-2337, www.snakeriverbrewing.com, daily 11:30 A.M.–2 A.M., food served till 11 P.M.). The bright, cavernous setting fills with a convivial—and very loud—crowd of young

© DON PITCHER

Snake River Brewing Co. and Restaurant

outdoors enthusiasts most evenings, and the bar generally has seven or eight of their award-winning beers on tap, along with 40 or so from other brewers. Particularly notable—they've all won gold medals at many international brew festivals—are Zonker Stout, A.K. Session, and Snake River Pale Ale. The lunch and dinner café menu includes delicious thin-crust pizzas baked in the apple-wood–fired oven, flavorful appetizers, daily pasta specials, half-pound burgers, panini sandwiches, and salads. This is great food in a lively atmosphere, and one of *the* places to be seen in Jackson. Most entrées run $9–15, but the brewery also serves a number of $7 lunch specials. While this is a brewpub, it's also completely family friendly, with a kids' menu and so much background noise nobody will know when the baby starts screaming. Happy-hour (4–6 P.M.) beers are just $2.50, and you can add a big homemade soft pretzel for another buck or tasty chicken wings for a few more. There's free Wi-Fi, too.

WINE SHOPS

The most complete local wine and beer shops are **Westside Wine and Spirits** (307/733-5038) in the Aspens along Teton Village Road, **The Liquor Store** (next to Albertson's on W. Broadway Ave., 307/733-4466, www.wineliquorbeer.com), and **Dornan's Wine Shoppe** (307/733-2415, ext. 202, www.dornans.com) in Moose. The Liquor Store features an impressive upstairs wine department, plus a wine bar with free tastings of a half-dozen wines Fridays 4–7 P.M. **Jackson Hole Wine Company** (200 W. Broadway Ave., 307/739-9463, www.jacksonholewinecompany.com) also has a fine selection, with Koshu Wine Bar in the back.

GROCERIES AND NATURAL FOODS

Get groceries from the large **Albertson's** (307/733-5950, www.albertsons.com) on the south end of town at the corner of Buffalo Way and Broadway Avenue. Inside you'll find a bakery, pharmacy, deli, one-hour photo lab, bank branch, and coffee bar. This is the most lucrative Albertson's in the entire chain of 2,300 stores; sales are said to be three times higher than the second-most-successful store! A few blocks farther south (right in front of the high school) is an even larger **Smith's** (1425 S. U.S. Hwy. 89, 307/733-8908, www.smithsfoodanddrug.com), with the same features as Albertson's and a deli serving fresh sushi.

In Powderhorn Mall, **Jackson Whole Grocer** (974 W. Broadway Ave., 307/733-0450, www.jacksonwholegrocer.com, daily 7 A.M.–11 P.M.) is a hybrid of sorts between an organic grocer and a traditional supermarket. The emphasis is upon fresh and local items, but there's also a great bakery, full deli, fresh-squeezed juices, and espresso.

The popular **Jackson Hole Farmers Market** (www.jacksonholefarmersmarket.org) comes to Town Square Saturdays 8–11 A.M. July–mid-September. Shop for fresh veggies, fruits, food, and flowers. Live music and cooking demonstrations add to

JACKSON HOLE

the attraction. A separate **People's Market** (307/690-0705, www.jhpeoplesmarket.org) takes place on Wednesday 4–7 P.M. at the Lutheran Church on the corner of Gill and Willow Streets.

In business since 1947, **Jackson Hole**

Buffalo Meat Company (1325 S. Hwy. 89, 307/733-4159 or 800/543-6328, www.jhbuffalomeat.com) sells smoked buffalo salami, jerky, sausage, steaks, and burgers, along with buffalo meat gift packs and elk steaks. It's in the Smith's mall.

Getting There and Around

Access to Jackson Hole has become easier in recent years, with several airlines and daily buses now serving the valley. Most summer visitors arrive by car, although a few more adventurous souls pedal in on bikes. If you're looking for or offering a ride, KMTN (96.9 FM, 307/733-4500, www.kmtnthemountain.com) has daily ride-finder announcements during its Trash and Treasure radio program. Tune in weekdays 9:30–9:50 A.M.

Several local travel agencies offer reservation services for those who prefer to leave the planning to someone else. They can set up airline tickets, rental cars, lodging, horseback riding, fishing trips, whitewater rafting, ski vacations, and all sorts of other packages. The biggest is the long-established **Jackson Hole Central Reservations** (307/733-4005 or 800/443-6931, www.jacksonholewy.com), which produces a slick glossy publication of featured properties. **Jackson Hole Reservations** (307/733-6331 or 800/329-9205, www.jacksonhole.net) has an equally complete listing of local places.

BY AIR

Jackson Hole Airport (307/733-7682, www.jacksonholeairport.com) is eight miles north of Jackson inside Grand Teton National Park. The remodeled airport is small and cozy but offers daily jet service to several U.S. cities. It's the only commercial airport within any national park, and the Grand Teton Association maintains a gift shop here. Stop by the **Ground Transportation Information Desk** (open daily 9 A.M.–5 P.M. year-round) for helpful maps and advice. Nearby are courtesy phones for local

businesses and racks of brochures. You'll also find free Wi-Fi and a restaurant.

Delta/SkyWest (800/221-1212, www.delta.com) has year-round flights from Salt Lake City, with summer and winter service from Minneapolis/St. Paul and Atlanta. **American** (800/433-7300, www.aa.com) has summer and winter flights to Dallas and Chicago. **United/United Express** (800/864-8331, www.united.com) offers year-round service from Denver and Chicago, plus summertime flights out of Los Angeles. **Frontier Airlines** (800/432-1359, www.frontierairlines.com) has summer-only flights from Denver; these are turboprops, not jets. (Some Delta/SkyWest and United/United Express flights from Denver and Salt Lake City are also on these smaller planes.) In addition, the tarmac is often crowded with Lear and Gulfstream jets and other noisy transportation symbols of the elite.

Amazingly, there are no flights into Jackson from Seattle or Portland. If you're flying in from the Pacific Northwest, you will need to go through Salt Lake City, a 275-mile rental car drive from Jackson.

Airport Shuttles and Taxis

Alltrans/Gray Line of Jackson Hole (307/733-3135 or 800/443-6133, www.jacksonholealltrans.com) provides airport shuttle service to and from motels in Jackson ($16 one-way or $31 round-trip per person) and Teton Village ($26 one-way or $47 round-trip per person). The shuttles meet nearly all commercial airline flights in winter and most summertime flights, but you should make reservations to be sure of an airport pickup. Make outgoing reservations for a motel pickup 24 hours in advance.

From the airport, one-way taxi rates for one or two people are $32 to Jackson, or $55 to Teton Village. At last count there were 24(!) local taxi companies, including **Buckboard Transportation** (307/733-1112 or 877/791-0211, www.buckboardtrans.com), **Bullseye Taxi** (307/730-5000), **Cowboy Cab** (307/413-1000, www.cowboycab.net), **Old West Taxi** (307/690-8898), **Old Faithful Taxi** (307/699-4020, www.oldfaithfultaxi.com), **Teton Taxi** (307/733-1506), and **Westbank Cab** (307/690-0112).

BY BUS
Long-Distance Buses

Greyhound buses don't come even close to Jackson; the nearest stopping place is the regional hub at Salt Lake City. **Mountain States Express/Alltrans** (307/733-3135 or 800/652-9510, www.mountainstatesexpress.com) has year-round daily service connecting Jackson with Salt Lake City ($70 one-way) and Idaho Falls ($35 one-way) daily. Along the way, vans pass through Star Valley, Cokeville, Kemmerer, Evanston, Park City, Rexburg, Tetonia, Driggs, and Victor, and you can also get on or off at any of these towns.

Salt Lake Express (208/656-8824 or 800/356-9796, www.saltlakeexpress.com) runs shuttle vans connecting Jackson with Idaho Falls three times daily for $39 one-way. The company also has daily service south to Salt Lake ($67), north to West Yellowstone and Butte, and west to Twin Falls and Boise.

START Buses

Local buses are operated by Southern Teton Area Rapid Transit (START, 307/733-4521, www.startbus.com) and serve Jackson and Teton Village all year. START fares are **free** within town and $3 one-way to Teton Village ($1.50 for seniors and children). Discount coupons are available for multiple rides. Hours of operation are generally 6 A.M.–10:30 P.M. During summer and winter, buses run seven days a week, with in-town service every half-hour. Service to Teton Village is hourly (more

or less) in summer and two or three times an hour in winter. Reduced bus service is available in fall and spring. Get schedules and route maps in the visitor center. Buses stop near most Jackson hotels and motels and are equipped to carry skis (in winter) and bikes (in summer) on outside racks. Unfortunately, START buses do not run to the airport, Kelly, or Moose, but commuter buses ($8 one-way) provide morning and evening service to Teton Valley, Idaho (Driggs and Victor), as well as Star Valley.

CAR AND RV RENTALS

Most of the national chains offer rental cars in town or at the airport. These include **Alamo** (307/733-0671 or 888/426-3299, www.alamo.com), **Avis** (307/733-3422 or 800/831-2847, www.avis.com), **Budget** (270 W. Pearl St., 307/733-2206 or 800/237-7251, www.budget.com), **Dollar** (345 W. Broadway Ave., 307/733-9224 or 877/222-7736, www.dollar.com), **Hertz** (307/733-2272 or 800/654-3131, www.hertz.com), **National** (220 N. Millward St., 307/733-7961 or 888/868-6204, www.nationalcar.com), and **Thrifty** (307/734-9306 or 800/847-4389, www.jackson.thrifty.com). Alamo, Avis, Hertz, and National all have counters at the airport, while the others provide a free shuttle to their in-town offices. **Leisure Sports** (1075 S. Hwy. 89, 307/733-3040, www.leisuresportsadventure.com) also has a few rental cars.

The best deals are often from Dollar or Thrifty, but check one of the online reservation sources (www.travelocity.com or www.expedia.com) to see who currently has the best rates. You may be better off getting a car in town, where you don't have to pay the additional taxes imposed at the airport. Taxes and fees (especially for airport rentals) can add another 21 percent to your charges, so read the fine print! Reserve cars at least one month ahead during summer and two months ahead for midsummer or the Christmas–New Year's holiday period. Be sure to mention any discounts; an AAA membership generally cuts 10 percent from the bill.

JACKSON HOLE

PARK TOURS

Summertime bus tours of Grand Teton and Yellowstone national parks are available several times a week from **Gray Line of Jackson Hole/Alltrans** (307/733-3135 or 800/443-6133, www.graylinejh.com). Yellowstone tours last 11 hours and cost $115, while eight-hour Grand Teton tours are $100; rates for kids are half-price. Add a $12 park entrance fee to both tours. During winter, Gray Line/Alltrans has daily bus runs to Flagg Ranch Resort for $106 round-trip, arriving in time to meet the snowcoach departures for Yellowstone. Reservations required. Jackson taxi companies also offer shuttle services within the park and guided tours.

Operated by Teton Science School, **Wildlife Expeditions** (307/733-2623 or 888/945-3567, www.wildlifeexpeditions.org) leads an array of wildlife-viewing safaris throughout the region, from four-hour sunset trips for $125 to four-day tours through Yellowstone and Grand Teton for $1,995. Their trips change seasonally—depending upon which animals are visible—and are offered in customized vehicles with multiple roof hatches for better wildlife viewing.

Get a geologist's perspective on the area from **Earth Tours** (307/733-4261, www.earth-tours.com), with outstanding tours and hikes led by Dr. Keith Watts. He also guides full-day trips into Yellowstone and longer trips to southern Utah parks.

Other companies with guided van tours of the area include **Ana's Grand Excursions** (307/690-6106, www.anasgrandexcursions.com), **Brushbuck Guide Services** (888/282-5868, www.brushbuckphototours.com), **Callowishus Park Touring Company** (307/413-5483, www.callowishus.com), **EcoTour Adventures** (307/690-9533, www.jhecotouradventures.com), **Upstream Anglers and Outdoor Adventures** (307/739-9443 or 800/642-8979, www.upstreamanglers.com), **Grand Teton Adventure Company** (307/734-4454 or 800/700-1558, www.grandtetonadventures.com), **The Hole Hiking Experience** (307/690-4453 or 866/733-4453, www.holehike.com), and **VIP Adventure Travel** (307/699-1077, www.vipadventuretravel.com).

Information and Services

INFORMATION

On the north side of town is the **Jackson Hole & Greater Yellowstone Visitor Center** (532 N. Cache Dr., 307/733-3316, www.jacksonholechamber.com, open daily). Brochures are also available at the airport, the stagecoach stop on Town Square, next to the downtown public restrooms at Cache and Gill, and at the Mangy Moose in Teton Village. Immediately south of the visitor center is an impressive building housing the **Wyoming Game and Fish** (307/733-2321) offices.

The **Bridger-Teton National Forest** supervisor's office (340 N. Cache Dr., 307/739-5500, www.fs.fed.us/r4/btnf) is open Monday–Friday 8 A.M.–4:30 P.M. Get information and Forest Service maps at the visitor center.

Kid-Friendly Jackson

During summer, older kids will enjoy hiking, mountain biking, Snake River float and whitewater trips, the shoot-out, and the putting course at Alpine Miniature Golf. In winter, snowboarding and skiing are favorites of older kids, but sleigh rides, dogsledding, ice-skating, and snowshoeing are also fun. While in town, be sure to pick up a copy of the free *Teton Family Magazine* (www.tetonfamily.wordpress.com), with articles on life beneath these majestic peaks.

For those traveling with tots, **Baby's Away** (307/739-4711 or 888/616-8495, www.babys-away.com) and **Babies on the Go** (307/690-6746, www.babiesonthego-jh.com) rent all sorts of baby supplies, including car seats, cribs, gates, joggers, backpacks, swings, and high chairs.

You'll find more stroller and backpack rentals—along with trendy kids' clothing—at **Teton Kids** (130 E. Broadway Ave., 307/739-2176). **Second Helpings** (141 E. Pearl Ave., 307/733-9466) has an excellent selection of quality used baby and children's clothes.

For child care, contact **Jackson Hole Babysitting** (307/732-7720, www.jackson-holebabysitting.com), **Playtime in the Tetons** (307/734-0153, www.playtimeinthetetons.com), or **Snake River Babysitting & Nannies** (307/699-1195, www.facebook.com).

Jackson Hole Mountain Resort (307/733-2292 or 888/333-7766, www.jacksonhole.com, Mon.–Sat. mid-June–early Sept. and daily late Nov.–early Apr.) operates a Kids Ranch day camp with activities and child care for ages 6 months–11 years old. Programs are geared to different ages and cost $89 per day.

Library

Spacious **Teton County Library** (125 Virginian La., 307/733-2164, www.tclib.org) is the kind of library every town should have. Inside this modern building is a large collection of books about Wyoming and the West, plus a great kids' section (complete with a fenced-in children's garden with a tepee). Computers provide free Internet access and are available by reservation or on a walk-up-and-wait basis. In the summer the queue can get long if you don't have a reservation. The library takes reservations up to one week in advance. Library hours are 10 A.M.–8 P.M. Monday–Thursday, 10 A.M.–5:30 P.M. Friday, and 1–5 P.M. Saturday–Sunday. If you plan to be in the Jackson area for a week or more, it may be worth your while to get a visitor's library card. For a one-time fee of $10 you can check out up to four books at a time. (Completion of a major library addition is expected in 2013.)

JACKSON HOLE FOR KIDS

Those traveling with children will find an abundance of kid-friendly options in Jackson Hole. A few noteworthy examples include:

- the hands-on **Children's Discovery Gallery** at the **National Museum of Wildlife Art**

- playgrounds at **Mike Yokel Jr. Park** (Kelly and Hall Streets), **Miller Park** (Powderhorn Lane and Maple Way), and **Baux Park** (base of Snow King Mountain)

- the excellent swimming pool and corkscrew water slide at the **Teton County Recreation Center**

- the fine children's section of the library

- chuck-wagon dinners at **Bar-T-Five** or **Bar J**

- pizzas at the **Calico** (where the lawn is great for kids)

- melodramas at **Jackson Hole Playhouse**

- the **Alpine Slide** at **Snow King Resort**

- the chairlifts, bungee trampoline, climbing wall, and pop-jet fountain at **Jackson Hole Resort**

- the evening shootouts at **Town Square**

- horseback or wagon rides

- float trips down the Snake River

- a trip to the fish hatchery

- a night at the rodeo (including the kids-only calf chase)

- the weird and wacky collection of oddities at **Ripley's Believe It or Not!**

- a boat ride and hike at **Jenny Lake** inside Grand Teton National Park

- day camp at the recreation center (grades 1-6)

JACKSON HOLE

Newspapers

Jackson's outstanding local newspaper—the *Jackson Hole News and Guide* (307/733-2047, www.jhnewsandguide.com)—is produced in tabloid format. Free Monday–Saturday editions can be found all over the valley, and a fat weekly edition ($0.50) comes out on Wednesdays with more detailed local and regional coverage, including the weekly entertainment paper, *Stepping Out*. The free *Jackson Hole Weekly* (307/732-0299, www.planetjh.com) focuses on local music, art, and entertainment, with a variety of topical stories about the region.

Radio

Find **National Public Radio's KUWJ** on your dial at 90.3 FM (www.wyomingpublicradio.net). The locals' commercial station is **KMTN** (www.kmtnthemountain.com) at 96.9 FM.

At 89.1 FM, radio station **KHOL** (www.jhcr.org) is a nonprofit community station with a wide variety of music—free from ads—hosted by local DJs. Other Jackson Hole radio stations are KZJH 95.3 FM and KSGT 1340 AM. See www.jacksonholeradio.com for details on the commercial stations.

Weddings

Jackson Hole makes a wonderful spot for a mountain wedding, with a grand setting, an abundance of fine lodging places and upscale caterers, plus easy access from anywhere in the nation. You can choose the simple back-to-nature version with a couple of family members along Jenny Lake or the full-blown variety at such places as Rancho Alegre Lodge (over $10,000 with the four-night minimum). A local company produces a slick 100-page free magazine called *A Grand Wedding* (www.jacksonholewedding.com), packed with advice and ads for Jackson Hole caterers, locations, musicians, DJs, photographers, wedding consultants, spas, tent and carriage rentals, wedding cakes, limos, and yes, even portable toilets. Pick up a copy at the visitor center or order one from their website.

Also check out **Destination Jackson Hole** (307/734-5007, www.destinationjacksonhole.com) for wedding planning.

Looking for a stunning natural setting to tie the knot? Book your wedding at **Chapel of the Transfiguration** (307/733-2603, www.stjohnsjackson.org) or **Chapel of the Sacred Heart** (307/733-2516, www.olmcatholic.org) within Grand Teton National Park, but be ready to drop $1,500 or so to reserve a date.

For specifics on obtaining marriage licenses, contact the Teton County Clerk (307/733-7733, www.tetonwyo.org).

SERVICES

Jackson's main **post office** (1070 Maple Way, 307/733-3650) near Powderhorn Lane is open 8:30 A.M.–5 P.M. Monday–Friday and 10 A.M.–1 P.M. Saturday. Other post offices are downtown (220 W. Pearl Ave., 307/739-1740), in Teton Village (307/733-3575), in Wilson (307/733-3335), and in Kelly (307/733-8884).

For shipping, packaging, and copying needs, head to the **UPS Store** (970 W. Broadway Ave., 307/733-9250, www.theupsstore.com).

Wash clothes at **Broadway Laundry** (860 W. Broadway Ave., 307/734-7627).

Showers ($6 with a towel) are available from **Anvil Motel** (215 N. Cache Dr., 307/733-3668 or 800/234-4507, www.anvilmotel.com).

Banking

Get fast cash from **ATMs** at many locations around town, including banks, grocers, downtown shops, the airport, plus in Teton Village and the Aspens.

International travelers will appreciate the currency exchange where you can swap those euros, Japanese yen, or colorful Canadian dollars at all four **Wells Fargo** (307/733-3737, www.wellsfargo.com) locations: 112 Center Street, 50 Buffalo Way, Teton Village, and in the Aspens on Teton Village Road.

Internet

To keep in touch with folks via email, use the

SAVING JACKSON HOLE

Over the last 30 years, Jackson has grown from a sleepy burg to a national focal point for outdoor fun. The population nearly doubled between 1990 and 2000. Growth has since slowed – especially with the recession that began in 2008 – but by 2010 almost 10,000 people lived in Jackson. Expensive homes have spread across old ranch lands, retailers such as Kmart moved in, and development now reaches for miles south from Jackson itself. Surrounding towns such as Alpine, Driggs, and Afton have become bedroom communities for those willing to endure the long commute to Jackson, and their growth spreads the problems outward.

Although 97 percent of the land in Teton County is in the public domain, the 70,000 acres of private land that remain are rapidly being developed, and Jackson Hole is in grave danger of losing the wild beauty that has attracted visitors for more than a century. This dilemma is immediately obvious to anyone arriving in Jackson. The edges of town have fallen under a proliferation of trophy homes, real-estate offices, chain motels, fast-food outlets, mega-marts, gas stations, and elaborate banks, all competing beneath a thicket of signs. Summertime traffic jams are becoming all too common in this once-quiet place, where more than 35,000 visitors can be found on a summer afternoon.

Way back in 1994, Jackson voters got fed up with the pace of development and voted to scrap the town's 2 percent lodging tax, which had provided more than $1 million per year in funding to promote Jackson Hole around the world. Despite this lack of promotional effort, growth has continued. A moratorium on large commercial developments went into effect in 2008, but smaller developments with housing for employees were allowed.

The **Jackson Hole Conservation Alliance** (307/733-9417, www.jhalliance.com) is a 1,800-member environmental group that works to preserve the remaining natural areas of Jackson Hole. Membership starts at $30 per year and includes biannual newsletters and a chance to help control the many developments that threaten this still-beautiful valley.

Another influential local group is the **Jackson Hole Land Trust** (307/733-4707, www.jhlandtrust.org). Established in 1980, this nonprofit organization obtains conservation easements to maintain ranches and other land threatened by development. The group has protected more than 20,000 acres in the valley in this way, including the 1,740-acre Walton Ranch, visible along the highway between Jackson and Wilson.

JACKSON HOLE

free terminals in the **public library.** Many local restaurants and coffee shops—even the Albertson's grocery store—provide free Wi-Fi.

Check out the current conditions around Jackson at the following **Web camera** sites: www.wyoroad.info and www.alltravelcams.com; the latter includes cameras in Town Square, the airport, Spring Creek Ranch, and Teton Valley, plus other regional webcams.

A great place to begin your Web tour is the chamber of commerce site: www.jacksonholechamber.com. Also very useful are www.jacksonholetraveler.com and www.jacksonholenet.com. All three of these contain links to dozens of local businesses of all types. You may also want to check out the Teton County website, www.tetonwyo.org. Federal government websites for the local area include Grand Teton National Park at www.nps.gov/grte, Yellowstone National Park at www.nps.gov/yell, Bridger-Teton National Forest at www.fs.fed.us/r4/btnf, and Caribou-Targhee National Forest at www.fs.fed.us/r4/caribou-targhee.

Medical

Because of the abundance of ski and snowboard accidents, orthopedic specialists are in high demand in Jackson and are some of the best around. The experts at **Teton Orthopaedics** (555 E. Broadway Ave., 307/733-3900 or 800/659-1335, www.tetonortho.com) are official physicians for the U.S. national ski team! **St. John's Medical Center** (625 E. Broadway Ave., 307/733-3636, www.tetonhospital.org) has emergency medical services. They also operate a winter-only ski-in (hobble in?) clinic at Teton Village (307/739-2650), along with a walk-in clinic next to the Smith's store, **Urgent Care of Jackson Hole** (1415 S. Hwy. 89, 307/739-8999). Another option is **Emerg-A-Care** (982 W. Broadway Ave., 307/733-8002) in the Powderhorn Mall.

Pets

Several local kennels in Jackson will keep an eye on Fido for you. **Happy Tails Pet Resort/ Spring Creek Animal Hospital** (1035 W. Broadway Ave., 307/733-1606, www.springcreekanimalhospital.com) provides veterinary care and kennels. **Rally's Pet Garage** (520 S. Hwy. 89, 307/733-7704, www.rallyspetgarage.com) is a unique service with "doggie daycare," boarding, dog baths, and grooming.

Photography

D. D. Camera Corral (60 S. Cache, 307/733-3831) is the local photo shop, with a good selection of professional and point-and-shoot equipment.

Serious professional or semipro photographers should not miss **Photography at the Summit** (303/295-7770 or 800/745-3211, www.photographyatthesummit.com), an extraordinary five-day series of workshops led by internationally famous photographers and photo editors. The staff always includes a contingent of *National Geographic* photographers.

Evening talks—held at the National Museum of Wildlife Art—are open to the public. Also notable are photography workshops through **Jackson Hole Center for the Arts** (240 S. Glenwood, 307/734-8956, www.jhcenterforthearts.org).

Recycling

Jackson has been at the forefront of the movement to practice the three R's: reduce, reuse, and recycle. Many businesses have attempted to go green (or at least to gain good publicity by saying all the right things). Even the ski resorts have gotten in on the action. Jackson Hole Mountain Resort—one of the largest users of energy in the valley—is committed to getting 50 percent of its energy from renewables such as wind, biomass, small hydro, and geothermal. **Reduce, Reuse, Recycle Jackson Hole** (www.howdoyourrr.com) recognizes local businesses that promote conservation.

Just because you're on vacation doesn't mean you should just chuck everything in the trash. If you don't need that extra plastic bag or napkin, don't take it. Bring your coffee mug instead of getting a throwaway cup. Walk or bike instead of driving around town. Even the small steps add up.

Jackson has a good recycling program and accepts newspaper, aluminum cans, glass, tin cans, plastic milk jugs, magazines, catalogs, cardboard, and office paper. The **recycling center** (307/733-7678, www.tetonwyo.org/recycling) is the big brown building two miles south of the high school on U.S. Highway 89, but bins are also located on the rodeo grounds on the corner of Snow King Avenue and Flat Creek Drive, the recreation center on East Gill, and in Teton Village.

Bridger-Teton National Forest

One of the largest national forests in the Lower 48, Bridger-Teton ("the B-T") National Forest stretches southward for 135 miles from the Yellowstone border and covers 3.4 million acres. In Jackson Hole, the two areas of most interest for recreation are the Teton Wilderness and the Gros Ventre Wilderness, but nonwilderness areas offer additional opportunities for recreation.

The Bridger-Teton National Forest **supervisor's office** (307/739-5500, www.fs.fed.us/r4/btnf) is at 340 North Cache Drive in Jackson. The **Jackson Hole & Greater Yellowstone Visitor Center** (532 N. Cache Dr., 307/733-3316, www.jacksonholechamber.com, open daily), a couple of blocks north on Cache, has a Forest Service worker on duty who can provide recreation information. The center usually sells Bridger-Teton maps and has a good choice of outdoor books. Local ranger stations are the **Jackson Ranger District** (directly behind the supervisor's office, 307/739-5400) and the **Buffalo Ranger District** (nine miles east of Moran Junction, 307/543-2386).

TETON WILDERNESS

The Teton Wilderness covers 585,468 acres of mountain country, bordered to the north by Yellowstone National Park, to the west by Grand Teton National Park, and to the east by the Washakie Wilderness. Established as a primitive area in 1934, it was declared one of the nation's first wilderness areas upon passage of the 1964 Wilderness Act. The Teton Wilderness offers a diverse mixture of rolling lands carpeted with lodgepole pine, spacious grassy meadows, roaring rivers, and dramatic mountains. Elevations range from 7,500 feet to the 12,165-foot summit of Younts Peak. The Continental Divide slices across the wilderness, with headwaters of the Yellowstone River draining the eastern half and headwaters of the Buffalo and Snake Rivers flowing down the western side. Teton Wilderness has a considerable amount of bear activity, so make sure you

know how to avoid bear encounters and bring pepper spray.

One of the most unusual places within Teton Wilderness is **Two Ocean Creek,** where a creek abruptly splits at a rock and the two branches never rejoin. One branch becomes Atlantic Creek, and its waters eventually reach the Atlantic Ocean, while the other becomes Pacific Creek and its waters flow to the Snake River, the Columbia River, and thence into the Pacific Ocean! Mountain man Osborne Russell described this phenomenon in 1835:

On the South side about midway of the prairie stands a high snowy peak from whence issues a Stream of water which after entering the plain it divides equally one half running West and other East thus bidding adieu to each other one bound for the Pacific and the other for the Atlantic ocean. Here a trout of 12 inches in length may cross the mountains in safety. Poets have sung of the "meeting of the waters" and fish climbing cataracts but the "parting of the waters and fish crossing mountains" I believe remains unsung yet by all except the solitary Trapper who sits under the shade of a spreading pine whistling blankverse and beating time to the tune with a whip on his trap sack whilst musing on the parting advice of these waters.

Natural events have had a major effect on the Teton Wilderness. On July 21, 1987, a world-record high-elevation tornado created a 10,000-acre blowdown of trees around the Enos Lake area, and it took years to rebuild the trails. A series of fires followed—including the Huck and Mink Creek fires that burned 200,000 acres. Don't let these incidents dissuade you from visiting; this is still a marvelous and little-used area, and more than 60 percent of the land was not burned. Herds of elk graze in alpine areas, and many consider the Thorofare country abutting Yellowstone

National Park the most remote place in the Lower 48. This is prime grizzly habitat and you may well encounter them, so be very cautious at all times. Poles for hanging food have been placed at most campsites, as have bear-resistant boxes or barrels. Use them, and always keep a clean camp. You can rent bear-resistant backpacker food tubes or horse panniers from the Buffalo Ranger District (307/543-2386), but it's a good idea to make reservations for these items before your trip.

Access

Three primary trailheads provide access to the Teton Wilderness: Pacific Creek on the southwestern end, Turpin Meadow on the Buffalo Fork River, and Brooks Lake just east of the Continental Divide. Campgrounds are at each of these trailheads. Teton Wilderness is a favorite of Wyomingites, particularly those with horses, and in the fall elk hunters from across the nation come here. Distances are so great and some of the stream crossings so intimidating that few backpackers head into this wilderness area. No permits are needed, but it's a good idea to stop in at the **Buffalo Ranger District** (307/543-2386), nine miles east of Moran Junction on U.S. Highway 26/287, for topographic maps and information on current trail conditions, bear problems, regulations, and a list of permitted outfitters offering horse or llama trips.

For a shorter trip, you could take a guided horseback ride at the Turpin Meadow Trailhead with **Yellowstone Outfitters** (307/543-2418 or 800/447-4711, www.yellowstoneoutfitters.com) or **Buffalo Valley Ranch** (307/543-2062 or 888/543-2477, www.buffalovalleyranch.com). **Teton Horseback Adventures** (307/730-8829, www.horsebackadv.com) heads out from the Pacific Creek Trailhead. All three of these outfitters offer pack trips into the Teton Wilderness.

Unfortunately, USGS maps don't show the many Teton Wilderness trails built and maintained (or not maintained) by private outfitters and hunters. These can make hiking confusing, since not every junction is signed. Forest Service maps for the wilderness have been updated with most trail locations. A few of the many possible hikes are described as follows.

Whetstone Creek

Whetstone Creek Trail begins at the Pacific Creek Trailhead, on the southwest side of Teton Wilderness. An enjoyable 20-mile round-trip hike leaves the trailhead and follows Pacific Creek for 1.5 miles before splitting left to follow Whetstone Creek. Bear left when the trail splits again another three miles upstream and continue through a series of small meadows to the junction with Pilgrim Creek Trail. Turn right here and follow this trail two more miles to Coulter Creek Trail, climbing up Coulter Creek to scenic Coulter Basin and then dropping along the East Fork of Whetstone Creek. This rejoins the Whetstone Creek Trail and returns you to the trailhead, passing many attractive small meadows along the way. The upper half of this loop hike was burned in 1988; some areas were heavily scorched, while others are patchy. Flowers are abundant in the burned areas, and this is important elk habitat.

South Fork to Soda Fork

A fine loop hike leaves Turpin Meadow and follows South Buffalo Fork River to South Fork Falls. Just above this point, a trail splits off and climbs to Nowlin Meadow (excellent views of Smokehouse Mountain) and then down to Soda Fork River, where it joins the Soda Fork Trail. Follow this trail back downstream to huge Soda Fork Meadow (a good place to see moose and occasionally grizzlies) and then back to Turpin Meadow, a distance of approximately 23 miles round-trip. For a fascinating side trip from this route, head up the Soda Fork into the alpine at Crater Lake, a six-mile hike above the Nowlin Meadow–Soda Fork Trail junction. The outlet stream at Crater Lake disappears into a gaping hole, emerging as a large creek two miles below at Big Springs. It's an incredible sight.

Cub Creek Area

The Brooks Lake area just east of Togwotee Pass is a popular summertime camping and fishing place with magnificent views. Brooks Lake Trail follows the western shore of Brooks Lake and continues past Upper Brooks Lakes to Bear Cub Pass. From here, the trail drops to Cub Creek, where you'll find several good campsites. You can make a long and scenic loop by following the trail up Cub Creek into the alpine country and then back down along the South Buffalo Fork River to Lower Pendergraft Meadow. From here, take the Cub Creek Trail back up along Cub Creek to Bear Cub Pass and back out to Brooks Lake. Get a topographic map before heading into this remote country. Total distance is approximately 33 miles round-trip.

GROS VENTRE WILDERNESS

The 287,000-acre Gros Ventre Wilderness was established in 1984 and covers the mountain country just east of Jackson Hole. This range trends mainly in a northwest-southeast direction and is probably best known for Sleeping Indian Mountain (maps now call it Sheep Mountain, but locals never use that appellation), the distinctive rocky summit visible from Jackson Hole. Although there are densely forested areas at lower elevations, the central section of the wilderness lies above timberline, and many peaks top 10,000 feet. The tallest is Doubletop Peak at 11,682 feet. The Tetons are visible from almost any high point in the Gros Ventre, and meadows line the lower-elevation streams. Elk, mule deer, bighorn sheep, moose, and black bears are found here, and a few grizzlies have been reported. The Forest Service office in Jackson has more information on the wilderness, including brief trail descriptions and maps.

Access and Trails

Several roads provide good access to the Gros Ventre Wilderness: Gros Ventre River Road on the northern border; Curtis Canyon Road on the western margin; and Granite Creek Road to the south. Flat Creek is rough and accessible only in a 4WD vehicle. Hikes beginning or ending in the Granite Creek area have the added advantage of nearby Granite Hot Springs, a great place to soak tired muscles.

For a beautiful hike, follow **Highline Trail** from the Granite Creek area across to Cache Creek, a distance of 16 miles. This route passes just below a row of high and rugged mountains, but because it isn't a loop route, you'll need to hitchhike or set up a shuttle back. Plan on three days for this hike. The area is crisscrossed with game and cattle trails, making it easy to get lost, especially on the headwaters of Little Granite Creek. Talk with Forest Service folks before heading out, and make sure that you know how to read a map and compass.

A third hike begins at the **Goosewing Ranger Station,** 12 miles east of Slide Lake on Gros Ventre River Road. Take the trail from here to Two Echo Park (a fine camping spot) and then continue up to Six Lakes. You can return via the same trail or take the Crystal Creek Trail back to Red Rock Ranch and hitch back to Goosewing. The trail distance is approximately 23 miles round-trip.

GRANITE HOT SPRINGS

At the head of a gorgeous mountain valley, Granite Hot Springs (307/734-7400, http:// granitehotsprings.mountainmancountry.com) is a wonderful escape both summer and winter. Get here by driving south from Jackson 12 miles to Hoback Junction and then another 12 miles east on U.S. Highway 189 to the turnoff at Granite Creek Road. This well-maintained gravel road follows Granite Creek for 10 miles, affording impressive views of the Gros Ventre Range and the 50-foot drop of **Granite Falls.** The road ends at a parking lot just a short walk from the hot springs. The deep pool was built in 1933 by the Civilian Conservation Corps and recently improved with a deck and changing rooms. The pool stays around 93°F in the summer but rises to 112°F in winter when the water flow slows. The springs are open daily (10 A.M.–8 P.M. June–Oct., 10 A.M.–5 P.M. Dec.–Mar., $6 adults, $4 ages 3–12, and free for infants), but are closed in the fall and

© DON PITCHER

Granite Hot Springs

spring. No showers or running water are available at the pool, but vault toilets are nearby. Suits and towels can be rented, and a few snacks are sold here. Granite Canyon Road is not plowed in winter but is groomed for use by both snowmobilers and cross-country skiers. A nearby campground (mid-May–Sept., $15, no reservations) is managed by folks from the hot springs and almost never fills up. Dispersed camping is allowed on the road to Granite Hot Springs, except along the final 1.3 miles before the springs.

Caribou-Targhee National Forest

Covering nearly three million acres, Caribou-Targhee National Forest extends from Montana to Utah. Most of the forest lies within Idaho, but it also includes the western edge of Wyoming along the Tetons. Much of the forest is heavily logged, but two wilderness areas protect most of the Wyoming section. Contact the Forest Service office in Driggs, Idaho (208/354-2312, www.fs.fed.us/r4/caribou-targhee) for more recreation information.

Hiking

Many short hiking options are available on the west side of the Tetons, and the Forest Service office in Driggs has a handout that describes more than 20 of these hikes. A few of the best include the following. From Darby Canyon Trailhead, you can choose either the **Aspen Trail** (3.6 miles one-way; especially pretty in the fall) or the **South Darby Trail** (2.7 miles one-way; with nice waterfalls and flowered meadows). The latter leads to two remarkable caves that extend deep into the mountains: **Wind Cave** and **Ice Cave.** Hikers with flashlights can go a short distance into these caves, but very experienced spelunkers (with proper gear) have discovered miles of passageways connecting the two.

From the South Teton Trailhead, you can opt to climb **Table Mountain** (6.4 miles one-way), visit gorgeous **Alaska Basin** (7.7 miles one-way), or ascend the **Devil's Stairs** to Teton Shelf (6.8 miles one-way). All three of these hikes take you high into the alpine, but many families just hike until the kids get tired, eat lunch, and then head back to the car.

Several trails take off from the Teton Pass area along Wyoming Highway 22/Idaho Highway 33, including **Moose Creek Trail,** which leads to Moose Meadows (5.4 miles one-way), and the **Teton Crest Trail** if you're feeling very ambitious (nine miles one-way). It joins another popular hiking route, the **Coal Creek Trail,** for an alternative return route to the highway.

JEDEDIAH SMITH WILDERNESS

The 123,451-acre Jedediah Smith Wilderness lies on the west side of the Teton Range, facing Idaho but lying entirely within Wyoming. Access is primarily from the Idaho side, although trails breach the mountain passes at various points, making it possible to enter from Grand Teton National Park. This area was not declared a wilderness until 1984. A second wilderness area, the 10,820-acre **Winegar Hole Wilderness** (pronounced WINE-a-gur), lies along the southern border of Yellowstone National Park. Grizzlies love this country, but hikers will find it uninteresting and without trails. In contrast, the Jedediah Smith Wilderness contains nearly 200 miles of paths and some incredible high-mountain scenery.

Several mostly gravel roads lead up from the Driggs and Victor areas into the Tetons. Get a map showing wilderness trails and access points from the Caribou-Targhee National Forest ranger station in Driggs, Idaho (208/354-2312) or from the Forest Service offices in Jackson. Be sure to camp at least 200 feet from lakes and 100 feet from streams. Group size limits are also in place; check with the Forest Service for specifics on these and other backcountry regulations. In addition, anyone planning to cross into Grand Teton National Park from the west side will need to get a park camping permit in advance. Wilderness permits are not required for the Jedediah Smith Wilderness. Both grizzly and black bears are present throughout the Tetons, so all food must be either hung out of reach or stored in bear-resistant containers.

Hidden Corral Basin

At the northern end of the wilderness, Hidden Corral Basin provides a fine loop hike. Locals (primarily those on horseback) crowd this area on late-summer weekends. Get to the trailhead by driving north from Tetonia on Idaho Highway 32 to Lamont, then turn north on a gravel road. Follow it one mile and then turn right (east) onto Coyote Meadows Road. The trailhead is approximately 10 miles up, where the road dead-ends. An eight-mile trail parallels South Bitch Creek (the name Bitch Creek comes from the French word for a female deer, *biche*) to Hidden Corral, where you may see moose. Be sure to bring a fishing pole to try for the cutthroats.

Above Hidden Corral you can make a pleasant loop back by turning north onto the trail to Nord Pass and then dropping along the Carrot Ridge and Conant Basin Trails to Bitch Creek Trail and then on to Coyote Meadows, a distance of 21 miles round-trip. Note that this is grizzly and black bear country, and bear-resistant containers are required. By the way, Hidden Corral received its name in the outlaw days, when rustlers would steal horses in Idaho, change the brands, and hold the horses in this natural corral until the branding wounds healed. The horses were then sold to Wyoming ranchers. Owen Wister's *The Virginian* describes a pursuit of horse thieves through Bitch Creek country.

◖ Alaska Basin

The most popular hiking trail in the Jedediah Smith Wilderness begins near the **Teton Canyon Campground** (518/885-3639 or 877/444-6777 for reservations, www.reservations.gov, open late May–mid-Sept., $10) and leads through flower-bedecked meadows to mountain-rimmed Alaska Basin. It's great country, but don't expect a true wilderness experience, because many others will also be hiking and camping here. Get to the campground by following the Grand Targhee Ski Resort signs east from Driggs, Idaho. A gravel road splits off to the right approximately three miles beyond the little settlement of Alta. Follow it to the campground. (If you miss the turn, you'll end up at the ski area.) For an enjoyable loop, follow Alaska Basin Trail up the canyon to Basin Lakes and then head southwest along the Teton Crest Trail to the Teton Shelf Trail. Follow this trail back to its junction with the Alaska Basin Trail, dropping down the Devil's Stairs—a series of very steep switchbacks. You can then take the Alaska Basin Trail back to Teton Campground, a round-trip distance of approximately 19 miles. You could also use these trails to reach the high peaks of the Tetons or to cross the mountains into Death Canyon within Grand Teton National Park (camping permit required). Campfires and horse camping are not allowed in Alaska Basin.

Moose Meadows

For a somewhat less crowded hiking experience, check out the Moose Meadows area on the southern end of the Jedediah Smith Wilderness. Get to the trailhead by going three miles southeast of Victor on Idaho Highway 33. Turn north (left) on Moose Creek Road and follow it to the trailhead. The trail parallels Moose Creek to Moose Meadows, a good place to camp. You'll need to ford the creek twice, so this trail is best hiked in late summer. At the meadows, the trail dead-ends into Teton Crest Trail, providing access to Grand Teton National Park through some gorgeous alpine country. A nice loop can be made by heading south along this trail to flower-covered Coal Creek Meadows. A trail leads from here past 10,068-foot Taylor Mountain (an easy side trip with magnificent views), down to Taylor Basin, through lodgepole forests, and then back to your starting point. This loop hike will take you 15 miles round-trip.

Teton Valley, Idaho

The west side of the Tetons differs dramatically from nearby Jackson Hole. As the road descends from Teton Pass into Teton Valley, Idaho (a.k.a. Pierre's Hole), the lush farming country spreads out before you, 30 miles long and 15 miles across. This, the "quiet side" of the Tetons, offers a slower pace than bustling Jackson, but the Teton Range vistas are equally dramatic.

In recent years the growth in Jackson Hole has spilled across the mountains. The potato farms, horse pastures, and country towns are now undergoing the same transformation that first hit Jackson in the 1970s. As land prices soar and affordable housing becomes more difficult to find in Jackson, more people have opted to move over the pass and commute from Idaho. Glossy ads now fill *Teton Valley Magazine,* offering ranchland with a view, luxurious log homes, cozy second homes, private aircraft hangars, espresso coffee, mountain-bike rentals, and handmade lodgepole furniture. Despite these changes, Teton Valley remains a laid-back place, and spud farming is still a part of the local economy. The primary town here—it's the county seat—is Driggs, with Victor nine miles south and tiny Tetonia eight miles north.

History

The area now known as Teton Valley was used for centuries by various Indian tribes, including the Bannock, Blackfeet, Crow, Gros Ventre, Shoshone, and Nez Perce. John Colter—a member of the Lewis and Clark expedition—was the first white man to reach this area, wandering through in the winter of 1807–1808. In 1931, an Idaho farmer claimed to have plowed up a stone carved into the shape of a human face, with "John Colter 1808" etched into the

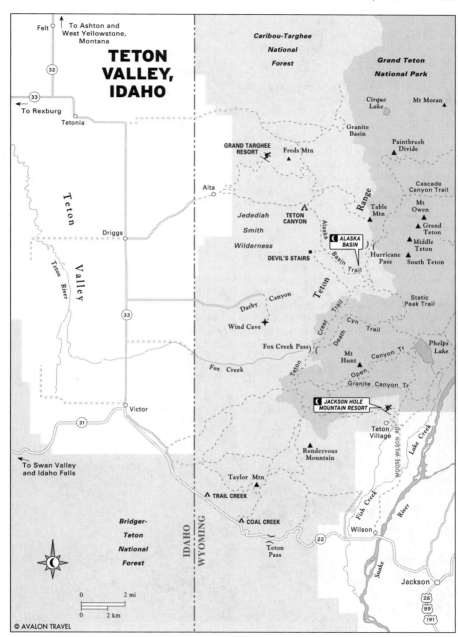

Felt

To Ashton and
West Yellowstone,
Montana

**TETON
VALLEY,
IDAHO**

32

33

To Rexburg

Tetonia

Teton

Valley

Teton River

Driggs

Alta

33

Darby *Canyon*

Wind Cave

Fox Creek Pass

Fox Creek

Victor

31

To Swan Valley
and Idaho Falls

*Bridger-
Teton
National
Forest*

0   2 mi

0   2 km

© AVALON TRAVEL

Caribou-Targhee

National

Forest

Grand Teton

National Park

Cirque
Lake

Mt Moran

Granite
Basin

Paintbrush
Divide

**GRAND TARGHEE
RESORT**

Freds Mtn

Cascade
Canyon Trail

Range

Table
Mtn

Mt
Owen

Jedediah

**TETON
CANYON**

Smith

Wilderness

DEVIL'S STAIRS

Alaska

**ALASKA
BASIN**

Grand
Teton

Middle
Teton

Hurricane
Pass

South Teton

Basin

Trail

Static
Peak Trail

Teton

Crest Trail

Cyn Trail

Death

Canyon Tr

Phelps
Lake

Mt
Hunt

Open

Granite *Canyon Tr*

**JACKSON HOLE
MOUNTAIN RESORT**

Teton
Village

MOOSE WILSON RD

Lake Creek

Rendezvous
Mountain

Taylor Mtn

Fish Creek

River

TRAIL CREEK

COAL CREEK

Wilson

22

Teton
Pass

IDAHO

WYOMING

Snake

Jackson

26

89

191

JACKSON HOLE

sides. The rock later turned out to be a hoax created by a man anxious to obtain a horse concession with Grand Teton National Park. He got the concession after donating the rock to the park museum.

Vieux Pierre, an Iroquois fur trapper for the Hudson's Bay Company, made this area his base in the 1820s, but was later killed by Blackfeet Indians in Montana. Many people still call the valley Pierre's Hole. Two fur trapper rendezvous took place in Pierre's Hole, but the 1832 event proved pivotal. About 1,000 Indians, trappers, and traders gathered for an annual orgy of trading, imbibing, and general partying. When a column of men on horseback appeared, two white trappers headed out for a meeting. The column turned out to be a group of Gros Ventre Indians, and the meeting quickly turned sour. One trapper shot the Gros Ventre chief point-blank, killing him. A battle quickly ensued that left 38 people dead on both sides and forced rendezvous participants to scatter. Later rendezvous were held in valleys where the animosities were not as high. For the next 50 years, virtually the only whites in Pierre's Hole were horse thieves and outlaws. Hiram C. Lapham was the first to try his hand at ranching in the valley, but his cattle were rustled by three outlaws, including Ed Harrington, alias Ed Trafton.

In 1888, a lawyer from Salt Lake City, B. W. Driggs, came to the valley and liked what he found. With his encouragement, a flood of Mormon settlers arrived in the next few years, establishing farms along the entire length of Teton Valley. By the 1940s the valley was home to a cheese factory, sawmills, a railroad line, and numerous sprawling ranches. Teton Valley's population plummeted in the 1960s, but in 1969 development began at Grand Targhee Ski Resort, and the economy started to turn around. Recent years have seen the area come into its own as tourism-related businesses began to eclipse farming and ranching. Over the last decade or so the valley has boomed, making Teton County, Idaho one of the fastest-growing counties (on a percentage basis) in the nation.

Teton Valley Recreation

Outdoor enthusiasts will discover all sorts of activities at all times of the year in the Driggs

© DON PITCHER

Teton Range, as seen from Teton Valley

area. The Teton River runs the entire length of Teton Valley and is renowned among fly-fishing enthusiasts, canoeists, and bird-watchers. A plethora of hikes can be found both to the east in the Tetons and to the west in the Big Hole Mountains. The Forest Service office in Driggs has details on other hiking options if you're looking for a less crowded experience.

The nonprofit **Friends of the Teton River** (36 E. Little Ave., 208/354-3871, www.tetonwater.org) works to preserve the Teton Basin.

The **National Outdoor Leadership School** (NOLS, 166 E. 200 S., 208/354-8443, www.nols.edu) has an office off the main road south of Driggs; headquarters is in Lander, Wyoming. The Driggs office—housed in an old Mormon church—runs summertime backpacking and whitewater training, plus backcountry skiing classes in the winter. Courses last 2–3 weeks.

Kids and their parents will appreciate the **Driggs Town Park,** with an attractive playground and sprinklers that make for impromptu summer fun. It's on Ashley Street. A paved **bike path** parallels Highway 33 between Victor and Driggs, providing a pleasant running, cycling, or inline skating opportunity. A wide bike lane heads east from Driggs all the way to the Targhee Resort. The nonprofit **Teton Valley Trails & Pathways** (208/201-1622, www.tvtap.org) has online maps showing local routes.

Peaked Sports (70 E. Little Ave., 208/354-2354 or 800/705-2354, www.peakedsports.com) rents mountain bikes, bike trailers, and kayaks in the summer, along with skis, snowboards, and snowshoes in the winter. Stop by for a helpful biking map ($12) of the area.

High Peaks Health and Fitness Center (50 Ski Hill Rd., 208/354-3128, www.highpeakspt.com) has $10 day passes.

The Links at Teton Peaks (127 N. 400 W., 208/456-2374) is a Scottish-style nine-hole golf course.

Horseback rides and pack trips are available from **Dry Ridge Outfitters** (208/354-2284, www.dryridge.com) or nearby Grand Targhee Ski Resort (in Alta, 307/353-2300 or 800/827-4433, www.grandtarghee.com). For horseback rides and winter sleigh rides, head to **Linn Canyon Ranch** (130 E. 600 S., 208/787-5466, www.linncanyonranch.com).

Bagley's Teton Mountain Ranch (265 W. 800 S., 208/787-9005 or 866/787-9005, www.elkadventures.com) raises more than 100 elk as breeding stock and for their antlers. It offers summertime wagon rides and wintertime sleigh rides among the elk for $9, plus horseback rides (starting at $35 for a one-hour ride).

Teton Aviation Center (208/354-3100 or 800/472-6382, www.tetonaviation.com) is best known for its scenic glider flights ($250 for a one-hour flight) past the Tetons, but it also offers airplane rides and has an impressive collection of vintage military aircraft.

Teton Balloon Flights (208/787-5500 or 866/533-6404, www.tetonballooning.com) offers one-hour hot-air balloon flights over Teton Valley for $265 per person in the summer.

Teton Valley Events

The main summer event, the **Teton Valley Summer Festival** (208/354-2500), comes on Fourth of July weekend. Highlights include hot-air balloon launches (more than 40 balloons) and tethered rides for the kids at the airport, a parade and crafts fair in Victor, a rodeo in Tetonia, arts exhibits, a pig roast, live music, and evening fireworks in Driggs.

Grand Targhee Ski Resort pulls out the stops for the always-popular **Targhee Bluegrass Festival** (307/353-2300 or 800/827-4433, www.grandtarghee.com) in mid-August, with nationally known acts. The music attracts a throng, so make camping or lodging reservations well ahead of time.

In mid-August, the **Teton County Fair** (208/354-2961) brings down-home fun with livestock judging, arts and crafts, quilts, and pies, jams, and other fare on display.

On Thursday evenings in July and August, **Music on Main** (208/201-5356, www.tetonvalleyfoundation.org) brings free concerts (two bands nightly) to Victor City Park. This is a surprisingly big deal, attracting nationally known acts.

VICTOR

Twenty-four miles west of Jackson, the town of Victor, Idaho, was—until recently—little more than the proverbial wide spot in the road. But things have changed dramatically as the population doubled in just five years and an ugly sprawl of homes and businesses covered former ranchland. Despite this, the town does have a couple of places worth noting.

Accommodations

Trails End Motel (208/787-2973, $80 d) rents simple four-person log cabin units with microwaves and fridges and is open May–mid-October.

Two miles south of town on Pole Canyon Road, **Kasper's Kountryside Inn** (208/787-2726, www.kasperskountrysideinn.com, $89–109 for up to four) is a barnlike building with two modern apartments with full kitchens.

Teton Springs is more evidence of the spillover effect from Jackson. This private club for the moneyed class includes 500 homes and condos, a golf course, a spa, tennis courts, a swimming pool, and an "old town village" with shopping, dining, lodging, and more. A heliport waits for those who can afford the helicopter flight over to Jackson for the evening. Various lodging options are offered at **Teton Springs Lodge & Spa** (208/787-7888 or 877/787-8757, www.tetonspringslodge.com), including luxurious hotel rooms ($237 d) and suites ($336–504 d). Condos and sprawling four-bedroom "cabins" are also available on a nightly or weekly basis.

On the north end of town, **Cowboy Roadhouse Lodge** (381 N. Agate St., 208/787-2755, www.cowboyroadhouselodge.com, $119 d) is a modern two-story motel with log beds, Wi-Fi, and two queen or one king bed.

Set on four acres and surrounded by cottonwood trees, **Fox Creek Inn Bed and Breakfast** (27 E. 550 South, 208/787-3333, www.thefoxcreekinn.com) has three guest rooms with queen beds and private baths ($139 d), plus a more spacious room with king bed, private bath, and indoor Jacuzzi ($185 d). All include a full breakfast, access to the outdoor hot tub, and Wi-Fi. Fox Creek is halfway between Victor and Driggs.

Camping

The Forest Service's pleasant **Trail Creek Campground** (518/885-3639 or 877/444-6777, www.recreation.gov, open mid-May–mid-Sept., $10) is six miles southeast of Victor and just across the Wyoming state line. **Teton Valley Campground** (208/787-2647 or 877/787-3036, www.tetonvalleycampground.com), one mile west of Victor on Idaho Highway 31, has RV hookups ($28–41), tent sites ($22), basic cabins ($45), plus a small heated outdoor pool, a playground, and Wi-Fi.

Food

Victor Emporium (208/787-2221, www.victoremporium.com, daily 8 A.M.–6 P.M.) houses an old-fashioned soda fountain with huckleberry shakes in season, plus sundaes, banana splits, and cones year-round. It's been in business since 1949, and also sells fishing supplies and Idaho souvenirs.

Housed in an old one-car garage, **Grumpy's Goat Shack** (37 S. Main St., 208/787-2092, www.goatshack.com, daily 11 A.M.–9 P.M. Apr.–Oct., till 11 P.M. summer weekends) is a fun hot-dog stand/wine bar where Mike and Liz serve the best brats you'll ever taste, along with hot Italian beef sandwiches, chili-cheese dogs, charbroiled burgers, and Chicago-style hot dogs. They're the real deal; even true Chicagoans love 'em. The owners' goat produces milk for homemade goat cheese, served with roasted garlic and bread. The ceiling is crowded with bras and panties left by previous female customers (free drinks are the incitement). Sit outside around the patio tables. Credit cards are not accepted, but everything's under $9.

A cozy little brunch nook, **Sun Dog Café** (208/787-3354, daily 7 A.M.–3 P.M., $6–10) has a full espresso bar, with delicious pastries and local chocolates filling the display case. Eggs Benedict or French toast with bacon are good breakfast choices. For lunch, try a mahimahi taco or grilled steak salad.

Also in Victor is **Knotty Pine Supper Club** (208/787-2866, www.knottypinesupperclub.com, 11 A.M.–10 P.M., bar open until 1 A.M.), with hearty ribs, steaks, and rack of lamb. Most entrées are $10–25, but you can always choose the $10 dinner of hot turkey, meatloaf, mashed potatoes, and gravy. Knotty Pine is an old-fashioned place with low ceilings, log walls, and a dark interior brightened by blue Christmas lights. Dining is also available on the outside deck. Live bands crank out the dance tunes most nights and the bar is entirely smoke-free.

Amazingly, there are two microbreweries in Victor. In existence since 1988, **Grand Teton Brewing Company** (208/787-9000, www.grandtetonbrewing.com, 1–8 P.M. Mon.–Fri., 2–7 P.M. Sat.–Sun.) is on the east end of town. Drop by to sample Teton Ale, Old Faithful Ale, Bitch Creek ESB, Howling Wolf Weisse Bier, or Sweetgrass IPA. The gift shop (9 A.M.–5 P.M. Mon.–Fri.) sells T-shirts, glasses, and beer to go.

Much smaller is **Wildlife Brewing and Pizza** (208/787-2623, www.facebook.com, daily 4–11 P.M., $14–18), a busy spot with crunchy pizzas by the slice or pie, plus fresh beers from the on-the-premises brewery, darts, horseshoes, a pool table, and an outdoor beer garden.

DRIGGS

Driggs (pop. 1,500) is an odd conglomeration, mixing an old-time farming settlement and newfangled recreation mecca. It's also fast becoming a bedroom community for commuters to Jackson Hole. A major development on the south end of town brought many more homes and businesses, and the airport keeps expanding with giant hangars for all those private jets. There isn't much to downtown Driggs, so it's pretty easy to find your way around. After a decade of rapid growth, things have slowed in the last few years—much to the relief of some locals who feared another Jackson Hole scenario.

Sights

New in 2011, the **Greater Yellowstone Regional Geotourism Center** (60 S. Main St., www.yellowstonegeotourism.org, daily in summer, reduced winter hours) provides an outstanding introduction to the region. Historical

JACKSON HOLE

© DON PITCHER

the Spud Drive-In, Driggs

exhibits cover the original Native American inhabitants, mountain men, emigrants, Mormon settlers, and the rise of agriculture. Other exhibits focus on scenic byways and a National Geographic display on geotourism around Yellowstone. Especially notable are 24 prints and reproductions of Yellowstone paintings by Thomas Moran and historical photos by William Henry Jackson. One of these is a beautiful reproduction of *The Three Tetons;* the original hangs in the Oval Office of the White House. Also inside the center is a gift shop and visitor information kiosk.

Find local information at **Teton Valley Chamber of Commerce** (255 S. Main St., 208/354-2500, www.tetonvalleychamber. com, 10 A.M.–3 P.M. Mon.–Fri.) in downtown Driggs.

A mile south of Driggs is the delightfully amusing **Spud Drive-In** (208/354-2727 or 800/799-7783, www.spuddrivein.com), here since 1953 but now with a Dolby sound system. You can't miss the big truck out front with a flatbed-size "potato" on the back. The drive-in even attracts folks from Jackson, who cross the pass for an evening of fun beneath the stars. The drive-in is locally famous for Gladys burgers and Spud buds—served by carhops. The Spud also serves as a venue for summer concerts.

Spacious **Teton Valley Museum** (137 N. Hwy. 33, 208/354-6000, 10 A.M.–5 P.M. Tues.–Sat. late May–Oct., $5 adults, $2 kids, $15 families) houses historical displays from the valley's past on two floors, with a separate building containing old farm equipment. It's on the north side of town just beyond the Super 8 Motel.

At the airport just north of town, **Warbirds Museum** houses an interesting collection of restored historic planes in a hangar at the Teton Aviation Center (208/354-3100 or 800/472-6382, www.tetonaviation.com, free). Access is through the adjacent Warbirds Café. The collection contains several unusual fighter aircraft—including a T-28 Trojan and a Mig 15—but only four are displayed at any given time.

Shopping

Yöstmark Mountain Equipment (285 E. Little Ave., 208/354-2828, www.yostmark. com) sells a wide range of outdoor equipment. They also rent cross-country skis, skate skis, snowboards, telemark and alpine touring skis, and guide backcountry ski tours in winter.

Browse the eclectic selection of regional books at friendly **Dark Horse Books** (76 N. Main St., 208/354-8882 or 888/424-8882). Adjacent to the airport, the **Community Art Center** (8 Rodeo Dr., 208/354-4278, www. tetonartscouncil.com) exhibits works by regional artists.

A few miles north of Driggs, **Drawknife Billiards** (5146 N. Hwy. 33, 800/320-0527, www.drawknife.com) creates one-of-a-kind pool tables using hand-carved lodgepole bases and top-quality tabletops.

Accommodations

Just a block from the center of town is a delightful European-style guesthouse built in 1900, **The Pines Motel Guest Haus** (105 S. Main St., www.thepinestetonvalley.com, 208/354-2774 or 800/354-2778). The Neilson family provides seven rooms with private baths, each different but all nicely appointed with tasteful touches such as handmade quilts, along with Wi-Fi and an outdoor hot tub. Rates are very reasonable ($55–65 d or $110 for a two-room suite that sleeps eight) and kids are welcome.

On the north side of Driggs, **Super 8 Motel** (133 Hwy. 33, 208/354-8888 or 800/800-8000, www.super8.com) has standard rooms ($88 d) and suites that sleep four ($150). Amenities include an indoor pool, sauna, hot tub, Wi-Fi, and continental breakfast.

On the north side of Driggs, **Best Western Teton West** (476 N. Main St., 208/354-2363 or 800/528-1234, www.bestwestern.com, $120–130 d) features a light breakfast, indoor pool, hot tub, and Wi-Fi. Closed mid-October–mid-November.

Located a mile east of town, **Teton Valley Cabins** (34 E. Ski Hill Rd., 208/354-8153 or 866/687-1522, www.tetonvalleycabins.com,

$79–99 d) rents comfortable, modern duplex cabins. Most have kitchenettes, and families appreciate units with bunk beds. A hot tub is available, along with Wi-Fi.

Short-term bookings for town houses, homes, cabins, and condos in the area are provided by **Grand Valley Lodging** (208/354-8890 or 800/746-5518, www.grandvalleylodging.com). Rates range $80–500 per night, higher around Christmas and the Fourth of July. These accommodations are popular with families and groups heading to Grand Targhee Ski Resort.

Camping

The nearest public campsites are at **Teton Canyon Campground** (reserve at 518/885-3639 or 877/444-6777, www.recreation.gov, $9 fee, late May–mid-Sept., $10 per site), 11 miles east of Driggs in the Tetons. This is a delightful camping spot, and the trailhead into beautiful (and very popular) Alaska Basin is nearby.

Food

One benefit of Teton Valley's growth is a dramatic improvement in the local restaurant scene. Driggs now has several excellent dining places.

Teton Thai (18 N. Main St., 208/787-8424, www.tetonthai.com, daily 11:30 A.M.–2:30 P.M., 5:30–9:30 P.M.), a Jackson Hole favorite, has expanded and offers the same menu of South Asian favorites—including noodle, rice, and curry dishes—in a busy downtown Driggs setting. Most entrées are $12–14, but lighter options such as satay chicken or tom kha gai soup are about $8.

After a spicy Thai dinner, nothing hits the spot like something cold. Head a few doors up the street to **Teton Valley Creamery** (20 N. Main St., 208/354-0404, noon–9 P.M. Tues.–Sun. in summer, 2–9 P.M. Thurs.–Sun. in winter) for a gelato ($2.50). Made on the premises from local milk, gelato flavors include huckleberry, raspberry, and dulce de leche, plus the standard chocolate and vanilla. The owners also produce a variety of raw-milk artisanal cheeses.

Tiny **Wrap and Roll** (65 S. Main St., 208/354-7655, www.facebook.com, 11 A.M.–4 P.M. Mon.–Fri., $6–8) is a good lunch spot, with Greek chicken wraps, shrimp spring rolls, rice bowls, and more. Get it to go or take a seat at the picnic table out front.

On the north end of town across from the airport, **Hacienda Ccuajimalpa** (528 Valley Centre Dr., 208/354-0121, daily 10 A.M.–10 P.M., $4–8) serves inexpensive and authentic Mexican meals: chile rellenos, chimichangas, enchiladas, quesadillas, tamales, burritos, and tostadas.

Best place for an organic latte, fruit smoothie, or gourmet hot chocolate? Head over to **Cocoa Grove** (180 S. Main St., 208/354-2899, www.facebook.com, 6 A.M.–7 P.M. Mon.–Sat., 8 A.M.–5 P.M. Sun.); it's in the mall with Broulim's. The owners hail from Seattle, and really know coffee.

You won't find burgers or steaks at **Miso Hungry Café** (165 N. Main St., 208/354-8015, www.facebook.com, 11 A.M.–3 P.M. Mon.–Sat., 5:30–9 P.M. Mon.–Tues. and Thurs.–Fri., $14–20), a playful spot with covered tables on the front porch and a flavorful globe-trotting fare. The lunch menu includes Thai noodle bowl, Greek Athenian plate, Philly cheese steaks, and a variety of soups, salads, homemade breads, espresso, and desserts. Even the potato chips are made on the premises from local (of course) Idaho potatoes. Dinner features paella, chicken sorrentino, rack of lamb, and curried shrimp. Check the chalkboard for daily specials.

An aviation-themed restaurant at—appropriately enough—Driggs Airport just north of town, **Warbirds Café** (208/354-2550, www.tetonaviation.com, 11 A.M.–2 P.M. Mon.–Fri., 5–9 P.M. Tues.–Sat., $15–28) has windows facing the taxiway, and several tables on the patio provide an even closer view. The dinner menu includes such treats as bacon-wrapped beef tenderloin, buffalo burgers, and big Caesar salads. Several restored old planes fill the adjacent hangar. Warbirds Café is popular with pilots, who can fly in for lunch with a view and an upscale meal. Or, as one local pointed out,

JACKSON HOLE

Warbirds Museum

© DON PITCHER

it represents "all the things we ran away from when we moved here from Jackson." Dinner reservations are recommended.

Find Martha Pendl's amazing Austrian pastries and other treats at **Pendal's Bakery & Café** (40 Depot St., 208/354-5623, www.pendlspastries.com, 7 A.M.–4 P.M. Mon.–Fri., 7 A.M.–3 P.M. Sat., 8 A.M.–3 P.M. Sun.). Ignore the official address; it's actually at the back of the public parking lot on Bates Road (and almost directly behind the bookstore). Get a coffee and one of the incredibly delectable treats: Nussknacker, Linzertorte, or Florentiner pastries. Lunchtime soups, sandwiches, and quiches follow. Pendl's is occasionally open for dinner in the summer.

Get malts, shakes, and hot fudge sundaes at the old-fashioned soda fountain inside **Corner Drug** (10 S. Main St., 208/354-2334, www.facebook.com, 9 A.M.–6:30 P.M. Mon.–Sat.). Lime freezes and huckleberry shakes ($4) are their claim to fame.

For late-night foraging and all-around wonderful meals, head to **Forage Bistro & Lounge** (385 Little Ave., 208/354-2858, www.forageandlounge.com, 4–10 P.M. Tues.–Sun.,

$10–22) a few blocks east of downtown. This trendy and very hip spot has a brick-paved deck out front and a curvy bar inside with a handful of tables. The limited, moderately priced menu changes seasonally, but typically includes noodles with coconut, garlic, ginger, and peanuts, a cheeseburger with chive aioli, red pepper, onion, and potato wedges, halibut with rice noodle salad, and an "everything" salad.

Shop for groceries at **Broulim's** (52 S. Main St., 208/354-2350, www.broulims.com, 7 A.M.–11 P.M. Mon.–Sat.). There's also a sushi bar, deli, and pizza by the slice. Just up the street is **Barrels and Bins Community Market** (36 S. Main St., 208/354-2307, daily 9 A.M.–7 P.M.), selling health foods, organic produce, and other earthy fare. The **Teton Valley Open Air Market** (208/351-4317, mid-June–Sept.) comes to downtown Driggs Fridays 9 A.M.–2 P.M., with produce, crafts, flowers, and baked goods.

Services

Get Caribou-Targhee National Forest information from the **Teton Basin Ranger District Office** (just south of town at 525 S. Main St.,

208/354-2312, www.fs.fed.us/r4/caribou-targhee).

Wash clothes at **Extra Sock Laundry,** next to Subway on the north end of town.

Teton Valley Hospital (120 E. Howard Ave., 208/354-2383, www.tetonvalleyhospital.com) is available for emergencies.

Rent cars from **Basin Auto Rental** (180 N. Main St., 208/354-2297, www.basinautorental.com).

Catch a ride with **Teton Valley Taxi** (208/313-2728).

START Buses (307/733-4521, www.startbus.com, $8 one-way) provide year-round weekday service connecting Driggs and Victor with Jackson.

TETONIA

Eight miles north of Driggs, sleepy Tetonia is dominated by a big LDS church, with dirt side streets. Potato farms and grand old barns spread across the surrounding landscape; it's a good place to see kids riding horseback. The crest of the tourist wave is just starting to lap at the shores of Tetonia, and at last check no local place sold espresso, focaccia, or cell phones.

Three miles south of Tetonia, **Blue Fly Gallery** (208/456-0900, www.kenmorrisonfineart.com) exhibits the colorful paintings and sculptures of Ken Morrison.

Steve Horn Mountain Gallery (112 S. Main St., 208/456-2719, www.stevehorn.com) crafts rugged Old West-style furniture and relief carvings.

Accommodations and Food

Teton Mountain View Lodge & RV Park (208/456-2741, www.tetonmountainlodge.com) has comfortable motel rooms ($79–89 d) with Wi-Fi, continental breakfast, and hot tub access. RV spaces are $29, and tent sites cost $10.

North End Bar & Grill (208/456-2202, daily 7 A.M.–10 P.M. in summer, 8 A.M.–9 P.M. in winter, $10–25) attracts local farmers (and travelers) with filling biscuits-and-gravy breakfasts (along with some lighter fare), lunchtime buffalo burgers, Cajun chicken sandwiches, and fish tacos, plus dinners that include blackened halibut, rib-eye steak, and weekend prime rib.

GRAND TARGHEE SKI RESORT

On the west side of the Tetons 42 miles from Jackson, Grand Targhee Ski Resort (in Alta, 307/353-2300 or 800/827-4433, www.grandtarghee.com) offers the friendliness of a small resort with the amenities and snow you'd expect at a major one. To get here you'll need to drive into Idaho and turn east at Driggs. The resort sits at the end of a beautiful road 12 miles east of Driggs and just six miles inside Wyoming. Its motto says it all: "Snow from heaven, not from hoses." With an annual snowfall topping 500 inches (42 feet!)—most of which is champagne powder—Targhee became the spot where powderhounds got all they could ever want. Ski magazines consistently rank it as having North America's best (or second-best) snow. In fact, the resort guarantees its snow: If you find conditions not to your liking, you can turn in your ticket within an hour of purchase and get a "snow check" good for another day of skiing. By the way, the official name is Grand Targhee Ski and Summer Resort, but most folks call it Grand Targhee, or simply Targhee.

The biggest drawback to Grand Targhee Ski Resort is the same thing that makes it so great—the weather. Lots of snow means lots of clouds and storms, and because it snows so much there are many days when the name cynics apply—"Grand Foghee"—seems more appropriate. Many folks who have returned to Targhee year after year have still not seen the magnificent Grand Teton backdrop behind the ski area! Be sure to bring your goggles. The quad lift up Peaked Mountain provides intermediate skiing on slopes that are more protected and suffer less wind and fog.

Skiing and Snowboarding

The resort has two quads, one double chairlift, and a surface lift on Fred's Mountain, plus a quad on adjacent Peaked Mountain. The top

JACKSON HOLE

elevation is 10,230 feet, with the longest run dropping 2,822 feet over almost three miles. About 750 acres are groomed, but you'll always find track-free skiing on the remaining 2,250 acres of ungroomed powder, so bring your snorkel. In addition, snowcat skiing ($349 per day including lunch) is offered on a 1,000-acre section of Peaked Mountain reserved for powderhounds.

Lift tickets at Grand Targhee cost $69 per day ($49 half-day) for adults and $29 per day for children ages 6–14 and seniors (free under age six). Substantial discounts are offered for multi-day lift tickets or lodging-and-ski packages.

Fully 70 percent of Targhee's groomed runs are intermediate to advanced-intermediate, but advanced skiers will find an extraordinary number of deep-powder faces to explore. The ski school offers lessons for all abilities, and children's programs make it possible for parents to leave their kids behind. Cross-country skiers enjoy the Nordic center, and ski and snowboard rentals are available at the base of the mountain. The ski area usually opens in mid-November and closes in mid-April, although some years you may be able to ski even into July. Lifts operate daily 9 A.M.–4 P.M.

Winter Activities

Teton Ice Park (307/690-1385 or 888/864-8029, www.tetonice.com) is a 40-foot ice waterfall where you can learn climbing techniques. Half-day guided climbs (with all gear) are $225 for one person or $300 for two.

Excellent guided **snowshoe wildlife tours** (free if you have snowshoes, $10 to rent them) will appeal to amateur naturalists, and on the **sleigh-ride dinner** ($40 adults, $15 kids), you'll ride in a horse-drawn sleigh to a yurt where a Western-style meal is served. Targhee's **tubing park** (opens at 5 P.M.; $10) is a fun place for kids to slide down a snowy hill. A **Kid's Club** at Targhee provides supervised child care for children under six, and teens can join special programs that include skiing and other fun on the mountain.

Summer Activities

Not far from Grand Targhee are several popular summertime hiking trails within the Jedediah Smith Wilderness.

The resort is a popular place to relax in the summer and offers many activities. A quad chairlift ($15 adults, $6 kids) takes you up the 10,200-foot summit of Fred's Mountain for strikingly close views of the Tetons. The lift operates daily late June–mid-September. A Forest Service naturalist leads guided walks twice daily.

Horseback rides and lessons are a favorite Targhee summertime activity; one-hour rides are $39. The area is also a fun mountain-biking destination, with bike rentals; you can also take them up the chairlift ($20). The big climbing wall ($10 for an introductory climb) is open to all abilities and is a good place to learn some basic—or advanced—moves. Other summer activities and facilities at Targhee include basketball courts, an outdoor swimming pool and hot tubs, a fitness center, horseshoes, tennis, disc golf, archery, and volleyball. The nine-hole **Targhee Village Golf Course** (208/354-8577 or 307/353-8577, www.targheevillage.com) is just down the road. After all this excitement, you'll probably want to relax with a massage, aromatherapy, facial, or steam bath at the on-site spa.

Events

End the year—and start a new one—with **Torchlight Parades** at Grand Targhee on the evenings of December 25 and 31. Also on New Year's Eve is a fireworks display over the mountain. Each March, the resort celebrates telemark skiing with the **Targhee Tele Fest.** Ski races of all sorts take place, and Targhee rocks to great music, an outdoor barbecue, and fun events. Close out winter with mid-April's **Cardboard Box Derby,** where participants swoosh down the ski hill on bizarre cardboard creations.

The resort pulls out the stops for two very popular musical events: **Targhee Fest** in mid-July with a mix of nationally known rock and folk artists—from Michael Franti to Los Lobos—plus **Targhee Bluegrass Festival** in mid-August. Bring your dancin' shoes! The music attracts hundreds of people, so call the resort well ahead of time for camping or lodging reservations.

Accommodations

Three lodges at the base of the mountain— Targhee Lodge, Teewinot Lodge, and Sioux Lodge—offer ski-in, ski-out access, a large heated outdoor pool, a hot tub, and a workout room. Rates quoted are for the winter holiday season; they're approximately 40 percent lower in summer. Contact Targhee (307/353-2300 or 800/827-4433, www.grandtarghee.com) for details on lodging options at or near the resort. Most lodging places are closed October–mid-November and mid-April–mid-June.

Get standard motel accommodations at **Targhee Lodge** with holiday winter rates of $179–199 for up to four. Deluxe hotel rooms ($245–270 d) with lodgepole furnishings and access to an indoor hot tub are at **Teewinot Lodge.** The lobby here is a fine place to relax in front of the fire on winter evenings. **Sioux Lodge** continues the Western theme with lodgepole furnishings, and it also has kitchenettes, adobe-style fireplaces, and small balconies. Studio units are $289–319 for up to four people, loft units $359–395 for four people, and two-bedroom units run $495–545.

Off-site lodging (approximately 10 miles downhill from Grand Targhee) includes one-, two-, and three-bedroom condominiums and town houses. Nightly holiday-season rates start at $230 d for one-bedroom condos and go up to $485 for three-bedroom town houses. The minimum stay at all Targhee-managed lodging places is two nights most of the year, or five nights during peak winter periods.

You can cut these lodging rates by avoiding the Christmas–New Year's and Spring Break rush periods. More substantial discounts are available if you ski or snowboard during the value season before mid-December or after late March.

Ski packages are a fine bargain, starting around $188 per day at Targhee Lodge (unavailable Dec. 25–Jan. 1). Packages include lodging and lift tickets for two adults and two kids under age 13, plus two free ski lessons. Summer lodging is surprisingly reasonable, with such options as rafting trips, scenic chairlift, and spa amenities.

Food

At the base of Grand Targhee is a compact cluster of shops. You won't have to walk far to find a cafeteria, pizza place, sandwich shop, burger joint, and general store. The nicest place is **Branding Iron Grill** (7:30 A.M.–9 P.M. daily in summer) serving hearty breakfasts and lunches, along with cozy dinners. Grand Targhee's social center is the **Trap Bar** (Thurs.–Sat. 11 A.M.–8:30 P.M., Sun. 11 A.M.–5 P.M. in summer) featuring live music all winter (Thurs.–Sat.), sporting events on the flat-screen TVs, and pub grub on the menu all the time. Guests at Targhee can also take a **horse-drawn sleigh** on a 15-minute ride to a Mongolian-style yurt for a home-cooked steak or chicken dinner. The price is $40 ($15 for kids ages 5–12), and reservations are required. Other shops here sell groceries, ski and snowboard gear, clothing, and gifts.

Getting There and Around

Grand Targhee is 42 miles northwest of Jackson on the western side of the Tetons in Alta, Wyoming. Get there by driving over Teton Pass (occasionally closed by winter storms), north through Victor and Driggs, Idaho, and then east back into Wyoming.

The **Targhee Express/Alltrans** bus makes daily wintertime trips (90 minutes each way) to Grand Targhee from Jackson Hole. Buses pick up skiers from Jackson and Teton Village hotels shortly after 7 A.M., returning from Targhee at 4:30 P.M. for a round-trip fare of $88, including a full-day lift ticket. Round-trip bus fare without a lift ticket costs $44. Reservations are required; make them before 9 P.M. on the night before by calling 307/733-3135 or 800/443-6133, or book online at www.jacksonholealltrans.com. Van service is also available year-round to airports in Jackson, Salt Lake City, and Idaho Falls.

GATEWAYS TO YELLOWSTONE

Yellowstone National Park is most commonly entered via one of several Wyoming or Montana towns. From the south, people generally arrive from the energetic town of Jackson. Three Montana towns are just outside Yellowstone National Park entrance roads. Immediately west of the park is the appropriately named West Yellowstone, a popular and family friendly town with moderately priced motels, RV parks, restaurants, and trinket shops. West (as it's called) has a fine museum, the Yellowstone Historic Center, but it is better known for the IMAX Theatre that shows big-screen movies about Yellowstone, and the zoolike Grizzly and Wolf Discovery Center.

The smaller town of Gardiner, Montana lies just outside Yellowstone's northwest corner and five miles from Mammoth Hot Springs.

A dramatic stone structure, Roosevelt Arch, provides a grand entry point into the park, and Gardiner offers a full range of services, from lodging and dining to horseback rides and rafting down the Yellowstone River. If you exit the park from the wooded northeast corner, you'll pass through a pair of rustic settlements: Silver Gate, where virtually all the buildings are built from logs, and the larger burg of Cooke City. Food, lodging, gas, and other basics are here, but the main draw is their homespun and genuine feel.

Yellowstone's east entrance road drops through the wilds of Shoshone National Forest and past the dude ranches and summer homes within scenic Wapiti Valley before emerging into the prosperous and busy town of Cody, Wyoming. It's named for Buffalo Bill Cody, and

© DON PITCHER

HIGHLIGHTS

◖ Yellowstone Historic Center: There's a fine historical collection inside this stone-and-log building that once served as a railroad depot (page 247).

◖ Beartooth Highway: Some call this the most scenic highway in America. It's high (10,947 feet) and dramatic; closed September–May (page 278).

◖ Buffalo Bill Historical Center: The center started with items from Buffalo Bill's life but now covers 300,000 square feet in five distinct museums focusing on Western art, the Plains Indians, natural history, firearms, and, of course, Buffalo Bill. It's one of the finest museums in North America (page 286).

◖ Trail Town: The perfect counterpoint to the Historical Center, with old wagons, rustic cabins – including one used by Butch Cassidy and the Sundance Kid – plus a treasure trove of other items. Check out the dugout canoe that just might have been used by Lewis and Clark (page 291).

◖ Heart Mountain Interpretive Center: This newly opened facility commemorates the thousands of Japanese-Americans interned at this remote spot during World War II (page 294).

◖ Cody Nite Rodeo: Still going strong after more than seven decades, these popular rodeos take place nightly all summer. Get there early for a seat in "buzzards roost" (page 300).

◖ National Bighorn Sheep Center: After exploring the museum, displays, and

theater, head out to Whiskey Basin to see the live version (but they're in the high country by June) (page 311).

◖ Togwotee Pass: One of the prettiest mountain passes in Wyoming, Togwotee provides a grand entryway into Grand Teton and Yellowstone National Parks (page 320).

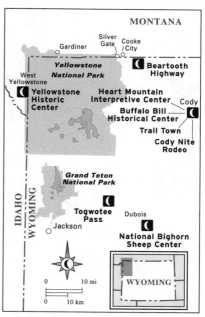

LOOK FOR **◖** TO FIND RECOMMENDED SIGHTS, ACTIVITIES, DINING, AND LODGING.

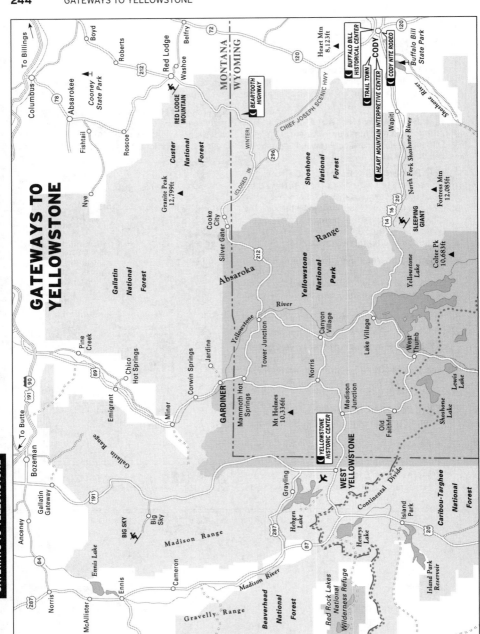

GATEWAYS TO YELLOWSTONE

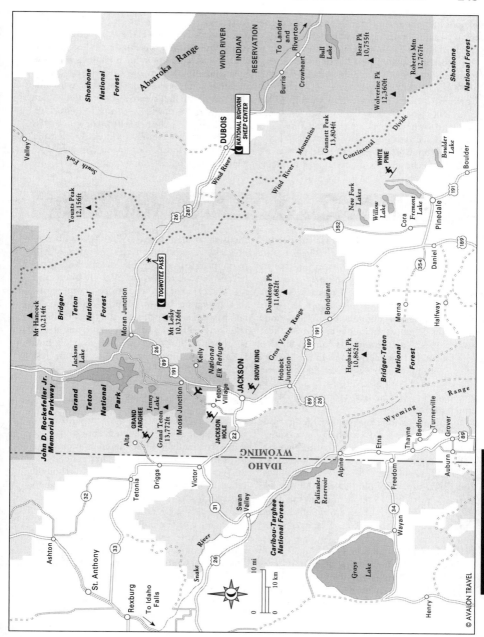

© AVALON TRAVEL

his old lodging place (Irma Hotel) is a downtown fixture. The main draw, however, is massive Buffalo Bill Historical Center, which houses five museums focusing on Plains Indians, the life of Buffalo Bill, Western art, natural history, and firearms. Up the road is the low-key Trail Town with historic cabins and wagons. The Cody Nite Rodeo takes place nightly all summer, and whitewater rafting on the Shoshone River lets visitors do their own bucking.

The Upper Wind River Valley town of Dubois, Wyoming, is a fine stopping place for travelers heading into Grand Teton and Yellowstone National Parks from the east. The town hosts a small museum and the National Bighorn Sheep Center, with exhibits on these majestic animals that live in the surrounding mountains. Dubois is unpretentious, with old-time dude ranches nearby and a good choice of family restaurants. East from Dubois, U.S. 26/287 climbs over beautiful Togwotee Pass into the parks. Visitors could easily spend at least two days in Cody or one in Dubois before heading into Yellowstone.

West Yellowstone, Montana

West Yellowstone (elev. 6,650) is the definitive Western tourist town. With a year-round population of only 1,000 (three times that in the summer) but more than 50 places to stay, it's pretty easy to see what makes the West Yellowstone cash registers ring. The West Entrance gate—most popular of all Yellowstone entrances—lies just a couple of hundred feet away. "West," as the town is known locally, isn't particularly attractive, and in the 1990s a major development brought several corporate hotels and other ugly additions to an already crowded mix of restaurants, motels, T-shirt stores, and gift shops.

West Yellowstone may be decidedly middle-brow, but the surrounding land is anything but, with Gallatin (GAL-a-tin) National Forest lying north and west, Caribou-Targhee National Forest just a few miles to the south, and Yellowstone National Park just a few feet to the east. It's just a couple of miles east from West Yellowstone to the Wyoming border, and the Idaho border lies only nine miles west.

HISTORY

In 1907, the Union Pacific Railroad completed laying tracks for its Oregon Short Line to the western border of Yellowstone. The following summer, Yellowstone Special trains began rolling in from Salt Lake City, dropping tourists for their stagecoach tours of the park. A small town—West Yellowstone—quickly developed on the margins of the park, providing lodging, meals, and tourist trinkets. After World War II, interest in rail travel declined and more people came to Yellowstone by automobile. Although the last passengers stepped off the train in 1960, the Union Pacific's historic stone depot and neighboring buildings still stand; they now house a museum, library, police station, jail, medical clinic, and other offices.

The West Yellowstone area was rocked by a devastating magnitude-7.5 earthquake on August 17, 1959. One of the most powerful temblors ever recorded in the Lower 48 states, the quake cracked Hebgen Dam and caused a massive landslide (estimated at more than 80 million tons of debris!) that generated a 20-foot-high tsunami and created Earthquake Lake. Twenty-eight people died, and the geysers and hot springs of Yellowstone were dramatically affected for years.

Evidence of the powerful 1959 earthquake is still visible north of West Yellowstone along Hebgen Lake. The Forest Service has an **Earthquake Visitor Center** (daily 8:30 A.M.–6 P.M. late May–late Sept. only). Get there by heading eight miles north on U.S. Highway 191 and turning left on U.S. Highway 287; continue another 17 miles west to the center.

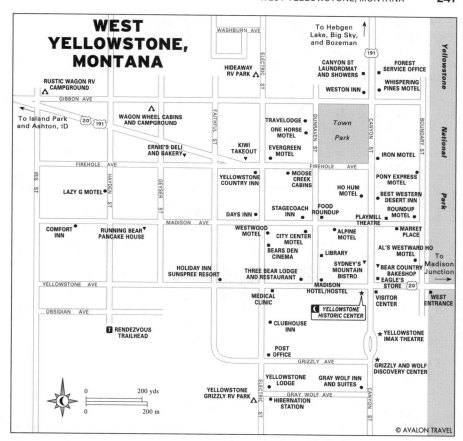

SIGHTS
Visitor Center

The **West Yellowstone Chamber of Commerce Visitor Center** (30 Yellowstone Ave., 406/646-7701, www.destinationyellowstone.com, daily 8 A.M.–8 P.M. late May–early Sept., daily 8 A.M.–6 P.M. May and early Sept.–Oct., 8 A.M.–5 P.M. Mon.–Fri. the rest of the year) is a one-stop destination for regional information. The office (406/646-4403) is staffed by Park Service employees whenever Yellowstone is open. Daily **ranger talks** (9:30 A.M. May–early Sept., free) are a summer feature; in winter, rangers lead twice-weekly snowshoe walks (call ahead for these). Forest Service employees are on-site Saturday in the summer, providing details on nearby Gallatin National Forest. A guest computer and free Wi-Fi are available. Pick up the historic walking tour brochure for an interesting introduction to the town.

◖ Yellowstone Historic Center

The Yellowstone Historic Center (104 Yellowstone Ave., 406/646-1100, www.yellowstonehistoriccenter.org, daily 9 A.M.–9 P.M. mid-May–early Sept., 9 A.M.–6 P.M. the rest of Sept.–mid-Oct., and closed the rest of the year,

$5 adults, $4 seniors, $3 ages 13–18, $2 ages 3–12, and free for kids under three) is a stone-and-log structure from the railroad days that served for decades as the town's train depot. Inside are exhibits on the history of park transportation, the 1959 Hebgen Lake earthquake, the fires of 1988, regional air travel, and "Old Snaggletooth" the grizzly. Videos and movies about Yellowstone are shown in the theater, and the museum offers historic-district walking tours (Mon., Wed., and Fri.–Sat. in summer) for museum visitors.

Right next door is another wonderful stone structure (built in 1925) that served until the late 1950s as an elegant Union Pacific Dining Lodge. The building has a spacious dining hall containing an enormous fireplace, a 45-foot-tall vaulted ceiling, and handmade light fixtures. Also worth a look-see is an **Oregon Short Line Railroad car** housed at the Holiday Inn (315 Yellowstone Ave., 406/646-7365, www.visityellowstonepark.com). Built in 1903, the beautifully restored railroad car forms a centerpiece for the restaurant and lounge here.

Grizzly and Wolf Discovery Center

The Grizzly and Wolf Discovery Center (201 S. Canyon St., 406/646-7001 or 800/257-2570, www.grizzlydiscoveryctr.com, daily 8:30 A.M.– dusk year-round) is home to seven Alaskan and Canadian grizzlies and eight captive-born gray wolves. Not all of the bears are visible at any given time, but visitors are bound to see at least one in the pseudo-natural habitat. This center attracts throngs of visitors and photographers who might otherwise never see a grizzly or wolf, and there's always a staff member out to answer any questions. Park Service rangers provide daily presentations in the summer. The center remains controversial, however. Scientists note that the bears here are genetically distinct from those in Yellowstone, and anyone who has spent time around grizzlies in the wild will be dismayed to see them in captivity, even in a facility less oppressive than traditional zoos. The folks at Grizzly and Wolf Discovery Center counter that all these bears were either raised in captivity or were "problem" bears that would

Yellowstone Historic Center museum

© DON PITCHER

almost certainly have been killed had they not been moved here. In addition to the bears and wolves, the center has wildlife exhibits, bear safety tips, a video on bears, plus the obligatory gift shop. Entrance—good for two consecutive days—is $11 adults, $10 seniors, $6 ages 5–12, free for kids under five.

Yellowstone IMAX Theatre

Directly in front of the Grizzly and Wolf Discovery Center is the Yellowstone IMAX Theatre (406/646-4100 or 888/854-5862, www.yellowstoneimax.com, daily 8:30 A.M.–9 P.M. late May–early Oct., reduced hours the rest of the year, $9 adults, $6.50 ages 4–12, free for younger children), where you can watch the big-budget production of *Yellowstone* on the 60-by-80-foot screen; other movies typically are on wolves, bears, or some other nature or Old West topic. The featured attraction is a 35-minute movie that presents Yellowstone history and geology, complete with stirring music and a cast of dozens. If you haven't seen IMAX flicks before, hold onto your seat—lots of jaw-dropping scenes here. The movie packs in the crowds on summer days, but the film seems to be a Disneylandish version of reality, ignoring many of the things you're likely to see in the park—such as burned forests and crowds of visitors—and putting history into a pretty little box. Reality wasn't—and isn't—quite like this. Even more disconcerting is that this glorification of the park stands right next to the park. To me, it symbolizes the make-a-buck attitude that holds Yellowstone up as an attraction while developing a massive complex on its very margin. But hey, the movies are still fun to watch.

SUMMER RECREATION

Birders should pick up the *West Yellowstone Birding Trail* brochure from the visitor center. It provides a map and helpful descriptions of nearby locations.

Horses and Bikes

Horseback trail rides are available from **Parade Rest Guest Ranch** (seven miles north of town,

406/646-7217 or 800/753-5934, www.paraderestranch.com), **Diamond P Ranch** (seven miles to the west, 406/646-7246 or 800/709-1358, www.yellowstonehorses.com), and **Yellowstone Mountain Guides** (406/646-7230, www.yellowstone-guides.com). Diamond P and Parade Rest both also offer evening wagon rides with Old West chuck-wagon suppers.

The 30-kilometer Rendezvous Trail System becomes mountain-bike central when summer rolls around. It starts from the southern edge of town; get a map at the visitor center. Rent mountain bikes from **Free Heel and Wheel** (40 Yellowstone Ave., 406/646-7744, www.freeheelandwheel.com). Free Heel also rents strollers and child-carrier backpacks.

Fishing

You'll find seven fly-fishing shops in town, a reflection of the sport's importance in the Yellowstone area. In business for nearly 60 years, **Bud Lilly's Trout Shop** (39 Madison Ave., 406/646-7801 or 800/854-9559, www.budlillys.com) is the best-known local place, with fishing tackle, clothing, guides, and even a gallery. Also well worth a look are **Arrick's Fly Shop** (37 Canyon St., 406/646-7290, www.arricks.com), **Blue Ribbon Flies** (305 Canyon St., 406/646-7642, www.blueribbonflies.com), **Eagle's Tackle Shop** (3 Canyon St., 406/646-7521), **Jacklin's Fly Shop** (105 Yellowstone Ave., 406/646-7336, www.jacklinsflyshop.com), **West Yellowstone Fly Shop** (140 Madison Ave., 406/646-1181, www.wyflyshop.com), and **Madison River Outfitters** (117 Canyon St., 406/646-9644, www.flyfishingyellowstone.com). All offer guided fishing float trips ($460 for two people per day) and equipment.

Rafting and Kayaking

Two rafting companies run all-day and half-day whitewater trips down the Gallatin River approximately 50 miles north of West Yellowstone (near Big Sky). The rafting season is generally late May–September, and you'll pay about $85 adults, $68 kids for all day or $51 adults, $41 kids for a half-day adventure.

The companies are **Geyser Whitewater Expeditions** (406/995-4989 or 800/914-9031, www.raftmontana.com) and **Montana Whitewater** (406/763-4465 or 800/799-4465, www.montanawhitewater.com). Both offer sit-on-top kayaks for those who'd rather paddle it themselves. Montana Whitewater also leads trips down the challenging Madison River northwest of West Yellowstone, and Geyser Whitewater has gentle scenic floats for those who'd rather relax.

Two local companies have guided kayak trips to Hebgen Lake (but not into Yellowstone): **Lava Creek Adventures** (406/646-5145, www.lavacreekadventures.com) and **Yellowstone Alpen Guides** (406/646-9591 or 800/858-3502, www.yellowstoneguides.com). Lava Creek also has rentals and a kayaker shuttle service.

WINTER RECREATION
Cross-Country Skiing
West Yellowstone is infamous for its bitterly cold winters, when the thermometer can drop to -50°F. Fortunately, it doesn't always stay there, and by March the days have often warmed to a balmy 20°F. In November, West Yellowstone becomes a national center for cross-country skiers, with the U.S. Nordic and biathlon ski teams training here. Pick up a map of local ski trails at the visitor center.

Two trail systems provide a wide variety of Nordic skiing conditions, with trails groomed for both classical and skate skiing. The 50-kilometer **Rendezvous Ski Trail** system (www.rendezvousskitrails.com) takes off from the southern edge of town and is groomed early November–April. The nine-kilometer **Riverside Trail** begins on the east side of town and leads to the Madison River within Yellowstone National Park. This trail provides a good opportunity to see bison, elk, and possibly moose. You can also ski the snowpacked streets in winter. Find many more places for flat tracking or telemarking in adjacent Yellowstone National Park and the Gallatin and Caribou-Targhee national forests. Before heading out into remote areas, get

recorded avalanche-safety information from the **Avalanche Advisory Hotline** (406/587-6981, www.mtavalanche.com). It's updated daily in the winter.

Rent skinny skis from **Bud Lilly's Trout Shop** (39 Madison Ave., 406/646-7801 or 800/854-9559, www.budlillys.com) or **Free Heel and Wheel** (40 Yellowstone Ave., 406/646-7744, www.freeheelandwheel.com). Free Heel also rents snowshoes and sleds.

The closest downhill ski and snowboard area is the world-class **Big Sky Resort** (800/548-4486, www.bigskyresort.com), 57 miles north of West Yellowstone. The resort features 15 lifts and more than 3,500 acres of terrain. You will find excellent cross-country trails at **Lone Mountain Ranch** (406/995-4644 or 800/514-4644, www.lmranch.com) near Big Sky.

The Forest Service leads Hebgen Lake **snowshoe walks** during the winter months.

Dogsledding
For a delightfully different way to explore the Gallatin National Forest backcountry, take a sled dog tour from **Spirit of the North Sled Dog Adventure** (406/682-7994, www.huskypower.com). Half-day tours are $125 adults or $80 kids. **Klondike Dreams Sled Dog Kennel** (406/646-4988, www.klondikedreams.com) offers two-hour trips for $75 adults or $50 kids.

Snowcoach Trips
Yellowstone Alpen Guides (406/646-9591 or 800/858-3502, www.yellowstoneguides.com) leads snowcoach tours from West Yellowstone. All-day trips are $110 adults, $100 seniors, and $90 kids to either Grand Canyon of the Yellowstone or Old Faithful. Guests on the latter run have an option of getting dropped at Biscuit Basin, where they can ski to Old Faithful and meet up with others. Ski or snowshoe rentals are available. The company's eight classic Bombardier snowcoaches—one built in 1953—have been modernized but are still a charming anachronism.

Other companies offering wintertime van tours into Yellowstone include **All Yellowstone**

Sports/Yellowstone Van Tours (406/646-7556 or 800/548-9551, www.allyellowstone.com), **Yellowstone Tours & Travel** (406/646-9310 800/221-1151, www.seeyellowstone.com), **Back Country Adventure** (406/646-9317 or 800/924-7669, www.backcountry-adventures.com), and **Snowcoach Yellowstone/Buffalo Bus Touring Co.** (406/426-7669 or 800/426-7669, www.yellowstonevacations.com).

For a truly unique experience, book a winter trip with another West Yellowstone–based company, **Yellowstone Expeditions** (406/646-9333 or 800/728-9333, www.yellowstoneexpeditions.com). The company has day tours of the park ($95), but specializes in homey yurts at the Canyon area during the winter. Choose from a variety of multi-night adventures for skiers; a four-day trip is $1,900 for two people.

Snowmobiles

Enthusiasts refer to West as the "snowmobile capital of the world," and each winter day hundreds of 'bilers show up to roar across nearby Forest Service lands or to join Yellowstone tours. All trips inside the park must be with guided groups, and a number of local companies provide these tours. Drop by the West Yellowstone Chamber of Commerce (406/646-7701, www.westyellowstonechamber.com) office for current snow and trail conditions, a detailed map of local trails, and brochures from companies that offer guided snowmobile trips.

Snowmobile rentals for use on Forest Service lands outside the park are available from several local companies; see the Chamber of Commerce website (www.destinationyellowstone.com) for specifics. Hundreds more folks bring in their own machines to ride on national forest lands, and local motels offer snowmobile/lodging packages.

ENTERTAINMENT AND EVENTS

During summer, you can attend light-hearted comedies and musicals such as *Hello Dolly* or *Beauty and the Beast* for the whole family at **Playmill Theatre** (124 Madison Ave., 406/646-7757, www.playmill.com). It's been in operation for more than 50 years.

Watch flicks at **Bears Den Cinema** (15 Electric St., 406/646-7777). **Yellowstone IMAX Theatre** (406/646-4100 or 888/854-5862, www.yellowstoneimax.com) shows movies specially formatted for the three-story screen.

The bar at **Stage Coach Inn** (209 Madison Ave., 406/646-7381) has a pool table and the occasional live band, or try **Iron Horse Saloon** inside Holiday Inn (315 Yellowstone Ave., 406/646-7365).

On the shores of Hebgen Lake 15 miles north of West Yellowstone, **Happy Hour Bar and Restaurant** (406/646-5100 or 800/400-4564, www.happyhourbar.com) is a party destination for country meals of steaks, burgers, and shrimp. The ceiling is coated with ball caps, and two walls are dedicated to pix of bare boobs and butts (don't ask). Open May–September and late December–mid-March.

On the second weekend of March, the **Rendezvous Marathon Ski Race** (406/646-7265, www.rendezvousrace.com), a nationally known Nordic ski race, attracts hundreds of participants. Motorheads arrive the following weekend for the **World Snowmobile Expo** (406/646-7001, www.snowmobileexpo.com), with races, demos, and other activities.

A fun parade, live music, barbecue, and fireworks highlight the town's **Fourth of July** festivities. The **Yellowstone Rod Run** (www.yellowstonerodrun.com) on the first full weekend of August brings vintage cars of all types to the oldest such event in the Pacific Northwest; it's been a summer staple since 1970. On summer Saturdays, bring your blankets and lawn chairs to Town Park for **Music in the Park**.

The **Wild West Yellowstone Rodeo** (406/560-6913, www.yellowstonerodeo.com, $12 adults, $6 kids) features bareback riding, team roping, saddle bronc riding, bull riding, barrel racing, calf roping, a calf scramble, and more in the rodeo arena six miles west of town. Rodeos start at 8 P.M. Thursday–Saturday evenings June–August.

The ever-popular **Knothead Jamboree** attracts more than 1,000 square-dancing enthusiasts for calling, clapping, and fun on Labor Day weekend; it's been happening annually since 1955.

Thanksgiving week in November means **Yellowstone Ski Festival** (www.yellowstoneskifestival.com), attracting hundreds of spandex-clad cross-country ski enthusiasts. The event also attracts major Nordic ski manufacturers, giving the public a chance to demo their latest toys.

SHOPPING

Many West Yellowstone shops sell the obligatory Yellowstone souvenirs, corny T-shirts, and other items with mass appeal. You'll probably get bored after one or two of these gift shops, but many more await your exploration. Fortunately, the town does have several more distinctive places.

Family-run **Eagle's Store** (406/646-9300, daily 8 A.M.–8 P.M.), on the corner of Canyon and Yellowstone, is definitely worth a stop. Built in 1927 and on the National Register of Historic Places, this beautiful log building contains all the standard tourist knickknacks, along with quality Western clothing, jewelry, fishing tackle, and a delightful old-fashioned soda fountain open in summer.

Seldom Seen Knives (115 Yellowstone Ave., 406/646-4116, www.seldomseenknives.com) is worth a look, not only for Steve Hulett's distinctive knives, but also for his multicolor wooden letter openers and other locally crafted items, including offbeat fencepost vases.

A book-lover's shop, **Bookworm Books** (14 Canyon St., 406/646-9736) is packed with both new and used titles, including many first editions. Don't miss the extraordinary collection of Yellowstone memorabilia, notably the postcards, collectable spoons, plates, and stereo views. Owner Scott Clewell also carries English stained glass from the 1890s. The shop is open late: daily till 11 P.M. in the summer and 10 P.M. at other times of the year when the Yellowstone National Park entrance is open.

In business for more than 30 years, **The** **Book Peddler** (106 Canyon St., 406/646-9358, daily 7 A.M.–10 P.M. in summer, 9 A.M.–5 P.M. the rest of the year) is a large and attractive bookstore with an abundance of regional titles. A pleasant café sells espresso in the back.

Free Internet access is at the modern **West Yellowstone Library** (23 N. Dunraven St., 406/646-9017, www.facebook.com, 10 A.M.–6 P.M. Tues. and Thurs., 10 A.M.–8 P.M. Wed., 10 A.M.–5 P.M. Fri., 10 A.M.–3 P.M. Sat.).

ACCOMMODATIONS

The proximity to Yellowstone makes the town of West Yellowstone an extremely popular stopping place for vacationers in both summer and winter. More than 1,700 rooms are available, starting around $75 in midsummer. The streets are lined with more than three dozen motels, so I won't try to describe all of them, although you'll find general information and links from the **West Yellowstone Chamber of Commerce** (406/646-7701, www.westyellowstonechamber.com). Add a 10 percent lodging tax to all rates quoted below.

Although rooms are generally available most summer nights, reservations are advisable; motels can be full even on late-September weekends. To ensure your best choice of accommodations, reserve a room in May for the peak summer season. **West Yellowstone Central Reservations** (406/646-7077 or 888/646-7077, www.yellowstonereservation.com) books rooms at many local places and can also set up a range of activities, from snowcoach tours to whitewater rafting.

Hostel

Budget travelers will be happy to discover the West Yellowstone International Hostel (not affiliated with AYH) in the historic **Madison Hotel** (139 Yellowstone Ave., 406/646-7745 or 800/838-7745, www.madisonhotelmotel.com). On the National Register of Historic Places, the hotel has friendly owners and a delightfully rustic lobby crowded with deer and moose heads. Presidents Harding and Hoover stayed here (though it wasn't a hostel at the time, of course). Travelers stay in clean and comfortable bedrooms (three beds in each, with bedding provided) that have been furnished with handmade lodgepole furniture. The classic hotel rooms are a delightful mix of old and new, providing the ambience of a place that has been here since 1912. The creaky floors and burled log railings add to the charm. No televisions or phones are provided in the rooms, but there is a small fridge and microwave for hostelers in the back, plus a TV in the lobby and a barbecue grill out back. A computer is available to check your email ($5 per day), and free Wi-Fi is available in some rooms. Lodging costs $30 per person in three-bed dorm rooms. Make hostel reservations a few days ahead in midsummer or get here before evening to be sure of a space in the dorms.

In addition to hostel rooms, the hotel has a range of other economical options. Rooms with a bath down the hall and no TV or phone are $49 s or $59 d. Larger units with private baths and space for four cost $89. Behind the hotel is a separate building with standard motel accommodations (private baths, TVs, and phones) for $72–99 d or $149 for a room with three double beds. The Madison Hotel is open late May–early October only.

$50-100

A fine economy choice, **Lazy G Motel** (123 Hayden, 406/646-7586, www.lazygmotel.com, $68–79 d) offers clean and quiet rooms with fridges, Wi-Fi, and phones (but no air-conditioning); kitchenettes are $15 extra. Friendly owners, too. It's a five-block walk from town center. Closed mid-October–mid-November and the month of April.

Alpine Motel (120 Madison Ave., 406/646-7544, www.alpinemotelwestyellowstone.com, $80–100 d) is similar and equally popular. The Alpine also has a family suite that sleeps six with a full kitchen for $155. No phones, but it does have air-conditioning, Wi-Fi, and gracious owners. Open mid-May–mid-October.

Pony Express Motel (4 Firehole Ave., 406/646-7644 or 800/323-9708, www.yellowstonevacations.com, $69 one queen bed,

$79 two queens) has a quiet location and rustic knotty-pine decor. A kitchenette is $99 for up to four people, and a deluxe two-bedroom suite with space for eight costs $179. Rooms are clean, but very simple, with old furnishings, no phones or air-conditioning, and Wi-Fi if you're lucky—basic, but a good value. If you're looking for something a bit nicer, the same owners run Brandin' Iron Inn (201 Canyon St., 406/646-9411 or 800/217-4613, www. yellowstonevacations.com), right across the street. Pony Express is open mid-May–mid-October.

A little nicer but still reasonably priced is another property with the same owners, **City Center Motel** (214 Madison Ave., 408/646-7337 or 800/742-0665, www.yellowstonevacations.com), where the big rooms (air-conditioning but no phones) are $89 for one queen bed or $99 for two. Family suites sleep up to eight for $129. A community kitchen, indoor hot tub, and Wi-Fi are available for guests. Open mid-May–mid-October.

Over $100

You'll find very nice accommodations at **Brandin' Iron Inn** (201 Canyon St., 406/646-9411 or 800/217-4613, www.yellowstonevacations.com). Spacious, clean rooms include fridges, a big hot breakfast, Wi-Fi, and access to two indoor hot tubs. Standard rooms are $139–149; suites are $149–155.

Family-run **One Horse Motel** (216 N. Dunraven St., 406/646-7677 or 800/488-2750, www.onehorsemotel.com, $119–129 d) is another good bargain, where all rooms contain microwaves, fridges, air-conditioning, and Wi-Fi, but no phones. Open May–September. The same owners run the nearby **Evergreen Motel** (229 Firehole Ave., 406/646-7655 or 800/488-2750, www.theevergreenmotel.com, $129 d), with comfortable and clean rooms. It has fridges, microwaves, Wi-Fi, air-conditioning, and a couple of kitchenettes ($139), but no phones. Open year-round.

Rebuilt after a 2008 fire, **Three Bear Lodge** (217 Yellowstone Ave., 406/646-7353 or 800/646-7353, www.threebearlodge.com)

has a variety of contemporary rooms in a motel and lodge, plus two indoor hot tubs, Wi-Fi, an exercise room, and a seasonal outdoor pool. Rates start at $159 for standard four-person motel rooms, or $169 d with a king bed and jet tub. Two-room family units are $189 in the motel or $249–279 in the lodge; the largest unit sleeps six. Open year-round.

Days Inn (118 Electric St., 406/646-7656 or 800/548-9551, www.allyellowstone.com) is a large motel with standard older rooms ($154 d), suites containing two queen beds, a sleeper sofa, microwave, and fridge ($215 d), and rooms with king beds and in-room hot tubs ($219 d). Days Inn also has Wi-Fi, plus two hot tubs and an indoor pool that features the star attraction: a 100-foot corkscrew water slide. Hotel guests receive a coupon for two free breakfasts at Trappers Family Restaurant, downstairs.

One of the newest places in town, **Yellowstone Lodge** (251 Electric St., 406/646-0020 or 877/239-9298, www.yellowstonelodge.com), has oversized rooms, an indoor pool, hot tub, Wi-Fi, guest computer, fridges, microwaves, and a light breakfast. Standard rooms with two queens or a king cost $169–179 d. Suites are $199 d, and a big family unit sleeps six for $209.

Extending for almost an entire downtown block, **Stage Coach Inn** (209 Madison Ave., 406/646-7381 or 800/842-2882, www.yellowstoneinn.com) features an impressive Western-style lobby with fireplace, plus a restaurant and heated underground parking (a big plus in winter). Nothing-special older rooms go for $130 d, while updated, larger units are $160 d. All rooms include Wi-Fi, fridges, a light breakfast, and access to the sauna and two hot tubs.

At **Hibernation Station** (212 Gray Wolf Ave., 406/646-4200 or 800/580-3557, www.hibernationstation.com) the 50 modern cabins—each a bit different inside—feature handmade log furniture and down comforters. Half also contain kitchenettes. Prices start at $119 d for a cabin with a queen bed. Spacious suites with fireplace, king bed, jetted tub, and kitchenette run $239 d, or check out the unique

six-person units (cabins 37 and 38) with queen bunk beds, kitchenettes, jet tubs, and fireplaces for $269. Families not on a budget will appreciate the large condo unit with room for six, a full kitchen and dining area, fireplace, and jetted tubs for $299. A big outdoor hot tub is available for all guests, along with a guest computer and Wi-Fi. Pets are $10 extra.

One of the better chain motels is **Comfort Inn** (638 Madison Ave., 406/646-4212 or 888/264-2466, www.westyellowstonecomfortinn.com), with the biggest indoor pool in town. Other amenities include large rooms, a hot tub, guest computer, hot breakfasts, and Wi-Fi. Rates are $199–209 d in standard rooms, or $269 for six-person suites.

Yellowstone Clubhouse Inn (105 S. Electric St., 406/646-4892 or 800/565-6803, www.yellowstoneclubhouseinn.com, $199 d for standard rooms, $249 d for king rooms with jetted tub, $259 for family suites) is an attractive hotel with modern rooms, fridges, microwaves, an indoor pool and whirlpool bath, small fitness center, guest computer, Wi-Fi, and light breakfast (with waffles). Closed late October–April.

Another place with a fine reputation is **Kelly Inn West Yellowstone** (104 S. Canyon St., 406/646-4544 or 800/259-4672, www.yellowstonekellyinn.com), featuring huge rooms, fridges, microwaves, an indoor pool, hot tub, sauna, Wi-Fi, guest computer, and hot breakfast. Rates average $200 for standard rooms, $240 for suites with king beds and jetted tubs, but may fluctuate widely throughout the summer.

The large **Gray Wolf Inn and Suites** (250 S. Canyon, 406/646-0000 or 800/852-8602, www.visityellowstonepark.com) features a hot tub, sauna, and small indoor pool, plus a breakfast buffet. An added attraction—especially in the winter—is the heated underground parking garage. Rates are egregious: $289 d for standard rooms, $309–369 for one- and two-bedroom suites that come with full kitchens.

The most elaborate local place is the **West Yellowstone Holiday Inn** (315 Yellowstone

Ave., 406/646-7365 or 888/633-1724, www.visityellowstonepark.com), where spacious—and spendy—rooms have fridges and microwaves; there's Wi-Fi, an indoor pool, exercise room, and hot tub. Standard rooms cost $229–239 d, two-room family suites are $279 and sleep six, and luxurious executive suites (king bed, jetted tub, and wet bar) run $289. Both Holiday Inn and Gray Wolf Inn and Suites are managed by Delaware North, one of the park's primary concessioners.

Cabins

■ Wagon Wheel Cabins and Campground (408 Gibbon, 406/646-7872, www.wagonwheelrv.com) has a unique collection of nine attractive cabins, most containing full kitchens. The cabins are on large lots surrounded by trees, and each has a barbecue grill and picnic table. Basic bring-your-sleeping-bag cabins ($70 d) have no water (a bathhouse is nearby); far nicer are the well-appointed one-bedroom units with full kitchens, private baths, gas grills, and screened porches ($114–139 d). Two- and three-bedroom cabins are $145–202 d, and the largest unit (cabin 7) is really a small log house with three bedrooms, a full kitchen, and a den with fireplace; it sleeps six for $243. There's a four-night summer minimum for the larger cabins and three-night minimum for the smaller ones. Cabins at Wagon Wheel fill early, so book several months ahead, especially for cabins 1 and 7. The cabins are usually closed in winter.

Offering a variety of rooms and cabins, **Moose Creek Cabins & Inn** (406/646-9546, www.moosecreekcabin.com) is an excellent West Yellowstone choice with reasonable prices and friendly owners. Four 1950s-era cabins ($175) have been attractively updated and are popular with families who appreciate the kitchenettes, knotty-pine walls, and two queen beds. Western-themed motel-style rooms are $107 d, or choose the spacious six-person loft unit with kitchen for $185. A separate property houses the inn, with spotless rooms for $100 d. All units at Moose Creek have microwaves, fridges, and Wi-Fi, but no phones.

Bed-and-Breakfasts

Four miles west of town, **West Yellowstone Bed and Breakfast** (20 Crane Lane, 406/646-7754, www.westyellowstonebandb.com, $155–159 d) has three rooms, all with private baths and entrances, along with a home-cooked breakfast and Wi-Fi. Kids welcome.

Six miles west of West Yellowstone and right along the Madison River, **Bar N Ranch** (Hwy. 20, 406/646-0300, www.bar-n-ranch.com) offers a luxurious way to rough it. The main lodge features a three-sided fireplace in the great room, with windows framing the mountains. Guests stay in elegant cabins ($285–460 d) with private hot tubs, or in rooms ($210–250 d) in the main lodge. Other amenities include jet tubs and wood-burning fireplaces in all units, a heated outdoor pool, hot tub, Wi-Fi, filling breakfasts, and a restaurant on the premises. Friendly owners, too. A three-night minimum is required in the summer. Open early May to late October.

Guesthouses and Rentals

Many companies rent homes, cabins, condos, and townhouses of all types, ranging from simple cabins ($95) and two-bedroom homes ($175) up to an 18-person log home with eight bedrooms and five baths ($550). Local companies include **Yellowstone Townhouses** (406/646-9331 or 866/252-6636, www.yellowstonetownhouses.com), **Moose Haven Vacation Cabin** (714/397-6486, www.moosehaven.com), **Angler's Rest** (301/461-0902, www.burkinc.net/anglersrest), **Brook Trout Inn** (406/646-4254, www.brooktroutinn.com), **LL Western Adventures** (406/646-9730, www.llwesternadventures.com), **Pine Shadows Motel and Condo Rentals** (406/646-7541 or 800/624-5291, www.pineshadowsmotel.com), **Faithful St. Inn** (406/646-1010 or 866/646-4329, www.faithfulstreetinn.com), **Eino's Tavern** (406/646-9344), **Yellowstone Wildlife Cabins** (406/646-7675, www.yellowstonewildlifecabins.com), **Two Feathers Cabin Lodging** (406/646-9764, www.twofeatherscabinlodging.com), and **Yellowstone Village Condominiums** (406/646-7335 or

800/276-7335, www.westyellowstonerentals.com). A three-night minimum stay is required for most of these places.

CAMPING
Public Campgrounds
The nearest Park Service camping place is inside Yellowstone at **Madison Campground** (307/344-7311 or 866/439-7375, www.yellowstonenationalparklodges.com), 14 miles east of West Yellowstone. The cost is $20, and it's open early May–late October. Reservations are advised.

Gallatin National Forest (406/823-6961, www.fs.fed.us/r1/gallatin) has several campgrounds in the West Yellowstone area. The closest camping spot is **Baker's Hole Campground** (open mid-May–mid-Sept., $16), just three miles north of West Yellowstone. Because of bear problems, it's open to RVs and other hard-sided vehicles only. Tent campers will need to go north of town to **Hebgen Lake,** where five different areas are strung westward along the lake; closest is the **Rainbow Point Campground** (open mid-May–mid-Sept., $16), 10 miles from West Yellowstone. No reservations are taken at these Forest Service sites.

The Forest Service maintains four public-use cabins ($30 a night for four people) in the country around West Yellowstone. Three of these are open year-round. Closest is **Basin Station Cabin** 518/885-3639 or 877/444-6777, www.recreation.gov, $9 reservation fee), eight miles west of town.

RV Parks
West Yellowstone has a half-dozen private campgrounds right in town, and several more are west or north of town. Most of the in-town places are just RV parking lots. Far nicer are two places with shady trees and quiet sites: **Rustic Wagon Campground** (634 U.S. Hwy. 20, 406/646-7387, www.rusticwagonrv.com, mid-Apr.–mid-Nov.) and **Wagon Wheel Cabins and Campground** (408 Gibbon Ave., 406/646-7872, www.wagonwheelrv.com, late May–Sept.). Rates are $35 for tents or $42–47 for RVs; noncampers can shower at either of

these for a few dollars. Both are owned by the same family and are recommended.

The other in-town RV parks (all have Wi-Fi) are **Pony Express RV Park** (4 Firehole Ave., 406/646-7644 or 800/217-4613, www.yellowstonevacations.com, $39 RVs, no tents, year-round), **Hideaway RV Park** (310 Electric St., 406/646-9049, www.hideawayrv.com, $20 tents, $34 RVs, May–mid-Oct.), **Yellowstone Cabins and RV Park** (504 U.S. Hwy. 20 W., 406/646-9350 or 866/646-9350, www.yellowstonecabinsandrv.com, $35 RVs, no tents, year-round), and **Yellowstone Grizzly RV Park** (210 S. Electric, 406/646-4466, www.grizzlyrv.com, $30 tents, $47 RVs, May–Oct.).

For a quiet in-the-country location, head to **Yellowstone Park KOA** (406/646-7606 or 800/562-7591, www.yellowstonekoa.com, $37–51 tents, $51–81 RVs, May–Sept.), six miles west of town on U.S. Highway 20. Amenities include an indoor pool, hot tub, game room, and Wi-Fi. Seven miles west of West Yellowstone is **Lionshead RV Park** (406/646-7662, www.lionsheadrv.com, $60–65 for RVs, $35 d for tents, May–Sept.); it's adjacent to Super 8 Motel. **Yellowstone Holiday RV Campground & Marina** (406/646-4242 or 800/643-4227, www.yellowstoneholiday.com, $39–49 RVs, mid-May–mid-Oct.) is an RV campground along Hebgen Lake, 13 miles north of West Yellowstone. Cabins are also available; $67 for simple units or $115 for nicer cabins.

FOOD
West Yellowstone has a decidedly mediocre dining reputation, so don't expect anything like what you'll find in Jackson—or even Gardiner, Driggs, Dubois, Cody, and other regional towns. Of course, you can always head to the Dairy Queen if milkshakes and burgers fill your hunger pangs.

Breakfast and Lunch
For omelets, buckwheat pancakes, biscuits and sausage gravy, or other breakfast favorites, run over to ◖ **Running Bear Pancake House** (538 Madison Ave., 406/646-7703, daily

7 A.M.–2 P.M., $3–10), but be ready for a long wait in midsummer. Five blocks from town center on the west side, this is a family place with plenty of kid-friendly choices (not to mention the kid-generated noise) and substantive portions. Menu options range from buttermilk pancakes to the full-cholesterol chicken-fried steak with sausage, gravy, eggs, hash browns, and toast. (The pancake sandwich is especially popular—ham or bacon between two pancakes topped with an egg. Only in America.) For lunch, try a turkey sandwich, made with turkey roasted on the premises.

A bit off the beaten path but worth the detour, **Ernie's Deli and Bakery** (406 U.S. Hwy. 20 W., 406/646-9467, www.erniesbakery. com, daily 7 A.M.–3 P.M.) is open for reasonable breakfasts ($6 for two eggs, hash browns, bacon, and a buttermilk biscuit), doughnuts, burritos, and unbeatable lunchtime sandwiches ($7–9) on freshly baked bread. Heading into the park? Ernie's will put together a box lunch ($10) if you want to leave the sandwiches to the experts. There's free Wi-Fi, too.

On the corner of Electric and U.S. Highway 20, **Kiwi Takeaway** (406/646-7040, www.kiwitakeaway.com, 10 A.M.–8 P.M. Mon.–Fri. in summer, reduced hours the rest of the year) has to be the only New Zealand restaurant for hundreds of miles in any direction. Join the locals inside or on one of the tables out front and check the chalkboard for the daily handmade meat pies ($6–7, try the chicken curry); they often sell out early. Buffalo burgers, fish and chips, and banana fritters are all popular, and there's even veggie-friendly toasted cheese with pineapple sandwiches. Take-away park lunches cost $10.

Coffee and Sweets

Stop by **Bear Country Bake Shop & Eatery** (29 Canyon St., 406/646-9737, www.facebook.com, 7 A.M.–2 P.M. Mon.–Sat., 7 A.M.–noon Sun. late May–Oct., 8 A.M.–2:30 P.M. Mon.–Fri. in winter) for a morning latte and fresh-from-the-oven pastry. Also here are Baja burritos and bagel sandwiches for breakfast, along with unusual lunch sandwiches such as the black bear wrap (chicken, mango-peach salsa, black beans, and cheese wrapped in a tortilla and toasted). Order a fisherman's lunch to go ($11) if you're really hungry and heading out for a day in Yellowstone.

Another very good espresso destination is **The Book Peddler** (106 Canyon St., 406/646-9358, daily 7 A.M.–8 P.M. in summer, 9 A.M.–5 P.M. the rest of the year) with several tables in the back for bagels, sweets, and coffee.

For sweet treats, head to **Arrowleaf Ice Cream Parlor** (29 Canyon St., 406/646-9776, 11 A.M.–10 P.M. Mon.–Sat. late May–Oct., 11 A.M.–5 P.M. Mon.–Sat. in winter). Arrowleaf blends its own flavors, and is best known for shakes, banana splits, and waffle cones.

Free Heel and Wheel (40 Yellowstone Ave., 406/646-7744, www.freeheelandwheel.com, 9 A.M.–6 P.M. Sun., 9 A.M.–7 P.M. Mon.–Sat. in summer; 1–5 P.M. Sun., 9 A.M.–5 P.M. Mon.–Sat. in winter) also serves espresso and pastries all day.

American

With a downtown location, friendly service, and an eclectic menu, ◖ **Sydney's Mountain Bistro** (38 Canyon St., 406/646-7660, www. sydneysbistro.com, daily 11 A.M.–3 P.M. and 5–10 P.M. May–Oct., closed in winter, $15–24) is a local standout. The butternut squash ravioli is made on the premises, and daily seafood specials are always worth a look. Order a three-cheese melt for lunch, or try Panang chicken or a porterhouse pork chop for dinner. Patio seating is available.

Beartooth BBQ (111 Canyon St., 406/646-0227, daily 11 A.M.–10 P.M. May–Oct., closed in winter) is a justly popular eatery with a top-carnivore menu of pulled beef brisket sandwiches, finger-lickin' spare ribs, and smoked sausage. Consistently good, it's a favorite of both locals and travelers. Sandwiches are $9, ribs are $14–18.

Three Bear Restaurant (205 Yellowstone Ave., 406/646-7811, www.threebearlodge.com, daily 6:30–11 A.M. and 5–10 P.M. in summer, reduced hours in winter, $12–27) is a friendly place with an upmarket dinner menu featuring bison rib steak, shrimp, rainbow trout, and roast chicken. It has a good salad-and-soup bar (all you can eat, $10), nightly specials, a children's menu, and apple brown Betty à la mode for dessert. Open for breakfast and dinner.

Outpost Restaurant (115 Yellowstone Ave., 406/646-7303, daily 6:30 A.M.–10:30 P.M. mid-Apr.–mid-Oct., closed in winter) serves three family meals daily, with a decent salad bar ($9) and all the dinner favorites—steaks, pork chops, salmon, chicken Parmesan, buffalo burgers, and country-fried steak ($17–25). "Old Faithfuls" ($10) include baked chicken or homemade beef stew. The restaurant's odd rules and extra charges may annoy some folks.

The most unusual local eatery is the eccentric **Eino's Tavern** (406/646-9344, open lunch and dinner year-round), nine miles north of town on U.S. Highway 191. It's a cook-your-own steak, burger, and chicken place with a big indoor grill and a motley, hard-drinking crowd. The bartender is famous for his Bloody Marys. Prices are reasonable ($6–25), *but you are cooking your own food after all.* The patio faces Hebgen Lake, and the bar has a big-screen TV and pool tables.

Located six miles west of town, **Bar N Ranch** (406/646-0300, www.bar-n-ranch. com) is opening a new seasonal restaurant in 2011, and the gourmet menu is sure to please.

Right in the heart of the action, **Dairy Queen** (40 N. Canyon St., 406/646-4106, $4–8) is the quintessential American joint. Join the line on a warm summer evening for burgers, onion rings, parfaits, and blizzards. DQ is open until midnight daily in the summer, with a couple of picnic tables out front.

Asian

Chinatown (110 Madison Ave., 406/646-7088, daily 11 A.M.–10 P.M., $9–10) serves okay Chinese meals and has $6 lunch specials—best deal in town.

Italian

Unlike other local pizza joints, **Wild West Pizza** (20 Madison Ave., 406/646-4400, www.wildwestpizza.com, daily 11 A.M.–midnight, $23) makes from-scratch pizzas with fresh dough and some odd toppings. I'm not sure how they came up with the pizza names, but somehow the "Sacajawea" has fresh spinach, feta, kalamata olives, and artichoke hearts! The menu also includes lasagna, calzones, and hot sandwiches on garlic bread. Local delivery is free after 5 P.M.

Groceries

Market Place (22 Madison Ave., 406/646-9600) and **Food Roundup Supermarket** (107 Dunraven, 406/646-7501) are the local grocery stores. Market Place also contains a deli and bakery. Both places are open daily 7 A.M.–10 P.M. in the summer, with reduced winter hours.

INFORMATION AND SERVICES

The **West Yellowstone Chamber of Commerce Visitor Center** (30 Yellowstone Ave., 406/646-7701, www.destinationyellowstone.com, daily 8 A.M.–8 P.M. late May–early Sept., daily 8 A.M.–6 P.M. May and early Sept.–Oct., 8 A.M.–5 P.M. Mon.–Fri. the rest of the year) provides useful information for travelers. The visitor center has a computer to surf the Web and free Wi-Fi. The **West Yellowstone Library** (23 N. Dunraven St.) also provides free computers and Wi-Fi. Other options for Wi-Fi and computer rentals include **Madison Hotel** (139 Yellowstone Ave., 406/646-7745 or 800/838-7745, www.madisonhotelmotel. com) and **Send-It-Home** (30 Madison Ave., 406/646-7300, www.send-it-home.com). Drop by the latter to check out the largest keychain collection in the area—600 at last count! A number of local restaurants have Wi-Fi, including Ernie's Deli, Bullwinkle's, and Trappers Restaurant. Online travel sources include www. westyellowstonetraveler.com and Yellowstone Park's www.westyellowstonenet.com.

The **Hebgen Lake Ranger District Office** (406/646-7369, www.fs.fed.us/r1/gallatin, 8 A.M.–4:30 P.M. Mon.–Fri.) is just north of town on U.S. Highway 191/287. Pick up maps of Gallatin National Forest, along with an interesting brochure on the Madison River Canyon Earthquake Area.

West Yellowstone's **post office** (406/646-7704) is at 209 Grizzly Avenue.

Wash clothes at **Swan Cleaners and Laundromat** (520 Madison Ave., 406/646-7892) or **Canyon Street Laundromat & Showers** (312 Canyon St., 406/646-7220).

Canyon Street, Grizzly RV Park, and Madison Hotel all have public showers.

West Yellowstone Family Medical Clinic (236 Yellowstone Ave., 406/646-0200) takes walk-in patients. It generally has a nurse practitioner or a doctor on duty, and it is open weekdays.

GETTING THERE AND AROUND
By Air
Yellowstone Airport (406/646-7631, www.yellowstoneairport.org) is two miles north of West Yellowstone off Highway 141. **Delta/Skywest** (406/646-7351 or 800/453-9417, www.delta.com) has daily flights from Salt Lake City, June–September. The rest of the year, the closest air service is in Bozeman, Idaho Falls, or Jackson Hole.

By Bus and Car
Karst Stage (406/556-3500 or 800/287-4759, www.karststage.com) provides daily shuttles between Bozeman airport and West Yellowstone ($64 one-way, $95 round-trip). Shuttles operate mid-December–mid-March. There are no scheduled shuttles in the summer, but Karst provides charters from Bozeman to West Yellowstone: $186 one-way for one person, dropping to $118 one-way per person for three travelers. For all Karst trips, be sure to make reservations at least three days ahead.

Salt Lake Express (208/656-8824 or 800/356-9796, www.saltlakeexpress.com) runs shuttle vans connecting West Yellowstone with Rexburg, Pocatello, Boise, Jackson, Salt Lake City, and Butte. The cost is $66 one-way to Salt Lake City.

West Yellowstone has some of the highest gas prices in the region; fill up before you get here! Rental cars are available at the airport from **Avis** (406/646-7635 or 800/831-2847, www.avis.com) and **Budget** (406/646-7882 or 800/527-0700, www.budget.com), or in town from **Big Sky Car Rentals** (415 Yellowstone Ave., 406/426-7669 or 800/426-7669, www.yellowstonevacations.com).

Yellowstone Roadrunner Taxi (406/640-0631, www.yellowstoneroadrunner.com) provides local transport, airport and trailhead shuttles, and bicycle drop-offs and pick-ups.

Park Tours
Buffalo Bus Touring Co. (429 Yellowstone, 406/646-9564 or 800/426-7669, www.yellowstonevacations.com) has summertime tours of Yellowstone, with daily lower park loop tours to Old Faithful, plus upper-and-lower loop tours on Mondays, Wednesdays, and Fridays. Rates are $65 adults and $49 kids for the lower loop, or $120 adults and $98 kids for tours that include both loops.

Yellowstone Tours & Travel (406/646-9310 or 800/221-1151, www.seeyellowstone.com) takes smaller groups (maximum 12) on van tours of the park for a bit more: $70 for the lower loop, $75 for an evening wildlife tour of the upper loop (including Lamar Valley), and $90 for a tour to Grand Teton and Jackson Hole.

Linda Wallace of **Yellowstone Country Adventures** (406/581-7476, www.yellowstonecountry-adventures.com) provides personalized tours, with more than 40 years' experience in the park. Also offering small-group van tours or private trips from West Yellowstone are **Yellowstone Alpen Guides** (406/646-9591 or 800/858-3502, www.yellowstoneguides.com), **Yellowstone Tour Guides** (406/646-1092 or 888/493-2260, www.yellowstonetourguides.com), **Lava Creek Adventures** (406/646-5145, www.lavacreekadventures.com), **Back Country Adventure** (406/646-9317 or 800/924-7669, www.backcountry-adventures.com), and **All Yellowstone Sports/Yellowstone Interpretive Van Tours** (406/646-9022 or 800/548-9551, www.allyellowstone.com).

Gardiner, Montana

The little tourist town of Gardiner, Montana (pop. 800) lies barely outside the northwest entrance to Yellowstone, just three miles from the Wyoming line. The Yellowstone River slices right through town. Park headquarters at Mammoth Hot Springs is just five miles away, and the large warehouses of park concessioner Xanterra Parks and Resorts dominate the vicinity. Gardiner is the only year-round entrance to Yellowstone, and the Absaroka-Beartooth Wilderness lies just north of here. The town sits at an elevation of 5,300 feet—about 900 feet lower than Mammoth—and has warm, dry summers and relatively mild winters.

SIGHTS
Roosevelt Arch

Gardiner was founded in 1880, and three years later the Northern Pacific Railroad extended a line to the edge of Yellowstone, making the town the first major entryway into the park. A reporter of that era described Gardiner as having "200 hardy souls, with 6 restaurants, 1 billiard hall, 2 dance halls, 4 houses of ill-fame, 1 milk man and 21 saloons." Today, the most distinctive structure in town is the monumental stone park entryway—similar to France's Arc de Triomphe—that was the primary entry point into Yellowstone for many years. Built in 1903, Roosevelt Arch was dedicated by President Theodore Roosevelt, a man regarded by many as Yellowstone's patron saint. A tablet above the keystone is inscribed, "For the Benefit and Enjoyment of the People." (The arch was actually built to offset the park visitors' initial disappointment at finding the rather ordinary country in this part of Yellowstone!) Just downhill from the arch is a small park with picnic tables.

Yellowstone Association

Headquarters for the Yellowstone Association (308 Park St., 406/848-2400, www.yellowstoneassociation.org, daily 8 A.M.–8 P.M. late May–early Sept., 8 A.M.–5 P.M. in winter) is in a lovingly restored historic structure near

Roosevelt Arch

© DON PITCHER

GATEWAYS TO YELLOWSTONE

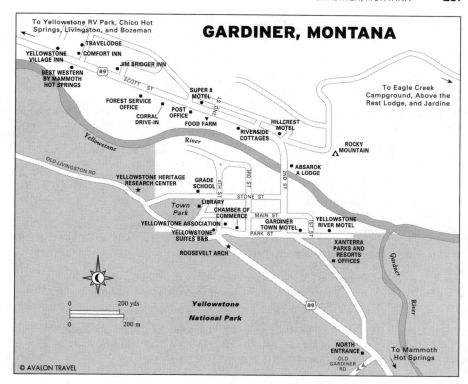

To Yellowstone RV Park, Chico Hot Springs, Livingston, and Bozeman

GARDINER, MONTANA

TRAVELODGE
YELLOWSTONE VILLAGE INN
COMFORT INN
JIM BRIDGER INN
BEST WESTERN BY MAMMOTH HOT SPRINGS
89
SCOTT ST
FOREST SERVICE OFFICE
CORRAL DRIVE-IN
POST OFFICE
SUPER 8 MOTEL
FOOD FARM
RIVERSIDE COTTAGES
HILLCREST MOTEL
2ND ST
To Eagle Creek Campground, Above the Rest Lodge, and Jardine
ROCKY MOUNTAIN
Yellowstone   River
OLD LIVINGSTON RD
ABSAROK A LODGE
YELLOWSTONE HERITAGE RESEARCH CENTER
GRADE SCHOOL
4TH ST
3RD ST
STONE ST
2ND ST
Town Park
LIBRARY
CHAMBER OF COMMERCE
MAIN ST
YELLOWSTONE ASSOCIATION
GARDINER TOWN MOTEL
1ST ST
YELLOWSTONE RIVER MOTEL
YELLOWSTONE SUITES B&B
PARK ST
ROOSEVELT ARCH
XANTERRA PARKS AND RESORTS OFFICES
Gardner
0   200 yds
0   200 m
Yellowstone
National Park
89
River
NORTH ENTRANCE
OLD GARDINER RD
To Mammoth Hot Springs
© AVALON TRAVEL

Roosevelt Arch. Constructed in 1903, the building operated as a general store until the 1950s. You can still see the words "We Sell Everything. WA Hall" on the brick facade. Inside are a few displays about Hall's Store, along with a large shop selling natural history books and maps. Stop by the information desk for details on Yellowstone Association classes and tours. The volunteer staff can also answer any questions you have about Yellowstone. Enjoy a picnic lunch on the side patio.

Yellowstone Heritage and Research Center

On the edge of town is the Park Service's massive 32,000-square-foot Yellowstone Heritage and Research Center (307/344-2664, www.nps.gov/yell/historyculture/collections.htm), home to archives, museum collections, and the park library. The 5.3 million (!) artifacts include Thomas Moran watercolors, rare books, early park souvenirs and postcards, more than 90,000 historic photos, and even wolf skulls. It's hard to miss the building, just below the Roosevelt Arch, as it's easily the largest structure in town. The lobby houses an exhibit about the park's early history, and the library (9 A.M.–4 P.M. Tues.–Fri.)is primarily for research purposes. Free one-hour tours (10 A.M. Tues. and Thurs.) are offered in the summer.

RECREATION

Kids will appreciate the **playground** behind the K-12 school in Gardiner; it's just downhill from the arch.

Get fishing gear at **Park's Fly Shop** (406/848-7314, www.parksflyshop.com).

During the winter, the store also rents cross-country skis.

For horseback rides and backcountry pack trips, contact **Rendezvous Outfitters** (406/848-7697 or 800/565-7110), **Hell's A-Roarin Outfitters** (406/848-7578, www.hellsaroarinoutfitters.com), and **Yellowstone Wilderness Outfitters** (406/223-3300, www.yellowstone.ws).

River Rafting

During summer, four rafting companies offer whitewater trips from Gardiner down the Yellowstone River, along with a variety of other adventures. **Yellowstone Raft Company** (406/848-7777 or 800/858-7781, www.yellowstoneraft.com) has been running trips since 1978. Other good companies are **Flying Pig Adventure Company** (406/848-7510 or 866/807-0744, www.flyingpigrafting.com), **Montana Whitewater** (406/763-4465 or 800/799-4465, www.montanawhitewater.com), and **Wild West Rafting** (406/848-2252 or 800/862-0557, www.wildwestrafting.com).

The rapids in this stretch of the Yellowstone River are relatively gentle, in the Class II–III range, and featured attractions are half-day eight-mile trips or all-day 17-mile trips. Expect to pay about $40 adults, $30 kids for three-hour trips, or $80 adults, $65 kids for a full-day voyage. Sit-on-top kayaks are a fun option, along with paddle-and-saddle trips ($90) that combine rafting with horseback rides. Wild West offers scenic float trips in Paradise Valley north of Gardiner, and Flying Pig has overnight trips ($200) that include a night of riverside camping, along with two-hour horseback rides for $50.

Mountain Biking

No local bike rentals, but if you brought your mountain bike, be sure to check out the **Old Gardiner Road.** This narrow dirt road gains 900 feet in elevation on the five-mile ride to Mammoth and makes for a speedy ride back down—not recommended for children. (Cars are allowed only in the downhill direction.) Also worth a ride is the old road to Livingston,

a gravel road that follows the west side of the Yellowstone River out of Gardiner. It starts near the arch and passes an interesting cemetery with century-old graves a few miles up.

ENTERTAINMENT AND EVENTS

The big annual event in town is the **Gardiner Rodeo,** which comes around the third weekend of June. It's part of the National Rodeo Association circuit, and includes bareback and saddle bronco riding, calf and team roping, bull riding, steer wrestling, breakaway roping, and barrel racing. A parade takes place the same day.

End summer with a Labor Day blast at the **Yellowstone Music Festival** (www.yellowstonemusicfest.com), offering plenty of live folk, bluegrass, rock, and roots music in Arch Park. In late September, return for the **Gardiner Brewfest,** an event that combines food with beers from regional breweries.

SHOPPING

Tumbleweed Bookstore and Café (501 Scott St., 406/848-2225) sells new and used titles and serves panini, wraps, sandwiches, espresso, salads, and smoothies. It has rental computers for Web surfing, too, but lacks Wi-Fi. You'll also find Western books and gifts—along with espresso—downtown on Park Street at **High Country Trading** (406/848-7707).

Yellowstone Gallery and Frameworks (406/848-7306, www.yellowstonegallery.com) is an excellent place for pottery, jewelry, paintings, and photography.

Open seasonally, **Flying Pig Camp Store** (406/848-7510 or 866/807-0744, www.flyingpigrafting.com) sells quality outdoor gear and guides river-rafting trips.

ACCOMMODATIONS

Gardiner has many places to stay, but be sure to make reservations in the summer; rooms may be hard to find even in mid-September. Rates plummet after (and before) the gold rush of seasonal tourists; $120 summertime rooms suddenly go for $60! For a complete listing of local lodging options, visit the Gardiner Chamber of Commerce website, www.gardinerchamber.com.

Under $100

Yellowstone River Motel (14 Park St., 406/848-7303 or 888/797-4837, www.yellowstonerivermotel.com, open May–Oct.) has a garden patio overlooking the river, plus microwaves, fridges, and Wi-Fi. Very well-maintained economy rooms in the older building are just $85 d, or $145 for up to six people in a three-bedroom family unit with full kitchen. Rooms (with fridges and microwaves) in the newer building are $105 d.

For economical lodging, **Westernaire Motel** (406/848-7397 or 888/273-0358, www.yellowstonemotel.com, $85–95 d) has attractive grounds and clean rooms but ancient furnishings. You're likely to see elk hanging out here most of the summer; guess they like the owner's plants better than the surrounding places. The motel has air-conditioning but no Wi-Fi. If you want something more upscale, try their sister property, Absaroka Lodge (310 Scott St. W., 406/848-7414 or 800/755-7414, www.yellowstonemotel.com).

Originally built in the 1950s but brought up to date with newer furnishings, **Hillcrest Cottages** (200 Scott St., 406/848-7353 or 800/970-7353, www.hillcrestcottages.com) has 17 cozy little units, all with functional kitchenettes and picnic tables. Most have tiny showers, but a few contain tubs. Rates are $80 d in the smaller units, $100 d or $115 for six in a two-room cottage, and $160 for a duplex unit that sleeps eight in two adjoining rooms. No phones, but the cottages have Wi-Fi and air conditioning. Open May–mid-October.

$100-150

Jim Bridger Motor Court (901 Scott St. W, 406/848-7371 or 888/858-7508) is a classic Western place with cute log cabins built in 1937 (but remodeled in 2010). Smaller cabins are $99 d or $127 for four, and two room units sleep up to six for $138. No phones or air-conditioning in the cabins, but they do have

fans and the larger rooms include small fridges. Open late May–mid-October.

On the north end of town next to the rodeo grounds, **Yellowstone Village Inn** (406/848-7417 or 800/228-8158, www.yellowstonevinn.com) features attractive rooms for $135–169 d and suites for $199–259 d; the larger suites sleep six ($10 extra per person for more than two guests). Amenities include a quiet location, an indoor pool, Wi-Fi, fridges, and a continental breakfast. Open mid-April–mid-October.

A newer motel close to the bridge, **Absaroka Lodge** (310 Scott St. W., 406/848-7414 or 800/755-7414, www.yellowstonemotel.com) has immaculate rooms for $110 d, and suites with kitchenettes (including range, microwave, fridge, dishes, pots, and pans) at $125 d, or $135 for four people. All rooms have balconies or decks with a great view of the Yellowstone River. The hotel is especially popular with families. Free Wi-Fi, too.

Totally remodeled in 2010, **Riverside Cottages** (406/848-7719 or 877/774-2836, www.riversidecottages.com) includes a mix of four-plex motel units ($120–130 d), cottages ($150–180 d) with full kitchens, and a family suite ($186 for up to six) with a jet tub and kitchen. All units include flat-screen TVs, granite counters, modern furnishings, and Wi-Fi. Guests appreciate the deck out back with a large hot tub overlooking the Yellowstone River and a staircase down to the river. Open year-round.

Over $150

On the north side of the river, **Best Western by Mammoth Hot Springs** (406/848-7311 or 800/828-9080, www.bestwestern.com/mammothhotsprings) has a fine indoor pool, two saunas, a hot tub, microwaves, fridges, and Wi-Fi. Rooms are $170–190 d, while large family suites with kitchens cost $250–280. Ask for a room on the first level with a balcony facing the river. Pets are welcome ($5 fee).

Out in the country four miles northwest of Gardiner, **Yellowstone Basin Inn** (406/848-7080 or 800/624-3364, www.yellowstonebasininn.com) is a charming contemporary lodge with a variety of accommodations. Standard rooms start at $180 d, and other options include one-bedroom and two-bedroom suites ($250–300), up to a three-bedroom cottage suite ($395) with space for five. Most units have private decks where you can sit on a rocking chair with a view of Electric Peak inside Yellowstone. An outdoor hot tub is available, along with Wi-Fi, and a light breakfast is served in the lobby. The inn is open mid-May–mid-October, with limited availability in the off-season. Well-behaved children are welcome.

It may be a chain hotel, but the four-story **Travelodge** (406/848-7520 or 800/578-7878, www.travelodge.com) gets rave reviews from many travelers. Clean rooms, an attentive management, filling hot breakfasts, comfy beds, in-room fridges, and Wi-Fi are all featured. Standard rooms with one or two queen beds are $149–159 d, but your best bet is a fourth-floor deluxe room facing the park ($179–199 d). (Note, however, that these rooms have one queen bed and a sofa bed rather than two standard queens.)

Bed-and-Breakfasts

Yellowstone Suites B&B (506 4th St., 406/848-7937 or 800/948-7937, www.yellowstonesuites.com, $112–158 d) is an attractive stone house built in 1904. Features include Victorian antique furnishings, hardwood floors, a veranda, full breakfasts, and Wi-Fi. The four guest rooms have shared or private baths; one contains a kitchenette. Kids are welcome, and it's open year-round.

A large house on three acres of land along the Yellowstone River, **(** **Headwaters of the Yellowstone B&B** (406/848-7073, www.headwatersbandb.com) is a mile north of the Gardiner airport. Inside are four guest rooms ($140 d), and nearby find two modern cabins with full kitchens ($165 for four and $195 for up to six); the riverview cabin fills quickly, so call ahead. All these units have private baths and Wi-Fi, and the rate includes a large homemade breakfast for guests in the rooms and suites (but not the cabins). Headwaters has a quiet location next to the park, with a fine view of Electric Peak from the deck and vintage Yellowstone souvenirs inside. Owners Tim and Charissa Reid are especially knowledgeable about the area; she's the author of an authoritative Yellowstone book, and both of them work for the Park Service. Kids are welcome.

Located in the heart of town, **(** **Gardiner Guest House B&B** (112 Main St., 406/848-9414, www.gardinerguesthouse.com) is a classic 1903 stone house—think grandma's place. Owners Nancy and Richard Parks have a sterling reputation as hosts. She's fluent in French and he owns the Parks Fly Shop, which offers summertime fly-fishing plus winter cross-country ski rentals. Two rooms in the main house ($90 d) share a bath, and a third ($125 d) has its own bath. Out back is a cozy little "Hobbit" cabin ($165 d) with a loft sleeping area and downstairs kitchen and living room. There's a TV in the parlor (but not in the rooms), along with Wi-Fi and a big hot breakfast. Kids are welcome.

Guesthouses and Rentals

Located two miles north of Gardiner on Jardine Road, **Above the Rest Lodge** (406/848-7747 or 800/406-7748, www.abovetherestlodge.com) has a cute cabin with loft, bath, kitchen, woodstove, and laundry ($135 d). Open May–September. (Adjacent cabins are used as housing for Yellowstone Association guests.)

A delightful country place, **North Yellowstone Cabins** (406/848-7651, www.northyellowstone.com, $120) has two modern log cabins two miles up Jardine Road that sleep up to six. No phones, but the cabins have private baths, small fridges, microwaves, TVs, and barbecue grills. Outside, weeping willow trees provide shade and gorgeous sagebrush country heads out in all directions. Open May–September. A two-bedroom vacation home ($225 for up to eight) is also available with a four-night minimum stay.

Five miles up Jardine Road from Gardiner, **Bear Lair Lodge** (406/223-7939, www.yellowstonevacationrental.net) is equally remote. The original lodge ($350) sleeps groups of eight comfortably, while a timber-frame 3,000-square-foot home ($395) contains four bedrooms, three baths, and a view into Yellowstone from the deck; it sleeps up to eight. A smaller one-bedroom cabin is also available ($175). All three places include full kitchens, woodstove, Wi-Fi, laundry, and comfortable beds.

Yellowstone Riverbend Cabin (406/586-0600, www.yellowstoneriverbendcabin.com) is a recently constructed cabin along the river with two bedrooms, a gas fireplace, flat-screen TV, porch, and kitchen. It sleeps up to eight for $185. Open May–mid-October with a three-night minimum.

Chico Hot Springs

Besides lodging in Gardiner, several places are available in Paradise Valley, 20 miles to the north. Farther away, but worth a visit if you're heading north, is Chico Hot Springs (406/333-4933 or 800/468-9232, www.chicohotsprings.com), 30 miles north of Gardiner in Pray, Montana. This classic old hotel sits adjacent to a hot springs–fed pool (open 8 A.M.–11 P.M., $6.50 adults, $4.50 kids, $2 seniors), and the restaurant is an attraction in its own right. Rooms in the main hotel start at $50 d for those with a bath down the hall ($89 d with private bath), while nicer ones in the Fisherman's Lodge or Lower Lodge run $115–125 d. A variety of suites, cabins, and houses are also available, all the way up to a five-bedroom log home (popular with wedding parties and family reunions) that sleeps 13 for $355 per night. There's a day spa on the premises, along with summertime horseback rides, fly-fishing, and whitewater rafting, plus wintertime dogsledding. The saloon swings to live bands on weekends year-round.

CAMPING

Yellowstone National Park's **Mammoth Campground** (open year-round, $14) is five miles up the hill at Mammoth Hot Springs. The campground sits close to a busy road and is often full, even in winter. No reservations are accepted.

Closer—and more peaceful—is the little **Eagle Creek Campground** (open year-round, $7), less than two miles northeast of Gardiner up the gravel road on the way to Jardine. This Gallatin National Forest campground (406/848-7375, www.fs.fed.us/r1/gallatin) is approximately 500 feet higher than Gardiner, and you will need to bring water from town or treat water from the creek here. Two other Forest Service campgrounds (mid-June–Oct., free) are a few miles up Jardine Road.

Park RVs at **Rocky Mountain Campground** (406/848-7251 or 877/534-6931, www.rockymountaincampground.com, mid-Apr.–Sept., $45–55 RVs, no tents), with Wi-Fi and a coin laundry. Simple cabins cost $45–80 d.

Campsites are also available in crowded, along-the-river sites at **Yellowstone RV Park** (406/848-7496, www.ventureswestinc.com, May–Oct., $42 RVs, $26 tents) on the northwest end of town. Laundry and Wi-Fi are available.

FOOD

For a town this small, Gardiner delivers a fine selection of dining options. **K-Bar & Café** (202 Main St., 406/848-9995, daily 11 A.M.–2 A.M.) doesn't look like much either outside or inside, but the from-scratch pizzas are very good in this locals' hangout; kids and families are welcome. Pizzas start at $9 for the mini version, up to $20 for a 16-inch combo.

Family-friendly **Outlaw's Pizza** (in the Outpost Mall on the northwest end of town, 406/848-7733, daily 11 A.M.–11 P.M. in summer, 4–9 P.M. Wed.–Sun. in winter) serves pizzas ($14 for a medium), pasta, and calzones.

The downtown **Sawtooth Deli** (220 W. Park St., 406/848-7600, 8 A.M.–4 P.M. Tues.–Sat. May–Sept., $6–8) serves breakfast burritos, huevos rancheros, and other morning fare, along with lunchtime subs, Reubens, cheesesteak subs, burgers, Polish dogs, and salads. Dine on the covered patio.

Corral Drive Inn (711 Scott St. W., 406/848-7627, daily 11 A.M.–11 P.M., late May–Sept., $7–14) serves the biggest, juiciest, and messiest (grab a handful of napkins) hamburgers anywhere around. Elk and buffalo burgers, chicken, fish and chips, grilled cheese sandwiches, and shrimp baskets fill out the menu.

A little hole-in-the-wall on the north side of the river, **The Silvertip Restaurant** (505 Scott St., 406/600-4730, www.the-silvertip. com, daily 11 A.M.–9 P.M. late May–mid-Sept., $6–9) loads your paper plate with big burritos, tacos, quesadillas, and nachos. The decor is funky and basic. Grab a beer and join the college kids and river guides at a picnic table out front.

With great food, friendly service, and a bright pine interior, **Ⓒ Rosie's** (204 West Park St., 406/848-9198, www.redsbluegoosesaloon.com, daily 7 A.M.–2 P.M. and 5:30–10 P.M. May–Oct.) is a favorite of locals and travelers. Meaty dinner specials ($14–28) such as buffalo meatloaf and rib-eye steak are popular, along with spicy shrimp linguini. Dinners come with a big house salad and fresh-baked bread. Breakfast items (about $8) include biscuits and gravy, French toast, and chicken-fried steak with eggs and hash browns. For lunch, try the turkey bacon avocado wrap. The same owner runs the adjacent **Red's Blue Goose Saloon** (406/848-7434), with a fantastic rooftop deck. Get a drink at the upstairs bar or order your food from Rosie's and have them bring it up in a to-go box. Picnic tables provide a view into Yellowstone, and the deck fills with young folks on sunny summer evenings.

The presentation is simple—picnic tables and paper plates—but meat-lovers should not miss **Ⓒ Raven Grill** (107 Hwy. 89 S, 406/848-7743, daily 5–10 P.M. late May–early Oct., $13–22). Owner/chef Philip Currie grills choice steaks, including buffalo sirloin, and also has Jamaican jerk chicken, jumbo shrimp (is that an oxymoron?), marinated garden vegetables, and other affordable meals. Entrées come with Cajun corn on the cob, baked beans, garlic bread, and fresh strawberries. Seating is within a screened porch or inside Two Bit Saloon (directly behind). This one's a real find!

The **Chico Dining Room** (in Pray, 406/333-4933 or 800/468-9232, www.chicohotsprings. com, 7–10:30 A.M. and 5:30–10 P.M.) serves $9 breakfast buffets ($16 on Sun.) along with fine dining in the evenings ($25–29). Dinner reservations are required.

Shop for groceries, fresh baked goods, and deli items at **Food Farm** (406/848-7524, 7 A.M.–9 P.M. Mon.–Sat., 8 A.M.–8 P.M. Sun.) across the river on the northwest end of town.

INFORMATION AND SERVICES

The **Gardiner Chamber of Commerce** (222 W. Park St., 406/848-7971, www.gardinerchamber.com, 9 A.M.–5 P.M. Mon.–Fri. and 9 A.M.–1 P.M. Sat., late May–early Sept., and 10 A.M.–5 P.M. Mon.–Thurs. the rest of the year) has local information.

Located adjacent to Arch Park, tiny **Gardiner Library** (406/848-7835, 10 A.M.–5 P.M. Tues. and 6–8 P.M. Thurs.) has a computer with Internet access and Wi-Fi.

For computer rentals and Wi-Fi, head to **Yellowstone Perk** (208 Park St., 406/848-2240), **Tumbleweed Bookstore and Café** (501 Scott St., 406/848-2225), **High Country Trading** (406/848-7707), or **The Silvertip** (505 Scott St., 406/600-4730, www.the-silvertip.com).

The **Gardiner District Office** of Gallatin National Forest (406/848-7375, www.fs.fed. us/r1/gallatin) has maps and information on the 930,584-acre **Absaroka-Beartooth Wilderness**. The area around Gardiner is lower in elevation and covered with forests, while farther east are the alpine peaks of the Beartooth Mountains.

The **post office** is on the north end of town (along U.S. Hwy. 89, 406/848-7579). Get fast cash at the ATM inside the Cenex station just north of the river, the Sinclair station in town, or from the First Interstate Bank on the northwest end of town. Wash clothes or take a shower at the **North Entrance Wash Tub** (209 Main St. W., 406/848-9870). The closest medical facility is in Mammoth Hot Springs.

GETTING THERE AND AROUND

Car rentals are not available in Gardiner. **Karst Stage** (406/388-2293 or 800/287-4759, www.karststage.com) has year-round shuttles between Bozeman airport and Gardiner for $84 one-way or $158 round-trip per person. There's a two-person minimum; make reservations at least three days ahead.

Late May–mid-September, **Xanterra Parks and Resorts** (307/344-7311 or 866/439-7375, www.yellowstonenationalparklodges.com) operates full-day bus tours of Yellowstone out of Gardiner. Rates are $70 adults, $35 ages 3–11, and free for younger kids; park entrance fees are extra. These tours are a bit grueling, because you leave at 7:30 A.M. and don't get back until 6:30 P.M.

Cooke City and Silver Gate, Montana

Shortly after you exit Yellowstone's northeast corner along U.S. Highway 212, the road widens slightly as it passes through two settlements: Silver Gate and the larger Cooke City, Montana. The towns are just three miles apart and almost within spitting distance of the Wyoming line. The area code—406—is larger than the combined population of both settlements! Although they depend on tourism, these quiet, homespun places lack the hustle and bustle of West Yellowstone and have a more authentic feel. No leash laws exist here, so you're likely to see dogs sleeping on the sidewalks or wandering lazily down the middle of the road. Most establishments are built of log, befitting the mining heritage of this area. Silver Gate even has a building code that requires all structures to be of log or rustic architecture—it's the only municipality in the country with such a code. Pilot Peak and Index Peak are the prominent rocky spires visible along the highway east of Cooke City. Dramatic Amphitheater Peak juts out just south of Silver Gate.

During winter, the road is plowed all the way from Gardiner, through the northern part of Yellowstone, and into Cooke City, making this a popular staging area for snowmobilers and skiers heading into the Beartooth Mountains. East of Cooke City, the Beartooth Highway across 10,947-foot Beartooth Pass is closed by the first of November (often earlier) and doesn't open again until late May.

HISTORY

The town of Cooke City was first called Shoo-Fly, but the name was changed in honor of Jay Cooke Jr., a promoter of the Northern Pacific Railroad. The promised railroad never materialized, but the name stuck. Cooke City had its start in 1882 when the boundaries of the Crow Reservation were shifted to the east, opening this area to mining. A small gold rush ensued, and by the following summer, Cooke City had grown to hold several hundred miners, along with two smelters, two sawmills, and a cluster of businesses. At its peak, the town was also home to 13 saloons. As with many 19th-century mining towns, the population of Cooke City had wild swings, with up to 1,000 people at one time but just 20 souls a few years later. The isolation, modest gold and silver strikes, and high transportation costs (no railroad was ever built into the settlement) kept mining from ever really booming. Today fewer than 100 people live in Cooke City year-round, but the population triples with the arrival of summer residents.

The town of Silver Gate has a briefer history. The land here was first homesteaded in the 1890s, but the town didn't appear until 1932 when John Taylor and J. J. White founded it as a haven for summer residents looking for a home close to Yellowstone. Only a handful of folks live here in the winter, but that swells to 100 or so when the long days of summer return.

The country around Silver Gate and Cooke City was torched in the Storm Creek Fire of 1988, leaving charred hills just a couple of hundred feet to the north and prompting alterations in the road signs to read "Cooked City." More than two decades later, the hillsides behind town are still barren. Today, tourism is the ticket to ride for both Cooke City and Silver Gate. In summer, the towns are crowded with folks en route to (or from) Yellowstone. Both Soda Butte Lodge and Miners Saloon in Cooke City have one-armed bandits with slot-machine poker and keno gambling, along with live poker. In the fall, hunters head into the surrounding mountains, and when the snow flies, the snowmobiles come out of hibernation.

Reminders of the mining era abound in the surrounding country, but not all of it is benign. Reclamation ponds catch toxic runoff from some of these old mines.

SIGHTS

It's hard to miss the red **Cooke City Store** (406/838-2234, www.cookecitystore.com, daily 8 A.M.–9 P.M. in July and Aug., till 6 P.M. May, June, and Sept.), one of the oldest buildings in the area. Built in 1886, this classic country market sells groceries, quality T-shirts, and gifts. It also carries Yellowstone and Wyoming fishing licenses. Open May–September only.

In Silver Gate, look for the seasonal **Sun Dog Trading** (406/838-2321), selling unique slumped bottles made in their own kiln.

The towns have a fun **Fireman's Picnic and Fourth of July fireworks.**

RECREATION

Yellowstone is less than four miles away, and it's the obvious site for recreation in the Cooke City–Silver Gate area during the summer. The **Absaroka-Beartooth Wilderness** is accessible from Cooke City and various points to the east along the gorgeous Beartooth Highway. One of the more unusual sights is **Grasshopper Glacier,** eight miles north of Cooke City and 4,000 feet higher. The glacier contained the remains of a swarm of locusts that was apparently caught in a snowstorm while flying over the mountains. Unfortunately, most have now melted out and decayed.

Summertime horseback rides, multi-day pack trips into the Absaroka-Beartooth Wilderness, and guided fly-fishing expeditions are provided by **Beartooth Plateau Outfitters** (406/445-2328 or 800/253-8545, www. beartoothoutfitters.com), **Castle Creek Outfitters** (406/838-2301), **K Bar Z Guest Ranch** (307/587-4410, www.agonline.com/kbarz), **Skyline Guest Ranch & Guide Service** (406/838-2380 or 877/238-8885, www.flyfishyellowstone.com), and **Stillwater Outfitters** (406/855-0016 or 888/341-2267, www.stillwateroutfitters.com).

Hiking, Skiing, and Snowshoeing

Visit **Silvertip Mountain Center** (406/838-2125 or 800/863-0807, www.silvertipmountaincenter.com) in Silver Gate for outdoor gear, climbing equipment, bear spray, maps, and other supplies. They rent skis and snowshoes in winter, along with all sorts of other gear (from tents to rock-climbing shoes) in summer. The owners also run Log Cabin Café (across the street), and can provide details on nearby hiking and snowshoe trails, plus vehicle drop-offs. Open daily in summer and on winter weekends.

Snowmobiling

Cooke City has become a hub for winter sports. Pick up a map of groomed cross-country ski trails and snowmobile routes from local businesses. The area consistently ranks among the top snowmobiling destinations in America. Snowmobile rentals (and summertime ATV rentals) are available from **Cooke City Exxon** (406/838-2244, www.cookecityexxon.com) and **Cooke City Motorsports** (406/838-2231, www.cookecitymotorsports.com). The local snowmobile club grooms approximately 60 miles of trails in the surrounding mountains. Be sure to also check the **Avalanche Advisory Hotline** (406/587-6981, www.mtavalanche.com) for the latest on backcountry conditions before heading out.

ACCOMMODATIONS

Cooke City and Silver Gate have quite a few old-fashioned motels and cabins that provide a delightful Old West feeling. As with other towns surrounding Yellowstone, reservations are always a good idea in midsummer or midwinter. Add a 10 percent lodging tax to all the rates.

Cooke City

You'll find spacious, clean, and comfortable rooms and cabins at **High Country Motel** (406/838-2272, www.cookecityhighcountry.com, $75–85 d). Some units contain kitchenettes, and Wi-Fi is available. Open year-round.

Alpine Motel (406/838-2262 or 888/838-1190, www.cookecityalpine.com) is also open all year and has rooms for $78–92 d, plus apartment-style units with two bedrooms and full kitchens for $115 d; add $10 per person for additional guests (max of five). Free Wi-Fi. **Hoosier's Motel** (406/838-2241, $120 d) has clean older rooms and is open mid-May–mid-October.

Three miles east of Cooke City, **Big Moose Resort** (406/838-2393, www.bigmooseresort.com) has four modern cabins, each with two queen beds, access to an outdoor hot tub, and Wi-Fi, but no phones. Rates are $95 for two of these, or $110 for units with kitchenettes. Open mid-May–October and January–March.

Right across the road, **Stillwater Outfitters Lodge** (406/838-2267 or 888/341-2267, www.stillwateroutfitters.com) is primarily a fishing, hiking, and hunting lodge but offers nightly accommodations throughout the year. Guests stay in six older but well-kept log cabins ($80 d), each with two double beds and private baths. Open May–September. Stillwater Outfitters leads all sorts of horse-based trips, including day rides and horse-packing into Yellowstone National Park.

Also on the east end of town, **Super 8 Motel** (406/838-2070 or 877/338-2070, www.cookecitysuper8.com, $100–125 d) is a modern and clean place where amenities include a light breakfast and Wi-Fi.

Friendly **Elk Horn Lodge** (406/838-2332, www.elkhornlodgemt.com) features attractive and spotless motel rooms ($89 d) with microwaves and fridges, plus two cabins ($109 d or $119 for four guests) with kitchenettes. Open year-round, with free Wi-Fi.

Antler's Lodge & Cabins (406/838-2432 or 866/738-2432, www.cookecityantlerslodge.com, $85–155 d) has 18 cabins in a variety of sizes and configurations, most with two queen beds and a kitchen. Some contain lofts, and Wi-Fi is available. Closed October–November.

Skyline Guest Ranch (406/838-2380 or 877/238-8885, www.flyfishyellowstone.com) has five spacious guest rooms in a three-story lodge, each with private bath, Wi-Fi, and access to a hot tub on the deck. Rates with a full breakfast are a reasonable $88 d or $110 for four guests. Open June–October and January–March. The ranch is popular for horseback rides, fly fishing, and backcountry adventures.

A few miles north of Cooke City and 1.5 miles up a Jeep/hiking trail, the Forest Service's **Round Lake Cabin** (518/885-3639 or 877/444-6777, www.recreation.gov, mid-July–mid-Sept. and mid-Dec.–Mar., $25, $9 reservation fee) sleeps four.

A number of vacation rentals are found in the Cooke City area. Located three miles east of town, **Montana Rocky Top Cabin** (863/465-2966, www.montanarockytopcabin.com) is an elegant log home with a bedroom and loft; it sleeps up to five for $225 nightly with a four-night minimum stay. Also well worth a look is **Yellowstone Cabin** (406/721-6986, www.vrbo.com/35554, $220 nightly with a three-night minimum).

Silver Gate

For a quiet step into the past, book one of the 26 cabins maintained by ◖ **Silver Gate Lodging** (406/838-2371, www.pineedgecabins.com), just a few minutes from the entrance to Yellowstone National Park. Many of these were built in the 1930s, but they've been updated with small private baths and Wi-Fi, though no TVs or phones. Most include kitchenettes with dishes and pans, and pets are welcome. The cabins vary widely, from rustic two-person units ($90) to an attractive six-person cabin ($198). The five motel units are $79 d. Outside, you'll find barbecue grills, volleyball,

© DON PITCHER

Silver Gate

and horseshoes. Some cabins remain open year-round. This is a quiet place where snowmobiles and four-wheelers are not allowed. Also on the premises is **Silver Gate General Store** (406/838-3043, May–Sept.) with supplies, a good selection of books, and Montana-made products. The store rents high-quality **spotting scopes** ($30 a day) and binoculars for folks heading into Yellowstone to watch wolves. Adjacent **Range Rider Lodge**—a classic log building from 1937—is open for weddings and other events.

Right on the river and close to the Yellowstone border in Silver Gate, **Grizzly Lodge** (406/838-2219, www.yellowstonelodges.com, $73–87) centers around a 1937 log building with a comfortable lounge and woodstove. Guests stay in a variety of rather basic motel-style rooms (some have kitchenettes or two bedrooms) with access to a sauna, and limited Wi-Fi. Open May–September.

Log Cabin Café (406/838-2367 or 800/863-0807, www.thelogcabincafe.com, $99 d, mid-May–mid-Sept.) rents two restored cabins

from the 1930s. A shower house is nearby, and guests are served a delicious free breakfast at the café.

All Seasons Cabin (406/838-2433, www.allseasonscabin.com, $245 for up to six people) is a very comfortable home with three bedrooms, a full kitchen, and glassed-in hot tub. A three-night minimum stay is required.

Lamar Valley Cabin (307/413-1990, www.lamarvalleycabin.com, $220–245) consists of two newly built cabins with room for six.

CAMPING

Heading east from Cooke City, you'll find four Forest Service campgrounds (open July–Sept., $8–9) within 10 miles of town. Closest is **Soda Butte Campground,** just 0.5 mile from town; another mile to the east is **Colter Campground** (406/848-7375, www.fs.fed.us/r1/gallatin). Showers are available from Soda Butte Lodge in Cooke City. In 2010, a grizzly bear killed one camper and injured two others at Soda Butte Campground during a nighttime attack. The bear was later captured and killed.

No RV parks are in the area, but **Big Moose Resort** (406/838-2393, www.bigmooseresort. com) has a few summertime RV sites with water, showers, and electric hookups.

FOOD

Inside Cooke City's Soda Butte Lodge, **Prospector Restaurant** (406/838-2251 or 800/527-6462, www.cookecity.com, daily 7 A.M.–10 P.M. in midsummer, $16–30) is well known for steak and prime rib cooked to perfection, but it's also open for breakfast and lunch. Also here is the **Ore House Saloon,** with sports on the TV and video poker and keno machines to take your money. Everything at Soda Butte Lodge is open year-round, and they pull out the poker tables in winter. (Note that all bars and restaurants in Montana are now entirely smoke-free.)

In the heart of Cooke City, the popular **Loving Cup Café** (406/838-2412, 8 A.M.–3 P.M. Mon.–Fri., 8 A.M.–4 P.M. Sat.–Sun., $5–7) cranks out espresso, and also serves fresh-baked goods, breakfast burritos, sandwiches, bagels, and ice cream. Wi-Fi is available. The big front deck has several tables for a sunny morning tea.

Cooke City's **Bistro Café** (406/838-2160, daily 7:30 A.M.–10 P.M. in midsummer, 8 A.M.–8 P.M. in winter, $15–28) serves American standards for breakfast and lunch, but dinner is when this bistro shines, with quality steaks, pork chops, and rack of lamb. Closed mid-October–December.

In business since 1979, **◖ Beartooth Café** in Cooke City (406/838-2475, www. beartoothcafe.com, daily 11 A.M.–10 P.M. mid-May–Sept.) is a perpetually busy place all summer. The lunch menu includes soups, salads, burgers, and sandwiches; try the half-pound funk burger with minced garlic and pepper-jack cheese. Dinners ($16–25) include hand-cut sirloin steaks, barbecue pork ribs, Angus prime rib, teriyaki chicken, and a popular rainbow trout, served with all the fixin's. Everything is freshly made on the premises. Beer connoisseurs can choose from 130 brews from all over the planet, including many from Montana and Wyoming. Eat out on the front patio for the full-on Beartooth experience.

Next door is **Buns 'N Beds Deli** (406/838-2030, www.home.earthlink.net/~bunsnbeds, daily 9 A.M.–7 P.M. in summer, 8 A.M.–5 P.M. in winter, $8–11), with hot or cold deli sandwiches, soups, and salads. The bread is baked fresh daily.

In peaceful Silver Gate, **Log Cabin Café** (406/838-2367, www.thelogcabincafe.com, daily 7 A.M.–10 P.M. mid-May–mid-Sept., $12–24) is a consistent favorite, serving locally famous rainbow trout, steak Oscar, and organic salads for dinner, along with big breakfasts and lunches featuring burgers, sandwiches, wraps, and homemade soups. The café has been here since 1937. Owners Laurie Hinck and Jay Schifferdecker are longtime residents with a deep knowledge of the area.

For tasty finger food in Cooke City, head to **Miner's Saloon** (406/838-2214, www.minerssaloon.com, daily noon–10 P.M. in summer, 4–10 P.M. in winter, bar till 2 A.M.). At this classic Old West bar the stools are filled with locals and tourists. Pull the handles on the keno and poker machines, or try a game of pool or foosball. The menu includes surprisingly good pizzas, steak sandwiches, fish tacos (highly recommended), and brisket sliders for $8–20.

Historic **Cooke City Store** (406/838-2234, www.cookecitystore.com) has a limited selection of groceries and supplies.

INFORMATION AND SERVICES

The **Cooke City, Colter Pass, and Silver Gate Chamber of Commerce** (406/838-2495, www. cookecitychamber.org, daily 10 A.M.–6 P.M. late May–mid-Sept., noon–5 P.M. Mon.–Fri. in winter) visitor center is housed within a newly built log building on the west end of Cooke City, and is staffed. Stop here for helpful info, gold-mining exhibits, and to use the only public restrooms in the area. Put away your **cell phone** in Cooke City and Silver Gate; there's no service here. If you're heading here from other areas, fill your tank, because gas prices here are some of the highest in the region. The Exxon station's website (www.cookecityexxon.com) has live webcams if you want to see what's happening in Cooke City right now.

Despite its remoteness, you'll discover several ATMs in Cooke City. Laundry facilities are inside Soda Butte Lodge, and **Cooke City Sinclair** (406/838-2000, www.cookecitysinclair.com) has Internet access.

Shoshone National Forest

Shoshone National Forest encompasses more than 2.4 million acres and extends along a 180-mile strip from the Montana border to the Wind River Mountains. Sagebrush dominates at the lowest elevations, but as you climb, lodgepole, Douglas fir, Engelmann spruce, and subalpine fir cover the slopes. Above 10,000 feet, the land opens into alpine vegetation and barren rocky peaks. The **Shoshone National Forest Supervisor's Office** (307/527-6241, www.fs.fed.us/r2/shoshone) is in Cody. Get information and forest maps there or from ranger stations in Cody, Dubois, and Lander.

History

Shoshone is America's oldest national forest. On March 30, 1891, President Benjamin Harrison signed a proclamation creating Yellowstone Park Timberland Reserve adjacent to Yellowstone National Park. At first this title meant very little, but in 1902 President Theodore Roosevelt appointed rancher and artist A. A. Anderson to control grazing and logging and catch poachers. His strong management almost got him lynched. Three years later under Gifford Pinchot, the forest reserves were transferred to the Department of Agriculture and renamed national forests. The land was renamed Shoshone National Forest in 1908.

Recreation

More than half of Shoshone National Forest lies inside wilderness boundaries; the Absaroka-Beartooth, North Absaroka, and Washakie wilderness areas cover much of the country

east of Yellowstone National Park, while the Wind River Mountains contain the Fitzpatrick and Popo Agie wildernesses. Part of the credit for the surprising expanse of wilderness areas in the national forest goes to Buffalo Bill. By bringing people into the area to hunt, fish, and explore, he helped create what one author called a "dude's forest." In addition, the Buffalo Bill Dam (which he vociferously supported) prevented logs from being sent down the North Fork of the Shoshone River and thus made logging less important.

More than 1,500 miles of trails offer hiking and horseback access to much of this country. Shoshone has more than 30 developed campgrounds for $10–15 per night. Once the water has been shut off for winter (generally Oct.–Apr.), you can camp for free but will have to haul out your own trash. Space is generally available even at the busiest times of year. In addition, free dispersed camping is possible at undeveloped sites throughout the forest, with the exception of heavily traveled U.S. Highway 14/16/20, where you must be 0.5 mile off the road.

Although uncommon, black bears roam throughout the forest, and grizzlies are found within the northern sections, including the North Absaroka and Washakie wilderness areas. Be sure to take the necessary bear precautions anywhere in the backcountry. Bears also sometimes wander into campgrounds along U.S. Highway 14/16/20 near Yellowstone National Park. You are much more likely to encounter mosquitoes, deer flies, and horse flies in midsummer, so be sure to bring insect repellent.

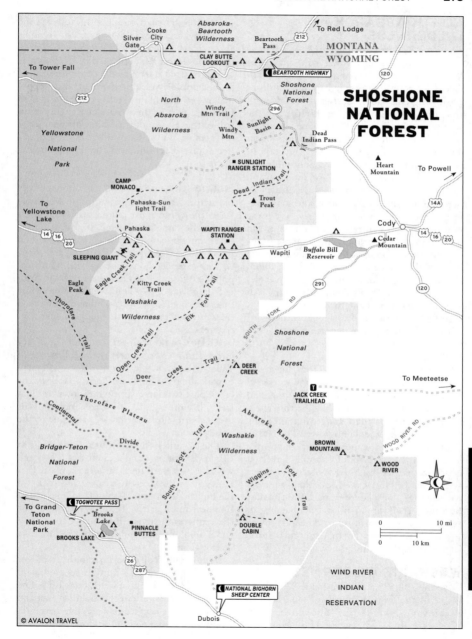

© AVALON TRAVEL

NORTH ABSAROKA WILDERNESS

The 350,488-acre North Absaroka Wilderness is one of the lesser-known wild places in Wyoming. It abuts Yellowstone National Park to the west and is bordered by the Sunlight Basin Highway and Beartooth Highway to the north and U.S. Highway 14/16/20 to the south. North Absaroka Wilderness is primarily used by hunters who arrive on horseback. The few hikers here tend to be quite experienced with backcountry travel and willing to tolerate the lack of trail signs and the steep and frequently washed-out paths. Much of the wilderness is relatively inaccessible, and snow may be present on passes until mid-July. Ask at the ranger stations for current trail conditions, and be sure to get topographic maps before heading out. Large populations of grizzly and black bears, bighorn sheep, moose, and elk are found in the Absaroka Mountains, and golden eagles are a common sight. The tough landscape is of volcanic origin, and the topsoil erodes easily, turning mountain creeks into churning rivers of mud after heavy summer rainstorms.

Hiking

The 1988 Clover-Mist Fire that began in Yellowstone burned through a large section of the North Absaroka Wilderness, but the land is recovering. Many hikers begin from trailheads near the Crandall Ranger Station along the Chief Joseph Scenic Highway. The **North Crandall Trail** is the most popular, a 16-mile hike up the North Fork of Crandall Creek. It is primarily used by horsepackers and offers great views of Hurricane Mesa along the way. Another popular wilderness path is **Pahaska-Sunlight Trail,** an 18-mile trek that begins at Pahaska Campground on U.S. Highway 14/16/20 and heads north through historic Camp Monaco to Sunlight Basin.

WASHAKIE WILDERNESS

Covering 704,529 acres, Washakie Wilderness is one of the largest chunks of wild land in Wyoming. Named for Shoshone chief Washakie, it lies between U.S. Highway 14/16/20 (the road connecting Yellowstone and Cody) and U.S. Highway 26/287 (Dubois area). To the west are Yellowstone National Park and Teton Wilderness. The Washakie is a land of deep narrow valleys, mountains of highly erodible volcanic material, and steppe-like buttes. The mountains—a few top 13,000 feet—are part of the Absaroka Range. About half of the land is forested. One of the unique features of Washakie Wilderness is a petrified forest, a reminder of the region's volcanic past.

Hiking

Numerous trails run through the Washakie Wilderness, but most require that you either return the same way or end at a location far from your starting point. Several trails stretch into Yellowstone National Park and are popular with extended horsepacking trips. The most popular Washakie Wilderness hikes are from U.S. Highway 14/16/20 in Wapiti Valley. Most folks use them for short day hikes or horseback rides rather than attempting longer backcountry treks.

Kitty Creek Trail leaves from the Kitty Creek summer home area, nine miles east of Yellowstone. Low-clearance vehicles will need to park along the highway. The trail follows the creek past two large scenic meadows to Flora Lake, 6.5 miles and 2,500 feet higher. This is the shortest hike in the area and one of the most popular.

The 21-mile-long **Elk Fork Trail** starts at Elk Fork Campground and crosses Elk Creek several times en route to remote Rampart Pass at nearly 11,000 feet. It is steep and rocky in the higher elevations. West of the Continental Divide you enter the Teton Wilderness. For the really ambitious, the Open Creek Trail and Thorofare Trail continue into Yellowstone National Park.

Deer Creek Trail departs from the free Deer Creek Campground, 42 miles southwest of Cody on Highway 291 (South Fork Rd.). The trail switchbacks very steeply uphill at first and after two miles reaches an attractive waterfall. Continue another eight miles from here to the

Continental Divide and the Thorofare section of the Teton Wilderness. This is probably the quickest route into this remote country and is popular with both horsepackers and hikers.

South Fork Trail takes off from the South Fork Guard Station across the creek from Deer Creek Campground. (Take a signed spur road to get there.) It climbs up along South Fork Creek to Shoshone Pass on the Continental Divide (9,858 feet). From here you can continue on several trails to the south, rambling over three more passes to eventually reach Double Cabin Campground, 27 miles north of Dubois. Another long hike into Washakie Wilderness leaves from this campground and follows the **Wiggins Fork Trail** up into a connecting series of paths: Absaroka, Nine Mile, East Fork, and Bug Creek Trails. It ends back at Double Cabin Campground. Total length is 60 miles. Along the way you're likely to see hundreds of elk in the high country as well as bighorn sheep.

SUNLIGHT BASIN

The **Chief Joseph Scenic Highway** (Hwy. 296) is a 46-mile route through a magnificent Wyoming landscape. Popularly known as Sunlight Basin Road, it is paved and most of it remains open year-round, providing access for backcountry skiers and snowmobilers to the beautiful Beartooth Pass area. (An eight-mile section between Cooke City, Montana and Pilot Creek, Wyoming is not plowed in the winter. It typically opens by early May.) Chief Joseph Highway begins 17 miles north of Cody off Highway 120, with Heart Mountain prominent to the southeast, and climbs sharply from the dry east side, passing a brilliant red butte en route to **Dead Indian Pass,** named for an incident during an 1878 fight between Bannocks and the U.S. Army. After the battle, Crow scouts found a wounded old Bannock warrior here. They killed and scalped him, burying the body under a pile of rocks. Other tales claim that the name came from the body of an Indian propped up as a ruse to trick the army during Chief Joseph's attempted escape to Canada in 1877. Chief Joseph *did* lead the

Nez Perce through this country, avoiding the cavalry by heading up Clarks Fork Canyon, a route the army had considered impassable. An overlook on top of Dead Indian Pass provides a panoramic vista of the rugged mountains and valleys below. The river forms a boundary between the volcanic Absarokas to the south and the granitic Beartooth Mountains to the north.

Indians weren't the only ones killed in this era. In 1870, two miners, Marvin Crandall and T. Dougherty, headed into the Upper Clarks Fork after reports of gold in the area. When they failed to meet up with other miners, a search party was sent out. The searchers were themselves attacked by Indians, but they later found the bodies of Crandall and Dougherty—scalped and decapitated, with their heads atop mining picks. In a macabre bit of humor, tin cups sat in front of each skull and the right hand of each man held a spoon. The men had apparently been killed while eating and the bodies were left as a warning against further white exploration of the area.

West of the overlook, the road switchbacks down hairpin turns into remote and beautiful Sunlight Basin. The name came about in the 1840s. Fur trappers worked this area for beaver and discovered a place flooded with light, but it was so remote that "the only thing that can get into this valley most of the year is sunlight." Today it is considerably more accessible but still just as beautiful. A gravel side road leads seven miles up the valley to **Sunlight Ranger Station,** built in 1936 by the Civilian Conservation Corps. It's open summers only. This is some of the finest elk winter range anywhere and the home of several scenic old guest ranches.

Back on the main road, a bridge—the highest in Wyoming, at 300 feet above Sunlight Creek—spans deep, cliff-walled **Sunlight Gorge.** Sorry, no bungee jumping allowed. The highway then continues northwest past Cathedral Cliffs and through a scenic ranching and timbering valley, offering views into the deep gorge that belongs to the Clarks Fork of the Yellowstone River. In some sections, sheer cliffs tower 1,200 feet above the water. Part of the area burned by the 1988 Clover-Mist Fire is visible near **Crandall Ranger Station.** This area also contains the only large herd of mountain goats in Wyoming. Eventually you reach the junction with U.S. Highway 212, the Beartooth Highway.

Camping and Hiking

The Forest Service's Lake Creek, Hunter Peak, and Dead Indian campgrounds (open mid-May–Sept., $10–15) are found along Chief Joseph Scenic Highway. Sites at **Hunter Peak Campground** can be reserved online (www.recreation.gov, $9 fee). **Dead Indian Trail** (just uphill from Dead Indian Campground) goes two miles to a fine overlook into Clarks Fork Canyon. Also of interest is **Windy Mountain Trail**, which climbs 10,262-foot Windy Mountain. It starts from a trailhead four miles east of the Crandall Ranger Station (interesting old log buildings here), is approximately seven miles one-way, and gains 3,700 feet in elevation. Windy Mountain can also be climbed from the other side near the Sunlight Ranger Station. Trailheads into the North Absaroka Wilderness are at the Crandall Ranger Station and beyond the **Little Sunlight Campground** (open year-round, free) on Forest Road 101.

River-Running

Clarks Fork of the Yellowstone River (named for William Clark, of the Lewis and Clark expedition) is Wyoming's only designated Wild and Scenic River. Experienced kayakers will find a couple of great stretches of Class IV–V whitewater in the upper Clarks Fork; however, use considerable caution because there are several big drops. Be sure to pull out before dangerous Box Canyon, which is considered unrunnable. Find more Class IV waters farther down the river. Check with the Forest Service for specifics. Below the rapids are quieter stretches.

Accommodations

In the heart of beautiful Sunlight Basin, **7D Ranch** (307/587-9885 or 888/587-9885, www.7dranch.com) is a family-oriented guest ranch offering horseback rides, cookouts, fly-fishing, hiking, pack trips, and something parents will really appreciate: child care for tots during riding periods, along with a special program for older kids. The setting is spectacular—it's where some of the Marlboro ads were shot—and the cabins are comfortable and cozy. Weekly all-inclusive rates are $3,220 for two people. The ranch has space for a maximum of 32 guests. Open early June–late September; adults only in September.

K Bar Z Guest Ranch (307/587-4410, www.agonline.com/kbarz) is off the Chief Joseph Scenic Highway in the Crandall Creek area. Nightly log-cabin accommodations are available for $95 d (lodging only), or two people can stay for six nights for $3,000, including meals, lodging, horseback rides, and Yellowstone sightseeing; extra charge for backcountry pack trips and guided fishing trips. The ranch is open May–mid-December and has room for a maximum of 30 guests.

Hunter Peak Ranch (4027 Crandall Rd., 307/587-3711, www.hunterpeakranch.com) is on the banks of the upper Clarks Fork River and offers lodging in rustic log cabins or motel-style rooms. Unlike most dude ranches, this one operates on an à la carte basis. Lodging starts at $135 d per night or $810 d per week, with extra charges for meals, horseback rides, and pack trips. The main lodge was built from hand-hewn logs in 1917. Open May–November.

Also in Sunlight Basin, **Elk Creek Ranch** (307/587-3902 in summer or 307/587-8828 in winter, www.elkcreekranch.com) provides a unique coed opportunity for teenagers to gain a wide range of ranching and wilderness skills. Ranch stays include lots of time on horseback (each kid has his or her own horse the entire time); guests also build cabins, cut hay, and learn other ranch work. The backpacking adventures give kids plenty of time in the backcountry, where they learn a range of outdoor and mountain-climbing skills. Two month-long sessions are offered each summer with a maximum of 30 kids at a time. The cost is $4,100 per person for all-inclusive four-week sessions.

Services

The minuscule settlement called **Crandall** is 21 miles southeast of Cooke City on Chief Joseph Highway and right along the Clarks Fork River. Here you'll find a convenience store, liquor, and gas, along with year-round campsites ($17–33 for RVs, $11 for tents) and lodging at **Painter Outpost** (307/527-5510, www.painteroutpost.com, $60). Its restaurant, named—appropriately enough—**Clark's Fork and Spoon** (daily 8 A.M.–7 P.M.), serves three home-style meals a day. Dine on the deck with a view overlooking the river. Showers are $6 if you aren't camping here.

SOUTH FORK AREA

South Fork Road heads southwest from Cody and follows the South Fork of the Shoshone River for 42 miles to the edge of the Washakie Wilderness. It's a beautiful drive through definitive Western country with tree-covered mountains and the rich valley below. During winter, the South Fork area has one of the largest collections of frozen waterfalls in the Lower 48, with more than 200 world-class multi-pitch climbs. Ice climbers are here all winter, and the **Water Fall Ice Festival** (www.southforkice.com) takes place each February.

Rustler's Roost Guest House (307/899-8171 or 800/667-6352, www.rustlersroost.homestead.com/guesthouse.html) is a small furnished house with a deck overlooking the South Fork, plus a full kitchen and a bath with jetted tub. It sleeps four for $150, with a two-night minimum stay.

BEARTOOTH MOUNTAINS

Spectacular Beartooth Highway (U.S. Hwy. 212) connects Cooke City and Yellowstone National Park with the historic mining town of **Red Lodge, Montana** (www.redlodge.com). Along the way, it passes through the Beartooth Mountains on a road built by the Civilian Conservation Corps in the 1930s. Some have called this the most scenic route

© DON PITCHER

Shoshone River near Cody

in America. If you like alpine country, towering rocky spires, and a landscape dotted with small lakes and scraggly trees, you're going to love this drive. A small corner (23,750 acres out of a total of 945,334) of the **Absaroka-Beartooth Wilderness** lies in Wyoming just north of the highway—the rest is right across the Montana border.

C Beartooth Highway

Designated both as a National Scenic Byway and as All-American Road, the Beartooth Highway sails across a high plateau and then over the twin summits of **Beartooth Pass.** The east summit is 10,936 feet, and a short distance farther is the west summit at 10,947 feet. A scenic overlook at the west summit provides views of the Absarokas to the south and west, the Beartooths to the north, and Bighorn Basin to the east. Majestic rock faces rise in all directions, the most obvious being Beartooth Mountain (its sharp point resembles the tooth of a bear), Pilot Peak, and Index Peak. This is the highest highway pass in Wyoming and one of the highest in North America. A major reconstruction of the highway won't be completed until 2015. Call 888/285-4636 for details on construction delays, or visit www.wfl.fhwa.dot.gov/projects/beartooth.

As the road enters Montana, it passes Beartooth Mountain and begins a rapid elevator ride down folded ribbon curves into the resort town of Red Lodge. On top, keep your eyes open for moose, mule deer, mountain goats, bighorn sheep, marmots, and pikas. Be ready for strange weather at this elevation, including snow at any time of year. The highway is closed with the first heavy snowfall (generally in September) and doesn't open until May. The flowers don't really get going until mid-July.

Red Lodge International Ski and Snowboard Camp (www.facebook.com), near the Wyoming-Montana border, provides Olympic ski training for teens in June and July. South of the summit is the Top of the World Store, and another mile or so farther south is the turnoff to an old fire lookout tower at **Clay Butte,** where you'll discover horizon-to-horizon views of the surrounding countryside. A narrow gravel road climbs three miles to the tower, perched at an elevation of 9,811 feet. The small visitor center here is staffed July–mid-September.

Hiking

The open country at this elevation is dotted with whitebark pines and Engelmann spruce, and it delivers marvelous cross-country hiking opportunities. Anglers should bring a fishing pole to take a few casts for the brook, cutthroat, and rainbow trout in the alpine lakes. Two major trail systems are found in the High Lakes area.

The **Beartooth High Lakes Trail**—actually a series of trails—connects Island Lake, Beartooth Lake, Beauty Lake, and many smaller alpine ponds and puddles. A good place to start is from the boat ramp at Island Lake; see topographic maps for specific routes. This is a very popular late-summer area for day hiking or for access to the Absaroka-Beartooth Wilderness. Be sure to bring a compass, topo map, and warm clothes before heading out on a day hike; the weather can close in very quickly at this elevation, and afternoon thunderstorms are frequent. Always be aware of lightning activity when hiking in this exposed country.

Beartooth Loop National Recreation Trail is just two miles east of Beartooth Pass. This 15-mile loop traverses alpine tundra and passes several lakes and a century-old log stockade of unknown origins.

Camping and Services

There are four developed campgrounds (open July–Sept., $15) along this stretch of U.S. Highway 212, and more once you drop into Montana. **Beartooth Lake** and **Island Lake** campgrounds border alpine lakes. In addition, dispersed camping is allowed for free once you get off the main roads. Grizzlies inhabit this country, so be sure to store your food safely.

A popular stopping point for cyclists and other travelers crossing the pass, **Top of the World Store** (307/587-5368, www.topoftheworldresort.com) sits along the highway between the two Forest Service campgrounds. The general store has a limited selection of food, gifts, camping supplies, gas pumps, and canoe rentals. Three rustic motel rooms ($55 d, add $15 for additional guests) and a handful of RV spaces ($24 with water and sewer) are also available. The store and motel are open daily mid-May–mid-October.

Wapiti Valley

Wapiti Valley provides one of the most popular and scenic routes into or out of Yellowstone National Park, connecting Cody with the park's East Entrance. President Theodore Roosevelt came here often and called it "the most scenic 50 miles in the U.S." The valley is bisected by the North Fork of the Shoshone River, which U.S. Highway 14/16/20 parallels for the entire 50 miles from Yellowstone to Cody. Heading east out of Yellowstone, the highway drops through high forests and past an array of volcanic pinnacles and cliffs as the country becomes drier and more open. Cottonwoods line the gradually widening river,

© DON PITCHER

Holy City Rocks, North Fork of the Shohone River

and Douglas firs intermix with sage, grass, and rock at lower elevations. Trailheads provide access to two backcountry areas that border the highway: North Absaroka Wilderness and Washakie Wilderness. The road is in excellent condition the entire distance from Cody to Yellowstone.

Wapiti Valley is dotted with lodges, dude ranches, and resorts, many of which offer family-style meals, barbecue cookouts, horseback rides, pack trips, fishing, hiking, river rafting, and other outdoor recreation. If you aren't staying on an all-inclusive plan, most of these perks will cost extra, and some—such as meals or horseback rides—are often available to both guests and the general public. The lodges generally do not have TVs or phones in the rooms. Most will provide transportation from Cody on request. Get additional lodge information from the **Wapiti Valley Association** (307/587-9595, www.yellowstone-lodging.com).

On the western end of the valley are Shoshone National Forest campgrounds and hiking trails. The fishing is great in the river and at Buffalo Bill Reservoir on the eastern end of Wapiti Valley.

SIGHTS

Heading east from the Yellowstone National Park's East Entrance, U.S. 14/16/20 drops in elevation, passing Pahaska Teepee and Sleeping Giant Ski Area, before descending toward Wapiti Valley. Along the way, the road passes a whole series of delightfully weird volcanic rock formations. Signs point out several of the most obvious.

Warning: The wide, smooth highway through the upper Wapiti Valley has a 50-mph speed limit, and it's tempting to speed. State

GATEWAYS TO YELLOWSTONE

troopers are waiting for you. The speed limit rises to 65 mph once you reach the western end of the valley.

Stop at the **Firefighters' Memorial,** which honors 15 firefighters who were killed nearby in the Blackwater Fire of 1937. The picnic area here has a special pond for anglers with disabilities.

Eight miles farther east is the historic **Wapiti Ranger Station.** Built in 1903, it was the nation's first Forest Service ranger station. Just a few hundred feet away and right along the highway is **Wapiti Wayside Visitor Center** (10 A.M.–4 P.M. Fri.–Sun. late May–early Sept.). Pull in for details on local camping and recreation opportunities, and to watch the informative video on safety in bear country. A few miles to the west (not marked) is **Mummy Cave,** where a 1,300-year-old mummified body was discovered in 1957. The site contains 38 different levels of Indian occupation covering 9,000 years.

Next up is a parking area at **Holy City,** an impressive group of dark red volcanic rocks with the North Fork of the Shoshone River cutting away at their base. Try to pick out Anvil Rock, Goose Rock, and Slipper Rock here. The highway leaves Shoshone National Forest and then passes the scattered settlement called **Wapiti**—an Indian word meaning "elk"—20 miles east of Cody. As you might guess, a large elk herd winters in this valley. An unusual volcanic rock ridge near here is locally called the Great Wall of China; scan the slopes for bighorn sheep. The eastern half of the road between Cody and Yellowstone passes through this broad and fertile valley; it's quite a change from the rock-lined route to the west. On the east end, the road borders Buffalo Bill Reservoir before plunging through three tunnels on the descent into Cody.

Pahaska Tepee

Less than three miles from Yellowstone's East Entrance (48 miles west of Cody), Pahaska Tepee (307/527-7701 or 800/628-7791, www.pahaska.com) was built in 1904 to house Buffalo Bill's guests and others on their way to the park. Pahaska (pa-HAZ-ka) was Buffalo Bill's nickname, a Crow Indian word meaning "Long Hair."

The original Pahaska Tepee is a two-story log building that contains a few of Buffalo Bill's original items, including an old buffalo skull over the stone fireplace and several flags that were given to him. Although it is no longer used and is in need of major repairs, the remarkable main lodge is open for fascinating tours (donation requested) on most summer days. The bar inside Pahaska Tepee is small but contains a stunning Thomas Molesworth chandelier crafted in 1938; it's said to be worth $1 million. Look around for other furnishings from Molesworth along with a beautiful stained-glass window.

On one of Buffalo Bill's many hunting treks with European royalty, he led the Prince of Monaco into the North Fork country. **Camp Monaco,** 15 miles up the Pahaska-Sunlight Trail from Pahaska Tepee, was named in his honor. Unfortunately, the old spruce tree inscribed with the words "Camp Monaco" was killed when the Clover-Mist Fire burned through here in 1988.

Pahaska Tepee Resort has a mix of old and newer cabins, along with A-frame motel rooms and duplexes. Summer rates start at $119 d in a little housekeeping cabin up to $575 for a two-bedroom condo (two-night minimum for this one). Also here are a full-service restaurant, gift shop, gas pumps, and limited supplies. Pahaska is open early May–mid-October, but a few cabins are available in the winter. The highway is not plowed beyond Pahaska.

RECREATION

Just four miles from Yellowstone's East Gate and 46 miles from Cody, **Sleeping Giant Ski Area** (307/527-3182, www.skisg.com, late Nov.–early Apr.) has one double chair, a triple chair, and a kiddie magic carpet, along with a terrain park for snowboarders, snowmaking capabilities, ski and snowboard rentals, and a 1,000-foot vertical drop. Rates are $29 adults ($24 half-day), $24 for youth ages 13–17 and seniors, $12 for kids ages 6–12, and free for

© DON PITCHER

horse and mule, Wapiti Valley

younger children. The Grizzly Grill serves meals and beer and has a big TV for sports fans. Bus transportation is available from Cody ($4 round-trip).

Not far away are more than 25 kilometers of groomed trails maintained by the **Park County Nordic Ski Association** (307/587-6281, www.nordicskiclub.com) for both classical and skate skiing. There's no charge (but donations are welcome), and the grooming is generally completed in time for the weekend rush of skiers. Trails cover a widely varied terrain along the river and right to the edge of Yellowstone National Park. Access is from Pahaska Tepee or Sleeping Giant.

ACCOMMODATIONS
Upper North Fork Ranches

More than a dozen lodges, motels, and guest ranches line the road between Yellowstone and Cody. Lodging places west of the midpoint between Cody and Yellowstone are in the more secluded and wooded canyon country of the upper North Fork of the Shoshone River.

These places are listed as follows, arranged by their distance from downtown Cody on U.S. Highway 14/16/20, starting with those nearest the East Entrance to Yellowstone. Places east of the midpoint between Cody and Yellowstone are situated in the broad and beautiful Wapiti Valley and are typically visible from the highway. Pahaska Tepee (above) is the closest lodge to Yellowstone.

A classic mountain lodge, **Shoshone Lodge** (46 miles west of Cody, four miles east of Yellowstone, 307/587-4044, www.shoshonelodge.com) has rustic log cabins and home-cooked meals ($11–20) served in the main lodge. Cabins have been updated with Western furnishings, and range in size from 1–3 rooms; some contain kitchens. Nightly lodging rates start at $130 d, although the nicest cabins are considerably more expensive (up to $300 for a three-bedroom cabin that sleeps seven). Horseback rides are available, and Shoshone Lodge is open May–mid-October. The restaurant is open to the public nightly in the summer.

GATEWAYS TO YELLOWSTONE

Established in 1898, **Crossed Sabres Ranch** (307/587-3750 or 888/587-3750, www.crossedsabresranch.com), 42 miles west of Cody or eight miles east of Yellowstone, operates as a B&B, with lodging and a big hot breakfast buffet for $145 d nightly. The ranch has a beautiful main lodge, plus space for 50 guests in modern two-bedroom cabins with log furniture and Western decor. Horseback rides and guided fly-fishing are available for an additional fee. Dinners are available ($15–18), and the restaurant opens to the general public in the evening. Open late May–mid-September.

Forty miles west of Cody or 10 miles east of Yellowstone, **Elephant Head Lodge** (307/587-3980, www.elephantheadlodge.com) is a no-frills dude ranch with a gracious main lodge built in 1910. Guests stay in 15 modernized cabins, all with private baths and most with decks. Because of its proximity to the park, Elephant Head makes a good base for exploring Yellowstone. Peak-season lodging-only rates start at $153 d per day, and the largest cabin—it's actually more like a luxury apartment—sleeps eight people comfortably and has a full kitchen for $320. Elephant Head's restaurant is open for breakfast and dinner ($12–31) with locally famous steaks, pork chops, and other carnivorous fare. It's a frequent destination for Cody folks looking for an evening out. Horseback rides are also available for both guests and the general public. The ranch is open mid-May–October.

Find old-time hospitality and adventure at **Absaroka Mountain Lodge** (307/587-3963 in summer, 406/932-6895 in winter, www.absarokamtlodge.com), 38 miles west of Cody or 12 miles east of Yellowstone. Guests stay in comfortable log cabins with private baths and dine in the historic main lodge, built in 1910. Nightly rates start at $129 for a cabin with one king bed, up to $209 for a two-bedroom cabin that sleeps eight. Open mid-May–September. Folks who aren't staying here can join the trail rides of all types, including four-hour lunch cookout rides ($89). The restaurant is open for breakfast and dinner daily (7–9 A.M.

and 6–8 P.M., $7–23), serving everything from burgers to rib-eye steaks. All-you-can-eat Wednesday-night outdoor barbecues ($18) and Saturday-evening Dutch oven beef stew ($12) are favorites.

Thirty-five miles west of Cody (15 miles east of Yellowstone), **Blackwater Creek Ranch** (307/587-5201, www.blackwatercreekranch.com) is a fine place to relax amid the natural beauty of the area. Featured attractions include horseback rides, trout fishing, hiking, games, barbecues, and plenty of kids' activities. The gracious log cabins contain fireplaces, and meals are served in the modern Old West–style lodge. Also here are an outdoor pool, a large hot tub, and a game room with pool and Ping-Pong tables. All-inclusive one-week stays cost $2,900 for two people, and the ranch is open May–September.

Halfway between Cody and Yellowstone—25 miles in either direction—**Bill Cody Ranch** (307/587-2097 or 800/615-2934, www.bill-codyranch.com) has attractive log cabins, a comfortable lodge, horseback rides, creekside cookouts, a playground, and trout fishing. All-inclusive stays (lodging, meals, and horseback riding) are $350 for two people per night; lodging-only rates range widely depending upon the cabin and the number of guests, starting at $125 d. Looking for additional room and privacy? The ranch also rents out two comfortable fully furnished homes with space for eight guests at $430 per day, with a three-night minimum stay. Horseback rides, meals (breakfast and dinner daily, $7–23), and chuck-wagon barbecue cookouts ($6–19) on Wednesday and Saturday nights are also available for those not staying at Bill Cody Ranch. The guest ranch is open mid-May–September.

Similarly positioned halfway between Cody and Yellowstone, **Rimrock Dude Ranch** (307/587-3970, www.rimrockranch.com) is a classic Western ranch with creekside log cabins, horseback riding, a heated swimming pool and hot tub, river rafting, hearty family-style meals, and grand mountain country. Weekly all-inclusive stays are $3,300 for two people. Open May–mid-September.

Lower Wapiti Valley

The places listed below are east of the midpoint between Yellowstone and Cody, in the broad and open part of Wapiti Valley.

Green Creek Inn and RV Park (307/587-5004 or 877/587-5004, www.greencreekinn. com), 22 miles west of Cody or 28 miles east of Yellowstone, has roadside motel rooms with rustic log furniture for $94 d, Wi-Fi included. Also available is a six-person log cabin with bunk beds for $152. The setting is pretty, and children will appreciate the playground and horseshoe pit. RV sites (no tents) are $40, but they lack showers or a restroom. Open April–September.

In the heart of Wapiti Valley 20 miles west of Cody or 30 miles east of Yellowstone, **Rand Creek Ranch** (307/587-3200 or 877/587-3201, www.randcreekranch.com) has seven refurbished cabins available on a nightly basis. Two-person cabins are $149, four-person units cost $175, and one cabin sleeps six for $250. Guests get a continental breakfast basket and access to the stocked fishing pond. Horseback rides ($35 for one hour), lunches ($9), and twice-weekly dinner barbecues ($22) are available for guests and the general public. Open mid-May–mid-October.

At **Yellowstone Valley Inn** (307/587-3961 or 877/587-3961, www.yellowstonevalleyinn. com), 18 miles west of Cody or 32 miles east of Yellowstone, small cabins and hotel rooms are $99–129 d, tent spaces are $22, and RV sites with full hookups run $35. Guests add $5 for a big breakfast buffet. The attractive inn—often filled with RVs—sits right on the North Fork Shoshone River and has an outdoor heated pool (the only heated pool in Wapiti Valley), indoor hot tub, restaurant, laundry, and lounge. Open mid-May–September. The restaurant is open daily for breakfast and dinner (7–10 A.M. and 5–10 P.M., $8–27) and specializes in steak, burgers, pasta, and seafood (including crab).

Red Pole Ranch (307/587-5929 or 800/587-5929, www.redpoleranch.com), 11 miles west of Cody or 39 miles east of Yellowstone, has eight pleasant log cabins starting for $89–99 d, up to $125 for units that sleep five and include a full kitchen.

CAMPING

Nine different Shoshone National Forest campgrounds provide rustic accommodations along the North Fork of the Shoshone River. Most of these are open mid-May–September (some remain open through Oct.) and cost $10–20 per site; no reservations are taken. All sites have picnic tables, fire rings, potable water, and outhouses. The **Wapiti Campground** has tent sites ($15) and RV sites with electricity ($20). In areas where bears are a problem, the campgrounds also contain bear-proof food-storage boxes. All of these Forest Service campgrounds are on the west half of the 50-mile stretch of highway between Cody and Yellowstone. Of these, **Big Game Campground** is closest to Cody at 25 miles to the west, and **Three Mile Campground** is closest to the park, just three miles from Yellowstone's East Gate. Three of these campsites can be reserved (518/885-3639 or 877/444-6777, www.recreation.gov, $9 fee).

Get details on public campgrounds from the Forest Service's seasonal Wapiti Wayside Visitor Center (10 A.M.–4 P.M. Fri.–Sun. late May–early Sept.). Dispersed camping outside designated campsites is not allowed anywhere between Cody and Yellowstone along U.S. Highway 14/16/20.

Two campgrounds are within Buffalo Bill State Park. There are also two Wapiti Valley lodges that have RV campgrounds: **Green Creek Inn and RV Park** (307/587-5004 or 877/587-5004, www.greencreekinn.com, Apr.–Sept., $40) and **Yellowstone Valley Inn** (307/587-3961 or 877/587-3961, www.yellowstonevalleyinn.com, $22–35).

Cody

The city of Cody (pop. 9,000, elev. 5,095 ft) marks the transition point between the forested mountains of northwest Wyoming and the sage-covered plains of Bighorn Basin. It's a favorite stopping place for Yellowstone tourists. The park is just 50 miles due west of town, and other magnificent country spreads in all directions—the Beartooth Mountains and Sunlight Basin to the north, the Absaroka Range and Wapiti Valley to the west and south. Established as an agricultural and tourism center, Cody retains both roles today, although

tourism gains in importance with each passing year.

Cody has several attractions, including the justly famous Buffalo Bill Historical Center, along with Trail Town and other local sights. The Shoshone River flows right through town, providing the opportunity for scenic float trips. Lots of events crowd the summer calendar, from nightly rodeos and shoot-outs to parades and powwows; biggest of all is the annual Cody Stampede in July. The town also takes pride in a long list of artists that includes Charles Cary

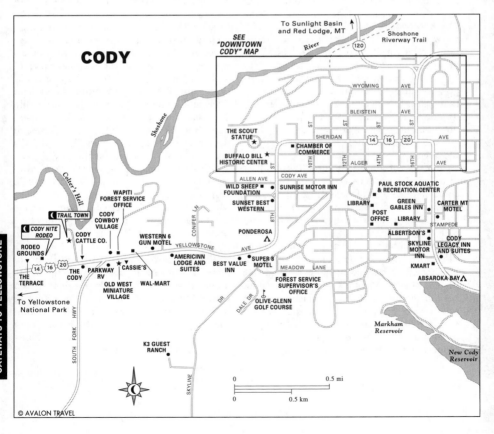

Rumsey and Harry Jackson. Famed abstract expressionist Jackson Pollock was born here but achieved his reputation in New York and never returned to his birthplace.

HISTORY

Just west of Cody—past the Walmart, RV parks, fireworks stands, and gas stations—are the Absaroka Mountains, named for the Native Americans who first lived here. They called themselves the Absaroka, or "Children of the Large Beaked Bird." Whites interpreted this as "crow," and the natives have been called Crow Indians ever since. Explorer John Colter passed through this region in 1808 while

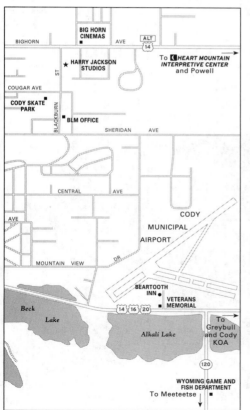

recruiting Indians to supply beaver furs. When Colter returned to the semblance of civilization called Fort Manuel Lisa, everyone laughed at his tales of a spectacular geothermal area along the "Stinkingwater River." Soon everyone was calling it "Colter's Hell." But the geysers were real, and they still steam along the Shoshone (formerly the Stinkingwater) just west of present-day Cody. Other mountain men came later, followed by miners who found copper and sulfur in Sunlight Basin. The first real settler in the area was a Prussian, Otto Franc, who developed a large cattle spread at the famous Pitchfork Ranch. (Franc is said to have helped finance the Wyoming Stock Growers during the infamous Johnson County War. He was later murdered, and some blamed men affiliated with the homesteaders.)

Because of desertlike conditions, Bighorn Basin was one of the last parts of Wyoming to be settled, and most of the towns did not spring up until the 1890s, when passage of the Carey Act brought a flood of irrigation speculators, investors, and farmers. In 1895, William F. "Buffalo Bill" Cody and two partners began plans for the Shoshone Land and Irrigation Company, with headquarters along the Shoshone River just west of the present city of Cody. Cody had spent much time in the Bighorn Basin, guiding parties of wealthy sportsmen, and was convinced that a combination of tourism and irrigated farming could transform this desert land. The name Cody was a natural choice for this new settlement, officially founded in 1896. At the urging of Buffalo Bill, the Chicago, Burlington, and Quincy Railroad arrived in 1901, bringing in thousands of tourists who continued west up Shoshone Canyon to Yellowstone by stagecoach. Between 1904 and 1909, construction of massive Buffalo Bill Dam employed hundreds of workers, and the reservoir later provided water to irrigate farmland in Bighorn Basin. Oil was first discovered near Cody in 1904, and Park County remains an important oil producer. Other local businesses include a wallboard manufacturing plant and a pharmaceutical manufacturer. One of the biggest employers (after the hospital, the school district, and Walmart) makes—I kid you not—insecticidal ear tags for livestock. Tourism remains a cornerstone of Cody's economy, fueled both by its status as an entry point into the park, and also because of the world-famous Buffalo Bill Historical Center. Interestingly, the town is also attracting quite a few retirees who appreciate the mild weather and abundant recreational opportunities.

◖ BUFFALO BILL HISTORICAL CENTER

Each year, more than 220,000 people visit Cody's main attraction, the Buffalo Bill Historical Center (BBHC). The center actually houses five separate museums covering Buffalo Bill, the Plains Indians, Western art, firearms, and natural history, plus a research library, the boyhood home of Buffalo Bill, and two sculpture gardens. This is the largest and most impressive museum in Wyoming and the finest Western museum in the world. Nowhere else in America is such a major museum situated in a town with so few people. The late author James Michener once labeled the BBHC "the Smithsonian of the

DOWNTOWN CODY

Buffalo Bill Historical Center

© DON PITCHER

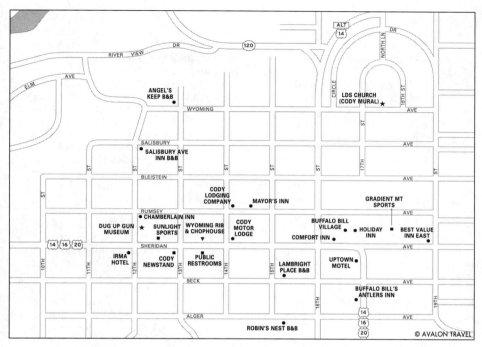

© AVALON TRAVEL

West," and his term is even truer today with the addition of a natural-history wing a few years back. The museum's collection focuses—not surprisingly—on the Western frontier and includes thousands of artifacts and works of art, culture, and natural history spread throughout more than 300,000 square feet of space.

The original Buffalo Bill Museum opened in 1927 in what is now the chamber of commerce log cabin. Opening in 1959, the Whitney Gallery of Western Art formed a nucleus for the current museum location; later additions included the Buffalo Bill Museum, the Plains Indian Museum, the Cody Firearms Museum, and the Draper Museum of Natural History.

Buffalo Bill Historical Center (307/587-4771, www.bbhc.org) is open year-round. It's open daily in the busy summer season (8 A.M.–6 P.M. May–mid-Sept.). At other times, hours are reduced: daily 8 A.M.–5 P.M. mid-September–October; daily 10 A.M.–5 P.M. November; 10 A.M.–5 P.M. Thursday–Sunday, December–February; and daily 10 A.M.–5 P.M. March–April Closed Thanksgiving, Christmas, and New Year's Day.

Admission is $15 adults, $13 seniors, $10 ages 6–17, and free for children under six. The $45 family rate is a great value. Admission is good for two days, and it may well take you that long to explore this massive collection! Tours are generally offered only for school groups and VIPs, but the historical center often has summertime demonstrations, and the helpful docents can provide additional information. If you have kids in tow, be sure to pick up the Art Gallery Family Guide, with activities specifically directed at children.

Buffalo Bill Museum

The Buffalo Bill Museum is a real joy. In it, the life of Buffalo Bill Cody is briefly sketched with all sorts of memorabilia from his Wild West Show, including the famous Deadwood Stage, silver-laden saddles, enormous posters,

GATEWAYS TO YELLOWSTONE

furniture, guns, wagons, and buffalo-hide coats. Be sure to look for "Lucretia Borgia," the Springfield rifle that helped William Cody gain his nickname. Also here are some of the gifts given to Buffalo Bill by European heads of state—including a fur carriage robe from Czar Alexander II—and by Wild Bill Hickok and Sitting Bull. Original film footage from the Wild West Show runs continuously, offering a fascinating and sometimes unintentionally comical glimpse into the past. Amazingly choreographed marching soldiers, fake Indian battles, sign-language conversations, and bucking broncos make it easy to see how the Wild West Show helped inspire Western movies.

Whitney Gallery of Western Art

The Whitney Gallery contains a stunning collection of masterworks by such Western artists and sculptors as Charles Russell, Frederic Remington, Carl Bodmer, George Catlin, Maynard Dixon, Harry Jackson, Thomas Moran, Albert Bierstadt, Alfred Jacob Miller, Edgar Paxson, N. C. Wyeth, and others. The paintings include a striking mix of works by old masters juxtaposed with more recent interpretations. Especially notable are two massive paintings: *Custer's Last Stand,* a famous 1899 painting by Edgar Paxson, and facing it, Allen Marden's modernistic *Battle of Greasy Grass* from 1996 (Greasy Grass was the Indian name for the same battle).

The studios of Frederic Remington and Alexander Phimister Proctor have been re-created, and Gertrude Vanderbilt Whitney's *The Scout* is visible from a large window on the north end. The collections of both "cowboy artist" Charles Russell and Frederic Remington—best known for his paintings of battles during the Indian wars—are the most complete here; the museum has more than 100 of each man's paintings. Next to the Whitney Gallery is the **Joseph Henry Sharp Garden,** where you'll find his "Absarokee Hut" filled with the painter's paraphernalia.

Plains Indian Museum

The largest exhibition space in the historical center encloses the Plains Indian Museum, with items from the Sioux, Cheyenne, Blackfeet, Crow, Arapaho, Shoshone, and Gros Ventre tribes. At first it may seem incongruous that a museum featuring the man once called the "youngest Indian slayer of the plains" should include so much about the culture of Indians, but Cody's later maturity forced him to the realization that Indians had been severely mistreated and that their culture was of great value. His Wild West Shows re-created some semblance of that lost society, if only for show. Some of the more important items here were given to Buffalo Bill by various Indian performers through the years, and the collection of artifacts is now one of the finest in America.

On exhibit are an extraordinary painted buffalo robe from 1890 that depicts the Battle of Little Big Horn, Red Cloud's shirt, elaborately decorated baby carriers, a ghost-dance dress, beaded arrow quivers, dance shields, leather garments, war bonnets, ceremonial pipes, a sundance buffalo skull, and even a Pawnee grizzly claw necklace. One of the more unusual items is Lone Dog's Winter Count, with figures representing a 71-year sequence of events affecting the Sioux; it was created in 1877. The Hitatsa earth lodge is another highlight.

Walking through this remarkable collection always leaves me with mixed emotions. I'm impressed at the beauty of the items and their historical and cultural significance, but I'm saddened by the way all museums—of necessity—remove things from their environments and create a visually enticing setting, yet one that is devoid of the living, breathing people who created these objects. If only we could step back into the past to see how life really was, dirt and all.

Draper Museum of Natural History

Covering some 55,000 square feet, this state-of-the-art exhibition covers the Greater Yellowstone Ecosystem and the integral role of humans. Guests begin at a pair of cabins, one of which serves as a naturalist's field station. The other serves as a classroom (of sorts),

YOUNG BUFFALO BILL CODY

For many people today, the name "Buffalo Bill" brings to mind a man who helped slaughter the vast herds of wild bison that once filled the West. But William F. Cody cannot be so easily pigeonholed, for here was one of the most remarkable men of his or any other era – a man who almost single-handedly established the aura of the "Wild West." More than 800 books – many of them the dimestore novels that thrilled generations of youngsters – have been written about Cody. In many of these, the truth was stretched far beyond any semblance of reality, but the real life of William Cody contains so many adventures and plot twists that it seems hard to believe one person could have done so much.

Born to an Iowa farm family in 1846, William Cody started life much as had many others of his era. His parents moved to Kansas when he was six, but his abolitionist father, Isaac Cody, soon became embroiled in arguments with the many local slaveholders. While defending his views at a public meeting, Isaac Cody was stabbed in the back and fled for his life. When a mob learned of his father's whereabouts, the eight-year-old Will Cody rode on his first venture through enemy lines, galloping 35 miles to warn him of the impending attack. Three years later, when Isaac Cody died of complications from the stabbing, 11-year-old Will Cody became the family's breadwinner. There were four other children to feed. He quickly joined the company of Alexander Majors, running dispatches between army supply wagons and giving his $40 monthly wages to his mother. In Cody's autobiography he claimed to have killed his first Indian on this trip, an action that gave him the then-enviable title "youngest Indian slayer of the plains."

On his first long wagon trek west, the army supply wagons were attacked by Mormon zealots who took all the weapons and horses, forcing Cody to walk much of the thousand miles back to his Kansas home. It was apparently on this walk that Cody met Wild Bill Hickok. At Wyoming's Fort Laramie, young Will sat in awe as famed scouts Jim Bridger and Kit Carson reminisced about their adventures. The experience was a turning point in Cody's life; he resolved to one day become a scout. Cody's next job offered excellent training: he became a rider for the Pony Express. At just 15 years of age he already was one of the finest riders in the West and a crack shot with a rifle. On one of his Pony Express rides, Cody covered a total of 320 miles in just 21 hours and 40 minutes – the longest Pony Express ride ever. The Civil War had begun, and at age 18 Cody joined the Seventh Kansas Regiment, serving as a scout and spy for the Union Army.

In 1867, Cody found work hunting buffalo to supply fresh meat for the railroad construction crews, a job that soon made him famous as "Buffalo Bill" and paid a hefty $500 per month. With 75 million bison spread from northern Canada to Mexico, and herds so vast that they took many days to pass, it seemed impossible that they could ever be killed off. Cody was one of the best hunters in the West; in just eight months, he slaughtered 4,280 buffalo, often saving transportation by driving the herd toward the camp and dropping them within sight of the workers. Cody's name lives on in a jingle: "Buffalo Bill, Buffalo Bill; never missed and never will; always aims and shoots to kill; and the company pays his buffalo bill..."

After this stint, Cody finally got the job he wanted – chief scout for the U.S. Army in the West – a job packed with excitement and danger. Conflicts with Indians had reached a fever pitch as more and more whites moved into the last Indian strongholds. Cody worked as scout for General Philip Sheridan, providing information on the Indians' movements, leading troops in pursuit of the warriors, and joining in the battles, including one in which he supposedly killed Chief Tall Bull. His men considered Buffalo Bill good luck because he managed to keep them out of ambushes.

with a seismograph and computer stations to learn about glaciers, volcanoes, and other natural forces. The main section of the Draper starts in an alpine setting, descending a spiraling path through forests, meadows, and lowland plains ecosystems in the Yellowstone landscape. It's like taking a virtual safari through the area.

Multidisciplinary exhibits invite interaction, with lots of kid-friendly audio and video stations, a walk-in beaver lodge, a wolf den, a prairie dog colony, a re-created buffalo jump site, and much more. The winding path ends at a colorful tile map of the Yellowstone ecosystem and an exhibition of children's art.

Cody Firearms Museum

The Cody Firearms Museum houses one of the most comprehensive collections of American firearms in the world, including everything from 16th-century matchlocks to self-loading semiautomatic pistols. This is one museum where the men outnumber the women. The entire firearms collection is remarkably informative and well worth taking time to view—even for those of us who consider the proliferation of guns a national menace.

The museum displays more than 2,700 weapons at any given time, but these aren't just rows of guns in glass cases. Some of the more unusual items include a 10-shot repeating flintlock rifle made for the New York Militia around 1825 and a 17th-century windlass crossbow. There are all sorts of displays to explore, including a colonial gun shop, a Western stage station, an early-1900s firearms factory, and a truly extraordinary collection of embellished arms. The Boone and Crockett Club's collection of trophy animal heads is here, including an elephant-sized moose housed in a re-created hunting lodge. Take the elevator to the basement for even more gun displays. All told, this museum houses more implements of destruction and mayhem than you're likely to see at an NRA convention. And if this isn't enough, kids (and adults) can try a bit of target practice at the "shooting gallery."

Additional Exhibits

Downstairs from the Buffalo Bill Museum is a spacious gallery used for special exhibitions (always worth a look), along with the **Harold McCracken Research Library** (8 A.M.–noon and 1–5 P.M. Mon.–Fri. May–Oct., or by appointment). The library houses 250,000 historical photos and 15,000 books, including more than 300 volumes about Buffalo Bill—mostly dime novels and comic books. Buffalo Bill's **boyhood home**—a tiny yellow building built in 1841 by Isaac Cody—is in the garden area. The house stood in LeClaire, Iowa, for almost a century. In 1933 it was sawed in half, loaded on two railcars, and hauled to Cody to be reassembled and refurbished. The **Photography Gallery** near the entrance to the Draper features changing exhibits.

Other facilities at the Buffalo Bill Historical Center include an excellent **gift shop and bookstore,** plus the Mustang Grill and an espresso stand. Get your lunch and take the

The Scout statue by Gertrude Vanderbilt Whitney

© DON PITCHER

kids outside to the **sculpture garden** for a peaceful picnic beneath the aspen trees.

Flanking the museum on the right side is *The Scout,* a dramatic, larger-than-life statue of larger-than-life Buffalo Bill. This tall bronze piece was created by New York sculptor Gertrude Vanderbilt Whitney and was unveiled in 1924. Her family later donated 40 acres of surrounding land to the Buffalo Bill Museum. Directly in front of the historical center are three colorfully painted tepees, a treat for kids.

Activities and Events

During summer you'll find a wide range of demonstrations every day, including wool-spinning demonstrations, historical talks, cowboy singing, storytelling, and various lectures. Get a brochure at the front desk for the day's activities. The **Larom Summer Institute in Western American Studies** is an in-depth two-week history course with two sessions offered each June. The BBHC also hosts many events.

TRAIL TOWN

Point your horses toward the mountains and head 'em two miles west of Cody to a unique collection of historic buildings at Trail Town (307/587-5302, www.oldtrailtown.us, open daily 8 A.M.–7 P.M. mid-May–Sept. only, $8 adults, $7 seniors, $4 for kids ages 6–12, tots free). Trail Town is the creation of Bob Edgar, the man who discovered Mummy Cave—one of the most important archaeological finds in the West—in 1957. Edgar bought the old Arland and Corbett trading post, and then began dragging in other historic Wyoming cabins. Some were transported whole; others were disassembled and then put back together at Trail Town. The site now holds 26 buildings dating from 1879 to 1901, along with 100 wagons.

For those who love history, Trail Town is an incredible treasure trove without the fancy gift shops and commercial junk that tag along with most such endeavors. This is the real thing, low-key and genuine. Visitors enter through a small gift shop in a cabin salvaged from the old town of Marquette, now beneath the waters of Buffalo Bill Reservoir. The most famous building here is an 1883 cabin from the Hole-in-the-Wall country that Butch Cassidy and the Sundance Kid used as a rendezvous spot. Also at Trail Town is the oldest saloon (another hangout of the gang) from this part of Wyoming, complete with bullet holes in the door, and a cabin where Jim White—one of the most famous buffalo hunters—was murdered in 1879. The log home of Crow Indian scout Curley stands along the main street, too. (Curley was the only one of General Custer's command who escaped alive from the Battle of the Little Big Horn.) Be sure to step inside **Museum of the Old West,** a more recent log cabin filled with artifacts that include a black hearse, rifles found at Indian battlefield sites, arrowheads, beaded necklaces, cradleboards, and items from the fur traders—including a gravestone from 1811, when only a few Anglo trappers were in the region. There's a quiver, bow, and arrow found in a mountain cave and a prehistoric fishing net. Look above the display cases for what may be the most significant discovery, a dugout canoe that had been buried along the Yellowstone River in Montana. It might have belonged to a trapper but is remarkably similar to the ones used by Lewis and Clark. They buried canoes while heading west, planning to dig them up on their return trip. The wood dates to that era; could this be one they left behind?

The bodies of buffalo hunter Jim White and several other historic figures have been re-interred in a small graveyard at Trail Town. One of the most interesting of these is Belle Drewry, a prostitute known as "The Woman in Blue." After bouncing around several 19th-century mining towns, she ended up in the lawless and now-abandoned town of Arland, northwest of Meeteetse. One night in 1897 she shot and killed a cowboy during a dance. The following night his outlaw friends took retribution by murdering her. Belle was buried in the blue dress that she always wore. Also buried in the cemetery is **John "Liver Eating"**

Johnson, the mountain man portrayed by Robert Redford in the movie *Jeremiah Johnson.* Those who have seen the film will be surprised to learn that Johnson died in 1900 at the Old Soldiers' Home in Los Angeles! Friends sent him there by train from Montana when his health deteriorated, but he spent only a month in California before his death at the age of 76. After the movie came out, schoolchildren in Los Angeles helped promote moving Johnson's body closer to his mountain home. Nearly 2,000 people showed up for the reburial in 1974, including Robert Redford. A memorial to explorers John Colter and Jim Bridger also stands near the graveyard. The historic buildings, artifacts, and graves at Trail Town provide a fine counterpoint to the glitzier Buffalo Bill Historical Center. Directly in front of Old Trail Town is **Colter's Hell Trail,** a pleasant 0.5-mile loop through the prairie within Stampede Park.

IRMA HOTEL

Named for Buffalo Bill Cody's daughter, the Irma Hotel was built in 1902 to house tourists arriving by train and was one of three way stations to Yellowstone that Cody built. The luxurious saloon has a French-made cherrywood back bar given to Buffalo Bill by Queen Victoria. The queen spent $100,000 to have it built—no doubt helping to fuel rumors of a romance between her and Buffalo Bill. Many famous people have gathered at the bar through the years.

The **Cody Gunfighters** (307/587-4221, www.codygunfighters.com) perform in front of the Irma Monday–Saturday, June–September. Cody was established long after the era of gunfights in the streets, so this isn't particularly authentic, but it does attract a crowd each evening. The gunfight officially starts at 5:30 P.M., but the first 15 minutes or so are typically wasted on ads for local businesses. You know you're in America when advertising delays even a gunfight!

HARRY JACKSON STUDIOS

Cody's most famous living artist, Harry Jackson, has a large and interesting gallery in an unlikely industrial park setting (602

Buffalo Bill's Irma Hotel

Blackburn St., 307/587-5508, www.harryjackson.com, Monday–Friday 8 A.M.–5 P.M., free). It doesn't look like much outside, but inside you'll discover an amazing diversity of works, covering the palette from abstract expressionist paintings, dark World War II pieces, collages, and cubist studies to his more recent paintings and sculptures (many of which contain distinctively painted surfaces). His other sculptures include the monumental *Sacajawea* at the Buffalo Bill Historical Center and *Horseman* in Beverly Hills. Jackson's pieces have been exhibited throughout the United States and in Italy, where his works are cast. Now something of a living legend, Jackson divides his time between Cody and Italy. Some bronzes (but not his paintings) displayed here are for sale, but they're only for serious art patrons willing to spend thousands of dollars—a 10-foot painted *Sacajawea* goes for $400,000.

ART GALLERIES

The **Buffalo Bill Historical Center** houses a large gift shop with art prints, Indian jewelry, and reproductions of bronze sculptures. Next to the chamber of commerce office, the **Cody Country Art League** (836 Sheridan Ave., 307/587-3597, www.codyart.vcn.com) has paintings, sculptures, photos, and crafts for sale. It also offers workshops and juried art shows.

Simpson Gallagher Gallery (1161 Sheridan Ave., 307/587-4022, www.simpsongallaghergallery.com) is one of the best in Cody, with works that go well beyond the standard Western clichés. View M. C. Poulsen's romanticized visions of the West at **Poulsen Studio Gallery** (2319 Larkspur Ct., 307/587-6862, www.mcpoulsen.com). His paintings have been exhibited in galleries across America, and even in the Capitol Rotunda. Also worth a look are **Big Horn Gallery** (1167 Sheridan Ave., 307/527-7587, www.bighorngalleries.com) and **Cody Fine Art** (1361 Sheridan Ave., 307/527-5380, www.codyfineartgallery.com).

Two photographic galleries are across from each other downtown: **Open Range Images** (1201 Sheridan Ave., 307/587-8870, www.openrangeimages.com), with works from various photographers, and the more distinctive **Traces of Light Gallery** (1280 Sheridan Ave., 307/527-6912 or 877/527-6912, www.tracesoflight.com), showing the large-format (film, not digital) pieces by Leslie and Jimmy Wilson.

DUG UP GUN MUSEUM

Cody seems to specialize in offbeat collections from the Old West, but this has to be the most unusual. Operated by Hans and Eva Kurth, the Cody Dug Up Gun Museum (1020 12th St., 307/587-3344, www.codydugupgunmuseum.com, daily 9 A.M.–9 P.M. May–Sept.) is a little one-room upstairs collection of once-buried guns. I know you're thinking this has to be a total waste of time, but it's actually worth a visit, especially since there's no charge (donation requested) and the 170 or so weapons include everything from rusty War of Independence rifles to a Civil War buckle hit by a bullet. Kids are enthralled by the collection, but they're likely to be found digging up your backyard afterward.

OLD WEST MINIATURE VILLAGE

Another unusual attraction that's worth a visit is Old West Miniature Village and Museum, a.k.a. Tecumseh's Trading Post (142 W. Yellowstone Ave., 307/587-5362, www.tecumsehs.com, open daily 8 A.M.–8 P.M. June–Aug., with reduced hours the rest of the year, donation requested). Owner Jerry Fick spent decades creating an enormous diorama that offers a truncated version of Wyoming and Montana history. Although the term "kitsch" quickly enters your head when you step inside, you've got to appreciate the effort that went into creating thousands of hand-carved figures and an array of fanciful miniature villages. It's said to contain the West's largest model train layout. Of considerably more interest is his collection of artifacts, which includes a knife from the Battle of Little Bighorn, old-time cowboy garb, and many Plains Indian artifacts.

◖ HEART MOUNTAIN INTERPRETIVE CENTER

Opened in 2011, this $5 million facility commemorates a sad chapter in American history, the forced internment of 120,000 Japanese Americans during World War II at remote places around the country, including Heart Mountain Relocation Center. The nonprofit **Heart Mountain Wyoming Foundation** (307/250-5542, www.heartmountain.org, daily Mar.–Oct., donation requested) works to preserve the memory of this painful era lest it be repeated.

The interpretive center is 13 miles northwest of Cody along U.S. Highway 14A, at the site of the old internment camp. Covering 11,000 square feet, the center mimics the design of the wartime barracks that confined internees. Inside are artifacts from the camp, historical photos, a small theater with a film about the camp, and a lovely room where large windows face Heart Mountain. Take a walking tour of the grounds, and be sure to visit the memorial to the many Japanese-American veterans who died while fighting for the U.S. Army in Europe during the war.

Future plans include reconstruction of a guard station and moving one of the surviving barracks back to the site. (A surprising number of the old barracks are still standing on nearby ranches.)

BUFFALO BILL STATE PARK

In 1899, Buffalo Bill Cody acquired the rights to build canals and irrigate 60,000 acres of land near the new town of Cody. With passage of the Reclamation Act of 1902, the project was taken over by the Reclamation Service and an enormous concrete-arch dam was added to provide water. The 328-foot-high dam was begun in 1904 and required five years to finish. It cost nearly $1 million and when finally completed was the tallest dam in the world. Seven men died along the way, including a chief engineer, and the first two contractors were forced into bankruptcy as a result of bad weather, floods, engineering difficulties, and labor strife. A lack of sand and crushed gravel forced them to manufacture it from granite, and 200-pound boulders were hand-placed into the concrete to save having to crush more gravel.

Originally named Shoshone Dam, the impoundment was renamed in honor of Buffalo Bill in 1946. A hydroelectric plant and a 25-foot addition to the top were completed in 1993, bringing the total dam height to 353 feet and increasing water storage by 50 percent. The dam irrigates more than 93,000 downstream acres through the Shoshone Reclamation Project, making it one of the only Wyoming irrigation schemes that actually benefits the state's farmers to a large extent.

Buffalo Bill State Park (six miles west of Cody on U.S. Hwy. 14/16/20, 307/587-9227, http://wyoparks.state.wy.us) encompasses the reservoir and includes two campgrounds ($17 for nonresidents or $10 for Wyoming residents, open May–Sept.) on the north shore. Make campsite reservations ($9) at 877/996-7275. Day use of the park is $6 for nonresident vehicles or $4 for those with Wyoming plates.

Atop the dam, the impressive **Buffalo Bill Dam Visitor Center** (307/527-6076, www.bbdvc.org, free) has historical displays and jaw-dropping views into the canyon, which plummets 350 feet below you. Watch the video on the dam, or borrow the headphones for a 30-minute audio tour ($3) of the area. The center is open 8 A.M.–7 P.M. Monday–Friday, 9 A.M.–5 P.M. Saturday–Sunday, June–August; 8 A.M.–6 P.M. Monday–Friday, 9 A.M.–5 P.M. Saturday–Sunday, May and September; closed the rest of the year. Even if it's shut, stop for the view over the dam.

Buffalo Bill Reservoir is a popular place for local boaters and fishermen. There's good fishing for rainbow, cutthroat, brown, and Mackinaw trout. The lake also offers some of the finest **sailboarding** conditions anywhere, with nearly constant 30 mph winds; *Outside* magazine once rated it among the country's 10 best spots. The water's cold and you'll need a wet suit.

HEART MOUNTAIN RELOCATION CENTER

For Americans of Japanese ancestry, Heart Mountain might as well have been called Broken Heart Mountain. After the Japanese attack on Pearl Harbor in 1941, Japanese-Americans found their patriotism under increasing suspicion, and the following spring President Roosevelt signed an executive order establishing the War Relocation Authority to move them away from the coasts. The authority built 10 remote "relocation centers" to imprison anyone of Japanese ancestry; one such center went up just east of Heart Mountain and housed nearly 11,000 Japanese-Americans (two-thirds of them born in America). The camp became Wyoming's third-largest settlement. It took just 62 days to complete the 468 barracks; 40 laundry-toilet buildings; Buddhist and Christian churches; a high school, fire station, recreation hall, power station, mess hall, hospital, and sewage plant; administrative offices, and numerous other structures. (No environmental impact reports on this baby!) Barbed wire surrounded the perimeter, and military police staffed nine guard towers with high-beam searchlights and machine guns.

CAMP LIFE

Most of the Japanese-Americans took the forced relocation with remarkable aplomb, realizing the futility of any escape attempt. It almost seemed the patriotic thing to do; *shikata-ga-nai* ("I guess it cannot be helped") became the accepted phrase. Although life in the camp maintained a sense of normalcy — some kids came to enjoy their peaceful high-school years and the picnics in Yellowstone — the camp was far from idyllic. Three or four people were jammed into each room, fur-

niture was minimal, people had to share communal bathhouses, and the winter winds blew through the uninsulated tar-paper buildings. Local folks resented the Japanese-Americans but appreciated the cheap farm labor that they provided while Wyoming's sons were off fighting the Germans and Japanese.

AFTER THE WAR

With the war's end in 1945, the camp was closed and the internees were given $25 and a one-way bus ticket home (or rather, to what remained; many found their homes ransacked or sold to others). Over the next four years the 740 acres of land was opened to homesteading, and the barracks were sold at two for $1. Most of the buildings ended up as temporary homes for the new settlers. None of the Japanese-American internees remained in the area, and most of the survivors have little desire to even visit what seemed such a desolate, godforsaken place. They would rather try to forget. See Gretel Ehrlich's *Heart Mountain* for a fictional treatment of life inside the camp.

THE CAMP TODAY

Today, only three buildings remain from the original camp, the largest of which is the old hospital heating plant with its tall brick chimney. Several plaques mark the camp's site, one noting the more than 600 men who left Heart Mountain facility to join the U.S. Army in Europe. Twenty-one internees and a camp teacher died while fighting in Europe. The excellent **Heart Mountain Interpretive Center** (307/250-5542, www.heartmountain.org) has opened on the site of the old Relocation Camp, providing a fascinating look into the lives of Japanese-Americans at the camp.

OTHER SIGHTS

Southeast of Cody near Beck Lake is the **Wyoming Veterans Memorial Park,** where memorials commemorate those who were killed or declared missing in action in the Vietnam War, the Korean War, and World War II.

The **Wild Sheep Foundation** (720 Allen Ave., 307/527-6261, www.wildsheepfoundation.org, 7 A.M.–5 P.M. Mon.–Fri., free) has its national headquarters just south of Buffalo Bill Historical Center. A favorite of wealthy trophy hunters, this nonprofit group funds wild sheep

BUFFALO BILL CODY: HUNTER AND SCOUT

During the Indian campaigns, Ned Buntline began writing of Cody's exploits for various New York papers, giving Buffalo Bill his first taste of national acclaim. Soon Buntline had cranked out several romantic novels loosely based on Cody's adventures. America had a new national hero. European and Eastern gentry began asking Cody to guide them on buffalo hunts. On the trips, he referred to them as "dudes" and to his camps as "dude ranches" – perhaps the first time anyone had used the terms for such hunters. One of the West's most unusual businesses had begun. Cody's knowledge of the land and hunting impressed the men, but they were stunned to also discover in him a natural showman. In 1872, the Grand Duke Alexis of Russia came to the United States and was guided by Cody on a hunt that made national headlines and brought even more fame to the 26-year-old. On a trip to New York in 1872, Cody met Buntline again and watched a wildly distorted theater production called Buffalo Bill. Amazingly, Cody adjusted quickly to the new surroundings. Dressed in the finest silk clothes but with his long scout's hair under a Western hat, Cody suddenly entered the world of high society.

In a short while, Cody was on the stage himself, performing with Ned Buntline and fellow scout Texas Jack in a play called Scouts of the Plains. Although meant to be serious, the acting of all three proved so atrocious that the play had audiences rolling in the aisles with laughter. A New York reviewer called the play "so wonderfully bad it was almost good. The whole performance was so far aside of human experience, so wonderful in its daring feebleness, that no ordinary intellect is capable of comprehending it." Audiences packed the theaters for weeks on end. But Cody was suddenly called back west, for the Sioux were again on the warpath.

Shortly after Cody had returned to guide General Eugene Carr's forces, they learned of the massacre of Custer's men at the Battle of the Little Big Horn. In revenge, Carr's men set out to pursue Indians along the border between Nebraska and Wyoming. Under Cody's guidance, they surprised a group of warriors at War Bonnet Creek. Cody shot the chief, Yellow Hand, and immediately scalped him, rais-

---

research and conservation. Visitors can view an interesting 15-minute video on bighorn sheep, or check out the wild sheep exhibits and habitat maps.

If you're really desperate for something to do, visit the **Cody Murals** (307/587-3290, www.codymural.com) on the domed ceiling of the Latter-day Saints (Mormon) church at 1719 Wyoming Avenue. Tours are available daily during summer. No, it isn't the Sistine Chapel. The mural—painted in 1951 by Edward Grigware—offers a rosy-tinted version of Mormon Church history and the Bighorn Basin pioneers.

Wild Horses

The McCullough Peaks area, approximately 20 miles east of Cody on U.S. Highway 14/16/20, is home to some 120 wild horses with a variety of coat colors. Some horses are believed to have descended from those brought back from England by Buffalo Bill Cody. The easiest way to see these wild horses is via a tour from **Red Canyon Wild Mustang Tours** (307/587-6988 or 800/293-0148, www.wildmustangtours.com, $24 adults or $21 kids). Photographer Ken Martin leads these highly informative two-hour trips. The **Friends of a Legacy** (FOAL, www.friendsofalegacy.org) is a nonprofit group working to protect these horses and to develop an education center nearby.

RECREATION

Paul Stock Aquatic and Recreation Center (1402 Heart Mountain St., 307/587-0400, www.cityofcody-wy.gov) is an impressive center on the south side of town, housing a large indoor pool with a 150-foot spiral slide, a hot ing the scalp above his head with the cry "first scalp for Custer!" The Sioux immediately fled. If Cody had been famous before, this event propelled him to even more acclaim. It became the grist for countless dime-store novels and was embellished in so many ways over the years that the true story will never be known.

THE WILD WEST SHOW

Buffalo Bill's days in the real Wild West were over, and he returned to staging shows, eventually starting his famed Wild West extravaganza. This was unlike anything ever done before – an outdoor circus that seemed to transport all who watched to the frontier. One newspaper remarked that Cody had "out-Barnumed Barnum." There were buffalo stampedes, cowboy bronco riding, Indian camps, a Deadwood stage and outlaws, crack shooting by Annie Oakley, and, of course, Buffalo Bill. At its peak in the late 1890s, Buffalo Bill was arguably the world's best-known man. Queen Victoria was a special fan, although rumors of an affair are probably false. The show traveled across America and Europe, attracting crowds of up to 40,000 people and making Cody more than a million dollars in profit each year. Unfortunately, as movies replaced outdoor extravaganzas the show fell out of favor and eventually went bankrupt. By the time of his death in 1917, Cody was plagued by mounting debts and was working for another Western show.

Amazingly, Sitting Bull and Buffalo Bill became good friends. Cody, who had earlier bragged of his many Indian killings, eventually said: "In nine cases out of ten when there is trouble between white men and Indians, it will be found that the white man is responsible." Cody went on to criticize the buffalo hunters for their reckless slaughter, and he became an ardent supporter of game preserves and limitations on hunting seasons.

Cody's life spanned one of the most remarkable eras in American history, and his impact on American culture is still felt today – not just in the image of the West that he created, which lives on in hundreds of Western movies and rodeos, but also in the Boy Scouts (an organization inspired by his exploits), in the city of Cody (which he helped found), and in the dude ranches that dot the West.

---

tub, a wading pool, basketball and racquetball courts, a suspended indoor track, exercise machines, and child care. Nonresident rec center passes are $11 adults, $6 youths. Next door is the **Victor J. Riley Arena and Community Events Center** (307/587-1681, www.parkcountyhockey.org), which serves as a summertime convention center and winter ice rink. The entire recreation complex is known as the Cody Quad Center.

Next to Kmart on the east side of town, **Absaroka Bikes** (2201 17th St., 307/527-5566, www.facebook.com) has mountain-bike rentals and bike trail maps. Skateboarders will appreciate the impressive **Cody Skate Park** in Mentock Park on Blackburn Street in east Cody.

The 18-hole **Olive Glenn Golf and Country Club** (802 Meadow Ln., 307/587-5308, www.oliveglenngolf.com) is a PGA championship course with a complete golf shop and upscale restaurant. Families enjoy playing at the seasonal **miniature golf course** (307/587-3685, $4) in the downtown city park near the Chamber of Commerce office.

Pick up a copy of *Cody Parks & Pathways* from the visitor center for details on local hiking paths, including the 1.3-mile **Shoshone Riverway Trail** on the north side of town.

River Rafting

One of the most popular summertime activities in Cody is floating the Class I and II Shoshone River. Beware, however, that even with these mild conditions, you should plan on getting soaked in the rapids. Expect to pay about $30 for a seven-mile run that lasts 90 minutes, or $40 for a 13-mile (three-hour) float. Both Wyoming River and Red Canyon offer 90-minute inflatable kayak trips ($47) for those who want to run the rapids on their own power. In addition, Red Canyon leads scenic float trips down the Clarks Fork ($62). The rafting companies offer half-day whitewater trips down the North Fork above the reservoir for $70 including lunch. These trips run only late May–July, when the water level is high.

Founded in 1978, Wyoming River Trips is the most experienced company in Cody. Red Canyon River Trips is newer, but the guides are also very experienced and use smaller rafts for a more personalized trip. For details, contact **Wyoming River Trips** (233 Yellowstone Hwy., 307/587-6661 or 800/586-6661, www.wyomingrivertrips.com), **River Runners** (1491 Sheridan Ave., 307/527-7238 or 800/535-7238, www.riverrunnersofwyoming.com), or **Red Canyon River Trips** (1374 Sheridan Ave., 307/587-6988 or 800/293-0148, www.imt.net/~rodeo/raft.html).

If you want to try rafting or kayaking on your own, you'll find several miles of technical Class IV water with some Class V drops below the dam and above DeMaris Springs. Above the dam are stretches of Class I and II water with good access from the main highway. Ask locally for flow conditions before heading out, because snowmelt and dam releases can dramatically affect water levels.

Most rafters put in three miles west of Cody off Demaris Street. Just upstream from the put-in point is DeMaris Springs, a part of "Colter's Hell" that is on private property and not open to the public. The area was once far more active, with hot springs bubbling out of the river and sulfurous smoke rising all around. People actually died from the poisonous gas. Today the geothermal activity has lessened, but the air still smells of sulfur and small hot springs color the cliff faces. Miners worked over nearby hillsides in search of sulfur; the diggings are still apparent. It's also pretty obvious why they first called this the Stinkingwater River.

Next to the Holiday Inn, **Gradient Mountain Sports** (1723 Sheridan Ave., 307/587-4659, www.gradientmountainsports.net, open late May–early Sept.) has kayak rentals and sales, gear, lessons, and guided trips to local lakes and the Shoshone River.

Hiking

Located 13 miles northwest of Cody on U.S. Highway 14, the distinctively shaped Heart Mountain with it 8,123-foot peak is a good spot for an adventurous day hike. Besides the (slightly) heart-shaped summit, the mountain is also an oddity, with older limestone formations atop younger strata, a mystery that has led to all sorts of geological theories. Access is via County Road 19, which connects with Road 13H, continuing west to a trailhead. The Heart Mountain Interpretive Center is nearby.

The Nature Conservancy manages a 15,000-acre preserve at the mountain, with a base at **Heart Mountain Ranch** (307/754-8446, www.nature.org). This preserve encompasses a variety of rare plants and is occasionally traversed by grizzlies. Sign in at the ranch for the 3.5-mile hike to the summit. You'll gain 2,500 feet in elevation along the way, so be sure to bring warm clothes since the top may be dramatically chillier than below. The Conservancy also has an office in Cody (1235 16th St.) where you can get additional details on Heart Mountain. **Jackson Hole Mountain Guides** (307/250-0763 or 877/587-0629, www.jhmg.com) leads day hikes up Heart Mountain in the summer.

Fishing

North Fork Anglers (1107 Sheridan Ave., 307/527-7274, www.northforkanglers.com) has anything you might need for fly-fishing, including a full-service retail shop, professional fishing guides, and fly-tying clinics. Also of note is **The Humble Fly** (1183 Sheridan Ave., 307/587-2757, www.thehumblefly.com). A full day of guided float fishing on nearby rivers costs $400 for two people.

Horse and Wagon Rides

Excellent horseback rides are available from **Cedar Mountain Trail Rides** (307/527-4966), a mile west of the rodeo grounds. Hour-long trail rides are $30. Many of the lodges in Wapiti Valley and the Upper North Fork also offer horseback rides and backcountry pack trips. Get a complete listing from the chamber of commerce (www.codychamber.org).

Jerry Kinkade of **K3 Guest Ranch** (33 Nielsen Trail, 307/587-2080 or 888/587-2080, www.k3guestranch.com) offers half-day ranch adventures for wannabe cowboys, including time with two trick horses, a visit to the wild mustangs, lunch, and other activities. He really has fun with this, and so do the guests—especially children. The cost is $79 for adults, or $49 for kids under 10. Call ahead for reservations.

Climbing

Jackson Hole Mountain Guides (307/250-0763 or 800/239-7642, www.jhmg.com) has a summertime operation out of Cody, leading climbing classes in nearby Shoshone River Canyon, plus Heart Mountain day hikes. Waterfalls in the South Fork area (www.codyice.com) are popular for ice climbing in the winter.

Caving

Cedar Mountain, the 7,889-foot-tall summit overlooking Cody from the west, is where Buffalo Bill had wanted to be buried. A winding 4WD trail climbs to the top, but there's no public access at present. Also here is **Spirit Mountain Cave,** one of the first national monuments ever designated (1909). A lack of interest caused the designation to be withdrawn, and Spirit Mountain's lower depths were blocked by a cave-in in the 1980s, but spelunkers can explore three levels of the cave. Get permission to enter and a key from the BLM office in Cody, 307/578-5900.

ENTERTAINMENT AND EVENTS

Pick up a copy of *Cody Pulse,* a free bimonthly paper listing local events, arts, and entertainment. The downtown City Park band shell is the place to be for Friday evening **Concerts in the Park** during July and August. These free musical performances—in a variety of genres—start at 6 P.M.

On the West Strip, **Cassie's** (214 Yellowstone Ave., 307/527-5500, www.cassies.com) has been here since 1922. Stop by for country-and-western tunes on Friday and Saturday nights year-round, and Monday-night lessons on the big dance floor. Hang around the bar long enough and you can join in that old Cassie's favorite, barroom brawling.

Silver Dollar Bar (1313 Sheridan Ave., 307/527-7666, www.codysilverdollarbar.com, daily 11 A.M.–2 A.M.) serves great burgers and pub grub (till 9 P.M.) and accompanies them with rock or C&W bands nightly all summer. Two pool tables are in the back, with a big side deck for when the smoke gets too thick. Happy hours are weekdays 5–7 P.M.

Find flicks at **Big Horn Cinemas** (2525 Big Horn Ave., 307/587-8001 or 888/878-3549); it's on the east end of town.

Don't miss **Dan Miller's Cowboy Music Revue** (1171 Sheridan Ave., 307/272-7855, www.cowboymusicrevue.com, $15 per person, May–Sept.) at the Cody Theater. Dan and his talented band perform nightly at 8 P.M., with cowboy music and poetry and lots of humor. (Miller hosted championship rodeo events on TNN for 18 years.) Combine the music revue with dinner ($32) at the Irma Hotel across the street.

Also check out the popular-with-tourists **Cody Cattle Company** (1910 Demaris St., 307/272-5770, www.thecodycattlecompany.com), featuring cowboy entertainment and a big dinner buffet.

Events

Summer is a busy time in Cody, with special events nearly every weekend. The **Cody Gunfighters** (www.codygunfighters.com) perform downtown in front of the Irma Hotel Monday–Saturday at 6 P.M. in the summer. These free mock gunfights are Western-style entertainment. They're worth a look if you haven't seen one before, but still corny and quite out of character for settled-down Cody.

One of the most unusual local events is the **What Festival** (www.whatfest.com), held in late July at Edelweiss Bar & Grill (2900 Hwy. 120, Powell, 307/645-3223), 30 miles north of Cody. This popular music festival attracts 15 or so acts—from reggae and funk to electronica and jazz—along with big jam sessions. It's entirely free, with camping on the grounds.

Held in the Robbie Powwow Garden in front of the Buffalo Bill Historical Center in mid-June, the **Plains Indian Museum Powwow** (307/587-4771, www.bbhc.org/events) attracts several hundred participants from all over the Rockies and Canada vying for $30,000 in prize money. It includes daylong singing and dancing in tribal regalia and various dance competitions. Visitors can buy Indian arts and crafts and taste Indian tacos and fry bread.

There's more Western fun at the annual **Day of the American Cowboy,** celebrated at the BBHC with cowboy music, poetry, and talk in late July. The **Yellowstone Jazz Festival** (www.yellowstonejazz.com) in mid-July brings both regional and national jazz groups.

In late September, the **Rendezvous Royale** encompasses a number of major events, including the largest art event of the year, the **Buffalo Bill Art Show and Sale** (307/587-5002 or 888/598-8119, www.buffalobillartshow.com), with exhibitions, a symposium, receptions, and an auction. Also featured is **Cody High Style,** with Western furniture, metalwork, and a Western-wear fashion show.

Cody Nite Rodeo

Cody calls itself the "Rodeo Capital of the World," packing the calendar with nightly summertime rodeos, plus the famous Cody Stampede. After over 70 years of operation, the Cody Nite Rodeo (307/587-5155 or

THE CRUSADING CAROLINE LOCKHART

The West overflows with famous men, and women sometimes get unjustly shunted aside in the accolades. One of the most interesting was Caroline Lockhart (1871-1962), a woman who began her career as an actress but turned quickly to journalism as a writer for a Boston newspaper. Using the pen name "Suzette," she became one of the country's first female newspaper reporters. The job led her into all sorts of adventures, from entering a circus cage with a lion that had killed his trainer the previous day to testing the Boston Fire Department's new fire nets by jumping out of a fourth-story hotel window. When she heard of a "Home for Intemperate Women" where the women were being severely mistreated, Caroline decided to investigate by posing as a derelict. She got her story all right, but it took considerable convincing from her editor to get her out. "Release!" shouted the matron running the house. "We can't! She's not cured yet." One of Lockhart's most lasting impacts was the creation of Mother's Day. Although Anna Jarvis came up with the concept, Caroline Lockhart made it a reality by tirelessly promoting the idea in the newspapers.

In 1904, Lockhart took a bold step. After an interview with Buffalo Bill Cody in the town named for him, she decided to move to Wyoming. She bought the local newspaper, the *Cody Enterprise,* and quickly made a name for herself as a crusader against Prohibition and "game hogs" (hunters who killed everything in sight). She also founded the Cody Stampede, the big annual event in Bighorn Basin. Lockhart wrote seven novels, including *The Lady Doc,* a book that managed to ruffle local feathers with its too-close-to-the-truth descriptions of real-life Cody people. Despite this controversy, her witty, humorous, and insightful writing gained a national reputation.

In 1925, Lockhart sold the *Cody Enterprise* and acquired a ranch that eventually included 7,000 acres of land along the Bighorn River north of Lovell, dividing her time between her Cody home (now the Lockhart Bed and Breakfast) and her ranch. She died at the age of 92. Today her old ranch lies within Bighorn Canyon National Recreation Area.

800/207-0744, www.codystampederodeo. com) is still one of the best in a state filled with rodeos. Shows begin at 8 P.M. nightly June–August and always attract a crowd. A favorite is the calf scramble, starring kids from the stands. Tickets cost $18 adults and $8 children; free for kids under seven. For top-of-the-action seats, be sure to get there early and follow the signs to the "buzzards roost" section. The rodeo grounds are one mile west of town on U.S. Highway 14/16/20, and a rodeo bus (307/272-5573, www.codytransportation. com) provides transportation from local hotels and RV parks for $4 round-trip; it's free for kids under 12.

Cody Stampede

Independence Day sets the stage for Cody's main event, the Cody Stampede (307/587-5155 or 800/207-0744, www.codystampederodeo. org), held July 1–4. Established in 1919—more than 90 years ago—it attracts thousands of visitors from all over the nation. Parade fans are treated to one each morning (including a kiddie parade), with dozens of marching bands, mountain men, vintage autos, floats, cowboys, and enough free candy to keep dentists busy for decades. Special PRCA rodeo performances, craft shows, running events, and fireworks complete the schedule.

SHOPPING

As you might expect from a tourist town, Cody has more than its share of shops dealing in clunky jewelry, crass T-shirts, and fake Indian trinkets. Fortunately, it's also home to several places with a bit more class. Get fancy Western duds at **Custom Cowboy Shop** (1286 Sheridan Ave., 307/527-7300, www.customcowboyshop. com), or saunter over to **Boot Barn** (1625 Stampede Ave., 307/587-4493, www.bootbarn. com, 9 A.M.–8 P.M. Mon.–Sat., 11 A.M.–5 P.M. Sun.) for inexpensive hats and clothes.

Traditions West Antique Mall (1137 12th St., 307/587-7434), next to Irma Hotel, and **Cowboy Story** (1215 Sheridan Ave., 307/587-7592, www.cowboystory.com) are good places to look for Western antiques. **Indian Territory** (1212 Sheridan Ave., 307/527-5522, www.doublehheaddresses.com) sells authentic Native American jewelry and museum replicas.

Cody Newsstand (1121 13th St., 307/587-2843) sells books and features the best magazine selection in Bighorn Basin.

Popular with locals, **Reindeer Ranch** (1241 Sheridan Ave., 307/587-6890 or 800/816-1640, www.reindeer-ranch.com) has three floors of home furnishings, gifts, and Christmas collectibles.

Check out the **Wyoming Dinosaur Center** (1210 Sheridan Ave., 307/864-2997 or 800/455-3466, www.wyodino.org), where you'll see a T-Rex casting and can purchase dinosaur toys, unusual fossils, and specimens. Daily tours of the fascinating dig site near Thermopolis are offered in the summer.

Outdoor Gear

Sunlight Sports (1131 Sheridan Ave., 307/587-9517, www.sunlightsports.com) is the largest outdoors shop in town, selling tents, climbing equipment, clothes, topographic maps, and more. It also rents cross-country and downhill skis, snowboards, and snowshoes during the winter.

Sierra Trading Post (1402 8th St., 307/578-5802 or 800/713-4534, www.sierratradingpost.com) has an outlet store in the large log building across from the Buffalo Bill Historical Center.

ACCOMMODATIONS

The tourist town of Cody is packed with places to stay, but be ready to pay more than anyplace in Wyoming except Jackson Hole. The town's hostel has closed, and budget accommodations are hard to find during the summer, although rates plummet with the first cold nights of fall. Most of the year, finding lodging in Cody is not a problem as long as you check in before 4 P.M., but during July and August you should reserve a week ahead—and longer for the Cody Stampede in early July. The **Park County Travel Council**'s website (www.yellowstonecountry.org) has details and links to most local lodging places.

In addition to the places below, you will find many dude ranches and lodges in the mountain country around Cody. Add a 9 percent lodging tax to all rates.

Under $100

Skyline Motor Inn (1919 17th St., 307/587-4201 or 800/843-8809, www.skylinemotorinn.com, $75 s or $84–97 d) has large rooms, Wi-Fi, updated furnishings, and a fenced play area for children.

Uptown Motel (1562 Sheridan Ave., 307/587-4245, www.uptowncody.com) is a 10-unit motel with well-maintained rooms; rates are $86 for one queen bed or $92 for two. Half the units contain microwaves and fridges, and Wi-Fi is available. A separate two-bedroom cottage with kitchenette is popular with families ($98 for up to six).

Carter Mountain Motel (1701 Central Ave., 307/587-4295, www.cartermountainmotel.net), atop the hill near Albertson's, features very nicely maintained rooms. Standard units (all with fridges, microwaves, and Wi-Fi) are $89 d. Two-, three-, and four-bedroom suites with full kitchens cost $145–242; the largest can sleep nine.

A decent older motel in a quiet part of town, **Budget Host** (1807 Sheridan Ave., 307/587-4258 or 800/283-4678, www.budgethost.com), is open May–mid-October. Standard rooms are $94–105 d, and a family room sleeps six for $134. All rooms contain small fridges and Wi-Fi access.

$100-200

For large older rooms with reasonable rates, check out **Cody Motor Lodge** (1455 Sheridan Ave., 307/527-6291 or 800/340-2639, www.codymotorlodge.net, $100 d). Amenities include fridges, microwaves, Wi-Fi, and continental breakfast. Pets are welcome.

The **Sunrise Motor Inn** (1407 8th St., 307/587-5566 or 877/587-5566, www.sunriseinncody.com, $100 d) has a heated outdoor pool (seasonal), fridges, some microwaves, a continental breakfast, and Wi-Fi. Open May–early October.

At **Buffalo Bill's Antlers Inn** (1213 17th St., 307/587-2084 or 800/388-2084, www.antlersinncody.com) rooms are decorated with handcrafted burlwood furniture. Look for the big waterfall out front; you can't miss it. The large and clean accommodations run $100 d for standard rooms, or $150 d for the honeymoon suite with a king bed and jet tub. There's free Wi-Fi. The hotel is closed mid-October–April.

One of the older local places, **Big Bear Motel** (139 W. Yellowstone Ave., 307/587-3117 or 800/325-7163, www.bigbearmotel.com) has updated, clean rooms and friendly owners. No phones in the rooms (use your cell phone), but there is Wi-Fi and half the units contain fridges and microwaves. Families love the large outdoor pool and pony rides for kids (small fee). Standard rooms are $114 d, and newer family suites can sleep six or more for $159.

On the National Register of Historic Places, Buffalo Bill Cody's **Irma Hotel** (1192 Sheridan Ave., 307/587-4221 or 800/745-4762, www.irmahotel.com) has a downtown location and all the ambience you could want. It's the real thing—a classic Old West hotel. Given the historic importance of the Irma, standard guest rooms ($100–114 d) here are a major disappointment. Considerably nicer are the unique and spacious rooms in the historic section of the hotel ($157 d or $172 for four), all named after famous guests. Book the Buffalo Bill suite a year in advance for the peak of summer. It has corner windows and historic Victorian decor. Be sure to ask about the ghost (of Buffalo Bill?) that supposedly haunts the Irma.

One of the newest local hotels, **Cody Legacy Inn and Suites** (1801 Mountain View Dr., 307/587-6067, www.codylegacyinn.com) features 50 plush rooms, most with two queen beds for $148 d. A king suite with jetted tub is $168 d, and luxurious two-bedroom suites cost $188–238. Amenities include an outdoor heated pool (seasonal), indoor hot tub, sauna, Wi-Fi, and light breakfast.

Green Gables Inn (1636 Central Ave., 307/587-6886, www.codysgreengables.com) is a modern and tidy 15-unit motel on the south side of Cody with fridges, microwaves, and pillowtop beds in all units. Standard rooms cost $129 d, with suites running $142 for up to six guests. A continental breakfast is served each morning. Open mid-May–mid-October. The hotel is owned by Kit Cody, a great grandson of Buffalo Bill; his daughter owns Cody Legacy Inn and Suites.

AmericInn Lodge and Suites (508 Yellowstone Ave., 307/587-7716 or 800/634-3444, www.americinn.com) is one of the better places to stay in Cody, with 66 large and quiet rooms (king or two queen beds) for $189–199 d. Suites, some with jetted tubs and fireplaces, cost $225–275. Amenities include an indoor pool, hot tub, sauna, plus a light breakfast.

Buffalo Bill Village Resort consists of three separate operations that total nearly 350 rooms: Holiday Inn, Comfort Inn, and Buffalo Bill Village Resort. All three are in the heart of Cody at 1701 Sheridan Avenue and share the same toll-free number and website: 800/527-5544, www.blairhotels.com. Guests at all three facilities can use the outdoor heated pool at the Holiday Inn and are welcome to join the free reception with snacks and sodas each evening. The attractively remodeled 189-room **Holiday Inn at Buffalo Bill Village Resort** (307/587-5555, $159–189 d) has rooms with two double beds or one king bed. Amenities include Wi-Fi, a guest computer, and fitness center. Rooms at **Comfort Inn at Buffalo Bill Village Resort** (307/587-5556, $140–190 d) include a filling breakfast and free Wi-Fi (but thin walls). The most distinctive of this Cody lodging triumvirate is **(Buffalo Bill Village Cabins** (307/587-5544), which consists of 83 cozy log cabins. These cabins were built in the 1920s to house workers and their families for nearby Buffalo Bill Dam. They were later moved here and have since been updated to include phones, TVs, private baths, and air-conditioning. Small cabins are decorated in a playful cowboy theme and have a queen or king bed ($109–149 d). Family cabins ($129–169) contain two bedrooms with three or four double beds. The cabins are open May–September, and Wi-Fi is available.

One of Cody's nicer motels, **Beartooth Inn** (2513 Greybull Hwy., 307/527-5505 or 800/807-8522, www.beartoothinn.com) is a mile east of town near the airport. Spacious standard rooms (biggest in town) are $125 d, six-person family rooms go for $139–149, and mini-suites with hot tubs cost $149 d. Hotel amenities include a sauna and indoor hot tub, exercise equipment, Wi-Fi, guest computer, airport shuttle, and a big breakfast (fresh waffles), plus microwaves and fridges in all rooms. Ground-floor rooms have both outside and interior entrances.

You'll find excellent accommodations at **Best Western Sunset Motor Inn** (1601 8th St., 307/587-4265 or 800/624-2727, www.bestwestern.com/sunsetmotorinn), where standard rooms start at $185 d, up to $235 for family suites that sleep six. Amenities include indoor and outdoor pools, a hot tub, continental breakfast, Wi-Fi, guest computers, a playground, and fitness facility. The adjacent restaurant (Sunset House) serves family-style meals.

(Cody Cowboy Village (203 W. Yellowstone Ave., 307/587-7555, www.codycowboyvillage.com) has 40 log cabin–style rooms ($145–159 d) and 10 luxury cabin suites ($199 for up to six) on the west end of town near the rodeo grounds. All rooms are furnished with high-end beds and linens, and guests appreciate the big outdoor hot tub with a waterfall, flat-screen TVs, light breakfast, concierge service, and Wi-Fi. Ultra-friendly management, too.

Over $200

With its concierge service, luxurious linens, turndown service, robes, microwaves, fridges, flat-screen TVs, indoor pool, hot tub, sauna, Wi-Fi, guest computers, shuttle service, iPod docking stations, and a hot breakfast buffet, **The Cody** (232 W. Yellowstone, 307/587-5915, www.thecody.com) would seem more at home in Jackson Hole than Cody. Choose from large rooms—some with private patios—for $209–219 d, up to king suites with electric (!) fireplaces and jet tubs for $249–259 d. There's a player grand piano in the lobby and a patio with a small waterfall and fireplace for chilly evenings. The indoor pool, hot tub, and sauna are open 24 hours.

When it first opened in 1903, the Chamberlin Hotel was one of Cody's finest lodging places, and its guests included Ernest Hemingway, who stayed here in 1932 after completing *Death in the Afternoon*. In later years the hotel was renamed the Pawnee Hotel, but the luster had long passed by the time new owners bought the neglected property in 2005. A year later the hotel reemerged with its original moniker, but entirely transformed into a luxurious boutique hotel. Today, **❖ Chamberlin Inn** (1032 12th St., 307/587-0202 or 888/587-2020, www.chamberlininn. com) provides elegant downtown lodging just a block off the main route through town. Each of the 23 rooms has its own personality. Standard queen rooms with shower start at $165–185 d, with king rooms for $215–255 d and suites costing $285–325 d. A shady, flower-filled courtyard is a relaxing focal point

for the hotel, and three smaller buildings are set up as more spacious units, ranging from a cozy garden cottage ($245 d) to a building that once housed Cody's courthouse. The latter has French beveled-glass doors, fireplaces, a full kitchen and bar, three baths, a living room, and office. It sleeps six in comfort for $550 nightly with a two-night minimum. Other amenities available to all guests include a library, central kitchen, Wi-Fi, silk linens, Belgian chocolates, fresh flowers in all rooms, and flat-screen TVs. Check out Hemingway's signature in the guest register and a cigar box he left behind, or spend a night where he once slept.

Bed-and-Breakfasts

Several historic buildings are now part of the Cody B&B scene, offering a taste of the genteel past. The website for **Cody Country Bed and Breakfast Association** (www.codybedandbreakfast.com) has links to local B&Bs.

Built in 1924 by Cody Mayor P. E. Markham, **Lambright Place B&B** (1501 Beck Ave., 307/527-5310 or 800/241-5310,

the courtyard of Chamberlin Inn

www.lambrightplace.com) exudes an old-fashioned charm. Three rooms in the large main house are available for $100–140 d, and a Western-themed cottage/bunkhouse sleeps five for $165. All rooms have private baths and Wi-Fi, and the breakfasts are memorable. Kids are welcome, and the bunkhouse works well for families and small groups.

For lodging in a classic Cody home, stay at (**The Mayor's Inn** (1413 Rumsey Ave., 307/587-0887 or 888/217-3001, www.mayorsinn.com), built in 1909 by Frank Houx, the town's first mayor. In 1997 it was moved to the present site and restored to its original opulence. The four guest rooms ($125–215 d) include private baths with jetted tubs, down comforters, terry-cloth robes, heated floors, and Wi-Fi. The nicest room has a king bed and jet tub. A full breakfast is served each morning. Also available is a separate cottage ($140) with full kitchen for families (no breakfast).

Also recommended is **Robin's Nest B&B** (1508 Alger Ave., 307/527-7208 or 866/723-7797, www.robinsnestcody.com, $135–145 d). On a quiet street just a few blocks from the heart of town, this 1928 brick-and-frame home features a relaxing and shady backyard, a large living room, and four guest rooms with queen or king beds, private baths, plus a guest computer and Wi-Fi. Unique is the tree-house suite, situated on an upstairs porch. A full breakfast is served each morning, and well-behaved kids are accepted. The owners have two Labrador retrievers and pets are sometimes accepted, but call ahead.

Built in 1914, **Salsbury Avenue Inn B&B** (1226 Salsbury Ave., 307/587-1226, www.salsburyinncody.com, $80–95 d) is a reasonably priced and attractive option close to downtown. Four guest rooms share an upstairs bath (hence the low rates), but two more are available downstairs. The home has Wi-Fi and a full breakfast is served. Kids over age 10 are welcome.

Angel's Keep B&B (1241 Wyoming Ave., 307/587-6205 or 877/320-2800, www.angelskeep.com, $109–145 d) is housed within a restored 1930s Assembly of God church and has three rooms with queen beds and a filling country breakfast, evening snacks, and Wi-Fi. A gift shop offers locally made items.

(**K3 Guest Ranch** (33 Nielsen Trail, 307/587-2080 or 888/587-2080, www.k3guestranch.com) sits on 33 acres of land along the outskirts of Cody. The modern home has three Western-themed guest rooms ($159–175 d), all with private baths and windows facing the hayfield. Add $24 for additional guests (max of six). The most unusual spot is an old sheepherder wagon ($159 d) from the 1890s with air-conditioning (!) and its own bath. The ultra-friendly owners, Jerry and Bette Kinkade, cook a big ranch breakfast over an open fire each morning and also offer a day ranch for wannabe cowboys ($69 for guests).

A rambling 8,000-square-foot home eight miles southwest of town near Buffalo Bill Reservoir, **Southfork Bed and Breakfast** (797 Southfork Rd., 307/587-8311, www.southforkbb.com) has two guest rooms ($125 d) with private baths and entrances. Guests are served a full breakfast by the owner, who is also a professional chef. A third room ($65 extra) can be combined with the others for families. Additional amenities include a home theater, full bar, outdoor pool, indoor lap pool and hot tub, and spacious great room with a stone fireplace. Horse lodging is available, or you can just visit with the owner's (formerly) wild mustangs.

Vacation Rentals

Cody has an abundance of vacation rentals available on a nightly or weekly basis. For an overview of the options, contact **Cody Lodging Company** (307/587-6000 or 800/587-6560, www.codylodgingcompany.com), which offers more than 85 furnished homes, cottages, condos, and mountain lodges. Prices range from $125 for a two-person guest cottage up to $2,000 nightly for a luxurious four-bedroom home near Heart Mountain. Other companies with vacation rentals include **Moose Alley Lodging** (307/587-6159 or 877/511-4438, www.moosealleylodging.com), **Cody Vacation Housing** (307/272-8524, www.codyvacationhousing.com), and **Duck Inn** (307/250-3189, www.duckinncody.com).

CAMPING

The closest public campgrounds are in **Buffalo Bill State Park** (877/996-7275, http://wyoparks.state.wy.us, $17 for nonresidents, $10 for Wyoming residents, $9 reservation fee). The park's North Shore and North Fork Campgrounds are nine miles west and 14 miles west of Cody, respectively. Most sites are first-come, first served. Find many more campgrounds in Shoshone National Forest (www.fs.fed.us/r2/shoshone, $10–20); the nearest is 28 miles west of Cody in the upper North Fork.

Cody's finest RV park is **Ponderosa Campground** (1815 8th St., 307/587-9203, www.codyponderosa.com, mid-Apr.–mid-Oct.), with shady sites ($22 tents or $31–36 RVs) along with tepees ($25) and simple cabins ($42 for four people). There's free Wi-Fi.

Cody KOA (two miles east on U.S. Hwy. 14/16/20, 307/587-2369 or 800/562-8507, www.codykoa.com, May–Oct.) opened in 1964 as the first franchised KOA. Rates are $30 for tents and $53 for RVs, $73–86 for simple cabins, or $165 for six-person cottages. Amenities include a large heated outdoor pool, wading pool, hot tub, playground, Wi-Fi, free pancake breakfasts, and a free rodeo shuttle.

Other good places are **Gateway Motel and RV Park** (203 W. Yellowstone Ave., 307/587-2561, www.gatewaycamp.qwestoffice.net, $28 for RVs, $17 for tents, May–mid-Sept.) and **Absaroka Bay RV Park** (U.S. Hwy. 14/16/20 S., 307/527-7440 or 800/557-7440, www.cody-wy.com, 30 RVs, $20 tents). You can also park RVs at several of the Wapiti Valley lodges, including **Green Creek Inn and RV Park** and **Yellowstone Valley Inn.** Noncampers can take showers at Gateway Campground or Ponderosa Campground.

FOOD

Because Cody is a tourist town, it's no surprise to find many fine places to eat, covering the spectrum from buffalo burgers to sushi. All Cody restaurants are entirely nonsmoking.

Breakfast and Lunch

Although ◖ **Peter's Café Bakery** (1219 Sheridan Ave., 307/527-5040, www.peterscafe.com, daily 6:45 A.M.–10 P.M. in summer, till 7 P.M. in winter) is open for dinner, the main attractions come earlier, with inexpensive breakfasts (two eggs, two pancakes, and bacon for $6) served all day, along with lunchtime subs ($6–10) on freshly baked breads, plus homemade soups, buffalo burgers, and 32-plus flavors of ice cream. Banana splits, smoothies, and malts are big draws on hot summer afternoons. Heading into the park? Let Peter's pack you a peck of picnic lunches ($9).

The Beta Coffeehouse (1132 12th St., 307/587-7707, 7 A.M.–6 P.M. Mon.–Fri., 7 A.M.–4 P.M. Sat.–Sun.) is the best local espresso joint, with a hip setting, fruit smoothies, iced coffees, homemade pastries (cinnamon rolls, scones, and muffins), and free Wi-Fi.

Secreted away in a suburban neighborhood on the east side of town, **Willow Fence Tea Room** (1913 Stampede Ave., 307/587-0888, 11 A.M.–2 P.M. Tues.–Fri.) serves steaming pots of tea, along with a limited menu of homemade soups, sandwiches, and desserts. Reservations are advised.

American

◖ **Proud Cut Saloon** (1227 Sheridan Ave., 307/587-7343, 11 A.M.–11 P.M. Mon.–Sat., noon–10 P.M. Sun.) is a fine Wyoming bar and restaurant offering unusual lunchtime sandwiches and burgers (try the bleu cheese burger) and outstanding steak and prime rib for dinner, or as the saloon calls it, "kick ass cowboy cuisine." It's the real thing, with a rustic and woodsy Old West decor, and mercifully, no smoke. Most dinners are $17–30, but burgers and sandwiches cost $7–9.

It's dark inside Buffalo Bill's old-time **Irma Hotel** (1192 Sheridan Ave., 307/587-4221, www.irmahotel.com, daily 6 A.M.–10 P.M. in summer, daily 7 A.M.–8:30 P.M. in winter), an old favorite for lunch and dinner. You can order à la carte with such dinner choices as chicken teriyaki, baby back ribs, or buffalo rib-eye for $16–22, but the Irma's sprawling buffets are a far better deal: $10 adults ($5 kids) for breakfast or lunch, or $23 adults, $10 kids for a slow-roasted prime-rib dinner buffet. These all-you-can-eat affairs are great for families with picky eaters.

Besides these dinner options, several Wapiti Valley/North Fork lodges serve outstanding meals and attract both locals and tourists. **Absaroka Mountain Lodge** (307/587-3963, www.absarokamtlodge.com) has Wednesday outdoor ribs barbecue ($18) and Saturday-night all-you-can-eat Dutch oven beef stew ($12) feasts. Both take place under the trees at this historic old lodge. Another mountain lodge (38 miles west of Cody) is **Elephant Head Lodge** (307/587-3980, www.elephantheadlodge.com, $12–31), with fine steaks in a rustic setting. Reservations are recommended.

On the west edge of town near the rodeo grounds, **Cody Cattle Company** (1910 Demaris St., 307/272-5770, www.thecodycattlecompany.com, daily 5:30–9 P.M. late May–mid-Sept.) blends cowboy-style family entertainment and a filling chuck-wagon dinner buffet spread of chicken, beef, potatoes, baked beans, cornbread, brownies, and lemonade. It's hard to beat the price: get 'em both for $24 adults or $12 kids (add $6 for steaks). There are two shows most summer nights at 6:30 and 8:30 P.M.

Asian, Italian, and Mexican

For authentic Chinese food, including a big lunch buffet ($9) and family-style dinners, visit **Hong Kong Restaurant** (1201 17th St., 307/587-6420, www.codychinese.com, 11 A.M.–9:30 P.M. Mon.–Sat., $9–11).

Adriano's Italian Restaurant (1244 Sheridan Ave., 307/527-7320, daily 11 A.M.–10 P.M., $17–20) may not have the fastest service, but this is the real thing, with a big menu featuring veal *calabrese,* shrimp scampi, chicken Marsala, burgers, and pizzas—try the white pizza.

For authentic south-of-the-border burritos, tacos, enchiladas, *rellenos,* and tamales in an unpretentious setting, slip into **Tacos el Taconozo** (610 Yellowstone Ave., 307/587-

4045, 11 A.M.–3 P.M. and 5–8:30 P.M. Mon.–Sat., $8–13). Mexican tunes spill from the speakers, the chips and salsa keep coming, and the bar cranks out margaritas (but the dishes are a bit heavy on the lard).

Fine Dining

Wyoming Rib and Chop House (1367 Sheridan Ave., 307/587-7731, www.ribandchophouse.com, 11 A.M.–10 P.M. Mon.–Sat., 10–A.M.10 P.M. Sun., $16–30) specializes in buffalo rib-eye steaks, jambalaya, fresh seafood, and award-winning baby back pork ribs. The atmosphere is upscale and romantic, but you can also get buffalo burgers and other munchies ($6 and up).

Also of particular note is **The Mayor's Inn** (1413 Rumsey Ave., 307/587-0887 or 888/217-3001, www.mayorsinndinnerhouse.com), where gourmet dinners are served Thursday–Saturday evenings (starting at 5 P.M., with the last seating at 8 P.M.) in a quaint Victorian setting. The limited menu changes every couple of weeks but always includes Wyoming lamb, buffalo, and beef, along with other regional fare. Prices are reasonable, with most entrées at $16–24. Open May–October only. Reservations recommended.

Right on the western end of town beyond the rodeo grounds, **The Terrace** (525 W. Yellowstone Ave., 307/587-5868, www.codyterrace.com, 4–10 P.M. Mon.–Sat. in summer, 5–10 P.M. Tues.–Sat. in winter, $16–35) has an open interior and big windows facing the foothills of Cedar Mountain. It's a classy night-on-the-town dining place with great appetizers (try the Reuben egg roll) and a menu encompassing London broil, southwestern chicken alfredo Florentine, seared scallops, and nightly specials. There's a full bar with 21 beers on draught ($1 happy-hour beers), along with a memorable flourless chocolate torte for dessert.

Groceries and Natural Foods

Cody's grocers include an **Albertson's** (on the south side of Cody at 1825 17th St., 307/527-7007) and a big **Walmart SuperCenter**

(321 Yellowstone Ave., 307/527-4673) on the west end. For natural foods and supplements, head to **Whole Foods Trading Co.** (1239 Rumsey Ave., 307/587-3213, www. wholefoodstradingco.com). **Wyoming Buffalo Company** (1270 Sheridan Ave., 307/587-8708 or 800/453-0636, www.wyomingbuffalocompany.com) specializes in buffalo jerky, salami, sausage, and fresh meat, with a variety of gift packages. Stop in for a free sample.

On the north end of town, **Juniper Wine & Spirits** (30 Pearson Ave., 307/587-4472, www.junipershop.com) has an excellent selection of wines, single-malt scotches, bourbons, and beers. Sample 10 wines daily in the tasting room; it's especially popular on "Thirsty Thursdays," with extended hours and several more-expensive wines to taste.

INFORMATION AND SERVICES

Get local information and an armload of brochures from the always-helpful folks at **Cody Country Chamber of Commerce** (836 Sheridan Ave., 307/587-2777 or 800/393-2639, www.codychamber.org). Hours are Monday–Friday 8 A.M.–6 P.M., Saturday 9 A.M.–5 P.M., and Sunday 10 A.M.–3 P.M. Memorial Day–September; Monday–Friday 8 A.M.–5 P.M. the rest of the year. This log building—on the National Register of Historic Places—housed the original Buffalo Bill Museum from 1927 to 1969 and was built as a replica of Cody's TE Ranch. A regional tourism organization, **Park County Travel Council** (307/587-2297 or 800/393-2639, www.yellowstonecountry.org), is also based here. Another useful Web source is www. codywyomingnet.com.

Government offices include the **BLM's Cody Field Office** (1002 Blackburn Ave., 307/578-5900, www.wy.blm.gov), **Shoshone National Forest Supervisor's Office** (808 Meadow Lane, 307/527-6241, www.fs.fed.us/r2/shoshone), and the **North Zone Ranger District Office** (203 W. Yellowstone, 307/527-6921).

Just down from the rec center, and up the street from the post office, the **Park County**

Library (1500 Heart Mt. St., 307/527-8820, www.parkcountylibrary.org, 9 A.M.–8 P.M. Mon.–Thurs., 9 A.M.–5:30 P.M. Fri., 9 A.M.–5 P.M. Sat., 1–4 P.M. Sun.) has regional titles, computers, and Wi-Fi. Coffee up at **Biblio Bistro** (307/527-1887, www.bibliobistro.com), housed within the library.

Cody's **West Park Hospital** (707 Sheridan Ave., 307/527-7501 or 800/654-9447, www. westparkhospital.org) is the largest in Bighorn Basin and one of the finest in the state. The hospital's **Urgent Care Clinic** (702 Yellowstone Ave., 307/587-7207) is open daily, with no appointment needed.

Wash clothes at **Eastgate Laundry** (1813 17th St., 307/587-5355) next to Albertson's, or **Cody Laundromat** (1728 Beck Ave., 307/587-8500); the latter is open 24 hours.

GETTING THERE AND AROUND

Yellowstone Regional Airport (www.flyyra. com) is just east of town on U.S. Highway 14/16/20. **SkyWest/Delta** (307/587-9740 or 800/221-1212, www.delta.com) has daily flights to Salt Lake City, while **United Express** (307/587-9740 or 800/864-8331, www.united.com) has daily service to Denver. **Spirit Mountain Aviation** (307/587-6732) offers scenic flights and charter service.

Rent cars at the airport from **Avis** (307/587-4082 or 800/331-1212, www.avis.com), **Budget** (307/587-6066 or 800/527-0700, www.budget.com), **Dollar** (307/587/3608 or 800/800-4000, www.dollar.com), **Hertz** (307/587-2914 or 800/654-3131, www.hertz. com), or **Thrifty** (307/587-8855 or 800/847-4389, www.cody.thrifty.com).

Unfortunately, there is absolutely **no bus service** to Cody, around Cody, or from Cody into Yellowstone.

Tours

Cody Trolley Tours (307/527-7043, www. codytrolleytours.com) can take you on a very informative hour-long cruise through town and up to Buffalo Bill Dam ($24 adults, $10 kids, $22 seniors). A combo ticket ($36) includes entrance to the Buffalo Bill Historical Center. Tours are offered several times daily June–September.

For a more personalized trip, call **Grub Steak Expeditions** (307/527-6316 or 800/527-6316, www.grubsteaktours.com). The company leads 12-hour auto tours of the park, along with visits to Sunlight Basin, Wapiti Valley, and the South Fork. One-day tours cost $490 for two people, plus $125 for each additional

guest. These are popular with families looking for a unique perspective on the park, and some are led by co-owner Bob Richard, a retired Yellowstone park ranger.

Yellowstone tours are also available from **Wyoming Touring Adventures** (307/587-5136) and **Yellowstone Wildlife & Photo Tours** (307/587-6988 or 800/293-0148, http://cu.imt.net/~rodeo). **Cody Cab** (307/272-8364) is the local taxi company.

Dubois

Approaching Dubois (pop. 1,000, elev. 6,917 feet) from either direction, you drive through the extraordinary red, yellow, and gray badlands that set this country apart. The luxuriant Wind River winds its way down a narrow valley where horses graze in the irrigated pastures and old barns and newer log homes stand against the hills, while the tree-covered Absaroka and Wind River Mountains ring distant views. The town of Dubois consists of a long main street that makes an abrupt elbow turn and then points due west toward the mountains. The log buildings and snatches of wooden sidewalks give the place an authentic frontier feel. Locals live in cabins, trailer homes, and simple frame houses. Dubois weather is famously mild; warm Chinook winds often melt any snow that falls. Grand scenery reigns in all directions. Snowmobilers, hunters, and anglers have discovered that Dubois provides a good place to relax in Wyoming's "banana belt" while remaining close to the more temperamental mountains. The area basks in an average of 300 days of sunshine each year. By the way, Dubois is pronounced "DU-boys"; other pronunciations will reveal your tenderfoot status. Locals sometimes jokingly call it "Dubious."

HISTORY

Dubois began in the 1880s when pioneer ranchers and more than a few rustlers, including Butch Cassidy, settled in the area, followed

by Scandinavian hand-loggers who cut lodgepole for railroad ties. The town that grew up along the juncture of Horse Creek and the Wind River was first known as Never Sweat, but when citizens applied for a post office the Postal Service refused to allow the name and suggested Dubois instead—the name of an Idaho senator who just happened to be on the Senate committee that provided funding for the post office.

© DON PITCHER

Be sure to obey this sign!

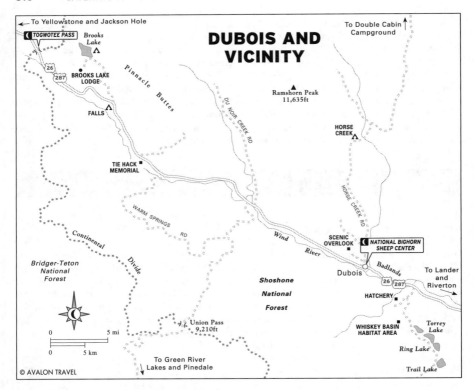

Like many edge-of-the-mountain towns, Dubois moved from a logging and ranching past to one focused on tourism. The visitor-oriented economy certainly has its downside—elaborate "trophy" log summer homes have overrun lush pastures on both ends of town—but so far this pretty little place has been spared the onslaught of "industrial tourism." Still, old attitudes die hard, and you'll see pickup trucks with bumper stickers saying "Save Wyoming's wildlife. Shoot a tree hugger" or "Wolves—Government sponsored terrorists."

SIGHTS

One thing you certainly would not expect to find in Dubois is a training center for lawyers, but famed Wyoming attorney Gerry Spence has one on his Thunderhead Ranch east of town. His nonprofit (!) **Trial Lawyers College** (760/322-3783 or 800/688-1611, www.trial-lawyerscollege.com) puts about 50 lawyers through an intense four-week session each summer, with mock trials and professional actors. Watch your step with all these lawyers around Dubois.

It's hard to miss the **Country Store Exxon** station (404 W. Ramshorn, 307/455-2677) on the west side of town with the **Jackalope** out front. Head inside for ice cream or a slice of pie and the chance to plunk your kid on the giant Jackalope inside for a goofy photo. Only in Wyoming!

Dubois Museum

The Dubois Museum (909 W. Ramshorn, 307/455-2284, www.duboismuseum.org,

© DON PITCHER

bighorn sheep in Whiskey Basin Wildlife Habitat Area

$2 adults, $1 kids, $5 for families) is open daily 9 A.M.–6 P.M. June–September and Tuesday–Saturday 10 A.M.–4 P.M. the rest of the year. The small collection includes exhibits on the Sheepeater Indians and their pictographs, with other displays on ranch life, geology, and wildlife. Surrounding the museum are 10 historic log cabins and other old structures, all containing interesting displays. Free interpretive programs take place on Monday evenings mid-June–mid-August. Next to the museum is the **Headwaters Arts and Conference Center,** where an upstairs gallery (307/455-2687, www.wrvag.org) exhibits works by regional artists. It's open daily in the summer.

◖ National Bighorn Sheep Center

Just steps from the town museum, The National Bighorn Sheep Interpretive Center (907 W. Ramshorn, 307/455-3429 or 888/209-2795, www.bighorn.org, $2.50 adults, $0.75 kids under 12, $6 families, 9 A.M.–7 P.M. Mon.–Sat., 9 A.M.–5 P.M. Sun. late May–early Sept., 9 A.M.–5 P.M. Tues.–Sat. rest of the year) houses a small collection of displays

on desert bighorn, Rocky Mountain bighorn, stone sheep, and Dall sheep. The museum details how the population was brought back from the brink of extinction, and it includes hands-on exhibits and interactive displays on the lives of bighorns. Also here is a diorama of a Sheepeater Indian trap and mounted specimens around a 16-foot-high central "mountain." A small theater shows an 18-minute video on bighorn sheep biology and behavior, while a gift shop sells books and other items.

The center offers **wildlife tours** (Nov.–Mar.) of the Whiskey Basin Habitat Area just west of town. These 3–4-hour van-and-hiking trips cost $25 per person and include binoculars and spotting scopes to view the animals. There's a two-person minimum, and reservations are required at least 24 hours in advance. The center also has an excellent brochure describing self-guided tours of Whiskey Basin.

Whiskey Basin

Approximately five miles east of Dubois, a sign points the way to Whiskey Basin. Follow the gravel road two miles to the **Dubois State Fish Hatchery** (307/455-2431, open daily

TIE HACKS

Many of the trees cut in Wyoming's forests between 1870 and 1940 went to supply railroad ties for an ever-expanding network of rails throughout the Rockies. The men who cut these ties – tie hacks – spent long, hard months in the mountains, working through the winter. Most of the woodsmen were emigrants from Sweden, Norway, Finland, Austria, and Italy. Tie hacks first felled a suitable lodgepole pine using a bucksaw, then limbed the tree and used a broadax to hew the tie into shape, finally peeling the remaining bark from the sides and cutting it to length. Hundreds of thousands of ties – each eight feet long and at least five inches on each side – were produced annually by tie hacks. Horses dragged the ties down to a creek bank or flume to await high spring flows, when thousands of ties could be sent downriver at once. The enormous logjams that resulted sometimes required dynamite to loosen. Downstream booms caught the logs, where they could be hauled up and loaded onto railway cars.

Tie hacks found work in many parts of Wyoming, but especially in the Medicine Bow Mountains, Laramie Mountains, Sierra Madre, Big Horn Mountains, and Wind River Mountains, where major streams provided a way for the ties to reach the railheads. In the upper Wind River country, the industry spanned three decades, from 1914 to 1946. During this time, more than 10 million ties were cut and floated downstream to Riverton, where the Chicago and Northwestern Railroad used them. A stone monument to the tie hacks stands along U.S. Highway 26/287 approximately 18 miles west of Dubois. The visitor center in Dubois has a handout that provides a self-guided tour of historical sights associated with the tie hacks.

---

8 A.M.–5 P.M.), where rainbow, cutthroat, golden, brook, and brown trout as well as grayling are raised. The bucolic setting is hard to beat: a tree-lined creek surrounded by sage, mountains, and badlands.

A short distance up the road is a wildlife-viewing kiosk for the **Whiskey Basin Wildlife Habitat Area.** During winter the valley is home to the largest population of **Rocky Mountain bighorn sheep** anywhere on earth. Some 650 sheep congregate here because of the mild winters and the shallow snow. Although you're likely to find sheep all winter, the best time to photograph them is in the breeding season, from late November–December. During this period you'll see rams charging head-first into each other over the chance to mate. It's enough to give you a headache. The lambs are born in late May and early June high up on rocky slopes. Bighorn sheep are also sometimes seen in the meadows along the highway or in the hills just above Dubois. The National Bighorn Sheep Interpretive Center in Dubois leads wildlife tours of Whiskey Basin.

Beyond the wildlife-viewing kiosk, the road follows Torrey Creek up past a string of three small bodies of water: Torrey, Ring, and Trail Lakes. These lakes were created by retreating glaciers centuries ago, but low dams have enlarged them. State Game and Fish **campsites** (free) are located along Ring and Trail Lakes. **Ring Lake Ranch** (307/455-2663 or 888/458-5253, www.ringlake.org) houses an ecumenical religious facility used for a variety of retreats, seminars, and other activities throughout the summer.

You'll discover quite a few **Indian pictographs** on large boulders in the Trail Lake vicinity; look for them along the hillside between Trail Lake and the south end of Ring Lake. (Unmarked wooden posts are near some of them.) These figures—some four feet tall—are elaborate otherworldly creations with horns and headdresses, and are believed to represent shamans performing ceremonies under altered states of consciousness. While their age is unknown, they are probably at least 2,000 years old and of Athapaskan (a Canadian tribe) rather than Shoshonean origin. This is some of the oldest rock art in Wyoming. Do not touch, make rubbings, or put anything in contact with the pictographs, since it could cause damage to these irreplaceable symbols from the past.

Badlands

Just west of Dubois is a signed turnoff to a **scenic overlook.** The gravel road climbs sharply (no RVs) for approximately one mile to an extraordinary viewpoint, where displays note the surrounding peaks. Enjoy marvelous views of 11,635-foot Ramshorn Peak from here, but bring warm clothes for the inevitable wind.

The magnificent badlands on both sides of Dubois, but especially to the east, are well worth exploring. The fascinating **Badlands Interpretive Trail** heads up Mason Draw, 2.4 miles northeast of town. Pick up a booklet describing the trail (not well maintained) at the chamber of commerce office.

Rock hounds will find all sorts of petrified wood, agates, and other colorful rocks up the Wiggins Fork and Horse Creek drainages; ask at the chamber of commerce for directions.

RECREATION

Dubois sits at the confluence of the Wind River and Horse Creek, and both streams provide good trout fishing right in town. Hot springs keep the Wind River flowing all year. Directly behind the National Bighorn Sheep Center is a shady riverside **Town Park** with picnic tables, a playground, tennis courts, and a skate park. The visitor center has descriptions of local fishing holes and brochures from local outfitters who offer pack trips and horseback rides.

Sixteen miles west of Dubois is **Mackenzie Highland Ranch** (307/455-3415, www.mackenziehighlandranch.com), with horseback rides and ATV rentals in the summer.

The nine-hole **Antelope Hills Golf Course** (307/455-2888) is on the western end of Dubois.

Winter Activities

The Absarokas and Wind River Mountains

badlands along the Wind River near Dubois

© DON PITCHER

around Dubois are crowded with **snowmobilers** during winter, and several places rent "sleds" in town and nearby. Don't expect peace and quiet with all of these machines roaring through the backcountry! More than 300 miles of trails head out in all directions, with the Union Pass area a particular focus.

For something quieter, **cross-country skiers** will find trails near Falls Campground and Brooks Lake (both 23 miles west of town) and Togwotee Mountain Lodge (40 miles west), and in backcountry wilderness areas off-limits to snowmobiles.

ENTERTAINMENT AND EVENTS

Find country-and-western bands at **Rustic Pine Tavern** (119 E. Ramshorn, 307/455-2430, www.rusticpinetavern.com), a classic Western bar with elk and moose heads, cowboy-hatted locals, plenty of old wood, and a pool table. Check out the ashtrays, which note, "God spends his vacation here." Bring your dance boots for Tuesday-night square-dance sessions all summer.

Whiskey Creek Saloon (204 W. Ramshorn, 307/455-2387) has a DJ or live music Tuesday and Thursday nights all summer long, plus pool tables and dart boards.

Events

The first weekend of February brings **Winterfest,** with sled dog and skijoring races (cross-country skiing while being pulled by a dog). In mid-May, **Dubois Antler Rendezvous** has five days of elk antler sales in Dubois's Town Park. The **Swedish Smorgasbord** in June celebrates the Scandinavian tie hacks (men who cut railroad ties between 1870 and 1940) with a big dinner of Scandinavian favorites.

The town's biggest festivities take place over **Fourth of July** weekend, with a parade, ice-cream social, rodeo, games, Western barbecue, fireworks, and rubber-ducky races down the river. In mid-July, **Dubois Museum Day** is a folk art festival with Indian dancing, frontier crafts demonstrations, and lectures.

A **National Art Show** comes to town on the last week of July, attracting both professionals and amateurs. It's been going on for more than 50 years. Also don't miss the always popular Dubois firefighters' **Buffalo Barbecue,** held the second Saturday of August. A big quilt festival takes place that same weekend. Get specifics on these and other events from the Dubois Chamber of Commerce, 307/455-2556.

On Friday evenings mid-June–mid-August, you'll find **rodeos** (www.duboisrodeo.org) at the town arena on the west end of Dubois.

SHOPPING

Drop by **Wind River Gear** (19 N. 1st St., 307/455-3468, www.windrivergearshop.com) for quality outdoor clothing and backpacking gear. Find traditional Western wear at the old-time **Welty's General Store** (113 W. Ramshorn, 307/455-2377), and fishing supplies at **Whiskey Mountain Tackle** (1428 Warm Springs Dr., 307/455-2587).

Two Ocean Books (128 E. Ramshorn, 307/455-3554, www.cowboybookseller.com) is a fine local bookshop, and **Water Wheel Gift Shop** (113 E. Ramshorn, 307/455-2112, www.waterwheelgiftsandbooks.com) also carries a selection of regional titles.

Galleries

Several downtown galleries are worth a visit. **Trapline Gallery** (120 E. Ramshorn, 307/455-2800) sells Indian-crafted beadwork, jewelry, and artwork. **Tukadeka Traders/Horse Creek Gallery** (104 E. Ramshorn, 307/455-3345) has an impressive collection of antique trade beads, along with tacky antler carvings and Indian trinkets. Find works by a dozen local and Wyoming artists at **Silver Sage Gallery** (124 E. Ramshorn, 307/455-3002, www.silversagegallery.com). On the north side of town, **Antler Workshop and Gallery** (1404 Warm Springs Dr., 307/455-2204, www.antlergallery.com) has a big wagon filled with elk antlers out front and an unusual variety of antler furniture, chandeliers, and lamps inside, all crafted by Kurt Gordon.

ACCOMMODATIONS

Dubois makes an excellent stopping point on the way to Yellowstone and Grand Teton National Parks, with lodging prices well below those in Jackson Hole. All places are open year-round unless noted otherwise.

Branding Iron Inn (401 Ramshorn, 307/455-2893 or 888/651-9378, www.brandingironinn.com) features cozy, well-maintained duplex log cabins that were built in the 1940s. They've been substantially updated, with standard rooms for $75–85, kitchenette units for $90, and an apartment for $100. All units contain fridges, microwaves, and Wi-Fi. Folks traveling with horses will appreciate the adjacent corral. No air-conditioning, but some units contain ceiling fans and the thick log walls help keep the heat out.

Located on a beautiful woodsy bend in the Wind River three miles east of town, **Longhorn Ranch Lodge and RV Resort** (307/455-2337, www.thelonghornranch.com) has two dozen modern and spotless motel rooms, cabins, and suites, all with fridges, microwaves, continental breakfast, and Wi-Fi. Weekend summer rates for rooms are $112–123 d, studio kitchenette cabins are $146, and two-bedroom cabins with full kitchens cost $186. Weekday prices are about $15 less. Check out the Aussie owners' prize longhorn cattle in an adjacent pasture.

Another place that gets high marks from travelers, **Trail's End Motel** (511 Ramshorn, 307/455-2540 or 888/455-6660, www.trailsendmotel.com) has knotty-pine interiors and a Western theme. Clean, remodeled rooms start at $79 d, and the nicest units ($99–149 d) include cedar decks facing the Wind River along with in-room fridges and microwaves. Also available are two-room family units that sleep eight for $149. There's free Wi-Fi. Open May–October.

For historic rooms, stay at **Twin Pines Lodge and Cabins** (218 Ramshorn, 307/455-2600 or 800/550-6332, www.twinpineslodge.com). Built in 1934 and on the National Register of Historic Places, the lodge has both modern and rustic cabins. Rates are $90–120 d in cabins or rooms in the main lodge, or $110–140 d for two larger suites in the lodge, both with jetted tubs. Twin Pines amenities include a filling breakfast, fridges, microwaves, Wi-Fi, and DVD players with a big video library. Everything is immaculate in this place that gracefully blends old and new.

Find attractive accommodations at the largest motel in town, **Stagecoach Motor Inn** (103 Ramshorn, 307/455-2303 or 800/455-5090, www.stagecoachmotel-dubois.com). Rates are $82–95 d, king suites run $90–95 d, and six-person kitchenettes cost $100–140. Wi-Fi is available, and families appreciate the seasonal heated outdoor pool, year-round hot tub, and shady backyard playground.

Along the river on the west end of town, **Rocky Mountain Lodge** (1349 W. Ramshorn, 307/455-2844 or 800/682-9323, www.rockymountainlodge-dubois.com) is a family-run motel with standard rooms for $84 d, along with larger units at $89–94. All include microwaves, fridges, and Wi-Fi; add $10 for kitchenettes. A horse corral is available out back, and pets are accepted.

Bed-and-Breakfasts

Constructed from red clay blocks in the 1940s, **The Stone House B&B** (207 S. 1st St., 307/455-2555, www.duboisbnb.com) is just two blocks from downtown Dubois. Guests can stay in one of the upstairs rooms ($80 d with a private bath) or four people can rent both rooms ($135 with a shared bath). Adjacent is a small guest cottage with two bedrooms, each with a queen bed ($95 d or $135 d for four). A full breakfast is served each morning, and the sitting room faces Whiskey Mountain, a good place to watch for bighorn sheep. Wi-Fi is available. Open May–October.

Jakey's Fork Homestead (307/455-2769, www.frontierlodging.com, $135 d) has B&B accommodations in a delightful century-old homestead four miles east of town. It's close to the bighorn sheep refuge in Whiskey Basin and offers extraordinary views of both the Wind

River Mountains and nearby badlands. Guests can stay in three guest rooms within the home (shared bath) or a rustic sod-covered cabin. A full breakfast is served.

Guest Ranches and Mountain Lodges

Quite a few dude ranches/mountain lodges are found around Dubois, including the country west of here on the way to Togwotee Pass.

Ten miles out East Fork Road, **Lazy L&B Ranch** (307/455-2839 or 800/453-9488, www.lazylb.com) is a century-old ranch offering creekside log cabins, horseback riding, an outdoor swimming pool and hot tub, stocked fishing ponds, kids' programs, volleyball, fly-fishing, and a rifle range. The ranch's horseback-riding program is excellent, and guests can choose trips through the badlands or high into the mountains. Lazy L&B is open late May–mid-September, with all-inclusive six-night rates of $2,950 for two people. The ranch also operates **Bear Basin Wilderness Camp** (www.bearbasincamp.com, $240 daily per person), a wonderful base from which to explore the Washakie Wilderness on horseback. A maximum of eight guests stay in wall tents during these backcountry trips.

Located 16 miles up East Fork Road, **Bitterroot Ranch** (307/455-2778 or 800/545-0019, www.bitterrootranch.com) emphasizes horseback riding for riders at all levels of ability; each guest gets to ride several different horses. The owners breed Arabian horses and offer centered riding clinics, a cross-country jumping course, pack trips, cattle drives, and fly-fishing. Both French and German are spoken here, attracting an international clientele. The ranch is open June–September and has space for 32 guests in a dozen cabins. All-inclusive weekly rates are $4,200 for two people. The owners also run Equitors (www.equitours.com), a travel agency specializing in horseback rides all over the globe.

South of Dubois in beautiful Jakeys Fork Canyon, **CM Ranch** (307/455-2331 or 800/455-0721, www.cmranch.com) is one of Wyoming's oldest dude ranches; it's been here since 1927.

The ranch offers dramatic badlands topography and a variety of fossils, making it a favorite of geologists (and amateur rock hounds). Trails lead into the adjacent Fitzpatrick Wilderness, a destination for horseback trips. Fishing is another popular activity, and a fishing guide is available. The immaculate lodge buildings have space for 55 guests, and kids love the big outdoor pool and a hot tub. All-inclusive weekly rates at this delightful old-time ranch are $3,250–3,400 for two people. Open June–mid-September. The ranch is owned by the Kemmerer family, whose ancestors founded the town of Kemmerer, Wyoming. They also own Jackson Hole Mountain Resort.

Operating as a dude ranch since 1920, **T-Cross Ranch** (307/455-2206 or 877/827-6770, www.tcross.com) is 15 miles north of Dubois near Horse Creek and is open mid-June–mid-September. Surrounded by the Shoshone National Forest, this remote ranch has weekly accommodations at $3,100 for two people, including horseback riding, all meals, activities for kids, trout fishing, and a hot tub. Backcountry pack trips and other activities are also available. Lodging is in eight comfortable log cabins, and the main lodge has a massive stone fireplace and spacious front porch.

Ramshorn Guest Ranch (307/455-3921 in summer or 307/333-4430 in winter, www.ramshornguestranch.com) has three cabins on a 250-acre ranch bordered on three sides by Forest Service land. Nearby trails lead into the Washakie Wilderness, making this a fine base for hikers and backpackers. Ignore "guest ranch" in the name; no horses or dudes here, just comfortable cabins with private baths and full kitchens for $65–100 nightly with a three-night minimum. Tent sites are $12 (shower house nearby), RV hookups cost $25, and a couple of bring-your-sleeping-bag tepees take you back in time for $20. Ramshorn is nine miles west of Dubois on U.S. 26/287, and another six miles up a dirt road. The ranch has Wi-Fi, but no phones or TVs; you don't need them up here in God's Country. Open mid-June–late August only.

Sixteen miles west of Dubois is **Mackenzie Highland Ranch** (307/455-3415, www.mackenziehighlandranch.com), where accommodations are offered in a variety of cabins and other rustic buildings. The simplest (very basic) cabins share a bathhouse and cost $45 for up to four people. Considerably nicer are the two-bedroom cabins with space for seven, full kitchens, baths, and living rooms that sleep up to four for $225–245. The finest is a modern four-bedroom home (it sleeps 10) with two baths and a full kitchen, for $275. There's a three-night minimum for most cabins. RVs can park for $45 per night with full hookups, and Wi-Fi is available. This isn't an all-inclusive dude ranch, so meals aren't available, but trail rides, ATV rentals, and guided fishing trips are offered in the summer. The ranch becomes a base for snowmobilers, cross-country skiers, and hunters at other times of the year.

Right along Highway 26/268 and 18 miles west of Dubois, **Triangle C Ranch** (307/455-2225 or 800/661-4928, www.trianglec.com) was established as the first tie-hack camp in the region. It now operates as a guest ranch where the main emphasis is horseback riding, but guests will also enjoy fishing, hiking, activities for kids and teens, wagon rides, and evening entertainment, plus the outdoor pool and hot tub. Weekly rates are $4,500 for two people. The ranch is open late May–mid-October and mid-December–mid-April. In winter, Triangle C offers dogsledding adventures and snowmobiling.

Twenty miles west of Dubois, **Lava Mountain Lodge** (307/455-2506 or 800/919-9570, www.lavamountainlodge.com) has motel rooms ($88 d), newly built cabins with bedroom, loft, full kitchen, and bath ($135–145 for four guests), plus a large rental house that sleeps up to 10 ($325). You'll also find a restaurant serving home-cooked meals three times a day, along with camping spaces ($15 tents, $35 RVs), basic camper cabins ($45 d, bring sleeping bags, shower house close by), plus a convenience store, bar, and laundry with coin-op showers. Open year-round, with a corral in the back for folks traveling with horses.

Vacation Rentals

For a beautiful in-town option, stay at **Cabin on the Wind** (615 W. Ramshorn, 307/455-3472, www.vrbo.com/98864), a lovingly refurbished cabin with a deck overlooking the Wind River. Inside are three bedrooms with queen beds, a full kitchen and living room, log furnishings, hardwood floors, washer, dryer, and Wi-Fi. It rents for $145 with a three-night minimum stay.

Next door is **Flying W Vacation Rental** (650/363-0473, www.vrbo.com/99558), a simple but comfy riverside place with four bedrooms. It sleeps eight for $200 nightly with a three-night minimum.

Mountain Pinnacle Properties (307/455-3735 or 866/738-4814, www.mountainpinnacleproperties.com) has additional vacation homes in the Dubois area.

CAMPING

The closest public camping spot is **Horse Creek Campground** (www.fs.fed.us/r2/shoshone, open late May–early Sept., $15), 12 miles north of Dubois on Horse Creek Road.

Dubois Wind River KOA (225 W. Welty, 307/455-2238 or 800/562-0806, www.koa.com, open May–Sept., $25 tents, $48 RVs, $50–60 cabins) is one of Wyoming's better private campgrounds, with an indoor pool, a playground, a game room, Wi-Fi, and a riverside location, plus chuck-wagon dinner shows on Monday and Thursday evenings. Showers for noncampers are $7.

In a quiet spot three miles east of town, **Longhorn Ranch Lodge and RV Resort** (307/455-2337, www.thelonghornranch.com, open May–mid-Oct.) has full hookup sites ($45–50) along the river and tent spaces ($22–27), including Wi-Fi.

FOOD
Breakfast and Lunch

Popular with both locals and tourists, **[** Cowboy Café** (115 E. Ramshorn, 307/455-2595, daily 7 A.M.–9 P.M., closed Wed. in winter, $10–22) serves home-style breakfasts with big helpings of biscuits and gravy, along with delicious burgers for lunch and chicken-fried black Angus steaks for dinner. Cowboy Café's pies are famous throughout the region, with 15 or so variations daily. There's a reason they sell 1,000 pies a month here!

Hang out with the locals at **Village Café/ Daylight Donuts** (515 W. Ramshorn, 307/455-2122, daily 6 A.M.–9 P.M.), where homemade doughnuts, coffee, and conversation are the morning attractions.

Kathy's Koffee (306 W. Ramshorn, 307/455-3862, 7 A.M.–3 P.M. Mon.–Fri., 7 A.M.–2 P.M. Sat., 7 A.M.–1 P.M. Sun.) operates from a little log cabin with a deck and picnic tables in the back, and a light menu of salads, sandwiches, wraps, smoothies, shakes, espresso (including iced lattes), and bagels. This is where the fishing outfitters hold court. Free Wi-Fi is available for customers.

American

Next to the bar of the same name, **Rustic Pine Steakhouse** (119 E. Ramshorn, 307/455-2772, www.rusticpinetavern.com, daily 5–10 P.M. in summer, 5–10 P.M. Tues.–Sat. in winter, $12–29) is a carnivore's delight, with steaks, London broil, Thai shrimp nachos, and big salads. Summer visitors can dine outside on the big corner patio.

For an Old West treat, head over to **Circle Up Chuckwagon Dinner Shows** at Dubois Wind River KOA (225 W. Welty, 307/455-2238 or 800/562-0806, www.circleupchuckwagondinnershow.com, 6:30–9 P.M. Mon. and Thurs. late June–late Aug.). You'll find filling Dutch oven meals (barbecue brisket, baked potato, coleslaw, baked beans, and cobbler) plus twangy cowboy music for $22 adults or $6 kids. You don't need to stay at KOA to enjoy the show.

Fine Dining

For fine dining in rustic Dubois, you won't go wrong at **The Sundance Café** (106 E. Ramshorn, 307/455-3989, www.sundancecafeduboiswyoming.com, daily 7:30 A.M.–2:30 P.M. and 5:30–9 P.M. year-round, $17–27). The little log cabin has a shady wraparound

deck right on Horse Creek, perfect for a sunny afternoon. Everything is fresh and made to order; no deep-fryer here! Try the chicken salad sandwich for lunch (with cranberries, almonds, and celery). Dinner faves include spicy plum shrimp kabobs, Baja fish tacos, and delicious rack of lamb. There's wine, beer, cocktails, and a full bar, plus Wi-Fi.

Also notable is **Nostalgia Bistro** (202 E. Ramshorn St., 307/455-3528, www.nostalgiabistrowy.com, 11 A.M.–2 P.M. and 5–9 P.M. Tues.–Sun. in summer, 11 A.M.–2 P.M. Tues.–Fri. and 5–9 P.M. Wed.–Sat. in winter, $18–29), with an eclectic mix of Rocky Mountain and Asian cuisine. Try a "flapper" (grilled steak) sandwich for lunch, or the dinnertime OMG chimichanga packed with crab and lobster. Other treats include seared scallops, tempura, sushi, and venison loin. The bakery sells home-style breads, tarts, and other treats.

Paya Deli, Pizza, and Catering (112 E. Ramshorn St., 307/455-3331, www.facebook.com/payadeli, 11 A.M.–8 P.M. Wed.–Sun.) has a pleasant front porch and a good selection of sandwiches, daily soups, and quiches, a big salad bar, and notable wood-oven pizzas. Everything is made from scratch. A large Mediterranean pizza with garlic, chicken, feta cheese, spinach, kalamata olives, pumpkin seeds(!), and sun-dried tomatoes costs $20, or you can get a little flatbread mini-pizza for under $6. There are lovely desserts, too.

Two places are fine-dining destinations near the top of Union Pass, 13 scenic miles west of Dubois: **Line Shack Lodge** (307/455-3232, www.lineshack.com) and **The Sawmill Lodge** (307/455-2171 or 866472-9645, www.thesawmill.org). Both are open for three meals a day; Sawmill is probably a better bet.

Groceries and Sweets

Get groceries at **Dubois Super Foods** (610 W. Ramshorn, 307/455-2402). If the kids are begging for a cone, take them to the **Country Store Exxon** (404 W. Ramshorn, 307/455-2677) for ice cream or slice of pie ($1) and a Jackalope ride.

riding the wild Jackalope

Get malts and sundaes from the old-time soda fountain inside the **Dubois Drug Store** (126 E. Ramshorn, 307/455-2300, daily 9 A.M.–6 P.M.).

INFORMATION AND SERVICES

The **Dubois Chamber of Commerce** (616 W. Ramshorn, 307/455-2556 or 888/518-0502, www.duboiswyoming.org) is—theoretically—open daily 8 A.M.–6 P.M. mid-May–mid-August, and Monday–Friday 1–5 P.M. the rest of the year. However, it's run by volunteers, so you may well find nobody home even during these hours. Stop by the Shoshone National Forest **Wind River Ranger District** office (307/455-2466, www.fs.fed.us/r2/shoshone, 8 A.M.–4:30 P.M. Mon.–Fri.) two miles west of town for maps of Shoshone and Bridger-Teton National Forests, information on local trails, and a listing of local horsepacking outfitters.

Open weekdays, the **Dubois Medical Clinic** (307/455-2516), just east of town on Highway 26, has a part-time doctor and nurse practitioners.

Wash clothes at the **Laundromat** at 408 W. Ramshorn (across from Branding Iron Inn).

Check your email or surf the Web for free at the lovely **Dubois Library** (202 N. 1st St., 307/455-2992, www.fremontcountylibraries. org, 11 A.M.–7 P.M. Mon., Tues., and Thurs., 11 A.M.–8 P.M. Wed., 11 A.M.–3 P.M. Fri.–Sat.), or for a fee at **Cyber Café** (308 W. Ramshorn, 307/455-4011).

DUBOIS VICINITY

Anyone who loves the outdoors will discover an abundance of pleasures around Dubois. There's good fishing for rainbow, cutthroat, brown, and brook trout in Wind River and for rainbow, brook, and Mackinaw trout in the many alpine lakes. You'll also see lots of deer, elk, and bighorn sheep. Hikers and horsepackers will find hundreds of miles of Forest Service trails in the area. Photographers love the brilliantly colored badlands that frame Dubois on both the east and west sides. Each winter, hundreds of snowmobilers climb on their "sleds" and cross-country skiers strap on their boards to enter the world of deep powder in the Absarokas.

Horse Creek Area

Horse Creek Road heads north from Dubois, with scenic views of the Absarokas and nearby badland country. Several dude ranches are in the area. **Horse Creek Campground** (open late May–early Sept., $15) is 12 miles north. Forest Road 504 continues another five miles, providing access to the Washakie Wilderness via Horse Creek Trail. Forest Road 508 splits off near Horse Creek Campground and leads another 17 miles to **Double Cabin Campground** (open late May–early Sept., $15). Several trails head into the wilderness from here; the most popular are Frontier Creek Trail and the Wiggins Fork Trail. You'll find remnants of a petrified forest six miles up the Frontier Creek Trail, but they have been rather picked over by illegal collectors. (It's unlawful to remove petrified wood from a wilderness area. Please leave pieces where you find them.) For other

Washakie Wilderness trails information, ask at the Dubois Ranger Station.

Union Pass

The first road across the Absarokas headed through Union Pass southwest of Dubois. The pass forms a divide between the waters of the Columbia, Colorado, and Mississippi Rivers and marks the boundary of the Absaroka, Wind River, and Gros Ventre mountain ranges. Near the pass are an interpretive sign and a nature trail through a flower-filled meadow. Union Pass Road (gravel) leaves U.S. Highway 26/287 eight miles northwest of Dubois and climbs across to connect with Highway 352 north of Pinedale. A major reconstruction project has dramatically improved the road in recent years, providing a beautiful over-the-mountains connection between Pinedale and Dubois in the summer. The road isn't plowed in winter, but it is popular with snowmobilers.

A scenic 20-mile side road begins a few miles up Union Pass Road, heads along Warm Springs Creek, and eventually reconnects with U.S. Highway 26/287. Find fantastic views of the Absaroka and Wind River ranges along this route. The remains of an old tie-hack logging flume are visible, and a warm spring (85°F) flows into the creek.

The Union Pass area is popular with mountain-bikers, cross-country skiers, and hordes of wintertime snowmobilers. Five miles up the road near the 8,600-foot summit, **Line Shack Lodge** (307/455-3232, www.lineshack.com) has a wonderful setting, an inviting interior with tall windows facing the mountains. It's closed in summer, but open for winter snowmobilers.

One-quarter mile downhill from Line Shack is **The Sawmill Lodge** (307/455-2171 or 866/472-9645, www.thesawmill.org), with attractive condo-style rooms ($110 d) and two-level suites ($150 d). A restaurant ($16–21) and bar are on the premises. Closed May and November.

The nonprofit **Teton Valley Ranch Camp** (307/733-2958, www.tvrcamp.org) provides a summertime Western experience for boys and girls. Formerly in Jackson Hole, the ranch moved to a 2,300-acre spread 10 miles west of Dubois in 2005.

◖ TOGWOTEE PASS

The enjoyable drive west from Dubois first cuts through the colorful badlands, playing tag with the Wind River as it begins a long ascent to 9,658-foot Togwotee Pass (TOE-go-tee). The pass is named for a subchief under Chief Washakie. Togwotee was one of the last independent Sheepeater Indians—a branch of the Shoshones—and the man who led a U.S. government exploratory expedition over this pass in 1873. He even guided President Chester Alan Arthur on his monthlong visit to Yellowstone in 1883.

Togwotee Pass (877/996-8724, www.go-togwoteetrail.com) is one of the most scenic drives imaginable, with Ramshorn Peak peeking down from the north for several miles until the road plunges into dense lodgepole forests within Shoshone National Forest, with lingering glimpses of the Pinnacle Buttes.

U.S. 20/287 at Togwotee Pass

© DON PITCHER

Unfortunately, bark beetles are wreaking havoc on these forests, leaving brown swaths of dead trees in their wake.

At the crest, the highway emerges into grass-, willow-, and flower-bedecked meadows with Blackrock Creek winding through. Whitebark pine and Engelmann spruce trees cover the nearby slopes. As the highway drops down the western side into the Bridger-Teton National Forest, another marvelous mountain range—the Tetons—dominates the horizon in dramatic fashion. Snow lies along the roadsides until early July; notice the high posts along the road used by snowplows. Togwotee Pass is a complete shock after all the miles of sagebrush and grassland that control the heartland of Wyoming. It's like entering another world—one of cool, forested mountains and lofty peaks instead of the arid land with horizon-wide vistas.

The highway over Togwotee Pass has been undergoing reconstruction in a process that will not be completed until 2012. New sections of the road have better shoulders, more passing lanes, and a wildlife underpass, but expect 15-minute delays somewhere along your route.

Pinnacle Buttes and Brooks Lake

Dominating the view along U.S. Highway 26/287 for perhaps 15 miles are the castlelike Pinnacle Buttes. Twenty-three miles west of Dubois, you'll come to the turnoff to Brooks Lake, elevation 9,100 feet. Take it, even if you don't plan on camping here. A five-mile gravel road leads to the cliff-rimmed lake, and a clear creek flows east and south from here. The Forest Service's excellent **Pinnacles** and **Brooks Lake** campgrounds (www.fs.fed.us/r2/shoshone, $10–15, open July–Sept.) are along the lakeshore. Facing the lake is historic **Brooks Lake Lodge** (307/455-2121, www.brookslake.com).

Back on the main highway, you'll want to stop at **Falls Campground** (open late May–early Sept., $15–20). Here, Brooks Creek tumbles into a deep canyon. Catch impressive views of **Brooks Creek Falls** along the short trail beginning from the parking lot. In winter, cross-country skiers will find an easy but ungroomed ski trail that heads out two miles from here. **Wind River Lake** is another five miles up the hill, just below the pass. It's a gorgeous place for picnics and fishing, with deep blue water and the sharp cliffs of Pinnacle Buttes behind. There's even a wheelchair-accessible float for anglers.

Continuing west over the pass the vista abruptly opens up, with magnificent Teton vistas from a pullout. A half-mile down the road is the popular **Togwotee Mountain Lodge** (307/543-2847 or 800/543-2847, www.togwoteelodge.com).

BACKGROUND

The Land

The term Greater Yellowstone Ecosystem is broadly applied to the high plateau and mountain ranges inside and surrounding Yellowstone National Park. Covering approximately 19 million acres, this high-elevation country includes two national parks—Yellowstone and Grand Teton—along with sections of six surrounding national forests—Beaverhead-Deerlodge, Bridger-Teton, Caribou-Targhee, Custer, Gallatin, and Shoshone—plus other public lands managed by the Bureau of Land Management (BLM) and national wildlife refuges managed by the U.S. Fish and Wildlife Service. This vast landscape centers on the northwest corner of Wyoming but also includes parts of Montana and Idaho. All together, this is one of the largest relatively intact temperate-zone ecosystems on the planet.

The official websites for Yellowstone (www.nps.gov/yell) and Grand Teton (www.nps.gov/grte) national parks are both packed with detailed information about plants, animals, geology, and other aspects of the Greater Yellowstone Ecosystem.

GEOGRAPHY

The Greater Yellowstone Ecosystem is a mountainous region, with several peaks topping 13,000 feet. The nation's Continental Divide cuts diagonally across the region from

© DON PITCHER

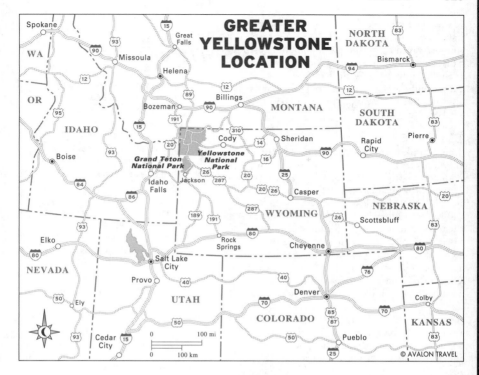

GREATER YELLOWSTONE LOCATION

the southeast to the northwest. Wyoming's highest summit, 13,804-foot Gannet Peak, is on the southern margin of the ecosystem in the Wind River Mountains, and the second-highest peak, Grand Teton (13,770 feet), forms the crown of the Tetons. Montana's tallest summit is 12,799-foot Granite Peak in the Absaroka-Beartooth Wilderness just northeast of Yellowstone. The little burgs of Cooke City and Silver Gate are not far away.

The heart of Yellowstone National Park is a high and rolling plateau that averages about 8,000 feet in elevation, but the eastern and northern sections of the park are considerably more rugged. The park's highest mountain is 11,358-foot Eagle Peak, on the southeastern border, and the lowest point (5,300 feet) is on the northwest corner near Gardiner, Montana. The eastern and northern borders of Yellowstone National Park front on the Absaroka Range, which contains many peaks topping 12,000 feet. To the west and northwest of the park are the lower-elevation Gallatin, Madison, and Centennial ranges and the town of West Yellowstone, while the Caribou Range lies to the southwest. The Yellowstone gateway town of Cody sits at the eastern margin of the Absarokas within Bighorn Basin, and another gateway town, Dubois, occupies the upper end of protected Wind River Valley.

Grand Teton National Park and Jackson Hole lie just south of Yellowstone. The Teton Range creates an incredible western skyline, and the less grandiose, but still impressive, Gros Ventre Range is to the east. Jackson Hole is a relatively flat intermountain basin through which the Snake River flows, with the town of Jackson on its southern end. South of Jackson Hole are the Wyoming and Salt River Ranges, while to the west of the Tetons lies Teton Valley,

Idaho. The massive Wind River Mountains have many peaks over 13,000 feet and reach southeastward from Union Pass to South Pass, a distance of 100 miles. Areas south of Jackson Hole, including the Wind River Mountains, are beyond the scope of this book; for details, see Don Pitcher's *Moon Wyoming* (www.don-pitcher.com).

CLIMATE

The complex and mountainous nature of the Greater Yellowstone Ecosystem creates widely varying microclimatic conditions. It may be a beautiful, sunny summer day in the town of Jackson, while backpackers 2,000 feet higher in the Tetons are getting drenched in a long and lightning-filled storm just a few miles away. The following overall weather description applies to Jackson Hole and the Yellowstone plateau (including the Old Faithful area). Temperatures may be a bit cooler along Yellowstone and Jackson Lakes and are often warmer in the lower-elevation towns of Gardiner, Cody, and Dubois. Killing frosts are possible in any month of the year; I've awakened to new snow on the ground in late June! Total precipitation also varies across the region, from a low of just 11 inches annually at Gardiner to an estimated 70 inches or more in the Lewis Lake area of Yellowstone National Park. Most of the precipitation falls in the winter as snow; summers are relatively dry. (The exceptions to this are low-elevation areas on the north side of Yellowstone, where spring and early summer rains are more important.)

Get detailed climate data at www.wrcc.dri.edu/summary/climsmwy.html, and for daily weather forecasts, visit the National Weather Service's site for western and central Wyoming, www.crh.noaa.gov/riw. Most visitor centers inside and outside the parks have updated forecasts.

Summer

In general, summers are short but pleasant throughout the region, with warm, sunny days and cool nights. Lower-elevation hiking trails

TROPICAL WYOMING

Sometimes I wish that Wyoming had more vegetation and less catarrh, more bloom and summer and fragrance and less Christmas and New Year's through the summer. I like the clear, bracing air of 7,500 feet above the civilized world, but I get weary of putting on and taking off my buffalo overcoat for meals all through dog days. I yearn for a land where a man can take off his ulster and overshoes while he delivers a Fourth of July oration, without flying into the face of Providence and dying of pneumonia.... As I write these lines I look out across the wide sweep of brownish gray plains dotted here and there with ranches and defunct buffalo craniums, and I see shutting down over the sides of the abrupt mountains, and meeting the foothills, a white mist which melts into the gray sky. It is a snow storm in the mountains.

I saw this with wonder and admiration for the first two or three million times. When it became a matter of daily occurrence as a wonder or curiosity, it was below mediocrity. Last July a snow storm gathered one afternoon and fell among the foothills and whitened the whole line to within four or five miles of town, and it certainly was a peculiar freak of nature, but it convinced me that whatever enterprises I might launch into here I would not try to raise oranges and figs until the isothermal lines should meet with a change of heart.

19th-century humorist Bill Nye

are usually free of snow mid-June–mid-October, but some high areas may not melt until late July. You may need both shorts and a light jacket in the same day. Midsummer daytime temperatures in Jackson Hole are typically in the upper 70s or low 80s F, with nighttime lows around 40°F. It's several degrees warmer in low-elevation places such as Gardiner, and 5–10 degrees cooler in many road-accessible parts of Yellowstone. The warmest temperature recorded for Jackson was 101°F in 1934, and for Gardiner it was 103°F in 1960. Cody gets even hotter, and summer days over 90°F hit several times per month.

The air is generally dry, and most summer rain falls during afternoon thundershowers, when the rain can come down in torrents for brief periods, particularly in the mountains. Average rainfall for July and August in Jackson Hole is just one inch each month. The frequent proximity of sunshine and showers makes for an abundance of rainbows. I've seen many days where a late-afternoon storm over the Tetons tapers off to a glorious display of colors arching into the sky.

Fall

Autumn provides a beautiful transition period from the warm summer days to the surprisingly cold winters. Nights are crisp and chilly, sending many folks scurrying for warmer climes. In Jackson Hole during September you can expect daytime highs around 55–65°F and nighttime lows around 25–30°F. Temperatures are 5–10 degrees cooler in the central sections of Yellowstone, where nighttime lows may reach into the single digits by late fall.

The peak of fall colors takes place around the first week of October in Jackson Hole and Grand Teton National Park, where aspens and cottonwoods turn a bright yellow (with a few orange trees). Although most of Yellowstone is covered with evergreen trees, you will find colorful deciduous stands in some areas, primarily on the north side of the park. You can expect to find snow on the ground anytime after late October, and earlier at high elevations.

Winter

Winter brings snow and cold weather throughout the Greater Yellowstone Ecosystem, although again, local microclimatic conditions vary widely. You'll face the coldest conditions in January, when a typical Jackson Hole day is in the 20s, with nights dropping to about 0–5°F. When the sky is clear, conditions can sometimes turn severely cold, with temperatures below zero for days at a time; the record low was recorded at West Yellowstone in 1933: -66°F. Fortunately, the relative humidity is quite low, making these temperatures easier to tolerate and creating fluffy powder snow conditions. The town of Jackson receives less summertime rain and wintertime snow than the nearby mountains. In a typical January you'll find a foot of snow on the ground, but nearby Jackson Hole Mountain Resort gets 38 feet of snow annually. Even more impressive is Grand Targhee Ski Resort on the west side of the Tetons, which gets an average of 42 feet of snow per year!

At Old Faithful in Yellowstone the snow is typically about 30–40 inches deep in midwinter, but in Mammoth Hot Springs (park headquarters) you're likely to see just 6–9 inches on the ground and much milder temperatures. At the other extreme, the Lewis Lake area may see 50 feet of snow in a typical winter. Temperatures at Old Faithful average in the 20s in the day but often drop well below zero at night. At Mammoth Hot Springs, day temperatures approach 30°F, with nights dropping to about 10°F.

One surprising winter feature is the presence of temperature inversions in intermountain valleys such as Jackson Hole. These often occur on cold, clear nights when the cold air sinks into the valley floors. Skiers who leave the lodge bundled in down parkas and polypro long johns are often surprised to find temperatures 20 degrees warmer at the top of the mountain.

Spring

Spring in the Greater Yellowstone Ecosystem is a transitional period, as the snow gradually melts and the plants reappear after a long winter. For many locals, this is the time to escape mud season for a week or two in southern Utah. Snow often remains on the ground until late April in Jackson Hole and doesn't melt from the higher mountains until late July. In addition, a few snowfields and glaciers remain year-round in the highest and most protected areas. Spring is when you'll meet the fewest travelers because the roads may not be plowed yet, snow blocks hiking trails, skiing gets worse by the day, and many summertime recreation operations haven't yet opened. Expect daytime temperatures in the 40s and 50s in early May, but warming up rapidly as the long days of June appear.

ENVIRONMENTAL ISSUES

One of the largest intact temperate-zone ecosystems on the planet, Yellowstone was for decades viewed as an island of nature surrounded by a world of human development. Unfortunately, this attitude has led to a host of problems. Despite its size, Yellowstone alone is not large enough to support a viable population of all the animals that once existed within its borders, and developments outside the park pose threats within. In recent years, there have been increasing calls to treat the park as part of the larger Greater Yellowstone Ecosystem—18 million acres of land at the juncture of Wyoming, Montana, and Idaho covering both public and private lands. With each year that passes it has become more obvious that Yellowstone can never be simply an island. Most of the issues that have made headlines in the last decade or so—from fisheries' problems to snowmobile use—have been ones that spread beyond the artificial park boundaries.

Within surrounding lands, conflicts between development and preservation are even more obvious than within the park itself. Logging is one of the most apparent of these, and along the park's western border aerial photos reveal a perfectly straight line, with lodgepole pines on the park side and old clearcuts on the Forest Service side. One of these clearcuts involved the largest timber sale ever made outside of Alaska. Near the park boundaries, housing developments, the massive growth of the tourism industry, oil and gas drilling, mining, a grizzly bear and wolf theme park, and other factors all create potential problems within the park and for the Yellowstone ecosystem as a whole.

Controversy on the Northern Range

Wildlife has always been one of the big drawing cards at Yellowstone, and early on there were constant charges against poachers and market hunters of mass slaughter. It was not until 1894 that Congress passed the Lacey Act, finally making it illegal to hunt within the park. Unfortunately, predators such as wolves, coyotes, mountain lions, and wolverines were regarded as despoilers of the elk, deer, and moose, and they became fair targets for poisoning and shooting by early park managers. (This happened throughout the West, not just in the park.) The campaign proved all too successful, devastating the wolf and mountain lion populations. In recent years, wolves have returned in a spectacular way, although mountain lion numbers remain low.

A recurring area of strife in Yellowstone has been the suggestion that elk and bison are overgrazing and destroying the Lamar and Yellowstone River Basins, an area known as the northern range. The issue periodically flares up, fed in part by the efforts of Montana ranchers and others who suffer from bison and elk that migrate out of Yellowstone onto their land each winter. They—and a few researchers—believe that the Park Service has allowed too many animals to survive and that overgrazing is damaging the land. Most research, however, points in the opposite direction—that the land is not overgrazed, and that ecological processes are working fine in a system termed "natural regulation." The populations of elk and bison fluctuate through time; some years numbers are up, and other years they drop because of harsh winters, predation, hunting outside the park, or other factors.

Flora

Several vegetation types predominate in the Greater Yellowstone Ecosystem. Within Grand Teton National Park, sagebrush flats cover the valley floor, with riparian corridors and wetlands lining the Snake River and smaller creeks. Northern Yellowstone National Park also has sagebrush-dominated areas, but much of Yellowstone and the surrounding mountain country is covered with forests dominated by lodgepole pine. Other common trees within the Greater Yellowstone Ecosystem include quaking aspens, whitebark and limber pine, Engelmann spruce, Douglas fir, and subalpine fir. The tree line is approximately 10,000 feet, and above this point, only low-growing alpine species survive the harsh conditions and brief summers.

Yellowstone National Park is primarily a series of high plateaus ranging 7,500–8,500 feet in elevation. Surrounding this gently rolling expanse are the Absaroka Mountains along the east and north sides and the Gallatin Range in the northwestern corner. Elevations are lowest along the northern end of the park, where the Yellowstone River and other rivers cut through, and highest on the eastern and northwestern margins. The plants that carpet Yellowstone are predominantly determined by the amount of precipitation and the type of soils in which they grow: Areas underlain by Absaroka volcanic bedrock have more nutrient-rich soils than areas with Yellowstone rhyolites. Vegetation types within the park include sagebrush-steppe, lodgepole pine forests, spruce-fir forests, and subalpine areas.

Bark beetle infestations have spread across the Western United States in the last decade, and visitors to the Yellowstone area will see extensive areas of dead or dying trees. Different beetles attack different species of trees, but the impact can be devastating. The problem is particularly severe in high-elevation forests, where whitebark pines are already under stress from a warming climate and blister rust fungus. In Yellowstone, whitebark pines face the threat of near extinction over the next few decades, and the cones are an important food source for grizzlies, Clark's nutcrackers, and other animals. Learn more about bark beetles at www.fs.fed.us/r1-r4/spf/fhp/publications.

SAGEBRUSH-STEPPE

These habitats dominate dry areas of the region. Here the precipitation totals less than 20 inches annually, and one finds open country with sagebrush, grasses, and shrubs, along with pockets of aspen and Douglas fir. A dry sagebrush-steppe vegetation type can be seen in the Gardiner area, where you'll even find prickly pear cactus.

LODGEPOLE PINE

Forests of lodgepole pine cover much of the region. In these forests lodgepoles dominate, although you may find a sprinkling of whitebark pine, spruce, and fir trees. Lodgepole forests are mostly even-aged, having been established after a forest fire that destroyed the previous generation of trees. Some lodgepole cones are serotinous, meaning that they can hang on the tree for years, only opening to release the seeds when a fire melts the gluelike material holding them shut. After a fire, the seedlings grow rapidly if conditions are right. Young trees established after the 1988 fires are dense in many areas, with some already topping 20 feet. Lodgepole roots are shallow, making them susceptible to being blown over in windstorms.

SPRUCE-FIR

Higher elevations have cooler temperatures and forests dominated by Englemann spruce and subalpine fir. These sites get more precipitation than lodgepole forests and are underlain by better soils.

SUBALPINE

On mountain slopes between 8,000 and 10,000 feet you'll find whitebark pine trees. Although these trees seldom top 40 feet, their seeds are an important food source for red squirrels, Clark's nutcrackers, and more surprisingly, grizzlies. Above timberline (approximately 10,000 feet), even these trees give way, and only low-growing forbs, grasses, and shrubs survive. Mount Washburn is a good place to find an easily accessible subalpine area.

OTHER HABITAT TYPES

Several other types of vegetation exist in the Yellowstone Ecosystem, including areas dominated by Douglas fir trees within the sagebrush-steppe. Stands of aspen (beautiful in the fall) are present throughout Grand Teton, on the north end of Yellowstone, in the Bechler region, and near the Snake River. Both Yellowstone and Grand Teton contain extensive areas of wet meadows and willow flats where the water table is high, and cottonwood-lined riparian areas along creeks and rivers. Yellowstone's geyser basins have given rise to plants that are specially adapted to heat and disturbance, including a species of grass (Ross' bentgrass) that grows where the temperature is 100°F just an inch below the surface.

Fauna

The Greater Yellowstone Ecosystem is famous as a place to view wildlife, particularly elk, bison, wolves, moose, and grizzlies. Because of its abundant animal populations, you'll sometimes hear the term "America's Serengeti" applied to Yellowstone, home to the largest concentration of large mammals in the Lower 48.

In summer, the best times to see wildlife are from sunrise to early morning or from late afternoon to early evening. At other times of the year the animals tend to be equally visible in the middle of the day. Bring a pair of binoculars for a close-up view, but make sure your behavior isn't disturbing the animals or causing them to move away. This is particularly true in midwinter, when any unnecessary movements lessen their chance for survival. Always stay at least 100 yards from bears and 25 yards from other wildlife. Park visitor centers have handouts showing where you're most likely to see wildlife in Yellowstone and Grand Teton.

Yellowstone National Park contains about 60 species of resident mammals, varying from shrews and bats to bison and grizzlies. In addition, 309 species of birds have been recorded, along with 18 species of fish (five of which are nonnative), four of amphibians, and six of reptiles. The only poisonous animal is the prairie rattlesnake, found at low elevations in the northern end of Yellowstone. Oh yes—countless insect species live here, too. Some Yellowstone critters are friendlier than others, most notably the mosquitoes that show up in large numbers early in the summer. By mid-August they're much less of a hassle, and winter visitors will have no problems at all.

BEARS

During Yellowstone's early years, bears were commonly viewed as either pets or nuisances. Cubs were tethered to poles in front of the hotels, and other bears fed on the garbage piles that grew up around the camps and hotels. Older folks still recall the bear-feeding grounds at the garbage dumps, where visitors might see 50 bears pawing through the refuse. The feeding shows continued until 1941, but it wasn't until 1970 that the park's open-pit dumps were finally sealed off and the garbage cans bear-proofed. Closure of the dumps helped create confrontations between "garbage bears" and humans; the bears nearly always lost. Between 1970 and 1972, dozens of grizzlies died in show-downs with humans in the park or surrounding areas. Fortunately, careful management in the intervening years has helped the population rebound. Today there are believed to be at least 650 grizzlies in the Greater Yellowstone

Ecosystem, and their numbers have been increasing fairly steadily since the 1980s.

One unusual aspect of the Yellowstone grizzlies was just discovered in recent years: the importance of moths as a food source in the grizzly diet. Millions of army cutworm moths congregate on Yellowstone's high alpine slopes during summer, where they feed on nectar from the abundant flowers. Bears are attracted to this food source because of the insect's abundance and high fat content. Researchers have sometimes seen two dozen bears feeding on a single slope!

Old-timers joke that bears are easy to differentiate: A black bear climbs up the tree after you, whereas a grizzly snaps the tree off at the base. Black bears live in forested areas throughout Wyoming, but grizzlies exist mainly in the northwest corner of the state, primarily within and around Yellowstone National Park. Both grizzlies and black bears pose potential threats to backcountry travelers, although you are considerably more likely to be involved in a car accident while driving to a wilderness area than to be attacked by a bear once you arrive.

Grizzlies once ranged across the entire Northern Hemisphere, from Europe across what is now Russia and through the western half of North America. When Europeans arrived, there were perhaps 50,000–100,000 grizzlies in what would become the Lower 48 states. Unfortunately, as white settlers moved in, they came to view these massive and powerful creatures (average adult males weigh 500 pounds) as a threat to themselves and their livestock. The scientific name, *Ursus arctos horribilis,* says much about human attitudes toward grizzlies.

Grizzlies still have healthy populations in Alaska and western Canada, but elsewhere they were shot, trapped, and poisoned nearly to the brink of extinction. In the Lower 48 states, grizzlies survive in only a few of the most remote parts of Montana, Wyoming, Idaho, and Washington. By 1975, when the U.S. Fish and Wildlife Service listed them as threatened, fewer than 1,000 grizzlies survived south of Canada.

BIGHORN SHEEP

These stocky mountain dwellers are named for the massive curling horns of the males (rams). They have a tan-colored coat with a white rump patch. Bighorns were once abundant throughout the western United States, and early trappers in the mountains east of Yellowstone reported finding thousands of sheep in and around the present-day park. They were also an important source of food for the Sheepeater Indians who lived in Yellowstone before the arrival of whites. Bighorn sheep were virtually wiped out by hunters in the late 19th century, and domestic sheep overran their lands and brought deadly diseases. Within a few decades, the millions of sheep that had roamed the West were reduced to a few hundred survivors, though the population has since rebounded.

Both the rams and ewes (females) have horns that remain for life, but only the rams get the curl for which bighorn sheep are known. Rams are 125–275 pounds in size, with ewes 75–150 pounds. During the mating season in November and December, you're likely to see the original head-bangers in action as rams clash to establish dominance. The clashes can be surprisingly violent, and to protect the brain, bighorns have a double cranium that absorbs much of the shock. Those with the larger horns are typically the dominant bighorns and the primary breeders. Lambs are born in May and June. In summer the sexes separate, with the ewes and lambs remaining lower while the bachelor herds climb higher into the mountains. Bighorns use their ability to climb steep and rocky terrain as protection from predators such as coyotes, wolves, and mountain lions. Winter often finds bighorns in mixed herds at lower elevations. About 250 bighorns live within Yellowstone National Park, with much larger populations in the surrounding national forests.

BISON

The bison is the definitive frontier animal and Wyoming's state mammal—its outline graces the state flag. Weighing up to 2,000 pounds, these are the largest land mammals in the New World. Bison live 45 years or more, with

© DON PITCHER

bison in Yellowstone National Park

females bearing calves until they are in their 40s. The calves weigh 30–40 pounds at birth and within minutes are standing and able to graze. Two races of bison exist: the plains bison, primarily east of the Rockies, and the mountain bison (sometimes called wood bison) in the higher elevations. Technically, these huge, hairy beasts are bison—the only true buffalo are the water buffalo of Southeast Asia—but the name buffalo is commonly used.

With their massive heads, huge shoulder humps, heavy coats of fur, and small posteriors, buffalo are some of the strangest animals in North America. They look so front-heavy as to seem unstable, ready to topple forward onto their snouts at any time. Despite this impression, buffalo are remarkably well adapted to life on the plains. A bison will use its strong sense of smell to find grass buried in a deep snowdrift and then sweep the snow away with a sideways motion of its head. The animals are also surprisingly fleet-footed, as careless Yellowstone photographers have discovered. In addition, the buffalo is one very tough critter.

In 1907, a buffalo was pitted against four of the meanest Mexican bulls at a bullring in Juárez, Mexico. After knocking heads several times with the buffalo, the bulls fled and were saved only when bullfighters opened the chute gates to let them escape.

Yellowstone is the only place in the Lower 48 states where free-ranging bison have lived since prehistoric times. Before their virtual annihilation in the 19th century, about 60 million bison were spread across America. When Yellowstone was established in 1872, hundreds of mountain bison (also called wood bison) still ranged across this high plateau. Sport and meat hunting—legal until 1894—and later poaching reduced the population, so that by 1902 only 23 remained in the park. That year, 21 plains bison were brought in from private ranches in Montana and Texas to help restore the Yellowstone herd, and today there are more than 4,000 in the park, making this the largest free-ranging herd of bison anywhere on earth. Another 500 live in Grand Teton National

Park. Unfortunately, interbreeding between the mountain and plains bison means that the animals in Yellowstone today are genetically different from the original inhabitants. In any case, the population has rebounded dramatically in the last century, and today 30,000 wild bison roam across America, with another 400,000 raised as livestock.

A favorite time to see bison in Yellowstone is late May, just after the new calves have been born. The calves' antics are always good for laughs. Be sure to use caution around bison; many people have been gored when they've come too close. Always stay at least 25 yards away, preferably farther. You'll find some entertaining (and simultaneously scary) wildlife safety videos of bison encounters with foolish tourists on the Yellowstone website (www.nps.gov/yell).

Cattle versus Bison

Bison are carriers of brucellosis, a disease that causes cows to abort calves and is the source of undulant fever in humans. Brucellosis can be spread when other animals lick a contaminated fetus or birthing material, a situation that is unlikely given the timing of bison movements. In 1985, Yellowstone's bison began wandering north into the Gardiner area for the winter. Montana and Wyoming are certified as "brucellosis-free" states, and although there is no evidence that wild bison have ever transmitted the disease to cattle, ranchers feared that the bison might threaten Montana's brucellosis-free status. If cattle become infected, ranchers might be prohibited from shipping livestock out of state.

A highly controversial "hunt" during the late 1980s let hunters shoot bison when they wandered outside the park. After a public outcry, the job was turned over to the Montana state Division of Livestock (DOL), an agency accustomed to dealing with cattle, not wildlife. Ironically, Yellowstone's far more numerous elk also carry brucellosis, but you won't hear Montana authorities talking about slaughtering all of the elk that wander across the park's borders! There are no known cases of bison transmitting brucellosis to domestic cattle, though elk have repeatedly infected cattle in Wyoming and Montana over the last decade.

Today, the Park Service, Montana DOL, and U.S. Forest Service operate under a controversial bison-management plan that attempts to simultaneously maintain a free-ranging bison population while reducing the risk of transmission of brucellosis to cattle. Under this plan, some bison are tolerated on outside lands when cattle aren't present, but if the population continues to be high, others can be captured in pens and slaughtered when they wander outside the park, even if they haven't been tested for brucellosis. It's not a pleasant situation, especially for a national park that was established in part to help protect wild bison. Even a Yellowstone publication admits:

Many park visitors are confused about why the National Park Service is a partner in a plan that often results in killing bison, a natural resource the National Park Service goes to great lengths to protect within the boundaries of the park and an animal so representative of the agency's successful protection of wildlife that it is prominently featured on the National Park Service's familiar "arrowhead" logo.

In heavy-snow winters (such as 2007–2008) fully one-third of Yellowstone's bison can be sent to slaughter, leading to a widespread outcry from advocacy groups. The long-term impact is relatively minor since the bison population rebounds quickly, typically reaching the old level of 4,000 within eight years or so. You can find much more about this issue on the Yellowstone National Park website, www.nps.gov/yell, or in a variety of publications from the visitor centers.

Buffalo Field Campaign (www.buffalo-fieldcampaign.org) is a West Yellowstone–based environmental group that has been at loggerheads with the Park Service and DOL over bison management for years.

COYOTES

Although wolves get the media attention, visitors to Yellowstone are probably more likely to see another native of the dog family: the coyote. Differentiating coyotes from wolves can be a bit tricky, especially from a distance without binoculars. Coyotes are considerably smaller animals; adult male coyotes weigh around 30 pounds, whereas wolves are far more massive, with many weighing 100 pounds or more. The wolf has a large head, short and rounded ears, and a broad and blocky muzzle, whereas the coyote has a small head, large and pointy ears, and a narrow, pointy nose. From a distance coyotes are more delicate in appearance, with smaller feet and thin legs.

The coyotes within Yellowstone generally live in packs containing 6–7 animals led by a dominant pair called the alpha male and female. Most packs have a long family lineage and a well-defined territory; some coyote packs have been using the same denning areas for at least 50 years! The average coyote lives about six years. The alphas mate in early February, and pups are born in early April. Other members of the pack guard the den from wolves and other predators and regurgitate food to feed the pups.

Top Dog No More

Before the reintroduction of wolves, coyotes were the big dogs (so to speak) in northern Yellowstone, and the primary predators of elk calves, killing about 1,200 each year. Wolves occupy a similar ecological niche as coyotes do, and their return has led to a 50 percent reduction in coyote numbers in northern Yellowstone. Some of this decrease comes from outright killing of coyotes by the far larger wolves, particularly alpha coyotes. The ever-resourceful coyotes have responded by banding together in larger packs, denning in rocky areas, becoming more wary, and staying on the margins of wolf territories. Despite competition, coyotes remain common and are certainly in no danger of being displaced from Yellowstone; after all, both species were here for thousands of years

before the extermination of wolves in the 20th century.

DEER

Mule deer (also known as black-tailed deer) are common in many parts of Yellowstone during summer, but most migrate to lower elevations when winter comes. They are typically found in open areas containing sagebrush or grass. Mule deer are named for their long mulelike ears. They also have black-tipped tails and a peculiar way of pogoing away when frightened. Adult males (bucks) grow antlers each summer, and mating season arrives in November and December. Fawns are born in May or June.

The smaller **white-tailed deer** are occasionally seen within Yellowstone but are far less common. You are most likely to find them along rivers or in brushy areas at low elevations, such as around Mammoth Hot Springs or in Lamar Valley. Other places to watch for them are along Yellowstone Lake and in the Upper Geyser Basin.

ELK

A majestic member of the deer family, elk—some biologists prefer the term "wapiti"—are a favorite with both tourists and hunters. In summer, nearly 100,000 elk can be found within the Greater Yellowstone Ecosystem. Bull elk can top 700 pounds, whereas the cows (females) weigh about 500–525 pounds, making elk the second-largest members of the deer family after moose.

Elk spend summers high in the mountains, feeding in alpine meadows and along forest edges. The young males and cows with their calves—generally born in late May and early June—group in large herds for protection. Meanwhile, the bachelor bulls hang out on their own, watching baseball games on TV while drinking Heineken (just kidding; they drink Teton Ale). Bulls grow massive antlers that can weigh 30 pounds or more, which prove useful in the fall mating season as bulls spar with each other.

When the fall rutting season arrives, bulls herd 25 or so cows and calves around, mating

© DON PITCHER

elk in Grand Teton National Park

when cows come into estrus and defending their harem from other rivals. Approximately 90 percent of the elk cows become pregnant each year. During the fall, the bugling of bull elk is a common sound in the mountains (particularly noticeable at Mammoth Hot Springs), a challenge to any bull within ear-shot. It's a strange sound that starts out low, followed by a trumpetlike call and then a series of odd grunts. When a competitor appears, a dominance display often follows—complete with bugling, stomping, and thrashing of the ground—to show who is the baddest bull around. In a fight, bulls lock their massive ant-lers and try to push and twist until one finally gives in and retreats. These battles help ensure that the healthiest bulls produce the most off-spring, although other bulls often wait in the wings during battles over harems, and then rush in to mate with the cows while the larger bulls are sparring. The mating season ends by mid- to late November, and the snows of late fall and winter push elk to lower elevations on the north side of Yellowstone or out of the park

into surrounding areas, notably at the National Elk Refuge in Jackson Hole, where they are fed.

When spring comes, the bulls drop their antlers and immediately begin to grow new ones. The elk head back into the high coun-try, following the melting snowline. Calves are born in late May or early June (sometimes dur-ing the migration) and weigh 25–40 pounds at birth. Elk—particularly young calves—are an important food source for predators in the Yellowstone ecosystem; almost one-third of the calves are killed each year by wolves, grizzly and black bears, coyotes, and golden eagles.

Elk and bison both can be infected with brucellosis, a bacterium causing spontane-ous abortions. Brucellosis is transmitted to other animals by contact with the dead fetus or birthing material and can cause undulant fever in humans. Ranchers worry that brucello-sis can spread from elk and bison to cattle, par-ticularly around elk feeding grounds in western Wyoming. To lessen the incidence of the dis-ease, state employees now routinely vaccinate elk at the feeding grounds, shooting them in the hindquarters with vaccine-loaded pellets.

MOOSE

The largest member of the deer family, moose are typically seen eating willow bushes in riparian areas. They are the loners of the deer world, and only during the fall mating season are you likely to see males (bulls) and females (cows) together or to see bulls jousting. Bulls can reach 1,300 pounds, while cows grow to 800 pounds and give birth to up to three calves. In addition to enormous racks, the bulls have a distinctive dewlap or "bell" that hangs below their throat but apparently serves no physical purpose. Both Yellowstone and Grand Teton support moose; look for them along streams, willow flats, and other wet places in the summer.

During winter, these moose migrate into high-elevation forests where the snow isn't as deep (tree branches hold the snow) or as crusty as in the open. In these forests they browse on subalpine fir and Douglas fir. The fires of 1988 burned through many of the forests, and the loss of cover has hurt the Yellowstone moose population.

PRONGHORN ANTELOPE

Antelope (biologists prefer the name "pronghorn" because they are not true antelopes) are sleek ungulates with beautiful reddish-brown coats accented by white throat patches and rumps. Antelope survive on grasses, forbs, and plants that other animals avoid, notably sagebrush—perhaps Wyoming's most abundant plant. They are almost never seen in wooded areas. Antelope are built for speed: Oversized lungs and windpipes give them the ability to run for miles at 30 mph, and they can accelerate up to 45 mph for short bursts. To watch for predators, they have the largest eyes by body weight of any mammal. Despite this speed, antelope have an innate inquisitiveness that makes them relatively easy to hunt, an attribute that nearly drove them to extinction by market hunting in the 20th century. One surprising trait in antelope is their inability to jump fences; instead they crawl under them.

Fences that are too low will completely halt their migrations.

Both males and females grow horns, and those on the males typically have a prong (hence the name). Dominant males (bucks) gather harems of females (does) and fawns and fight off other bucks in the late-summer rutting season. In May or June, does give birth to 1–2 fawns.

Antelope are abundant in many parts of Wyoming, and more than 400,000 of them live in the state. They are not nearly as common in the northwest corner, where the habitat is more marginal. You'll see small herds in open country within Grand Teton National Park and on the north side of Yellowstone National Park, from Lamar Valley to the Gardiner area.

Pronghorn antelope populations declined sharply in the 1990s within Yellowstone, where they now number about 200 animals. Coyotes and other predators take many newborn fawns each spring and may be a significant factor in the decline, combined with several other factors such as inbreeding caused by the small population, changes in vegetation, loss of habitat to development in their Paradise Valley wintering area north of the park, increasing numbers of fences across their range, and hunting.

WOLVES

Wolves are the largest members of the canids (dog family), with males averaging 70–120 pounds and stretching up to six feet long from head to tail. They are much more massive than coyotes, although the two are sometimes confused. Wolves live in packs of 2–8, led by an alpha male and female, and establish territories to exclude other wolf packs. Most pack members are from an extended family, but they may include outside members. The alphas are the only ones that generally mate, and a litter of six or so pups is born in early spring. Once they are weaned, the pack feeds pups regurgitated meat until they are large enough to join the hunt. Wolves hunt primarily in the evening and morning hours, when their prey—elk, deer, moose, bison, and pronghorn—are feeding.

The reintroduction of wolves to Yellowstone has brought back one of the park's top predators, and for many visitors, it's been a howling success. Today, Yellowstone is one of the few places in the Lower 48 where wolves can be viewed in the wild. Wolves once ranged across nearly all of North America, but white settlers regarded them—along with mountain lions, grizzly bears, and coyotes—as threats to livestock and unwanted predators on game animals. Even in Yellowstone, wolves were hunted and poisoned by both the army and the Park Service. By 1940, the wolf was probably gone from the park, although a few lone animals turned up briefly again in the early 1970s.

In the United States, until 1995, wolves could be found only in Alaska, in northern Minnesota, and in Isle Royale and Glacier National Parks. With the more enlightened public attitude evident in recent years, ecologists and conservationists began pushing for the reintroduction of wolves to Yellowstone, considered one of the few remaining areas in the Lower 48 that could support a viable wolf population.

The proposal to return wolves to Yellowstone set off a firestorm from ranchers (with ardent support from Wyoming's Republican senators), who feared that the wolves would wander outside the park to destroy sheep and cattle. Opponents said hundreds of livestock would be killed each year around the park and that the reintroduction cost might reach $1.8 million per wolf, a figure that proved grossly inflated.

Despite these dire predictions, the U.S. Fish and Wildlife Service began reintroducing wolves to Yellowstone in 1995, initially releasing 14 gray wolves that had been captured in British Columbia. Additional wolves were set free the following spring. During subsequent years, things have gone far better than anyone had predicted. By 2010, biologists estimated a population of 99 wolves inside Yellowstone National Park, spread across 14 different packs. Approximately 400 wolves inhabit the entire Greater Yellowstone Ecosystem from north and west of Yellowstone to the Pinedale area on the south, and eastward into Shoshone National Forest.

In 2008, the U.S. Fish & Wildlife Service (under the Bush administration) removed wolves from the Endangered Species list, and limited hunting is now allowed in Idaho and Montana. In Wyoming, another court decision in 2010 reinstated their protected status, though exceptions are made when wolves attack cattle and livestock on private lands. For the latest on the ongoing saga, visit the **U.S. Fish and Wildlife Service's gray wolves homepage** (http://westerngraywolf.fws.gov). The Yellowstone National Park website (www.nps.gov/yell) has additional details on wolves and tips for watching them, and regional information is updated weekly. For a different perspective, check out the **Greater Yellowstone Coalition** (www.greateryellowstone.org), the environmental group that helped keep wolves listed as an Endangered Species in Wyoming.

History

YELLOWSTONE NATIONAL PARK

Yellowstone National Park has a rich and fascinating history that reaches back through thousands of years of settlement. The most thorough source for history is *The Yellowstone Story* (University Press of Colorado, www.up-colorado.com), an excellent two-volume set by former park historian Aubrey L. Haines. For an engaging and personal journey through the past, read *Searching for Yellowstone* by Paul Schullery (Houghton Mifflin, www.hmco.com).

Sheepeater Indians

The last major glaciation ended about 15,000 years ago, and the first peoples may have reached Yellowstone while the ice was still retreating. There is good evidence that the country was occupied for at least 10,000 years, although the tribes apparently changed through time. By the mid-19th century, the country was surrounded by Blackfeet to the north, Crow to the east, and Shoshone and Bannock to the south and west. These tribes all traveled through and hunted in Yellowstone, building temporary shelters, called wickiups, made of aspen poles covered with pine boughs; a few of these still exist in the park. The primary inhabitants of this high plateau were the Sheepeater Indians, who may have been here for more than 2,000 years. Of Shoshone stock, the Sheepeaters hunted bighorn sheep (hence the name) and made bows from the sheep horns, but their diet also included other animals, fish, roots, and berries. Because they did not have horses, the Sheepeaters used dog-pulled travois to carry their few possessions from camp to camp. Summers were spent in high alpine meadows and along passes, where they hunted migrating game animals or gathered roots and berries. They wintered in protected canyons.

The Sheepeaters were smaller than other Indians and have achieved an aura of mystery because so little is known of their way of living.

Yellowstone was at the heart of their territory, but with the arrival of whites came devastating diseases, particularly smallpox. The survivors joined their Shoshone brothers on the Wind River Reservation or the Bannock Reservation in Idaho. The last of the tribe left Yellowstone in the 1870s.

Fur Trappers

The word "Yellowstone" appears to have come from the Minnetaree Indians, who called the river "Mi tsi a-da-zi," a word French-Canadian trappers translated into "Rive des Roche Jaunes"—literally, "River of Yellow Rock." The Indians apparently called it this because of the yellowish bluffs along the river near Billings, Montana (not because of the colorful Grand Canyon of the Yellowstone). The term "Yellow Stone" was first used on a map made in 1797. When the Lewis and Clark Expedition traveled through the country north of Yellowstone in 1805–1806, the Indians told them tales of this mysterious place: "There is frequently heard a loud noise like thunder, which makes the earth tremble, they state that they seldom go there because children Cannot sleep—and Conceive it possessed of spirits, who were adverse that men Should be near them." (This certainly was not the attitude of all the native peoples, for the park had long been inhabited.) The first white man to come through Yellowstone is believed to be John Colter, a former member of the Lewis and Clark Expedition who wandered through the region in the winter of 1807–1808. A map based on Colter's recollections shows Yellowstone Lake ("Eustis Lake"), along with an area of "Hot Spring Brimstone."

As fur trappers spread through the Rockies in the 1820s and 1830s, many discovered the geysers and hot springs of Yellowstone, and stories quickly spread around the rendezvous fires. The word of the trappers was passed on to later settlers and explorers but not entirely believed. After all, mountain man Jim Bridger described not just petrified trees, but petrified birds singing petrified songs! His tales of a river that "ran so fast that it became hot on the bottom" could well have referred to the Firehole River. When Bridger tried to lead a party of military explorers into Yellowstone, they were stymied by deep snows. Still, word gradually got out that something very strange could be found in this part of the mountains. Little remains today from the mountain-man era, although in 1880 the letters "J.O.R. Aug. 19, 1819" were found carved in a tree near the Upper Falls of the Yellowstone, and later a cache of iron beaver traps similar to those used by the Hudson's Bay Company was discovered near Obsidian Cliff.

Mountain Men

The era of the fur trapper is one of the most colorful slices of American history, a time when a rough and hardy breed of men took to the Rockies in search of furs and adventure. Romanticized in such films as *Jeremiah Johnson,* the trappers actually played but a brief role in history and numbered fewer than 1,000 individuals. Their real importance lay in acting as the opening wedge for the West, a vanguard for the settlers and gold miners who would follow their paths—often led by these same mountain men.

THE FUR BUSINESS

Fashion sent men into the Rockies in the first place, since the waterproof underfur of a beaver could be used to create the beaver hat, which was all the rage in the early part of the 19th century. (It cost a month's wages for a man in England to buy a fine beaver hat in the 1820s!) Beavers in the eastern United States were soon trapped out, forcing trappers to head farther and farther west. Several companies competed for the lucrative fur market, but John Jacob Astor's American Fur Company proved the most successful. In 1811, Astor sent a party of men across the Rockies to the mouth of the Columbia to build a trading post and then set up a chain of posts across the West. The men—known as the Astorians—were probably the first whites

to follow the route that would later become the Oregon Trail.

John Jacob Astor's trappers went head to head against the Rocky Mountain Fur Company, which was owned at various times by some of the most famous mountain men—Jedediah Smith, David Jackson, William and Milton Sublette, Jim Bridger, Thomas Fitzpatrick, and others. Competition for furs became so intense that Astor's men began following Jim Bridger and Tom Fitzpatrick to discover their trapping grounds. After trying unsuccessfully to shake the men tailing them, Bridger and Fitzpatrick deliberately headed into the heart of Blackfeet country, where Indians killed the leader of Astor's party and managed to leave Bridger with an arrowhead in his shoulder that was not removed until three years later.

A large number of Indians (particularly from the Flathead and Nez Perce tribes) were also involved in the fur trade, and a standard Indian trade value was 240 beaver pelts for a riding horse. In the mountains, anything from the world back east had considerable value: guns sold for $100 each, blankets for $40 apiece, tobacco for $3 per pound, and alcohol (often diluted) for up to $64 per gallon. After just two years of such trading, William Ashley retired with an $80,000 profit. Control of the fur market continued to change hands as the Rocky Mountain Fur Company and the American Fur Company competed with each other and with a mysterious company headed by Captain Benjamin Bonneville, which some believe was a front for the U.S. Army to explore the West.

Most of the men who trapped in the Rockies were hired and outfitted by the fur companies, but others worked under contract and traded furs for overpriced supplies. Many men found themselves in debt to the company at the end of a season. At the top of the heap were the free trappers, men who worked either alone or with others but who sold their furs to whoever offered the highest prices. Some men, primarily those who brought trade goods to the rendezvous, became rich in the process. Others, such as John Colter, Jim Bridger, James Beckwourth,

THE NEZ PERCE WAR

One of the saddest episodes in the history of Yellowstone took place in 1877 and involved the Nez Perce Indians of Oregon's Wallowa Valley. When the government tried to force the people of Chief White Bird and Chief Joseph onto an Idaho reservation so that white ranchers could have their lands, the Indians stubbornly refused. A few drunken young Indians killed four whites, and subsequent raids led to the deaths of at least 14 more. The army retaliated but was turned back by the Nez Perce. Rather than face government reinforcements, more than 1,000 Nez Perce began a 1,800-mile flight in a desperate bid to reach Canada. A series of running battles followed, as the Indians managed to confound the inept army using their geographic knowledge and battle skills. The Nez Perce entered Yellowstone from the west, and a few hotheads immediately attacked vacationing tourists and prospectors. Two whites were killed in the park, others were kidnapped, and another man nearly died from his wounds.

The Nez Perce exited Yellowstone two weeks after they arrived, narrowly missing an encounter with their implacable foe, General William T. Sherman, who just happened to be vacationing in Yellowstone at the time. East of the park, the Indians plotted a masterful escape from two columns of army forces, feinting a move down the Shoshone River and then heading north along a route that left their pursuers gasping in amazement – straight up the narrow Clarks Fork Canyon, "where rocks on each side came so near together that two horses abreast could hardly pass." Finally, less than 40 miles from the international border with Canada, the army caught up with the Nez Perce, and after a fierce battle the tribe was forced to surrender (although 300 did make good their escape).

Chief Joseph's haunting words still echo through the years: "Hear me, my chiefs, I am tired; my heart is sick and sad. From where the sun now stands, I will fight no more forever." Despite promises that they would be allowed to return home, the Nez Perce were hustled onto reservations in Oklahoma and Washington while whites remained on their ancestral lands. Chief Joseph spent the rest of his life on Washington's Colville Reservation and died in 1904, reportedly of a broken heart. Yellowstone's Nez Perce Creek, which feeds the Firehole River, is named for this desperate bid for freedom.

Jedediah Smith, Thomas Fitzpatrick, and Kit Carson, would achieve fame for their rich knowledge of the land and their ability to survive against insurmountable odds. Many trappers married Indian women, learned sign language and various Indian tongues, and lived in tepees.

Trappers worked through the winter, when the beaver pelts were at their finest; most summers were spent hunting and fishing, or hanging out with fellow trappers or friendly Indians. A good trapper could take in more than 150 beaver in a year, worth $4–6 apiece. It was an arduous job, and the constant threat of attacks by the Blackfeet Indians made it even more difficult. The great letting-go came with the summer rendezvous, an event anticipated months ahead of time.

THE RENDEZVOUS

William H. Ashley, founder of the Rocky Mountain Fur Company, was one of the most important figures in the fur trade. In 1822, he ran an ad in a St. Louis paper that read:

To Enterprising Young Men. The subscriber wishes to engage ONE HUNDRED MEN, to ascend the river Missouri to its source, there to be employed for one, two or three years.–For particulars enquire of Major Andrew Henry, near the Lead Mines, in the County of Washington, (who will ascend with, and command the party) or to the subscriber at St. Louis.

–Wm. H. Ashley.

Ashley's company of men—along with $10,000 in supplies—made it up into the Yellowstone River country that summer, and the success of the trappers led to the first rendezvous in 1825 on the Henrys Fork near its confluence with the Green River, along the present-day Wyoming–Utah border. Thus began the first rendezvous. They would take place every summer until 1840. Ashley failed to bring booze that first summer, and the rendezvous lasted only two days. In future years, however, the whiskey flowed freely, and the festivities lasted for weeks.

The rendezvous—a French word meaning "appointed place of meeting"—was a time when both white and Indian trappers could sell their furs, trade for needed supplies and Indian women (who had little say in the matter), meet with old friends, get rip-roaring drunk, and engage in storytelling, gambling, gun duels, and contests of all sorts. Horse racing, wrestling bouts, and shooting contests were favorites—Kit Carson killed Shunar, a big French bully, in a duel during one of the Green River rendezvous. Debauchery reigned supreme in these three-week-long affairs, and by the time they were over, many of the trappers had lost their entire year's earnings.

During the heyday of the fur trade, a common saying was "all trails lead to the Seedskeedee [Green River]." Six rendezvous were held here in the 1830s; others were held in the Wind River/Popo Agie River area, on Ham's Fork of the Green River, and in Idaho and Utah. Sites were chosen where there was space for up to 500 mountain men and 3,000 Indians, plenty of game, ample grazing for the thousands of horses, and good water. Not coincidentally, all were held in Shoshone country rather than farther east or north, where the hostile Sioux, Blackfeet, and Crow held sway. Despite such precautions, more than half of Ashley's men were scalped by Indians.

CHANGING TIMES

The end of the rendezvous system—and most of the Rocky Mountain fur trapping—came about for a variety of reasons: overtrapping, the

financial panic of 1837, and the growing use of other materials, particularly South American nutria and Chinese silk, for hats. In addition, permanent trading posts such as Fort Laramie drew Indians away from the mountains to trade for buffalo robes instead of beaver furs. By 1840, when the last rendezvous was held on the banks of the Green River near present-day Pinedale, it was obvious there would be no more.

Expeditions

National attention finally came to Yellowstone with a series of three expeditions to check out the wild claims of local prospectors. In 1869, David E. Folsom, Charles W. Cook, and William Peterson headed south from Bozeman, finding the Grand Canyon, Yellowstone Lake, and the geyser basins. When a friend pressured them to submit a description of their travels for publication, the *New York Tribune* refused to publish it, noting that the paper "had a reputation that they could not risk with such unreliable material."

The adventures of this first expedition led another group of explorers into Yellowstone the following year, but this time money was the motive. Jay Cooke's Northern Pacific Railroad needed investors for a planned route across Montana. A good public-relations campaign was the first step, and it happened to coincide with the visit of a former Montana tax collector named Nathaniel P. Langford, who had heard of the discoveries of Folsom, Cook, and Peterson. The party of 19 soldiers and civilians, including Langford, headed out in August of 1870 under General Henry D. Washburn. They were thrilled by what they discovered and proceeded to give the geysers names—Old Faithful, Castle, Giant, Grotto, Giantess—which became permanently attached to the features. The joy of the trip was marred when one man—Truman Everts—became separated from the others and lost his horse. He was not found until 37 days later, by which time he weighed just 50 pounds. His rescuer did not even recognize him as human. Amazingly, Everts survived and recovered.

With the return of the Washburn Expedition, national newspapers and magazines finally began to pay attention to Yellowstone, and Langford began lecturing in the East on what they had found. One of those listening was Dr. Ferdinand V. Hayden, director of the U.S. Geological Survey. Hayden asked Congress to fund an official investigation. With the help of Representatives James G. Blaine (coincidentally a supporter of the Northern Pacific Railroad) and conservationist Henry M. Dawes, Congress appropriated $40,000 for an exploration of "the sources of the Missouri and Yellowstone Rivers." Thus began the most famous and influential trip into Yellowstone—the 1871 Hayden Expedition. The troop included 34 men, an escort of cavalry, painter Thomas Moran, and photographer William H. Jackson.

Establishing the Park

When Hayden returned to Washington to prepare his report, he found a letter from railroad promoter Jay Cooke. In the letter, Cooke proposed that "Congress pass a bill reserving the Great Geyser Basin as a public park forever—just as it has reserved that far inferior wonder the Yosemite valley and big trees." (Abraham Lincoln had established Yosemite earlier as a state park.) In an amazingly short time, a bill was introduced to set aside the land, and Hayden rushed to arrange a display in the Capitol rotunda of geological specimens, sketches by Moran, and photos by Jackson. The bill easily passed both houses of Congress and was signed into law on March 1, 1872, by President Ulysses S. Grant. The first national park had come into existence, a culmination not just of the discoveries in Yellowstone but also of a growing appreciation for preserving the wonders of the natural world.

Congress saw no need to set aside money for this new creation because it seemed to be doing fine already. Besides, it was thought that Jay Cooke's new railroad would soon arrive, making it easy for thousands of vacationers to explore Yellowstone. In turn, concessioners would build roads and hotels and pay the government

franchise fees. The park was placed under the control of the Secretary of the Interior, with Nathaniel P. Langford as its unpaid superintendent. Meanwhile, the planned railroad fizzled when Jay Cooke and Co. declared bankruptcy, precipitating the panic of 1873.

Roads and Railroads

Because of the difficult access, fewer than 500 people visited in each of Yellowstone's first few years as a park, most to soak in tubs at Mammoth Hot Springs. Not a few decided to take home souvenirs, bringing pickaxes and shovels for that purpose. Meanwhile, hunters—including some working for the Mammoth Hotel—began shooting the park's abundant game. Two brothers who had a ranch just north of the park killed 2,000 elk in a single year. Superintendent Langford did little to stop the slaughter and bothered to visit the park only twice. Finally, in 1877, the Secretary of the Interior fired him, putting Philetus W. Norris in charge instead. Norris proved a good choice, despite a knack for applying his name to everything in sight. (Most of his attempts at immortality have been replaced by other titles, but Norris Geyser Basin, Norris Road, and even the town of Norris, Michigan, remain.)

Norris oversaw construction of the first major road in Yellowstone, a rough 60-mile route built in just 30 days to connect Upper Geyser Basin with Mammoth and the western entrance. All of this was precipitated by the raids of the Nez Perce Indians earlier that summer and threats that the Bannock Indians would strike next. In addition, Norris began, but never completed, the Queen's Laundry, a bathhouse that is considered the first government building constructed for the public in any national park. The log walls are still visible in a meadow near Lower Geyser Basin.

By 1882, Norris had managed to alienate the company that helped found the park, the Northern Pacific Railroad. The company announced plans to build a railroad line to the geysers and construct a large hotel, "being assured by the Government of a monopoly therein." Norris's opposition led to his being fired and replaced by railroad man Patrick H. Conger. Soon, however, the scheme began to unravel. The Yellowstone Park Improvement Company—whose vice president happened to be construction superintendent for the Northern Pacific's branch line into Gardiner—had planned not just a lodging monopoly but also a monopoly on all transportation, timber rights, and ranching privileges in the park. Later it was discovered that the company had contracted for 20,000 pounds of venison (killed in the park) to feed the construction crews. As one newspaper writer commented, "It is a 'Park Improvement Company' doing this, and I suppose they consider it an improvement to rid the park, as far as possible, of game."

Finally, in 1884 Congress acted by limiting the land that could be leased—thus effectively ending the railroad's plans—and adding funding to hire 10 assistants to patrol Yellowstone. Unfortunately, it neglected to include any penalties for the poachers and despoilers other than expulsion, so even the few assistants who did decent work found the culprits quickly returning. The problems were myriad. Cooke City miners were fishing with spears, seine nets, and even dynamite. Guides were throwing rocks into the geysers, squatters had ensconced themselves on prime land in Lamar Valley, and visitors were leaving fires unattended and breaking off specimens from the geysers.

Superintendent Conger was later replaced by Robert E. Carpenter, a man about whom historian Hiram Chittenden noted, "In his opinion, the Park was created to be an instrument of profit to those who were shrewd enough to grasp the opportunity." Carpenter lobbied Congress to remove lands from the park so that the Northern Pacific could construct a railroad along the Yellowstone and Lamar Rivers to Cooke City. In return, friends promised to locate claims in his name along the route so that he, too, might profit from the venture. The land grab fell apart when the Senate vetoed the move, and Carpenter was summarily removed from office. Not long thereafter, Congress flatly refused to fund the civilian administration of Yellowstone, and the Secretary of the Interior was forced to request the aid of the military in 1886. It proved a fortuitous step.

The Army Years

The U.S. Army finally brought a semblance of order to Yellowstone, eliminating the political appointees who viewed the park as a place to get rich. That first year, a temporary fort—Camp Sheridan—was thrown up and a troop of soldiers arrived, but it wasn't until 1891 that work began on a permanent Fort Yellowstone at Mammoth. By 1904, the fort consisted of some 26 buildings housing 120 men. The soldiers had clear objectives—protecting wildlife (or at least bison and elk) from poachers, fighting fires, stopping vandalism, and generally achieving order out of chaos. These goals were accomplished with a fervor that gained widespread respect, and in a way that would later influence the organization of the National Park Service. One of the major accomplishments of the soldiers was completion of the Grand Loop Road, which passes most of Yellowstone's attractions. The basic pattern was completed by 1905.

Fort Yellowstone was a favorite station for soldiers, and it was considered something of an honor to be sent to such a setting. The life of the soldiers was not always easy, however, and some died in the bitter winters or in accidents. A series of 16 soldier stations—actually little more than large cabins—was established around the park, and each was manned year-round, usually by four soldiers.

Before the arrival of cars, many visitors to Yellowstone were wealthy people from the East Coast or Europe intent on doing the grand tour of the West. The railroads (the Northern Pacific to the north, Union Pacific to the west, and Burlington to the east) deposited them near park borders, where they were met by carriages, Tallyhos (26-passenger stagecoaches), and surreys. In 1915, some 3,000 horses were in use within the park! Most "dudes" paid approximately $50 for a six-day tour that included transportation, meals, and lodging at the hotels. They paid another $2.50 for the privilege of sailing across Yellowstone Lake on the steamship *Zillah*. By contrast, another group, the "sagebrushers," came to Yellowstone in smaller numbers, arriving in their own wagons or hiring a coach to transport them between the "Wylie Way" campgrounds. These seasonal tent camps were scattered around the park, providing an inexpensive way to see the sights—just $35 for a seven-day tour. Even as early as 1908, Yellowstone was being seen by 18,000 visitors per year.

The Northern Pacific was still intent on carving Yellowstone into a moneymaking resort, even going so far as to propose an electric railroad, to be powered by a dam at the falls of the Yellowstone River. Fortunately, equally powerful forces—notably General Philip Sheridan and naturalist Joseph Bird Grinnell—saw through their designs and thwarted each attempt to bring railroads into Yellowstone. Still, the Northern Pacific's interests were represented by its indirect control of many of Yellowstone's hotels, stagecoaches, wagons, and other vehicles used to transport tourists.

All of this changed when the first car was allowed through the gate on August 1, 1915. (Entrance fees were a surprisingly stiff $5— about $100 in today's dollars—for single-seat vehicles and $7.50 for five-passenger cars.) Almost immediately, it became clear that horses and cars could not mix, and motor buses replaced the old coaches. From then on, the park would be increasingly a place for "autoists." Interestingly, within a year the park would come under the jurisdiction of the newly created National Park Service.

The Park Service Takes Over

After years of army control, supporters of a separate National Park Service finally had their way in 1916. The congressional act created a dual role for the new park system: to "conserve the scenery" and to "provide for the enjoyment of the same," a contradictory mandate that would later lead to all sorts of conflicts. The first couple of years were tenuous, as management flip-flopped between the army and civilians; the final changeover came in 1918 and ended three decades of military supervision. The management of Yellowstone fell on the shoulders of two men, Horace M. Albright and his mentor, Stephen Mather, both of whom had been heavily involved in lobbying to create the new agency. Mather became the Park Service's first director, while Albright served as superintendent at Yellowstone and later stepped into Mather's shoes to head the agency.

Albright quickly upgraded facilities to meet the influx of motorists, who demanded more camping facilities but also cabins, lodges, cafeterias, and bathhouses. Forty-six camps of one sort or another were constructed (only 12 survive today), fulfilling Albright's dream of "a motorist's paradise." The focus of the new Park Service was clearly visitation rather than preservation. Albright assembled a first-rate force of park rangers and instituted the environmental-education programs that have been the agency's hallmark ever since.

As the automobile took over Yellowstone, the railroads gradually lost their sway, and the final passenger train to the park's gateway towns stopped in 1960. In the 1950s, the Park Service initiated "Mission 66," a decade-long project to upgrade facilities and add lodging. By the late 1960s, a growing appreciation for the natural world was shifting public opinion away from such developments, and the 1973 master plan scaled back proposed developments. From day one, Yellowstone National Park had been set up for what Edward Abbey called "industrial tourism." The park had come into existence in part because of a railroad promoter who hoped to gain from its development, and it grew to maturity on a diet of roads, hotels, and curio shops. In recent years, Americans have taken a second look at this heritage and have begun to wonder which matters more: providing a public playground or preserving an area that is unique on this planet. The inherent conflict between the need for public facilities and services in Yellowstone and the survival of a functioning ecosystem will continue to create a tug-of-war between various factions.

Certainly the most famous recent event was the series of massive fires that swept across nearly half of Yellowstone in 1988. The land has recovered surprisingly well since then, and in recent years other issues came to the fore: wolf reintroduction, the killing of bison on the park boundaries, snowmobile and other winter use, and problems caused by global warming, exotic species, and bark beetle infestations. There's always something stewing in the mud pots of Yellowstone! Some things have been improving in recent years, including efforts to repair aging roads and to replace outdated buildings in the park. Despite any problems or controversies, the park is just as fascinating as ever. The geysers never cease to amaze visitors, the scenery remains majestic, the Grand Canyon of the Yellowstone is still just as stunning, and the superb wildlife-viewing continues to make this the Serengeti of America.

The Yellowstone Fires of 1988

Many will long remember the summer of 1988 as the time that fires seared Yellowstone National Park. TV reporters flocked to the park, pronouncing the destruction of America's most famous national wonder as they stood before trees turned into towering torches and 27,000-foot-high clouds of black smoke. Newspaper headlines screamed, "Park Sizzles," "Winds Whip Fiery Frenzy Out of Control," and "Firestorms Blacken Yellowstone." Residents of nearby towns complained of lost tourism dollars, choking smoke, and intentionally lit back fires that threatened their homes and businesses; Wyoming politicians berated the Park Service's "Let Burn" policy; President Reagan expressed astonishment that fires were ever allowed to burn in the national parks, although the policy had been in place for 16 years. Perhaps the most enduring image is from a forest that had been blown down by tornado-force winds in 1984 and then burned by the wind-whipped fires of 1988. The media ate it up, with one headline reading, "Total Destruction: Intense Heat and Flames from the Fires in Yellowstone Left Nothing but Powdered Ash and Charcoal Near Norris Junction." Unfortunately, the real story

© DON PITCHER

young lodgepole trees in an area burned by 1988 fires

behind the fires of '88 was lost in this media feeding frenzy.

A CENTURY OF CHANGE

In reality, these fires were not unprecedented; we were just fortunate enough to witness a spectacle of nature that may not occur for another 300 years. When Yellowstone National Park was established in 1872, most of the land was carpeted with a mixture of variously aged stands of lodgepole pine established after a series of large fires. Fewer large fires, partly because of a fire-suppression policy in effect until 1972, meant that by the 1980s one-third of the park's lodgepole stands were more than 200 years old. Yellowstone was ripe to burn.

Since the early 1950s, Smokey the Bear had drummed an incessant message: "Only You Can Prevent Forest Fires." Forest fires were viewed as dangerous, destructive forces that had to be stopped to protect our valuable public lands. Unfortunately, this immensely effective and generally valid ad campaign convinced the public that *all* fires were bad. Ecological research has shown not only that this is wrong, but also that putting out all fires can sometimes create conditions far more dangerous than if fires had been allowed to burn in the first place. Fire, like the other processes that have affected Yellowstone—cataclysmic volcanic explosions, geothermal activity, and massive glaciation—is neither good nor evil. It is simply a part of the natural world that national parks are attempting to preserve. Unfortunately, national parks are no longer surrounded by similarly undeveloped land, so when fires burned in Yellowstone and on adjacent Forest Service lands, they also affected nearby towns and the people who made a living from tourism or logging.

FIRE IN LODGEPOLE FORESTS

Fire has played an important role in lodgepole pine forests for thousands if not millions of years, and as a result the trees have evolved an unusual adaptation. Some of the cones are sealed with a resin that melts in a fire, thus releasing the seeds. The parent trees are killed, but a new generation is guaranteed by the thousands of pine seeds released to the bare, nutrient-rich soil underneath the blackened overstory. Within five years the landscape is dotted with thousands of young pines, competing with a verdant cover of grasses and flowers.

Although some animals are killed in the wildfires (including, in 1988, at least 269 of Yellowstone's 30,000 elk), and others, weakened by the lack of food available immediately after the fire, succumb to the rigors of the next succeeding winter, the early decades after major fires create conditions that are unusually rich for many animals. Wildlife diversity in lodgepole forests reaches a peak within the first 25 years after a fire as woodpeckers, mountain bluebirds, and other birds feed on insects in the dead trees, and elk and bears graze on the lush grasses.

As the forest ages, a dense thicket of trees develops, keeping light from reaching the forest floor and making it difficult for understory plants to survive. These trees are eventually thinned by disease and windthrow, creating openings in the forest, but after 200–300 years without fire, lodgepole forests become a tangle of fallen trees that are difficult to walk through, are of lesser value to many animals, and burn easily. They also become susceptible to attacks by bark beetles, such as those that killed thousands of acres of trees in Yellowstone starting in the 1960s and continuing through the 1980s. These beetle-killed trees added to the fuel available to burn once a fire started.

YELLOWSTONE IN 1988

Yellowstone's 1988 fires were caused by not just the heavy fuel loading from aging forests, but also weather conditions that were the driest and windiest on record. The winter of 1987–1988 had been a mild one, and by spring there was a moderate-to-severe drought in the park, lessened only by above-normal rainfall in April and May. Since 1972, when Yellowstone Park officials first began allowing certain lightning fires to burn in backcountry areas, the acreage burned had totaled less than 2 percent of the park. (Mistakenly called a "Let Burn" policy, the natural fire program actually involved close monitoring of these lightning-ignited fires to determine when and if a fire should be suppressed. All human-caused fires were immediately suppressed, as were any that threatened property or life.)

When the first lightning fires of the 1988 season began in late May, those in the backcountry areas were allowed to burn, as fire management officials anticipated normal summer weather conditions. Many fires went out on their own, but when June and July came and the rains failed to materialize, the fires began to spread rapidly. Alarmed park officials declared them wildfires and sent crews to put them out. (Ironically, the largest fire, the North Fork/Wolf Lake Complex, was started by a logger outside the park who tossed a lit cigarette to the ground. Although firefighters immediately attacked the blaze, it consumed more than 500,000 acres.) As the summer progressed, more and more firefighters were called in, eventually totaling more than 25,000 personnel, at a cost exceeding $120 million. Firefighters managed to protect most park buildings but had little effect on the forest fires themselves. Experts say that conditions in summer 1988 were so severe that even if firefighters had immediately responded to all of the natural fires, it would likely have made little difference. Yellowstone has experienced these massive fires in the past and will again in the future, no matter what humans do.

OUT OF CONTROL

August brought worsening conditions with each passing day. Winds blew steadily at 20–40 miles per hour, and gusts up to 70 mph threw firebrands two miles in beyond the fire front, across fire lines and roads, and even over the Lewis River Canyon. The amount of moisture in the large logs was less than that in kiln-dried wood. By mid-August, more than 25 fires were burning simultaneously across the park and in surrounding national forests, with many joining together to create massive complexes, such as the Clover-Mist Fire, the Snake River Complex, and the North Fork/Wolf Lake Complex. On a single day—September 7—more than 100,000 acres burned. Also torched that day were 20 cabins and outbuildings in the vicinity of Old Faithful (out of the more than 400 structures there). Fortunately, all of the major historical buildings were spared. The fires seemed poised to consume the remainder of Yellowstone, but four days later the season's first snow carpeted the park. Within a few days, firefighters had the upper hand.

A TRANSFORMED LANDSCAPE

The fires had burned nearly 800,000 acres—more than one-third of the park—plus another 600,000 acres on adjacent Forest Service lands. Of the park total, 41 percent was consumed in canopy fires in which all of the trees were killed, and another 35 percent burned in a mixture of ground fires and canopy fires. The remaining acreage suffered lighter burns. Less than one-tenth of 1 percent of the land was burned hot enough to sterilize the soil. The fires killed countless small mammals, along with at least 269 elk, nine bison, six black bears, four deer, and two moose. The drought of 1988 followed by the severe winter of 1988–1989 led to a large die-off of elk and bison, but their carcasses provided food for predators. Since then, wildlife populations have rebounded and may even exceed pre-fire levels.

It's been more than two decades since the massive fires were put out, and much has changed, including the park's natural-fire program. It was replaced by a somewhat more conservative version that requires managers to provide daily certifications that fires are controllable and that they will remain "in prescription" for another 24 hours. Visitors to Yellowstone today will find dense thickets of young lodgepole pines—some 20 feet tall—in many areas that burned, and other evergreen species are starting to emerge. In other places, grasses, colorful wildflowers, forbs, and other plants dominate. Not everything burned, of course, so you'll also see many green older forests next to burned stands, creating a complex mosaic of habitats that supports a high diversity of animal life. Once you grow accustomed to the burned areas and understand that they are a part of the natural process, they actually add interest to the park and help you appreciate Yellowstone as a functioning ecosystem rather than a static collection of plants and animals.

Take a hike through one of the burned areas to discover the wealth of new life within Yellowstone. Vistas that were long blocked by forests are now more open and will gradually become even more so, and most of the fire-killed trees have fallen. The Park Service has placed signboards at sites around Yellowstone describing the fires of 1988 and the changes they brought about. The **Grant Village Visitor Center** has an informative exhibit and film about the fires. The fires of 1988 are, of course, not the last to strike these forests, and scientists warn that global warming may well lead to more intense fires in the future. Since 1988, thousands of acres have burned in a series of Yellowstone wildfires, and visitors will see evidence of these, especially on the east side of the park, where fires in the last decade burned more than 80,000 acres. Even in low fire years, several thousand acres burn within Yellowstone.

GRAND TETON NATIONAL PARK

Once the wonders of Yellowstone came to widespread public attention, it took only a few months for Congress to declare that area a national park. But the magnificent mountain range to the south proved an entirely different story. Early on, there were suggestions that Yellowstone be expanded to include the Tetons, but it would take decades of wrangling before Jackson Hole would finally be preserved.

"Damning" Jackson Lake

Jackson Lake represents one of the sadder chapters in the history of northwestern Wyoming. Jackson Lake Dam was built in the winter of 1910–1911 to supply water for Idaho potato and beet farmers. The town of Moran was built to house construction workers for Jackson Lake

Dam and at one time included more than 100 ramshackle structures. Virtually nothing remains of the town. The 70-foot-tall dam increased the size of the natural lake, flooding out more than 7,200 acres of trees and creating a tangle of floating and submerged trunks and stumps. To some, the dam seemed like the serpent in the Garden of Eden, a symbol of the development that would destroy the valley if not stopped. The trees remained in Jackson Lake for many years, creating an eyesore until the Park Service and the Civilian Conservation Corps finally launched a massive cleanup project in the 1930s. The dam was completely rebuilt in 1988–1989, and while the lake now looks attractive, it remains yet another example of how Wyoming provides water for farmers in surrounding states. Late in the fall, especially in dry years, the lake can drop to a large puddle with long stretches of exposed bottom at the upper end. Fortunately, Idaho irrigators did not succeed in their planned dams on Jenny, Leigh, and Taggart Lakes in what is now Grand Teton National Park.

Dudes and Development

Because of the rocky soils and long winters, Jackson Hole has always been a marginal place for cattle ranching, and only in the southern end of the valley are the soils rich enough to support a decent crop of hay. This poor soil and harsh climate saved Jackson Hole from early development and forced the ranchers to bring in dudes to supplement their income. (One old-timer noted, "Dudes winter better than cattle.")

Louis Joy established the first Jackson Hole dude ranch, the JY, in 1908 along Phelps Lake. It was followed a few years later by the Bar BC Ranch of Struthers Burt, an acclaimed East Coast author who had come west as a dude but learned enough to go into the business for himself. The dude ranchers were some of the first to realize the value of Jackson Hole and to support its preservation. Burt proposed that the valley and mountains be saved not as a traditional park but as a "museum on the hoof," where ranching and tourism would join hands

© DON PITCHER

Teton Range from Buffalo Valley, Grand Teton National Park

to stave off commercial developments. The roads would remain unpaved, all homes would be log, and Jackson would stay a frontier town. Needless to say, that didn't happen.

The movement to save Jackson Hole coalesced in a 1923 meeting at the cabin of Maude Noble. Horace Albright, superintendent of Yellowstone National Park, was there, along with local dude ranchers, businessmen, and cattlemen who were eager to save the remote valley from exploitation. To accomplish this goal, they proposed finding a wealthy philanthropist who might be willing to invest the $2 million that would be needed to buy the land. Fortunately, one of Struthers Burt's friends happened to be Kenneth Chorley, an assistant to John D. Rockefeller Jr. Burt used this contact to get Rockefeller interested in the project.

Rocky to the Rescue

In 1926, Rockefeller traveled west for a 12-day trip to Yellowstone. Horace Albright used the opportunity to take him on a side trip into Jackson Hole and to proselytize for protection of the valley. What they saw portended badly for the future: the Jenny Lake dance hall, roadside tourist camps and hot-dog stands, rusting abandoned cars, and a place that billboards proclaimed "Home of the Hollywood Cowboy." Rockefeller was angered by the prospect of crass commercial developments blanketing Jackson Hole and quickly signed on to the idea of buying the land and giving it to the Park Service.

To cover his tracks as he bought the land, Rockefeller formed the Snake River Land Company; if ranchers had known that the Rockefeller clan was behind the scheme, they would have either refused to sell or jacked up the price. Only a few residents—mostly supporters—knew of the plan. The local banker, Robert Miller, served as land-purchasing agent, although even he opposed letting the Park Service gain control of the valley. Miller used his position to buy out ranches with delinquent mortgages at his Jackson State Bank and then resigned, claiming the whole thing was part of a sinister plot to run the ranchers out and halt "progress." In 1929, Congress voted to establish a small Grand Teton National Park that would encompass the mountains themselves, which stood little chance of development, but not much else. Conservationists knew that without preservation of the valley below, the wonderful vistas would be lost.

A National Battleground

Rockefeller and Albright finally went public with their land-buying scheme in 1930, releasing a tidal wave of outrage. Anti-park forces led by Senator Milward Simpson (father of recently retired Senator Alan Simpson) spent the next decade fighting the park tooth and nail, charging that it would destroy the economy of Jackson Hole and that ranchers would lose their livelihoods. Rockefeller's agents were falsely accused of trying to intimidate holdouts with strong-arm tactics. Congress refused to accept Rockefeller's gift, and local opposition blocked the bill for more than a decade.

Finally, in 1943, President Roosevelt made an end run around the anti-park forces; he accepted the 32,000 acres purchased by Rockefeller, added 130,000 acres of Forest Service land, and declared it the Jackson Hole National Monument. The move outraged those in the valley, prompting more hearings and bills to abolish the new national monument. Wyoming's politicians attacked Roosevelt's actions. A bill overturning the decision was pocket-vetoed by the president, but for the next several years, the Wyoming delegation kept reintroducing the measure.

Things came to a head when Wallace Beery—a Reaganesque Hollywood actor—threatened to "shoot to kill" park officials. Beery, who had to use a stepladder to climb on his horse, organized a cattle drive across the monument. Unable to find anyone to fire on in the new monument, his cadres sat on a creek bank and drank a case of beer, cussing out the damn bureaucrats. So much for the Wild West.

By 1947, the tide had turned as increasing

postwar tourism revitalized the local economy. Finally, in 1950, a compromise was reached, granting ranchers lifetime grazing rights and the right to trail their cattle across the park en route to summer grazing lands. The new-and-improved Grand Teton National Park had finally come to fruition.

Postmortem

Some of the early fears that Rockefeller would use the new park for his own gain seemed partly justified. For many years his descendants owned the old JY Ranch and used Phelps Lake as something of a semiprivate playground, though it has now been generously donated to the Park Service. Rockefeller also built the enormous Grand Teton Lodge along Jackson Lake and facilities at Colter Bay Village and Jenny Lake, leading some to accuse the family of attempting to monopolize services within the park. The company, Grand Teton Lodge Company, is now owned by Vail Resorts, which manages Jackson Lake Lodge, Jenny Lake Lodge, and Colter Bay Village, along with Jackson Hole Golf and Tennis Club (near Jackson).

Looking back on the controversial creation of Grand Teton National Park, it's easy to see how wrong park opponents were. Teton County has Wyoming's most vibrant economy, and millions of people arrive each year to enjoy the beauty of the undeveloped Tetons. As writer Nathaniel Burt noted, "The old enemies of the park are riding the profitable bandwagon of unlimited tourism with high hearts and open palms." Park opponents' claims that the Park Service would "lock up" the land ring as hollow as similar anti-wilderness claims today by descendants of the same politicians who opposed Grand Teton National Park half a century ago. Without inclusion of the land purchased by Rockefeller, it is easy to imagine the valley covered with all sorts of summer-home developments, RV campgrounds, souvenir shops, motels, billboards, and neon signs. Take a look at the town of Jackson to see what might have been without Rockefeller's philanthropy.

JACKSON HOLE

The first people to cross the mountain passes into Jackson Hole probably arrived while the last massive glaciers were still retreating. Clovis stone arrowheads—a style used 12,000 years ago—have been found along the edges of the valley. These early peoples were replaced in the 16th and 17th centuries by the Shoshone, Bannock, Blackfeet, Crow, and Gros Ventre tribes, who hunted bison from horseback. When the first fur trappers tramped into Jackson Hole, they found Indian trails throughout the valley.

John Colter

Transport yourself back to the early 19th century, a time when people from the new nation called America saw the world west of the Mississippi River as just a blank spot on the map. In 1803, Thomas Jefferson bought the Louisiana Territory from France, and to learn more about this gigantic piece of real estate he sent Meriwether Lewis and William Clark on a military expedition to the Pacific coast, a trip that took nearly 2.5 years. Although the expedition skirted around Wyoming—heading across Montana instead—it proved the opening wedge for the settlement of the West and, indirectly, the discovery of Jackson Hole. On the return trip, the party met two fur trappers en route to the upper Missouri River. One of Lewis and Clark's respected scouts, John Colter, was allowed to join the trappers, "provided no one of the party would ask or expect a similar permission."

After a winter of trapping with his partners, Colter headed alone down the Platte River, but before he could get back to civilization he met a company of trappers led by Manuel Lisa. They were on their way to the Rockies, determined to cash in on the huge demand for beaver furs by trapping the rich beaver streams that Lewis and Clark had described. Wealth beckoned, and John Colter gladly turned around again, guiding Lisa's men up to the mouth of the Big Horn River, where they built a small fort. From there Colter was sent on a mission: Contact

Indians throughout the region, trading beads and other items for beaver furs.

His wanderings in the winter of 1807–1808 were the first white exploration of this region. A map produced by William Clark in 1814 and based on Colter's recollections shows an incredible midwinter journey around Yellowstone and Jackson Lakes, across the Tetons twice, and up through Jackson Hole. He did not get back to the fort until the following spring, telling tales of huge mountain ranges and a spectacular geothermal area that others quickly laughed off as "Colter's Hell."

Colter went on to become one of the most famous of all mountain men, and his later harrowing escape from the Blackfeet in Montana has become the stuff of legend. After being captured and stripped naked, he was forced to literally run for his life. Somehow he managed to outdistance his pursuers for six miles before hiding in a pile of logs until dark. He walked barefoot the 300 miles back to Manuel Lisa's fort, surviving on roots and tree bark. Shortly thereafter, Colter was reported to have thrown his hat on the ground, declaring, "I'll be damned if I ever come into [this country] again." He returned to St. Louis, married, and established a farm near that of fellow explorer Daniel Boone. Colter lived long enough to give William Clark a description of the country he had visited, but he died from jaundice just three years later, in 1813.

Because of the abundance of beavers along tributaries of the Snake River, Jackson Hole became an important crossroads for the Rocky Mountain fur trade. Although no rendezvous was ever held in the valley, many of the most famous mountain men spent time here. They first trapped beavers in Jackson Hole in 1811, but it was not until the 1820s that fur trapping really came into its own as mountain men fanned throughout the wilderness in search of the "soft gold." This quest continued for the next two decades, finally dying out when overtrapping made beavers harder to find and silk hats replaced fur hats. After the last rendezvous in 1840, most of the old trappers headed on to new adventures, the best becoming guides for those en route to Oregon and California. Because Jackson Hole was not near the Oregon Trail or other routes west, the area remained virtually deserted until the late 19th century.

Settlers

The first Jackson Hole homesteaders arrived in 1884, followed quickly by a handful of others fleeing the law. The settlers survived by grazing cattle, harvesting hay, and acting as guides for rich hunters from Europe and Eastern states. Gradually they filled the richest parts of the valley with homesteads. Conflicts soon arose between the Bannock Indians, who had been hunting in Jackson Hole for more than 100 years, and the new settlers who made money guiding wealthy sportsmen.

By 1895, Wyoming had enacted game laws prohibiting hunting during 10 months of the year. Claiming that the Indians were taking elk out of season, Constable William Manning and 26 settlers arrested a group of 28 Indians (mostly women and children) who had been hunting in Hoback Canyon. When the Bannocks attempted to flee, an elderly Indian was shot four times in the back and died. Most of the others escaped. Settlers in Jackson Hole feared revenge and called in the cavalry, but the Indians who had been hunting in the area all returned peaceably to their Idaho reservation. Astoundingly, *The New York Times* headlined its report of the incident, "Settlers Massacred—Indians Kill Every One at Jackson's Hole—Courier Brings the News—Red Men Apply the Torch to All the Houses in the Valley." Absolutely none of this was true, but the attack by whites succeeded in forcing the Indians off their traditional hunting grounds, an action eventually upheld in a landmark U.S. Supreme Court case.

Jackson Hole Comes of Age

By the turn of the 20th century, the Jackson Hole settlements of Jackson, Wilson, Kelly, and Moran had all been established. The

THE WHITE SHOSHONE

The little Jackson Hole town of Wilson is named for one of Wyoming's most fascinating characters, "Uncle Nick" Wilson. Born in 1842, Wilson grew up in Utah, where he made friends with a fellow sheepherder, an Indian boy, and learned to speak his language. Then, suddenly, Nick's life took a strange twist. The mother of Chief Washakie (from Wyoming's Wind River Reservation) had recently lost a son, and in a dream she was told that a white boy would come to take his place. Unable to convince her otherwise, Washakie sent his men out to find the new son. They came across Nick and offered him a pinto pony and the chance to fish, hunt, and ride horses all he wanted. It didn't take much persuading, and for the next two years he lived as a Shoshone, learning to hunt buffalo, to use a bow and arrow, and to answer to his new name, Yagaiki. He became a favorite of Chief Washakie, but when word came (falsely) that

Nick's father was threatening to attack the Shoshones with an army of men to retrieve his son, the chief reluctantly helped Nick return home.

At age 18, Nick Wilson became one of the first Pony Express riders, a job that nearly killed him when he was struck in the head during a Paiute Indian attack. A doctor managed to remove the arrow point, but Wilson remained in a coma for nearly two weeks. Thereafter, Wilson always wore a hat to cover the scar, even inside buildings. He went on to become an army scout and a driver for the Overland Stage before returning to a more sedate life as a farmer. Many years later, in 1889, Nick Wilson led a party of five Mormon families over steep Teton Pass and down to the rich grazing lands in Jackson Hole. The town that grew up around him became Wilson. In later years, "Uncle Nick" recounted his adventures in *The White Indian Boy*.

towns grew slowly; people survived by ranching, guiding, and engaging in the strange new business of tending to wealthy "dudes" from back East. Eventually, tourism would vastly eclipse raising cattle in importance, but even today Teton County has nearly as many cattle as people.

Jackson, Jackson Hole's primary settlement, was named by Maggie Simpson, who opened a post office here in 1894. Three years later Grace Miller—wife of a local banker known derisively as "Old Twelve Percent"—bought a large plot of land and planned a townsite, but the town wasn't officially incorporated until 1914. In an event that should come as no surprise in "The Equality State," Jackson later became the first town in America to be entirely governed by women. The year was 1920, and not only was the mayor a woman (Grace Miller), but so were all four council members, the city clerk, the treasurer, and even the town marshal. They remained in office until 1923.

Jackson Today

Through the years Jackson has grown, spurred on by the creation of Grand Teton National Park and the development of Jackson Hole Mountain Resort. In the last three decades, Jackson Hole has seen almost continuous growth; tourists have flooded the region to play, investors have built golf courses and ostentatious hotels, and wealthy families have snatched up their own parcels of paradise. Today, Teton County has the highest per capita income of any county in America (over $130,000), and locals quip that the billionaires are buying land so fast that they're driving the millionaires out of Jackson Hole.

Although much of the area is public land and will remain undeveloped, rapid growth on private land is transforming Jackson Hole into the Wyoming version of Vail or Santa Fe. Even the formerly quiet town of Wilson failed to fight off the development onslaught, with a massive new grade school and a collection of modest new homes that locals call Whoville (after those in the Dr. Seuss book). As a former resident of Wilson, I can appreciate the joke going the rounds: How many Wilsonites does it take to change a light bulb? Seven. One to screw it in, and the other six to talk about how good the old one used to be.

Growth in Jackson Hole has forced land values sky-high, and affordable housing has become an oxymoron, unless you consider $1 million—the median single-family home price—affordable. Despite all of the problems brought on by growth, the area is still remarkably beautiful, and the surrounding public lands will remain wild. Locals like to point out that this is more than a place to visit; for them it is a place to live surrounded by the best of the Old (and new) West.

ESSENTIALS

Getting There

Yellowstone National Park fills the northwest corner of Wyoming, with Grand Teton National Park and Jackson Hole immediately to the south. Although bus tours and limited public transportation are available, you will probably want a car to explore the Yellowstone area at your own pace. The vast majority of visitors arrive by car, either by driving their own vehicle or renting one at a regional airport. No interstates lead into this part of Wyoming, but year-round highways provide access from all directions. The closest interstates are I-80 across southern Wyoming, I-25 through eastern Wyoming, I-15 through Idaho, and I-94 across southern Montana.

BY AIR

Commercial airline service is available directly to three towns covered in this book: Cody, Jackson, and West Yellowstone (seasonal). The main regional hub is in Salt Lake City, but many travelers fly into closer airports in Billings and Bozeman, Montana or Idaho Falls, Idaho. The regional carriers are **American** (800/433-7300, www.aa.com), **Allegiant Air** (702/505-8888, www.allegiantair.com), **Delta/SkyWest** (800/221-1212, www.delta.com), **Frontier Airlines** (800/432-1359, www.frontierairlines.com), and **United/United Express** (800/864-8331, www.united.com).

© DON PITCHER

Jackson Hole

A number of carriers provide nonstop service to **Jackson Hole Airport** (www.jacksonholeairport.com): Delta/SkyWest from Salt Lake City year-round, plus summer and winter service to Minneapolis/St. Paul and Atlanta; American, with summer and winter service from Dallas and Chicago; United/United Express from Denver and Chicago year-round and in the summer from Los Angeles; and Frontier Airlines in summer from Denver. Many travelers opt to fly either to Salt Lake (275 miles away) or Idaho Falls (90 miles away) and pick up a rental car for the drive to Jackson.

Other Regional Airports

Delta/SkyWest has direct summer-only flights connecting Salt Lake City with **Yellowstone Airport** (www.yellowstoneairport.org) in West Yellowstone, Montana. Cody's **Yellowstone Regional Airport** (www.flyyra.com) is served by Delta/SkyWest from Salt Lake City and by United Express from Denver.

A 90-mile drive from Jackson, the airport at **Idaho Falls, Idaho** (www.idahofallsidaho.gov) is served by Delta/Sky West from Salt Lake City, United from Denver, and Allegiant Air from Las Vegas and Los Angeles.

It's an 84-mile drive from **Bozeman, Montana** (www.gallatinfield.com) to Mammoth Hot Springs on the northwest corner of Yellowstone, or 225 miles from Bozeman to Jackson. Several airlines serve Bozeman: Allegiant Air from Las Vegas, Delta from Salt Lake City and Minneapolis, Frontier from Denver, Horizon Air from Seattle, and United from Denver, Los Angeles, San Francisco, and Chicago.

Karst Stage (406/388-2293 or 800/287-4759, www.karststage.com) provides daily wintertime shuttles from the Bozeman airport to West Yellowstone, Gardiner, Mammoth Hot Springs, and Big Sky. There are no scheduled summertime shuttles, but Karst has custom service from Bozeman to Old Faithful, Mammoth Hot Springs, West Yellowstone, and Big Sky. For all Karst trips, be sure to make reservations at least three days ahead.

BY BUS AND TRAIN

The closest **Greyhound** (800/231-2222, www.greyhound.com) stations are in Salt Lake City, Rock Springs, Bozeman, and Billings. Unfortunately, Greyhound does not serve Jackson, Cody, West Yellowstone, Idaho Falls, or other towns in the region. In fact, there is no bus service of any kind into Cody! **Mountain States Express/Alltrans** (307/733-3135 or 800/652-9510, www.mountainstatesexpress.com) has daily shuttle vans to Jackson from Salt Lake City Airport and Idaho Falls. A wide variety of park bus tours are available from surrounding towns.

Amtrak's (800/872-7245, www.amtrak.com) California Zephyr runs between Chicago and Oakland but does not come close to Jackson Hole or Yellowstone. The nearest train station is in Salt Lake City, 275 miles from Jackson. Those traveling by train will need to take a bus, rental car, or plane from Salt Lake into Jackson.

FROM SALT LAKE CITY
Airport

Salt Lake City International Airport (www.slcairport.com) is served by most of the major national carriers and is a hub for Delta/SkyWest, with hundreds of flights daily from around the country. Other large carriers include Southwest, United, Frontier, American, Jet Blue, SkyWest, and US Airways. The airport is seven miles west of downtown and has two terminals and all the amenities travelers expect, including ATMs, Wi-Fi, and play areas for kids. The ground transportation desk is at the far end of baggage claim in both terminals.

Bus

Mountain States Express/Alltrans (307/733-3135 or 800/652-9510, www.mountainstatesexpress.com) has daily buses between Jackson and Salt Lake City Airport.

Salt Lake Express (208/656-8824 or 800/356-9796, www.saltlakeexpress.com) operates daily shuttle vans connecting Salt Lake with Jackson, Idaho Falls, West Yellowstone, Butte, Twin Falls, and Boise.

Greyhound has a regional terminal (300 South 600 West) in Salt Lake City, but no runs to the Yellowstone area.

Car Rentals

All the major companies have rental counters on the ground floor of the short-term parking garage, directly across from the terminal. These include **Advantage** (801/322-6090 or 800/777-5500, www.advantage.com), **Alamo** (801/575-2211 or 800/462-5266, www.alamo. com), **Avis** (801/575-2847 or 800/230-4898, www.avis.com), **Budget** (801/575-2821 or 800/527-0700, www.budget.com), **Dollar** (801/575-2580 or 800/800-4000, www.dollar. com), **Enterprise** (801/537-7433 or 800/261-7331, www.enterprise.com), **Fox** (801/401-0281 or 800/225-4369, www.foxrentacar. com), **Hertz** (801/575-2683 or 800/654-3131, www.hertz.com), **National** (801/575-2277 or 800/227-7368, www.nationalcar.com), and **Thrifty** (801/265-6677 or 800/847-4389, www.thrifty.com).

RV Rentals

A number of companies rent recreation vehicles in Salt Lake City, including **Access RV** (220 S. Hwy. 89, 801/936-1200 or 800/327-6910, www.accessrv.com), **Cruise America** (4125 S. State St., 801/288-0930 or 800/983-3184, www.cruiseamerica.com), **Hugh's RV** (250 S. Hwy. 89, 801/936-1010, www.elmonterv.com), and **Pappy's Motorhome Rentals** (8201 S. State St., 801/262-2100 or 800/888-2230, www.rentmotorhomes.com).

Accommodations

It's an all-day drive to Jackson Hole or West Yellowstone from Salt Lake City, so if your flight gets in late, find a room locally or in a town along the way. Check the Salt Lake City Chamber of Commerce website (www. saltlakechamber.org) for an extensive listing of lodging choices. A number of comfortable mid-priced places are close to the airport, including **Hampton Inn & Suites** (307 N. Admiral Byrd Rd., 801/530-0088 or 800/426-7866, www.hamptoninn.com), **Airport Hilton** (5151 Wiley Post Way, 801/539-1515 or 800/999-3736, www.hilton.com), and **La Quinta Inn and Suites** (1965 N. 1200 W., 801/776-6700 or 866/725-1661, www.lq.com). All three of these have outdoor pools, Wi-Fi, hot tubs, and full breakfasts.

Suggested Driving Routes

There are several ways to drive from Salt Lake City to **Jackson,** but the shortest route (via Evanston and Afton) is a rather circuitous 274-mile journey. Take I-80 east from Salt Lake to Evanston, Wyoming (84 miles), and turn north on Wyoming Highway 89, which wanders back over the border as Utah Highway 16 before slicing back into Wyoming. Turn north on U.S. Highway 30 shortly after crossing the Wyoming state line and follow it west into Idaho, where you turn north again on U.S. Highway 89 in the town of Montpelier. The rest is pretty straightforward: drive U.S. Highway 89 through Star Valley and Alpine, along the Snake River, through Hoback Junction, and finally into Jackson.

An alternate—and slightly longer, at 294 miles—route to Jackson follows the Green River Valley, with the Wind River Mountains providing a snowcapped horizon. From Salt Lake City, take I-80 east to Wyoming exit 18 (13 miles east of Evanston), and turn north on U.S. Highway 189 through Kemmerer (stop to see Fossil Butte National Monument) and Big Piney. You may want a side trip to Pinedale before heading into the mountains along the Hoback River to Hoback Junction and Jackson.

The most direct route to **West Yellowstone** is a relatively easy 319 miles. Follow I-84 north to Tremonton, Utah, and turn onto I-15 to Idaho Falls, where U.S. Highway 10 continues the rest of the way to West Yellowstone.

FROM BILLINGS, MONTANA
Airport

Montana's largest airport, **Billings Logan International Airport** (www.flybillings. com), has daily nonstop flights by Frontier from Denver; Delta from Salt Lake City and

Minneapolis; Allegiant Air from Las Vegas, Phoenix, and Los Angeles; Frontier from Denver; Horizon Air/Alaska Air from Seattle, and United Express/United from Denver and Chicago. The airport sits atop a local geological formation called the Rim Rocks just north of town. Billings Logan houses a restaurant and bar, Montana-made gift shop, and children's play area, with Yellowstone County Museum directly across the parking lot.

Bus and Shuttle

Greyhound (800/231-2222, www.greyhound. com) has daily service connecting Billings with points west all the way to Seattle. If you're heading east to Fargo, North Dakota, take **Rimrock Stages Trailways** (800/255-7566, www.rimrocktrailways.com). **Phidippides Shuttle Service** (307/527-6789 or 866/527-6789, www.codyshuttle.com) provides vans to Cody, Wyoming.

Car Rentals

Most companies have counters inside the airport terminal, including **Alamo** (406/252-3556 or 877/222-9075, www.alamo.com), **Enterprise** (406/294-2930 or 800/261-7331, www.enterprise.com), **Hertz** (406/248-9151 or 800/654-3131, www.hertz.com), **National** (406/252-7626 or 800/227-7368, www.nationalcar.com), and **Thrifty** (406/248-9993 or 800/847-4389, www.thrifty.com). **Avis** (406/252-8007 or 800/230-4898, www.avis.com) has a shuttle to its downtown location.

RV Rentals

Rent recreational vehicles locally from **Pierce RV Center** (3800 Pierce Pkwy., 406/655-8000 or 888/881-2745, www.piercerv.com) or **Tour America RV Center** (2220 Old Hardin Rd., 406/248-7481 or 800/735-1330, www.touramericarv.com).

Accommodations

A number of Billings places provide lodging if you want to overnight before starting out for Yellowstone. The Billings Chamber of Commerce website (www.billingschamber.com) has links to many of these. **Dude Rancher Lodge** (415 N. 29th St., 406/259-5561 or 800/221-3302, www.duderancherlodge.com) is a good bargain place with Old West styling and an attached restaurant. The downtown **Riversage Billings Inn** (880 N. 29th St., 406/252-6800 or 800/231-7782, www.billingsinn.com) is a reasonably priced place with large rooms, fridges, microwaves, and a continental breakfast. Just a couple of minutes from the airport, **Country Inn and Suites** (231 Main St., 406/245-9995 or 888/201-1746, www.countryinns.com) provides nice rooms, an indoor pool, continental breakfast, and Wi-Fi.

Suggested Driving Routes

It's a 127-mile drive from Billings to the **northeast corner of Yellowstone National Park.** From Billings, take I-94 16 miles west to Laurel and turn south onto U.S. Highway 212, which goes through the pretty mountain town of Red Lodge before climbing over spectacular **Beartooth Pass** (10,947 feet; closed Nov.–May) and down to the tiny twin settlements of Cooke City and Silver Gate, Montana, before entering Yellowstone.

From Billings to **Cody,** the drive is 104 miles, plus another 52 miles to the **Yellowstone's East Entrance.** From Billings, take I-94 west to Laurel and turn south on U.S. Highway 310 to Bridger, where the road divides. Continue south on Montana Highway 72 to Cody; the road becomes Wyoming Highway 120 when you cross the state line. Spend a couple of days seeing the sights in Cody, and then turn west on U.S. Highway 14/16/20 through pretty Wapiti Valley to the East Entrance of Yellowstone, a total distance of 156 miles from Billings.

The town of **Gardiner, Montana** can be reached by driving west 125 miles on I-94 from Billings to Livingston, and then south on U.S. Highway 89 to Gardiner; stop at Chico Hot Springs in appropriately named Paradise Valley along the way. The total distance is 178 fairly easy miles.

Getting Around

BY CAR

Most summer travelers to the Yellowstone–Grand Teton area—and a substantial number of winter visitors—arrive by car. Some fly into Jackson Hole, Salt Lake City, Billings, or Idaho Falls and rent a vehicle, whereas others head out on a grand road trip from home. The northwest corner of Wyoming is accessible from all sides in the summer, but most roads inside Yellowstone National Park are closed when the snow flies.

Maps

Free state highway maps can be found at visitor centers in Wyoming, Montana, and Idaho, but map aficionados should also buy one of the excellent statewide topographic map books published by DeLorme Mapping (800/511-2459, www.delorme.com). These maps are indispensable for travelers heading off main routes and are sold in most local bookstores. National forest maps are also helpful for mountain driving in many parts of Wyoming; buy them in local Forest Service offices.

Car Rentals

You can rent cars, SUVs, and vans in all of the larger towns, and those with airports generally have Hertz, Avis, and other national chains. The best rental rates tend to be in the larger cities, where there's more competition. If you plan to rent a car for an extended period, check travel websites such as www.travelocity.com, www.expedia.com, or www.orbitz.com to see which company offers the best rates. Note, however, that these quotes may not include taxes, which can be substantial, especially if you rent from an airport office. Even if you've made a reservation, it pays to call around once more after you arrive. On one visit I saved hundreds of dollars by getting a last-minute quote. If you're visiting in the summer, try to get a light-colored car; dark ones can get incredibly hot.

Highway Conditions

The national phone number for up-to-date road and travel information is **511.** Dial this number almost anywhere and it will link to regional conditions. In addition, state highway departments provide detailed information on construction delays and current road conditions for Wyoming (888/996-7623, www.wyoroad.info), Montana (800/226-7623, www.mdt511.com), and Idaho (888/432-7623, www.511.idaho.gov). Roadwork is ongoing within Yellowstone National Park (307/344-7381, www.nps.gov/yell). Get today's regional **weather forecast** at www.crh.noaa.gov/cys.

Winter Closures

Jackson Hole remains accessible by highway year-round, but most roads in Yellowstone National Park close to cars when the first heavy snows block the passes. By the first of November, things are generally shut down all over except for the 56 miles between Gardiner and Cooke City. This is the only road within Yellowstone that remains open all year. The roads are groomed for snowcoaches (a delightfully old-fashioned way to travel) and guided snowmobiles mid-December–mid-March. Plowing starts in March, but most park roads don't open for cars again until mid-May and sometimes not until early June. If you're planning a trip early or late in the season, contact the park (307/344-7381, www.nps.gov/yell) for current road conditions.

Within Grand Teton National Park (307/739-3399, www.nps.gov/grte), U.S. Highway 89/191/287 is plowed from Moran Junction to Flagg Ranch throughout the winter, providing a starting point for snowcoaches and guided snowmobiles heading into Yellowstone. Most other roads in Grand Teton are not plowed and are generally closed to cars November–April.

Outside the parks, most regional roads are plowed all winter, including Teton Pass (west of Jackson), Togwotee Pass (northeast

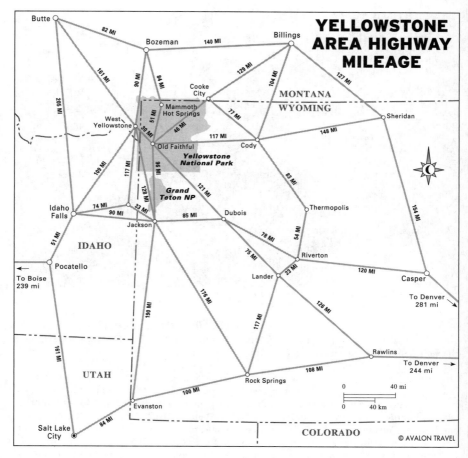

YELLOWSTONE AREA HIGHWAY MILEAGE

of Jackson), and U.S. Highway 14/16/20 from Cody to Pahaska Tepee near the East Entrance to Yellowstone. Two roads that are not plowed are U.S. Highway 212 over Beartooth Pass (between Cooke City and Red Lodge, Montana) and an eight-mile stretch of Chief Joseph Scenic Highway east of Cooke City and northwest of Cody.

Winter Travel

Winter travelers need to take special precautions. Snow tires are a necessity, but you should also have emergency supplies, including tire chains, a shovel and bag of sand in case you get stuck, a first-aid kit, booster cables, signal flares, a flashlight with extra batteries, a lighter and candle, chemical hot packs, a transistor radio, nonperishable foods (granola bars, canned nuts, or dried fruit), a jug of water, an ice scraper, winter clothes, blankets, a sleeping bag, an ax, and tow strap. The most valuable tool may well be a cell phone to call for help—assuming you're in an area with reception.

© DON PITCHER

tracked oversnow vehicle in West Yellowstone, Montana

If you become stranded in a blizzard, stay in your car. You're more likely to be found, and the vehicle provides shelter from the weather. Run the engine and heater sparingly, occasionally opening a downwind window for ventilation. Don't run the engine if the tailpipe is blocked by snow—you may risk carbon monoxide poisoning. For up-to-date road and travel conditions in Wyoming, call 307/772-0824 or 888/996-7623, or log onto www.wyoroad.info for information, webcams, and construction advisories. Get weather forecasts at www.crh.noaa.gov/cys.

BUSES AND TOURS

Greyhound (800/231-2222, www.greyhound.com) has buses to Salt Lake City, Bozeman, Billings, and the southern Wyoming cities of Rock Springs, Rawlins, and Laramie, but not to Jackson, West Yellowstone, or other cities in the region. Both **Mountain States Express/Alltrans** (307/733-3135 or 800/652-9510, www.mountainstatesexpress.com) and **Salt Lake Express** (208/656-8824 or 800/356-9796, www.saltlakeexpress.com) provide daily van connections among Salt Lake City, Jackson, and West Yellowstone.

Recreation

Northwest Wyoming is famous for its year-round recreational opportunities. In the summertime, hiking, camping, horseback rides, river rafting, mountain biking, and other adventures top the charts, and winter brings out the skis, snowboards, skates, snowshoes, and snowmobiles. Each part of the region has its own attractions, from whitewater rafting through the Snake River Canyon, to mountain climbing within Grand Teton National Park, to family day hikes in Yellowstone. If outdoor adventure is what you crave, you've come to the right place!

FISHING

Outstanding fishing opportunities abound throughout the Greater Yellowstone Ecosystem, and several rivers have achieved an almost mythical status among fly-fishers.

Fishing Licenses

Nonresident Wyoming fishing permits cost $14 for one day or $92 for a season. Resident fishing licenses are $24 for the year. Nonresident youths (ages 14–17) pay $15 for the year ($3 for resident youths). With the exception of the one-day rate, you will also need to buy a $12.50 mandatory conservation stamp. Kids younger than 14 don't need a license if they're with an adult who has a valid fishing license. Buy permits at most sporting-goods stores or from Game and Fish offices. For detailed fishing information, contact the **Wyoming Game and Fish Department** (307/777-4600 or 800/548-9453, http://gf.state.wy.us).

Get Montana fishing information from the **Montana Fish, Wildlife & Parks Department** (406/444-2535, www.fwp.m.t.gov/fishing/license). Nonresident two-day licenses cost $15, 10-day licenses are $44, and season licenses cost $60; you're required to also have a $10 conservation license. No license is required for children younger than age 15 if accompanied by an adult with a Montana fishing license (but special restrictions apply).

In Idaho, nonresident fishing licenses are $13 for one day plus $6 per day for additional days, or $98 for an annual license. Kids under 18 pay $22 annually. Get details from **Idaho Fish and Game** (208/334-3700 or 800/554-8685, www.fishandgame.idaho.gov).

Within **Grand Teton National Park,** only a Wyoming fishing license is required, but separate regulations apply in Yellowstone National Park. There, anglers don't need a state fishing license but must obtain a special **Yellowstone National Park permit,** available from visitor centers, ranger stations, and Yellowstone General Stores, plus fishing shops in surrounding towns. The adult fishing fee is $15 for a three-day permit, $20 for a seven-day permit, or $35 for a season permit. Kids under age 15 can get a free permit, or can fish without a permit under the supervision of an adult who has one. Park visitor centers and ranger stations have copies of current fishing regulations.

Fishing Information

Several good books provide detailed information for fishing enthusiasts. Try one of the following: *Bud Lilly's Guide to Fly Fishing the New West* by Bud Lilly and Paul Schullery (Frank Amato Publications), *Yellowstone Fishes: Ecology, History, and Angling in the Park* by John Varley and Paul Schullery (www.stackpolebooks.com), *Fishing Yellowstone* by Richard Parks (www.falcon.com), or *Fishing the Beartooths* by Pat Marchuson (www.falcon.com). For broader coverage, see *Fishing Wyoming* by Kenneth Graham (www.falcon.com), or Ken Retallic's *Flyfisher's Guide to Wyoming* (Wilderness Adventures Press). Several other books detail the multitude of fishing options on surrounding lands in Montana and Idaho. In Jackson, stop by **Jack Dennis Sports** (50 E. Broadway, 307/733-3270 or 800/570-3270, www.jackdennisoutdoors.com) to pick up a copy of the free *Flyfisher's Guider to Wyoming,* with descriptions of regional fishing areas and which lures to try.

An exceptionally helpful online source for fishing information is the *Wyoming Fishing Network,* www.wyomingfishing.net. Here you'll find details on where to fish, lures, local guides, and up-to-date fishing reports for various rivers and lakes.

A variety of exotic plants and animals threaten the Yellowstone ecosystem, including New Zealand mud snails, zebra mussels, and Eurasian water-milfoil. Help prevent the arrival or spread of these pests by carefully cleaning boots, clothing, waders, gear, and boats. Find out more at www.cleaninspectdry.com and www.protectyourwaters.net.

BOATING

Jackson Hole's most popular summertime recreational activity is floating Wyoming's largest river, the Snake. Almost 20 different rafting companies offer dozens of trips each day of the summer, and on a busy day you'll see several thousand folks floating the placid upper sections or blasting through the boiling rapids of Snake River Canyon. Whitewater and float trips are also available from the towns of Cody, Gardiner, and West Yellowstone.

Two Jackson-based kayaking schools teach a full range of classes in river kayaking, sea kayaking, and canoeing. These and other companies also offer sea-kayak trips on Jackson Lake in Grand Teton National Park and Lake Yellowstone within Yellowstone National Park. They're available in a variety of flavors, from quick half-day paddles to multi-night kayaking and camping trips. Motorboat rentals are also available on Lake Yellowstone and Jackson Lake.

HORSEBACK AND WAGON RIDES

Horseback day rides are available throughout the region, including within both Yellowstone and Grand Teton National Parks.

Two companies lead overnight wagon-train rides into the country around Jackson Hole: **Wagons West** (307/543-2418 or 800/447-4711, www.wagonswestwyo.com) and **Teton**

Wagon Train/Double H Bar (307/734-6101 or 888/734-6101, www.tetonwagontrain.com).

In addition to these trips, very popular **chuck-wagon cookouts** are offered in Jackson Hole and at Roosevelt Lodge within Yellowstone National Park. These outings combine a ride in a Conestoga-style wagon with a big Old West feast and cowboy entertainment.

BIKING

Bicycles are available for rent in Jackson, Cody, Moose (Grand Teton National Park), and West Yellowstone, and at Old Faithful Snow Lodge inside Yellowstone National Park. Excellent paved paths can be found in Grand Teton National Park, around Jackson, and within Teton Valley, while hiking/mountain-biking trails and dirt roads crisscross the region, particularly on Forest Service lands. A few of these trails are described in this book; for others, contact local bike shops or get trail information from Forest Service or Park Service offices. Bikes are prohibited on backcountry trails in both Yellowstone and Grand Teton National Parks but are allowed on most main roads and certain other paths.

Bike Touring

Many cyclists ride through this part of Wyoming, Montana, and Idaho, but conditions are not the safest, particularly within Yellowstone, where traffic is heavy and the roads are narrow and winding with little or no shoulders. During summer, the best times to ride are in the morning before traffic thickens or late in the afternoon before the light begins to fade and you become less visible to motorists. September and October are far less crowded than midsummer.

Backroads (800/462-2848, www.backroads.com) leads six-day tours of the Greater Yellowstone area that include biking, hiking, rafting, and kayaking. Park websites (www.nps.gov/yell and www.nps.gov/grte) list additional bike touring companies.

The Wyoming Department of Transportation publishes a useful *Bicycle Guidance Map*—on

© DON PITCHER

cyclists near Mammoth Hot Springs, Yellowstone National Park

waterproof paper—showing the amount of traffic on each paved road, the width of paved shoulders, profiles of the steeper road grades, and general wind patterns. Anyone touring on a bike will find this map immensely valuable. Get a copy by calling the WYDOT Bicycle Coordinator at 307/777-4719, or online at www.dot.state.wy.us.

INTO THE BACKCOUNTRY

To get a real feel for the Greater Yellowstone Ecosystem, you need to abandon your car, get away from the towns, and head out into the vast and undeveloped public lands. The region contains some of the most remote country in the Lower 48 and one of the largest intact temperate-zone ecosystems anywhere.

Many campers prefer to use horses for longer trips, but backpacking is popular on the shorter trails, especially in the national parks. Backcountry permits are required only within Yellowstone and Grand Teton National Parks. It is, however, a good idea to check in at a local Forest Service ranger station to get a copy of the regulations, because each place is different in such specifics as how far your tent must be from lakes and trails and whether wood fires are allowed. Be sure to take insect repellent along on any summertime trip because mosquitoes, deerflies, and horseflies can be thick, especially early in the summer.

Trail Information

This book describes several hiking trips, mostly two- or three-day hikes, for Yellowstone and Grand Teton National Parks, along with nearby Forest Service wilderness areas. Recommended hiking guides for the Tetons and Jackson Hole are *Jackson Hole Hikes* by Rebecca Woods (White Willow Publishing) and *Teton Trails* by Katy Duffy and Darwin Wile (www.grandtetonpark.org). For Yellowstone, there are two fine guidebooks: *Yellowstone Trails* by Mark Marschall (www.yellowstoneassociation.org) and *Hiking Yellowstone National Park* by Bill Schneider (www.falcon.com). The National Park Service and the U.S. Forest Service can also provide specific trail information, and they post much of this information on their websites.

The **Continental Divide National Scenic Trail** (303/838-3760 or 888/909-2382, www.cdtrail.org) stretches for 3,100 miles from Mexico to Canada, including across the Teton Wilderness and Yellowstone National Park.

Horses

For many people, the highlight of a Western vacation is the chance to ride a horse into wild country. Although a few folks bring their own steeds, most visitors leave the driving to an expert local outfitter instead. (If you've ever worked around horses in the backcountry, you'll understand why.) Horsepacking is an entirely different experience from backpacking. The trade requires years of experience in learning how to properly load horses and mules with panniers (large baskets), which types of knots to use for different loads, how to keep the packstrings under control, which horses to picket and which to hobble, and how to awaken when the horses decide to head down the trail on hobbles at three in the morning. Add to this a knowledge of bear safety, an ability to keep guests entertained with campfire tales and ribald jokes, a complete vocabulary of horse-cussing terms, and a thorough knowledge of tobacco chewing, and you're still only about 10 percent of the way to becoming a packer.

Get a complete listing of local backcountry outfitters from the **Wyoming Outfitters and Guides Association** (307/265-2376, www.wyoga.org), **Montana Outfitters and Guides Association** (406/449-3578, www.moga-montana.org), or **Idaho Outfitters and Guides Association** (208/342-1438 or 800/494-3246, www.ioga.org). Not all of these guides and outfitters may be permitted in a given backcountry area; contact the Park Service or Forest Service to see which ones are licensed to use the places you plan to visit.

Although horses are far more common, **llamas** are used in some backcountry areas. You can't ride them, but they're easier to control than horses and do not cause as much damage to trails and backcountry meadows. Llamas are perfect for folks who want to hike while letting a pack llama carry most of the weight. Contact local Forest Service and Park Service offices for permitted llama-packers.

Trail Etiquette

Because horses are so commonly used in the Yellowstone region, hikers should follow a few rules of courtesy. Horses and mules are not the brightest critters on this planet, and they can spook at the most inane thing, even a bush blowing in the breeze or a brightly colored hat. Hikers meeting a packstring should move several feet off the trail and not speak loudly or make any sudden moves. If you've ever seen what happens when just one mule in a string decides to act up, you'll appreciate the chaos that can result from sudden noises or movements. Anyone hiking with a dog should keep it well away from the stock and not let it bark. Last of all, never walk close behind a horse, unless you don't mind spending time in a hospital. A horse's kick is *definitely* worse than its bite.

Backcountry Ethics

The wilderness areas of northwest Wyoming are places to escape the crowds, enjoy the beauty and peace of the countryside, and develop an understanding of nature. Unfortunately, as more and more people head into backcountry areas, these benefits are becoming endangered. To keep wild places wild, always practice **leave no trace** principles when hiking and camping:

- Use existing campsites and fire rings.
- Locate your campsite well away from trails and streams.
- Stay on designated trails; don't cut across switchbacks.
- Burn only dead and down wood.
- Extinguish all fires.
- Wash dishes 200 feet from lakes and creeks.

- Dig "cat holes" at least 200 feet from lakes or streams.

- Hang all food well above the reach of bears.

- Don't litter the ground with toilet paper; instead, bury it deep or burn it in your campfire. (Do not, however, try to burn toilet paper in the woods; more than one person has started a forest fire in this way.)

Your tent site should be 100 yards from the food storage and cooking areas to reduce the likelihood of bear problems. Wood fires are not allowed in many areas, so be sure to bring along a portable gas stove. And, of course, haul your garbage out with you. Burning cans and tinfoil in the fire lessens their weight (and the odors that attract bears), but be sure to pick them out of the fire pit before you depart. And make sure that fire is completely out.

For detailed leave-no-trace brochures on minimizing your impact and treating the land with respect, contact the **Leave No Trace Center** (800/332-4100, www.lnt.org).

WINTER SPORTS
Downhill Skiing and Snowboarding

Jackson Hole is the primary skiing and snowboarding area in Wyoming. This area includes one of America's top winter destinations, **Jackson Hole Mountain Resort** in Teton Village, 12 miles from the town of Jackson. For ease of access, it's hard to beat the smaller (but surprisingly steep) **Snow King Resort,** just seven blocks from Town Square. On the other side of Teton Pass—42 miles from Jackson—is **Grand Targhee Ski Resort,** famous for its deep powder skiing. **Sleeping Giant Ski Area** is a family area 50 miles west of Cody near Yellowstone. During winter, call the Wyoming Travel and Tourism Division at 800/225-5996 for the statewide ski report, or visit www.wyomingtourism.org.

Many more ski resorts can be found in Montana, including those at Red Lodge (northeast of Yellowstone) and Big Sky (south of Bozeman and west of Yellowstone).

Cross-Country Skiing

Skinny-skiers have an overwhelming choice of places to ski in the Yellowstone–Grand Teton–Jackson Hole area. Developed Nordic areas are in Jackson Hole, west of Cody, and at West Yellowstone, Montana. In addition, Yellowstone and Grand Teton National Parks have cross-country skiing with views to die for, and some trails in Grand Teton are groomed. Adjacent Forest Service lands provide deep snow and inexhaustible opportunities for those with backcountry skiing experience.

Snowmobiling

An extensive network of snowmobile trails leads through northwest Wyoming and nearby parts of Montana and Idaho, including the **Continental Divide Snowmobile Trail** (www.sledwyoming.com) in the Wind River Mountains. Yellowstone National Park is open only to guided snowmobile tours; check with the Park Service for details.

Snowmobile trail maps and listings of snowmobile rental companies are available from local visitor centers. Find detailed snowmobile information—and current trail reports—at http://wyotrails.state.wy.us/snow.

Snowcoaches

Yellowstone snowcoaches provide a fine alternative to snowmobiling through the park. These 10-passenger machines are old-fashioned and gawky, but they provide a delightful way to explore the sights. The Yellowstone concessioner (Xanterra) runs a wide variety of snowcoach trips, including ones that drop you off to cross-country ski or explore. Another company (Yellowstone Expeditions) leads snowcoach trips to a remote yurt near Grand Canyon of the Yellowstone. Here you stay overnight and can explore the winter wonderland at a slower pace. Several other West Yellowstone and Jackson companies offer tours on jacked-up vans with tracks.

AVALANCHE SAFETY

Backcountry skiing is becoming increasingly popular in the mountains surrounding Jackson Hole. Unfortunately, many skiers fail to take the necessary precautions and more than a few have paid with their lives. Between 2000 and 2010, avalanches killed 37 people in Wyoming, and many of these were snowmobilers or backcountry skiers in the Tetons. Given the enormous snowfalls that occur, the steep slopes the snow piles up on, and the high winds that accompany many storms, it should come as no surprise that avalanches are a real danger.

Nearly all avalanches are triggered by the victims. If you really want to avoid avalanches, ski only on groomed ski trails or "bombproof" slopes that, because of aspect, shape, and slope angle, never seem to slide. Unfortunately, this isn't always possible, so an understanding of the conditions that lead to avalanches is imperative for backcountry skiers. The Forest Service produces a useful booklet called *Basic Guidelines for Winter Recreation,* available in many of its offices around Wyoming.

The best way to learn about backcountry safety is through an avalanche class. These are offered in the Jackson Hole area by **American Avalanche Institute** (307/733- 3315, www.americanavalancheinstitute. com), **Exum Mountain Guides** (307/733- 2297, www.exumguides.com), **Jackson Hole Mountain Guides** (307/733-4979 or 800/239-7642, www.jhmg.com), and **Rendezvous Backcountry Tours** (307/353-2900 or 877/754-4887, www.skithetetons.com). Failing that, you can help protect yourself by following these precautions when you head into the backcountry:

- Before leaving, get up-to-date avalanche information. Visit www.avalanche.org for links to avalanche forecasting sites throughout the Western states. For the Jackson Hole area, check the Forest Service's 24-hour **Backcountry Avalanche Hazard and Weather Forecast** (307/733- 2664, www.jhavalanche.org). For areas around Yellowstone – including West Yellowstone and Cooke City on the margins and the Washburn Range inside the park – contact the **Gallatin National Forest Avalanche Advisory Center** (406/587-6981, www.mtavalanche.com) in Bozeman. If the message says avalanche danger is high, ski on the flats instead.

- Be sure to carry extra warm clothes, water, high-energy snacks, a dual-frequency ava-

Other Winter Activities

Several companies offer **dogsled** rides in the Greater Yellowstone area, including ones to delightful Granite Hot Springs and overnight trips to a remote yurt. You'll find them in Jackson, Grand Targhee, and West Yellowstone. **Sleigh rides** are also available in Jackson Hole and at Grand Targhee, and some are combined with a meal at a remote cabin.

Unique sleigh rides take visitors among the elk on the National Elk Refuge.

Snowshoeing is popular and a good way to get to places others don't go. Guided snowshoe hikes are offered in both Grand Teton and Yellowstone National Parks.

You'll find **ice-skating rinks** at the three big Jackson Hole ski areas, in the towns of Jackson and Cody, and at Mammoth Hot Springs within Yellowstone.

lanche transceiver (make sure it's turned on and that you know how to use it!), a lightweight snow shovel (for digging snow pits or excavating avalanche victims), an emergency snow shelter, a cell phone, first-aid supplies, a Swiss Army or Leatherman knife, a topographic map, an extra plastic ski tip, a flashlight, matches, and a compass or GPS unit. Many skiers also carry that cure-all, duct tape, wrapped around a ski pole. Let a responsible person know exactly where you are going and when you expect to return. It's also a good idea to carry special ski poles that extend into probes in case of an avalanche. Check with local ski shops or talk to Forest Service or Park Service folks for details on specific areas.

- Check the angle of an area before you ski through it. Slopes of 30-45 degrees are the most dangerous; lesser slopes do not slide as frequently.

- Watch the weather; winds over 15 miles per hour can pile snow much more deeply on lee slopes, causing dangerous loading on the snowpack. Especially avoid skiing on or below cornices.

- Avoid the leeward side of ridges, where snow loading can be greatest.

- Be aware of gullies and bowls; they're more likely to slip than flat open slopes or ridgetops. Stay out of gullies at the bottom of wide bowls; these are natural avalanche chutes.

- Look out for cracks in the snow, and listen for hollow snow underfoot. These are strong signs of dangerous conditions.

- Look at the trees. Smaller trees may indicate that avalanches rip through an area frequently, knocking over the larger ones. Avalanches can, however, also run through forested areas.

- Know how much new snow has fallen recently. Heavy new snow over older weak snow layers is a sure sign of extreme danger on potential avalanche slopes. Most avalanches slip during or immediately after a storm.

- Learn how to dig a snow pit and how to read the various snow layers. Particularly important are the very weak layers of depth hoar or surface hoar that have been buried under heavy new snow.

Accommodations

Lodging in the Yellowstone and Jackson Hole area is generally at a premium during summer and the Christmas–New Year's holiday. During peak summer or winter seasons in Jackson Hole, you should expect to pay at least $130 for a decent room. Rates are somewhat lower in West Yellowstone, Gardiner, Cody, Driggs, Cooke City, and Dubois, but not nearly as cheap as in less-touristy towns in Wyoming, Montana, or Idaho.

Throughout this book I have typically listed only one price for most accommodations:

double, or "d," for two people. Prices listed are the peak-season summertime rates, which are generally the highest of the year. These prices do not include state and local taxes, which run 4–9 percent. The prices are also, of course, not set in concrete and will certainly increase in time due to inflation.

If you're in doubt about where to stay, visit **Trip Advisor** (www.tripadvisor.com) or **Yahoo Travel** (www.travel.yahoo.com) to see what other travelers say, or see the annual *AAA TourBook* for Idaho, Montana, and Wyoming;

it's free to AAA members (www.aaa.com), who often get discounted rates.

HOTELS AND MOTELS

The motel and hotel scene in the Greater Yellowstone area is geared to travelers with cash to spend, although there are inexpensive hostels in Jackson and West Yellowstone. If you are visiting the region and planning to save money by camping the entire time, *do* make one or two modifications to your plan by booking at least one night in Yellowstone's Old Faithful Inn or Lake Yellowstone Hotel. Both of these are classics, and Old Faithful Inn occupies a league of its own. Rates are surprisingly reasonable if you're willing to walk down the hall for a shower. Call far ahead for reservations at these places.

BED-AND-BREAKFASTS

Wyoming Homestay and Outdoor Adventures (WHOA, www.wyomingbnbranchrec.com) produces a brochure listing most state B&Bs; get a copy from any visitor center. For Montana listings, contact the **Montana Bed and Breakfast Association** (www.mtbba.com). Find connections to Idaho B&Bs on the Web at www.visitid.org.

Favorites of 30- and 40-something professional couples, bed-and-breakfasts are a fine way to get acquainted with a new area. They're also a good choice if you're traveling alone because you'll have opportunities to meet fellow travelers in the library, over tea, and at breakfast. Note, however, that the single-person rate frequently differs little, if at all, from the price for couples.

One problem with B&Bs is that they sometimes get a bit too homey and lack the privacy afforded by motels. I've stayed at places where the owner sits by your table in the morning, feeling it is his duty to hold a conversation. This may be fine sometimes, especially if you want to learn more about the local area, but it's not so great if you're looking for a romantic place or you just want to read the newspaper in peace. In some places the intense personal attention and strict rules (no hard-soled shoes,

no noise after 10 P.M., and so on) get to be a bit much, making you feel less a guest than an intruder. Also, in some B&Bs hosts serve breakfast at precisely 8 A.M., and guests who sleep in miss out. Other B&Bs are more flexible, and some even offer separate cottages or suites for honeymooners seeking privacy.

Several regional B&Bs don't allow kids, and almost none allow pets or smoking inside. Most guest rooms have private baths, but if they don't, one is probably just a few steps away.

GUEST RANCHES

An old and respected Western tradition is the dude ranch, or guest ranch, which began as a sideline to the business of raising cattle. Friends from back East would remember old Jake out there in wild Wyoming, where the buffalo roam and the antelope play, and would decide it was time for a visit. So off they would head, living in the rancher's outbuildings and helping with the chores. The "dudes," as they became known, soon told their friends, and Jake found his ranch inundated. After a couple of years of this arrangement, the next step was obvious: Get those Eastern scoundrels to fork over some cash for the privilege of visiting. Pretty soon the dude-ranching business was born. At its peak in the 1920s, dude ranching spread throughout much of the West. It saved many cattle ranches from extinction by providing a second source of income and simultaneously brought these magnificent lands to the attention of people who had the money to prevent their development (most notably John D. Rockefeller Jr. in Grand Teton National Park).

At the older ranches, generations of families have returned year after year for a relaxing and rejuvenating vacation in the "Wild West." Many dude ranches now call themselves guest ranches, a term that reflects both the suspicious way people view the word "dude" and the changing nature of the business. Most city folks today lack the desire or skill to actually saddle up their own horses, much less push cattle between pastures. As a result, guest/dude ranches tend to emphasize grand scenery, horseback riding—the centerpiece of

© DON PITCHER

Spring Creek Ranch Resort, Jackson

nearly every ranch—campfires, hiking, fishing, hearty meals, chuck-wagon cookouts, sing-alongs, and evenings around the fireplace. A few ranches still offer the chance to join in on such activities as cattle drives, branding, pregnancy testing, shot-giving, calving, and roundups. For some folks it's a great chance to learn about the real West; others view it as paying good money (sometimes a lot of good money!) to work as a cowhand.

Practicalities

Dude-ranch stays generally cost about $3,500 for two people per week, with lower rates for kids and surcharges for those staying by themselves. The price includes all meals, lodging, and horseback rides, but you'll usually pay more for features such as airport shuttles, rafting trips, guided fishing, beer and wine, or backcountry pack trips, not to mention local taxes and tips. The fanciest resort, Lost Creek Ranch in Jackson Hole, will set you back more than $13,000 for two people per week! Many guest ranches offer discounted rates in early

June and late September and for repeat guests. A few also have special adults-only weeks. Most require that you stay a week, or at least three nights, although a few places offer overnight accommodations. To really get into the comfortably slow pace of ranch life, try to set aside at least a week.

Ask plenty of questions before you visit, such as what activities are available, what to bring in the way of clothing, what sort of meals to expect (vegetarians may have a hard time on some ranches), whether there are additional charges, whether it accepts credit cards (many don't), what the living accommodations are like, and how many other guests will likely be there at the same time—some house up to 125, others fewer than a dozen. Also note that some places provide six nights' lodging, while others include seven nights in their weekly stays. Upon request, all ranches will provide lists of references from previous clients. Note that it is considered proper to tip the ranch hands, kitchen help, and others who work hard to keep the ranch running. The standard gratuity is 15 percent of your bill, and many ranches add this automatically to the total. For many workers, this is a way to fund their college education (or a big vacation in New Zealand).

Finding a Ranch

A good source for detailed information about guest ranches in Wyoming (and elsewhere) is **Gene Kilgore's Ranch Vacations** by Gene Kilgore (www.ranchweb.com).

The **Wyoming Dude Rancher's Association** (307/455-2084, www.wyomingdra.com) has a useful website with links to more than 30 dude ranches in the state. Other useful sources are the national **Dude Ranchers' Association** (307/587-2339 or 866/399-2339, www.duderanch.org), along with www.guestranches.com and www.duderanches.com. Nearly all dude ranches have their own website, filled with beautiful photos of their ranch, glowing reports from past clients, and details on the packages available and their costs.

CAMPING

The Greater Yellowstone Ecosystem is dotted with several dozen Forest Service and Park Service campgrounds. Most of these have drinking water, garbage pickup, and outhouses, but they generally do not have showers. The fee is typically $10–15 per night, with a 14-day limit on camping at any one location. It's generally legal to camp for free on undeveloped Forest Service land throughout the region, but check with local ranger district offices for any restrictions. Dispersed camping is not allowed in the Snake River Canyon south of Jackson or the North Fork of the Shoshone River west of Cody.

Campsite reservations are available for some Yellowstone National Park sites, but all of those within Grand Teton National Park are on a first-come basis. In addition, several Forest Service campgrounds in the area are on a reservation system; for an extra service charge of $9 you can reserve a site up to six months in advance. Get details from **Recreation.gov** (518/885-3639 or 877/444-6777, www.recreation.gov).

RV PARKS

Every Yellowstone-area town of any size contains at least one private RV park and so-called campground. Most of these are little more than vacant lots with sewer and electrical hookups, showers, and toilet facilities, but a few are quite nice. These private campgrounds generally charge $5 for showers if you're not camping there. A better deal in many towns is to use the shower at the local public swimming pool, where you get a free swim thrown in for the entrance charge.

Tips for Travelers

When planning a trip to the Yellowstone area, always err on the side of too much time if at all possible. Although the distances are not great, this isn't freeway driving, and you'll want sufficient time to savor the sights and soak up the beauty of this magical place. If you have only a few days, pick one place and explore it well rather than trying to see all the sights. A week is sufficient time to see many regional highlights, but set aside more if you plan to visit Cody and Jackson or take a backcountry trek. Those with the time (and money) should consider booking a week at a Jackson Hole or Wapiti Valley guest ranch.

Begin planning your travels by contacting Yellowstone National Park (307/344-7381, www.nps.gov/yell) and Grand Teton National Park (307/739-3600, www.nps.gov/grte) for park newspapers and the helpful *Yellowstone National Park Trip Planner*. Also request a copy of the *Jackson Hole Explorer* from the Jackson Hole Chamber of Commerce (307/733-3316, www.jacksonholechamber.com).

picnic sign, Yellowstone National Park

WHAT TO TAKE

When you visit dictates what you need to bring. Summers in the mountains are mild (often in the 70s and 80s °F), and often gloriously sunny (with afternoon thunderstorms). Shorts and Tevas are ubiquitous, but bring pants and long-sleeved shirts for cooler evenings. Carry a light Gore-Tex jacket for rainy days or on-the-water trips. For other seasons, carry several layers of non-cotton clothing to adjust to varying temperatures. If you plan to spend time in Yellowstone in midwinter, come prepared; the thermometer at Old Faithful once hit -66°F!

As a general rule, keep it casual. However, a few of the fanciest restaurants in Jackson Hole and Grand Teton require a sports jacket or tie, and you may feel like Michael Moore at a Republican fund-raiser if you show up wearing shorts and a tie-dyed T-shirt when others are dressed for a night out. For summer travel, pack comfortable walking shoes, sunglasses, a hat, sunscreen, insect repellent, and prescription medications. Be sure to bring a bathing suit even if you don't plan to swim in local lakes or pools—many hotels and B&Bs have hot tubs.

TRAVELING BY RV

Yellowstone and Grand Teton National Parks are very popular destinations for RVers. Surrounding towns all have private RV parks with all the amenities; many have Wi-Fi and cable TV hookups. Motor-home rentals are available in Billings, Salt Lake City, and Idaho Falls.

Many Yellowstone roads are narrow and winding, making them a challenge for large RVs and a potential hazard for cyclists, who risk getting hit by side mirrors. Owners of large RVs should consider leaving their rigs at the campground and taking one of the park bus tours. A few roads are closed to RVs, including Terrace Drive and the Old Gardiner Road near Mammoth. In Grand Teton National Park, RVs and trailers are not allowed on Signal Mountain Road or the Moose-Wilson Road.

Motor homes are prohibited from Jenny Lake Campground in Grand Teton, and some other park campgrounds have a 30-foot size limit. Conversely, only hard-sided campers and RVs are allowed at Yellowstone's Fishing Bridge RV Park. Check with each park for regulations on generator use in the campgrounds.

TRAVELING WITH CHILDREN

Yellowstone is a major family destination in summer, and visiting the park has become something of a rite of passage for middle-class Americans (along with thousands of European and Japanese families). Families will especially appreciate the woodsy campgrounds, inexpensive cabins, stagecoach and horseback rides, and the reasonable cafeteria meals. Most lodges and hotels have cribs for those traveling with infants. Of special interest to kids ages 5–12 is the **Junior Ranger Program,** in which children attend a nature program, hike a trail, and complete other activities. They're rewarded with an official Junior Ranger patch and are sworn in. It's always a big hit, but your kids may later try to arrest you if you get too close to an elk.

The **Teton County Parks & Recreation Department** (307/739-9025, www.tetonwyo. org/parks) has a summertime day camp for children entering first through eighth grades; it costs $35 per day. Also check out the excellent natural history programs through **Teton Science Schools** (307/733-4765, www.tetonscience.org), and the family-friendly Lodging and Learning packages offered by **Yellowstone Association Institute** (307/344-2294, www. yellowstoneassociation.org).

The Yellowstone Association's four-day **Yellowstone for Families** program includes a mix of activities for both kids and parents. Yellowstone National Park's **Windows into Wonderland** (www.windowsintowonderland. org) is a great online source for kid-friendly park information, with details on wildlife, art, fires, history, geology, microorganisms, and more.

SENIOR TRAVELERS

An **Interagency Senior Pass** for all national parks is available to anyone over 62 for a one-time fee of $10. The card also provides for a 50 percent reduction in most camping fees. Many lodging places and attractions offer senior discounts. A variety of **Road Scholar** (formerly Elderhostel, www.roadscholar.com) educational adventure programs are also offered throughout the year in the Yellowstone region for travelers over age 55, including many programs at Teton Science Center in Jackson.

ACCESS FOR TRAVELERS WITH DISABILITIES

The Park Service's free **Interagency Access Pass** allows the blind and other people with permanent disabilities entrance to all national parks, historic sites, and recreation areas. The passport also provides a 50 percent discount for camping in the parks. Pick them up from any park visitor center or entrance station.

People with disabilities who are visiting Yellowstone will find that the park is making a concerted effort to provide accessible facilities, although it has a long way to go. Most of the major tourist areas, including Old Faithful, have at least some paths that are paved, and accessible accommodations can be found at Canyon, Grant Village, Old Faithful, and Lake. Accessible campsites are also available throughout the park. For details, see the *Visitor's Guide to Accessible Features in Yellowstone National Park* (307/344-2018, www.nps.gov/yell/planyourvisit/accessibility.htm).

Grand Teton National Park has some accessible campsites, and all park lodging places provide accessible units. Some hiking trails are paved. Get the park's "Accessibility" handout for complete details, or find it on the Web at www.nps.gov/grte.

Many hotels and B&Bs in Jackson and other gateway towns have wheelchair-accessible rooms. Contact **Wheelchair Getaways of Montana** (406/227-6524 or 800/630-8267, www.wheelchairgetaways.com) for accessible van rentals in the Yellowstone area.

TRAVELING WITH PETS

Pets must be leashed and are not allowed on trails or hydrothermal basins in Yellowstone and Grand Teton National Parks. They can't be more than 50 feet from roadways in Grand Teton or 100 feet from Yellowstone roads or parking areas. In Grand Teton, you cannot take pets on Snake River boats, inside visitor centers, or on ranger-led activities. Don't think of leaving a dog in your car or RV within Yellowstone; it's illegal. In other words, leave your dog at home or at one of the Jackson kennels. Some regional motels and hotels (but very few B&Bs) allow pets; call ahead for specifics.

Two kennels in Jackson will keep an eye on Fido for you: **Happy Tails Pet Resort/Spring Creek Animal Hospital** (307/733-1606, www.springcreekanimalhospital.com) and **Rally's Pet Garage** (520 S. Hwy. 89, 307/733-7704, www.rallyspetgarage.com).

WEDDING PLANNING

If you're looking for an outdoor wedding, it's hard to imagine a grander setting than Yellowstone and Grand Teton National Parks. Popular **Yellowstone** sites are Old Faithful, Lake Butte Overlook, and Grand Canyon of the Yellowstone River.

Grand Teton has a multitude of stunning wedding locations, including Schwabacher's Landing, Blacktail Ponds Overlook, Signal Mountain Summit, and Mormon Row. For indoor weddings with an amazing backdrop, check out **Chapel of the Transfiguration** (307/733-2603, www.stjohnsjackson.org), **Chapel of the Sacred Heart** (307/733-2516, www.olmcatholic.org), and **Jackson Lake Lodge** (307/543-3100 or 800/628-9988, www.gtlc.com). Rental fees are substantial, about $1,500 for the chapels and at least twice that at the lodge.

Both Yellowstone and Grand Teton National Parks require special permits ($50) for weddings, and you'll need to apply at least two weeks prior to the big day. Details are available online (www.nps.gov/yell/planyourvisit/weddinginfo.htm and www.nps.gov/grte/planyourvisit/weddings.htm).

The town of **Jackson** and nearby Teton Village deliver an array of wedding options, and it's just a short drive to Grand Teton National Park. There's an abundance of fine lodging places and upscale caterers, plus easy access from anywhere in the nation. Choose from the relaxed back-to-nature setting along the Snake River to the million-dollar extravaganza at Four Seasons Resort or Amangani. A local company produces a slick 100-page free magazine, *A Grand Wedding* (www.jacksonholewedding.com), filled with advice and ads for Jackson Hole caterers, locations, musicians, DJs, photographers, wedding consultants, spas, tent and carriage rentals, wedding cakes, limos, and yes, even portable toilets.

OPPORTUNITIES FOR EMPLOYMENT
Yellowstone National Park

During summer, both the National Park Service and private concessioners provide several thousand jobs in Yellowstone. These positions rarely last more than six months. You can find much more about Yellowstone jobs, both public and private, online (www.nps.gov/yell/parkmgmt/jobs.htm).

Yellowstone National Park hires more than 300 seasonal employees each year, but many more people apply, so the competition is stiff for new hires. Most seasonals start out as a park ranger (leading naturalist walks, working in entrance stations, etc.) or laborer (building trails, cleaning campgrounds and restrooms, etc.), but more specialized positions are available in the fields of natural resources and law enforcement. You must be a U.S. citizen to be employed by the Park Service.

Although there is a national register for seasonal rangers, specific vacancy announcements come out when jobs are available, and you will need to apply within the specified time frame and meet all qualifications. For details on seasonal Park Service jobs, call Yellowstone's human resources office (307/344-2052, www.usajobs.gov) for a listing of park jobs. The Department of the Interior's website (www.doi.gov/hrm/jobs.html) has additional employment information.

Unpaid volunteers do many jobs in Yellowstone and Grand Teton, and it isn't necessary to be a U.S. citizen to do volunteer work. The Park Service operates a **Volunteers in Parks (VIP)** program at Yellowstone that includes more than 300 people each year. To join the ranks of the employed but unpaid, call the park's VIP coordinator (307/344-2047, www.nps.gov/yell/supportyourpark/volunteer.htm). For Grand Teton, get details at 307/739-3397, www.nps.gov/grte/supportyourpark/volunteer.htm.

A national nonprofit organization, the **Student Conservation Association** or SCA (603/543-1700, www.thesca.org), provides workers for Yellowstone who do a wide variety of activities, from trail maintenance to answering visitors' questions. Volunteers get most expenses paid.

The park has two primary concessioners, Xanterra Parks and Resorts and Delaware North Parks and Resorts, along with the smaller Yellowstone Park Service Stations. Most employees of these companies are college students (who live in dorm-style accommodations), retired folks (who live in their RVs), or young people from other countries, including many from Asia and Latin America. Don't expect high pay; entry-level positions start at about $7.50 per hour, with meals and lodging deducted from this paltry sum. A good overall website for concessioner jobs inside Yellowstone is www.coolworks.com/yell.htm.

Xanterra Parks and Resorts (307/344-5324, www.yellowstonejobs.com) is in charge of lodging, restaurants, bus tours, boat rentals, horse rides, several campgrounds, and similar services within the park. It is also the largest park- and resort-management company in the nation, with operations in such diverse spots as Everglades National Park and Grand Canyon National Park. The company hires some 2,600 people each summer in Yellowstone. It's best to apply early for summer jobs. The more competitive winter positions often go to those with previous work experience in the park.

The 12 Yellowstone General Stores are operated by **Delaware North Parks and Resorts** (www.delawarenorth.com), with a regional office in Bozeman, Montana. The company employs about 800 folks seasonally in Yellowstone, with a handful more as year-round managers. Many of the seasonals are retirees who bring their RVs along for private accommodations. If you can start in April or May, you're considerably more likely to be hired. Employment details and applications are available from Yellowstone General Stores (877/600-4308, www.visityellowstonepark.com).

The third concessioner is **Yellowstone Park Service Stations** (406/848-7333, www.ypss.com), the folks who pump Conoco gas and wash your windshield at seven stations in the park. A few higher-level positions are available for auto repair or towing operations.

Jackson Hole

Jackson Hole is an increasingly popular place to live and work—a fact that angers many longtime residents who came here to escape crowds elsewhere. The surrounding country is grand, with many things to do and places to explore; the weather is delightful; and you're likely to meet others with similar interests, not to mention all the good-looking young people. Wyoming's lack of an income tax certainly doesn't hurt. Jobs such as waiting tables, driving tour buses, cleaning hotels and condos, and operating ski lifts are plentiful (but pay poorly). The unemployment rate generally hovers far below the national average, and housing can be scarce. Get to Jackson in mid-May and you'll find the papers filled with employment ads.

The best jobs are those that either offer such perks as housing or free ski passes or give you lots of free time to explore the area. To get an idea of available jobs, check local classified ads (www.jacksonholenewsandguide.com) and Craigslist (www.wyoming.craigslist.org), or stop by the **Wyoming Workforce Center** (155 W. Gill, 307/733-4091, www.wyomingworkforce.org).

Because of Jackson Hole's popularity, finding a place to live can be difficult, especially during the peak summer and winter tourist seasons. As the moneyed class has moved in, those who work in service jobs find it tougher and tougher to obtain affordable housing. Many Jackson workers now suffer long commutes from Victor or Driggs in Idaho, or from the Wyoming towns of Alpine or Afton. Land prices (and consequently housing costs) have risen for the past decade or so, and because of this, the median home price is more than twice what the median household income will buy! Two-bedroom furnished apartments often rent for $1,200 or more per month. The median single-family home in Jackson costs $1 million, and the median home in the area sells for a cool $1.75 million. More prestigious local homes sell for $3 million, and the very finest log mansions ("log cabins on steroids") can fetch more than $6 million.

The inflation of real estate has attracted the major players: both Christie's and Sotheby's (the auction folks) have offices in Jackson. As a side note, Teton County is the wealthiest county in America, with the nation's highest average taxable income. (These figures are, of course, skewed by a relatively small number of ultra-rich individuals; you'll find many folks working at $10-an-hour jobs.)

Because of the extreme difficulty in finding rental housing, many Jackson-area businesses include this perk as a way to lure workers. In 2008, the county imposed a moratorium on new commercial developments that don't provide worker housing. Those workers who are not so lucky are often forced to jam into too-small apartments or to join the commuters from Driggs, Alpine, and Afton. The best times to look for a place to live are in April and October. Check the local newspapers (or their online versions if you haven't yet arrived in the area), Craigslist (www.wyoming.craigslist.org), and local coin-laundry and grocery-store bulletin boards for apartments or cabins. The *Trash and Treasure* morning program on radio station KMTN (96.9 FM, www.kmtnthemountain. com) is another place to try.

Health and Safety

Medical clinics can be found in most towns in the Yellowstone region, with good hospitals in Jackson and Cody, plus a smaller hospital in Driggs, Idaho. A summer-only hospital is near Lake Yellowstone Hotel within Yellowstone, with clinics at Old Faithful and Mammoth. Inside Grand Teton National Park there's a summertime clinic near Jackson Lake Lodge. Both West Yellowstone and Dubois have medical clinics.

A common annoyance for travelers is insects, especially mosquitoes and blackflies. These pests are most prevalent in early summer in the mountains; by late August mosquito populations thin considerably. Use insect repellents containing DEET to help keep them away or wear a head net.

Beaver Fever

Although the lakes and streams of the Greater Yellowstone Ecosystem may appear clean, you could be risking a debilitating sickness by drinking the water without treating it first. The protozoan *Giardia lamblia* is found throughout the state, spread by both humans and animals (including beaver). The disease is curable with drugs, but it's always best to carry safe drinking water on any trip or to boil any water taken from creeks or lakes. Bringing water to a full boil for one minute is sufficient to kill *Giardia* and other harmful organisms. Another option—the one I much prefer—is to use one of the water filters sold in camping-goods stores. Make sure you buy one that filters out organisms such as *Campylobactor jejuni,* bacteria that are just 0.2 microns in size. Chlorine and iodine are not always reliable, taste foul, and can be unhealthy. The MSR Miox (www.cascadedesigns.com/msr, $140) purifier uses an oxidant—not filtration—to clean water with little aftertaste.

Hypothermia

Anyone who has spent much time in the out-doors will discover the dangers of exposure to cold, wet, and windy conditions. Even at temperatures well above freezing, hypo-thermia—the reduction of the body's inner core temperature—can prove fatal.

In the early stages, hypothermia causes uncontrollable shivering, followed by a loss of coordination, slurred speech, and then a rapid descent into unconsciousness and death. Always travel prepared for sudden changes in the weather. Wear clothing that insulates well and that holds its heat when wet. Wool and polypro are far better than cotton, and clothes should be worn in layers to provide better trap-ping of heat and a chance to adjust to chang-ing conditions more easily. Always carry a wool hat, because your head loses more heat than any other part of the body. Bring a waterproof shell to cut the wind. Put on rain gear *before* it starts raining; head back or set up camp when the weather looks threatening, and eat candy bars, keep active, or snuggle with a friend in a down bag to generate warmth.

If someone in your party begins to show signs of hypothermia, don't take any chances, even if the person denies needing help. Get the victim out of the wind, strip off his or her clothes, and put the person in a dry sleeping bag on an insulating pad. Skin-to-skin con-tact is the best way to warm a hypothermic person, and that means you'll also need to strip and climb into the sleeping bag. If you weren't friends before, this should heat up the relationship! Do not give the victim alcohol or hot drinks, and do not try to warm the person too quickly, because it could lead to heart fail-ure. Once the victim has recovered, get medi-cal help as soon as possible. Actually, you're far better off keeping close tabs on everyone in the group and seeking shelter *before* exhaustion and hypothermia set in.

West Nile Encephalitis

Most people who are infected with West Nile encephalitis show mild (or no) symptoms, but the disease can occasionally be fatal. The virus is transmitted through mosquito bites, and it can infect not just humans, but also horses, many species of birds, and other animals—even mountain lions. At least 16 Wyoming residents have died from West Nile infections in the last decade, though the inci-dences have dropped markedly in recent years. Reduce your chance of infection by applying insect repellents containing DEET. (A higher concentration lasts longer, but there's no ben-efit in using DEET in concentrations over 50 percent.) You can also spray your clothing with the repellent, wear long-sleeved shirts and long pants, and stay indoors at dusk and dawn, when the mosquitoes are their most ac-tive. The Wyoming Department of Health (877/996-2483, www.badskeeter.org) has de-tails on the virus.

Hantavirus

This potentially fatal respiratory disease is spread by rodents, particularly deer mice. Contact with them or their droppings can lead to such symptoms as fever, muscle aches, coughing, and difficulty breathing resulting from fluid buildup in the lungs within 1–5 weeks. Once the symptoms appear, the dis-ease progresses quickly, leading to hospitaliza-tion within 24 hours. Almost half of those who come down with hantavirus die, and in the last decade, it has killed at least five Wyoming res-idents. Avoid contact with rodents and their feces or urine to minimize your chances of in-fection. Campers should never sleep on bare ground and should avoid cabins if they find signs of rodents. Fortunately, the disease is not contagious from person to person.

Ticks

Ticks can be a bother in brushy and grassy areas in the spring and early summer. They drop onto unsuspecting humans and other animals to suck blood and can spread several potentially devastating diseases, including Rocky Mountain spotted fever, Ehrlichiosis, and Lyme disease. A few cases of these diseases have been reported in the Greater Yellowstone Ecosystem, but they are not common.

Avoid ticks by tucking pant legs into boots and shirts into pants, using insect repellents containing DEET, and carefully inspecting your clothes while outside. Light-colored clothing and socks are less attractive to ticks and make it easier for you to see them, while broad hats keep them out of your hair. Check your body while hiking and immediately after the trip. If possible, remove ticks before they become embedded in your skin. If one does become attached, use tweezers to remove the tick, making sure to get the head. Apply a triple-antibiotic ointment such as Neosporin to the area, and monitor the bite area for two weeks.

Lyme disease typically shows up as a large red spot with a lighter bull's-eye center and often causes muscle aches, fatigue, headache, and fever. Get medical help immediately if you show these symptoms after a tick bite. Fortunately, the disease can usually be treated with antibiotics. If untreated, it can cause a facial nerve palsy, memory loss, arthritis, heart damage, and other problems. A relatively effective vaccine has been developed for Lyme disease, but it requires a one-year regimen of doses and is expensive; check with your doctor for specifics. In northwest Wyoming, where the disease is relatively uncommon, the vaccine is probably not warranted, and it may give a false sense of security because ticks can still spread other—and more dangerous—diseases. No vaccinations are available against either Rocky Mountain spotted fever or Erlichia, both of which sometimes kill people. The best action is to prevent tick bites in the first place. For more on tick-borne diseases, see the Harvard Medical School's website at www.intelihealth.com.

SAFETY IN BEAR COUNTRY

Bears seem to bring out conflicting emotions in people. The first is an almost gut reaction of fear and trepidation: What if the bear attacks me? But then comes that other urge: What will my friends say when they see these *incredible* bear photos? Both of these reactions can lead to problems in bear country. "Bearanoia" is a justifiable fear but can easily be taken to such an extreme that one avoids going outdoors at all for fear of running into a bear. The "I want to get close-up shots of that bear and her cubs" attitude can lead to a bear attack. The middle ground incorporates a knowledge of and respect for bears with a sense of caution that keeps you alert for danger without letting fear rule your wilderness travels. Nothing is ever completely safe in this world, but with care you can avoid most of the common pitfalls that lead to bear encounters.

Avoiding Bear Hugs

Surprise bear encounters are rare but frightening experiences. There were just 32 bear-caused injuries in Yellowstone National Park between 1980 and 2002—one injury for every 1.9 million visitors. Avoid unexpected encounters with bears by letting them know you're there. Most bears hear or smell you long before you realize their presence, and they hightail it away. Surprising a bear, especially a sow with cubs, is the last thing you want to do in the backcountry. Before heading out, check at a local ranger station to see whether there have been recent bear encounters. If you discover an animal carcass, be extremely alert, because a bear may be nearby and may attack anything that appears to threaten its food. Get away from such areas. Do not hike at night or dusk, when bears can be especially active. Safety is also in numbers: The more of you hiking together, the more likely a bear is to sense you and stay away.

Make noise in areas of dense cover or when coming around blind spots on trails. If you're unable to see everything around you for at least 50 yards, warn any hidden animals by talking, singing, clapping your hands, tapping a cup, or rattling a can of pebbles. Some people tie bells to their packs for this purpose, but others regard this as an annoyance to fellow hikers. In general, bells are probably of little value because the sound does not carry far, and they might actually attract bears. If bears can't hear you coming, don't be shy—make a lot of noise! It might seem a bit foolish, but loud voices may prevent an encounter of the furry kind. Unfortunately, it will probably scare off other animals, so you're not likely to see many critters, and other hikers may not appreciate the noise. Personally, I reserve yelling "Hey Bear!" for situations where I'm walking in brushy bear country with low visibility and have to contend with other noises such as a nearby creek. I wouldn't recommend doing so while walking the paved path around Old Faithful Geyser; you might get carried off in a straitjacket.

Hunters and photographers are the main recipients of bear-hugs. Never under any circumstances approach a bear, even if it appears to be asleep. Move away if you see bear cubs, especially if one comes toward you, because mom is almost always close by. Dogs create dangerous situations by barking and exciting bears—leave yours at home (dogs are not allowed in the backcountry in national parks). Never leave food around for bears. Not only is this illegal, but it also trains the bears to associate people with free food. Fed bears become garbage bears, and that almost inevitably means that the bear gets killed. Remember, bears are dangerous wild animals. This is *their* country, not a zoo. By going in you accept the risk—and thrill—of meeting a bear.

At the Campsite

Before camping, take a look around the area to see if there are recent bear tracks or scat and to make sure you're not on a game trail. Bears are attracted to odors of all sorts, including food, horse feed, soap, toothpaste, perfume, and deodorants. Your cooking, eating, and food storage area should be at least 50 yards away from your tent. Keep your campsite clean and avoid such smelly items as tuna, ham, sausage, and bacon; freeze-dried food is light and relatively odorless (although also relatively tasteless). Store food away from your sleeping area in airtight containers or several layers of plastic bags, and be sure to hang all food and other items that bears may smell at least 12 feet off the ground and four feet from tree trunks. Bring 50 feet of rope for this purpose. Tie two cups

Sleeping Area

100 yards

Cooking and Eating Area

Hang at least 10' from the ground and 4' from the top and side supports

© BOB RACE

or pots to it so you will hear if it's moved. Some Forest Service and Park Service wilderness areas provide food storage poles at campsites. In Grand Teton National Park backcountry, campers must carry bear-proof containers. In the Teton and Bridger wilderness areas, you can also rent bear-resistant backpacker food tubes or horse panniers from Forest Service offices. Camping stores in Jackson, Cody, and elsewhere sell similar containers.

Researchers have reported no evidence that either sexual activity or menstrual odors precipitate bear attacks. It is, however, wise for menstruating women to use tampons instead of pads and to store soiled tampons in double ziplock bags above the reach of bears.

Encounters of the Furry Kind

If you do happen to suddenly encounter a bear and it sees you, try to stay calm and not make any sudden moves. Do not run, because you could not possibly outrun a bear; they can exceed 40 miles per hour for short distances. Bear researchers now suggest that quickly climbing a tree is also not a wise way to escape bears and may actually incite an attack. Instead, make yourself visible by moving into the open so the bear will (you hope) identify you as a human and not something to eat. Never stare directly at a bear. Sometimes dropping an item such as a hat or jacket will distract the bear, and talking calmly (easier said than done) also seems to have some value in convincing bears that you're a human. If the bear sniffs the air or stands on its hind legs, it is probably trying to identify you. When it does, it will usually run away. If a bear woofs and postures, don't imitate— this is a challenge. Keep retreating. Most bear charges are also bluffs; the bear will often stop short and amble off.

If a **grizzly bear** actually attacks, hold your ground and freeze. It may well be a bluff charge, with the bear halting at the last second. If the bear does not stop its attack, curl up facedown on the ground in a fetal position with your hands wrapped behind your neck and your elbows tucked over your face.

Your backpack may help protect you somewhat. Remain still even if you are attacked, because sudden movements may incite further attacks. It takes an enormous amount of courage to do this, but often a bear will only sniff or nip you and leave. The injury you might sustain would be far less than if you tried to resist. After the attack, prevent further attacks by staying down on the ground until the grizzly has left the area.

Bear authorities now recommend against dropping to the ground if you are attacked by a **black bear,** because they tend to be more aggressive in such situations and are more likely to prey on humans. If a black bear attacks, fight back with whatever weapons are at hand; large rocks and branches can be surprisingly effective deterrents, as can yelling and shouting. (This, of course, assumes you can tell black bears from brown bears. If you can't, have someone who knows—such as a park ranger— explain the differences before you head into the backcountry.)

In the rare event of a **nighttime bear attack** in your tent, defend yourself *very* aggressively. Never play dead under such circumstances, because the bear probably views you as prey and may give up if you make it a fight. Before going to bed, try to plan escape routes should you be attacked in the night, and be sure to have a flashlight and pepper spray handy. Keeping your sleeping bag partly unzipped also allows the chance to escape should a bear attempt to drag you away. If someone is attacked in a tent near you, yelling and throwing rocks or sticks may drive the bear away.

Protecting Yourself

Cayenne pepper sprays (sold in camping goods stores) have sometimes proven useful in fending off bear attacks. Note, however, that these "bear mace" sprays are effective only at close range (10–30 feet). This is particularly true in open country, where winds quickly disperse the mist or may blow it back in your own face. Another problem with bear mace is that you cannot carry it aboard commercial jets because

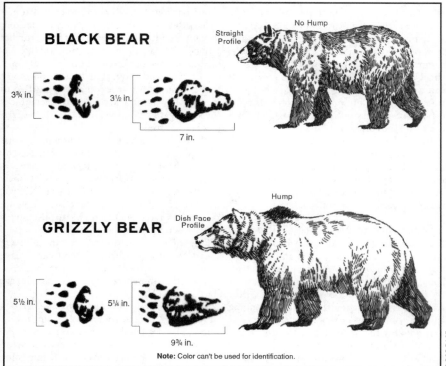

BLACK BEAR

Straight Profile

No Hump

3¾ in.   3½ in.

7 in.

GRIZZLY BEAR

Dish Face Profile

Hump

5½ in.   5¼ in.

9¾ in.

Note: Color can't be used for identification.

© BOB RACE

of the obvious dangers if a canister explodes. If you do carry a pepper spray, make sure it is readily available by carrying it in a holster on your belt or across your chest. Also be sure to test-fire it to see how the spray carries. Although they *are* better than nothing, pepper sprays are not a cure-all or a replacement for caution in bear country. It's far better to avoid bear confrontations in the first place.

The latest development for campers in bear country is the use of portable **electric fences** made by Electro Bear Guard (907/232-9758, www.electrobearguard.com) to surround your campsite; a backpacker unit runs on two AA batteries, weighs just two pounds, and costs $340.

A good source for up-to-date bear safety information is the Yellowstone National Park website, www.nps.gov/yell. Two recommended safety books are *Bear Attacks: Their Causes and Avoidance* by Stephen Herrero (www.globepequot.com) and *Bear Aware: Hiking and Camping in Bear Country* by Bill Schneider (www.falcon.com).

BACKCOUNTRY SAFETY TIPS

The most important part of enjoying—and surviving—the backcountry is to be prepared. Know where you're going; get maps, camping information, weather forecasts, and trail conditions from a ranger before setting out. Although I have often hiked alone, single hikers are at a greater risk of getting into trouble than those trekking with companions. Two are better than one, and three are better than two; if one gets hurt, one person can stay with the injured party and one can go for help. Bring more than enough food so hunger won't cause you to continue when weather conditions say stop. Tell a responsible person where you're going and when you'll be back.

Always carry the **10 essentials:** map, compass, water bottle, first-aid kit, flashlight, matches (or lighter) and fire starter, knife, extra clothing (a full set, in case you fall in a stream) including rain gear, extra food, and sunglasses—especially if you're hiking on

snow. To this list, you might want to add a cell phone. Most backcountry areas have no service, but in an emergency you might be able to find a high point where the phone can hit an antenna. GPS units have become much cheaper and easier to use in recent years, making them an excellent option.

Check your ego at the trailhead; stop for the night when the weather gets bad, even if it's 2 P.M., or head back. And don't press on when you're exhausted; tired hikers are sloppy hikers, and even a small injury can be disastrous in the woods.

Information and Services

TOURIST INFORMATION

Chamber of commerce information centers are described for each town in this book. Both parks have visitor centers, and the large Jackson Hole and Greater Yellowstone Visitor Center is in Jackson. You'll find chamber of commerce offices in even the tiniest towns in the Yellowstone area.

Wyoming

For a helpful overall guide to Wyoming, along with a listing of events, chamber of commerce offices, and lodging and camping places, request a copy of the free *Wyoming Travelers Journal* from the Wyoming Travel and Tourism Division (307/777-7777 or 800/225-5996, www.wyomingtourism.org). The agency also has free state maps, or pick them up at any regional visitor center.

For additional information, head to the Wyoming state homepage (www.wyoming. gov). See Don Pitcher's *Moon Wyoming* (www. donpitcher.com) for the full story on the Cowboy State.

Montana

For Montana travel information, check out the fat *Montana Vacation Planner* (406/841-2870 or 800/847-4868, www.visitmt.com). The maps in this publication are particularly

revealing, showing Yellowstone as a brown appendage to Montana, even though virtually all the park lies within Wyoming! Request a free *Yellowstone Country Travel Planner* (406/556-8680 or 800/736-5276, www.yellowstonecountry.net). The state of Montana's homepage is www.mt.gov. The most complete travel guide is *Moon Montana & Wyoming* (www.moon.com) by Carter Walker.

Idaho

Contact the Idaho Division of Tourism Development (208/334-2470 or 800/847-4743, www.visitid.org) for the official *Idaho Travel Guide* and a state map. For Eastern Idaho info, request a free *Yellowstone Teton Territory* booklet (800/634-3246, www.yellowstoneteton. com). The state of Idaho's homepage is www. idaho.gov. Find comprehensive Idaho coverage in *Moon Idaho* (www.moon.com) by James Patrick Kelly.

Land Management Agencies

The following phone numbers and websites provide contact information for major public land-management agencies in the Greater Yellowstone Ecosystem:

- **Grand Teton National Park,** Moose, 307/739-3300, www.nps.gov/grte

- **Yellowstone National Park,** Mammoth, 307/344-7381, www.nps.gov/yell
- **National Elk Refuge,** Jackson, 307/733-9212, www.fws.gov/nationalelkrefuge
- **Bridger-Teton National Forest,** Jackson, 307/739-5500, www.fs.fed.us/r4/btnf
- **Shoshone National Forest,** Cody, 307/527-6241, www.fs.fed.us/r2/shoshone
- **Caribou-Targhee National Forest,** Idaho Falls, Idaho, 208/524-7500, www.fs.fed.us/r4/caribou-targhee
- **Gallatin National Forest,** West Yellowstone, Montana, 406/823-6961, or Gardiner, Montana, 406/848-7375, www.fs.fed.us/r1/gallatin
- **Beaverhead-Deerlodge National Forest,** Dillon, Montana, 406/683-3900, www.fs.usda.gov/bdnf
- **Custer National Forest,** Red Lodge, Montana, 406/446-2103, www.fs.fed.us/r1/custer

COMMUNICATIONS AND MEDIA
Newspapers and Radio
Jackson's outstanding tabloid newspaper—the *Jackson Hole News and Guide* (307/733-2047, www.jhnewsandguide.com)—publishes a weekly edition with local news, along with freebie versions Monday–Saturday.

Wyoming's only statewide paper, the *Casper Star-Tribune* (www.casperstartribune.net), is ubiquitous throughout the area. Another paper you'll see in local racks (particularly within Yellowstone) is the *Billings Gazette* (www.billingsgazette.com).

Jackson, Cody, and other towns in the region have local radio stations of varying quality, offering the standard mix of top-40, rock, and country. For a bit more class, turn your dial to one of the **National Public Radio** stations that provide in-depth news, insightful call-in shows, and comedic relief. In Jackson, the local Wyoming Public Radio station is KUWJ 90.3 FM (www.wyomingpublicradio.net). In the Yellowstone area and Cody, you're also likely to hear "Yellowstone Radio" out of Bozeman, KBMC 102.1 FM. In Idaho's Teton Valley, listen to NPR on KRIC-FM 100.5 from Rexburg, Idaho.

On the Web
Internet addresses are listed in the text for local chamber of commerce offices and a multitude of businesses. Excellent places to begin your virtual voyage are the state tourism sites and land-management agencies. See specific town descriptions for listings of chamber of commerce websites.

Two particularly useful websites with abundant links to local businesses are the Jackson Hole Chamber of Commerce's site, www.jacksonholechamber.com, and the Cody-based Park County Travel Council, www.yellowstonecountry.org. Other websites worth browsing include www.jacksonholetraveler.com, www.jacksonholenet.com, www.westyellowstonechamber.com, www.westyellowstonetraveler.com, and www.westyellowstonenet.com.

Looking for live streaming **Web cameras** to see the Yellowstone–Grand Teton region in real time? The Wyoming Department of Transportation (www.wyoroad.info) has webcams for Teton Pass, Alpine, and Pinedale, while www.jacksonholenet.com/webcams shows more than 30 webcams scattered around Jackson Hole and Yellowstone (including Old Faithful).

All local libraries have computers with free Internet access, although you may need to sign up for a terminal. Find a listing of Wyoming libraries and links to their homepages at www.publiclibraries.com/wyoming.htm. In addition, the towns of Jackson, Cody, Gardiner, Cooke City, Dubois, and West Yellowstone all have Internet cafés or businesses with computers for rent by the hour. Most motels and many coffee shops also now provide **free Wi-Fi** access for those with laptops, smart phones, and iPads.

MONEY
Travelers checks (in U.S. dollars) are accepted without charge at most stores and businesses throughout the Yellowstone region. It's not

a good idea to travel with travelers checks in non-U.S. currency; they are accepted only at certain banks in Wyoming and are a time-consuming hassle. If you do arrive with pounds, yen, or euros, several banks in Jackson, along with the park hotels inside Yellowstone, will exchange foreign currency for greenbacks.

Tipping is expected for many services, with 15 percent or more for waitstaff at restaurants. In addition, tips are appreciated for other personal services, including those provided by river-rafting guides, taxi drivers, dude-ranch employees, and hotel maids. The amount varies widely, but it is common for a wildlife tour guide to receive at least a $20 tip at the end of a day's assistance.

RESOURCES

Suggested Reading

Note: A few of the following books are now out of print. You can find many of them in regional libraries, or check the Web for special orders or rare book auctions. Websites such as www.amazon.com, www.barnesandnoble.com, and others will search used bookstores for out-of-print titles.

YELLOWSTONE NATIONAL PARK

Several natural history and geology books encompass both Yellowstone and Grand Teton National Parks. See the suggested reading for Jackson Hole and Grand Teton National Park for additional titles with overlapping coverage.

The most authoritative, detailed, and up-to-date guide to Yellowstone is the fat, spiral-bound **Yellowstone Resources & Issues.** Published by the U.S. Park Service annually and sold in park visitor centers, it serves as a training manual for new park rangers and is a wonderful compendium for everything Yellowstone. The publication is also available online at www.nps.gov/yell. If you really want to know Yellowstone, get this book!

Geology

Bryan, Scott T. *The Geysers of Yellowstone.* Boulder: University Press of Colorado, www.upcolorado.com, 2008. The definitive guide to more than 400 geysers and other geothermal features in Yellowstone.

Fritz, William J. *Roadside Geology of the Yellowstone Country.* Missoula, MT: Mountain Press Publishing Co., www.mountain-press.

com, 1986. All of the park roads are covered in this easy-to-follow Yellowstone geology primer.

History

Bartlett, Richard A. *Yellowstone: A Wilderness Besieged.* Tucson: University of Arizona Press, www.uapress.arizona.edu, 1989. The history of Yellowstone and the fight to prevent its destruction by railroad magnates, concessioners, and others.

Haines, Aubrey L. *The Yellowstone Story: A History of Our First National Park.* Boulder: University Press of Colorado, www.upcolorado.com, 1996. A definitive two-volume history of the park. Volume one (history up to the park's establishment) is the more interesting.

Janetski, Joel C. *Indians of Yellowstone Park.* Salt Lake City: University of Utah Press, www.upress.utah.edu, 1987. A general overview of the earliest settlers in Yellowstone and later conflicts with incoming whites.

Milstein, Michael. *Yellowstone Album: 125 Years of America's Best Idea.* Billings, MT: The Billings Gazette, www.billingsgazette.com, 1996. A delightful book filled with historical photographs, along with photos of postcards, souvenirs, and other tourist artifacts.

Schreier, Carl (ed.). *Yellowstone: Selected Photographs 1870–1960.* Moose, WY: Homestead

Publishing, 1989. An outstanding collection of historical photographs from the park. Now out of print.

Whittlesey, Lee H. *Yellowstone Place Names: Mirrors of History.* Helena: Montana State Historical Press, www.montanahistoricalsociety.org, 2006. For the Trivial Pursuit enthusiast: 290 pages of detailed descriptions with every possible name from every obscure corner of Yellowstone.

Natural History

Craighead, Frank J. *Track of the Grizzly.* San Francisco, CA: Sierra Club Books, www.sierraclub.org, 1982. The life of grizzlies in Yellowstone, by one of the most famous bear researchers. Dated, but still a classic.

Halfpenny, James C. *Yellowstone Wolves in the Wild.* Helena, MT: Riverbend Publishing, www.riverbendpublishing.com, 2003. An excellent look at the reintroduction of wolves and their lives. It's scientific in scope and nicely illustrated with photos.

Krakell, Dean, II. *Downriver: A Yellowstone Journey.* San Francisco, CA: Sierra Club Books, www.sierraclub.org, 1987. An extraordinarily moving journey down the magnificent Yellowstone River.

McEneaney, Terry. *Birds of Yellowstone.* Boulder, CO: Roberts Rinehart, www.roberts-rinehart.com, 1988. A guide to Yellowstone birds and where to find them.

Schullery, Paul. *Searching for Yellowstone.* New York: Houghton Mifflin Co., www.hmco.com, 2004. An eloquently written book by a longtime park ranger whose knowledge of the park goes far beyond the hype. Must-reading for anyone who cares about Yellowstone.

Schullery, Paul (ed.). *Yellowstone Bear Tales.* Boulder, CO: Roberts Rinehart Publishers, www.roberts-rinehart.com, 2001. First-person stories of bear encounters from a range of travelers—including President Theodore Roosevelt—between 1880 and 1950.

Shaw, Richard J. *Wildflowers of Yellowstone and Grand Teton National Parks.* Salt Lake City, UT: Wheelwright Press, 1992. Color photos and short descriptions of more than 100 wildflowers in the Greater Yellowstone Ecosystem.

Smith, Douglas W., and Gary Ferguson. *Decade of the Wolf: Returning the Wild to Yellowstone.* Guilford, CT: The Lyons Press, www.lyonspress.com, 2005. The story of how wolves were reintroduced to Yellowstone and how it changed the park, as told by a naturalist at the center of the project.

Wuerthner, George. *Yellowstone: A Visitor's Companion.* Mechanicsburg, PA: Stackpole Books, www.stackpolebooks.com, 1992. A detailed natural history of Yellowstone.

Recreation

Anderson, Roger, and Carol Shively Anderson. *A Ranger's Guide to Yellowstone Day Hikes.* Helena, MT: Farcountry Press, www.farcountrypress.com, 2000. One of the best books for short Yellowstone hikes.

Bach, Orville E., Jr. *Hiking the Yellowstone Backcountry.* San Francisco, CA: Sierra Club Books, www.sierraclub.org, 1998. A pocket-size guide to hiking, canoeing, biking, and skiing in the park.

Butler, Susan Springer. *Scenic Driving Yellowstone and Grand Teton National Parks.* Guilford, CT: Falcon Guides, www.falcon.com, 2006.

Carter, Tom. *Day Hiking Yellowstone.* Garland, TX: Dayhiking Press, 1991. A pocket-size guide to 20 day-treks, coordinated with the Trails Illustrated topographic maps.

Henry, Jeff. *Yellowstone Winter Guide.* Boulder, CO: Roberts Rinehart Publishers, www.roberts-rinehart.com, 1998. A detailed guide to visiting Yellowstone in the winter; especially good for cross-country skiers.

Lilly, Bud, and Paul Schullery. *Bud Lilly's Guide to Fly Fishing the New West.* Portland, OR: Frank Amato Publications, 2000. The authoritative fishing source from the father of Western trout fishing.

Marschall, Mark C. *Yellowstone Trails: A Hiking Guide.* Yellowstone National Park, WY: The Yellowstone Association, www.yellowstoneassociation.org, 2008. An excellent, detailed guidebook to the park's 1,000 miles of hiking trails.

Nelson, Don. *Paddling Yellowstone and Grand Teton National Parks.* Guilford, CT: Falcon Guides, www.falcon.com, 1999.

Parks, Richard. *Fishing Yellowstone National Park.* Guilford, CT: Falcon Guides, www.falcon.com, 2007. One of several authoritative guides, this one provides details on fly- and lure fishing, along with descriptions of more than 100 sites.

Schneider, Bill. *Best Easy Day Hikes in Yellowstone National Park.* Guilford, CT: Falcon Guides, www.falcon.com, 2011.

Schneider, Bill. *Hiking Yellowstone National Park.* Guilford, CT: Falcon Guides, www.falcon.com, 2003. Clear maps and helpful trail profiles make this the most useful book for anyone heading out on Yellowstone hiking routes. Contains descriptions of more than 100 trails.

Varley, John D., and Paul D. Schullery. *Yellowstone Fishes: Ecology, History, and Angling in the Park.* Mechanicsburg, PA: Stackpole Books, www.stackpolebooks.com, 1998. The comprehensive guide to the fish of Yellowstone, written by two authorities in the field.

GRAND TETON NATIONAL PARK AND JACKSON HOLE

Good, John M., and Kenneth L. Pierce. *Interpreting the Landscape: Recent and Ongoing Geology of Grand Teton and Yellowstone National Parks.* Moose, WY: Grand Teton Association, www.grandtetonpark.org, 1997. This attractive book has the latest geologic research on the parks and presents it in an understandable format with excellent illustrations.

Love, David D., John C. Reed, Jr., and Kenneth L. Pierce. *Creation of the Teton Landscape: the Geologic Story of Grand Teton National Park.* Moose, WY: Grand Teton Association, www.grandtetonpark.org, 2003. A small but authoritatively detailed guide to the geology of Jackson Hole and the Tetons.

History

Betts, Robert B. *Along the Ramparts of the Tetons: The Saga of Jackson Hole, Wyoming.* Boulder: University Press of Colorado, www.upcolorado.com, 1978. A substantial, detailed, and beautifully written book about the history of Jackson Hole.

Burt, Nathaniel. *Jackson Hole Journal.* Norman: University of Oklahoma Press, www.oupress.com, 1983. Tales of growing up as a dude in Jackson Hole. Contains some very amusing stories.

Hayden, Elizabeth Wied, and Cynthia Nielsen. *Origins, A Guide to the Place Names of Grand Teton National Park and the Surrounding Area.* Moose, WY: Grand Teton Association, www.grandtetonpark.org, 1988. A guide to the obscure sources for place names in Grand Teton.

Huidekoper, Virginia. *The Early Days in Jackson Hole.* Moose, WY: Grand Teton Association, www.grandtetonpark.org, 1996. Filled with more than 100 photos from old-time Jackson Hole.

Righter, Robert W. *Crucible for Conservation: The Creation of Grand Teton National Park.* Boulder: University Press of Colorado, www. upcolorado.com, 1982. The story of how the Tetons were spared through a half-century battle.

Thompson, Edith M., and William Leigh Thompson. *Beaver Dick: The Honor and the Heartbreak.* Laramie, WY: Jelm Mountain Press, 1982. A touching historical biography of Beaver Dick Leigh, one of the first white men to settle in Jackson Hole. Out of print.

Natural History

Carrighar, Sally. *One Day at Teton Marsh.* Lincoln: University of Nebraska Press, www.unp. unl.edu, 1979. A classic natural history of life in a Jackson Hole marsh. Made into a movie by Walt Disney. Out of print.

Murie, Margaret, and Olaus Murie. *Wapiti Wilderness.* Boulder: University Press of Colorado, www.upcolorado.com, 1986. The lives of two of America's most-loved conservationists in Jackson Hole and their work with elk.

Travsky, Amber. *Mountain Biking Jackson Hole.* Guilford, CT: Falcon Guides, www.falcon. com, 2001. Thirty-one rides in Jackson Hole, Grand Teton National Park, and surrounding areas.

Vizgirdas, Ray S. *A Guide to Plants of Yellowstone and Grand Teton National Parks.* Salt Lake City: University of Utah Press, www. uofupress.com, 2007. The definitive guide to regional plants.

Recreation

Craighead, Charles. *Day Hikes and Short Walks of Grand Teton National Park.* Moose, WY: Grand Teton Association, www.grandtetonpark.org, 2005. A handy little guide with good trail information and plenty of photos.

Dufy, Katy, and Darwin Wile. *Teton Trails.* Moose, WY: Grand Teton Association, www. grandtetonpark.org, 1995. A useful guide to more than 200 miles of trails in the park.

Jackson, Reynold G. *A Climber's Guide to the Teton Range.* Seattle, WA: Mountaineers Books, www.mountaineerbooks.org, 1996. The definitive (415 pages!) climbing guide for the Tetons.

Prax, Brian, and Mark Schultheis. *The Book: Guide to Mountain Biking in the Jackson Hole Area.* Jackson, WY: Prax Photography and Productions, 2001. This spiral-bound book is the most complete guide to local cycling options, and includes coverage on Teton Valley.

Rossiter, Richard. *Teton Classics: 50 Selected Climbs in Grand Teton National Park.* Guilford, CT: Falcon Guides, www.falcon.com, 1994. A small and nicely illustrated guide to 50 climbing routes in the Tetons.

Schneider, Bill. *Best Easy Day Hikes Grand Teton.* Guilford, CT: Falcon Guides, www. falcon.com, 2005.

Schneider, Bill. *Hiking Grand Teton National Park.* Guilford, CT: Falcon Guides, www. falcon.com, 2005.

Stone, Robert. *Day Hikes in Grand Teton National Park and Jackson Hole.* Guilford, CT: Falcon Guides, www.falcon.com, 2004.

Watters, Ron. *Winter Tales and Trails: Skiing, Snowshoeing and Snowboarding in Idaho, the Grand Tetons and Yellowstone National Park.* Pocatello, ID: Great Rift Press, 1997. A book that combines lucid writing on the area's rich history with guides to winter trails. More than 350 pages of details from an expert in the field. Out-of-date, but still useful.

Woods, Rebecca. *Jackson Hole Hikes*. Jackson, WY: White Willow Publishing, 1999. An excellent guide that includes trails in Grand Teton National Park and surrounding national forest areas. Easy to use and informative.

CODY AND SHOSHONE NATIONAL FOREST

Cook, Jeannie (ed.). *Buffalo Bill's Town in the Rockies: A Pictorial History of Cody, Wyoming*. Cody, WY: Park County Historical Society, 1996. A photographic visit to Cody's interesting past.

Ehrlich, Gretel. *Heart Mountain*. New York: Viking Penguin, www.penguinputnam. com, 1988. A touching novel about life in the Heart Mountain Relocation Camp near Cody, the forced home for hundreds of Japanese-Americans during World War II.

Rosa, Joseph G., and Robin May. *Buffalo Bill and His Wild West*. Lawrence: University Press of Kansas, www.kansaspress.ku.edu, 1989. One of the newer books on Buffalo Bill, with a somewhat revisionist take on his life and times. Rich in detail on Cody's Wild West show.

Russell, Don. *The Lives and Legends of Buffalo Bill*. Norman: University of Oklahoma Press, www.oupress.com, 1979. The most complete biography on the life of Buffalo Bill Cody.

Stone, Robert. *Day Hikes in the Beartooth Mountains*. Guilford, CT: Falcon Guides, www.falcon.com, 2006.

REGIONAL TITLES

Birkby, Jeff. *Touring Montana and Wyoming Hot Springs*. Guilford, CT: Falcon Guides, www.falcon.com, 1999.

Blackstone, D. L., Jr. *Traveler's Guide to the Geology of Wyoming*. Laramie, WY: Geological Survey of Wyoming, www.wsgsweb.uwyo.

edu, 1988. An excellent overview of Wyoming's geological history and how to see it in today's landscapes.

Graham, Kenneth L. *Camping Wyoming and the Black Hills*. Guilford, CT: Falcon Guides, www.falcon.com, 2001.

Graham, Kenneth Lee. *Fishing Wyoming*. Guilford, CT: Falcon Guides, www.falcon.com, 1998. A 300-page tome that goes far beyond the standard coverage of Yellowstone and Jackson Hole.

Herrero, Stephen. *Bear Attacks: Their Causes and Avoidance*. Guilford, CT: The Lyons Press, www.globepequot.com, 2002. An authoritative volume on the lives of bears and staying safe in their country.

Kilgore, Gene. *Gene Kilgore's Ranch Vacations*. Berkeley, CA: Avalon Travel Publishing, www.avalontravelbooks.com, 2005. The definitive guide to dude and guest ranches in Wyoming and the rest of North America. Includes detailed, up-to-date descriptions of the best places to be a city-slicker cowboy.

Largeson, David R., and Darwin R. Spearing. *Roadside Geology of Wyoming*. Missoula, MT: Mountain Press Publishing Co., www. mountain-press.com, 1988. Wyoming is perhaps the most geologically interesting of all the states. This is an invaluable road guide for anyone wanting to know more about geology without resorting to dense textbooks.

Phillips, Wayne. *Central Rocky Mountain Wildflowers: Including the Yellowstone and Grand Teton National Parks*. Guilford, CT: Falcon Guides, www.falcon.com, 1999.

Retallic, Ken. *Flyfisher's Guide to Wyoming*. Gallatin Gateway, MT: Wilderness Adventures Press, www.wildadvpress.com, 2005. An excellent guide; particularly helpful for anglers headed to Yellowstone.

Schneider, Bill. *Bear Aware*. Guilford, CT: Falcon Guides, www.falcon.com, 2004. A handy pocket-size book that is easy to read and up to date.

ONWARD TRAVEL
The following is a shameless promotion for other Moon books (www.moon.com) covering the region. All of these are authoritative guides for their respective states or regions.

Kelley, James Patrick. *Moon Idaho*. Berkeley, CA: Avalon Travel, 2011.

Knopper, Steve. *Moon Colorado*. Berkeley, CA: Avalon Travel, 2009.

McRae, W. C., and Judy Jewell. *Moon Utah*. Berkeley, CA: Avalon Travel, 2011.

Pitcher, Don. *Moon Wyoming*. Berkeley, CA: Avalon Travel, 2006.

Walker, Carter. *Moon Montana & Wyoming*. Berkeley, CA: Avalon Travel, 2011.

Internet Resources

GENERAL TRAVEL
Don Pitcher
www.donpitcher.com
www.donpitcher.com/blog
Author Don Pitcher's website provides details on all his books and photographic projects, plus links to most websites found in this book. Visit his blog or Facebook page for updated comments and more.

Recreation.gov
www.recreation.gov
Head here to book reservations at Forest Service campgrounds.

U.S. Forest Service
www.fs.fed.us
This federal agency manages land within several national forests in the Greater Yellowstone Ecosystem. These include Bridger-Teton National Forest (www.fs.fed.us/r4/btnf), Shoshone National Forest (www.fs.fed.us/r2/shoshone), Caribou-Targhee National Forest (www.fs.fed.us/r4/caribou-targhee), Gallatin National Forest (www.fs.fed.us/r1/gallatin), Beaverhead-Deerlodge National Forest (www.fs.usda.gov/bdnf), and Custer National Forest (www.fs.fed.us/r1/custer).

GATEWAYS TO YELLOWSTONE
Buffalo Bill Historical Center
www.bbhc.org
Cody's famous museum now covers an incredible 300,000 square feet, making it easily the most impressive museum in the region.

Cooke City, Colter Pass, and Silver Gate Chamber of Commerce
www.cookecitychamber.org
Head here for details on these rustic and remote Montana towns on the northeast corner of Yellowstone National Park.

Dubois Chamber of Commerce
www.duboiswyoming.org
This is the best Web source for information on the Dubois area.

Gardiner Chamber of Commerce
www.gardinerchamber.com
Details on the little edge-of-Yellowstone town of Gardiner, Montana.

Park County Travel Council
www.yellowstonecountry.org
This regional tourism agency has a great website for travelers heading into Cody.

Tripadvisor
www.tripadvisor.com
A very useful site for the latest on hotels, restaurants, and more—but don't take all comments as the gospel truth.

Webcams
www.jacksonholenet.com/webcams
Check out the current activity at Old Faithful, Jackson's Town Square, and a multitude of other places with live webcams.

West Yellowstone Chamber of Commerce
www.westyellowstonechamber.com
The most complete Web source for West Yellowstone, Montana.

JACKSON HOLE
Grand Targhee Ski Resort
www.grandtarghee.com
This resort on the west side of the Tetons is a favorite of powderhounds.

Jackson Hole Chamber of Commerce
www.jacksonholechamber.com
This website is a fine starting point for travel to Jackson, with a multitude of weblinks to local businesses.

Jackson Hole Gallery Association
www.jacksonholegalleries.com
A fine Web source for more than 30 Jackson art galleries.

Jackson Hole Mountain Resort
www.jacksonhole.com
The big one, this is the primary ski and snowboard destination in Jackson Hole.

Jackson Hole Traveler
www.jacksonholetraveler.com
This private website is nicely designed and packed with useful information and links.

National Elk Refuge
www.fws.gov/nationalelkrefuge
This website details Jackson Hole's famous refuge with its picturesque sleigh rides among the elk.

National Museum of Wildlife Art
www.wildlifeart.org
This large Jackson museum exhibits the works of many internationally recognized artists.

Snow King Resort
www.snowking.com
Jackson's town hill, this small ski area is accessible and surprisingly challenging.

NATIONAL PARKS
Grand Teton National Park
www.nps.gov/grte
This official Park Service site has an abundance of background information about Grand Teton.

Yellowstone National Park
www.nps.gov/yell
A fine starting point for any exploration of the Yellowstone area.

WYOMING
Wyoming Department of Transportation
www.wyoroad.info
This website has updated road conditions, webcams, and details on road construction projects; call 511 for the phone version.

Wyoming Dude Rancher's Association
www.wyomingdra.com
This statewide organization's homepage has links to the websites of 30 different Wyoming guest ranches.

Wyoming Fishing Network
www.wyomingfishing.net
An exceptionally useful online source for Wyoming anglers.

Wyoming Game and Fish Department
http://gf.state.wy.us
Head to this website for details on fishing

licenses and seasons, along with current issues affecting fish. You can even download application forms.

Wyoming Homestay & Outdoor Adventures
www.wyomingbnb-ranchrec.com
Better known as WHOA, this organization maintains links to several dozen bed-and-breakfasts, dude ranches, guest cabins, and other distinctive lodging options.

Wyoming Outfitters and Guides Association
www.wyoga.org
Interested in a backcountry pack trip? Visit this website to find outfitters for the area you plan to visit.

Wyoming Public Radio
www.wyomingpublicradio.net
A good starting place for information on public radio around Wyoming.

Wyoming Travel & Tourism Division
www.wyomingtourism.org
The state's tourism site has everything you'd expect in the way of an interactive visitor center and much more.

Index

List of Maps

Acknowledgments

For Aziza Bali
Who still loves cats, snowboards, and Jumping Horse stories
May you always chase waves, snowflakes, and dreams
May you never lose your sense of wonder

It would be impossible to thank all those who helped me with this fifth edition of *Moon Yellowstone & Grand Teton,* but a number of individuals deserve special commendation. A big thank-you goes to the following people who opened doors to their hometowns or reviewed the manuscript for errors: Lee Anne Ackerman in Cody, Heather Falk in Jackson, Rick Hoeninghausen at Xanterra Parks & Resorts, Vicky Millspaugh in West Yellowstone, Donna Rowland in Cooke City, and Jackie Skaggs in Grand Teton National Park.

I also wish to thank Zahan Billimoria at Jackson Hole Mountain Resort, Samantha Stout Denny at Terra Resort in Teton Village, Ed Krajsky at The Lexington in Jackson, and Lisa Smith at Chamberlin Inn in Cody for their generous assistance with lodging. A special thanks goes to Tom and Mona Mesereau of Mesereau Communications for Yellowstone accommodations.

This book was shepherded through the production process by my helpful editor, Sabrina Young. Thanks to her and everyone else at Avalon Travel for getting the book into your hands.

I offer special gratitude to my wife, Karen Shemet, and our two live-wire children, Aziza and Rio, for keeping my priorities straight and adding a bit of levity.

www.moon.com

DESTINATIONS | ACTIVITIES | BLOGS | MAPS | BOOKS

MOON.COM is ready to help plan your next trip! Filled with fresh trip ideas and strategies, author interviews, informative travel blogs, a detailed map library, and descriptions of all the Moon guidebooks, Moon.com is all you need to get out and explore the world—or even places in your own backyard. While at Moon.com, sign up for our monthly e-newsletter for updates on new releases, travel tips, and expert advice from our on-the-go Moon authors. As always, when you travel with Moon, expect an experience that is uncommon and truly unique.

MOON IS ON FACEBOOK—BECOME A FAN!
JOIN THE MOON PHOTO GROUP ON FLICKR

MAP SYMBOLS

▬▬▬ Expressway	◖	Highlight	✗	Airfield	⚓	Golf Course
▬▬▬ Primary Road	○	City/Town	✈	Airport	🅿	Parking Area
▬▬▬ Secondary Road	◉	State Capital	▲	Mountain	◭	Archaeological Site
- - - - Unpaved Road	◉	National Capital	✚	Unique Natural Feature	⛪	Church
------ Trail	★	Point of Interest			⛽	Gas Station
············ Ferry	•	Accommodation	♨	Waterfall	◯	Glacier
-·-·-· Railroad	▼	Restaurant/Bar	▲	Park		Mangrove
▬▬ Pedestrian Walkway	■	Other Location	🚩	Trailhead		Reef
Stairs	⛺	Campground	🎿	Skiing Area		Swamp

CONVERSION TABLES

°C = (°F − 32) / 1.8
°F = (°C x 1.8) + 32
1 inch = 2.54 centimeters (cm)
1 foot = 0.304 meters (m)
1 yard = 0.914 meters
1 mile = 1.6093 kilometers (km)
1 km = 0.6214 miles
1 fathom = 1.8288 m
1 chain = 20.1168 m
1 furlong = 201.168 m
1 acre = 0.4047 hectares
1 sq km = 100 hectares
1 sq mile = 2.59 square km
1 ounce = 28.35 grams
1 pound = 0.4536 kilograms
1 short ton = 0.90718 metric ton
1 short ton = 2,000 pounds
1 long ton = 1.016 metric tons
1 long ton = 2,240 pounds
1 metric ton = 1,000 kilograms
1 quart = 0.94635 liters
1 US gallon = 3.7854 liters
1 Imperial gallon = 4.5459 liters
1 nautical mile = 1.852 km

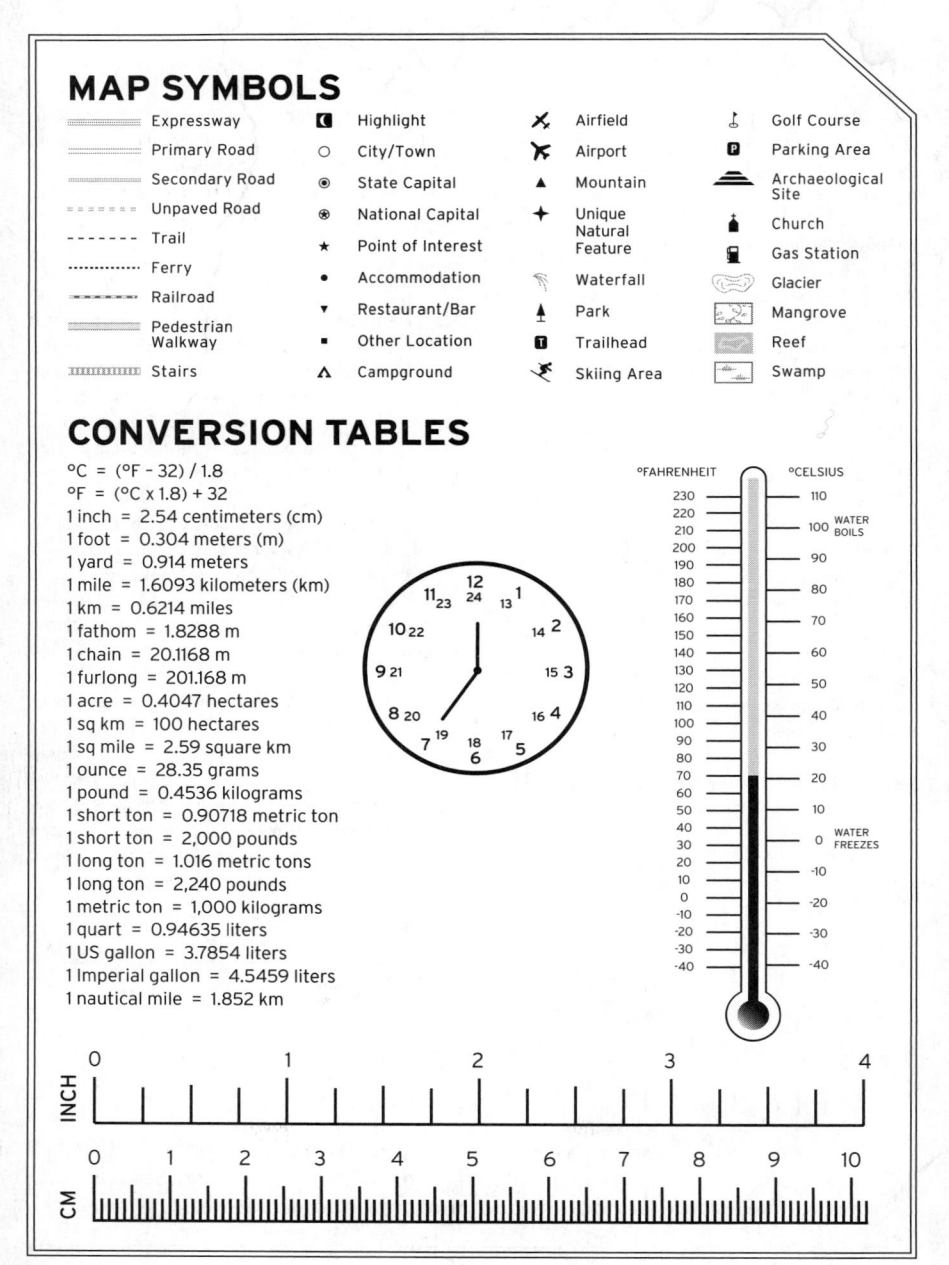

MOON YELLOWSTONE & GRAND TETON

Avalon Travel
a member of the Perseus Books Group
1700 Fourth Street
Berkeley, CA 94710, USA
www.moon.com

Editor and Series Manager: Sabrina Young
Copy Editor: Lisa Wolff
Production and Graphics Coordinator: Lucie Ericksen
Cover Designer: Lucie Ericksen
Map Editor: Brice Ticen
Cartographers: Kat Bennett, Andrea Butkovic,
  Chris Henrick
Indexer: Greg Jewett

ISBN-13: 978-1-59880-736-3
ISSN: 1542-8850

Printing History
1st Edition – 2000
5th Edition – May 2011
5 4 3 2 1

Front cover photo: © Don Pitcher
Title page photo: © Don Pitcher
Interior photos: pages 8, 9 left & right, 10, 11 bottom-
  left, 13-21, 23-24: © Don Pitcher; pages 9 middle,
  11 top & bottom-right: Photo Courtesy of
  Xanterra Parks & Resorts® in Yellowstone;
  page 22: © shaday365/123RF

Printed in Canada by Friesens

KEEPING CURRENT

If you have a favorite gem you'd like to see included in the next edition, or see anything
that needs updating, clarification, or correction, please drop us a line. Send your
comments via email to feedback@moon.com, or use the address above.